HISTORIC HOUSES
CASTLES & GARDENS

Open to the public

Editor: Deborah Valentine

Published by:
Reed Information Services Ltd.
Windsor Court, East Grinstead House, East Grinstead,
West Sussex RH19 1XA
Telephone: (0342) 326972 Fax: (0342) 335665
Telex: 95127 INFSER G

REED
INFORMATION
SERVICES

A Division of Reed Telepublishing Ltd.
A member of the Reed Elsevier group

Arundel Castle

Family home of the Dukes of Norfolk
For details see West Sussex Section

HISTORIC HOUSES CASTLES & GARDENS in Great Britain & Ireland

INTRODUCTION

Historic Houses Castles and Gardens has been published annually since 1954, and is recognised as the most comprehensive guide in its field. It gives details of over 1300 heritage properties open to the public, including those administered by The National Trust, English Heritage, CADW, National Trust for Scotland, Historic Scotland and HITHA, as well as those houses and gardens which are privately owned.

The fire which broke out in Hampton Court Palace in 1986 led to one of the largest and most complex restoration works undertaken, involving as it did the careful salvage and assimilation of thousands of fragments from the building. The scale and range of skills required in this "story of a phoenix rising from the ashes" are described in the introductory article on the restoration of the King's Apartments at Hampton Court Palace.

Restoration and conservation of a different kind is discussed in The Garden Landscape Heritage of Wales; the use of the country house for concerts, and the Stately Homes Music Festival is described in Music in Country Houses, and the ever widening remit of the Heritage Education Trust is demonstrated in Historic Houses and the Arts: Education with Inspiration.

Holker Hall was the winner of the Historic Houses Association/Christie's Garden of the Year Award and is featured on our title page. More information about Holker Hall can be found on page 29.

All admission charges quoted are subject to change without notice. All dates are inclusive i.e. May to September, Weds, means first Wednesday in May to last Wednesday in September. Opening times and dates apply to 1993 only.

CONTENTS

Restoring the King's Apartments at Hampton Court Palace	v
Music in Country Houses	xv
The Garden Landscape Heritage of Wales: Decay and Revival	xxi
Historic Houses and The Arts: education with inspiration	xxix
Sandford Awards	xxxii
Houses Castles and Gardens in County Order	1
The Garden Specialists	263
Universities	271
Supplementary List of Properties open by appointment only	273
Index of Houses Castles and Gardens	277
Maps – 12 page section following Index	282

Cover picture: Woburn Abbey
see Bedfordshire section.

Title Page picture: Holker Hall
winner – Christie's/HHA Garden of the Year Award presented in 1992.

The Banqueting House

Whitehall

The King's Grand Staircase
State Apartments
Kensington Palace

Restoring The King's Apartments at Hampton Court

On Wednesday, 8th July 1992, HM the Queen payed an official visit to Hampton Court Palace to re-open the King's Apartments following a massive six year restoration project after the tragic fire of Easter 1986, which left the wing severely damaged. Her Majesty's visit marked the completion of the most important restoration project in this country, at a total cost of £10 million which has involved not only returning the Apartments to their original state, but refurbishing the interiors exactly as they were in 1700.

Cleaning the Throne Canopy

Fire broke out in a Grace and Favour Apartment directly above the Cartoon Gallery at about 11 o'clock on the evening of March 31st, 1986. Thanks to the prompt action of the Palace Rescue Squad, most of the contents of the Apartments were saved. However, in the cold light of morning, it became apparent that the Cartoon gallery and the Audience Chamber were severely damaged by fire, and the rooms around them badly water damaged. Immediately after the fire, a meticulous salvage operation

The King's Apartments: Cartoon Restoration

was organised and a high proportion of the historic fragments were salvaged which could be reincorporated as part of the restoration work. In the months following the fire, the PSA were appointed to oversee the reconstruction.

Following the initial response to the fire, many months of discussion over the sensitive issues raised by the reconstruction were discussed and a decision was eventually made to rebuild on a like-for-like basis. In the following years. it was decided to undertake a more historically accurate restoration, on the basis of new information

which materialised as a direct result of the reconstruction.

The Textile Conservation Studios at Hampton Court Palace have spent the last five years repairing and restoring 2 badly damaged Throne Canopies which are now restored to their original glory. In addition to the two Throne Canopies, eight major tapestries have been conserved for the apartments, making the King's Apartments the foremost tapestry gallery and tapestry collection on shown in this country.

In a major coup, the Palace has obtained seven late seventeenth century copies of the Acts of the Apostles cartoons by Raphael from the Ashmolean Museum (the originals are in the V & A) for the Cartoon Gallery. These have now been conserved and re-hung so the Gallery now looks exactly as William III perceived it.

The restoration of the King's Apartments is one of the largest and most complex undertaken involving the meticulous saving of thousands of fragments from the original building and their assimilation into the restoration is a major feature of this project.

This is a story of a phoenix rising from the ashes. In 1986 the task facing the Palace seemed virtually impossible. In 1992 the Palace has been able to refurbish the interiors, re-open a new floor and bring the experience of the King's Apartments to life.

Refurbishing the Interiors
In the aftermath of the fire, the bold decision was taken not only to restore the King's Apartments exactly as they

Canopy Crimson Damask being woven by Neil Shuttlewood at Humphries Weaving Company in Essex

were beforehand but to recreate the splendour of William III's time, thereby providing an authentic impression of life inside a set of Baroque Royal Apartments.

At the time of the fire, the King's Apartments had been sparsely furnished, largely provided by the two magnificent Throne Canopies and the King's red velvet bed. Nothing remained of the rich silk wall hangings and the curtains commissioned by William III in 1700, which have been on show to the public since July 9, 1992. The refurbishment has been a remarkable achievement and ruthless accuracy has been applied throughout.

There are three critical reasons that enabled the Palace to perform this restoration:

1. The King's Apartments have not been altered architecturally in any way since they were built by Sir Christopher Wren in the 1690s.

Damaged Mirrors in Privy Chamber

2. The original furnishing bills survive virtually intact enabling staff to discover even the tiniest details such as the colour, width and yards of cord needed to pull the rich white silk damask curtains which hang in the main state rooms.

3. Unlike most other European collections which were dispersed and broken up after Revolution and war, the English Royal Collection still contains almost all the original furniture which belonged in the King's Apartments. With only one or two exceptions, there is no reproduction furniture.

The guiding principle throughout has been that whatever could be salvaged should be restored and replaced. Meticulous research since the fire has resulted in a wealth of knowledge, not only about the way these rooms looked, but their various uses in the context of life at William's Court. Notable "finds" along the way include two of the most valuable tapestries in the world, The Triumph of Bacchus and the Labours of Hercules, originally commissioned by Henry VIII for Whitehall Palace in 1542, which have not been seen this century.

For the very first time, visitors to the King's Apartments will not only see the original 300 year old furnishings and tapestries, brilliantly restored, conserved and replaced, but will gain an understanding of life in King William's Court, and how he lived both in public and in private.

Grinling Gibbons Carving damaged in fire

The Public and Private Life of William III

The rooms of the King's Apartments were planned in such a way so as to make the rules of etiquette which enforced the King's privacy as easy as possible to operate. These began with rooms which were relatively public, accessible to most members of court. They ended in a few very private rooms to which only William and his most trusted friend and Groom of the Stool, The Duke of Portland, held a key. Between the two were the main rooms of state in which the King would grant audiences and generally mingle with his court.

The 1992 representation creates an authentic impression of life inside a set of Baroque Royal Apartments as the rooms are decorated and furnished exactly as they would have been in 1700. The large, relatively plain public rooms in which William III received his courtiers are sparsely furnished for the simple reason that nobody sat in the King's presence. These rooms are mainly hung with

The Privy Chamber

open to the public. These rooms are reached by a back staircase which provided an easy escape for William from his public duties. An introductory exhibition houses a collection of items belonging to William including his watch and a shirt worn shortly before his death, as well as a fabulously ornate silver gilt toilet service inscribed with

The Great Bedchamber

important 16th century tapestries and paintings and lit with solid silver sconces. The Grinling Gibbons carvings, now cleaned, restored and, in some cases, re-carved, provide further decoration. Today, as visitors walk through William's State rooms, they will be amazed by the increasing opulence of these rooms culminating in the King's Little Bedchamber and Closet. These were the King's inner sanctum and are decorated with the most expensive material available. The King's Little Bedchamber, the room where he actually slept, is decorated with bright yellow silk damask trimmed with real silver lace. The walls are hung with priceless mirrors and the room is filled with gilded furniture.

Downstairs are three smaller rooms used by the King for private entertaining which, until now, have not been

Craftswoman restoring Grinling Gibbons' Carving

William and Mary's cipher. This was a present to William and Mary on their wedding and was made by Pierre Prevost in 1677. It consists of 23 pieces and was given to the 3rd Duke of Devonshire in the 1690's by the King. The present Duke of Devonshire has kindly loaned the service to the Exhibition.

In William's private closets themselves, in addition to the original furniture, chess and backgammon sets, decanters and glasses all create the effect that the King has just left the room for a few moments.

William's picture inventory survives so that many of the actual paintings of the great names of the period such as Van Dyck, Julio Romano, Titian, Veronese and Bassano are hung in 1992 exactly as they were in this 18th century Royal household.

In the last hitherto unseen private rooms, one gains a sense of how the King spent his time entertaining friends,

The Private Dining Room

The Little Bedchamber

returning from hunting trips or whiling away the archetypal wet afternoon. His study is lined with bookcases, globes and plans to create the look of a room that is still occupied rather than an atmosphere of a museum.

Royal Dining
King William III frequently dined privately with one or two friends. For the first time, the King's private dining room in which he entertained his friends can be seen as if an 18th century dinner party was in progress. The vast oval dining table is set for the desert or confectionery course with pyramids of fruit and meringues on salvers and marbled boards which the King's special confectioners would have made up for him. The sources for the table setting are William III's own court cook, Patrick Lamb, and the 17th century French cook, Massialot.

In the sideboard alcove is a splendid display of silver-gilt, piled three and four tiers high, known as the King's buffet and echoes that depicted in the painting above the King's Staircase at the entrance to the King's Apartments. This buffet was never actually touched by the King but was intended as a display of his wealth and magnificence. Some of this silverware is borrowed from the Victoria and Albert Museum and is a mid-19th century electrotype, ie made from a mould of the original piece. Pieces include a pair of flagons, a pair of ewers and several basins. There

The King's Bedchamber Canopy

are also two original wine cisterns with 17th century bottles cooling in them.

Possibly one of the most striking elements of William's private dining room are the paintings. For the first time since the 18th century, the famous Kneller portraits of the most beautiful women in Mary's Household, have been returned to their original position. These enormous paintings are now hung as William had them – touching the ceiling and cheek by jowl all the way around the room.

This is the room to "meet" the King sitting with his back to the fireplace, as was his custom, surrounded by silver and looking at "wall-to-wall beauties" whilst he ate.

Canopy, severely damaged by water, has likewise been resurrected from a very sorry state.

In addition to the two Throne Canopies, eight major tapestries have been conserved for the Apartments, making the King's Apartments the foremost tapestry gallery and tapestry collection on show in this country.

Live Interpretation at Hampton Court Palace
To coincide with the re-opening of the King's Apartments by HM The Queen on 8 July 1992, Hampton Court Palace introduced permanent live historical interpretation for the

The King's Presence Chamber

Textile and Tapestry Conservation
The Textile Conservation Studio, founded in the late nineteenth century by William Morris, has had a reputation for many years for undertaking work on large scale textiles and has been conserving the Royal Collection at Hampton Court Palace. The fire presented the Studio with its greatest challenge and, to cope with the work generated by the fire, the Studio moved to new premises within the Palace and commissioned the construction of an enormous washing machine, made by Woolard Development in Chichester.

New techniques have been pioneered by the Studio during the restoration work, including the cleaning of metal threads in tapestries. Both Throne Canopies passed through the Studio's hands. The Audience Chamber Throne Canopy, which was almost completely devastated and thought by many to be beyond salvage, has been miraculously restored. The Presence Chamber Throne

first time. Historical interpreters wearing, courtiers costumes of the early 18th century are positioned in the King's private rooms which, until now, have not been open to the public.

The interpreters have undergone an intensive programme into the historic life of the apartments and the philosophy behind their presentation. They will provide visitors with specific information on the public and private life of William III and bring to life themes such as dining, gardens and games.

The team of interpreters also include costumed musicians and dancers who make daily appearances throughout the palace.

Historic Royal Palaces Marketing Director, Dylan Hammond, commented, "This latest initiative at Hampton Court is designed to improve the visitor experience at the Historic Royal Palaces by bringing history to life".

The costumed interpreters in the King's Apartments

play an additional role to the team of guide lecturers already established at Hampton Court Palace.

Editor's Notes
Sir Christopher Wren (1632-1723), as Surveyor General of the King's works, built the State and Private Apartments at Hampton Court for William and Mary, soon after they came to the throne in 1689. After the death of George II in

The Cartoon Gallery

The Privy Chambers

1790, Hampton Court Palace was no longer used as Royal residence but continued to be occupied by members of the Royal Household and the grace and favour widows of distinguished servants of the Crown. The State Rooms were open to the public in 1838 by Queen Victoria and today Hampton Court is one of the leading popular attractions with over 1 million visitors annually to the Palace and its splendid gardens and parkland.

Hampton Court Palace is owned by HM The Queen and managed by the Historic Royal Palaces. Other Royal Palaces include: the Tower of London; Kensington Palace State Apartments; the Banqueting Hall, Whitehall Palace and Kew Palace with Queen Charlotte's Cottage.

HAMPTON COURT PALACE

Royal History by the Thames

FOR DETAILS SEE LONDON SECTION

300 Historic Properties

520 Miles of Coastline

½ Million Acres of Countryside

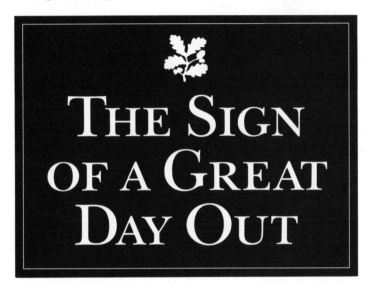

Whether you're an art-lover, nature lover or just an out-and-out explorer, the National Trust has something for you.

Magnificent houses and castles restored, with their priceless treasures, for all to enjoy.

Ancient woodlands and centuries-old gardens preserved for today's visitors.

THE SIGN OF A GREAT DAY OUT

And mile upon endless mile of unspoilt beaches and winding rustic lanes that lead to all sorts of wonderful and unexpected places.

Places you can find only with the National Trust as your guide.

Please 'phone the Membership Department on 081-464 1111 for more information.

The National Trust

Music in Country Houses

by Douglas Reed

Arch-Lute Flute, Kensington Palace, London

During the past few years, historic houses have increasingly been used for opera and concerts of classical chamber music. This resurgence is interesting for the owners, the performers and for the audiences who attend the concerts. Country houses were built as centres of social power but they were also places where artists and musicians could work for their wealthy patrons. As in those days music is being increasingly performed in the style of venues composers had intended, certainly as far as chamber music is concerned.

The Commercial Benefits that Concerts can Bring

While the country house will never quite return to the days when elegant soirees and music recitals arranged by the owner were virtually commonplace, many owners are today recognising the commercial benefits that concerts can bring. Some owners enjoy staging their own seasons of opera and concerts and occasionally, as at Glyndebourne, a permanent purpose built theatre is constructed adjoining the house.

The Stately Homes Music Festival

The business of promoting concerts and opera in country houses is specialised, and the majority of owners would prefer not to do it themselves. A small number of independent promoters exists to stage professional performances of opera and concerts in country houses and other heritage buildings. Heritage Events is responsible for presenting the Stately Homes Music Festival, the largest and most experienced promoter of historic house concerts. The Festival was first established in 1980 with the aim of presenting

The Great Hall, Longleat

the Festival to embrace other countries in Europe and to promote the concept of classical music in historic houses to audiences across many national frontiers.

In some cases, concerts can open the doors of historic houses and gardens, but most are also usually accessible during the day. Every country in Europe, including those formerly in the eastern bloc, has a large number of properties open to the public and while many of these are State owned, a very high proportion remain lived in by their private owners, often by the same families that built them. The continuance of private ownership of historic houses represents an important contribution to the health of each country's heritage. For those who enjoy visiting houses and gardens, the opportunities to explore in continental Europe are formidable.

Stately Homes Music Festival

La Villa Gulia, Rome

concerts of high artistic merit in settings that are both historic and appropriate for Chamber music. Audiences have the opportunity of privately viewing the house during the evenings before listening to music performed by world class artists and companies in the Great Hall, Ballroom, Gallery, Terrace and sometimes in the beautiful gardens. Much of the music included is designed to complement the fine architecture and interiors while audiences are restricted in order to achieve the comfortable and intimate ambience that can only be captured in such a country house setting.

Over the years, the Stately Homes Music Festival has evolved to become one of the major arts festivals in the UK and in 1992, concerts were also held in properties in France and Italy. It is the intention of

Blenheim Palace

Home of the 11th Duke of Marlborough, birthplace of Sir Winston Churchill.

Open daily 10.30am–5.30pm (last admission 4.45pm) mid March to 31st October 1993.
A visit to Blenheim is a wonderful way to spend a day. An inclusive ticket covers the Palace tour, Park and Gardens, Butterfly House, Motor Launch, Train, Adventure Play Area and Nature Trail. Optional are the new Marlborough Maze and Rowing Boat Hire on Queen Pool. Car parking is free for Palace visitors and there are Shops, Cafeterias and a Garden Centre. Events for 1993 include the Annual Grand Charity Cricket Match, in aid of the Oxfordshire Association of Young People, between a Celebrity XI and an Oxford University XI on 30th May and The Blenheim Audi International Horse Trials take place on 16th, 17th, 18th and 19th September. Further details from The Administrator, Blenheim Palace, Woodstock, Oxon OX20 1PX. Telephone: 0993-811091.

The right to close the Palace or Park without notice is reserved.

THE PAST:
SOMETHING TO LOOK FORWARD TO.

LINDISFARNE PRIORY, NORTHUMBERLAND

AUDLEY END, ESSEX

THE PAST IS ALL AROUND us waiting to be discovered. Throughout the countryside England's history is landmarked by standing stones, ruined abbeys, powerful castles and great houses. The properties and gardens for which we care each have their own unique atmosphere and most are open daily for you to visit. You'll find many of our properties listed in this book; you can also pick up our leaflets at a Tourist Information Centre or just follow the signs. Why not plan a few days out and look forward to the past.

DOVER CASTLE, KENT

RIEVAULX ABBEY, NORTH YORKSHIRE

Boscobel House

OSBORNE HOUSE, ISLE OF WIGHT

English ⊞ Heritage

FIND YOURSELF A PLACE IN HISTORY

THE GARDENS AT
HATFIELD HOUSE Hertfordshire

"There are nearly 14 acres of formal and informal gardens dating back to the late 15th century. From 1609 to 1611 John Tradescant the Elder laid out and planted the gardens for Robert Cecil, the builder of the House. Today the gardens, much embellished in the last years, contain many of the same plants growing in knot gardens typical of the period, arranged in the court of the 15th century Palace where Queen Elizabeth I spent much of her childhood. There are herb and sweet gardens, a parterre of herbaceous plants and roses, fountains, statuary and a foot maze or labyrinth, the whole enclosed in ancient rose-brick walls, topiaried yews, holly and pleached limes.

A wilderness garden, planted with forest and ornamental trees, blossoms in the spring with crabs, cherries, magnolias and rhododendrons underplanted with many flowers and bulbs, the whole providing colour and interest (for there are many rare and unusual plants) for all seasons."
"Photographs by Mick Hales, Garry Rogers and Jeremy Whitaker."

"I feel at home here as I gaze down and respond to the feeling of total delight which it gives me . . ."   Sir Roy Strong

"Hatfield's gardens are the most completely beautiful and fit for their purpose of any great house in England."
                      "Tradescant" of the RHS Journal.

FOR DETAILS SEE HERTFORDSHIRE SECTION

THE GARDEN LANDSCAPE HERITAGE OF WALES
Decay and Revival

Photograph John Savidge

Erddig in Clwyd. One of the most significant surviving gardens of the early 18th Century. On the brink of dereliction it was rescued, and is being revitalised, by the National Trust.

The misconception that Wales has no parks or gardens of interest or value is widespread and of long-standing: Bodnant, Erddig and Powis Castle are of course well known, but even some experts struggle to double that shortlist.

The Rationale for Conserving our Gardens

The rationale for conserving our garden landscape heritage rests on two propositions and one fact: firstly, that a great park or garden is as much a part of our heritage as any great work of art and if the nation is prepared to spend millions on buying and conserving a painting or sculpture, then there is every reason that the park or garden should benefit on a similar footing. Secondly, it has to be recognised that the best-known monuments in Wales – the castles and the relics of the industrial revolution – are symbols of effort and contention. But it is in the gardens and designed landscapes, as in the language, that other values predominate: reflecting accord, peace and the harmony of man and nature. Indeed the beauty of the natural setting in Wales was a source of particular inspiration to designers and, because gardens so often relate to the wider natural setting, we are concerned with an art both specific to Wales and one whose history and aesthetic significance goes far beyond the Principality.

The fact referred to is that visiting gardens is of economic importance in conservation, and will be returned to again.

Why then was that first list so small? Certainly (as Thomas Lloyd has noted) the habitable portion of Wales is not much bigger than the old county of Yorkshire, but within that territorial limitation there is a diversity of landscape that is as rich as anywhere in Britain. But the

Welsh garden, like the Welsh estate, tended to be on a smaller, less dominant scale, than was the usual case in England, and that led to a more intimate, harmonious relationship with the natural landscape: hence the flowering of the Picturesque movement in Wales and the technique of 'borrowing' the mountain landscapes that so often form the backdrop to vistas.

However the series of blows that have brought all but the most robust and well-endowed estates in Britain to their knees have been felt most acutely in Wales. Add to that the still widespread perception that Wales lacks sites of historic value, together with the vulnerability of gardens compared with buildings, and it is hardly surprising that too many of the finest gardens and landscapes in Wales lie dismembered, in decay, despoiled or threatened by unsympathetic development.

The now self-evident fact that they are as much a part of the Welsh heritage as the buildings and natural landscapes has only recently been brought on to the agenda, largely through the work of Cadw, together with a handful of indomitable owners, including the National Trust (it is no coincidence that all three gardens in that first list are in the custody of the Trust), a handful of local authorities and – since 1989 – the Welsh Historic Gardens Trust. One of the most tangible measures of the success of this raising of consciousness is that the provisional register of sites of special historic importance is now one hundred times longer than the number we first thought of!

Photograph John Savidge

Hafod, Cwmystwyth. The Cavern Cascade, a breath-taking artefact in the Picturesque tradition.

Photograph John Savidge

Hafod, Cwymstwyth in Dyfed. Thomas Johnes's archetypical Picturesque landscape of the late 18th Century, awaiting revitalisation under a partnership agreement between Forest Enterprise and the Welsh Historic Gardens Trust.

Research and Revival of Garden Landscapes

Raising consciousness through careful research is one thing; actually reviving a garden landscape that has been developed or left for dead is quite another, and financing its upkeep thereafter the most difficult task of all. Frequently the site is beyond revival and involvement has to be limited to archival research, surveys of 'humps and bumps' and other archaeological techniques. On occasion a site is found that, while overgrown and virtually forgotten, is all but intact in structure. What happens next depends very largely on the owner but having 'proved' the site through research and survey, it may well be necessary to leave the shrouds of vegetation largely in place until (or if) resources are available to start the work of revitalisation: an inexpert or half-completed restoration can be far more damaging than benign neglect, particularly if the site becomes the target for vandals.

Protective Policies

Unhappily there is no statutory protection for garden landscapes and conservationists therefore have to fall back on a limited arsenal of legislation, designed primarily for the protection of structures, although most local authorities are now including protective policies in their Local Plans. However the wielding of statutory instruments is usually left to the last resort because powers of persuasiveness, tact, understanding of owners' views and first-class research are usually far more effective in the long run. Indeed much of the time is spent at the interface between owners, local authorities, developers and central governmental agencies in order to raise consciousness of the existence and value of our garden heritage and to coordinate actions and limited resources.

An alternative use for a historic garden landscape is a controversial issue, but a necessary consideration when faced with heavy capital and revenue costs for conservation. Happily the recent wave of golf course applications has subsided because there is no surer way of destroying the character and substance of a park than through the reshaping of contours, the planting of alien species in unsympathetic lines and groups, together with the infra-structure of buildings, roads, services and ancillary facilities. However, whatever the proposal, experience shows that the conservationist (and not just of gardens) gets a much better hearing if he avoids saying, "don't", in favour of, "why not do it this way?" Handled sensitively develop-ment can coexist with conservation and often to mutual advantage, especially when grant-aid is available.

The Evolution of Gardens

Not all gardens and parks of historic importance are open to visitors; moreover some of those that are open may well be more of archaeological than horticultural interest. Nevertheless anyone wishing to trace the development of gardening in Wales throughout this millenium will find no difficulty in doing so and will certainly not be confined to our initial list. Elisabeth Whittle's recent book, 'The Historic Gardens of Wales', is an essential guide through the centuries which could start in the Roman fortress of Isca (Carleon) in Gwent, going on to the C14 park of the bishop of St David's at Lamphey in Pembrokeshire, back to Gwent to the Tudor gardens at Raglan Castle, across to the turf-covered remnants of a sophisticated Renaissance garden at Old Gwernyfed (now a country hotel) in South Powys, further north to the dramatic, Italianate gardens of Powis Castle; Tredegar House, Erddig, The Gnoll, Dynevor Park (where Capability Brown is said to have noted that "Nature has been truly bountiful and Art has done no harm"), the archetypical Picturesque landscape of Thomas Johnes and others at Hafod, Glynllifon in Gwynedd which is just one of many splendid C19 sites, Bodnant and Dyffryn which are outstanding representatives of this century.

The garden landscape heritage of Wales is as rich as it is diverse. Much of it has suffered from neglect, ignorance and unwitting damage, but that is now changing: in a number of instances decay is being replaced by revival through careful conservation. Discerning visitors have an important role to play in this transformation.

The Welsh Historic Gardens Trust, Plas Tyllwyd, Tanygroes, Cardigan SA43 2JD. Telephone 0239 810432.

Photograph John Savidge

Powis Castle, Montgomeryshire. One of the few Italianate gardens in Britain, largely unaltered and in magnificent condition, in the care of the National Trust.

"The loveliest Castle in the whole world."
LORD CONWAY

LEEDS CASTLE, KENT

Open every day from mid-March to
October; at weekends in winter; plus "Christmas Week"

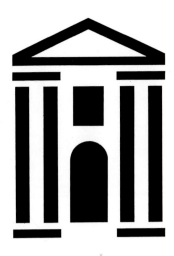

Become a Friend of the Historic Houses Association

over 270
Houses & Gardens
to
Visit Free

What is the HHA?

The Historic Houses Association was formed in 1973 by owners of some of Britain's best known Heritage properties. It has grown to represent over 1,400 owners and guardians of historic houses, parks and gardens in private ownership in the United Kingdom. The owners are responsible for looking after and financing their own properties. The HHA exists to provide practical advice and professional services to the owners and to represent them as a group. Private ownership is now widely recognised as the best way to preserve the Nation's great country houses, interiors and gardens and to maintain their atmosphere and sense of continuity.

Who are the Friends?

Friends are a small but important group of people who are interested in the heritage and enjoy visiting country houses. They can visit 280 HHA members' properties free of charge and become involved in the HHA's work at a regional level. They pay a subscription to the Association on an annual basis.

Please ask for information and subscription rates:
Mrs. Rachel Oakley,
Historic Houses Association, Membership Department
PO Box 21, Unit 7, Campus 5, The Business Park, Letchworth, Herts. SG6 2JF.
Tel: (0462) 675848

Come and enjoy two outstanding examples of 18th century genius near Ripon, North Yorkshire

Newby Hall

Newby Hall, the lived-in home of the Compton family contains wonderful and rare treasures. The glorious gardens cover some twenty-five acres and in 1986 received the Christies/Historic Houses Association "Garden of the Year" Award.

Fountains Abbey

and Gardens

The magnificent views of Fountains Abbey provide the dramatic focal point of the eighteenth century landscape garden at Studley Royal. Famous for its water gardens, ornamental buildings and vistas, this National Trust property has been awarded World Heritage Status.

& Studley Royal

For opening times see North Yorkshire section.

Palace of Holyroodhouse
Edinburgh

The ridge, known as the Royal Mile, that slopes downwards from Edinburgh Castle, comes to a majestic conclusion at Holyroodhouse where Palace and Abbey stand against the spectacular backdrop of Salisbury Crags.

See Lothian Section for further details.

Windsor Castle

For over 900 years, Windsor Castle has served as residence and fortress for the British Monarchy, acting as a spectacular backdrop for the important Ceremonies of State, including the gatherings of The Knights of The Garter.

See Berkshire section for further details.

HERITAGE EDUCATION TRUST

HISTORIC HOUSES AND THE ARTS: EDUCATION WITH INSPIRATION

ETHA in Action at Boughton House

On a glorious summer evening in June, 1992, Boughton House, and its grounds became the stage for Northamptonshire schoolchildren to bring history alive through music, art, drama, and dance. Thursday, 25th June was for Boughton the culmination of what everyone involved hopes is only the first instalment of the Heritage Education Trust's ETHA project – Education Through Heritage and the Arts.

Gareth Fitzpatrick, Director of the Living Landscape Trust at Boughton House and Bert Gill, County Arts Inspector, had put together an ETHA IN ACTION event involving over two hundred children drawn from all age ranges. The House, the grounds and the contents at Boughton provided settings for a series of events showing how an historic property, its contents and surroundings can be used to inspire children and enliven the curriculum.

The programme was devised to take place at various locations in and around the House and the audience was invited to move freely between one event and another. Thus guests arriving in the courtyard would see 'pilgrims' from Geddington Primary School enacting a mummers' play; passing through the archway to the lawns there was Barton Seagrave Primary School in fifteenth century costume performing an elaborate dance of the period drawn from the manuscripts in the Boughton music library. Meanwhile, from within, the sounds of music beckoned visitors who upon entering discovered pupils from All Saints Middle School playing music from the Library in Boughton House and members of the County Youth Choir singing madrigals all in the ideal setting of the Great Hall. One of the pieces had been composed by a pupil inspired by the contemporary music which she had studied on a visit to the House.

Of outstanding interest in the Great Hall are the Painted Ceiling depicting the marriage of Hercules and Hecuba and the family portraits including one of Ralph, first Duke of Montagu and his second wife, the Duchess of Albemarle. The children of Kingswood School constructed an ingenious costume drama inspired by the portraits and the Painted Ceiling based on an incident in which Ralph dressed as a Chinese emperor, wooed his second wife. As the audience left the Great Hall there on the lawns in the long shadows of the declining sun were four 'A' level students doing a Stately Dance – a very lively one – which they had themselves choreographed to the Music for the Royal Fireworks which the second Duke of Montagu had commissioned Handel to write while the composer was paying a visit to Boughton.

Pupils from Barton Seagrave Primary School rehearse their fifteenth century dance for ETHA in Action at Boughton House.

European Arts Festival

One of the most exciting developments for the Heritage Education Trust in 1992 was the approach from European Arts Festival with a request to set up educational events in historic properties during the six months July–December 1992 in celebration of the U.K. Presidency of the Community. Grants were to be available through HET for properties which could come up with imaginative Heritage Education schemes with a European focus. The Trust had exactly one month to draft, print and circulate information to properties and to deliver their finished proposals, fully documented and budgeted, to European Arts Festival. With the wholehearted co-operation of Reed Information Services Ltd., sponsors of the Sandford Award, and the positive response from properties, this seemingly impossible brief was accomplished. The Trust was able to announce thirteen European Arts Festival Awards, eight of which went to Sandford Award holders.

The whole exercise was an example of how a small voluntary body like the Heritage Education Trust and its network of Sandford Award holding properties can respond to challenge as pin-pointed in 'The Individual and the Community':

Silk-Screen printing of the European Arts Festival symbol was part of a Heritage Education 'European Fun Day'' at Culzean Castle and Country Park which also included dance & drama.

'Dedicated individuals and groups can act flexibly; they can spot and fill gaps in provision quickly. Their services are personally based and can be readily tailored to individual needs.'

(Section 1:3 – *The Individual and the Community*, issued by the Home Office and the Central Office of Information, and with a foreword by the Prime Minister.)

Opera North at Harewood House

One of the proposals to win a Heritage Education Trust European Arts Festival Award came from Diane Holloway, Education Officer at Harewood House. Sandford Award 1989. Diane had master-minded a brilliant ETHA IN ACTION event at Harewood earlier in the year, so her mind was attuned to the idea of Heritage Education working through the arts when the European Arts Festival opportunity arose. Opera North were already in-volved in European Arts Festival with their first ever staging of The Duenna, an opera by the Spanish composer Roberto Gerhard, so she asked their education team to put on a schools' workshop at Harewood.

The Opera North team came up with an idea which was daring in conception and brilliant in execution. Two schools, Pudsey Grangefield and Crawshaw School were asked to supply two teams fifteen children each. They were not to be selected for special music or drama ability. The challenge was to create their own version of 'The Duenna' using the setting of Harewood for their inspiration – very much an ETHA IN ACTION approach. They had to create everything – story line, characters, words and music – and then perform the results of their three-day effort before an adult audience in the magnificent gallery at Harewood House.

Stephen Page, Acting Community Officer for Opera North assembled a young group comprising an opera director Jonathan Alver, a music director Nick Skilbeck, an actor Paul Walton, and two singers, Clare Rutter soprano, and Michael Kinnerly tenor.

In co-operation with Diane Holloway, Education Officer at Harewood House, the team set about the unlikely task of getting two groups of British children from different schools to come together to explore the idea of choosing between money and love in finding happiness. Three days of intensive work resulted in this theme being presented in a musical performance of verve and beauty in surroundings of the utmost grandeur and in a way which touched the audience: hankies were out, tears flowed and the 'tingle factor' was palpable.

Susannah Daley directs Gondal theatre actresses in the roles of Charlotte and Emily Brontë in front of Haworth Parsonage. The Brontë Society's successful submission to the Heritage Education Trust for a European Arts Festival grant was for a drama presentation inspired by the Sisters' visit to Brussels in 1842.

The first job was to get the two groups to work with each other, so they played games. Then they were talked through the story of 'The Duenna'. Once they had got the hang of it – and The Duenna's twists and turns are as complicated as most opera plots – they were all given characters and taken round the House. They had to look at it through the

Opera North's Heritage Education European Arts Festival Workshop. Jonathan Alver in the Long Gallery, Harewood House directs the children of Pudsey Grangefield and Crawshaw Schools, Leeds, in 'Greed and Passion' – their version of Robert Gerhard's Spanish opera. The Duenna Michael Kennerly (tenor) and Clare Rutter (Soprano) are the professionals (centre) singing with the children.
Photo: Jack Hicks

eyes of their adopted characters and make observations on the way. These were all recorded by the accompanying tutors. Then all repaired to the Education Room where the mass of material was edited and shaped into a story.

Once the story was in place songs had to be created: words first, music second. Children came up with suggested lines to cover aspects of the plot and gradually the words of a song were shaped to advance the story. Then in a similar process the children were invited to sing the lines. Nick Skilbeck played the suggestions on the piano and steadily the music evolved. As each song was completed it was sung by all the children in chorus accompanied by the piano with Clare Rutter, soprano and Michael Kinnerly, tenor singing along too but holding themselves back until the final repeat. Then with stunning effect they unleashed the fullness of their voices: the children were overwhelmed by a power and beauty which they can never have heard before and will long to hear again.

When it was all over one of the teachers, Gillian Seward, Head of Music at Pudsey Grangefield School said, 'I feel rather shell-shocked: it was all so beautiful. It was such an amazing experience I shall never forget it and neither I am sure will the pupils.' With such words Gillian was surely speaking for everyone in the audience. As for the children, let one of them have the last word:
'Are *we* going to perform in the House? Whow!'

MARTIN DYER
Heritage Education Trust

The Heritage Education Trust has published a pamphlet, ETHA IN ACTION: Guidelines for Schools and Properties. £2.20 post free direct from the Heritage Education Trust, The University College of Ripon & York St. John, College Road, Ripon HG4 2QX.

Sandford Award Winners

Complete List, 1978–1992

The following properties received Sandford Awards in the years in brackets after their names in recognition of the excellence of their educational services and facilities and their outstanding contribution to Heritage Education. Two or more dates indicate that the property has been reviewed and received further recognition under the system of Quinquennial Review introduced by the Heritage Education Trust in 1986.

Any property which wishes to retain its listing must apply for review of its educational services and facilities five years after the date of its last award.

The closing date for initial applications and quinquennial review is 31st March.

AVONCROFT MUSEUM OF BUILDINGS, Bromsgrove, Worcs (**1988**)

*BASS MUSEUM, VISITOR CENTRE AND SHIRE HORSE STABLES, Burton on Trent, Staffs (**1990**)

BEAULIEU ABBEY, Nr. Lyndhurst, Hampshire (**1978**) (**1986**) (**1991**)

*BEDE MONASTERY MUSEUM, Jarrow, Tyne and Wear (**1988**)

BEWDLEY MUSEUM, Worcestershire (**1992**)

BICKLEIGH CASTLE, Nr. Tiverton, Devon (**1983**) (**1988**)

BLENHEIM PALACE, Woodstock, Oxfordshire (**1982**) (**1987**) (**1992**)

*BOLLING HALL, Bradford, West Yorkshire (**1978**) (**1987**)

BOUGHTON HOUSE, Kettering, Northants (**1988**)

BUCKFAST ABBEY, Buckfastleigh, Devon (**1985**) (**1990**)

CANTERBURY CATHEDRAL, Canterbury, Kent (**1988**)

CASTLE MUSEUM, York (**1987**)

CASTLE WARD, County Down, Northern Ireland (**1980**) (**1987**)

CATHEDRAL & ABBEY CHURCH OF ST. ALBAN, St. Albans, Herts (**1986**) (**1991**)

*THE CECIL HIGGINS ART GALLERY AND MUSEUM & THE BEDFORD MUSEUM, Bedford (**1989**)

*CHATTERLEY WHITFIELD MINING MUSEUM, Tunstall, Stoke on Trent (**1988**)

CLIVE HOUSE MUSEUM, Shrewsbury, Shropshire (**1992**)

*COLDHARBOUR MILL, Working Wool Museum, Cullompton, Devon (**1989**)

COMBE SYDENHAM, Nr. Taunton, Somerset (**1984**) (**1989**)

CRATHES CASTLE and GARDENS, Kincardineshire (**1992**)

CROXTETH HALL and COUNTRY PARK, Liverpool, Merseyside (**1980**) (**1989**)

CULZEAN CASTLE and COUNTRY PARK, Ayrshire, Scotland (**1984**) (**1989**)

*DOVE COTTAGE and THE WORDSWORTH MUSEUM, Grasmere, Cumbria (**1990**)

DRUMLANRIG CASTLE and COUNTRY PARK, Dumfriesshire, Scotland (**1989**)

DULWICH PICTURE GALLERY, London (**1990**)

ERDDIG HALL, Nr. Wrexham, Clwyd (**1991**)

GAINSBOROUGH OLD HALL, Gainsborough, Lincolnshire (**1988**)

GEORGIAN HOUSE, Edinburgh, Lothian Region (**1978**)

HAREWOOD HOUSE, Leeds, West Yorkshire (**1979**) (**1989**)

HELMSHORE TEXTILE MUSEUM, Lancashire (**1990**)

HOLDENBY HOUSE, Northampton, Northamptonshire (**1985**) (**1991**)

HOLKER HALL, Cark in Cartmel, Cumbria (**1982**) (**1988**)

HOPETOUN HOUSE, South Queensferry, Lothian Region (**1983**) (**1991**)

KINGSTON LACY HOUSE, Wimborne, Dorset (**1990**)

LEIGHTON HALL, Carnforth, Lancashire (**1982**)

LICHFIELD CATHEDRAL AND VISITORS' STUDY CENTRE, Lichfield, Staffordshire (**1991**)

MACCLESFIELD MUSEUMS, Macclesfield (**1988**)

MOSELEY OLD HALL, Wolverhampton, West Midlands (**1983**) (**1989**)

NATIONAL WATERWAYS MUSEUM, Gloucester (**1991**)

NORTON PRIORY, Cheshire (**1992**)

*OAKWELL HALL COUNTRY PARK, Birstall, West Yorkshire (**1988**)

PENHOW CASTLE, Nr. Newport, Gwent (**1980**) (**1986**)

QUARRY BANK MILL, Styal, Cheshire (**1987**) (**1992**)

ROCKINGHAM CASTLE, Nr. Corby, Northamptonshire (**1980**) (**1987**) (**1992**)

THE SHUGBOROUGH ESTATE, Stafford (**1987**) (**1992**)

TATTON PARK, Knutsford, Cheshire (**1979**) (**1986**) (**1991**)

*TOWER OF LONDON, Tower Bridge, London (**1978**) (**1986**) (**1991**)

*WIGAN PIER, Lancashire (**1987**) (**1992**)

WIGHTWICK MANOR, Wolverhampton, West Midlands (**1986**) (**1991**)

WIMPOLE HALL, Nr. Cambridge (**1988**)

*WILBERFORCE HOUSE and the GEORGIAN HOUSES, Hull (**1990**)

YORK MINSTER, York (**1984**) (**1989**)

1992 RESULTS

Full Sandford Awards

BEWDLEY MUSEUM
CLIVE HOUSE MUSEUM
CRATHES CASTLE and GARDENS
NORTON PRIORY MUSEUM and WALLED GARDEN

Highly Commended

SIR HAROLD HILLIER GARDENS and ARBORETUM

Quinquennial Review

At quinquennial review a successful applicant will receive either a second Sandford Award indicating that educational services and facilities have been developed and improved since the date of the last award, or continued listing indicating that the educational services have maintained their original level of excellence.

BLENHEIM PALACE	**Sandford Award**
QUARRY BANK MILL	**Sandford Award**
ROCKINGHAM CASTLE	**Sandford Award**
SHUGBOROUGH	**Sandford Award**
WIGAN PIER	**Sandford Award**

The Sandford Awards are administered by the Heritage Education Trust and sponsored by Reed Information Services Ltd.

Full details of the Sandford Award and the work of the **Heritage Education Trust** from: **Martyn Dyer, Chief Executive, Heritage Education Trust, The University College of Ripon & York St. John, College Road, Ripon, HG4 2QX. Tel: 0765 602691 Ext 297.**

For details of museums shown in the above list with a star, please refer to **Museums and Galleries in Great Britain and Ireland, 1993 edition.**

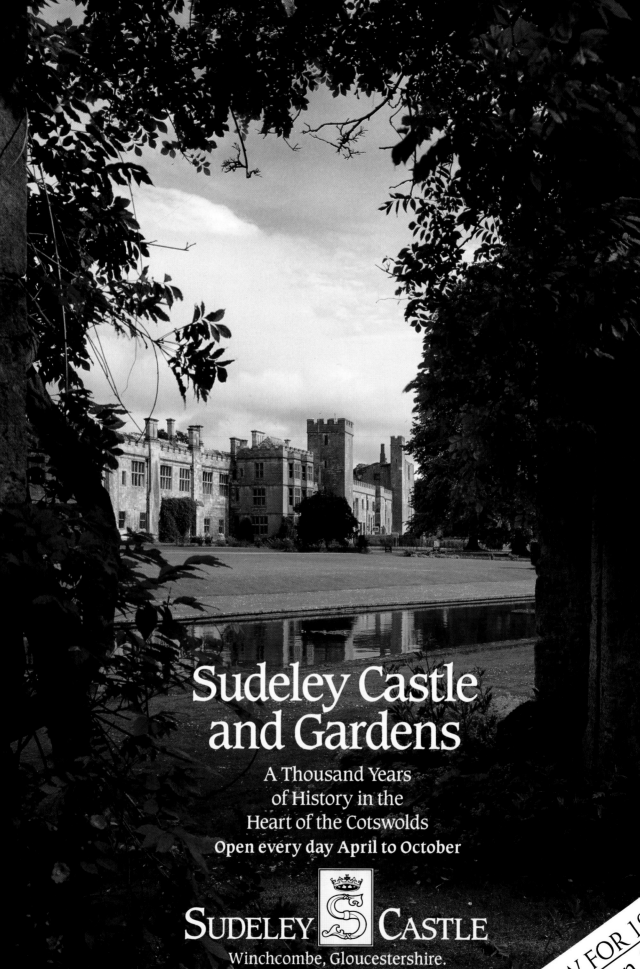

Sudeley Castle and Gardens

A Thousand Years
of History in the
Heart of the Cotswolds
Open every day April to October

SUDELEY 𝒮 CASTLE

Winchcombe, Gloucestershire.
Telephone: Cheltenham (0242) 602308

❖ NEW FOR 1993 ❖
Exhibition Centre

Historic Houses Castles & Gardens
in Great Britain and Ireland

△ Denotes guided tours of the Building

&. Denotes the major part of the property is suitable for wheelchairs

Ⓔ Denotes educational services recognised by the Heritage Education Trust

Ⓢ Denotes that all property is a recipient of the Sandford Award

🦡 **The National Trust**   Denotes properties in the care of The National Trust

Denotes properties in the care of The National Trust for Scotland

English✠Heritage   Denotes properties in the care of English Heritage

🏛 Denotes property owned and administered by a member of HHA

Denotes property in the care of CADW

Denotes property under the auspices of HITHA

AVON

BARSTAPLE HOUSE (TRINITY ALMSHOUSES)

Bristol map G4
Telephone: (0272) 265777 (Warden)
(Bristol Municipal Charities)

Victorian almshouse with garden courtyard.

Location: Old Market Street, Bristol; ½ m from City centre on A420.
Station(s): Bristol Temple Meads (¾ m).
Open: GARDEN & EXTERIOR OF BUILDINGS ONLY, now extensively renovated. All the year - Week-days 10-4.
Admission: Free.
The Almshouse is occupied mainly by elderly residents & their rights for privacy should be respected.

BECKFORD'S TOWER

Bath map G4
Telephone: (0225) 312917
(The Beckford Tower Trust)

Built 1827 by William Beckford of Fonthill. A small museum (first floor) illustrating Beckford's life; fine views from Belvedere (156 steps).

Location: 2 m from Bath Spa Station via Lansdown Road.
Station(s): Bath Spa (2 m).
Open: Apr to end Oct - Sats, Suns & Bank Hol Mons 2-5. Parties other days by arrangement.
Admission: £1, Chd & OAPs 50p.

BLAISE CASTLE HOUSE MUSEUM

Henbury map G4
Telephone: (0272) 506789
(City of Bristol)

CLAVERTON MANOR

nr Bath map G4 △ Ⓔ
Telephone: (0225) 460503
(The American Museum in Britain)

A Greek Revival House high above the valley of the River Avon. Completely furnished rooms showing American decorative arts from the late 17th to the mid 19th centuries. Galleries of special exhibits. Paintings, furniture, glass, silver, textiles, miniature rooms and Folk Art. Dallas Pratt Collection of Historical Maps. American gardens.

Location: 2½ m from Bath Station via Bathwick Hill; 3¼ m SE of Bath via Warminster Road (A36) & Claverton village. Bus 18 (to University) from bus station - alight The Avenue, 10 mins walk to Museum.
Station(s): Bath Spa (2½ m).
Open: 27 Mar to 7 Nov every day (except Mons) 2-5; Bank Hols Sun and Mon 11-5. Gardens open throughout the season 1-6pm *(except Mon).*
Admission: House and Grounds £4.50, Chd £2.50 and OAPs £4. (1992 prices) Grounds and Galleries only £1.50, Chd £1. Adult parties by previous arrangement with the Secretary. Free Car Park.
Refreshments: Tea with American cookies.

1

CLEVEDON COURT   🍂 The National Trust

nr Clevedon map F4
Telephone: (0275) 872257

A 14th century manor house incorporating a 12th century tower and a 13th century hall with terraced 18th century garden; rare shrubs and plants. The home of the Elton family. Important collections of Nailsea glass and Eltonware.

Location: 1½ m E of Clevedon on the Bristol Road B3130.
Station(s): Yatton (3 m).
Open: Apr 1 to Sept 30 - Weds, Thurs & Suns, also Bank Hol Mons 2.30-5.30 (last adm 5).
Admission: £3.20, Chd £1.60 (children under 17 must be accompanied by an adult).
Refreshments: Tea room in old kitchen open 2.30-5 (not NT).
No dogs. Unsuitable for wheelchairs. Coaches by appointment.

DYRHAM PARK   🍂 The National Trust

nr Bristol and Bath map G4   ♿
Telephone: (027237) 2501

Late 17th century house in a splendid deer park. The Blathwayt furniture and Dutch paintings in a fine series of panelled rooms.

Location: 12 m E of Bristol approach from Bath/Stroud Road (A46), 2 m S of Tormarton interchange with M4, 8 m N of Bath.
Open: Park - Daily 12-5.30 (or dusk if earlier), last adm 5. *Closed* Christmas Day. House & Garden: Apr 3 to Oct 31 - Daily (except Thurs & Frid) 12-5.30. Last adm 5, or dusk if earlier.
Admission: House, Gardens & Park £4.70, Chd £2.30. *Parties must book.* Park only: £1.50, Chd 75p.
Refreshments: In the Orangery.
Dog walking area provided but no dogs in deer park. Wheelchairs provided. Braille guide.

HORTON COURT   🍂 The National Trust

Horton map G4   ♿

A Cotswold manor house restored and altered in the 19th century. 12th century hall and late Perpendicular ambulatory in garden only shown.

Location: 3 m NE of Chipping Sodbury, ¼ m N of Horton, 1 m W of Bath/Stroud Road (A46).
Open: HALL & AMBULATORY ONLY: Apr 3 to Oct 30 - Weds & Sats 2-6 (or sunset if earlier). *Other times by written appointment with the tenant.*
Admission: £1.50, Chd 75p. *No reduction for parties.*
No dogs. Unsuitable for coaches. Wheelchairs - ambulatory only. No WCs.

THE MANOR HOUSE

Walton-in-Gordano map F4
Telephone: (0275) 872067
(Mr & Mrs Simon Wills)

4 acres, mainly shrubs and fine trees, bulbs, alpines and herbaceous plants.

Location: W of Bristol; via B3124 from Clevedon to Portishead; driveway on left before 1st houses in Walton-in-Gordano.
Open: GARDEN ONLY: Weds & Thurs Apr 14 to Sept 16 and Oct 20 to Nov 4, 10-4. Suns May 2, Jun 6, Jul 25, Aug 29. Mons Apr 12, May 3, Aug 30. By appointment all year.
Admission: £1, accompanied Chd free. *In aid of National Gardens Scheme and St. Peter's Hospice.*
Plants for sale. No dogs. Coaches by appointment only.

NUMBER ONE, ROYAL CRESCENT

Bath map G4
Telephone: (0225) 428126
(Bath Preservation Trust)

A Georgian Town House at the eastern end of Bath's most magnificent crescent; redecorated and furnished to show the visitor how it might have appeared in the late 18th century.
Location: Bath.
Open: Mar 2 - Oct 31 Tues to Sun 10.30-5, Nov 1 - Dec 12 Tues to Sun 10.30-4. Last adm half an hour before closing. Special tours by arrangement with Administrator.
Admission: £3, Chd/Students/OAPs/Adult Groups £2.20, School Groups £2.
Museum. Shop.

SHERBORNE GARDEN (PEAR TREE HOUSE)

Litton map G4
Telephone: (0761) 241220
(Mr & Mrs John Southwell)

3½ acres landscaped into several gardens of distinctive character. Cottage garden, rock garden, large ponds with moisture gardens, pinetum, mixed wood. Collections of acers, birches, species roses, clematis. Special collection of hollies (over 180 varieties). Featured on 'Gardeners World'. Picnic area.

Location: Litton, 8 miles N of Wells on B3114 off A39.
Open: Suns & Mons; June 14 - Sept 6. *for National Gardens Scheme;* also Apr 11, Jun 13, Oct 10. 11-6.30. Other times by appointment.
Admission: £1.50 Chd free. Parties by arrangement. Free car parking.
Refreshments: Home-made teas on National Gardens Scheme days (except in Apr) and for parties; at other times tea/coffee available.
Suitable for the disabled. Dogs on leads.

VINE HOUSE

Henbury, Bristol map G4
Telephone: (0272) 503573
(Professor & Mrs T. F. Hewer)

Two acres. Trees, shrubs, small water garden; bulbs; naturalised garden landscape.

Location: 4 m NW of Bristol centre next to 'Salutation' Bus stop.
Station(s): Bristol Parkway; Bristol Temple Meads each about 4 m from Henbury.
Open: GARDENS ONLY. Sat, Sun Apr 17, 18 and Sun, Mon May 30, 31 (2-6pm). Also open by appointment throughout the year.
Admission: £1, Chd & OAPs 50p. *In aid of National Gardens Scheme & 'Friends of Blaise. Dogs on leads.*

BEDFORDSHIRE

BUSHMEAD PRIORY   English ♯ Heritage

map K6
Telephone: (023 062) 614

The priory was a small house for Augustinian canons and founded in about 1195. The remains consist of the 13th century canon's refectory occupying one side of the former cloister. The timber-framed roof is a rare example of an almost complete crown-post construction of about 1250. The refectory contains wall-paintings and interesting stained glass.

Location: 4 m west of A1 at St Neots.
Open: Good Friday or Apr 1 (whichever is earlier) to Sept 30: Daily 10-6; Winter: Oct 1 to Maundy Thurs or Mar 31 (whichever is earlier) Tues to Sun 10-4.
Admission: £1.20, Concessions 90p, Chd 60p.

CHICKSANDS PRIORY

Shefford map K5
Telephone: (02302) 4195
(Ministry of Defence Property Administered by RAF Commander).

Chicksands Priory was founded by Payne De Beauchamp and his wife Countess Rohese for Nuns and Canons of the English Order of Gilbertines c 1150. Dissolved and surrendered 1538, it was sold by Henry VIII for £810 11s 8d to the Snowe family 1540. Acquired by the Osborne family in 1576, it so remained their family home until sold to The Crown, 1936. 13th and 15th century monastic remains survive with architectural work by Isaac Ware (1740) and James Wyatt (1813). Stained glass, Chinese wallpaper, Coade statuary have been uncovered since the Anglo-American Group of Friends opened the building to the public, 1975. The 18th century Venetian Prayer Book purchased by Sir Danvers Osborn, 3rd Baronet, is shown in the refurbished Private Chapel. Ghosts of former inhabitants are said to haunt the building; a plaque boasts of a walled up Nun within the cloisters and remains of monastic residents are buried in the still landscaped gardens. Game larder, Orangery and grapevines are on show exclusive of guided tour of the interior, which takes approximately 45 minutes. Past visitors to Chicksands include St Thomas Becket, King James I, HRH Princess Alice, Duchess of Gloucester, the Duke of Bedford, Terence, Cardinal Cooke. Following intensive external restoration by the Ministry of Defence, The Friends are decorating and restoring the interior.

Location: In RAF Chicksands 1¼ miles from Shefford. Entrances on A507 Shefford to Ampthill Road and on A600 Shefford to Bedford Road.
Open: 1st & 3rd Suns of Month Apr to Oct 2-5; last tour 4.30. Guided tours only.
Admission: No adm charge - donations for interior decoration requested, suggested donation £1 per adult. Parties by appointment only.
Refreshments: Light refreshments at Priory. Nearest hotels at Biggleswade, Bedford & Hitchin, all being 7 miles from Chicksands.
Car parking. Unsuitable for wheelchairs. *Friends of Priory licensed to open Priory to public and redecorate interior.*

CECIL HIGGINS ART GALLERY & MUSEUM

Castle Close, Bedford map J6   ♿
Telephone: (0234) 211222
(Gallery jointly owned and administered by the North Bedfordshire Borough Council and the Trustees of the Cecil Higgins Art Gallery)

Award-winning re-created Victorian Mansion, original home of Cecil Higgins. Rooms displayed to give 'lived-in' atmosphere, including bedroom with furniture designed by William Burges (1827-1881). Adjoining gallery with outstanding collections of ceramics, glass and watercolours. Situated in gardens leading down to the river embankment.

Location: Centre of Bedford, just off The Embankment.
Station(s): Bedford Midland (1 m). Bus Station: (½ m).Trains from London (St.Pancras), and King's Cross Thameslink - fast trains 36 mins. United Counties X4 Bedford/Milton Keynes - Buckingham - Bicester - Oxford; X3 Northampton - Bedford - Cambridge; Coach link from London Marylebone Station.
Open: Tues-Fri 12.30-5, Sat 11-5, Sun 2-5. *Closed* Mons (except Bank Hol Mons), Christmas Day, Boxing Day, Good Fri.
Admission: Free. Group bookings by prior arrangement.
Refreshments: By prior arrangement.
Facilities for the disabled.

LUTON HOO

Luton map K5
Telephone: (0582) 22955
(The Wernher Family)

WOBURN ABBEY

Woburn map J5
Telephone: (0525) 290666; Catering (0525) 290662; Antiques Centre (0525) 290350
(The Marquess of Tavistock and Trustees of the Bedford Estates)

Location: In Woburn 8½ m NW of Dunstable on A4012. 42 m from London off M1 at junctions 12 or 13.
Station(s): Leighton Buzzard and Bletchley (Euston) and Flitwick (Kings Cross Thameslink). The three local stations are between 6 and 7 miles from Woburn village, which is 1½m from the Abbey.
Open: HOUSE AND GARDENS. Jan 1 to Mar 28 - Sats & Suns only. House 11-4.45; Park 10.30-3.45. Mar 29 to Oct 31 - Daily. House: Weekdays 11-5.45; Suns 11-6.15. Park: Weekdays 10-4.45; Suns 10-5.45. Last adm to House 45 mins before closing time every day.
Admission: Including Private Apartments: House £6 Chd (12-16) £2, OAPS £5 (reduced rates apply when Private Apartments are in use by the Family). Group rates are available. Free car park.
Refreshments: Flying Duchess Pavilion Coffee Shop, Restaurants for pre-booked parties.

WREST PARK HOUSE AND GARDENS   English Heritage

Silsoe map J5
Telephone: (0525) 60718

Home of the Dukes of Bedford for over 350 years, the Abbey contains one of the most important private art collections in the world, including paintings by Canaletto, Van Dyck, Cuyp, Teniers, Rembrandt, Gainsborough, Reynolds, Velazques and many other famous artists. French and English 18th century furniture, silver and the fabulous Sevres dinner service presented to the 4th Duke by Louis XV of France. The 3,000 acre Deer Park has lots of wild life, including nine species of deer, roaming freely. One of these, the Pere David, descended from the Imperial Herd of China, was saved from extinction at Woburn and is now the largest breeding herd of this specie in the world. In 1985 twenty two Pere David were given by the Family to the People's Republic of China with the hope that the specie may become re-established in its natural habitat. The Marquess of Tavistock visited Beijing (Peking) to release the herd at Nan Haizi, the former Imperial hunting ground outside Beijing (Peking). The tour of the Abbey covers three floors including the Crypt. It is regretted that wheelchairs can only be accommodated in the House by prior arrangement with the Administrator but unfortunately the Crypt area is not accessible. The 40 shop Antiques Centre is probably the most unusual such centre outside London - the shop fronts having been rescued from demolition sites in various parts of Britain. Shipping can be arranged on a world wide basis. All catering is operated by ourselves with banqueting, conferences, receptions and company days out our speciality, in the beautiful setting of the Sculpture Gallery, overlooking the private gardens. There is a Pottery and summer weekend events are arranged. Extensive picnic areas with ample coach and car parking. Gift shops, Pottery and Camping Equipment Centre.

Here is a history of English gardening in the grand manner from 1700-1850, which would not, of course, be complete without some designs by 'Capability' Brown. Every whim of fashion is represented, whether it be for a Chinese bridge, artificial lake, classical temple or rustic ruin. The present house was built about 1839 by the Earl de Grey, whose family had lorded over the Manor of Wrest for 600 years. The State Rooms and gardens are open to the public.

Location: ¾ m (1 km) east of Silcoe.
Open: Good Friday or Apr 1 (whichever is earlier) to Sept 30, weekends and Bank Hols only 10-6.
Admission: £1.70, Concessions £1.30, Chd 85p.
Refreshments: Available.

BERKSHIRE

BASILDON PARK 🌺 The National Trust

Lower Basildon, Reading map J4
Telephone: (0734) 843040

Classical house built 1776. Unusual Octagon room; fine plasterwork; important paintings and furniture, Garden and woodland walks.

Location: 7 m NW of Reading between Pangbourne and Streatley on A329. Leave M4 at junction 12.
Station(s): Pangbourne (2½m); Goring and Streatley (3 m).
Open: Apr to end Oct - Weds to Sats 2-6; Suns & Bank Hol Mons 12-6. Grounds open at 12 on Sat. Last adm to house half-hour before closing. Closed Mons (except Bank Hols), Tues & Weds following Bank Hols and Good Friday.
Admission: House & Grounds £3.50 Grounds only £2.50 Child half price. Reductions (except Suns and Bank Hol Mons) to House and Grounds for parties of 15 or more (Booking essential).
Refreshments: Tea room in house accessible to wheelchairs.
Shop. Dogs in grounds only on leads. House unsuitable for wheelchairs.

FROGMORE GARDENS

Windsor map J4
(Her Majesty The Queen)

Beautifully landscaped gardens with trees, shrubs and lake.

Location: Entrance to garden through Long Walk Gate. *(Visitors are requested kindly to refrain from entering grounds of the Home Park).*
Station(s): Windsor & Eton Central; Windsor & Eton Riverside (both 20 mins walk).
Open: GARDEN ONLY. Open on Wed May 5 & Thurs May 6: 10.30-7 (last adm 6.30) .No dogs. Free car park. Coaches by appointment only (apply to National Gardens Scheme, Hatchlands Park, East Clandon, Guildford, Surrey GU4 7RT. Tel: (0483) 211535, stating whether am or pm pass is required). The Royal Mausoleum also open on above 2 days; (In addition Mausoleum open Wed May 26: 11-4, but *not* the gardens).
Admission: Garden only £1.50, accompanied Chd free. Mausoleum Free.
Refreshments: Tent at car park - May 5 & 6.

FROGMORE HOUSE

Windsor map J4
Telephone: (0753) 868286

One of the least known royal residences Frogmore House is situated within the private Home Park at Windsor Castle. Built in the late 17th century the house is particularly associated with Queen Charlotte and with the Duchess of Kent, Queen Victoria's mother. The house has been extensively restored and is furnished with many of its original contents reflecting the taste and interests of former residents.

Open: Early August to late September. Telephone above number for details.

MAPLEDURHAM HOUSE

See under Oxfordshire.

THE OLD RECTORY

Burghfield map J4
(Mr & Mrs R. R. Merton)

Garden of horticultural interest; roses, hellebores, lilies, many rare and unusual plants from China and Japan; old-fashioned cottage plants; autumn colour.

Location: 5½ m SW of Reading, between M4 junctions 11 & 12.
Station(s): Reading and Mortimer (3½m).
Open: GARDEN ONLY. Last Wed of every month except Nov, Dec, Jan, (11-4).
Admission: 50p, Chd 10p. *In aid of National Gardens Scheme.* (Share to Save the Children and NCCPG).
Plants and produce for sale. No dogs.

Lancelot 'Capability' Brown

Born 1716 in Northumberland, Capability Brown began work at the age of 16 in the vegetable gardens of Sir William and Lady Loraine at Kirharle Tower. He left Northumberland in 1739, and records show that he worked at Stowe until 1749. It was at Stowe that Brown began to study architecture, and to submit his own plans. It was also at Stowe that he devised a new method of moving and replanting mature trees.

Brown married Bridget Wayet in 1744 and began work on the estate at Warwick Castle in 1749. He was appointed Master Gardener at Hampton Court in 1764, and planted the Great Vine at Hampton Court in 1768. Blenheim Palace designs are considered amongst Brown's finest work, and the technical achievements were outstanding even for the present day.

Capability Brown died in February 1783 of a massive heart attack. A monument beside the lake at Croome Court was erected which reads "To the memory of Lancelot Brown, who by the powers of his inimitable and creative genius formed this garden scene out of a morass". There is also a portrait of Brown at Burghley.

Capability Brown was involved in the design of grounds at the following properties included in Historic Houses Castles and Gardens:

Luton Hoo	*Corsham Court*	*Stowe*	*Burton Constable*
Bowood	*Fawley Court*	*Weston Park*	*Sledmere House*
Burghley House	*Longleat*	*Wotton House*	*Syon House*
Chilham Castle (reputed)	*Moccas Court*	*Wrest Park*	*Warwick Castle.*
Claremont	*Nuneham Park*	*Broadlands*	
Chillington Hall	*Petworth*	*Berrington Hall*	

SAVILL GARDEN

Windsor Great Park map J4
Telephone: (0753) 860222
(Crown Property)

World renowned woodland garden of 35 acres with adjoining area of herbaceous borders, rose gardens, alpine raised beds and an extensive dry garden. The whole garden offering much of great interest and beauty at all seasons.

Location: To be approached from A30 via Wick Road & Wick Lane, Englefield Green.
Station(s): Egham (3 m).
Open: Daily 10-6. *Closed* for a short period at Christmas.
Admission: £3.00, OAPs £2.50. Parties of 20 and over £2.50, accompanied Chd (under 16) free.

SWALLOWFIELD PARK

Swallowfield map J4
(Country Houses Association)

Built by the Second Earl of Clarendon in 1678.

Location: In the village of Swallowfield 6 m SE of Reading.
Open: May to September - Weds & Thurs 2-5. Last entry 4.30.
Admission: £1.50, Chd 50p.
Free car park. No dogs admitted.

VALLEY GARDENS

Windsor Great Park map J4
Telephone: (0753) 860222
(Crown Property)

Extensive woodland gardens of 400 acres which include a large heather garden offering beauty and charm at all seasons of the year.

Location: To be approached from Wick Road off A30 (1 m walk).
Station(s): Egham (3 m).
Open: Open daily from sunrise to sunset.
Admission: Free to pedestrians.
Car park adjoining gardens. £2 per car.

WELFORD PARK

nr Newbury map H4
Telephone: (048838) 203
(Mrs. A. C. Puxley)

Queen Anne house with later additions. Attractive gardens and grounds.

Location: 6 m NW of Newbury and 1 m N of Wickham village off B4000.
Open: Spring and Summer Bank Hols and June 1-26 inclusive from 2.30-5.
Admission: £3, OAP's and under 16's £2.
Interior by prior appointment only.

THE SIGN OF A GREAT DAY OUT

WINDSOR CASTLE

Windsor map J4
Telephone: (0753) 868286
(Official residence of H.M. The Queen)

Windsor Castle

See entry for details

Perhaps the largest fortress of its kind in the world, Windsor Castle has belonged to the Sovereigns of England for over 900 years, and is by far, the oldest residence still in regular use. The State Apartments, the most magnificent rooms in the Castle, are open for the majority of the year. The Gallery, which hosts a series of changing exhibitions from the Royal Collection, Queen Mary's Dolls' House and the Exhibition of The Queen's Presents and Royal Carriages are open all year.

Location: 3m off J6 of M4.
Open: Open all year (State apartments closed when Her Majesty The Queen is in official residence). **Group Discounts:** Special group rates on application. This applies to the following: The State Apartments, Exhibition of The Queen's Presents and Royal Carriages, Queen Mary's Dolls' House. *Whilst there is every intention to adhere to the above schedule this cannot be guaranteed as Windsor Castle is always subject to closure, sometimes at short notice. Enquiries: Castle (0753) 831118; St. George's Chapel (0753) 865538.*
Admission: Group Discounts: Special group rates on application. This applies to the following: State Apartments, Exhibition of The Queen's Presents and Royal Carriages, Queen Mary's Dolls' House. Separate arrangements apply for St.George's Chapel.
Refreshments: Castle Hotel (opposite).

BUCKINGHAMSHIRE

ASCOTT 🍂 The National Trust

Wing, nr Leighton Buzzard map J5 △
Telephone: (0296) 688242

Anthony de Rothschild collection of fine pictures. French and English furniture, exceptional Oriental porcelain containing examples of the Ming, K'ang Hsi and Chun ware of the Sung dynasty. Gardens contain unusual trees, flower borders, topiary sundial, naturalised bulbs and water lilies.

Location: ½ m E of Wing; 2 m SW of Leighton Buzzard, on the S side of Aylesbury/Leighton Buzzard Road (A418).
Station(s): Leighton Buzzard (2 m).
Open: HOUSE & GARDENS. Apr 12-May 16; Sept 1-30, Tues to Suns 2-6. Bank Hol Mon, Apr 12 & May 3, 2-6 (but closed Apr 13 & May 4). Garden only: Apr 7 and May 19 to Aug 30. Every Wed and last Sun in each month and Bank Hol Mon, Aug 30 2-6. Last adm 5.
Admission: House & Gardens £5, Chd £2.50; Gardens only £3, Chd £1.50. *No reduction for parties.*
Dogs on leads, in car park only. Wheelchair access to ground floor and part of garden only. Enquiries: Estate Manager. NB Owing to large number of visitors, entry is by timed ticket. Occasionally there will be considerable delays in gaining admission to the House.

CHENIES MANOR HOUSE 🏛

Chenies map J5
Telephone: (0494) 762888
(Lt Col & Mrs MacLeod Matthews)

15/16th century Manor House with fortified tower. Original home of the Earls of Bedford, visited by Henry VIII and Elizabeth I. Home of the MacLeod Matthews family. Contains contemporary tapestries and furniture. Hiding places, 'secret' passages, collection of antique dolls; medieval undercroft and well. Surrounded by beautiful gardens which have featured in many publications - a Tudor sunken garden, a white garden, herbaceous borders, a fountain court, a physic garden containing a very wide selection of medical and culinary herbs, and and two mazes. The kitchen garden is in the Victorian style with unusual vegetables and fruit. Special exhibitions throughout open period. Flower drying and arrangements.

Location: Off A404 between Amersham & Rickmansworth (M25 - junction 18).
Station(s): Chorleywood (1½ m).
Open: First week in April to end of Oct Weds and Thurs 2-5. Also open Bank Hol Mons Apr 12, May 3 and 25 and Aug 31, 2-6.
Admission: £3.20, GARDENS ONLY £1.60, Chd (under 14) half price. Parties throughout the year by prior arrangement - min charge £50.
Refreshments: Home-made teas.
Free parking. No dogs.

Editor's Note: *To avoid disappointment, visitors should be aware of the fire at Windsor Castle which occurred as this publication went to press. Therefore some of the details may be incorrect.*

CHICHELEY HALL

Newport Pagnell map J5
Telephone: (023 065) 252
(Trustees of the Hon Nicholas Beatty)

Chicheley Hall, home of the Hon. Nicholas Beatty, is an exceptionally fine early Georgian House built 1719-1723 by Francis Smith of Warwick. Here is some of the most notable brickwork to be found in any house of the period, with the four sides of the house displaying a carefully graduated crescendo of architecural effect. The interior has a striking Palladian Hall designed by Flitcroft and beautiful panelled rooms including Sir John Chester's ingenious hidden library. The rooms are furnished with fine period furniture and pictures. The BEATTY NAVAL MUSEUM at Chicheley contains many mementoes of Admiral Earl Beatty and World War I at sea. The gardens contain a formal three-sided canal designed in 1700 by George London who also worked at Hampton Court. Recently renovated 18th century dovecote. Tea Rooms and Gift Shop.

Location: 2 m E of Newport Pagnell; 11 m W of Bedford on A422.
Open: Apr 11 - May 30, and Aug: every Sun. Also Bank Hol Mons 2.30-6. Last tour 5. Day or evening parties, with or without meals, by appointment at any time throughout the summer.
Admission: £3, Chd £1.50, parties (over 20) £2.40.
Refreshments: Tea room.

Thomas Gainsborough (1727–1787)

*His paintings can be seen at the following properties included in
Historic Houses Castles and Gardens:*

> *Althorp*
> *Arundel Castle*
> *Christchurch Manor*
> *Gainsborough's House*
> *Kenwood*
> *Shalom Hall*
> *Weston Park*

CHILTERN OPEN AIR MUSEUM

Newland Park, Gorelands Lane, Chalfont St Giles map J4
Telephone: (0494) 871117
(Chiltern Open Air Museum Ltd)

A museum of historic buildings, rescued from demolition, and which reflect the vernacular heritage of the Chilterns region. You can explore barns, granaries, cartsheds and stables, a blacksmith's forge, a toll house and a vicarage room - and the collection is growing all the time. Several of the buildings incorporate displays illustrating their original use, or house exhibitions on Chiltern life and landscape. The Museum occupies 45 acres of parkland and woodland which has an attractive Nature Trail running through it.

Location: At Newland Park, Chalfont St Giles; 4½ m Amersham, 8 m Watford, 6 m Beaconsfield; 2 m A413 at Chalfont St Peter, 4 m from junction 17 on the M25 via Maple Cross and the Chalfonts.
Station(s): Chorleywood.
Open: Apr to Oct - Weds to Suns & Bank Hols 2-6. Parties & School parties by arrangement weekdays all year round.
Admission: £2.50, OAPs £2, Chd under 16yrs £2, under 5 free. Family ticket (2 adults 2 children £8).
Refreshments: Home-made teas.

CLAYDON HOUSE   The National Trust

Middle Claydon, nr Buckingham map J5
Telephone: (0296) 730349/730693

Built mid 18th century as an addition to an earlier house. The stone-faced West front contains a series of magnificent and unique rococo state-rooms, also Florence Nightingale Museum, her bedroom and sitting room.

Location: In the village of Middle Claydon, 13m NW of Aylesbury, 3½ m SW of Winslow. Signposted from A413, A421 and A41.
Open: Apr to end Oct - Sat to Wed 1-5, Bank Hol Mons 1-5. Last adm 4.30. *Closed Thurs & Frid (inc Good Friday).* PLEASE NOTE: Essential repair work may delay the property opening in April.
Admission: £3.30, Chd £1.65. Parties write to Custodian.
Refreshments: Available at house.
Dogs in park on leads only.Wheelchairs provided (access to ground floor only, half price adm.)

CLIVEDEN   The National Trust

Taplow, Maidenhead (1851) map J4 △
Telephone: (0628) 605069

Gardens contain temples by Giacomo Leoni. Box parterre, fountain, formal walks; amphitheatre, water garden, rose garden, herbaceous borders. Views of Thames.

Location: 3 m upstream from Maidenhead; 2 m N of Taplow on Hedsor Road. Main entrance opposite Feathers Inn.
Station(s): Taplow (2½ m) (not Suns); Maidenhead (4¼ m).
Open: Grounds: Mar to end Oct - Daily 11-6 or sunset if earlier. Nov and Dec: daily 11-4. Closed Jan & Feb. House: (3 Rooms Open) Apr to Oct, Thurs & Suns 3-6 (last adm 5.30).
Admission: Grounds £3.50 House £1 extra (timed ticket), Chd half price. *Parties must book.*
Refreshments: Light lunches, coffee, teas in Conservatory Restaurant Apr to end Oct (Weds to Suns & Bank Hol Mons 11-5).
No dogs in House or in gardens, in specified woodlands only on lead. Shop Apr to end Oct, Weds to Suns (incl Good Friday) & Bank Hol Mons 1-5.30pm. Also pre-Christmas Nov to Dec 19, Weds to Suns 11-4.

COWPER & NEWTON MUSEUM

Olney map J6
Telephone: (0234) 711516

Personal belongings of William Cowper and Rev. John Newton. Bobbin lace and items of local interest.

Location: Market Place, Olney; N of Newport Pagnell via A509.

DORNEY COURT

nr Windsor map J4
Telephone: (0628) 604638
(Mr & Mrs Peregrine Palmer)

One of the finest Tudor Manor Houses in England' Country Life. A visit to Dorney is a most welcome, refreshing and fascinating experience. Built about 1440 and lived in by the present family for over 400 years, this enchanting, many gabled pink brick and timber house is a joy to behold. The rooms are full of the continuing atmosphere of history: early 15th and 16th century oak, beautiful 17th century lacquer furniture, 18th and 19th century tables, 400 years of family portraits and stained glass and needlework. Charles II came here to seek the charms of Barbara Palmer, Countess of Castlemaine - 'the most intelligent beautiful and influential

of ladies'. The 14th century church of St. James next door, is a lovely, cool, cheerful and very English Church. *Country Sports Fair - Sat Jun 12, 11-4pm.*

Location: 2 m W of Eton & Windsor in village of Dorney on B3026. Signposted from M4, exit 7.
Station(s): Burnham (2 m).
Open: Easter weekend Fri to Mon; May Suns & Bank Hol Mons; also Sun, Mon & Tues in June, July, Aug & Sept; 2-5.30. Last admission and last orders for teas at 5.
Admission: £3.50, Chd over 9 £1.75. 10% discount for National Trust and NADFAS members and OAPs. Parties at other times by arrangement.
Refreshments: Home-made cream teas.

HUGHENDEN MANOR   The National Trust

High Wycombe map J5 &
Telephone: (0494) 532580

Home of Benjamin Disraeli, Earl of Beaconsfield (1847-1881). Small formal garden.

Location: 1½ m N of High Wycombe on W side Gt Missenden Road (A4128).
Station(s): High Wycombe (2 m).
Open: House & Garden. Mar - Sats & Suns only 2-6, Apr to end of Oct - Weds to Sats 2-6; Suns & Bank Hol Mons 12-6. *Closed* Good Friday. Last Adm 5.30. Shop open as House and pre-Christmas Nov to Dec 19 Wed to Sun, 12-4. *Parties must book in advance.* Dogs in Park & car park only. Wheelchair provided. Parties Weds to Frid only if booked in advance.
Admission: £3.30, Chd half price.

MILTON'S COTTAGE

Chalfont St Giles map J5 &
Telephone: (0494) 872313
(Milton Cottage Trust)

The Cottage where John Milton completed 'Paradise Lost' and began 'Paradise Regained', contains many Milton relics and a library including first and early editions and many translations into other languages. Free car park for visitors. Two museum rooms and charming cottage garden open to the public.

Location: ½ m W of A413; on road to Seer Green and Beaconsfield.
Station(s): Gerrards Cross L.T. to Amersham or Chalfont and Latimer.
Open: Mar to Oct - Tues to Sats 10-1, 2-6; Suns 2-6. Spring & Summer Bank Hol Mons 10-1, 2-6. *Closed* Mons (except Bank Hols) & Jan, Feb, Nov & Dec.
Admission: £1.50, Chd (under 15) 60p, Parties of 20 or more £1.20.

NETHER WINCHENDEN HOUSE

Aylesbury map J5 &
Telephone: (0353) 290101
(Trustees of Will Trust of J. G. C. Spencer Bernard Dec'd)

Tudor manor house with 18th century additions. Home of Sir Francis Bernard, Governor of New Jersey and Massachusetts, 1760.

Location: 1 m N of A418 Aylesbury/Thame Road, nr village of Lower Winchendon, 6 m SW Aylesbury.
Station(s): Aylesbury (7½ m).
Open: May 4 to May 31; Aug 29 & 30. 2.30-5.30. Last party each day at 4.45. Parties at any time of year by written appointment.
Admission: £1.75, Chd (under 12) and OAPs £1.25 (not weekends or Bank Hols). Correspondance to Administrator, R.V. Spencer Bernard Esq.

PRINCES RISBOROUGH MANOR HOUSE

🍂 The National Trust

Princes Risborough map J5   ♿
17th century red-brick house with Jacobean oak staircase.

Opposite church off market square in town centre.

Location: Princes Risborough (1 m).
Station(s): Open by written arrangement only - Weds 2.30-4.30. Last adm 4. Principal rooms and staircase shown. No dogs. Wheelchair access.
Admission: £1, Chd 50p. No reductions for parties.

STOWE LANDSCAPE GARDENS   🍂   The National Trust

nr Buckingham map J5
Telephone: (0280) 822850

Splendid landscape gardens with buildings and temples by Vanbrugh, Kent and Gibbs. One of the supreme creations of the Georgian era. (N.B. the main house is in the ownership of Stowe School.)

Location: 3 m NW of Buckingham, via Stowe Avenue off the A422 Buckingham/Banbury Road.
Open: Mar 27 to Apr 18. Jul 4 to Sept 5, Oct 23-31, 18-23 & Dec 27-31, Jan 1-9 & Mar 27-Apr 17 1994. Daily 10-6 or dusk if earlier. Also Apr 19 to Jul 2, Sept 6 to Oct 20: Mon, Wed & Fri 10-5 or dusk if earlier. Last adm 1 hour before closing. *Closed* Good Friday, Dec 24, 25 and 26.
Admission: Entry to Gardens £3.50, Family ticket £9. The main house belongs to Stowe School and may be open during Stowe School holidays at an additional charge of £2 (inc NT members).
Refreshments: Light refreshments and teas as above 12-5 (12-4 during Dec and Jan).
Dogs on lead only. Batricar available for disabled visitors, telephone Administrator for details.

STOWE (STOWE SCHOOL) 🏛

Buckingham map J5

Famous 18th century house formerly the home of the Duke of Buckingham. Superb landscaped gardens with largest collection of garden buildings in England by Bridgeman, Kent, Gibbs, Vanburgh and 'Capability' Brown.

Location: 4 m N of Buckingham town.
Open: HOUSE ONLY: Mar 29 - Apr 6 and Apr 13 - 18; July 6 - Aug 26 and Aug 31 - Sept 6: 2-5. Closed Sats.**Please note** it may be necessary to close the house for private functions. Please check before visiting. Tel: (0280) 813650.
Admission: £2, Chd £1.
Refreshments: Pre-booked only. Guide books, postcards, souvenirs and prints available from the Stowe Bookshop.

THE THATCHED COTTAGE

Duck Lane, Ludgershall, nr Aylesbury map H5
Telephone: (0844) 237415
(Mr & Mrs D. A. Tolman)

WADDESDON MANOR   🍂   The National Trust

nr Aylesbury map J5   △   ♿
Telephone: (0296) 651211

In 1874 Baron Ferdinand de Rothschild acquired the Buckinghamshire hilltop which became the site for the Destailleur designed chateau, around which is set one of the finest late Victorian formal gardens and parks designed by Lain. Restoration plans for the gardens include shrubberies and additional bedding to the fountain terrace. The elegant cast iron rococo style aviary, built in 1889, contains mainly softbill birds and some parrots. House closed for refurbishment during 1993. Open again in 1994. Grounds, aviary, gift shop and tear room remain open during 1992.

Location: At W end of Waddeson village; 6 m NW of Aylesbury on Bicester Road (A41). *Station(s): Aylesbury (6 m). Buses: Red Rover 1, 15, 16, from Aylesbury. (Tel: Aylesbury 28686).*
Open: GROUNDS & AVIARY ONLY Mar 3 to Dec 23 - Wed to Fri 12-5, weekends and Bank Hol Mons 12-6. Free guided tours of the grounds and aviary (to include information about refurbishment) will be available to visitors, weather permitting.
Admission: £3, Chd (5-17) £1.50, Chd under 5 free.
Refreshments: Light lunches and teas in tearoom, open as grounds.
Free parking near the stables. Play area for young children. Dogs not admitted except guide dogs. Free entry to stables for gift shop and tea room.**Shops:** Gift shop which includes Christmas shopping, open as grounds.

WEST WYCOMBE PARK (1750)   The National Trust

West Wycombe map J4 △
Telephone: (0494) 524411

Palladian house with frescoes and painted ceilings. 18th century landscape garden with lake and various classical temples.
Location: At W end of West Wycombe, S of Oxford Road (A40), 2½ m W High Wycombe.
Station(s): High Wycombe (2½ m).
Open: Grounds only: Apr & May Suns & Weds 2-6, and Easter, May Day and Spring Bank Hols. Sun & Mon 2-6. Closed Good Friday. House and Grounds: June, July & Aug, Suns to Thurs 2-6 (last adm 5.15). Entry to house by timed tickets on weekdays.
Admission: House & Grounds £4; Ground only £2.50, Chd half price,*No reduction for parties.*
Dogs in car park only. House unsuitable for wheelchairs.

WINSLOW HALL

Winslow map J5 △
Telephone: (0296) 712323
(Sir Edward & Lady Tomkins)

Built 1698-1702. Almost certainly designed by Sir Christopher Wren. Has survived without major structural alteration and retains most of its original features. Modernized and redecorated by the present owners. Good eighteenth century furniture, mostly English. Some fine pictures, clocks and carpets. Several examples of Chinese art, notably of the Tang period. Beautiful gardens with many unusual trees and shrubs.
Location: At entrance to Winslow on the Aylesbury road (A413).
Open: Open all Bank Holiday weekends except Christmas 2-5. July and Aug: Wed and Thurs 2.30-5.30 or by appointment throughout the year.
Admission: £4, Chd free.
Refreshments: Catering by arrangement.

WOTTON HOUSE

nr Aylesbury map J5
Telephone: (Administrator Mrs Patrick Brunner)

Built 1704, on the same plan as Buckingham House, which later became Buckingham Palace Interior remodelled by Sir John Soane 1820. Wrought iron by Tijou and Thomas Robinson. 'Capability' Brown landscape 1757-1760.
Location: In Wotton Underwood 2 m S of A41 midway between Aylesbury and Bicester.
Open: Wed. Aug - Tour at 2 and 3.15. Sept - Tour at 2.30.

CAMBRIDGESHIRE

ANGLESEY ABBEY AND GARDEN   The National Trust

nr Cambridge map K6
Telephone: (0223) 811200

The Abbey, founded in the reign of Henry I, was later converted to an Elizabethan manor. Contains Fairhaven collection of art treasures. About 100 acres of garden including flower borders, trees, avenues, unique garden statuary and a working water mill that grinds corn.
Location: In village of Lode 6 m NE of Cambridge on B1102, signposted off A45.
Station(s): Cambridge (6 m).
Open: House: Mar 27 to Oct 17 - Wed to Sat 1.30-5.20; *closed* Good Fri. Sun & Bank Hol Mons 1-5.20. Pre-booked parties of 15 or more (Weds, Thurs, Fris and Sats only). Garden: Mar 27 to July 11 - Wed to Sun & Bank Hol Mons 11-5.30; July 12 to Sept 7 daily 10-5.30. Sept 8 to Oct 17 - Sat to Wed 11-5.30. Lode Mill: Mar 27 to Oct 17 Wed to Sun & Bank Hol Mons 1.30-5.15.
Admission: House and Garden: £4.50, Suns and Bank Hol Mon £5.50. Pre-booked parties £3.60. Garden: £2.50, Suns & Bank Hol Mon £3, Chd (with adult) half price. Free car park and picnic area.
Refreshments: Restaurant open same days as House 11-5, lunches and teas. Table license. Refreshments only Mon & Tues, July 11 to Sept 8.
No dogs. Wheelchair access (house difficult); chairs provided.

OLIVER CROMWELL'S HOUSE, ELY

Ely map K6
Telephone: (0353) 662062

The historic home of Cromwell and his family, beautifully restored to recreate a 17th century atmosphere. An audio visual presentation on Cromwell, and life size animated models are both informative and entertaining.
Location: 29 St Mary's Street, Ely.
Station(s): Ely (1 m).
Open: Oct 1 to Apr 1: Mon-Sat 10-5.15; May 1 to Sept 30: daily, including Sun and Bank Hols 10-6.
Admission: Charge. Party rates available and guided tours by arrangement.

DENNY ABBEY   English ⌗ Heritage

map K6
Telephone: (0223) 860489

After a brief life as a Benedictine priory, the abbey passed to the Knights Templar who used it as a hospital for their sick and aged members. In 1308 the Order was suppressed and the inmates arrested. The abbey remained empty until 1339 when the widowed Countess of Pembroke acquired it and moved the Franciscan nuns from her Abbey at Waterbeach to Denny. Most of the monastic buildings were demolished in the 16th century, but there are remnants of the 12th century church and 14th century additions.

Location: 6 m (9.7 km) north of Cambridge on A10.
Open: Good Friday or Apr 1 (whichever is earlier) to Sept 30: Open Daily 10-6. Oct 1 to Maundy Thursday or Mar 31 (whichever is earlier): Open Suns only 10-4. *Closed* Dec 24-26, Jan 1.
Admission: £1.20, Concessions 90p, Chd 60p.

DOCWRA'S MANOR

Shepreth map K6
Telephone: (0763) 261473, 261557 or 260235
(Mrs John Raven)

2 acres of choice plants in a series of enclosed gardens. Small nursery for hardy plants.

Location: Opposite War Memorial in centre of Shepreth village; ½ m W of Cambridge to Royston Rd (A10) bus stops at gate.
Station(s): Shepreth.(Hourly Service on Main King's Cross, London line incl Suns)
Open: GARDEN ONLY. All year Mon, Wed, Fri 10-4. Suns Apr 4, May 2, June 6, July 4, Aug 1, Oct 3 (2-5), also Bank Holiday Mons (10-4); Also Suns May 16, Sept 5 (2-6) £1.50 *in aid of National Gardens Scheme.* Also open by appointment.
Admission: £1.50, accompanied Chd free. Proceeds for garden upkeep.
Refreshments: Teas Suns May 16, Sept 5. Proceeds shared with Shepreth Church Funds. No dogs.

Become a Friend of the Historic Houses Association

over 270 Houses & Gardens to Visit Free

Who are the Friends?

Friends are a small but important group of people who are interested in the heritage and enjoy visiting country houses. They can visit 280 HHA members' properties free of charge and become involved in the HHA's work at a regional level. They pay a subscription to the Association on an annual basis.

Please ask for information and subscription rates:
Mrs. Rachel Oakley,
Historic Houses Association, Membership Department PO Box 21, Unit 7,
Campus 5, The Business Park, Letchworth, Herts. SG6 2JF. Tel: (0462) 675848

ELTON HALL 

nr Peterborough map J6
Telephone: (0832) 280 468
(Mr & Mrs William Proby)

Spanning five centuries, this romantic and gracious house has been the home of the Proby family for over 300 years. The house, with its mixture of medieval, gothic and classical styles, reflects the family's passion for collecting, and this is shown in the remarkable contents to be seen today - excellent furniture outstanding paintings by Gainsborough, Reynolds, Constable, Alma Tadema, Millais and other fine arts. There are over 12,000 books, including Henry VIII's prayer book. Attractive gardens, including restored Rose Garden, new knot and sunken gardens and recently planted Arboretum.

Location: On A605, 5 m W of Peterborough.
Open: Bank Hols during May and Aug, Sun, Mon 2-5; July - Weds & Suns 2-5; Aug - Weds, Thurs, Suns 2-5.
Admission: £3.50, Chd £1.75. Private parties by arrangement with House Manager, prices on application. Free parking.
Refreshments: Home-made teas. Lunches by arrangement. Shop.

🌳 THE SIGN OF A GREAT DAY OUT

ISLAND HALL

Godmanchester map K6
(Mr Christopher & The Hon Mrs Vane Percy)

An important mid 18th century mansion of great charm owned and being restored by an award winning Interior Designer. Lovely rooms with fine period detail and interesting possessions relating to the owners' ancestors since their first occupation of the house in 1800. Tranquil riverside setting with ornamental island forming part of the grounds.

Location: In centre of Godmanchester next to the car park. 1 m S of Huntingdon (A1); 15 m NW of Cambridge (A604).
Station(s): Huntingdon (1 m).
Open: June 13 to Sept 12 Suns only 2.30-5. Parties particularly welcome May to Sept by appointment.
Admission: Party rate £2 groups over 40. Adm House and Grounds £2.50, Chd £1 (grounds only). Grounds only £1.
Refreshments: Teas.

KIMBOLTON CASTLE

Kimbolton map K6
(Governors of Kimbolton School)

Tudor manor house associated with Katherine of Aragon, completely remodelled by Vanbrugh (1708-20); courtyard c. 1694. Fine murals by Pellegrini in chapel, boudoir and on staircase. Gatehouse by Robert Adam. Parkland.

Location: 8 m NW of St Neots on A45; 14 m N of Bedford.
Station(s): St Neots (9 m).
Open: Easter Sun & Mon; Spring Bank Hol Sun & Mon; Summer Bank Hol Sun & Mon also Suns only late July and Aug: 2-6.
Admission: 60p, Chd & OAPs 20p.

LONGTHORPE TOWER   English ⌗ Heritage

map K6
Telephone: (0733) 268482

This three-storey tower, added to an existing fortified manor house about 1300, is remarkable for the richness and completeness of its early 14th century wall-paintings. These were discovered less than 40 years ago under layers of limewash and distemper, and depict scenes from the Bible and of life in the East Anglian countryside; the most complete set of such paintings of the period in Northern Europe.

Location: 2 m (3.2 km) west of Peterborough on A47.
Open: Good Friday or Apr 1 (whichever is earlier) to Sept 30: Weekends 10-6.
Admission: £1.20, Concessions 90p, Chd 60p.

PECKOVER HOUSE AND GARDEN   🍃 The National Trust

Wisbech map K7 △ &
Telephone: (0945) 583463

Important example of early 18th century domestic architecture. Fine rococo decoration. Interesting Victorian garden contains rare trees, flower borders, roses. Under glass are orange trees. Georgian stables.

Location: Centre of Wisbech town on N bank of River Nene (B1441).
Station(s): March (9½ m).
Open: House & Gardens: Mar 27 to Oct 31, Sun, Wed & Bank Hol Mon. 2-5.30. Garden also open Mon, Tues, Sat. Parties also on Sat and Mon by appointment.
Admission: £2.30, Chd £1.15. Party rate £1.70. Garden only days, £1.
Refreshments: Teas on house open days.
No dogs. Wheelchairs garden only.

PRIOR CRAUDEN'S CHAPEL

The College, Ely map K6
Telephone: (0353) 662837
(The Bursar, The King's School)

Built as a private chapel in 1324/1325 for Prior Crauden, the Prior of the Mediaeval Benedictine Monastery from 1321 to 1341. Recently restored to show glimpses of coloured walls, painted glass and wall paintings. In 1649 Cromwell's Commissioners planned to destroy the Chapel, but it was saved by being turned into a dwelling house for two hundred years, until a restoration in 1850. Now on view to the public and used for services by the King's School, Ely.

Location: In the precincts of Ely Cathedral.
Open: Mon to Fri 9-5, excluding statutory and Bank Hols. Key available from Chapter Office in Firmary Lane.
Admission: Free.
Refreshments: Lamb Hotel, and restaurants in City of Ely.
Parking in Cathedral Car Park. Not suitable for disabled visitors.

WIMPOLE HALL   🍃 The National Trust

nr Cambridge map K5 ⓢ
Telephone: (0223) 207257

An architecturally refined house of aristocratic proportions, sumptuous 18th and 19th century staterooms, set in a beautifully undulating park devised by the best of the landscape architects. Exhibition at Stable Block.

Location: 8 m SW of Cambridge; signposted off A603 at New Wimpole.
Station(s): Shepreth (5 m) (not Suns); Royston (7 m).
Open: House, Garden & Park: Mar 27 to Oct 31, Tues, Weds, Thurs, Sat, Sun 1-5, Bank Hol Sun & Mon 11-5 also Frid July 23 to Aug 20.
Admission: £4.50, Chd £2. Pre-booked parties of 15 or more £3.50 (Tues to Thurs only). Joint ticket for Hall & Farm £6.
Refreshments: Lunches & teas in the Dining Room 12-5. Table license. Light refreshments at stable block 10.30-5.30.
Picnic area. Shop. Dogs allowed in park only on leads, Wheelchair access, 3 chairs provided.

WIMPOLE HOME FARM   The National Trust

nr Cambridge map K5
Telephone: (0223) 207257

An historic farm, faithfully restored by the National Trust, set in 350 acres of beautiful parkland. Approved Rare Breeds Centre. Children's corner. Agricultural museum. Adventure playground. Shop. Film loft.

Location: 8 m S of Cambridge; signposted off A603 at New Wimpole.
Station(s): Shepreth (5 m); Royston (7 m).
Open: Mar 27 to Oct 31: Tues, Wed, Thurs, Sat, Sun & Bank Hol Mon, 10.30-5. Also open Frid July 23 to Aug 20.
Admission: £3.50, NT members £1.50, Chd over 3 £1.50, parties (pre-booked) £2.50. Joint ticket for Hall and Farm £6.
Refreshments: Lunches & teas at Wimpole Hall. Snacks at Home Farm.

CHESHIRE

ADLINGTON HALL 🏛

Macclesfield map G8
Telephone: (0625) 829206
(Charles Legh, Esq.)

Adlington Hall is a Cheshire Manor and has been the home of the Leghs since 1315. The Great Hall was built between 1450 and 1505, the Elizabethan 'Black and White' in 1581 and the Georgian South Front in 1757. The Bernard Smith Organ was installed c 1670. A Shell Cottage', Yew Walk and Lime Avenue are features of the gardens.

Location: 5 m N of Macclesfield on the Stockport/Macclesfield Road (A523).
Station(s): Adlington (½ m).
Open: Good Friday to Oct 3 - Suns & Bank Hols: 2-5.30.
Admission: HALL AND GARDENS £2.70, Chd £1.25. GARDENS ONLY £1, Chd 50p.
Special parties by arrangement other days (over 25 people £2).
Refreshments: At the Hall.
Gift Shop. Car park free.

ARLEY HALL AND GARDENS 🏛

nr Great Budworth and midway between Warrington and Northwich map G8
Telephone: (0565) 777353, Fax: (0565) 777465
(The Hon M. L. W. Flower)

Victorian country house and private Chapel (c 1840). Gardens with magnificent displays throughout the open season and elegant woodland walk. Special features include award-winning herbaceous border, Ilex avenue, topiary, herb garden, fine yew hedges, walled gardens, azaleas.
Location: 5 m N of Northwich; 6 m W of Knutsford; 7 m S of Warrington; 5 m off M6 at junctions 19 & 20; 5 m off M56 at junctions 9 & 10. Nearest main roads A49 and A50.
Open: Apr to Oct - Tues to Suns & Bank Hol Mons 12-5, extended hours for group and party bookings.
Admission: GARDENS £2.60, HALL £1.60.
Refreshments: Lunches and light refreshments in converted Tudor barn.
Shop and Plant Nursery. Craft workers and farm for children nearby. Facilities for disabled visitors.

BEESTON CASTLE   English 🏛 Heritage

map F8
Telephone: (0829) 260464

Built on an isolated crag, Beeston Castle is visible for miles around. The view across the Cheshire plain extends to the Pennines in the east and westwards to Wales. Begun about 1220 by Ranulf de Blundeville, the castle was further fortified by Edward I. The ditch alone can have been no small task, as it is hewn from the solid rock. There is an exhibition on the history of the castle in the museum.

Location: 2 m (3.2 km) west of Bunbury. 11m (18 km) south east of Chester.
Open: Good Friday or Apr 1 (whichever is earlier) to Sept 30: daily 10-6. Oct 1 to Maundy Thursday or Mar 31 (whichever is earlier) Tues to Sun 10-4. *Closed* Dec 24-26, Jan 1.
Admission: £2, Concessions £1.50, Chd £1.

CAPESTHORNE

Macclesfield map G8
Telephone: (0625) 861221, 861779
Fax: (O625) 861619
(Mr and Mrs William Bromley-Davenport)

Capesthorne has been the home of the Bromley-Davenport family and their ancestors the Capesthornes and Wards since Domesday times. The family were originally Chief Foresters responsible for the law and order in the King's Forests of Macclesfield and Leek. The family crest, a felon's head with a halter of gold around his neck, denoted the power of life and death without trial or appeal. Later members of this same family were to serve as Speakers to the House of Commons and in the last and present centuries, as Members of Parliament. Recent research has revealed that Francis and William Smith of Warwick were almost certainly the original architects of this Jacobean style house built in 1722. Later alterations were made by Blore and Salvin. Pictures, furniture, Capesthorne collection of vases, family muniments and Americana. The extensive grounds include an arboretum, nature trail and delightful woodland walk. Other amenities include a Touring Caravan Park, fishing and children's play area, craft and souvenir shop. Capesthorne is available for Corporate entertaining and a brochure outlining the many advantages of using the hall and grounds is available on request. Enquiries to: Administrator, Capesthorne Hall, Macclesfield, Cheshire SK11 9JY. Telephone: (0625) 861221/861779. Fax: (0625) 861619.

Location: 7 m S of Wilmslow, on Manchester/London Road (A34); 6½ m N of Congleton, Junction 18 (M6).
Station(s): Chelford (3 m).
Open: PARK, GARDENS AND CHAPEL 12-6, HALL 2-4. April - Suns only; May: Suns & Weds; June/July: Tues, Weds, Thurs & Suns. Aug/Sept: Wed and Sun. *Open* All Bank Hols and Easter Tues. Caravan Park open Mar to Oct inc.
Admission: PARK, GARDENS & CHAPEL £2, Chd (5-16 years) 50p, OAP £1.75. PARK, GARDENS, CHAPEL & HALL £3.50, OAP £3, Chd £1. Budget Family ticket £8. Visitors £2, Chd 50p, at the desk in the Hall entrance. Chd under 5 years accompanied by an adult free. Coach and Car Park free. Dogs (exempt from government control regulations) are permitted in the Park area only. Organised parties are welcome on any open day plus Tues, Thur, May to Aug inc. by appointment (please send for booking form and coloured brochure). Special reductions for parties of 20 or more at £2.75 per person to Hall, Park, Gardens & Chapel. Evening parties are also welcome on any open day except Sun, May to Aug (by appointment). Evening party rate £3,25 per person, minimum number 20.
Refreshments: Garden Restaurant & Bromley room.

Sir Peter Lely – portrait painter

His paintings can be seen at the following properties included in Historic Houses Castles and Gardens:

Althorp
Aynhoe Park
Belton House
Browsholme Hall
Dalmeny House
Euston Hall
Goodwood House
Gorhambury

Hinwick House
Kedleston Hall
Ragley Hall
St Osyth Priory
Stoneleigh Abbey
Stanford Hall
Weston Park

CHOLMONDELEY CASTLE GARDENS

Malpas map F7
Telephone: (0829) 720383 or 720203
(The Marchioness of Cholmondeley)

Extensive pleasure gardens dominated by romantic Gothic Castle built in 1801 of local sandstone. Imaginatively laid out with fine trees and water gardens, it has been extensively replanted from the 1960's with rhododendrons, azaleas, cornus, acer and many other acid loving plants. As well as the beautiful water garden, there is a rose and lavender garden and herbaceous borders. Lakeside picnic area, rare breeds of farm animals including Llamas. Ancient private chapel in park.

Location: Off A41 Chester/Whitchurch Road and A49 Whitchurch/Tarporley Road.
Open: GARDENS & FARM ONLY. April 4 to Oct 17 - Suns & Bank Hols only 12-5.30. Weekday visits accepted by prior arrangement. Enquiries to: The Secretary, Cholmondeley Castle, Malpas, Cheshire. (House not open to public.)
Admission: £2.50, OAPs £1.50, Chd 75p.
Refreshments: Excellent tea room open for light lunches.
Gift Shop. Plants for sale.

DORFOLD HALL

Nantwich map G7 △
Telephone: (0270) 625245
(R. C. Roundell, Esq.)

Jacobean country house built 1616. Beautiful plaster ceilings and panelling. Attractive gardens. Guided tours.

Location: 1 m W of Nantwich on A534 Nantwich/Wrexham Road.
Station(s): Nantwich (1½ m).
Open: Apr to Oct - Tues & Bank Hol Mons 2-5.*At other times by appointment only.*
Admission: £2.50, Chd £1.50.

DUNHAM MASSEY   The National Trust

Altrincham map G8
Telephone: 061-941 1025

Fine 18th century house with Georgian and Edwardian interiors. Huguenot silver collection, fine furniture and family portraits. Large garden, extensively replanted with shade loving and waterside plants, with attractive woodland. Deer park and water mill.

Location: 3 m SW of Altrincham off A56; junction 19 off M6; junction 7 off M56.
Open: Apr 1 to End Oct: House: Sat to Wed 12-5, Last adm 4.30. Garden open daily 12-5. Outside normal hours guided tours of house by arrangement at an extra charge. Shop: Sat to Wed 12-5. Also open Nov 4 to Dec 19: Thurs to Sun 12-4; Jan 8 to Mar 27 1994: Sat, Sun 12-4. Park open until 7.30pm or dusk if earlier. Dogs in park only on lead. Wheelchairs provided - access to shop, coffee shop, garden and park. Limited access to house. Information from the Administrator, Dunham Massey Hall, Altrincham, Cheshire. WA144SJ.
Admission: House and Garden £4, Chd £2. Garden only £2. Family ticket £10. Reduced rates for pre-booked parties. Guided evening tours at an extra charge. Park only: Apr-Oct £2 per car, Nov-Mar 1994 £1.50 per car (NT Members free). Coaches free.
Refreshments: Licensed self-service restaurant for lunches & teas. Apr to Oct daily, 11-5.30 (lunches 12-2: limited service Thurs and Fri). Nov to Mar 1994: open as shop. Also open for booked parties, functions etc - by arrangement. Tel: 061-941 2815.
Shop.

GAWSWORTH HALL

Macclesfield map G8
Telephone: (0260) 223456
(Mr & Mrs Timothy Richards)

Tudor half-timbered manor house with tilting ground. Former home of Mary Fitton, Maid of Honour at the Court of Queen Elizabeth I, and the supposed 'dark lady' of Shakespeare's sonnets. Pictures, sculpture and furniture. Open air theatre with covered grand stand - June/July/August. Situated half-way between Macclesfield and Congleton in an idyllic setting close to the lovely medieval church. Open Air Theatre - Shakespeare play - June 17 to 26; Gilbert and Sullivan - Yeomen of the Guard - July 1 to 10; Heroic Brass Band Evenings July 15 to 17; Comedies and Concerts - July 21 to Aug 8. Audience seated in covered stand. Tel: (0260) 223456.

Location: 3 m S of Macclesfield on the Congleton/Macclesfield Road (A536).
Open: Apr 3 to Oct 3 - Daily 2-5.30. Evening parties by arrangement.
Admission: £3.20, Chd £1.60. Party rates on application.
Refreshments: In the Pavilion

HANDFORTH HALL

Handforth, nr Wilmslow map G8
(Dr & Mrs J. C. Douglas)

Small 16th century half-timbered manor house. Home of Sir William Brereton, Parliamentary General. Fine Jacobean staircase. Collection of oak furniture. Formal gardens.

Location: ½ m E of Handforth on B5358.
Open: June to Sept by written appointment only.

HARE HILL GARDEN   🍂 The National Trust

Over Alderley, nr Macclesfield map G8

Walled garden with pergola, rhododendrons and azaleas; parkland.
Location: Between Alderley Edge and Prestbury off B5087 at Greyhound Road. Link path to Alderley Edge 2 m in each direction. Free parking at Alderley Edge.
Station(s): Alderley Edge (3½ m); Prestbury (2½ m).
Open: Apr 1 to End Oct - Weds, Thurs, Sats, Suns and Bank Hol Mons 10-5.30. Special opening for rhododendrons and azaleas May 17 to June 4, daily 10-5.30.
Admission: £2. Entrance per car £1, refundable on entry to the garden. Parties by appointment to the Head Gardener, Garden Lodge, Oak Road, Over Alderley, Macclesfield SK10 4QB. Unsuitable for school parties.
Wheelchair access - some assistance needed. Wheelchair available.

LITTLE MORETON HALL   🍂 The National Trust

Congleton map G7 ♿
Telephone: (0260) 272018

Begun in the 15th century, one of the most perfect examples of a timber-framed moated manor house in the country. Remarkable carved gables. Restored 16th century wall paintings are on view. Attractive knot garden.

Location: 4 m SW of Congleton off Newcastle-under-Lyme/Congleton Road (A34).
Open: Apr 1 to Sept 30: Wed to Sun 12-5.30. Bank Hol Mon 11-5.30; (Closed Good Fri). Oct: Wed, Sat, Sun 12-5.30. Last adm 5. Special openings by arrangement with Administrator. School parties: Apr to end Sept: Wed to Fri mornings only by prior arrangement with Administrator (sae please). Optional guided tours most afternoons.
Admission: Weekends & Bank Hols £3.50; Family ticket £8.75. Weekdays £2.50; Family ticket £6.25. Pre-booked parties by arrangement.
Refreshments: Light lunches and home made teas. Limited seating.
Dogs in car park and grass area in front of Hall only. Wheelchairs provided. Shop.

LYME PARK   🍂 The National Trust

Disley, Stockport map G8 △
Telephone: (0663) 762023
(Financed and Managed by Stockport Metropolitan Borough Council)

An Elizabethan House with 18th and 19th century alterations, particularly by Giacomo Leoni in the 1730's. A lively visitor centre evokes the atmosphere of Edwardian times which carries through into the Hall with the guides as costumed servants of 1910. Formal gardens, including a spectacular Dutch Garden. Over 1377 acres of designated Country Park with breathtaking views of Peak District and Cheshire Plain. The Park contains Red and Fallow deer herds and Countryside Centre. The Hall, park and gardens, are available for filming, promotional use, functions or entertaining.

Open: Hall: Good Friday Apr 9 - Sun Oct 3 (inclusive). *Closed* Mon and Frids except Bank Hols. Guided tours weekdays and Saturdays. Freeflow Sundays. Last admission 4pm on tour days and 4.15pm on freeflow. Special Christmas openings. Please telephone for details.
Admission: HALL: £1.95, Chd and concessionaires £1. Family ticket (2 adults and up to 3 children) £5. PARK AND GARDENS: Pedestrians free, car/mini bus (up to 12 seats) £3.20 (N.T. members incl.) Motorcycle (incl. riders) £2.20. Coach passengers (N.T. members incl.) for Hall, Park and Gardens £1.50. GARDEN: All year daily except Dec 25,26. Summer (April 9 - Oct 3) 11-5, Winter (Oct 4 - Good Friday '94) 11-4.
Other Activities: Pitch & Putt Course, Adventure playground, Orienteering, Nature Trails, Fishing and Horse riding permits. Extensive Events Programme - ask for leaflet. Guided walks and Chapel Services throughout the year. For further information contact: The Marketing and Events Manager, Lyme Park, Disley, Stockport SK12 2NX - Telephone (0663) 762023.

NETHER ALDERLEY MILL 🌰 The National Trust

Nether Alderley map G8
Telephone: (0625) 523012

15th century corn-mill in use until 1939 and now restored; tandem overshot water wheels. Flour ground occasionally for demonstration.

Location: 1½ m S of Alderley Edge on E side of A34.
Station(s): Alderley Edge (2 m).
Open: Apr, May and Oct - Weds, Suns & Bank Hol Mons 1-4.30. June to Sept - Tues to Sun and Bank Hol Mons 1-5. Parties (maximum 20) by prior arrangement with Mrs Pamela Ferguson, 7 Oak Cottages, Styal, Wilmslow, SK9 4QJ.
Admission: £1.80, Chd 90p.
No dogs. Unsuitable for disabled or visually handicapped.

The National Trust
THE SIGN OF A GREAT DAY OUT

NORTON PRIORY MUSEUM

Runcorn map F8
Telephone: (0928) 569895
(Norton Priory Museum Trust)

The beautiful woodland gardens covering 30 acres with an 18th century award winning walled garden were the setting for the now demolished mansion of Sir Richard Brooke, built on the site of a former Augustinian priory. Excavated remains of the priory, the atmospheric 12th century vaulted under croft,can be found in the museum with displays on the mediaeval priory, which later became houses and gardens. A collection of contemporary sculpture is sited throughout the grounds.

Location: From M56 (junction 11) turn towards Warrington and follow Norton Priory road signs.
Open: Open daily all year. Apr to Oct - Sats, Suns & Bank Hols 12-6; Mons to Fris 12-5. Nov to Mar - Daily 12-4. Walled Garden open Mar to Oct. *Closed* Dec 24, 25 & 26, Jan 1. Special arrangements for groups.
Admission: All in ticket £2.40 (£1.20 concession).
Refreshments: Available.
Shop, picnic area and easy parking.

PEOVER HALL

Over Peover, Knutsford map G8
(Randle Brooks)

An Elizabethan House dating from 1585. Fine Caroline stables. Mainwaring Chapel. 18th century landscaped park. Large garden with Topiary work, also Walled and Herb gardens.

Location: 4 m S of Knutsford off A50 at Whipping Stocks Inn.
Open: Beginning of May to end of Sept (except Bank Holidays).
Admission: House, Stables & Gardens - Mons 2.30-4.30. £2.50, Chd £1.50. Stables & Gardens Only - Thurs 2-5. £1.50, Chd 50p. Enquiries: J.Stocks (0565) 722656.
Refreshments: Teas in the Stables on Mons.

QUARRY BANK MILL The National Trust

Styal map G8 ⑤
Telephone: (0625) 527468
(The National Trust & Quarry Bank Mill Trust Ltd)

Quarry Bank Mill

Award-winning museum of the cotton textile industry, set in rural parkland, with England's largest working waterwheel, producing cloth on historic looms. The Apprentice House recreates the 1830's, when it was home to pauper child millworkers, and its unique garden grows rare, historic fruits, vegetables and herbs. Large shop selling goods made from mill-woven cloth and National Trust gifts and books. Licensed restaurant with excellent homecooked menu, also catering for private and business functions. Open all year: 2 miles from Manchester Airport: full details under listing.
Enquiries: (0625) 527468

A National Trust property.

Kitchen in Apprentice House

Award-winning working museum of the cotton industry housed in a 200-year-old spinning mill. Skilled demonstrators spin and weave cotton which is then made into goods on sale in the Mill Shop. Exhibitions cover the way of life of the Mill Workers, dyeing, finishing and Water power. The Mill is powered by a 50 ton, 150 h.p. Water-wheel. The restored Apprentice House brings the life of child workers vividly to life. The museum is at the heart of a 275 acre country park and the nearby village is largely as it was in the 1850's complete with School, Chapels, Village Green and Pub. Former Museum of the Year and a winner in the 1991 Best Attraction in the North West Competition.

Location: 1½ m N of Wilmslow off B5166. 1 m from M56 exit 5. 10 m S of Manchester (log: SJ 35835).
Station(s): Styal (1/3 m); Wilmslow (2 m).
Open: Mill: All year. Apr to Sept daily 11-5; Oct to Mar - Tues to Sun 11-4. Open all Bank Hols. Pre-booked parties from 9.30 throughout the year (not Sun or Bank Hols) and specified evenings May to Sept. APPRENTICE HOUSE AND GARDEN: Mon *closed* except Bank Hol Mons. Tues to Fri: as Mill opening times during school holidays. Wed, Thurs, Fri: 2pm to Mill closing time during term time. Sat, Sun: as Mill opening times. Please note that due to fire and safety regulations a maximum of 30 people can be accommodated in the house at one time. Shop, newly sited and refurbished, open as Mill.
Admission: By timed ticket ONLY available from Mill Reception. Members wishing to avoid crowds are advised not to visit on Bank Hols and Sun afternoons in spring and summer. Adm charges not available at time of going to press. Advance booking essential for all groups of 10 or more, one in 20 free, but not in June or July; please apply for booking form at least three weeks in advance. Guides, fee per guide per 20 persons, may be booked at the same time.
Refreshments: Available during all Mill opening hours, licensed tearoom/refreshment for morning coffee, home-made soup, hot meals, regional dishes, vegetarian food and teas.
Stocks goods made from cloth woven in Mill. Disabled access: Exterior and special route through part of interior using step-lift. Please telephone for access details and leaflet. Cars may set down passengers in Mill yard. Disabled lavatory by Styal Workshop. Mill unsuitable for guide dogs. Shop.

STAPELEY WATER GARDENS LTD

London Road, Stapeley, Nantwich, Cheshire CW5 7LH
Telephone: Gdn Centre (0270) 623868; The Palms (0270) 628628

See under Specialist Growers Section.

TABLEY HOUSE COLLECTION

Tabley House, Knutsford map G8
Telephone: (0565) 750151
(Tabley House Collection Trust)

Grinling Gibbons (1648–1721)

Sculptor and wood carver. His work can be seen at the following properties included in Historic Houses Castles and Gardens:

> *Fawley Court Historic House and Museum*
> *Kentchurch Court*
> *Lyme Park*
> *Somerleyton Hall*
> *Sudbury Hall*

Fine Palladian mansion, designed in 1761 by John Carr of York for Sir Peter Byrne Leicester Bt. The State Rooms, including the spectacular Regency Picture Gallery, show furniture by Gillow, Bullock and Chippendale, and paintings by Lely, Turner, Lawrence and other English Masters from the 17th Century to the present day. Also on display is a varied collection including musical instruments and other family memorabilia. The XVIIth Century Chapel adjoins the House.

Location: 2 m W of Knutsford, entrance on A5033 (M6 Junction 19, A556).
Open: Apr to Oct: Thurs, Fri, Sat, Sun and Bank Hols 2-5.(Last entry 4.30). Free car park. Main rooms and the Chapel suitable for the disabled.
Admission: £3, Chd £1.
Refreshments: Tea room facilities. All enquiries to The Administrator.

WOODHEY CHAPEL

Faddiley, nr Nantwich map F7
Telephone: (027 074) 215
(The Trustees of Woodhey Chapel)

'The Chapel in the Fields.' A small private chapel, recently restored, dating from 1699.

Location: 1 m SW of Faddiley off A534 Nantwich/Wrexham Road.
Open: Apr to Oct - Sats & Bank Hol Mons 2-5. At other times by appointment.
Admission: 50p, Chd 25p.

CLEVELAND

THE CASTLE, Castle Eden

Hartlepool, Cleveland map H11

A Grade II listed Manor House principally dating from 1757, with 19th century additions.

Location: In the village of Castle Eden, Peterlee (2 m) Durham City (10 m).
Open: May 15 to Aug 31 - Wed & Thurs 2-5. Spring & Summer Bank Hol Mons 2-5.

GISBOROUGH PRIORY　English⌗Heritage

map H11
Telephone: (0287) 38301

Founded in the 12th century for Augustinian canons by Robert de Brus, the priory was among the richest and most magnificent in the north. The remains include an impressive gatehouse, and the wonderful east wall, an important example of early Gothic architecture.

Location: Guisborough, next to the parish church.
Open: Good Friday or Apr 1 (whichever is earlier) to Sept 30: Open Daily 10-6. Oct 1 to Maundy Thursday or Mar 31 (whichever is earlier): Open Tues to Sun 10-4. *Closed* Dec 24-26, Jan 1.
Admission: 80p, Concessions 60p, Chd 40p.

ORMESBY HALL　🌣　The National Trust

nr Middlesbrough map H11　△
Telephone: (0642) 324188

Mid-18th century house. Contemporary plasterwork. Small garden.

Location: 3 m SE of Middlesbrough.
Station(s): Marton (1½ m) (not Suns April, Sept & Oct).
Open: Apr 1 to Oct 31: Wed, Thurs, Sat, Sun, Bank Hol Mons & Good Friday 2-5.30. Last adm 5.
Admission: HOUSE & GARDENS £2, Chd £1, Adult party £1.60, Chd party 80p. GARDEN: 80p, Chd 40p.
Refreshments: Afternoon teas.
No dogs (except guide dogs). Wheelchair access to ground floor only. Shop and tea room open as house and some weekends in Nov & Dec.

CORNWALL

ANTONY　🌣　The National Trust

Torpoint map E2　△
Telephone: (0752) 812191

The home of Mr. Richard Carew Pole. Built for Sir William Carew 1718-1729. Unaltered early 18th century house, panelled rooms. Fine furniture. Extensive garden and woodland walks.

Location: 5 m W of Plymouth via Torpoint car ferry. 2 m NW of Torpoint, N of A374.
Open: Apr 1 to end of Oct - Tues, Weds & Thurs; also Bank Hol Mons and Suns in June, July and Aug 1.30-5.30 (last adm 4.45).
Admission: £3.40, Chd £1.70. Pre-arranged parties £2.60, Chd £1.30. Guided tours.
Refreshments: Tea room.
No dogs. Unsuitable for wheelchairs. Shop.

ANTONY WOODLAND GARDEN

Torpoint map E2　△
(Carew Pole Garden Trust)

A woodland garden and natural woods extending to 100 acres in an area designated as one of Outstanding Natural Beauty and a Site of Special Scientific Interest. The Woodland Garden established in the late 18th century with the assistance of Humphrey Repton features over 300 types of Camellias and a wide variety of Magnolias, Rhododen drons, Hydrangeas, Azaleas and other flowering shrubs together with many fine species of indigenous and exotic hardwood and softwood trees. Adjoining and contrasting with this long established woodland garden an additional 50 acres of natural woods bordering the River Lynher, featuring a 'Fishful' Pond, many wild flower species and birds make this an area to delight botanists, ornothologists, or those who merely enjoy peaceful woodland walks.

Location: 5 m W of Plymouth via Torpoint Car Ferry. 2 m NW of Torpoint off A374.
Open: ANTONY WOODLAND GARDEN and WOODLAND WALK: Mar 15 to Oct 31. Mon-Sat 11-5.30. Suns 2.30-5.30.
Admission: £1.50, Chd 50p. Special openings in aid of Charities by arrangement Car parking available. No dogs allowed.

BOSVIGO HOUSE (GARDENS)

Bosvigo Lane, Truro map C1
Telephone: (0872) 75774
(Wendy and Michael Perry)

A series of enclosed and walled gardens, still being developed, around Georgian house (not open). Mainly herbacious plants used for colour and foliage effect. Woodland Walk and Victorian Conservatory. Nursery open daily selling rare and unusual plants - see listing under the Garden Specialists Section.

Location: ¾ m from city centre. Take A390 towards Redruth. At Highertown turn right by Shell garage and drive 400 yards down Dobbs Lane.
Open: GARDEN ONLY. June to end Sept - daily 11-6.
Admission: £1.50, Chd 50p. Parties by appointment.
Sorry, no dogs.

CHYSAUSTER ANCIENT VILLAGE   English⌗Heritage

map C1
Telephone: (0736) 61889

Halfway up a hillside, through a stone passage, lie the stone houses erected by our prehistoric ancestors. By the time the Romans came the village had already existed for two centuries. Each house, built around a courtyard, had its own terrace. Were these the earliest gardens?

Location: 2½ m (3½ km) north west of Gulval, near Penzance.
Open: Good Friday or Apr 1 (whichever is earlier) to Sept 30: Open Daily 10-6. Oct 1 to Maundy Thursday or Mar 31 (whichever is earlier): Open Tues to Sun 10-4. *Closed* Dec 24-26, Jan 1.
Admission: £1.30, Concessions £1, Chd 65p.

COTEHELE   🌿 The National Trust

St. Dominick map E2
Telephone: (0579) 50434. Restaurant (0579) 50652.

Fine medieval house, the former home of Earls of Mount Edgcumbe. Armour, furniture, tapestries. Terrace garden falling to the sheltered valley, ponds, stream, unusual shrubs. Watermill and Cotehele Quay museum.

Location: On W bank of the Tamar, 1 m W of Calstock by footpath, (6 m by road). 8 m SW of Tavistock; 14 m from Plymouth via Saltash Bridge.
Station(s): Calstock (1½ m).
Open: Apr 1 to Oct 31- Garden, Shop and Quay every day, 11-5.30. House, Mill and Restaurant every day *except Friday,* but open Good Friday 12-5.30. 12-5 in Oct, (Mill and Restaurant open 11) closes dusk if earlier. Last adm ½ hr before closing. Nov to Mar - Garden open daily during daylight.
Admission: House, Gardens, Cotehele Mill and Quay £5. Chd £2.50. Gardens, Cotehele Mill and Quay £2.50, Chd £1.25.*Reduced fee of £4, Chd £2 for pre-booked coach parties. Organisers should book visits & arrange for meals beforehand with the Administrator.*
Refreshments: Coffee, lunch and tea in Barn (*closed* Fri) and on Quay (open daily) during season.
DOGS IN WOODS ONLY - on lead. Wheelchairs provided; house only accessible. Shop.

GLENDURGAN GARDEN   🌿 The National Trust

Mawnan Smith map C1
Telephone: (0326) 250906 (Opening hours only).

A valley garden of great beauty with fine trees and shrubs, overlooking Helford River. Giant's Stride much enjoyed by children.

Location: 4 m SW of Falmouth ½ m SW of Mawnan Smith on road to Helford Passage.
Open: Mar 1 to end of Oct - Tues-Sat incl (except Good Friday) but open Bank Hol Mons. 10.30-5.30 (last adm 4.30.)
Admission: £2.50, Chd £1.25.*No reduction for parties.*
No dogs. Unsuitable for wheelchairs.

GODOLPHIN HOUSE   🏛

Helston map C1
(Mrs. Schofield)

A Former home of the Earls of Godolphin and the birthplace of Queen Anne's famous Lord High Treasurer - Sidney, first Earl of Godolphin. Parts of the house are of early Tudor date and additions were made in Elizabethan and Carolean times. The unique front was completed shortly before the Civil War and rests on massive columns of local granite. The fine 'Kings Room' is traditionally said to have been occupied by Charles II (then Prince of Wales) at the time of his escape from Pendennis Castle to the Scilly Islands. Pictures include 'The Godolphin Arabian' by John Wootton. Display of Farm Waggons and Civil War Exhibition on show in the old stables.
Location: 5 m NW of Helston; between villages of Townshend and Godolphin Cross.
Open: Bank Hol Mons; May & June - Thurs 2-5. July & Sept - Tues 2-5, Thurs 2-5, Aug - Tues 2-5, Thurs 10-1, 2-5.
Admission: £3, Chd £1. Open at other times for pre-booked parties & all year round for arranged parties.

LANHYDROCK 🌳 The National Trust

nr Bodmin map D2 ♿
Telephone: (0208) 73320. Restaurant(0208) 74331.

The great house of Cornwall, with 42 rooms open to the public. 17th century long gallery. Fine plaster ceilings. Family portraits 17th to 20th centuries. The extensive kitchen and servants' quarters (1883) are also shown. Formal garden with clipped yews, and parterre, laid out in 1857. Rhododendrons, magnolias, rare trees and shrubs. Woodland garden and parkland setting. 17th century Gatehouse above.

Location: 2½ m SE of Bodmin on Bodmin/Lostwithiel Road (B3268).
Station(s): Bodmin Parkway (1¾ m by signposted carriage-drive to house; 3 m by road).
Open: House, Garden and Grounds - Apr 1 to Oct 31 - Daily except Mon when House only is closed (*open* Bank Holiday Mons) 11-5.30 (last adm 5) 11-5 in Oct. Last adm ½ hr before closing. Nov to end of Mar - Garden and Grounds - open daily during daylight hours.
Admission: £5.00, Chd £2.50; Garden only £2.50, Chd £1.25. Pre-booked parties £4, Chd £2. *Organisers should book visits and arrange for meals beforehand with The Administrator.*
Refreshments: Lunches and teas in restaurant at House; snacks in stable block (last adm 5). Dogs in park only on leads. Wheelchairs provided. Shop (also open Nov & Dec).

LAUNCESTON CASTLE   English ⌗ Heritage

map D2
Telephone: (0566) 772365

The impressive round keep stands high on its grassy mound within a circular wall. Inside, a tall cylindrical tower soars from the centre. The space between tower and keep was roofed. Like Launceston itself, the castle was important in the Middle Ages. Small site museum.

Location: Launceston.
Open: Good Friday or Apr 1 (whichever is earlier) to Sept 30: Open Daily 10-6. Oct 1 to Maundy Thursday or Mar 31 (whichever is earlier): Open Tues to Sun 10-4. *Closed* Dec 24-26, Jan 1.
Admission: £1.20, Concessions 90p, Chd 60p.

MOUNT EDGCUMBE HOUSE & PARK

nr Plymouth map E2
Telephone: (0752) 822236
(City of Plymouth & Cornwall County Council)

'This Mount all the Mounts of Great Britain surpasses. 'Tis the Haunt of the Muses, the Mount of Parnassus.' *David Garrick (1717-1779).* Mount Edgcumbe House, a restored Tudor Mansion with the Earls Garden, including the newly restored Victorian flower beds surrounding it, was the home of the Mount Edgcumbe family for 400 years. The House and furniture have recently been redecorated and restored to reflect the 18th century, the period at which this nationally important Historic Garden was at its peak. Stretching along 10 miles of spectacular coastline from Plymouth to Whitsand Bay, the Park contains one of only three Grade I Historic Gardens in Cornwall. The earliest landscape park in Cornwall, it was designed 240 years ago with wonderful woodland walks and views and includes a deer park and Formal Gardens in the Italian, French and English styles. Two new gardens have been established, a New Zealand Garden and American Plantation, reflecting family associations with these countries. It is the site for the collection of the National Camellia Society.

Location: On Rame Peninsula, 12 m from Torpoint or from Trerulefoot roundabout (A38) via A374 to Antony or Crafthole, and B3247 to Mount Edgcumbe, or by Cremyll (pedestrian) Ferry from Plymouth (Stonehouse) to Park entrance.
Open: PARK, including LANDSCAPED PARK and FORMAL GARDENS open every day, all year round, Free. HOUSE and EARLS GARDEN open Apr 1 to Oct 31 11-5.30 Wed to Sun and Bank Hol Mons.
Admission: £3.00, Chd £1.50, Concessions £2.15. Group rates - bonus discounts. Any booking made in advance with a value of £30 or more attracts a discount of 20%, which can be passed on to the booking agent (coach operator, driver, club secretary, group leader etc) to be used at their discretion.
Refreshments: Lunches, teas and light refreshments available in the Orangery Restaurant/Cafe, Apr 1 to Oct 31 daily. Reservations and enquiries telephone Plymouth (0752) 822586.
Visitor Centre and Shop selling guides and souvenirs open Apr 1 to Oct 31 every day. Gifts produced in Devon and Cornwall a speciality.

PENCARROW HOUSE AND GARDEN

Bodmin map D2 △ ♿
Telephone: (020 884) 369
(The Molesworth - St Aubyn Family)

Georgian house and listed gardens, still owned and lived in by the family. A superb collection of 18th century pictures, furniture and china. Mile long drive and Ancient British Encampment. Marked walks through beautiful woodland gardens, past the great granite Victorian Rockery, Italian and American gardens, Lake and Ice House. Approx 50 acres in all. Over 600 different species and hybrid rhododendrons and also an internationally known specimen conifer collection.

Location: 4 m NW of Bodmin off A389 & B3266 at Washaway.
Open: House, Tearooms and Craft Centre. Easter to Oct 15 - Every day *(except Fri and Sat)* 1.30-5 (Bank Hol Mon and from June 1 to Sept 10 from 11). GARDENS open daily.
Admission: HOUSE AND GARDENS £3, Chd £1.50. GARDENS ONLY £1.50, Chd (over 5 yrs) 50p. Coaches £2.50. (1992 prices) Guided tours.
Refreshments: Light lunches and cream teas.
Car park and toilet facilities for disabled. Dogs very welcome in grounds. Plant shop. Picnic area. Small children's play area, and pets corner. Self pick soft fruit in season.

PRIDEAUX PLACE

Padstow map D2
Telephone: (0841) 532411 and 532945
(The Prideaux-Brune family)

An Elizabethan Mansion House set in extensive grounds above the fishing port of Padstow. 20 acres of deer park. Guided tours through this family home include a visit to the Great Chamber with its interesting embossed plaster ceiling dating from 1585, dining room, morning room, drawing room, reading room and library. Newly restored Italian formal garden.

Location: 7 m from Wadebridge, 14 m from Newquay.
Open: HOUSE, SHOP, TEAROOM - Easter Sat for two weeks then Spring Bank Hol to end of Sept, Sun to Thurs inclusive, 1.30-5. Spring and Aug Bank Hol Mon from 11.
Admission: HOUSE AND GROUNDS £3.50. GROUNDS ONLY £1.50. Chd free. Special party rates. Open all the year round by appointment.
Concerts and exhibitions throughout the summer. Free parking for cars (not coaches) in grounds. Enquiries to the Administrator, Prideaux Place, Padstow PL28 8RP. Tel (0841) 532945 or 532411.

PENDENNIS CASTLE English ⌗ Heritage

Falmouth map C1
Telephone: (0326) 316594

Henry VIII's reply to the Pope's crusade against him was to fortify his coastline. Two castles guarded the Fal Estuary, Pendennis and St Mawes. Built high on a promon tory, Pendennis saw action in the Civil War when 'Jack-for-the-King' Arundell held the castle for five terrible months. It continued in military use until 1946. 1588 Gundeck tableau, exhibition, views and refreshments.

Location: Pendennis Head 1 m (1.6 km) south east of Falmouth.
Open: Good Friday or Apr 1 (whichever is earlier) to Sept 30, daily 10-6. Oct 1 to Maundy Thursday or Mar 31 (whichever is earlier) Tues to Sun 10-4. *Closed* Dec 24-26, Jan 1.
Admission: £2, Concessions £1.50, Chd £1.

RESTORMEL CASTLE English ⌗ Heritage

map D2
Telephone: (0208) 872687

Crowning a hill overlooking the River Fowey, the castle rises steeply above a dry but deep, wide moat. The outer 12th century wall is a perfect circle. Domestic buildings were later added inside and a rectangular chapel outside.

Location: 1½ m (2.4 km) north of Lostwithiel.
Open: Good Friday or Apr 1 (whichever is earlier) to Sept 30. Open Daily 10-6.
Admission: £1.20, Concessions 90p, Chd 60p.

❧ THE SIGN OF A GREAT DAY OUT

ST. MAWES CASTLE   English⌗Heritage

map C1
Telephone: (0326) 270526

Shaped like a clover leaf, this small 16th century castle, still intact, nestles among rock plants and tropical shrubs. During the Civil War the Governor capitulated without gunfire or bloodshed, unlike Pendennis on the opposite shore.

Location: St Mawes.
Open: Good Friday or Apr 1 (whichever is earlier) to Sept 30: Open Daily 10-6. Oct 1 to Maundy Thursday or Mar 31 (whichever is earlier): Open Tues to Sun 10-4. *Closed* Dec 24-26, Jan 1.
Admission: £1.30, Concessions £1, Chd 65p.

ST. MICHAEL'S MOUNT   🍂 The National Trust

Marazion, nr Penzance map C1
Telephone: (0736) 710507

Home of Lord St Levan. Mediaeval and early 17th century with considerable alterations and additions in 18th and 19th century.

Location: ½ m from the shore at Marazion (A394), connected by causeway. 3 m E Penzance.
Open: Apr 1 to end of Oct: Mons to Fri 10.30-5.30 (last adm 4.45). Nov to end of Mar: Guided tours as tide, weather and circumstances permit. *(NB: ferry boats do not operate a regular service during this period).*
Admission: £3, Chd £1.50, Family ticket £8. Prebooked parties £2.80.
Shop and restaurant - Apr 1 to end Oct, daily. No dogs. Unsuitable for wheelchairs. NB: Access to The Mount and opening arrangements are liable to interruption in foul weather.

TINTAGEL CASTLE   English⌗Heritage

map D2
Telephone: (0840) 770328

Amazing that anything has survived on this wild, windswept coast. Yet fragments of Earl Reginald's great hall, built about 1145, and Earl Richard's 13th century wall and iron gate still stand in this incomparable landscape. No wonder that King Arthur and his Knights were thought to have dwelt here. Site exhibition.

Location: ½ m (0.8 km) north west of Tintagel.
Open: Good Friday or Apr 1 (whichever is earlier) to Sept 30 daily 10-6. Oct 1 to Maundy Thursday or Mar 31 (whichever is earlier) Tues to Sun 10-4. *Closed* Dec 24-26, Jan 1.
Admission: £2, Concessions £1.50, Chd £1.

TINTAGEL - THE OLD POST OFFICE

🍂 The National Trust

Tintagel map D2 ♿
Telephone: (0840) 770024 (opening hours only)

A miniature 14th century manor house with large hall.

Location: Nos 3 & 4 in the centre of Tintagel.
Open: Apr 1 to Oct 31 - Daily 11-5.30. (11-5 in Oct). Last adm ½ hr before closing.
Admission: £1.90, Chd 95p. *No reduction for parties.*
No dogs. Wheelchair access. Shop

TREGREHAN

map D2
Telephone: (0726) 814389 or (0726) 812438
(Mr T. C. Hudson)

Woodland garden created since early 19th century by Carlyon family concentrating on species from warm-temperate regions. Fine glasshouse range in walled garden. Small nursery, also open by appointment, specialising in wild source material, and camellias bred by the late owner.

Location: 2 m E of St Austell on A390. 1 m W of St. Blazey on A390.
Open: Mid Mar to end of June and Sept: 10.30-5.
Admission: £2, Chd 75p. Guided tours for parties by prior arrangement.
Refreshments: Teas available.
Parking for cars and coaches. Access for disabled to half garden only. No dogs.

TRELISSICK GARDEN   The National Trust

nr Truro map C1   &
Telephone: (0872) 862090; Restaurant (0872) 863486

Large shrub garden. Beautiful wooded park overlooking the river Fal. Woodland walks. Particularly rich in rhododendrons, camellias and hydrangeas.

Location: 5 m S of Truro on both sides of B3289 overlooking King Harry Ferry.
Open: Gardens only: Mar 1 to 31 Oct - Mons to Sats 10.30-5.30 (or sunset if earlier), Suns 12.30-5.30 (or sunset if earlier), 10.30-5 in Mar and Oct. Last adm ½ hr before closing. Entrance on road to King Harry Passage.
Admission: £3, Chd £1.50. *No reduction for parties.*
Refreshments: In the barn Mon-Sat 10.30-5.30; Sun 12-5.30. (Closed 5 in Mar and Oct). Shop, with special plants section. Art and Craft gallery. Dogs in woodland walk and park only, on leads. Wheelchairs provided

TRELOWARREN HOUSE & CHAPEL   🏛

Mawgan-in-Meneage, Helston map C1   △
Telephone: (032 622) 366
(Sir John Vyvyan, Bt.)

Home of the Vyvyan family since 1427 part of the house dates from early Tudor times. The Chapel, part of which is pre-Reformation, and the 17th century part of the house are leased to the Trelowarren Fellowship, an Ecumenical Christian Charity. The Chapel and main rooms containing family portraits are open to the public with guided tours. Concerts take place, and Sunday Services are held in the Chapel during the holiday season. Exhibitions of paintings.

Location: 6 m S of Helston off B3293 to St Keverne.
Open: HOUSE & CHAPEL. Open from Apr 12 to Oct 6 - Weds & Bank Hol Mons. Always 2.30-5. Conducted tours. Concerts are held in Chapel and Chapel Services every Sun during the holiday season. Organised tours by arrangement.
Admission: £1, Chd 50p (under 12 years free), including entry to various exhibitions of paintings.
Ground floor only suitable for disabled.

TRENGWAINTON GARDEN   The National Trust

Penzance map C1   &
Telephone: (0736) 63021

Large shrub and woodland garden. Fine views. A series of walled gardens contain rare sub-tropical plants.

Location: 2 m NW of Penzance ½ m W of Heamoor on Morvah Road (B3312).
Station(s): Penzance (2 m).
Open: Mar 1 to end Oct - Weds, Thurs, Fris, Sats & Bank Hol Mons 10.30-5.30, 10.30-5 in Mar and Oct. Last adm ½ hr before closing.
Admission: £2.40, Chd £1.20.*No reduction for parties.*
No dogs. Wheelchair access.

TRERICE   The National Trust

nr. Newquay map C2   &
Telephone: (0637) 875404; Restaurant (0637) 879434

A small Elizabethan house, fine furniture, plaster ceilings and fireplaces, in a recently planted garden. A small museum in the Barn traces the development of the lawn mower.

Location: 3 m SE of Newquay A392 & A3058 (turn right at Kestle Mill).
Station(s): Quintrel Downs (1½ m).
Open: Apr 1 to Oct 31 - Daily (*except* Tues) 11-5.30, 11-5 in Oct. Last adm ½ hr before closing.
Admission: £3.60, Chd £1.80.*Reduced rate of £3, for pre-booked parties.*
Refreshments: In the barn, opening times as for House. *Parties must book.*
No dogs. Wheelchairs available; access to house only. Shop.

TREWITHEN HOUSE AND GARDENS

Probus map D1
Telephone: (0726) 882763/882764 (nurseries),(0726) 883794 (Garden Shop)

'Trewithen' means 'House of the Trees' which truly describes this exceptionally fine early Georgian house in its magnificent setting of wood and parkland. The origins of the house go back to the 17th century but it was the Architect Sir Robert Taylor, aided by Thomas Edwards of Greenwich, who were responsible for the splendid building and interiors we see today. Philip Hawkins bought the property in 1715 and began extensive rebuilding. The house has been lived in and cared for by the same family since that date. The magnificent landscaped gardens have an outstanding collection of magnolias, rhododendron and azaleas which are well known throughout the world. The gardens are particularly spectacular between March and the end of June and again in Autumn, although there is much to see throughout the year. A wide variety of shrubs and plants from the famous nurseries are always on sale. Other attractions include a children's playground and a 25-minute video of the house and gardens. The gardens are one of only two in this county to be awarded 3 stars by the Michelin Guide to the South West.

Location: On A390 between Probus and Grampound, adjoining County Demonstration Gardens.
Open: GARDENS: Open Mar 1 to Sept 30, Mon to Sat 10-4.30. *Closed* Sun. Nurseries: Open throughout the year 9-4.30.
Admission: Gardens: Mar-June £2, Chd (under 15) £1; July-Sept £1.75, Chd (under 15) £1. HOUSE: Guided tours Mon and Tues only Apr to July and Aug Bank Hol Mon (2-4.30) £2.80. Parties by arrangement please.
Refreshments: Tea shop for light refreshments.

CUMBRIA

ABBOT HALL ART GALLERY & MUSEUM OF LAKELAND LIFE & INDUSTRY

Kirkland map F10 &
Telephone: (0539) 722464
(Lake District Art Gallery & Museum Trust)

Impressive Georgian House with comprehensive collections of portraits by Romney and Gardner, and a new gallery of Lake District art over 250 years. Furniture by Gillows displayed in recently restored rooms. Lively programme of temporary exhibitions. Access for disabled throughout the Gallery. Adjacent Museum of Lakeland Life recaptures flavour of everyday social and industrial life in the Lakes. Arthur Ransome Room and John Cunliffe Room (Postman Pat). Also visit award-winning Kendal Museum of Natural History and Archaeology on Station Road.

Location: Off Kirkland nr Kendal Parish Church. From M6 exit 36.
Station(s): Oxenholme (1½m); Kendal (¾m).
Open: All the year - daily except Dec 25, 26 and Jan 1. Mon-Sat 10.30-5, Sun 2-5, **Reduced hours during winter/spring**
Admission: Charge; concessions for OAPs, Chd, Students and families. Disabled access. Free parking.

ACORN BANK GARDEN   🌿 The National Trust

Temple Sowerby, Penrith map F11
Telephone: (07683) 61893

This 2½ acre garden is protected by fine oaks under which grow a vast display of daffodils. Inside walls are two orchards with medlar, mulberry, cherries, quince and apples. Surrounding the orchards are mixed borders with herbaceous plants and many flowering shrubs and climbing roses. The adjacent herb garden has the largest collection of culinary, medicinal and narcotic herbs in the north. The red sandstone house is let to the Sue Ryder Foundation and is open on application.

Location: Just N of Temple Sowerby, 6 m E of Penrith on A66.
Open: GARDEN ONLY. Apr 1 to Oct 31 - Daily 10-5.30.
Admission: £1.50, Chd 80p. Reduction for pre-arranged parties.
No dogs. Wheelchair access to parts of garden only. Small shop. Plant sales.

Sir Joshua Reynolds
Portrait painter (1723–1792)
First President of the Royal Academy, knighted in 1769

His work can be seen in the following properties included in Historic Houses Castles and Gardens:

Arundel Castle
Dalmeny House (Roseberry Collection of Political Portraits)
Goodwood House

Kenwood
Shalom Hall
Weston Park

BRANTWOOD

Coniston map F10
Telephone: (05394) 41396
(Brantwood Educational Trust)

The home of John Ruskin from 1872-1900. Large collection of pictures by Ruskin and his associates. Ruskin's coach, boat, furniture and other associated items. Ruskin's woodland gardens are currently being restored. There is a delightful nature walk around the 250 acre estate.

Location: 2½ m from Coniston. Historic House signs at Coniston, Head of Coniston Water & Hawkshead.
Open: Open all year. Mid-Mar to mid-Nov - Daily 11-5.30. Winter season - Weds to Suns 11-4.
Admission: House, Exhibitions & Nature Walks £2.80, Chd free. Nature trails only £1 (including guide), Chd free. Free car park.
Refreshments: Licensed restaurant/tea room/coffee; light meals available.
Steam Yacht Gondola sails regularly from Coniston Pier. Parking for disabled near house. Toilets (incl for disabled). Craft gallery and shop.

BROUGH CASTLE   English⌗Heritage

map G11
Telephone: 091-261 1585 (Area Office)

The importance of Brough-under-Stainmore, lying between Carlisle and York, did not escape the Romans. So it is hardly surprising that the Normans built a stronghold on the site of that derelict Roman fort. The Scots destroyed it in 1174 and the present castle is a product of the rebuilding that followed. Until 1204 Brough was a royal castle; then King John granted it to Robert de Vipont, ancestor of the Lords Clifford. Part of the 11th century wall remains and much of the 17th century repair work carried out by that energetic restorer of castles, Lady Anne Clifford.

Location: 8 m (13 km) south east of Appleby.
Open: Good Friday or Apr 1 (whichever is earlier) to Sept 30: Open Daily 10-6. Oct 1 to Maundy Thursday or Mar 31 (whichever is earlier): Open Wed to Sun 10-4. *Closed* Dec 24-26, Jan 1.
Admission: 80p, Concessions 60p, Chd 40p.

BROUGHAM CASTLE   English✠Heritage

map F11
Telephone: (0768) 62488

The oldest part of the surviving building, the keep, was constructed in Henry II's reign after the Scots had relinquished their hold on the north west of England. The keep, later heightened, and its gatehouses formed an impregnable fortress, while also providing a lordly residence of spacious proportions. The castle was restored by Lady Anne Clifford in the 17th century.

Location: 1½ m (2.4 km) east of Penrith.
Open: Good Friday or Apr 1 (whichever is earlier) to Sept 30: Open Daily 10-6. Oct 1 to Maundy Thursday or Mar 31 (whichever is earlier): Open Wed to Sun 10-4. *Closed* Dec 24-26, Jan 1.
Admission: £1.20, Concessions 90p, Chd 60p.

CARLISLE CASTLE   English✠Heritage

Carlisle map F11
Telephone: (0228) 591922

Twenty-six years after the Battle of Hastings. Carlisle remained unconquered. In 1092 William II marched north, took the city and ordered the building of a stronghold above the River Eden. Since William's time the castle has survived 800 years of fierce and bloody attacks, extensive rebuilding and continuous military occupation. A massive Norman keep contains an exhibition on the history of the castle. D'Ireby Tower now open to the public, containing furnishings to authentic medieval design, an exhibition and shop. Guided tours are given by a local group of volunteers.

Location: North of town centre.
Open: Good Friday or Apr 1 (whichever is earlier) to Sept 30 daily 10-6. Oct 1 to Maundy Thursday or Mar 31 (whichever is earlier) daily 10-4. *Closed* Dec 24-26, Jan 1.
Admission: £2, Concessions £1.50, Chd £1.

CASTLETOWN HOUSE

Rockcliffe, Carlisle map F11
Telephone: (0228 74) 205
(Giles Mounsey-Heysham, Esq.)

Georgian Country House set in attractive gardens and grounds. Fine ceilings. Naval pictures, furnishings and model engines.

Location: 5 m NW of Carlisle on Solway coast, 1 m W of Rockcliffe village and 2 m W of A74.
Open: HOUSE ONLY. By appointment only.

CONISHEAD PRIORY

Ulverston map F11
Telephone: (0229) 584029

Victorian Gothic mansion, under restoration, on 12th century site. Now a Buddhist centre. Oak room, cantilever staircase, stained glass windows, cloister. Woodland trail to Morecambe Bay. Shop.

Location: 2 m Ulverston, A5089, coast road to Barrow-in-Furness.
Open: Easter to end Sept. 2-5, Sat, Sun and Bank Hols. CLOSED - 24/25 July & 31 July/1 Aug & 7/8 Aug.
Admission: Free. House tours £1.50.
Refreshments: Teas.

DALEMAIN

nr Penrith map F11
Telephone: (07684) 86450
(Mr Robert Hasell-McCosh)

Mediaeval, Tudor and early Georgian house and gardens lived in by the same family for over 300 years. Fine furniture and portraits. Countryside museum and picnic areas, Agricultural Museum, Westmorland and Cumberland Yeomanry Museum and Adventure Playground, Fell Pony Museum. Interesting garden as featured on BBC and in various publications. Plant Centre. Gift shop.

Location: 3 m from Penrith on A592. Turn off M6 exit 40 onto A66 (A592) to Ullswater.
Open: April 4 to Oct 3 - daily except Frid and Sats, 11.15-5.
Admission: Charged. Entry to car park, picnic area, shop and restaurant free.
Refreshments: Licensed Restaurant. Coffee from 11.15. Bar lunches 12-2.30. Home made teas from 2.30. High teas by arrangement. No dogs please.

FURNESS ABBEY   English✠Heritage

map F10
Telephone: (0229) 23420

At the time of its suppression in 1537, the abbey was one of the wealthiest monasteries in the land. Founded in 1124 by King Stephen, the abbey, set in a beautiful valley, belonged to the first Order of Savigny, then to the Cistercians. Ruined buildings of red sandstone evoke a vision of past splendour. Magnificent still are the canopied seats in the presbytery and the Chapter House. Exhibition in the museum at the entrance.

Location: 1½ m (2.4 km) north of Barrow-in-Furness.
Open: Good Friday or Apr 1 (whichever is earlier) to Sept 30: Open Daily 10-6. Oct 1 to Maundy Thursday or Mar 31 (whichever is earlier): Open Tues to Sun 10-4. *Closed* Dec 24-26, Jan 1.
Admission: £2, Concessions £1.50, Chd £1. Price includes a free Personal Stereo Guided Tour.

HADRIAN'S WALL   English✠Heritage

map G12

Snaking across the north of England, from Bowness to Wallsend, is Hadrian's remarkable wall, built between AD125-130 to demarcate the frontier of Britain and the northernmost limit of the Roman Empire at the time. With true Roman precision, a milecastle was constructed at every mile and two observation turrets between each milecastle, many sections have withstood the ravages of time. At strategic points great forts were built to garrison 500 or 1000 men. English Heritage has a well-preserved milecastle at Harrow's Scar, near Gilsland, and several turrets in the Brampton area, the best at Banks East. (See also Northumberland Section).

HOLKER HALL

Cark-in-Cartmel, nr Grange-over-Sands map F10
Telephone: (05395) 58328
(Lord and Lady Cavendish)

25 acres of National Award winning gardens with water features. (World Class Good Gardens Guide '92) Zanussi Victorian and wartime kitchen exhibition, patchwork/quilting displays; exhibitions; adventure playground, deer park. Former home of the Dukes of Devonshire and still lived in by members of the family.

Location: ½ m N of Cark-in-Cartmel on B5278 from Haverthwaite; 4 m W Grange-over-Sands.
Open: HOUSE, GARDENS & MOTOR MUSEUM. Apr 1 to Oct 31 - Daily (ex Sat) 10.30-4.30. Park open until 6.
Admission: Group rates for parties of 20 or more. Free Coach and Car Park.
Refreshments: Clock Tower Cafe serving salads, sandwiches, home made cakes and pastries, beverages including wine and beer. *Group catering by prior arrangement.*
Gift Shop.

HUTTON-IN-THE-FOREST

Penrith map F11
Telephone: (07684) 84449
(Lord and Lady Inglewood)

One of the ancient manors in the Forest of Inglewood, and the home of Lord Inglewood's family since the beginning of the 17th century. Built around a medieval pele tower with 18th and 19th century additions. Fine English furniture and pictures, ceramics and tapestries. Outstanding gardens and grounds with terraces, walled garden, dovecote, lake and woodland walk through magnificent specimen trees.

Location: 6 m NW of Penrith on B5305 Wigton Road (from M6 exit 41).
Open: Easter to Oct 3 - Thurs, Frid, Suns and all Bank Hol Mons, 1-4. GROUNDS open every day (*except* Sat) 11-5. Private parties by arrangement any day from Apr 1.
Refreshments: Fresh home-made teas available in the cloisters when house open. Lunch and supper menus available on request.

19/20 IRISH STREET

Whitehaven map E11   ♿
Telephone: (0946) 693111 Ext 285
(Copeland Borough Council)

1840-50 Italianate design, possibly by S. Smirke. Stuccoed 3-storey building now occupied by the Council Offices.

Location: In town centre
Station(s): Whitehaven.
Open: All the year during office hours. For details and appointments telephone Mr J. A. Pomfret.
Refreshments: Hotels and restaurants in town centre.
Ground floor only suitable for disabled.

LANERCOST PRIORY   English✠Heritage

map F11
Telephone: (06977) 3030

Just south of Hadrian's Wall, in the wooded valley of the River Irthing, stands this noble Augustinian priory founded by Robert de Vaux in the 12th century. Centrepiece is the priory church, 800 years old, and the nave is still a parish church. English Heritage cares for the area around the cloisters and the ruined East End of the church.

Location: 2 m (3.2 km) north east of Brampton.
Open: Good Friday or Apr 1 (whichever is earlier) to Sept 30: Open Daily 10-6.
Admission: 80p, Concessions 60p, Chd 40p.

LEVENS HALL

Kendal map F10 &
Telephone: (05395) 60321
(C. H. Bagot, Esq.)

This magnificent Elizabethan home of the Bagot family, with its famous topiary garden (c.1694) is a must for visitors to the Lake District. The garden is unique in age and appearance, beautifully maintained in its original design with colourful bedding and herbaceous borders. The house contains a superb collection of Jacobean furniture, fine plaster ceilings, panelling, paintings and needlework, including the earliest English patchwork (c.1708). A collection of working model steam engines shows the development of steam power from 1820 to 1920, with full-sized traction engines in steam on Sundays and Bank Holiday Mondays.

Location: 5 m S of Kendal on the Milnthorpe Road (A6); Exit 36 from M6.
Open: Apr 1 to Sept 30. House, Garden, Gift Shop, Tearooms, Plant Centre, Play Area and Picnic Area. Suns, Mons, Tues, Weds & Thurs 11-5. Steam Collection 2-5. Closed Frid & Sats.
Admission: Charge. Group rates for 20 or more.
Refreshments: Home-made light Lunches and teas.
Shop. Regret house not suitable for wheelchairs.

MIREHOUSE

Keswick map F11 &
Telephone: (076 87) 72287
(Mr & Mrs Spedding)

Seventeenth century Manor House with 19th century additions. Portraits and manuscripts of Francis Bacon and many literary friends of the Spedding family including Tennyson, Wordsworth, Southey. Children welcome. French, German and Spanish spoken. Walk through grounds to Bassenthwaite Lake. Adventure Playgrounds. Norman Lakeside Church of St. Bega.

Location: 4½ m N of Keswick on A591 (Keswick to Carlisle Road).
Open: Apr to Oct - Lakeside Walk, Adventure Playgrounds - Daily 10.30- 5.30. House - Suns, Weds & also Frid in Aug. 2-5. Parties welcome by appointment.
Refreshments: Old Sawmill Tearoom open daily 10.30-5.30; salads & sandwiches made to order, home baking. Parties please book (Tel: Keswick (07687) 74317).

MUNCASTER CASTLE

Ravenglass map F10 △
(Mrs P. Gordon-Duff-Pennington)

Seat of the Pennington family since the 13th century, this magnificent castle with its famous rhododendron gardens and superb views of Eskdale dates from early 14th century, although the Pele tower is built on Roman foundations. There is an excellent collection of family portraits, tapestry and porcelain, but its outstanding feature is the large collection of 16th and 17th century furniture in beautiful condition. The octagonal library is one of Salvin's finest works and contains over 6,000 books. It is a very special family home. The gardens offer a variety of walks which can all offer some of the finest views in England, including those over the Esk Valley (Ruskin's Gateway to Paradise). The Owl Centre houses a large collection of these mystical creatures and daily at 2.30 (Apr-Oct 31) a talk is given on the pioneering work of the Centre. Weather permitting, the birds fly.

Location: 1 m SE of Ravenglass village on A595 (entrance ½ m W of Church).
Station(s): Ravenglass (1 m).
Open: Gardens and Owl Centre daily throughout the year 11-5. Castle: Mar 28 to Oct 31 Tues to Sun 1-4. Open all Bank Holiday Mons.
Admission: Gardens and Owl Centre £2.90, Chd £1.60. Castle, Gardens and Owl Centre: £4.50, Chd £2.50, Family tickets (2 plus 2) Gardens and Owl Centre £8. Castle, Gardens and Owl Centre £12. Special Party Rates available. Write or telephone for Party Bookings and details of events during the season to: Muncaster Castle, Ravenglass, Cumbria. Telephone (0229) 717614; Fax (0229) 717010. SEASON TICKETS AVAILABLE - ADULT £12.50. FAMILY - £28 (2+3).

NAWORTH CASTLE

Brampton map F11
Telephone: (069 77) 3666
(The Earl of Carlisle MC)

Historic border fortress, built by the Dacres in 1335, acquired and renovated by the Howard Family in 1602, the Castle is currently the home of the Earl and Countess of Carlisle. A stronghold for the Wardens of the West March in the 16th century, an impressive residence for the powerful Earls of Carlisle in the 17th century, and an artistic centre for the pre-Raphaelites in the late 19th century, the Castle features: the Great Hall with Gobelin Tapestries and Heraldic Beasts, Lord William's Tower, the Long Gallery, the Library designed by Philip Webb & Burne-Jones, and the original 14th century dungeons.

Location: 12 m E of Carlisle, near Brampton, off the A69 to Newcastle.
Open: Easter Weekend to Sept 30 12-5, Weds, Sats and Suns; five days/week Wed to Sun in Aug only.
Admission: £2.50, OAPs/Chd £1.50. Family ticket £6. Special parties by arrangement. Free car and coach park.
Refreshments: Tea room and visitors' shop on premises.

RYDAL MOUNT

Ambleside map F10
Telephone: (05394) 33002
(Mrs Mary Henderson - nee Wordsworth)

Wordsworth home from 1813-1850. Family portraits and furniture, many of the poet's personal possessions, and first editions of his works. The garden which was designed by Wordsworth has been described as one of the most interesting small gardens to be found anywhere in England. Two long terraces, many rare trees and shrubs. Extends to 4½ acres.

Location: Off A591, 1½ m from Ambleside, 2 m from Grasmere.
Open: Mar 1 to Oct 31 - Daily 9.30-5. Nov 1 to Mar 1 - 10-4 (*Closed* Tues in winter). See Lake District National Park Visitor Centre for out of season package.
Admission: House & Gardens £2, Chd 80p, Parties £1.70.

SIZERGH CASTLE AND GARDEN 🍂 The National Trust

Kendal map F10
Telephone: (05395) 60070

The 14th century Pele tower (the oldest part of the castle) rises to 60 feet, contains some original windows, floors and fireplaces; 15th century Great Hall, extended in later centuries; 16th century wings; fine panelling and ceilings; contents include French and English furniture, china, family portraits. Extensive garden includes two thirds of an acre limestone rock garden, the largest owned by the Trust with large collection of Japanese maples, dwarf conifers, hardy ferns and many perennials and bulbs; water garden; herbaceous borders; wild flower banks; fine autumn colour.

Location: 3½ m S of Kendal NW of interchange A590/A591 interchange; 2 m from Levens Hall.
Open: CASTLE & GARDEN: Apr 1 to Oct 31 - Suns, Mons, Tues, Weds & Thurs; 1.30-5.30 (last admission 5). Garden & Shop open from 12.30 same days.
Admission: £3.30 (House and Garden), Chd £1.70. GARDEN ONLY: £1.70. Parties by arrangement with The Administrator, Sizergh Castle, Tel: Sedgwick 60070. Please send sae. Shop. No dogs. Wheelchairs (one provided) in garden only.

STOTT PARK BOBBIN MILL   English⌗Heritage

map F10
Telephone: (05395) 31087

The Victorian mill buildings forming Stott Park are virtually the same today as they were 150 years ago. The bobbin mill developed from man's ability to harness the power of the fast-flowing Lakeland streams to run machinery and also from the abundance of local coppice wood. Restored as a working industrial monument, much of the machinery still remains, including a turbine and steam engine.

Location: On unclassified road north of the village of Finsthwaite, 2 m (3.2 km) north of A590 Kendal/ Barrow-in-Furness Road at Newby Bridge (near east bank of Lake Windermere).
Open: Good Friday or Apr 1 (whichever is earlier) to Oct 31: Open Daily 10-6 (or dusk if earlier).
Admission: £2, Concessions £1.50, Chd £1. Guided tours are available.

TOWNEND 🍂 The National Trust

Troutbeck map F10
Telephone: (05394) 32628

17th century Lakeland farmhouse with original furnishings including much wood-carving in traditional style. Home of the Browne family for 300 years, and last remaining glimpse into the old farming way of life.

Location: At S end of Troutbeck village, 3 m SE of Ambleside.
Open: Apr 1 to Oct 31. Daily (except Mons & Sats but open Bank Hol Mons) 1-5 or dusk if earlier). Last adm 4.30.
Admission: £2.40, Chd £1.20. No reductions for parties. No dogs. No coaches. Unsuitable for wheelchairs.

WORDSWORTH HOUSE 🍂 The National Trust

Cockermouth map F11 △
Telephone: (0900) 824805

North country Georgian House built in 1745, birthplace of the poet Wordsworth, furnished in the style of his time, with some of his belongings. The pleasant garden is referred to in his 'Prelude'. Video displays.

Location: In Main Street.
Open: Apr 1 to Oct 29 - daily except Sat and Sun 11-5pm (last admission 4.30). Shop open winter: as summer but closed Sun and week after Christmas.
Admission: £2.40, Chd £1.20. Reductions for pre-booked parties except on Suns.
Refreshments: Light refreshments in the old kitchen (licensed).
No dogs. Unsuitable for wheelchairs.

DERBYSHIRE

BOLSOVER CASTLE   English ⌗ Heritage

map H8
Telephone: (0246) 823349

Castle in name only, the present mansion was built during the 17th century by Sir Charles Cavendish and his son William on the site of a 12th century castle. The Little Castle, separate and self-contained, is a delightful romantic Jacobean folly.

Location: Bolsover 6 m east of Chesterfield on A632.
Open: Good Friday or Apr 1 (whichever is earlier) to Sept 30 daily 10-6. Oct 1 to Maundy Thursday or Mar 31 (whichever is earlier) Tues to Sun 10-4. *Closed* Dec 24-26, Jan 1.
Admission: £2, Concessions £1.50, Chd £1.

CALKE ABBEY AND PARK   🌺   The National Trust

nr Derby map H7
Telephone: (0332) 863822 recorded information (0332) 864444

Baroque mansion built 1701-3. House virtually unaltered since death of last baronet in 1924. Unique Caricature Room, gold and white drawing room, early 18th century Chinese silk state bed. Carriage display in Stable Block. Calke Park is a fine landscaped setting (approx. 750 acres). Park accessible via Ticknall entrance only. (One-way system in operation).

Location: 9m S of Derby on A514 at Ticknall between Swadlincote and Melbourne.
Open: Apr 3 to end Oct: Sat-Wed including Bank Holiday Mon. *Closed* Good Friday. 1-5.30 (last adm 5).
Admission: By timed ticket only. Ticket office open at 11am. Visitors are advised that on busy days admission may not be possible. Long distance travellers are advised to contact the Calke office before setting out. Parties **must** book in advance with the Administrator. £4.20, Chd £2.10

CHATSWORTH

Bakewell map H8
Telephone: (0246) 582204
*(Chatsworth House Trust)*K2

Built by Talman for 1st Duke of Devonshire between 1687 and 1707. Splendid collection of pictures, drawings, books and furniture. Garden with elaborate waterworks surrounded by a great park. **Regret House impossible for wheelchairs, but they are most welcome in the garden.**

Location: ½ m E of village of Edensor on A623, 4 m E of Bakewell, 16 m from junction 29, M1. Signposted via Chesterfield.
Open: HOUSE & GARDEN. Mar 21 to Oct 31 - Daily 11-4.30. FARMYARD & ADVENTURE PLAYGROUND. Mar 21 to Oct 3 - Daily 10.30-4.30.
Admission: Charges not available at time of going to press.
Refreshments: Home-made refreshments. Coach Drivers' Rest Room.
Gift shops. Baby Room. All details subject to confirmation.

EYAM HALL

Eyam map H8
Telephone: (0433) 631976
(R. H. V. Wright)

Seventeenth century manor house situated in the famous 'plague village' of Eyam. Built and still occupied by the Wright family. A glimpse of three centuries through the eyes of one family. Great variety of contents, including family portraits, tapestries, clocks, costumes, and toys. Jacobean staircase and spectacular old kitchen.

Location: 100 yds W of church. Eyam is off A623, 12 m W of Chesterfield, 15 m SW of Sheffield. Parking in village car park.
Open: Mar 28 to Oct 24: Weds, Thurs, Suns and Bank Hol Mons. Tues for schools only. Open 11. Last tour 4.30.
Admission: £2.95, Chd 1.70, Over 60s £2.25, Family ticket £8. Advance booking essential for parties, reductions available.
Refreshments: Knivetons' Tea Shop: home-made teas, cakes and light lunches. 11-5.30.

HADDON HALL - *SEE PAGE 36*

HARDWICK HALL   The National Trust

Nr Chesterfield map H8
Telephone: (0246) 850430

Built 1591-1597 by 'Bess of Hardwick'. Notable furniture, needlework, tapestries. Gardens with yew hedges and borders of shrubs and flowers. Extensive collection of herbs. Information Centre in Country Park.

Location: 2 m S of Chesterfield/Mansfield Road (A617) 6½ m NW of Mansfield and 9½ m SE of Chesterfield. Approach from M1 exit 29.
Open: House and Garden: Apr 1 to end Oct. House - Weds, Thurs, Sats, Suns & Bank Hol Mons 12.30-5 (or sunset if earlier). Last adm 4.30. Garden open daily to end Oct, 12-5.30. *Closed* Good Friday. Access to Hall may be limited at peak periods.
Admission: House & Garden £5, Chd £2.50; Garden only £2, Chd £1.*No reduction for parties (including schools). School parties must book.*
Refreshments: In the Great Kitchen of Hall 2-4.45. Lunches 12-2 (last orders 15 mins before closing) on days when hall is open.
Car park (gates close 6). Dogs in park only, on leads. Wheelchairs in garden only.*Enquiries to The National Trust, Hardwick Hall, Doe Lea, nr Chesterfield, Derbys.*

KEDLESTON HALL   The National Trust

Derby map H7
Telephone: (0332) 842191

One of the best examples of neo-classical architecture in the country. Robert Adam designed the late 18th century house for Sir Nathaniel Curzon to house his fine collection of furniture, tapestries and portraits. Landscaped park includes further examples of Adam's work.

Location: 4 m NW of Derby on Derby/Hulland Road via the Derby Ring Road Queensway.
Open: House, Park and Gardens: Apr 3 to end Oct, Sats to Wed including Bank Holiday Mons. Park and Gardens: 11-6. Tea room: 12-5. House and Shop: 1-5.30 (last adm 5). Coach parties welcome on days when the property is open, but **must** book well in advance in writing to the Administrator. 1993 events-details from Administrator.
Admission: £3.90, Chd £1.90.

MELBOURNE HALL AND GARDENS

Melbourne map H7
Telephone: (0332) 862502
(Lord Ralph Kerr)

This beautiful house of history is the home of Lord and Lady Ralph Kerr. In its picturesque poolside setting, Melbourne Hall was once the Home of Victorian Prime Minister William Lamb who as 2nd Viscount Melbourne gave his name to the famous city in Australia. This delightful family home contains an important collection of pictures and antique furniture. One of the most famous formal gardens in Britain featuring Robert Bakewell's wrought iron 'Birdcage'.

Location: 9 m S of Derby off the A453 in village of Melbourne.
Open: HOUSE open every day of Aug only (except first 3 Mons) 2-5. Garden open: Apr to Sept: Weds, Sats, Suns, Bank Hol Mons 2-6.
Admission: Pre-booked parties in House - Aug only.
Refreshments: Melbourne Hall Tearooms - open throughout the year Tel: (0332) 864224/863469. Craft Centre & Gift Shop open at various times throughout the year. Car parking limited - none reserved. Suitable for disabled persons.

OLD HOUSE MUSEUM

Bakewell map H8
(Bakewell & District Historical Society)

An early Tudor house with original wattle & daub screen and open chamber. Costumes and Victorian kitchen, children's toys, craftsmen's tools and lacework.

Location: Above the church in Bakewell. ¼ m from centre.
Open: HOUSE ONLY. Apr 1 to Oct 31 - Daily 2-5. Parties in morning or evening by appointment (Telephone Bakewell (0629) 813647).
Admission: £1.50, Chd 50p.

PEVERIL CASTLE   English Heritage

map H8
Telephone: (0433) 20613

The castle was built to control Peak Forest, where lead had been mined since prehistoric times. William the Conqueror thought so highly of this metal - and of the silver that could be extracted from it - that he entrusted the forest to one of his most esteemed knights, William Peveril.

Location: In Castleton on A625, 15 m west of Sheffield.
Open: Good Friday or Apr 1 (whichever is earlier) to Sept 30: Open Daily 10-6. Oct 1 to Maundy Thursday or Mar 31 (whichever is earlier): Open Tues to Sun 10-4. *Closed* Dec 24-26, Jan 1.
Admission: £1.20, Concessions 90p, Chd 60p

HADDON HALL

Bakewell map H8
Telephone: (0629) 812855
(His Grace the Duke of Rutland)

HADDON HALL

Estate Office, Haddon Hall, Bakewell, Derbyshire DE45 1LA   Telephone: Bakewell **(0629) 812855**   Fax: **(0629) 814379**

The Derbyshire seat of the Duke of Rutland

One of our few remaining 12th century manor houses, perfectly preserved. Noted for its tapestries, wood carvings and wall paintings. Standing on a wooded hill overlooking the fast flowing River Wye, Haddon is totally unspoiled. The beautiful terraced gardens dating from the middle ages are famous for roses, old fashioned flowers and herbs. Banqueting and clay pigeon facilities available in Hall and Park. The House is extremely difficult for disabled visitors.

Location: 2 m SE Bakewell & 6½ m N of Matlock on Buxton/Matlock Road (A6).
Open: Apr 1 to Sept 30 - Tues-Sun, 11-6. *Closed* Mons except Bank Hols, also closed Suns in July and Aug except Bank Hol weekends.
Admission: £3.40, Chd £2, Party rate £2.80, OAPs £2.80 NB: These prices may vary - please ring to check for details.
Refreshments: Morning coffee, lunches, afternoon teas at Stables Restaurant.

Robert Adam – architect

His work can be seen at the following properties included in Historic Houses Castles and Gardens:

Bowood
Culzean Castle
Hatchlands
Kedleston Hall
Kenwood
Kimbolton Castle
Luton Hoo
Mellerstain

Moccas Court
Newby Hall
Nostell Priory
Osterley Park House
Papplewick Hall
Saltram House
Syon House

SUDBURY HALL AND MUSEUM OF CHILDHOOD

❧ The National Trust

nr Derby map H7 ⓢ
Telephone: (0283) 585305

A 17th century brick built house. Contains plasterwork ceilings. Laguerre murals staircase carved by Pierce and overmantel by Grinling Gibbons. Museum of Childhood.

Location: At Sudbury, 6 m E of Uttoxeter off A50 Road.
Open: Apr 1 to end of Oct - Wed to Sun. 1-5.30 (last adm 5). Museum 12-5.30.
Admission: £3, Chd £1.50. Pre-booked parties special rates. Museum £2.
Refreshments: Light lunches & teas in Coach House, same open days as property, 12.30-5.30.
Dogs in grounds only, on lead. Wheelchairs in garden only. 1993 events-details available from the Administrator.

WINSTER MARKET HOUSE   ❧ The National Trust

nr Matlock map H8
Telephone: (033 529) 245

A stone market house of the late 17th or early 18th century in main street of Winster.

Location: 4 m W of Matlock on S side of B5057.
Open: Easter to end Oct. Daily.
Admission: Free.
Information Room. No dogs. Unsuitable for wheelchairs.

DEVON

A LA RONDE   ❧ The National Trust

Exmouth map F2
Telephone: (0395) 265514

A unique 16 sided house built in 1796; fascinating interior decoration including shell encrusted and feather frieze; 18th century contents and collections from European Tour.

Location: 2 m N of Exmouth on A376.
Open: 1 Apr to 31 Oct. 11-5.30 daily, except Frid and Sat. Last admission ½hr before closing.
Admission: £3, Chd half-price.
Not suitable for coaches or visually handicapped. No dogs.

ARLINGTON COURT   ❧ The National Trust

Barnstaple map E3 ♿
Telephone: (0271) 850296

Regency house furnished with the collections of the late Miss Rosalie Chichester; including shells, pewter and model ships. Display of horse-drawn vehicles in the stables. Good trees. Victorian formal garden.

Location: 8 m NE of Barnstaple on E side of A39.
Open: Footpaths through park open all year daily during daylight hours. House, Victorian garden, Carriage Collection, Stables, Shop: Apr 1 to Oct 31 - Daily (except Sats but open Sats of Bank Hol Weekends) 11-5.30. (Last adm ½ hour before closing.)
Admission: House & Carriage Collection £4.60, Chd half-price. Gardens, Ground & Stables £2.40, Chd half-price. *Reduced fee of £3.50 for parties of 15 or more on application to the Administrator.* Parties who do not pre-book will be charged full rate.
Refreshments: Licensed restaurant at the House: Apr 1 to Oct 31 - days and times as for House.
Shop. Dogs in park only, on leads. Wheelchairs provided. Carriage rides.

AVENUE COTTAGE GARDENS

Ashprington, Totnes map E2
Telephone: (0803) 732 769
(R. J. Pitts Esq, R. C. H. Soans Esq)

11 acres of garden and woodland walks. Part of 18th century landscape garden under going recreation by Designers/Plantsmen.

Location: 3 m SE of Totnes 300 yds beyond Ashprington Church (Sharpham Drive).
Open: Apr 1 to Sept 30, Tues to Sat inclusive 11-5. Parties by arrangement.
Admission: £1, Chd 25p. Collecting box.
No coaches. Limited access for disabled persons. No wheelchairs available. Dogs on leads only.

BICKLEIGH CASTLE 🏛

nr Tiverton map E3 △ ♿
Telephone: (0884) 855 363
(Mr O. N. Boxall)

A Royalist Stronghold with 900 years of history and architecture and still lived-in. The 11th c detached Chapel, the Armoury featuring a Civil War display and Cromwellian arms and armour, the Guard Room with Tudor furniture and pictures, the Great Hall, Elizabethan bedroom, and the 17th c farmhouse - all are shown. Museum of 19th c domestic and agricultural objects and toys. Maritime Exhibition showing Bickleigh Castle's connection with the 'Mary Rose' and the 'Titanic'. World War 11 original spy and escape gadgets: the most complete collection known. Moated garden, 'Spooky' tower (57 steps). Spinning. Heritage Education Trust Award winner 1983 and 1988. Full of interest for all the family.

Location: 4 m S of Tiverton A396. At Bickleigh Bridge take A3072 and follow signs.
Open: Easter Week (Good Fri to Fri) then Weds, Suns & Bank Hol Mons to late Spring Bank Hol; then to early Oct 3 - Daily (except Sats) 2-5.30 *Parties of 20 or more by prior appointment only (preferably at times other than above) at reduced rates.*
Admission: £2.90, Chd £2.50. Free coach & car park.
Refreshments: Devonshire Cream Teas in the thatched Barn.
Souvenir shops. Popular for Wedding Receptions etc.

BICTON PARK GARDENS

nr Exeter   map E4
Telephone: (0395) 68465
(Bicton Park Trust Co.)

Bicton Park, regarded by many as one of the finest old gardens in England, is set in the beautiful wooded countryside of East Devon just 8 miles from Exeter. Sixty acres of formal gardens and parkland include the Italian Garden, designed by Andre le Notre, (designer of the gardens at Versailles), American, Oriental and the smaller Hermitage and Alpine gardens. Ornamental lakes and fountains are complemented with a fine display of statuary. Specialist glasshouses are a particular feature at Bicton and include displays of Fuchsias, Geraniums, Termperate and Tropical plants, the best known of these being the famous Palm House, a magnificent glass domed structure dating from 1840. Other notable aspects to be found in the gardens are the Bird Garden, Tropical House and a wonderful collection of agricultural and estate artifacts in the James Countryside Museum.

Location: 8 m S of Exeter near Budleigh Salterton. Signed off M5 Jct 30.
Open: Mar to Oct, daily. 10-6. 4pm in Mar and Oct.
Admission: £4.90, OAPs/Chd £3.50.
Refreshments: Self service Restaurant, Orangery and Licensed Bar.
Good disabled facilities. Dogs welcome *on leads.*

BRADLEY MANOR   The National Trust

Newton Abbot map E2

Small, roughcast 15th century manor house set in woodland and meadows.

Location: W end of town, 7½ m NW of Torquay. On W side of A381.
Open: Apr to Oct 1 - Weds 2-5; also Thurs, Apr 8 & 15, Sept 23 and 30. Last admission ½ hr before closing.
Admission: £2.60, Chd half-price.*No reduction for parties.* Parties of 15 or more must book in writing.
No indoor photography. No access for coaches - Lodge gates too narrow. No dogs. Unsuitable for disabled or visually handicapped.

BUCKLAND ABBEY   The National Trust

Yelverton map E2
Telephone: (0822) 853607
(The National Trust jointly managed with Plymouth County Council)

13th century Cistercian monastery bought by Sir Richard Grenville in 1541, altered by his grandson Sir Richard Grenville, of the 'Revenge', in 1576. Home of Drake from 1581 and still contains many relics of the great seaman, including Drake's drum. Exhibition to illustrate the Abbey's history. Restored buildings, including the monk's guesthouse and 18th century farm buildings. Great Barn. Craft workshops.

Location: 11 m N of Plymouth 6 m S of Tavistock between the Tavistock/Plymouth Road (A386) & River Tavy.
Open: Apr 1 to Oct 31: daily (except Thurs) 10.30-5.30. Last admissions 45 mins before closing time. Nov to Mar 1994: Weds, Sats and Suns 2-5 (Wed pre-booked parties only).
Admission: £4, Grounds, including Great Barn and Craft Workshops £2. Chd half price. Reduced rate for parties £3.20. Parties who do not pre-book will be charged at full rate.
Refreshments: Licensed Restaurant serving home-made lunches, teas and coffee. Apr 1 to Dec 19.
Dogs in designated areas only, on leads. Shop.

CADHAY 🏛

Ottery St Mary map F2 △
Telephone: (0404) 812432
(Lady William-Powlett)

Cadhay is approached by an avenue of lime-trees, and stands in a pleasant listed garden, with herbaceous borders and yew hedges, with excellent views over the original mediaeval fish ponds. Cadhay is first mentioned in the reign of Edward I, and was held by a de Cadehaye. The main part of the house was built about 1550 by John Haydon who had married the de Cadhay heiress. He retained the Great Hall of an earlier house, of which the fine timber roof (about 1420) can be seen. An Elizabethan Long Gallery was added by John's successor at the end of the 16th century, thereby forming a unique and lovely courtyard. Some Georgian alterations were made in the mid 18th century. The house is viewed by conducted tour. Photography is permitted outside.

Location: 1 m NW of Ottery St Mary on B3176.
Station(s): Feniton (2½ m) (not Suns).
Open: Spring (May 30 & 31) & Summer (Aug 29 & 30) Bank Hol Suns & Mons; also Tues, Weds & Thurs in July & Aug: 2-6 (last adm 5.30).
Admission: £2.50, Chd £1. *Parties by arrangement.*

CASTLE DROGO   The National Trust

nr Chagford map E2 ♿
Telephone: (064 743) 3306

Granite castle designed by Sir Edwin Lutyens, standing at over 900ft overlooking the wooded gorge of the River Teign. Terraced garden and miles of splendid walks.

Location: 4 m NE of Chagford; 6 m S of A30.
Open: Apr 1 to Oct 31 - Daily (except Fri, *Garden daily*) 11-5.30 (last adm ½ hour before closing).
Admission: £4.60; Grounds only £2. Chd half-price. *Reduced rates for parties.* (£3.60) *on application to the Administrator. Parties who do not pre-book will be charged at full rate.*
Refreshments: Coffee, lunches (licensed) & teas at the castle.
No dogs except guide dogs. Wheelchairs provided. Shop and Plant Centre. The restored croquet lawn is open. Equipment for hire from the shop.

COLETON FISHACRE GARDEN   The National Trust

Coleton map E2 ♿
Telephone: (0803) 752466

20 acre garden in a stream-fed valley. Garden created by Lady Dorothy D'Oyly Carte between 1925 and 1940; planted with wide variety of uncommon trees and exotic shrubs.

Location: 2 m from Kingswear; take Lower Ferry Road, turn off at tollhouse & follow Garden Open' signs.
Open: Mar 1 - Apr 1 - (Last admission ½ hr before closing) Suns 2-5; to Oct 31 - Weds, Thurs, Frid & Suns 10.30-5.30. Limited wheelchair access.
Admission: £2.60, Chd half price. Pre-booked parties £2.

COMPTON CASTLE   The National Trust

nr Paignton map E2
Telephone: (0803) 872112

Fortified manor house. Great Hall (restored), Solar, Kitchen, Chapel and rose garden.

Location: 1 m N of Marldon off A381.
Open: Apr to Oct 31 - Mons, Weds & Thurs 10-12.15, 2-5 (last adm 30 mins before closing).
Admission: £2.60, Chd half-price. Parties £2 -*organisers should please notify the Secretary.*
Refreshments: At Castle Barton.
No dogs except guide dogs. Additional parking at Castle Barton, opposite entrance.

DARTMOUTH CASTLE   English⚹Heritage

Dartmouth map E2
Telephone: (0803) 833588

Boldly guarding the narrow entrance to the Dart Estuary this castle was among the first in England to be built for artillery. Construction began in 1481 on the site of an earlier castle which was altered and added to over the following centuries. Victorian coastal defence battery with fully equipped guns, a site exhibition and magnificent views can all be seen at the castle.

Location: 1 m (1.6km) south east of Dartmouth.
Open: Good Friday or Apr 1 (whichever is earlier) to Sept 30 daily 10-6. Oct 1 to Maundy Thursday or Mar 31 (whichever is earlier) Tues to Sun 10-4. *Closed* Dec 24-26, Jan 1.
Admission: £1.70, Concessions £1.30, Chd 85p.

ENDSLEIGH HOUSE

Milton Abbot, Nr Tavistock map E2
Telephone: (0822) 87 248
(The Endsleigh Charitable Trust)

Arboretum, Shell House, Flowering Shrubs, Rock Garden.

Location: 4 m W of Tavistock on B3362.
Open: House and Gardens: Apr to Sept: weekends 12-4; Tues and Fris by appointment 12-4; Bank Hols 12-4.
Admission: Honesty Box in Aid of Trust.
Refreshments: Lunches and teas at Endsleigh House by appointment. No dogs.
Limited car parking. No coaches. No dogs. Not suitable for the disabled. No wheelchairs.

FLETE

Ermington, Ivybridge map E2
(Country Houses Association)

Built around an Elizabethan manor with alterations in 1879 by Norman Shaw.

Location: 11 m E of Plymouth at junction of A379 and B3210.
Station(s): Plymouth (12m), Totnes (14m). Bus Route: No 93 Plymouth-Dartmouth.
Open: May to Sept - Weds & Thurs, 2-5. Last entry 4.30.
Admission: £1.50, Chd 50p. Free car park.
No dogs admitted.

FURSDON

Cadbury, Thorverton map E3   △
Telephone: (0392) 860860
(E. D. Fursdon, Esq)

Fursdon is set in a beautiful rural landscape and the Fursdon family have lived here for over 700 years. It remains primarily a family home. There is a Regency library, a recently discovered oak screen from the mediaeval hall, family portraits and annual displays from the family costume collection including some fine 18th century examples. Attractive developing garden.

Location: 9 m N of Exeter, 6 m SW of Tiverton; ¾ m off A3072.
Open: Easter Mon to end Sept: Thurs and Bank Hol Mon only 2-4.30 (last adm 4). Parties over 20 by arrangement please.
Admission: House & Gardens £2.75. Reductions for children; under 10 years, free.
Refreshments: Home made teas in Coach Hall on open days.

HARTLAND ABBEY

Bideford, North Devon map D3
Telephone: (02374) 41264
(Sir Hugh Stucley, Bt.)

Abbey founded in 1157. Dissolved in 1539 and descended to the present day through a series of marriages. Major architectural alterations in 1705 and in 1779. Unique document exhibition dating from 1160 AD. Pictures, furniture and porcelain collected over many generations. Victorian & Edwardian photographic exhibition. Shrub gardens of rhododendrons, azaleas and camellias. Magnificent woodland walk to a remote atlantic cove with spectacular cliff scenery. Set in a designated area of outstanding natural beauty.

Location: NW Devon (Hartland Point); 15 m from Bideford; 5 m approx from A39.
Open: May to Sept incl - Weds 2-5.30. Sun 2-5.30 in July & Aug, and first 2 Suns in Sept. Bank Hols (Easter to Summer) Suns & Mons 2-5.30.
Admission: £2.50, Chd £1.50. Parties welcomed £2. Shrub garden and grounds only £1.
Refreshments: Cream teas provided at house.
Ample car parking close to house.

HEMERDON HOUSE

Plympton map E2   &
Telephone: (0752) 223816 (Office hours);(0752) 337350 (weekend & evenings)
(J. H. G. Woollcombe, Esq)

Regency house containing West country paintings and prints, with appropriate furniture and a Library.

Location: 2 m from Plympton.
Open: May - 22 days including Bank Holidays and Aug - 8 days including Bank Holiday 2-5.30. For opening dates please contact the Administrator.
Admission: £2.

KILLERTON   🌿   The National Trust

nr Exeter map F2   &
Telephone: (0392) 881345

Late 18th century house in a beautiful setting containing the Paulise de Bush Collection of Costume. Lovely throughout the year, with flowers from early spring, and splendid late autumn colours. 19th century Chapel and Ice House. Estate exhibition in Stables. Paths lead up the hill to the Dolbury, an isolated hill with an Iron Age hill fort site.

Location: 7 m NE of Exeter on W side of Exeter Cullompton (B3181 - formerly A38); from M5 s'bound exit 28/B3181; from M5 n'bound exit 29 via Broadclyst & B3181.
Open: House: Apr 1 to Oct 31 - Daily (except Tues) 11-5.30 (last adm ½ hour before closing). Park: All the year during daylight hours.
Admission: House and Garden £4.60 (tickets available at Stable Block), Chd half-price; Garden only £2.80. *Reduced rates for parties(£3.50) on application to the Administrator. Parties who do not pre-book will be charged at full rate.The Conference Room may be booked for meetings, etc. Applications (in writing) to: The Administrator, Killerton House, Broadclyst, Exeter, Devon.*
Refreshments: Licensed restaurant at House, entrance from garden - tickets necessary, available in Stables. Light refreshments and ice cream in Coach House, home baked bread and pastries for sale and to take away.
Shop, produce shop and plant centre in Stables. Dogs in Park only. Wheelchairs provided. Motorised buggy for disabled visitors to tour the garden.

KNIGHTSHAYES COURT   🌿   The National Trust

nr Tiverton map E3   &
Telephone: (0884) 254665

One of the finest gardens in Devon with specimen trees, rare shrubs, spring bulbs, summer flowering borders; of interest at all seasons. House by William Burges, begun in 1869, decorated by J D Crace.

Location: 2 m N of Tiverton; turn off A396 (Bampton/Tiverton Road) at Bolham.
Open: Apr 1 to Oct 31 - Garden daily 10.30-5.30. House -daily except Fri (but open Good Friday) 1.30-5.30 (last adm ½ hour before closing). *Nov and Dec: Sun 2-4; pre-arranged parties only.*
Admission: £4.80, Chd half-price. Garden & Grounds only £2.80. *Reduced rates for parties (£3.80) on application to the Administrator. Parties who do not pre-book will be charged at full rate.*
Refreshments: Licensed restaurant for coffee, lunches and teas. Picnic area in car park.
Shop. Plants available at garden shop. Dogs in park only on leads. Wheelchairs provided.

MARWOOD HILL

nr Barnstaple map E3
(Dr J. A. Smart)

Extensive collection of camellias under glass and in the open, daffodils, rhododendrons, rare flowering shrubs: rock and alpine garden, waterside planting. Bog garden. 18 acre garden with 3 small lakes. Many eucalyptus and NCCPG National Collection of astilbes and iris ensata (kaempferi).

Location: 4 m N of Barnstaple; opposite church in Marwood. Signs from A361 Barnstaple-Braunton Road.
Open: GARDENS ONLY. All the year - Daily (except Christmas Day) dawn to dusk.
Admission: £2, OAPs £1.50 Accompanied children under 12 no charge.*In aid of National Gardens Scheme.* Plants for sale. Dogs allowed, on leads only.
Refreshments: Teas. Apr to Sept, Suns & Bank Hols, or by prior arrangement for parties.

OKEHAMPTON CASTLE   English⚔Heritage

map E2
Telephone: (0837) 522844

Rebellion broke out in the south west after the Battle of Hastings and a stronghold was built here to subdue it. The castle passed from Baldwin FitzGilbert to Robert de Courtenay in 1172 and remained with this family, off and on, for 3½ centuries. The last Courtenay to own it, the Marquis of Exeter, was beheaded in 1538 and the castle dismantled.

Location: 1 m (1.6 km) south west of Okehampton.
Open: Good Friday or Apr 1 (whichever is earlier) to Sept 30: Open Daily 10-6. Oct 1 to Maundy Thursday or Mar 31 (whichever is earlier): Open Tues to Sun 10-4. *Closed Dec 24-26, Jan 1.*
Admission: £1.70, Concessions £1.30, Chd 85p. Price includes a Personal Stereo Guided Tour.

OVERBECKS MUSEUM & GARDEN

🌿   The National Trust

Sharpitor, Salcombe map E2
Telephone: (054 884) 2893 or (054 884) 3238

6 acres of garden with rare and tender plants and beautiful views eastwards over Salcombe Bay. Part of house forms museum of local interest and of particular interest to children.

Location: 1½ m SW of Salcombe signposted from Malborough & Salcombe.
Open: Garden: All the year - Daily 10-8, or sunset if earlier. Museum: Apr 1 to Oct 31 - Daily except Sat 11-5.30. Last adm ½ hour before closing.
Admission: Museum & Garden £3.40, Chd half-price. Garden only £2.*No reduction for parties.*
No dogs except Guide dogs. Shop. Picnicking allowed in gardens. Not suitable for coaches.

POWDERHAM CASTLE 🏛

nr Exeter map F2
(Lord and Lady Courtenay)

Originally built as a medieval castle by Sir Philip Courtenay (1390), the Castle is still lived in by his descendants. The siege of Powderham in the Civil War led to substantial alterations and restoration in the 18th and 19th centuries. A guided tour of the State Rooms brings alive the history of this lived in family home.

Location: 8 m S of Exeter off A379 in Kenton Village.
Station(s): Starcross 1½ m.
Open: Easter to Oct, every day except Sat from 10-6.
Admission: For details of prices, group booking discounts, private tours and booking of functions, events, receptions etc throughout the year please telephone the General Manager.
Refreshments: Light lunches and teas available in the Courtyard Tea rooms.

ROSEMOOR GARDEN

Great Torrington map E3
(The Royal Horticultural Society)

Important and internationally famous plantsmans' garden of 8 acres which is being expanded by the Royal Horticultural Society to 40 acres. New features include 2000 roses in 200 different varieties, colour theme gardens, herb garden and ornamental vegetable garden, stream and bog gardens, cottage garden, foliage and plantsman's garden and herbaceous borders. New Visitors Centre with restaurant, shop and plant sales centre with many interesting and unusual plants.

Location: 1 m SE of Great Torrington on B3220 to Exeter.
Open: Garden open all year. Visitors Centre open from Mar 1 to Oct 31 10-6.
Admission: £2.50, Chd 50p. Parties of over 20 persons £2 each.
Refreshments: Refreshments, light lunches and Devon cream teas available in new licensed restaurant.
Coaches welcome by appointment. Guide dogs only.

SALTRAM HOUSE 🍃 The National Trust

Plymouth map E2 ♿
Telephone: (0752) 336546

A George II house, built around and incorporating remnants of a late Tudor mansion, in a landscaped park. Two exceptional rooms by Robert Adam. Furniture, pictures, fine plasterwork and woodwork. Great Kitchen. Beautiful garden with Orangery. Octagonal summer-house, rare shrubs and trees. Shop in stables. Art Gallery in Chapel.

Location: 2 m W of Plympton 3½ m E of Plymouth city centre, between A38 & A379 main roads.
Open: House: Apr 1 to Oct 31. Suns-Thurs. House: 12.30-5.30. Garden, Kitchen, Shop & Art Gallery 10.30-5.30, Last adm ½ hour before closing. The Chapel may be booked for meetings, etc. Applications (in writing) to: The Administrator, Saltram House, Plympton, Plymouth.
Admission: £5, Chd half-price; Garden only £2.20.
Refreshments: Licensed restaurant in House (entrance from Garden). Light refreshments at Coach House near car park during peak periods.
Dogs in designated areas only. Wheelchairs provided.

SAND 🏛

Sidbury, nr Sidmouth map F2 △
(Lt Col P. V. Huyshe)

Lived in Manor house owned by Huyshe family since 1560, rebuilt 1592-4, situated in unspoilt valley. Screens passage, panelling, family documents, heraldry. Also **Sand Lodge** roof structure of late 15th century Hall House. Shady Car Park.

Location: ¾ m NE of Sidbury; 400 yds from A375, Grid ref 146925.
Open: Suns & Mons - Apr 11, 12; May 30, 31; Aug 1, 2; Aug 29, 30; 2-5.30. Last tour 4.45.
Admission: £2, Chd & Students 40p. Sand Lodge and outside of Sand by written appointment, £1.
Refreshments: Light teas in house, cream teas in Sidbury (free car parking).

SHUTE BARTON 🍃 The National Trust

Shute, nr Axminster map F3
Telephone: (0297) 34692

Manor house, built over three centuries and completed in late 16th century; grey stone with battlemented tower and late Gothic windows; gatehouse. The house is tenanted; there is access to most of interior for conducted visitors.

Location: 3 m SW of Axminster, 2 m N of Colyton on Honiton-Colyton road (B3161) [177(193): SY253974].
Station(s): Axminster 3 m.
Open: Apr to Oct 31: Wed & Sat 2-5.30. Last admissions ½hr before closing.
Admission: £1.60, pre-booked parties £1.20, Chd half price.
Refreshments: None available.
No dogs except guide dogs. Unsuitable for disabled or visually handicapped.

TIVERTON CASTLE

Tiverton map E3
Telephone: (0884) 253200 or 071-727 4854
(Mr and Mrs A. K. Gordon)

Historically important mediaeval castle commissioned by Henry I in 1106; magnificent mediaeval gatehouse and tower containing important Civil War armoury, notable clock collection, fine furniture and pictures, New World Tapestry. Comfortable holiday accommodation available.

Location: Next to St. Peter's Church. The Castle is well signposted in Tiverton.
Open: Good Friday to last Sun in Sept - Suns to Thurs 2.30-5.30.
Admission: £2.75, Chd under 7 free, 7-16 £1.75. Party bookings at special rates. Free parking inside.
Refreshments: Devon cream teas on Sundays. Light lunches, evening parties by prior arrangement.
Coach parties by appointment only.

TORRE ABBEY

Torquay map E2
Telephone: (0803) 293593
(Torbay Borough Council)

12th century monastery converted into a private residence after the Dissolution in 1539. Extensively remodelled in the early 18th century and currently undergoing complete renovation and restoration. Contains furnished period rooms, family chapel, extensive collection of paintings and other works of art, and the Dame Agatha Christie memorial room, containing many mementos of the Torquay born authoress. Over 25 rooms now open to the public including those in the newly restored South-West wing. Ruins of medieval Abbey also on show, including the remains of the Abbey Church, excavated in 1987/9. Formal gardens containing tropical palm house, summer bedding, rockeries and spring bulbs. Special exhibitions throughout the summer.

Location: On Torquay Sea front.
Station(s): Torquay (¼ m).
Open: HOUSE· Apr to Oct - Daily. Other times by appointment. GARDENS: All the year - Daily.
Admission: (1992 rates) HOUSE: £2, Chd/Senior Citizens £1. Family ticket £4.50 (2 adults and up to 3 children). GARDENS: Free.

TOTNES CASTLE   English⊞Heritage

map E2
Telephone: (0803) 864406

The Normans also built a stronghold here to overawe the townspeople. But they surrendered without a blow, as they did again in the Civil War. The remains date largely from the 14th century, although the huge earth mound on which the castle rests is Norman.

Location: Totnes.
Open: Good Friday or Apr 1 (whichever is earlier) to Sept 30: Open Daily 10-6. Oct 1 to Maundy Thursday or Mar 31 (whichever is earlier): Open Tues to Sun 10-4. *Closed* Dec 24-26, Jan 1.
Admission: £1.30, Concessions £1, Chd 65p.

UGBROOKE HOUSE

Chudleigh map E2
Telephone: (0626) 852179

Set in beautiful scenery and quiet parkland in the heart of Devon. The original House and Church built about 1200, redesigned by Robert Adam. Home of the Cliffords of Chudleigh, Ugbrooke contains fine furniture, paintings, beautiful embroideries, needlework and porcelain. Capability Brown landscaped Park with lakes, majestic trees, terraced gardens and scenic views to Dartmoor. Guided tours relate stories of Clifford Castles, Shakespeare's 'Black Clifford', Henry II's 'Fair Rosamund' Lady Anne Clifford who defied Cromwell, The Secret Treaty, the Cardinal's daughter, Charles II's Lord High Treasurer Clifford of the CABAL, and many more tales of intrigue, espionage and bravery.

Location: Chudleigh
Open: May 29, 30 and 31. Then July 25 - Aug 31 on Sun, Tues, Wed and Thurs. GROUNDS - 1-5.30. Guided tours of House at 2.00 and 3.45.
Admission: £3.80, Chd (5-16) £1.90. Groups (over 20) £3.50. Private party tours/functions by arrangement.
Refreshments: Afternoon teas at The Orangery 2 - 5pm.

YARDE

Malborough, nr Kingsbridge
Telephone: (054 884) 2367
(John and Marilyn Ayre)

Grade 1 Listed. An outstanding example of the Devon farmstead with a Tudor Bakehouse, Elizabethan Farmhouse and Queen Anne Mansion under restoration. Still a family farm.

Location: On A381 ½ m E of Malborough. 4 m S of Kingsbridge.
Open: Easter to Sept 31: Suns, Weds and Frid,2-5.
Refreshments: Cream teas. Coaches by appointment.

DORSET

ATHELHAMPTON

Athelhampton map G2
Telephone: (0305) 848492
(Lady Du Cann)

Athelhampton

HOUSE AND GARDENS

K5

- Five centuries of history in a family house built 1485 on the site of King Athelstan's Palace.
- Great Hall, Tudor Great Chamber, 18th Century Dining Room, State Bedroom and Wine Cellar all with fine furniture.
- Architectural and water gardens including Topiary Pyramids, Garden Pavilions and 15th Century Dovecote encircled by the River Piddle.

OPENING TIMES
Easter to end October
1-5.30pm on Wednesdays, Thursdays, Sundays and Bank Holidays
ALSO Tuesdays May to September
AND Mondays and Fridays in August
Gift Shop – Homemade Cream Teas
Telephone: 0305 848363

One of the finest medieval houses in England. Five centuries of history in a family house built in 1485 on the site of King Athelstan's Palace. Great Hall with unique roof, oriel window, heraldic glass and linenfold panelling. Fine furniture in the Tudor Great Chamber. 18th century Dining Room, State Bedroom, Wine Cellar and Exhibition Room. 12 architectural and Water Gardens with rate plants and trees in 10 acres encircled by the River Piddle. 15th century dovecote.

Location: 1m E of Puddletown on Dorchester/Bournemouth Road (A35); 5m NE of Dorchester.
Open: Easter to end October 12 - 5 on Weds, Thurs & Sun. Good Friday and Bank Holidays, also Mon and Fri in August and Tues from May to September.
Admission: House and Garden £3.80 (Chd half price) Special rate for pre booked parties £3.00.
Refreshments: In Old Stable Building.
Dogs admitted only to shaded car park. Guide Dogs accepted.

CHETTLE HOUSE

Chettle, Blandford map G3
Telephone: (0258 89) 209
(J. P. C. Bourke)

One of the finest examples of a Queen Anne House in the English Baroque style by Thomas Archer. Set in 5 acres of garden with many unusual herbaceous plants and shrubs.

Location: 6 m NE of Blandford on A354 & 1 mile W.
Open: Easter to 10 Oct (Except Tues and Sat) 11-5.
Refreshments: Many pubs within 2 miles. Picnic area available, teas usually. Plant Centre with unusual herb plants. No dogs.

CLOUDS HILL   The National Trust

nr Wool map G2

The cottage home of T. E. Lawrence (Lawrence of Arabia) after the first World War; contains his furniture and other relics.

Location: 1 m N of Bovington Camp, ½ m E of Waddock crossroads (B3390), 9 m E of Dorchester.
Open: Apr 1 to Oct 31 - Weds, Thurs, Frid, Suns & Bank Hol Mons 2-5. (No electric lighting available, *closed* dusk if earlier).
Admission: £2.20. *No reduction for children or parties.*
No photography. No dogs. Unsuitable for wheelchairs and coaches. No WCs.

CORFE CASTLE   The National Trust

nr Wareham map G2
Telephone: (0929) 481294

Ruins of former royal castle, sieged and sleighted by Parliamentary forces in 1646.

Location: In the village of Corfe Castle: on A351 Wareham-Swanage road.
Open: Feb 8 to end Oct daily 10-5.30pm or dusk if earlier, open Good Friday. Nov to Feb 1994; Sat and Sun 12-3.30.
Admission: £2.80, Chd £1.40, parties (15 or more) £2.30, Chd £1.20.
Refreshments: Available.
Not suitable for wheelchairs. NT Shop and Refreshments.

CRANBORNE MANOR GARDENS

Cranborne map H3
Telephone: (07254) 248

(The Viscount and Viscountess Cranborne)

Walled gardens, yew hedges and lawns; wild garden with spring bulbs, herb garden, Jacobean mount garden, flowering cherries and collection of old-fashioned and specie roses. Beautiful and historic gardens laid out in the 17th century by John Tradescant and much embellished and enlarged in the 20th century.

Location: 18 m N of Bournemouth, B3078; 16 m S of Salisbury, A354, B3081.
Open: GARDEN CENTRE open Tues-Sats 9-5, Suns 10-5. *Closed* Mons except Bank Holidays. Something for every gardener, but specialising in old-fashioned and specie roses, herbs, ornamental pots and garden furniture. GARDENS ONLY, Mar to Sept - Wed 9-5. Free car park.

THE SIGN OF A GREAT DAY OUT

DEANS COURT

Wimborne map H3 &
(Sir Michael & Lady Hanham)

Thirteen acres of partly wild garden, in a peaceful setting on the River Allen. Specimen trees, monastery fishpond. Peacocks. Herb garden with over 100 varieties. Organically grown herb plants for sale; also kitchen garden produce as available.

Location: 2 m walk South from Wimborne Minster & Square; nr car parks in town.
Open: Suns: Apr 11, May 3, 30, Aug 29, Oct 3 (2-6). Mons: Apr 12, May 4, 31, Aug 30 (10-6). Every Thurs: Apr 1 to Sept 30 (2-6). House open by prior written appointment only (not on garden open days). Possible daily openings Sun Jun 13 - Sat Jul 3. (10-6) for Sculpture Exhibition. Telephone Tourist Information Office (0202) 886116 for details.
Admission: Garden charges: £1.50, Chd 70p. *Sculpture Exhibition: Entrance charges would be different from those for normal garden openings. This would include Thurs falling within this period. To be confirmed later.* Groups welcome by arrangement.
Refreshments: Wholefood teas on all open days. Coffee on Bank Hol mornings.

EDMONDSHAM HOUSE AND GARDENS

Cranborne, nr Wimborne map H3
Telephone: (0725) 517207
(Mrs J. E. Smith)

A family home since the 16th century, and a fine blend of Tudor and Georgian architecture, with a Victorian stable block and dairy, interesting furniture, lace and other exhibits. The Gardens include an old-fashioned walled garden, cultivated organically, with an excellent display of spring bulbs, shrubs, lawns and herbaceous border.

Location: Between Cranborne and Verwood, off the B3081.
Open: HOUSE AND GARDENS: Easter Sun, all Bank Hol Mons, all Weds in Apr and Oct, 2-5. Groups by arrangement at other times. GARDENS: Open at all times when the House is open and on all Wed and Suns; Apr to Oct. 2-5.
Admission: House and Garden £2, Chd £1. Garden only £1, Chd 50p.

FORDE ABBEY AND GARDENS

nr Chard map F3
Telephone: (0460) 20231
(Trustees of Forde Abbey)

Cistercian monastery, founded 1140. Converted to private house mid 17th c. and unaltered since. Thirty acres of outstanding gardens - trees and shrubs, herbaceous borders, rock garden, bog garden and kitchen garden. Plants on sale.

Location: 1 m E of Chard Junction, 4 m SE of Chard signposted off A30.
Open: GARDENS AND NURSERY: open daily throughout the year 10-4.30; HOUSE: April to end Oct. Suns, Weds & Bank Hol, 1-4.30.
Admission: Our charges for 1993 are not yet finally decided.
Refreshments: Undercroft open for light lunches and teas 11.00 to 4.30 daily during summer months.

HARDY'S COTTAGE   🌿 **The National Trust**

Higher Bockhampton map G2 &
Telephone: (0305) 262366

Birthplace of Thomas Hardy 1840-1928. A thatched cottage, built by his grandfather; little altered.

Location: 3 m NE of Dorchester; ½ m S of Blandford Road (A35).
Open: Interior: by prior appointment with the custodian. Garden: daily (except Thurs) from 11-6 or dusk if earlier.
Admission: Interior £2.30. Garden free.
Approached by 10 mins walk from car park via woods. No dogs. Wheelchairs, garden only. No WCs.

HIGHBURY

West Moors map H3
Telephone: (0202) 874372
(Stanley Cherry Esq.)

Small Edwardian house (Listed, 1909) in half acre garden with much of rare and unusual botanical interest, with everything labelled.

Location: In Woodside Road off B3072 (last road at N end of village).
Open: April to September.
Admission: HOUSE AND GARDEN: Organised parties £1, (incl. Tea); otherwise by appointment, GARDEN ONLY: 75p. *In aid of National Gardens Scheme.*
Refreshments: Teas in the orchard when fine.

HORN PARK

Beaminster map G3
Telephone: (0308) 862212
(Mr & Mrs John Kirkpatrick)

Large Garden. Magnificent views. Rhododendrons, azaleas, camellias, bulbs. Rock and water gardens, herbaceous and unusual plants. Woodland Garden and walks with wild flowers. Good all seasons.

Location: 1½ m N. of Beaminster on A3066.
Open: Apr 1 to Oct 1 every Tues and Thur, 1st and 3rd Sun each month, Bank Hol Mons, 2-6pm
Admission: £2, (under 16 free).

ILSINGTON

Puddletown, Dorchester map G2
Telephone: (0305) 848454
(Mr & Mrs P. Duff)

Set in the centre of the village of Puddletown (Thomas Hardy's Weatherbury). A family home. A classical William and Mary mansion built by the 7th Earl of Huntingdon. Home of George III's illegitimate grandson, born to HRH Princess Sophia in 1800, kept a secret until the Royal Scandal of 1826. Ilsington was visited by many members of the Royal Family during George III's reign. Fine furniture and present owners' private collection of pictures and sculpture. A fully guided house tour given. 11 acres of formal and landscape gardens with probably the longest haha in Dorset. New gardens being redesigned and created.

Location: 4 m from Dorchester on the A35.
Open: May 2 to Sept 30, Wed, Thurs and Sun 2-6. Plus Bank Hol Mons. Parties by special arrangement. Last tour 5.
Admission: HOUSE & GARDENS: £3.
Refreshments: Lunch or tea for parties by arrangement in the House, teas available in the village.
Free car parking. Not suitable for disabled persons.

KINGSTON LACY 🌢 The National Trust

nr Wimborne Minster map G3 ⓢ
Telephone: (0202) 883402

17th century House designed by Sir Roger Pratt but with considerable alterations by Sir Charles Barry in the 19th century. Important Italian and English paintings collected by W. J. Bankes. Set in 250 acres of wooded park.

Location: on B3082 - Wimborne-Blandford Road, 1½ m W of Wimborne.
Open: Apr 3 to Oct 31 daily except Thurs & Frid. House: 12-5.30 (last adm 4.30). Park: 11.30-6.
Admission: House: £5, Chd £2.50. Park & Garden: £2, Chd £1. Parties by prior appointment with Administrator.
Refreshments: Lunches and cream teas. National Trust Shop.
House not suitable for wheelchairs. One wheelchair available for use in Garden. Guide dogs admitted to grounds. Parties by arrangement **only**. National Trust shop.

MACPENNYS

Bransgore, nr Christchurch map H3
Telephone: (0425) 72348
(Tim Lowndes, Esq)

Large woodland garden. Nurseries, camellias, rhododendrons, asaleas, heathers and herbaceous.

Location: 4 m NE of Christchurch; 1½ m W of A35. Halfway between Christchurch and Burley on Burley Road at Bransgore.
Open: Garden and nurseries open all year daily (except Christmas Hols and New Year). Mons to Sats 9-5; Suns 2-5.
Admission: Free but donations to the National Gardens Scheme welcomed.

MAPPERTON

Beaminster map G3
Telephone: (0308) 862645
(Montagu family)

Terraced and hillside gardens with topiary, formal borders and specimen shrubs and trees. Modern orangery in classical style, 17th century stone fish ponds and summer house. Tudor manor house, enlarged 1660s. Magnificent walks and views.

Location: 1 m off B3163, 2 m off B3066.
Open: Mar to Oct, daily 2-6.
Admission: £2.50, under 18 £1.50, under 5 free. House also open to group tours by appointment, £2.50 or £4 for house and gardens.

MILTON ABBEY

Milton Abbas, nr Blandford map G3
(The Council of Milton Abbey School Ltd)

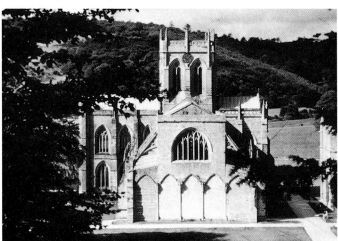

A fine Abbey Church (Salisbury Diocese) partially completed 15th century on site of 10th century Abbey. The magnificent Abbot's Hall, completed 1498, with fine hammerbeam roof and carved screen, is incorporated in the Georgian Gothic mansion (now Milton Abbey School). Architect Sir William Chambers with ceilings and decorations by James Wyatt. The ancient St. Catherine's Chapel looks down on this unique group set in secluded valley seven miles SW of Blandford. The little town of Milton, swept away in the late 18th century by the imperious owner of the house, in order to improve his park, was rebuilt as a charming model village nearby.

Location: 7 m SW of Blandford, just N of A354 from Winterborne Whitechurch or Milborne St Andrew.
Open: HOUSE & GROUNDS. Apr 3 to Apr 12 and July 12 to Aug 31 incl. - Daily 10-6.30. ABBEY CHURCH: Throughout the year.
Admission: £1.20, Chd free. ABBEY CHURCH - free except for above dates.
Refreshments: Available when House is open in summer only.

MINTERNE

Dorchester map G3
Telephone: (0300) 341370
(The Lord Digby)

Important rhododendron and shrub garden, many fine and rare trees, landscaped in the 18th century with lakes, cascades and streams.

Location: On A352 2 m N of Cerne Abbas; 10 m N of Dorchester, 9 m S of Sherborne.
Open: Apr 1 to Oct 31 - Daily 10-7.
Admission: £2, accom chd free. Free car park.

PARNHAM

Beaminster map G3
Telephone: (0308) 862204
(Mr & Mrs John Makepeace)

PARNHAM

Celebrating the Living Arts!

Furniture by John Makepeace : Evocative Architecture and Interiors : Romantic Terraces and Topiary

Inspiring 20th-Century craftsmanship in the home of John and Jennie Makepeace, who have restored and enlivened this fascinating historic house. Contemporary art exhibitions. Shop: books and exciting work by leading British craftsmen in textiles, ceramics and wood. Workshop: unique furniture in the making. Licensed Buttery: delicious home-made food all day.

Open: April to October – Suns., Weds., Bank Hols. 10-5

PARNHAM   BEAMINSTER   DORSET
On A3066, five miles north of Bridport

An Elizabethan manor-house, enlarged by John Nash in 1810; surrounded by fourteen acres of gardens extensively restored and replanted by Jennie Makepeace since 1980. In the workshop, furniture designed by John Makepeace is made for public and private collections.

Location: On A3066, 1 m S of Beaminster; 5 m N of Bridport.
Open: Apr 4 to Oct 31 -Weds, Suns & Bank Hols (incl. Gd Frid) 10-5. Group visits on these and other days by prior arrangement only.
Admission: To Principal rooms, gardens, workshop, picnic areas: £3, Chd (10-15) £1.50; under 10 free.
Refreshments: Morning coffee, lunches, teas etc in licensed 17th century buttery
Shop selling excellent range of high quality craft and books.

PORTLAND CASTLE   English ♯ Heritage

Portland map G2
Telephone: (0305) 820539

Built in the middle of the 16th century on the northern shore of the Isle of Portland, the castle was part of Henry VIII's coastal defences and is little altered. Unusually shaped, like a segment of a circle, it was seized by Royalists in the Civil War, changing hands twice before yielding to Parliament in 1646.

Location: Overlooking Portland Harbour, adjacent to RN helicopter base.
Open: Good Friday or Apr 1 (whichever is earlier) to Sept 30: Open Daily 10-6.
Admission: £1.70, Concessions £1.30, Chd 85p.

PRIEST'S HOUSE MUSEUM AND GARDEN

23 High Street, Wimborne Minster map H3
Telephone: (0202) 882533
(Priest's House Museum Trust)

A recently restored town house of medieval origin with many Tudor and Georgian features. Set in exquisite walled garden with new displays including reconstructed 1920's ironmonger's shop, working forge and Victorian kitchen, period rooms and regular special exhibitions.

Location: Centre of Wimborne Minster.
Open: Apr 1 to Oct 31 every day (Not Jul 28). Nov 1 to Christmas weekends only plus Christmas Exhibition. Mon - Sat 10.30-4.30; Sun 2-4.30.
Admission: Includes entrance to garden. Group bookings welcome.
Refreshments: Tea room in summer season and museum gift shop.

PURSE CAUNDLE MANOR

nr Sherborne map G3
Telephone: (0963) 250400
(Michael de Pelet, Esq)

Interesting 15th/16th century Manor House. Lived in as a family home. Great Hall with minstrel gallery; Winter Parlour; Solar with oriel; bedchambers; garden. Not commercialised! Come and visit us.

Location: 4 m E of Sherborne; ¼ m S of A30.
Open: Easter Mon, May to Sept '93, Thurs, Suns & Bank Hol Mons, 2-5, showing every half hour. Coaches welcomed by appointment.
Admission: £2, Chd Free. Free car park.
Refreshments: Home-made cream teas by prior arrangement at £2 each for coach parties.

SANDFORD ORCAS MANOR HOUSE

Sandford Orcas, Sherborne map G3
Telephone: (0963) 220206
(Sir Mervyn Medlycott, Bt)

Tudor Manor House with gatehouse, fine panelling. furniture, pictures. Terraced gardens, with topiary, and herb garden. Personal conducted tour by owner.

Location: 2½ m N of Sherborne, ent. next to Church.
Open: Easter Mon 10-6 then May to Sept - Suns 2-6 & Mons 10-6.
Admission: £1.80, Chd 80p. Pre-booked parties (of 10 or more) at reduced rates on other days if preferred.

SHAFTESBURY ABBEY RUINS AND MUSEUM

Shaftesbury map G3
Telephone: (0747) 52910
(Shaftesbury Abbey and Museum Preservation Trust Company Ltd)

Ruins of 9th century Abbey founded by Alfred the Great set in an attractive and peaceful garden. Museum displays finds from the site.

Location: 100 metres West of Shaftesbury Town Centre.
Open: Easter to Oct, daily 10-5.30.
Admission: 90p, concessions 60p, chd 30p.

SHERBORNE CASTLE

Sherborne map G3
Telephone: (0935) 813182
(Simon Wingfield Digby, Esq)

Built by Sir Walter Raleigh in 1594 and enlarged in 1625 by Sir John Digby, 1st Earl of Bristol. Home of the Digby family since 1617, the house contains fine furniture, porcelain and pictures by Vandyck, Gainsborough, Reynolds, Lely, Kneller and other famous artists. Twenty acres of lawns and pleasure grounds planned by 'Capability Brown' around the 50 acre lake are open to the public.

Location: 5 m E of Yeovil off A30 to S.
Station(s): Sherborne (few mins walk).
Open: Easter Sat to end of Sept - Thurs, Sats, Suns & Bank Hol Mons 2-5.30. Grounds open 12 noon Thurs, Sats, Suns and Bank Hol Mons.
Admission: Charges available on request by telephone.*Special terms and days for parties by arrangement.*
Refreshments: Tea at the house.
Gift shop.

SHERBORNE OLD CASTLE   English ✠ Heritage

Sherborne map G3
Telephone: (093581) 2730

The powerful and wealthy Bishop Roger de Caen built the castle in the early 12th century, but by 1135 it had been seized by the Crown. In 1592 the castle passed to Sir Walter Raleigh who built Sherborne Lodge in the grounds. The buildings were largely demolished after the Civil War, but a gatehouse, some graceful arcading and decorative windows survive.

Location: ½ m (0.8 km) east of Sherborne.
Open: Good Friday or Apr 1 (whichever is earlier) to Sept 30: Open Daily 10-6. Oct 1 to Maundy Thursday or Mar 31 (whichever is earlier): Open Tues to Sun 10-4. *Closed* Dec 24-26, Jan 1.
Admission: £1.20, concessions 90p, Chd 60p.

WOLFETON HOUSE

Dorchester map G2
Telephone: (0305) 263500
(Capt. N. T. L. Thimbleby)

Outstanding medieval and Elizabethan manor house with magnificent wood and stone work, fireplaces and plaster ceilings; Great Hall and stairs; parlour, dining room, Chapel and Cider House. The medieval gatehouse, French in appearance, has two unmatched and far older towers.

Location: 1½ m from Dorchester on Yeovil road (A37); indicated by Historic House signs.
Station(s): Dorchester South and West 1¾ m.
Open: May to Sept - Tues, Thur and Bank Hol Mons 2-6. At other times throughout the year, parties by arrangement.
Admission: Charges not available at time of going to press.
Refreshments: Ploughman's lunches, teas and evening meals for parties, by prior arrangement. Cider for sale.

COUNTY DURHAM

AUCKLAND CASTLE

Bishop Auckland map H11
Telephone: (0388) 601627
(The Church Commissioners)

Historic home of the Bishops of Durham with parts dating from 12th century. Very fine private Chapel remodelled by Bishop Cosin from 1660. Fourteenth century Hall, gothicised by James Wyatt in 1795. State Rooms include a Gothic Throne Room lined with portraits of past bishops. Also large public park and unusual 18th century deerhouse.

Location: In Bishop Auckland, at the end of Market Place.
Station(s): Bishop Auckland.
Open: CASTLE AND CHAPEL: Bank Hol Mons 2-5. May 3 to Sept 20: Tues 10-12. Suns, Wed and Thurs 2-5. Sats in Aug 2-5. PARK: Daylight hours throughout the year.
Admission: Please ring warden for opening times and adm charges.

BARNARD CASTLE   English ✠ Heritage

Durham map G11
Telephone: (0833) 38212

Named after it's founder, Bernard de Baliol, the castle overlooks the River Tees from a craggy cliff-top. It's ownership was disputed by the Bishops of Durham, one of whom seized it in 1296. He added a magnificent hall and refortified the castle. Part of the castle has recently been excavated to discover more of it's complex building history.

Location: In Barnard Castle.
Open: Good Friday or Apr 1 (whichever is earlier) to Sept 30: Open daily 10-6. Oct 1 to Maundy Thursday or Mar 31 (whichever is earlier): Open Tues to Sun 10-4. *Closed* Dec 24-26, Jan 1.
Admission: £1.70, Concessions £1.30, Chd 85p.

BOTANIC GARDEN, UNIVERSITY OF DURHAM

Durham map H11
Telephone: 091-3742671
(University of Durham)

18 acres of trees and shrubs, set in mature woodland.

Location: Take the Durham turn off at A167 at Cock o' the North Roundabout. 1 m from Durham, along Hollingside Lane.
Open: Gardens: 9-6 daily. Glasshouse: 9-4 daily. Visitor centre: Mar to Nov, 10-5 daily. Winter restricted to afternoons, weather permitting.
Admission: Under review.

Sir Edwin Landseer Lutyens Architect

His work can be seen at the following properties included in Historic Houses Castles and Gardens:

> Castle Drogo
> Goddards
> Great Dixter
> Great Maytham Hall
> Hestercombe House and Gardens
> Knebworth

Gertrude Jekyll writer and gardener (1843–1932)

Her designs were used at the following properties included in Historic Houses Castles and Gardens:

> Hestercombe House and Gardens
> Knebworth
> Vann

DURHAM CASTLE

Durham map H11 △
(The University of Durham)

Durham Castle, the former home of the Prince Bishops of Durham, was founded in the 1070's. Since 1832 it has been the foundation College of the University of Durham. With the Cathedral it is a World Heritage Site. Important features include the Norman Chapel (1072), the Great Hall (1284), the Norman Doorway (1540's). With its 14th century style Keep it is a fine example of a Motto and Bailey Castle. In vacations the Castle is a conference and holiday centre and a prestige venue for banquets etc.

Location: In the centre of the city (adjoining Cathedral).
Station(s): Durham (½ m).
Open: Guided tours only: July to Sept, 10-12 noon and 2-5pm. Oct to June 2-4pm.
Admission: £1.40, Chd 90p, Family ticket £3.20.

RABY CASTLE 🏛

Staindrop, Darlington map G11 &
Telephone: (0833) 60202
(The Lord Barnard, T.D.)

Principally 14th century, alterations made 1765 and mid-19th century. The Castle is one of the largest 14th century castles in Britain and was built by the Nevills although one of the towers probably dates back to the 11th century. Interior mainly 18th and 19th century; medieval kitchen and Servants' Hall. Fine pictures of the English, Dutch and Flemish Schools and good period furniture. Collection of horse-drawn carriages and fire engines. Large walled Gardens.

Location: 1 m N of Staindrop village, on the Barnard Castle/Bishop Auckland Road (A688).
Open: Easter weekend (Sat-Wed) *closed* remainder of April, then May 1 to June 30, Weds & Suns; July 1 to Sept 30, daily (except Sats); May, Spring and Aug Bank Hols, Sat-Tues; CASTLE 1-5; PARK & GARDENS 11-5.30.
Admission: CASTLE, PARK AND GARDENS £3, Senior Citizens £2.60, Chd £1.30. PARK AND GARDENS ONLY £1, Senior Citizens and Chd 75p. Separate adm charge for Bulmer's Tower when open. Rates may vary when charity events are held. Special terms for parties over 25 on above by arrangement (Tel Curator).
Refreshments: Tea at the Stables.
Picnic area.

ROKEBY PARK

nr Barnard Castle   map G11

Palladian House built by Sir Thomas Robinson in 1735. Fine rooms, furniture and pictures (including exceptional collection of 18th century needlework pictures by Anne Morritt).

Open: May 3, then each Mon & Tues from May 31 to Tues Sept 7, 2-5 (last adm 4.30). Parties of 25 or more will also be admitted on other days if a written appointment is made with the Curator.

ESSEX

AUDLEY END HOUSE AND PARK   English✠Heritage

Saffron Waldron   map K5
Telephone: (0799) 522399

James I is said to have remarked that Audley End was too large for a king but not for his Lord Treasurer, Sir Thomas Howard, who built it. The house was so large in fact that early in the 18th century about half of it was demolished as being unmanageable, but this still leaves a very substantial mansion. The interior contains rooms decorated by Robert Adam, a magnificent Jacobean Great Hall, a picturesque 'Gothic' chapel and a suite of rooms decorated in the revived Jacobean style of the early 19th century. Restaurant.

Location: ¾ m (1 km) west of Saffron Walden off B1383.
Open: Good Friday or Apr 1 (whichever is earlier) to Sept 30, Tues to Sun (except Bank Hols) 1-6. Park and Garden open 12 noon. Last admission 1 hr before closing.
Admission: House & Grounds: £4.90, Concessions £3.70, Chd £2.40. Grounds only: £2.70, Concessions £2. Chd £1.30.

BETH CHATTO GARDENS

Elmstead Market   map L5
(Mrs Beth Chatto)

5-acre garden, attractively landscaped with many unusual plants in wide range of conditions.

Location: 4 m E of Colchester on A133 Colchester/Clacton Road.
Station(s): Colchester.
Open: GARDEN ONLY. All the year - Mons to Sats 9-5 Mar to Oct. Mon-Fri 9-4 Nov to Feb. *Closed* Suns & Bank Hols also Sats Oct 30 to end of Feb. Adjacent nursery also open.
Admission: £1.50, Chd free.*In aid of National Gardens Scheme.Parties by arrangement.* No dogs please.

GOSFIELD HALL

Halstead map L5
(Country Houses Association)

Very fine Tudor gallery.

Location: 2½ m SW of Halstead on Braintree/Haverhill Road (A1017).
Station(s): Braintree. Bus route 310 Braintree-Halstead.
Open: May to Sept - Weds & Thurs 2-5. Last entry 4.30.
Admission: £1.50, Chd 50p. Free car park.
No dogs admitted.

HARWICH REDOUBT

Harwich Harbour, Harwich map L5
(The Harwich Society)

Commanding Harwich Harbour this substantial circular fort was built to keep Napoleon out. Now being restored by volunteers of The Harwich Society, with 11 different guns on the battlements and a variety of small museums in the casemates.

Location: Opposite 42A Main Road, Harwich.
Open: Jul and Aug, daily 2-5. Throughout the year, Suns only, 10-12 and 2-5. (Excluding 30 May and 26 Dec). Annual Fete 31 May, 2-5.
Admission: £1. Accompanied children free. No unaccompanied children.
Refreshments: Light drinks only.
Not suitable for disabled.

HEDINGHAM CASTLE

Castle Hedingham, nr Halstead map L5
Telephone: (0787) 60261
Fax: (0787) 61473
(The Hon Thomas & Mrs Lindsay)

One of the best preserved Norman keeps overlooking a beautiful village. Built by the famous medieval family the de Veres, Earls of Oxford. Visited by King Henry VII, King Henry VIII, and Queen Elizabeth I, and besieged by King John. See the Banqueting Hall with Minstrels' Gallery and the largest Norman arch in England. Peaceful woodland and lakeside walks ideal for family picnics. Close to Constable country within easy reach of M11 and A12.

Location: On B1058 4 m N of Halstead, turn off A604; 9 m N of Braintree; 30 m SE of Cambridge.
Open: Easter Weekend to Oct 31. 10-5 daily. Parties and Schools especially welcome all year by appointment.
Admission: £2.25, chd £1.25, Family ticket £6.
Refreshments: Light refreshments.

LAYER MARNEY TOWER

nr Colchester map L5 △ Ⓔ
Telephone: (0206) 330784
(Mr Nicholas Charrington)

Lord Marney's 1520 masterpiece is the tallest Tudor gatehouse in the country. Visitors may climb the tower for excellent views of the Essex countryside and the Blackwater estuary, explore the formal gardens and visit the Long Gallery. The adjoining Church has 3 effigy tombs of the Marney's and an original wallpainting of St. Christopher. There is a collection of rare breed farm animals and deer. A Farm walk starts from the Mediaeval Barn. Guided Tours are available by arrangement (minimum number 25 people). The Long Gallery and Carpenters Shop can be hired for Receptions, Banquets and Concerts.

Location: 6 m S of Colchester, signpost off the B1022 Colchester/Maldon Road.
Open: Apr, May, Jun and Sept, Sun and Thurs 2-6pm. July and Aug, Sun to Fri 2-6pm. Bank Hols 11-6pm. Parties other days by prior arrangement.

LOWER DAIRY HOUSE GARDEN

Water Lane, Nayland, Colchester map L5
Telephone: (0206) 262220
(Mr & Mrs D.J. Burnett)

1¾ acre plantsman's garden. Natural stream with waterside plantings, bog gardens and pond. Raised beds with rock plants. Collection of cistus, diascias and other sun loving plants. Herbaceous borders, roses and groupings of shrubs complete the informal design of this cottage style garden. Good displays of spring bulbs and blossom.

Location: 7 m N of Colchester off A134. A12 dual carriageway to Colchester.
Open: Apr 3, 4, 10, 11, 12, 24, 25. May 1, 2, 3, 8, 9, 22, 23, 29, 30, 31. Jun 5, 6, 12, 13, 26, 27. July 3, 4, 10, 11.
Admission: £1, Chd 50p. *In aid of National Gardens Scheme.* Paries by arrangement.
Refreshments: Teas provided. Hotel in Nayland.
Car park by house and nearby field. Suitable for the disabled but no wheelchairs available. Plants for sale.

THE MAGNOLIAS

18, St John's Avenue, Brentwood map L4
Telephone: (0277) 220019
(Mr & Mrs R. A. Hammond)

A plantsman's garden. The ground is intensively planted with trees, shrubs, climbers, herbaceous groundcover and bulbs, good collections of acer, magnolia, rhododendron, camellia and pieris. There are seven ponds including one in a green house, some with Koi Carp.

Location: 1 m from Brentwood High Street (A1023). At Wilsons Corner turn S down A128; after 300 yds turn R at traffic lights; over railway bridge: St. John's Ave 3rd on R.
Open: Suns Mar 28, Apr 11, 25; May 2, 16, 30; June 13, July 18; Aug 1, 29; Sept 19; Oct 24, 10-5.
Admission: £1, Chd 50p.*In aid of National Gardens Scheme.* Parties by appointment.
Refreshments: Teas.
Not suitable for disabled.

SIR ALFRED MUNNINGS ART MUSEUM

Castle House, Dedham map L5 &

Telephone: (0206) 322127

Home of the late Sir Alfred Munnings. KCVO, President of the Royal Academy 1944-1949. Exhibitions of paintings, drawings, sketches and other works by this famous East Anglian artist in the house and studios.

Location: ¾ m Dedham village, 7 m NE Colchester 2 m E of Ipswich Road (A12).
Open: May 2 to Oct 3 - Weds, Suns & Bank Hol Mons, also Thurs & Sats in Aug, 2-5.
Admission: £2, Chd 25p, OAPs £1. Private parties by arrangment. Free car park.

PARK FARM (GARDEN)

Great Waltham map L5
Telephone: (0245) 360871
(Mrs Jill Cowley & Mr Derek Bracey)

Young garden on farmyard site. 2 acres of bulbs, herbaceous plants and especially roses planted in separate rooms formed by new hedges. There is a newly-constructed pond garden.

Location: Take B1008 from Chelmsford: on Little Waltham Bypass turn W to Chatham Hall Lane: Park Farm ½ m on left.
Open: Sun & Mon, Apr 11, 12, 25, 26. May 2, 3, 16, 17, 30, 31. Jun 6, 7, 13, 14, 20, 21, 27, 28. Jul 11, 12, 25, 26. (2-6).
Admission: 80p, Chd 40p.*In aid of National Gardens Scheme.*
Refreshments: Teas.
Not suitable for disabled.

PAYCOCKE'S   The National Trust

Coggeshall (1500) map L5
Telephone: (0376) 561305

Richly ornamented merchant's house, dating from about 1500. Special display of local lace. Delightful garden leading down to small river.

Location: On A120; S side of West St. Coggeshall next to Fleece Inn; 5½ m E of Braintree. *Station(s): Kelvedon (2½ m)*
Open: Mar 28 to Oct 10 - Tues, Thur, Sun and Bank Hol Mons 2-5.30.
Admission: £1.40, Chd (accompanied) half-price.*Parties exceeding six should make prior arrangements with the tenant.* No reduction for parties.
No dogs.

THE SIGN OF A GREAT DAY OUT

ST. OSYTH PRIORY

St.Osyth map L5
Telephone: (0255) 820492
(Somerset de Chair)

The Great gatehouse c 1475, ('unexcelled in any monastic remains in the country',*Country Life*), was built 20 years before Christopher Columbus sailed. A unique group of buildings dating from the 13th, 15th, 16th, 18th and 19th centuries, surrounding a wide quadrangle like Oxford or Cambridge college. Gardens include Rose garden, Topiary garden, Water garden etc. Peacocks. Art collection in Georgian wing includes world-famous paintings by George Stubbs ARA.

Location: 65 m from London via A12, A120; A133 12 m from Colchester; 8 m from Frinton.
Open: Easter weekend, Then May 1 to Sept 30. Gardens and Ancient Monuments open 10-5. Art Collection 10.30-12.30, 2.30-4.30. Buildings and art collection *closed* Sat although the gardens will remain open. Parties by arrangement.
Admission: £3, Chd 75p, OAPs £1.50. Free car parking.
Refreshments: In village 100 yds from entrance.
Gardens suitable for disabled persons. Gardens overlook but do not include deer park on the estuary of the River Cole. Contact Mrs Colby, Tel (0255) 820242 (9-10 am)

SALING HALL

Great Saling, nr Braintree map L5
(Mr & Mrs Hugh Johnson)

12 acre garden; walled garden dated 1698; small park with fine trees, extensive new collection of unusual plants with emphasis on trees; water gardens.
Location: 6 m NW of Braintree; mid-way between Braintree & Dunmow (A120); turn off N at Saling Oak Inn.
Open: GARDEN ONLY. Weds in May, Jun and Jul 2-5. Sun Jun 27, 2-6. *Parties other days by arrangement.*
Admission: £1.50, accompanied Chd free.*In aid of National Gardens Scheme & Village Church Fund.*
No dogs please.

SHALOM HALL

Layer Breton, nr Colchester map L5
(Lady Phoebe Hillingdon)

19th century house containing a collection of 17th and 18th century French furniture and porcelain and portraits by famous English artists including Thomas Gainsborough, Sir Joshua Reynolds etc.
Location: 7 m SW of Colchester; 2 m from A12.
Open: Aug, Mon to Fri 10-1, 2.30-5.30.
Admission: Free.

TILBURY FORT   English ♯ Heritage

Tilbury map L5
Telephone: (0375) 858489

After an audacious raid up the Thames by the Dutch in 1667, Charles II commissioned plans for a defensive fort at Tilbury, on the site of Henry VIII's smaller fortification. It took 13 years to build but never saw the action for which it was designed. In the First World War a German Zeppelin was gunned down from the parade ground. Entry is now from the landward side across two restored bridges.

Location: ½ m SE of Tilbury.
Open: Good Friday or Apr 1 (whichever is earlier) to Sept 30: Open Daily 10-6. Oct 1 to Maundy Thursday or Mar 31 (whichever is earlier): Open Tues to Sun 10-4. *Closed* Dec 24-26, Jan 1.
Admission: £1.70, concessions £1.30, Chd 85p. Price includes a Personal Stereo Guided Tour.

GLOUCESTERSHIRE

BARNSLEY HOUSE GARDEN   🏛

Barnsley, nr Cirencester map H5   ♿
Telephone: (0285) 740281
(Rosemary Verey)

Garden laid out 1770, trees planted 1840. Re-planned 1960. Many spring bulbs. Laburnum avenue (early June). Lime walk, herbaceous and shrub borders. Ground cover. Knot garden. Autumn colour. Gothic summerhouse 1770. Classical temple 1780. House 1697 (not open). Vegetable garden laid out as decorative potager.

Location: 4 m NE of Cirencester on Cirencester to Bibury and Burford Road (B4425).
Open: GARDEN ONLY. All the year - Mon, Wed, Thurs, Sat 10-6 (or dusk if earlier);
Admission: (Mar to Nov inc) £2, OAPs £1, Season tickets £4. Guided Parties entrance plus £25. Dec to Feb free.
Refreshments: Morning coffee, lunch and supper - The Village Pub, Barnsley. Tea - Bibury & Cirencester.
Plants for sale.

BATSFORD ARBORETUM   🏛

Moreton-in-Marsh map H5
Telephone: (0386) 700409 or (0608) 50722.
(The Batsford Foundation)

Over 1000 species of different trees set in fifty acres of delightful Cotswold countryside overlooking the Vale of Evenlode, with a unique collection of exotic shrubs and bronze statues from the Orient.

Location: 1½ m NW of Moreton-in-Marsh on A44 to Evesham. Turn right into Park drive prior to Bourton-on-the-Hill.
Station(s): Moreton-in-Marsh (2½ m).
Open: GARDEN ONLY: Mar to mid-Nov - every day 10-5. Garden Centre open all year round (10-5).
Admission: £2, Chd & OAPs £1.50 (1992 prices). Parties by arrangement. Free parking.
Refreshments: Tea room for coffee, light lunches and teas (Apr to Oct except Mons). Picnic area.

BERKELEY CASTLE   🏛

nr Bristol map G4   △
Telephone: (0453) 810332
(Mr & Mrs R. J. Berkeley)

BERKELEY CASTLE
Gloucestershire

England's most Historic Home and Oldest Inhabited Castle

Completed in 1153 by Lord Maurice Berkeley at the command of Henry II and for nearly 850 years the home of the Berkeley family. 24 generations have gradually transformed a savage Norman fortress into a truly stately home.

The castle is a home and not a museum. Enjoy the castle at leisure or join one of the regular one-hour guided tours covering the dungeon, the cell where Edward II was murdered, the medieval kitchens, the magnificent Great Hall and the State Apartments with their fine collections of pictures by primarily English and Dutch masters, tapestries, furniture of an interesting diversity, silver and porcelain.

Splendid Elizabethan Terraced Gardens and sweeping lawns surround the castle. Tropical Butterfly House with hundreds of exotic butterflies in free flight – an oasis of colour and tranquility.

Facilities include free coach and car parks, picnic area and two gift shops, Tea rooms for refreshments, light lunches and afternoon teas.

Opening times and admission charges–see editorial reference. Evening parties by arrangement. Further information from the Custodian, Berkeley Castle, Glos. GL13 9BQ. Telephone: 0453-810 332

Location: Midway between Bristol and Gloucester, just off A38. M5 junctions 13 or 14.
Open: Apr - Daily (exc Mons) 2-5, May to Sept - Tues to Sats 11-5, Suns 2- 5; *closed Mons.* Oct - Suns only 2-4.30, also Bank Hol Mons 11-5. Grounds open same day as House, until 6 pm (5.30 in Oct).
Admission: £3.70, Chd £1.80, OAPs £3; Group rate (parties of 25 or over) £3.20, Chd £1.60, OAPs £2.70.
Refreshments: Light lunches (May to Sept) and teas at Castle.
Evening parties by arrangement. Further information from the Custodian.

BOURTON HOUSE GARDEN

Bourton-on-the-Hill map H5
Telephone: (0386) 700121
(Mr & Mrs R. Paice)

CHAVENAGE   🏛

Tetbury map G4
Telephone: (0666) 502329
(David Lowsley-Williams, Esq)

Elizabethan House (1576) with Cromwellian associations. 16th and 17th century furniture and tapestries. Family Chapel and medieval barn. Personally conducted tours.

Location: 2 m N of Tetbury signposted off A46 B4014.
Open: Easter Sun & Mon then May to end Sept - Thurs, Suns & Bank Hols 2-5.
Admission: £2.50, Chd half-price. Parties by appointment as above and also on other dates and times.

CHEDWORTH ROMAN VILLA   🌿 The National Trust

Yanworth, nr Cheltenham map H5   ♿
Telephone: (0242) 890256

The best exposed Romano-British villa in Britain. It was built about AD120 and extended and occupied until about AD400. There are good fourth century mosaics in the bath suits and triclinium (dining room). The villa was excavated in 1864, and a museum has a good range of household objects.

Location: 3 m NW of Fossebridge on Cirencester-Northleach road (A429).
Open: Feb: Parties by prior arrangement. Mar to end Oct: Tues to Sun & Bank Hol Mon 10-5.30. Last admissions 5. *Closed* Good Friday. 3 Nov to 5 Dec : Wed to Sun 11-4, also Dec 11, 12. March '94: Tues to Sun & Bank Hol Mon 10-5.30.
Admission: £2.50, Chd £1.25, Family £6.90. Parties by prior written arrangement only. Disabled - all parts accessible but some with difficulty. Disabled WC. Shop open on site - introductory film.

HAILES ABBEY   English ⌗ Heritage

map G5
Telephone: (0242) 602398

His life in danger at sea, Richard, Earl of Cornwall, vowed he would found a religious house if he lived. In 1245 his brother, King Henry III, gave him the manor of Hailes so that he could keep his pledge. After its establishment Richard's son, Edmund, presented the Cistercian monks of the abbey with a phial said to contain the Blood of Christ and from then until the Dissolution Hailes became a magnet for pilgrims. Extensive ruins survive and there is an excellent museum.

Location: 2 m (3.2 km) north east of Winchcombe.
Open: Good Friday or Apr 1 (whichever is earlier) to Sept 30: Open Daily 10-6. Oct 1 to Maundy Thursday or Mar 31 (whichever is earlier): Open Daily 10-4. *Closed* Dec 24-26, Jan 1.
Admission: £1.80, Concessions £1.30, Chd 90p.

HARDWICKE COURT

nr Gloucester map G5
Telephone: (0452) 720212
(C.G.M. Lloyd-Baker)

Late Georgian house designed by Robert Smirke, built 1816-1817. Entrance Hall, Drawing Room, Library and Dining Room open. Garden under course of restoration.

Location: 5 m S of Gloucester on A38 (between M5 access 12 S only and 13).
Station(s): 5 m S of Gloucester on A38 (between M5 access 12 S only and 13).
Open: Easter Mon to End Sept - Mons only 2-4. Other times by prior written appointment.
Admission: £1, Parking for cars only.
Not suitable for disabled.

HIDCOTE MANOR GARDEN   🌿 The National Trust

Hidcote Bartrim, nr Chipping Campden map H5
Telephone: (0386) 438333

One of the most beautiful English gardens.

Location: 4 m NE of Chipping Campden, 1 m E of A46 (re-designated B4632) off B4081.
Open: Apr to end of Oct - Daily (except Tues & Frid) 11-7 (last adm 6 or one hour before sunset).
Admission: £4.40, chd £2.20, Family ticket £12.10. *Parties by prior written arrangement only.*
Refreshments: Coffee, lunches 11-2. Teas 2.30-5. Light refreshments available from Tea Bar adjacent to car park 10.30-5.45
No dogs. No picknicking. Liable to serious overcrowding on Bank Hol weekends and fine Suns. Access: for the less able is limited in parts due to the nature of some informal stone paved paths. Wheelchair access to part of garden only, wheelchairs available.

KIFTSGATE COURT

nr Chipping Campden map H5
(Mr & Mrs J. G. Chambers)

Garden with many unusual shrubs and plants including tree paeonies, abutilons etc, specie and old fashioned roses.

Location: 3 m NE of Chipping Campden 1 m E of A46 and B4081.
Open: GARDENS ONLY. Apr 1 to Sept 30 - Weds, Thurs & Suns 2-6 also Sats in June and July, Bank Hols 2-6. Sat May 16, June 20 and Aug 22, 2-6.
Admission: £2.50, Chd £1. In aid of *National Gardens Scheme*.
Refreshments: Whit Sun to Sept 1.
Coaches by appointment only. *Unusual plants for sale on open days.*

LITTLE DEAN HALL

Littledean map G5
Telephone: (0594) 824213
(D. M. Macer-Wright, Esq.)

Sir John Van Brugh (1664–1726)

Architect. His work can be seen at the following properties included in Historic Houses Castles and Gardens:

Blenheim Palace
Castle Howard
Claremont
Grimsthorpe Castle

LYDNEY PARK

Lydney map G5
Telephone: (Office) (0594) 842844
(Viscount Bledisloe)

Extensive Woodland Garden with lakes and a wide selection of fine shrubs and trees. Museums and Roman Temple Site. Deer Park (picnics). Country shop.

Location: ½ m W of Lydney on A48 (Gloucester to Chepstow).
Open: Easter Sun and Mon; every Sun, Wed and Bank Hol from Apr 11 to June 6, but every day from Sun May 30 to Jun 6, 11-6. **Coaches and parties** on Open Days and on other days by appointment (minimum 25). Easter to mid June; thereafter to end Sept for Temple Site and Museum only.
Admission: Car park and accompanied chd free.
Refreshments: Teas in house (house not otherwise open).
Dogs on lead.

MISARDEN PARK GARDENS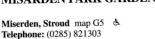

Miserden, Stroud map G5 &
Telephone: (0285) 821303
(Major M T N H Wills)

The garden has a timeless quality of a typically English Garden. A particular feature is the extensive yew topiary. To the south of the house is a wide Terrace laid with York paving. Sir Edward Lutyens Wing contains a Loggia overhung with Wisteria and on a lower terrace against the wing is a magnificent Magnolia 'Soulangeana'. On the south lawn are two flights of finely detailed grass steps. West of the main lawn are a series of terraced lawns leading to the Nurseries. To the east of these lawns is a broad grass walk lined by two substantial and very colourful herbaceous borders and beyond this is a traditional rose garden (many new introductions and features added recently). There are many fine specimen trees throughout the garden and the bulbs in variety and blossom in the Spring are other particular features. The garden stands high overlooking the wooded 'Golden Valley'. The Garden was featured in Country Life Spring Gardens Number 1992.

Location: Miserden 7 m from Gloucester, Cheltenham, Stroud & Cirencester; 3 m off A417 (signed).
Open: Every Tues, Wed & Thurs from Apr 1 to Sept 30, 9.30-4.30. Nurseries adjacent to garden open daily. *In aid of National Gardens Scheme* Suns Apr 4, July 4, 2-6.
Admission: £1.50 (includes leaflet), Chd (accompanied) free. Reductions for parties (of 20 or more) by appointment.
Car parking provided. Suitable for disabled. No wheelchairs available.

NEWARK PARK 🦋 The National Trust

Wotton under Edge map G4
Telephone: (0453) 842644

Elizabethan Hunting Lodge built on cliff edge, modified in 1790's by James Wyatt and rehabilitated by present tenant. Woodland garden.

Location: 1½ m E of Wotton under Edge, 1½ m S of junction of A4135 and B4058.
Open: Jun to Sept: Weds and Thur afternoons by 'prior appointment only' with the tenant. (Guided tour). Parties by written arrangment only.
Admission: £1.50, Chd 75p. No reductions for parties.
Not suitable for coaches or wheelchairs. No dogs. No WC's.

OWLPEN MANOR

Uley, nr Dursley map G5
Telephone: (0453) 860261
Fax: (0435) 860819
(Mr & Mrs Nicholas Mander)

Opening again for 1993, romantic Tudor manor house in 16th/17th century formal terraced gardens. Picturesque Cotswold manorial group - including Jacobean Court House and Watermill dated 1728 (now holiday cottages), Victorian church and medieval tithe barn - enclosed in its own lovely wooded valley. 'The epitome of romance' (Pevsner). The mellow stone manor dates from 1450-1616, with small improvements of 1719; uninhabited for over 100 years before 1925, when it was restored by Cotswold Arts & Crafts architect, Norman Jewson. Tudor Great Hall and Jacobean Oak Parlour. Contents include unique 17th C painted-cloth wall hangings in Queen Margaret of Anjou's bedroom, family and Cotswold Arts & Crafts furniture and pictures, and textiles. One of the oldest complete secular gardens in England, with parterres, topiary yews and mill pond. 'Owlpen, in Gloucestershire - ah, what a dream is there!' Vita Sackville-West.

Location: 3 m E of Dursley off B4066, 1 m E of Uley at Green by Old Crown pub.
Open: Apr 1 to Sept 30 incl. Tues, Thur, Suns and Bank Hol Mons 2-5.30. No dogs.
Admission: £2.80, chd £1.50. Guided tours for pre-booked groups of 20 or more.
Refreshments: Teas in Tithe Barn.

PAINSWICK ROCOCO GARDEN

Painswick map G5
Telephone: (0452) 813204
(Lord & Lady Dickinson)

This beautiful six acre garden, set in a hidden combe, is a rare and complete survivor of the brief eighteenth century taste for the Rococo in garden design. A restoration programme was begun in October 1984, based on a Thomas Robins painting of 1748, and this is now largely completed.

Location: ½ m from Painswick on B4073.
Open: GARDEN ONLY: Feb 1 to mid Dec: Wed to Sun incl Bank Hols, 11-5. Groups by appointment.
Admission: £2.40, OAPs £2, Chd £1.20.
Refreshments: In licensed restaurant, morning coffees and home made light lunches and afternoon teas. Present Collection shop.

RYELANDS HOUSE

Taynton map G5
(Captain & Mrs Eldred Wilson)

Fascinating sunken garden of 1½ acres with great variety of plants, many rare and unusual, in beautiful unspoilt country setting. Country walk to see abundance of wild flowers and spectacular views; landscaped lake in woodlands.

Location: 8 m NW of Gloucester; on B4216 between Huntley (A40) & Newent (B4215).
Open: Suns Apr 4, 11, 18, 25; Mon Apr 12, Sun May 2, 30, Mon May 3, 31. All dates 2-6. Parties by appointment. *In aid of National Gardens Scheme.*
Admission: £2, chd and parking free.
Refreshments: Home made teas Suns and Bank Hol Mons.
Dogs welcome on walk. Plants for sale.

SEZINCOTE

Moreton-in-Marsh map H5
(Mr & Mrs D. Peake)

Oriental water garden by Repton and Daniell with trees of unusual size. House in 'Indian' style inspiration of Royal Pavilion, Brighton.

Location: 1½ m W of Moreton-in-Marsh on A44 to Evesham; turn left by lodge before Bourton-on-the-Hill.
Open: GARDEN. Thurs, Frid & Bank Hol Mons 2-6 (or dusk if earlier) throughout year, except Dec. HOUSE May, June, July & Sept, Thurs & Frid 2.30-6. Parties by appointment. Open in aid of *National Gardens Scheme* Sun July 11, 2-6.
Admission: House & Garden: £3.50. Garden only: £2.50, chd £1.
Refreshments: Hotels & restaurant in Moreton-in-Marsh.
No dogs.

SNOWSHILL MANOR   The National Trust

nr Broadway map H5
Telephone: (0386) 852410

A Tudor house with c1700 facade; 21 rooms containing interesting collection of craftsmanship, including musical instruments, clocks, toys, bicycles and Japanese armour, with small formal garden.

Location: 3 m SW of Broadway off A44.
Open: Apr & Oct: Sat & Sun 11-1, 2-5. Easter Sat to Mon 11-1, 2-6. May to end Sept: Wed to Sun & Bank Hol Mon 11-1, 2-6. Last admissions to house ½ hour before closing.
Admission: £4, chd £2, Family ticket £11. Parties by prior written arrangment only. No coaches. No dogs. Liable to serious overcrowding on Suns and Bank Hol Weekends. Disabled - limited access to house (ground floor) and part of garden.

STANWAY HOUSE

nr Broadway map H5
Telephone: (038673) 469
(Lord Neidpath)

This jewel of Cotswold Manor houses is very much a home rather than a museum and the centre of a working landed estate which has changed hands once in 1275 years. The mellow Jacobean architecture, the typical squire's family portraits, the exquisite Gatehouse, the old Brewery, mediaeval Tithe Barn, the extensive gardens, arboretum pleasure grounds and formal landscape contribute to the timeless charm of what Arthur Negus considered one of the most beautiful and romantic houses in England.

Location: 1 m off B4632 Cheltenham/Broadway road; on B4077 Toddington/Stow-on-the-Wold road; M5 junction 9.
Open: June, July, Aug and Sept - Tues and Thurs 2-5.
Admission: £2.50, OAPs £2, Chd £1.
Refreshments: Teas in Old Bakehouse in village (Stanton 204).

SUDELEY CASTLE

Winchcombe map G5 △
Telephone: (0242) 602308
(Lord and Lady Ashcombe)

Set against the picturesque splendour of rolling Cotswold Hills, Sudeley Castle is one of Englands's most delightful historic houses. Once the magnificent palace of Queen Katherine Parr the Castle boasts an impressive collection of art treasures and fascinating relics. Also eight majestic gardens with avenues of trees, shrubs, wide stretches of water, grand yew hedges and fragrant old fashioned roses. Adventure Playground, Picnic Area, Exhibition Centre, Gift Shop, Restaurant, Specialist Plant Centre.

Location: 7 m NE of Cheltenham on B4632. Access A40, A438, M5 (junction 9, Tewkesbury).
Open: Apr 1 to Oct 31: daily (inc. Bank Hols). Grounds open: 11-5.30; Castle Apartments 12-5.
Admission: Inclusive: £4.75; Chd £2.50 + OAP £4.25. Ground adm: £3.10, Chd £1.40 + OAP £2.75. Special rates for parties of 20 persons or more. Free car parking.
Refreshments: The Old Kitchen Restaurant open for luncheon and afternoon tea.
Guided Tours available by prior arrangement. Full educational pack available. Also holiday cottages, conference centre, corporate activities, product launches, filming, weddings etc.

WESTBURY COURT GARDEN   🌳 **The National Trust**

Westbury-on-Severn map G5   ♿
Telephone: (0452) 760461

A formal Dutch water-garden with canals and yew hedges, laid out between 1696 and 1705; the earliest of its kind remaining in England.

Location: 9 m SW of Gloucester on A48.
Open: Apr to end Oct - Weds to Suns & Bank Hol Mons 11-6. *Closed* Good Friday.
Admission: £2, chd £1. Parties by prior written arrangement only.
Picnic area. No dogs. Wheelchairs provided.

WHITTINGTON COURT

Whittington, nr Cheltenham map G5
Telephone: (0242) 820218.
(Mrs R. J. Charleston)

Small Elizabethan stone-built manor house with family possessions.

Location: 4½ m E of Cheltenham on A40.
Open: Apr 10 to 25, Aug 14 to 30. Daily 2-5.
Admission: £2, OAPs £1.50, Chd £1. Open to parties by arrangement.

WOODCHESTER PARK MANSION

Nympsfield   map G4
Telephone: (0453) 860531 (for private bookings and info.) or (0453) 750455
(Woodchester Mansion Trust)

Woodchester Park Mansion is an unfinished masterpiece of Victorian building, abandoned over 120 years ago and hidden from time and the modern world within a secret Cotswold valley. Designed by brilliant, young, architect Benjamin Bucknall, for the wealthy Catholic merchant William Leigh. The Mansion is a curious mixture of European Gothic revival and Cotswold tradition. The building was started in 1856 and inexplicably abandoned in the early 1860s. Over the last century the building has suffered from neglect and decay. The Woodchester Mansion Trust, a registered charity purchased the lease of the building and are carrying out a ten year restoration programme, training courses are run for stonemasons, architects and conservators in the use of traditional building methods. The Mansion is run entirely by volunteers and all proceeds go towards the work of the Woodchester Mansion Trust.

Location: ½ m from the village of Nympsfield, on the B4066 Stroud-Dursley road, opposite the Coaley Peak picnic site.
Open: From Apr - Oct first weekend in the month, Bank Hol weekends & an openweek in July. Apr 3, 4, 10, 11, 12. May 1, 2, 3, 29, 30, 31. June 5, 6. July 3, 4, 5, 6, 7, 8, 9, 10, 11. August 7, 8, 28, 29, 30. Sept 4, 5. Oct 2, 3.
Admission: £3. Private parties on other days by arrangement. No children under 12 inside the mansion.
Refreshments: Teas.
No dogs. Shop open at the Mansion. Free mini-bus shuttle service available along 1 mile drive.

HAMPSHIRE

JANE AUSTEN'S HOUSE

Chawton   map J3
Telephone: (0420) 83262
(Jane Austen Memorial Trust)

Pleasant 17th century village house where Jane Austen lived from 1809 to 1817, and wrote or revised her six great novels. Many interesting mementoes of Jane and her family. Pretty, old fashioned garden, suitable for picnics.

Location: In Chawton, 1 m SW of Alton, sign-posted off roundabout at junction of A31 with A32.
Station(s): Alton (1¾ m).
Open: Daily Apr-Oct; Nov, Dec & Mar: Weds to Suns. Jan & Feb: Sats & Suns only, 11-4.30. *Closed Christmas Day & Boxing Day.*
Admission: £1.50, chd (8-18) 50p, Groups (15 plus) £1.
Refreshments: Available in village.
Bookshop.

AVINGTON PARK

map H3 △
Telephone: (0962) 779260
(Mr and Mrs J B Hickson)

William Cobbett wrote of Avington that it was 'one of the prettiest places in the County' and indeed it is true today. Avington Park, where Charles II and George IV both stayed at various times, is an old house enlarged in 1670 by the addition of two wings and a classical Portico surmounted by three Statues. The State Rooms on view include the Ballroom with its magnificent ceiling, the Red Drawing Room, Library etc. Avington Church, one of the most perfect Georgian Churches in Hampshire, is in the grounds close by and may be visited. The facilities are available for filming or still photography. The Library is also available for Wedding Receptions, Conferences etc.

Location: 4 m NE of Winchester, just S of B3047 in Itchen Abbas.
Open: May to Sept - Suns & Bank Hols 2.30-5.30 (last tour begins 5). *Other times for large parties by prior arrangement.*
Refreshments: Tea at the House during opening times.

BASING HOUSE

Basingstoke map J4
Telephone: (0256) 467294
(Hampshire County Council)

Basing House ruins were once the country's largest private house, the palace of William Paulet, 1st Marquess of Winchester who was Lord Treasurer of England under three Tudor monarchs. The Civil War brought disaster to Basing which fell to Oliver Cromwell in person after 2½ years of siege in 1645. The ruins, which cover about 10 acres, contain Norman earthworks, the remains of Tudor kitchens, cellars, towers, a 300 foot long tunnel, a spectacular barn, Civil War defences designed by Inigo Jones and a recently re-created 16/17th century formal garden. Special events in 1993 to commemorate 350th anniversary of the English Civil War.

Location: 2 m from Basingstoke Town Centre & 2 m from Junction 6 of M3.
Open: Apr 1 to Sept 26: Wed to Sun and Bank Hols 2-6 .Parties any time by prior arrangement.
Admission: £1.10, Chd and OAPs 60p.
Refreshments: Meals can be obtained at two public houses near main entrance. Tea shop usually open on site most Suns.
Car parking. Suitable for disabled persons.

Sir Joshua Reynolds
Portrait painter (1723–1792)
First President of the Royal Academy, knighted in 1769

His work can be seen in the following properties included in Historic Houses Castles and Gardens:

Arundel Castle
Dalmeny House (Roseberry Collection of Political Portraits)
Goodwood House

Kenwood
Shalom Hall
Weston Park

BEAULIEU

Beaulieu map H3   Ⓢ
Telephone: (0590) 612345
(The Lord Montagu of Beaulieu)

Palace House and Gardens; Beaulieu Abbey and Exhibition of Monastic Life; The National Motor Museum featuring more than 250 exhibits including motor cars, commercial vehicles and motorcycles; Wheels' - a fantastic ride on space age' pods through 100 years of motoring from 1895 to the present day. Monorail, veteran bus and miniature veteran car rides, Driving Experience' simulator and display; model railway, radio-controlled cars, mini racing car and motorcycle rides. Daily cavalcades of historic vehicles during peak summer season and many other events throughout the year.

Location: In Beaulieu 7 m SE of Lyndhurst; 14 m S of Southampton; 6 m NE of Lymington.
Open: All facilities open throughout the year. Easter to Sept - Daily 10-6; Oct to Easter - Daily 10-5. *Closed Christmas Day.*
Admission: Inclusive charge. Reduced rates for Chd and OAPs. *Parties at special rates.*
Refreshments: Lunches and teas at licensed Brabazon Restaurant.

BISHOP'S WALTHAM PALACE   English♯Heritage

map J3
Telephone: (0489) 892460

The Bishops of Winchester held Waltham since Saxon times, but they did not build here until about 1135. Heavily fortified, this was more castle than palace, and was dismantled by Henry II. Most of the present remains are from the spacious 15th century palace with its walled garden, all within this vast moated site. Forfeited by the bishops at the Reformation, the palace was reduced to a ruin in the Civil War, when it was held for the King against Parliament. The Dower House or Farmhouse was the medieval lodging of the Palace. It now houses an exhibition, carved stone display, and the downstairs rooms are furnished in the style of a 19th c Farmhouse.

Location: Bishop's Waltham.
Open: Good Friday or Apr 1 (whichever is earlier) to Sept 30 daily 10-6. Oct 1 to Maundy Thursday or Mar 31 (whichever is earlier) Tues to Sun 10-4. *Closed* Dec 24-26, Jan 1.
Admission: £1.70, Concessions £1.30, Chd 85p.

BRAMDEAN HOUSE

Bramdean, nr Alresford map J3
Telephone: (0962) 771214
(Mrs H. Wakefield)

Carpets of Spring bulbs. Walled garden with famous herbaceous borders, working kitchen garden and large collection of unusual plants.

Location: Bramdean. On A272 midway between Winchester & Petersfield.
Open: Suns Mar 21, Apr 11, May 16, June 20, July 18, Aug 15, Mon Apr 12, 2-5. Also by appointment.
Admission: £1, Chd free. *In aid of the National Gardens Scheme.*
Refreshments: Teas.
Car park. Not suitable for the disabled.

Gertrude Jekyll
writer and gardener
(1843–1932)

Her designs were used at the following properties included in Historic Houses Castles and Gardens:

Hestercombe House and Gardens
Knebworth
Vann

BREAMORE HOUSE

nr Fordingbridge map H3   △
Telephone: (0725) 22468
(Sir Westrow Hulse, Bt)

Elizabethan Manor House (1583) with fine collection of paintings, tapestries, furniture. Countryside Museum. Exhibition of Rural Arts and Agricultural machinery. Carriage Museum. 'The Red Rover', and other coaches.

Location: 3 m N of Fordingbridge off the main Bournemouth Road (A338) 8 m S of Salisbury.
Open: Easter Hol, Apr, Tues, Weds, Suns; May, June, July & Sept - Tues, Weds, Thurs, Sats, Suns and all Bank Hols; Aug - Daily, 2-5.30. *Other times by appointment.*
Admission: Combined ticket £4, chd £2.50. Reduced rate for parties and OAPs.
Refreshments: Home-made Teas. Food available. Bat and Ball, Breamore.

Robert Adam – architect

His work can be seen at the following properties included in Historic Houses Castles and Gardens:

Bowood
Culzean Castle
Hatchlands
Kedleston Hall
Kenwood
Kimbolton Castle
Luton Hoo
Mellerstain

Moccas Court
Newby Hall
Nostell Priory
Osterley Park House
Papplewick Hall
Saltram House
Syon House

BROADLANDS

Romsey map H3
Telephone: (0794) 516878
(Lord and Lady Romsey)

BROADLANDS

Famous for royal honeymoons and as the home of Lord Mountbatten, Broadlands has countless mementoes of the Mounbatten and Palmerston eras and of its many royal visitors.

One of the finest Palladian houses in England, Broadlands is also home to a magnificent collection of paintings and furniture.

Enjoying an idyllic setting on the banks of the Test with superb views from the riverside lawns.

The Mountbatten Exhibition traces the eventful lives of Lord and Lady Mountbatten, while history is brought vividly to life in 'The Life and Times of Lord Mountbatten' multi-screen audio-visual presentation.

SPECTACULAR MOUNTBATTEN AUDIO-VISUAL

Facilities include self-service restaurant, picnic area and two gift shops.

Open Easter to end September. Admission 10am - 4pm. Closed Fridays, except Good Friday and in August. All-inclusive admission charge. Children under 12 free when accompanied by parent. Free parking.

For further information, call Romsey (0794) 516878.

OFF A31, ROMSEY. SIGNPOSTED FROM JUNCTIONS 2 AND 3, M27

Famous in recent times as the home of Lord Mountbatten, Broadlands was also the country residence of Lord Palmerston, the great Victorian Prime Minister. Fine example of Palladian architecture set in Capability Brown parkland on the banks of the River Test. Visitors may view interior of house containing many fine works of art including several Van Dycks and furniture by Ince and Mayhew. Visitors may also relive Lord Mountbatten's life and times in the Mountbatten Exhibition and spectacular Mountbatten Audio-Visual Presentation housed in William and Mary stable block.

Location: 8 m N of Southampton (A3057); entrance from by-pass immediately S of Romsey (A31).
Station(s): Romsey (1 m).
Open: Easter to end Sept. Daily 10-5.30 (last adm 4). *Closed* Fri except Good Friday and in Aug.
Admission: £5, Chd (12-16) £3.40, Chd (under 12) accompanied by parent/guardian free, OAPs £4, Disabled £4, Students £4. Reduced rates for parties of 15 or more.
Refreshments: Self-service restaurant. Kiosk in picnic area.
Free coach and car park.

CALSHOT CASTLE   English❖Heritage

map H3
Telephone: (0703) 892023

Part of the chain of Henry VIII's coastal defences against the Catholic powers of Europe. Completed in 1540 and still virtually intact, the Castle has played an important role in England's defence from the 16th Century until World War II. From 1912 to the mid 1950's it formed part of a flying boat base, initially a Royal Naval Air station, then RAF Calshot. Site exhibition and restored WWI barrack room.

Location: On Spit 2 m (3.2 km) south-east of Fawley off B3053, 15 m (24 km) south east of Southampton.
Open: Good Friday or Apr 1 (whichever is earlier) to Sept 30: Open daily 10-6.
Admission: £1.20, Concessions 90p, Chd 60p.

EXBURY GARDENS

nr Southampton map H3
(E L de Rothschild, Esq)

Unique 200 acre woodland garden created by Lionel de Rothschild, with a superb display of rhododendrons, azaleas, camellias, magnolias, other fascinating flora and new plantings. Well stocked Plant Centre and Gift Shop, artist's studio, licensed tea rooms. Dogs welcome on leads.

Location: Exbury village, 15 m SW of Southampton close to New Forest. Turn W off A326 at Dibden Purlieu towards Beaulieu.
Open: Daily 10-5.30pm. Gardens: Mar to Oct. **Plant Centre and Gift Shop** open all year except Christmas and Boxing Day.
Admission: £3.50, OAPs and parties £3, Chd (10-16) £2.50. Early and late season discounts.
Refreshments: Licensed refreshments.
Also ample parking and toilet facilities. Dogs on short leads.

FORT BROCKHURST   English Heritage

Portsmouth map J3
Telephone: (0705) 581059

One of five forts known as the Gosport Advanced Line, Brockhurst was built in the mid-19th century to protect Portsmouth Dockyard. The traditional star shape was abandoned for a polygonal plan. Norman castles had become obsolete with the use of gunpowder, but some features were retained. Brockhurst has a moat and a drawbridge. It also has a keep, traditionally the point of last defence. There is an exhibition on the history of Portsmouth's defences.

Location: Off the A32 in Elson on the north side of Gosport.
Open: Good Friday or Apr 1 (whichever is earlier) to Sept 30: Open Daily 10-6. Oct 1 to Maundy Thursday or Mar 31 (whichever is earlier): Open Tues to Sun 10-4. *Closed* Dec 24-26, Jan 1.
Admission: £1.70, concessions £1.30, Chd 85p.

GILBERT WHITE'S HOUSE & GARDEN AND THE OATES EXHIBITIONS

Selborne map J3
Telephone: (042 050) 275
(Rev. Gilbert White, 1720-93)

Historic house with furnished rooms & glorious tranquil 5 acre garden. Home of famous 18th century naturalist Gilbert White, author of 'The Natural History of Selborne'. Displays on Gilbert White & Selborne. Events during the year to commemorate the bicentenary of his death. Also Exhibitions on Captain Lawrence Oates who accompanied Scott to the South Pole and Frank Oates, Victorian explorer and naturalist in South America and Africa.

Location: In Selborne
Open: 11-5.30 (last adm 5) Tues to Sun & Bank Hols from 13 Mar - 31 Oct. Sat & Sun from 6 Nov to 2 Jan. (Not 25/26 Dec). Parties by arrangement.
Admission: £2, OAPs & Sudents £1, Children (First child free) £1. Free adm to shop.
Refreshments: In village.
Shop.

THE SIGN OF A GREAT DAY OUT

HIGHCLERE CASTLE

nr Newbury map H4
Telephone: (0635) 253210
(The Earl of Carnarvon KCVO, KBE)

Highclere Castle is the ultimate in high Victorian exuberance. Designed by Charles Barry in the 1830s at the same time as he was building the Houses of Parliament, this soaring pinnacled mansion provided the perfect social setting for the 3rd Earl of Carnarvon, one of the great hosts of Queen Victoria's reign. Several prominent Victorian architects, including Barry, George Gilbert Scott and Thomas Allom, are responsible for the extravagant interiors in styles which range from church Gothic through Moorish flamboyance and rococo revival to the solid masculinity in the long library. Old master paintings mix with portraits by Van Dyck and 18th Century painters. Napoleon's desk and chair rescued from St. Helena sits with other 18th and 19th Century furniture. The 5th Earl of Carnarvon, passionate archaeologist and Egyptologist, was the discoverer of the tomb of Tutankhamun and a special display shows some of his early finds in Egypt which had laid hidden for over 60 years. GARDENS - The parkland with its massive cedars was designed by Capability Brown. The walled gardens also date from the earlier house at Highclere but the dark yew walks are entirely Victorian in character. The glass Orangery and Fernery add an exotic flavour and an impression of the complexity of the gardens at their peak. Walking through to the Secret Garden, the walled walks unexpectedly open up into a curving, densely planted herbaceous garden laid out in this Century with ornamental trees and flowering plants and shrubs.

Location: 4½ m S of Newbury on A34, junction 13 of M4 about 2 m from Newbury. M3. Basingstoke junction about 15 m. Heathrow via M4 1 hour. Rail from London (Paddington station) 1 hour.
Open: July, Aug, Sept, Wed, Thurs, Fri, Sat and Sun 2-6 (last entry 5). Easter, May and Aug Bank Holidays, Sun and Mon.
Admission: Rates not available at time of going to press. Special reductions for parties of 30 or more by application.
Refreshments: Traditional country cream teas, ices, soft drinks, etc.
Car park and picnic area adjacent to Castle. Suitable for disabled persons on ground floor only. One wheelchair available. Visitors can buy original items in Castle Gift Shop and visit the Plant Centre only a short distance away in the Park.

THE SIR HAROLD HILLIER GARDENS AND ARBORETUM

Ampfield, nr Romsey map H3
Telephone: (0794) 68787
(Hampshire County Council)

Begun by the famous nurseryman Sir Harold Hillier in 1953, and gifted to Hampshire County Council in 1977, the Gardens and Arboretum now extend to some 160 acres and contain the largest collection of different hardy plants in the British Isles. With this diversity in plants, the Gardens provide something of interest throughout the seasons, from the magnificent floral displays in the spring, followed by the pastel shades of summer which become overwhelmed by the riot of autumnal hues in October to the highly scented winter flowering Witch Hazels.

Location: 3 m north east of Romsey, off A31.
Open: Mon to Fri 10.30-5 (all year round). Weekends and Bank Hols 10.30-6 (Mar to end Nov). Suns 10.30 -dusk (Dec to Feb).
Admission: £2.50, OAPs £2 (under 16 yrs) £1. Groups over 30 £2 each.
Refreshments: Teas and light meals at weekends from March until Easter and also during November. Everyday from Easter until end October.
Regret NO DOGS.

HINTON AMPNER   The National Trust

nr Alresford map J3
Telephone: (0962) 771305

The house was remodelled in the Georgian style in 1936 by Ralph Dutton but decimated by fire in 1960. Rebuilt and re-furnished with fine regency furniture, pictures and porcelain. The gardens juxtapose formality of design and informality of planting, producing delightful walks and unexpected vistas.

Location: 1 m W of Bramdean Village on A272; 8 m E of Winchester.
Open: Apr 1 to end Sept. GARDEN: Sat, Sun, Tues and Wed (inc. Good Friday and Bank Holiday Mon) 1.30-5.30. HOUSE: Tues & Wed only and Sat & Sun in Aug 1.30-5.30 (last adm 5). Car park open at 1.15.
Admission: GARDEN: £2.20, HOUSE: £1.30 extra. Children half-price. Party reductions (£3 House & Gardens) by prior booking.
Refreshments: Teas same days as garden 2-5pm.
No dogs. Most of garden accessible by wheelchair.

HOUGHTON LODGE GARDENS

Stockbridge map H3 ⅋
Telephone: (0264) 810177 or (0264) 810502
(Captain & Mrs M W Busk)

Landscaped pleasure grounds surround unique 18th C 'Cottage Ornee' beside the River Test with lovely views over the tranquil and unspoiled valley. Within the traditional kitchen garden surrounded by rare chalkcob walls is the HAMPSHIRE HYDROPONICUM where flowers, fruits, herbs and vegetables grow WITHOUT SOIL. Believed to be the first Hydroponicum in England primarily intended to delight and inform the visitor. The ease of Hydroponic Gardening (no weeding, or digging, no soil borne pests) makes it an ideal method for the handicapped.

Location: 1½ m S of A30 at Stockbridge on minor road to Houghton village.
Open: Mar to Sept incl, 10-5 on Sat and Sun, 2-5 on Mon, Tues and Fri. Coach tours and parties welcome by prior appointment. Tel. for details.
Admission: Free parking.
Plants and produce for sale.

HURST CASTLE   English❖Heritage

map H2
Telephone: (0590) 642344

Built by Henry VIII to defend the Solent, Hurst Castle was completed in 1544, and had a garrison of 23 men. During the Civil War it was occupied by Parliamentary forces and Charles I was imprisoned here for a short time. A longer incarceration was that of an unfortunate priest called Atkinson, who was a prisoner here for 29 years in the 18th century. The castle was considerably modernised in the mid-19th century, under the fear of a French invasion, and was still useful in the Second World War. Café open during summer season.

Location: Approach by ferry from Keyhaven.
Open: Good Friday or Apr 1 (whichever is earlier) to Sept 30: Open Daily 10-6. Oct 1 to Maundy Thursday or Mar 31 (whichever is earlier): Open weekends 10-4. *Closed* Dec 24-26, Jan 1.
Admission: £1.70, concessions £1.30, Chd 85p.
Refreshments: Café open during summer season.

JENKYN PLACE

Bentley map J3
(Mrs G E Coke)

Beautifully designed garden with large collection of rare plants, old-fashioned roses and exceptionally fine, double herbaceous borders.

Location: In Bentley 400 yds N of cross roads Heritage signs on A31. Station: Bentley (1 m).
Open: GARDEN ONLY: Apr 8 to Sept 12 - Thur, Fri, Sat, Sun & Bank Hol Mons. 2-6. *Open on certain Suns in aid of the National Gardens Scheme.*
Admission: £2, Chd (5-15) 75p. Car park free.
No dogs.

THE MANOR HOUSE

Upton Grey, Basingstoke map J4
Telephone: (0256) 862827
(Mrs J Wallinger)

A 4 acre garden designed by Gertrude Jekyll in 1908 surrounds Arts and Crafts house built in 1907 by Ernest Newton for Charles Holme, Editor of 'The Studio'. The garden has been meticulously restored over the last 8 years to the original plans which are on display and plants are as Jekyll specified:- Nuttery, Tennis lawn, Bowling Green, Rose Garden, Formal Garden with herbaceous borders and dry-stone walling. Also Jekyll's only surviving wild garden with Pond.

Location: 6 m SE of Basingstoke in Upton Grey on hill immediately above the church.
Open: Garden only open. Every Wed in May, June and July. also by arrangement for groups. Guided tours available on the History of Jekyll and Arts and Crafts. No dogs.
Admission: £1.50. *In aid of National Gardens Scheme.*
Refreshments: Teas by prior arrangement. Local pub. 'The Hoddington Arms', Upton Grey (0256) 862371
No dogs. Parking in nearby Farmyard,

MEDIEVAL MERCHANTS HOUSE English❖Heritage

Southampton map H3
Telephone: (0703) 221503

A medieval merchant's house, built in the 1290s is now fully restored to its 14th century appearance. On the ground floor is the restored medieval shop stocked with traditional wines and other produce. The house is furnished with medieval reproductions based on contemporary illustrations.

Location: 58 French St between Castle Way and Town Quay.
Open: Good Friday or Apr 1 (whichever is earlier) to Sept 30: Open Daily 10-6. Oct 1 to Maundy Thursday or Mar 31 (whichever is earlier): Open Tues to Sun 10-4. *Closed* Dec 24-26, Jan 1.
Admission: £1.70, Concessions £1.30, Chd 85p. Price includes a Personal Stereo Guided Tour.

MOTTISFONT ABBEY GARDEN   🌳 The National Trust

Mottisfont   map H3   △   ♿
Telephone: (0794) 41220

With a tributary of the River Test flowing through, the garden forms a superb setting for a 12th century Augustinian priory, which, after the Dissolution became a house (tenanted). It contains the spring or 'font' from which the place name is derived, a magnificent collection of trees, and the Trust's unique collection of old roses within walled gardens.

Location: 4½ m NW Romsey ¾ m W of A3057.
Station(s): Mottisfont Dunbridge (¾ m).
Open: GARDEN: April to end Oct - Sat-Wed, 12-6; last adm 5. June: Sat-Wed, 12-8.30. HOUSE: (Whistler room and cellarium only) April to end Oct - Tues, Wed, Sun, 1-5.
Admission: GARDEN: £2.50, House 50p extra. No reduction for parties. Coaches please book in advance.
Shop. Dogs in car park only. Wheelchairs - grounds and cellarium only. Special parking area for disabled people and powered vehicles, please ask at kiosk on arrival.

NETLEY ABBEY   English ⌗ Heritage

map H3
Telephone: (0703) 453076

Extensive picturesque remains of a Cistercian abbey on the east bank of the Southampton Water. Netley Abbey was founded in 1239 by monks from Beaulieu. Remains include the church and cloister buildings.

Location: In Netley, 7 m SE of Southampton, facing Southampton Water.
Open: Good Friday or Apr 1 (whichever is earlier) to Sept 30: Open Daily 10-6. Oct 1 to Maundy Thursday or Mar 31 (whichever is earlier): Open Weekends only 10-4. *Closed* Dec 24-26, Jan 1.
Admission: £1.20, Concessions 90p, chd 60p.

PORTCHESTER CASTLE   English ⌗ Heritage

map J3
Telephone: (0705) 378291

A Roman fortress, a Norman castle and a Romanesque church share this same site on the north shore of Portsmouth harbour. The outer walls were built in the 3rd century when Britain was the vulnerable north-west frontier of a declining Roman Empire. Today they are among the finest Roman remains in northern Europe. Eight centuries - and very little repair work - later, the walls were sound enough to encompass a royal castle. Portchester was popular with the medieval monarchs but by the 15th century royal money was being spent on Portsmouth instead. The last official use of the castle was as a prison for French seamen during the Napoleonic wars. An exhibition tells the story of Porchester.

Location: South side of Portchester.
Open: Good Friday or Apr 1 (whichever is earlier) to Sept 30: Open Daily 10-6. Oct 1 to Maundy Thursday or Mar 31 (whichever is earlier): Open Tues to Sun 10-4. *Closed* Dec 24-26, Jan 1.
Admission: £1.70, Concessions £1.30, chd 85p.

ROTHERFIELD PARK

Alton   map J3
Telephone: (042 058) 204
(Lt Col Sir James and Lady Scott)

Victorian Gothic House, built 1820. Romanticised 1880s. Fine position, many original contents. Large garden. Plants for sale.

Location: On A32, East Tisted. 4½ m S of Alton.
Open: Suns, Mons of Bank Hol Weekends and June 1 to June 7, July 1 to July 7, Aug 1 to Aug 7 2-5. Also Garden open Easter to end Sept, Thurs and Sun 2-5. Other times for groups by appointment with Lady Scott (042 058) 204, or preferably in writing. Also available for wedding receptions, still photography and filming.
Admission: House/Garden £2.50. Garden only £1, Chd free.
Refreshments: Teas (often for charity, only when house is open). Picnic area. Plants for sale.

🌳 THE SIGN OF A GREAT DAY OUT

SANDHAM MEMORIAL CHAPEL  The National Trust

Burghclere, nr Newbury map H4 &
Telephone: (063 527) 292

Walls covered with paintings by Stanley Spencer depicting war scenes in Salonica.

Location: In village of Burghclere 4 m S of Newbury ½ m E of A34.
Open: Apr 1 to end Oct: Wed-Sun 11.30-6. Open Bank Holiday Mon. Nov 1993 and Mar 1994: Sat & Sun only 11.30-4. *Closed Dec - Feb.*
Admission: £1.20, Parties must book. No reduction for parties.
No cameras allowed in Chapel. No dogs. Wheelchair access via two small sets of steps.

STRATFIELD SAYE HOUSE

Reading map J4 &
Telephone: (0256) 882882
(The Duke of Wellington)

Homes of the Dukes of Wellington since 1817, Stratfield Saye is a living example of the classic English Country House tradition with the present Duke and Duchess in residence for much of the year. At the same time, the house and exhibition pay tribute to Arthur Wellesley, the first and great Duke - soldier, statesman and victor of the Napoleonic wars. THE HOUSE: Gift of a grateful nation, the house contains a unique collection of paintings, prints, furniture and personal effects belonging to the Great Duke. THE WELLINGTON EXHIBITION: Depicts the life and times of the Great Duke with displays of his maps, weapons, personal effects and clothes of infinite variety. It features his magnificent funeral carriage which celebrates a long and successful military career that culminated in the battle of Waterloo. THE GROUNDS: Include a wildfowl sanctuary, gardens and the grave of Copenhagen, the Dukes's favourite charger that carried him throughout the battle of Waterloo and lived on for many years in retirement at Stratfield Saye. The house and associated Wellington Country Park are situated on the Hampshire/Berkshire borders.

Location: 1 m W of A33 between Reading & Basingstoke (turn off at Wellington Arms Hotel); signposted. Close to M3 & M4.
Open: HOUSE AND GARDENS; open daily (except Fris) from May 1 to last Sun in Sept 11.30-4. Available for private and corporate functions by arrangement with The Wellington Office (Tel 0256 882882). Wellington Country Park (3 m from house) - nature trails, adventure playground, animals, boating, windsurfing, fishing, deer park, miniature railway, National Dairy Museum, Thames Valley Time Trail - Mar to Oct daily 10-5. Nov-Feb Sats & Suns only. (Tel 0734 326444).
Admission: Please telephone for charges to House and Park.
Refreshments: Tea and snacks, licensed restaurant.

THE VYNE  The National Trust

Basingstoke map J4 &
Telephone: (0256) 881337

House of diaper brickwork built by William 1st Lord Sandys in early 16th century, extensively altered in mid 17th century when John Webb added the earliest classical partico to a country house in England. Tudor chapel with Renaissance glass; Palladian staircase; garden with herbaceous borders, lawns and lakes; woodland walks.

Location: 4 m N of Basingstoke between Bramley & Sherborne St John (1½ m from each). *Station(s): Bramley (2½ m).*
Open: Apr 1 to Oct 31 daily except Mon and Fri (open Good Friday and Bank Hol Mon but closed Tues following). Apr 1 to Oct 24: HOUSE: 1.30-5.30; GARDEN: 12.30-5.30. Bank Hol Mons 11-5.30. Last adm 5. Oct 24 to Oct 31: HOUSE: 1.30-4. GARDEN: 12.30-4. Last adm 3.30.
Admission: House and Garden: £4. Garden only: £2, *Chd half-price. Reduced rates for pre-booked parties Tues, Weds & Thurs only £2.50.*
Refreshments: Light lunches and teas in the Old Brewhouse - April to Oct 23. 12.30-2 and 2.30-5.30. Oct 24 to Oct 31. 12.30-2 and 2.30-4.
Shop. Dogs in car park only. Wheelchair provided.

WOLVESEY: OLD BISHOP'S PALACE English⌗Heritage

map H3
Telephone: (0962) 54766

Ruins of an extensive palace of the Bishops of Winchester, built round a quadrangular courtyard.

Location: ¼ m (½ km) south east of Winchester Cathedral, next to the Bishop's Palace.
Open: Good Friday or Apr 1 (whichever is earlier) to Sept 30: Open Daily 10-6.
Admission: £1.20, Concessions 90p, Chd 60p.

HEREFORD & WORCESTER

ABBERLEY HALL

nr Worcester map G6
Telephone: (0299) 896634 (office hours only)
(Mrs Atkinson)

Five principal rooms show ornate decoration of mid-Victorian period.

Location: 12 m NW of Worcester on A443.
Open: HOUSE ONLY. May 31; July 21-23 and 26-30; Aug 2-6, 9-13, 16-20, 23-27 and 30, 1.30-4.30.
Admission: £1.
Refreshments: Unsuitable for wheelchairs. No dogs.

AVONCROFT MUSEUM OF BUILDINGS

Stoke Heath, Bromsgrove map G6   ⓢ
Telephone: (0527) 31886 or 31363
(Council of Management)

An open-air Museum containing buildings of great interest and variety. Exhibits include a working windmill, the magnificent 14th century Guesten Hall Roof from Worcester, a 15th century timber framed house, 1946 prefab: from the 18th century a cockpit theatre, an icehouse, an earth closet and a cider mill, and from the 19th century a toll house and a 3 cell lock-up.

Location: At Stoke Heath 2 m S of Bromsgrove off A38 between junctions 4 & 5 of M5 and 3½ m S of M42 junction 1.
Open: Mar & Nov 11-4.30, closed Mons & Frid; Apr, May, Sept & Oct 11-5 (11-5.30 weekends) *closed Mons;* June, July & Aug daily 11-5.30. Open Bank Holidays. *Closed Dec to Feb.*
Admission: £3, Chd £1.50, OAPs £2.10. Family ticket (2 adults and 2 chd) £8. Parties at reduced rates by arrangement. Free car park & picnic site.
Refreshments: Available at Museum tea room. Souvenir and Bookshop.

BERNITHAN COURT

Llangarron map G5
(M.J. Richardson Esq.)

William & Mary house built for Hoskyns family in 1692: some surviving panelling, fine staircase, walled gardens.

Location: 4 m Ross on Wye, 1½ m from A40 Ross-Monmouth road.
Open: By prior appointment, contact Mrs James, 1 Bernithan Farm Cottage, Llangarron, Ross on Wye HR9 6NG.
Admission: £2.

BERRINGTON HALL   🍂 The National Trust

Leominster map F6   △   ♿
Telephone: (0568) 615721

Built 1778-1781,designed by Henry Holland, the architect of Carlton House. Painted and plaster ceilings. 'Capability' Brown laid out the park.

Location: 3 m N Leominster, 7 m S of Ludlow, W of A49.
Open: Apr to end of Sept - Weds to Suns & Bank Hol Mons 1.30-5.30; (Closed Good Frid). Oct: Wed to Sun 1.30-4.30. Grounds & restaurant open from 12.30. Last admission ½hr before closing.
Admission: £3.20, Chd £1.60, grounds only £1.50. Family ticket £8.80. Parties by prior written arrangement only.
Refreshments: Licensed restaurant in the Servants Hall, serving homemade lunches and teas. Restaurant 12.30-2 (lunch), 2.30-5.30 (teas). Open same days as house and also Nov 6 to Dec 19, Sats and Suns 12.30-4.30.
No dogs. Wheelchair available. Wheelchair access grounds only. No photography.

🍂 THE SIGN OF A GREAT DAY OUT

BURFORD HOUSE GARDENS

Tenbury Wells map G6
Telephone: (0584) 810777
(Treasures of Tenbury Ltd.)

BURTON COURT

Eardisland map F6 &
Telephone: (05447) 231
(Lt-Cmdr & Mrs R. M. Simpson)

A typical squire's house, built around the surprising survival of a 14th century hall. The East Front re-designed by Sir Clough Williams-Ellis in 1912. An extensive display of European and Oriental costume, natural history specimens, and models including a working model fairground. Pick your own soft fruit in season.

Location: 5 m W of Leominster between A44 & A4112.
Open: Spring Bank Hol to end Sep - Weds, Thurs, Sats, Suns & Bank Hol Mons 2.30-6.
Admission: £2, chd £1.50, Coach parties £1.50.
Refreshments: Coach parties catered for. Teas.

CROFT CASTLE   The National Trust

nr Leominster map F6 &
Telephone: (056885) 246

Welsh Border castle mentioned in Domesday Book. Inhabited by the Croft family for 900 years. Fine 18th century Gothic interior. Extensive wooded parkland.

Location: 5 m NW of Leominster just N of B4362 signposted from Ludlow/Leominster road (A49), and from A4110 at Mortimers Cross.
Open: Apr & Oct Sat & Sun 2-5; Easter Sat, Sun & Mon 2-6, Closed Good Frid; May to end Sept - Weds to Suns & Bank Hol Mons 2-6. Last admission 30 mins before closing.
Admission: £2.80, chd £1.40, family ticket £7.70. Parties by prior written arrangement.
Refreshments: Picnics allowed in car park only.
Access for disabled to ground floor and part of grounds. Wheelchair available.

The gardens at Burford were created by John Treasure over a period of 35 years and are filled with a wealth of rare and interesting plants many of which are stocked by the adjoining world famous plant centre which bears his name.

Location: 1 m W of Tenbury Wells on the A456.
Open: All year.
Admission: £1.95, Chd 80p, Parties of 25 or more by prior arrangement £1.60 each.
Refreshments: Tea Rooms situated near entrance, serving morning coffee, light lunches and teas with locally baked cakes and scones.
No wheelchairs available.

CWMMAU FARMHOUSE, BRILLEY

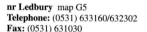 **The National Trust**

Whitney-on-Wye map F5

Early 17th century timber-framed and stone tiled farmhouse.

Location: 4 m SW of Kington between A4111 and A438. Approached by a long narrow lane.
Open: Easter, May, Spring & Summer Bank Hol weekends only -(Sats, Suns & Mons) 2-6. *At other times by prior written appointment with the tenant Mr D Joyce.*
Admission: £2, chd £1.*No reduction for parties.*
No dogs. Unsuitable for wheelchairs and coaches.

DINMORE MANOR

nr Hereford map F5   ♿
Telephone: (0432) 71322
(R.G. Murray)

Spectacular hillside location. A range of impressive architecture dating from 14th to 20th century. Chapel, Cloisters, Great Hall (Music Room) and extensive roof walk giving panoramic views of the countryside and beautiful gardens below. Large collection of stained glass. Interesting and unusual plants for sale in plant centre.

Location: 6 m N of Hereford on (A49).
Open: All the year - Daily 9.30-5.30.
Admission: £2, Chd (under 14) free when accompanied.
Refreshments: Available in the Plant Centre most afternoons.

EASTGROVE COTTAGE GARDEN NURSERY

Sankyns Green, nr Shrawley, Little Witley map G6
Telephone: (0299) 896389
(Mr & Mrs J. Malcolm Skinner)

A peaceful old world country flower garden displaying a specialist collection of hardy plants maintained by the owners since 1970. This cottage garden is sensitively arranged with great emphasis laid on colour and form, and with the 17th century cottage and timber framed barn, it blends into the unspoiled country of meadow and woodland. The owners are on hand to offer advice and a wide range of good quality and unusual plants are grown at the nursery.

Location: Near Shrawley - 4 m SW of Stourport; 8 m NW of Worcester on road between Shrawley (on B4196) and Great Witley (on A443).
Open: Open afternoons - Apr 1 to Jul 31, Thurs to Mon 2-5 *closed throughout Aug.* Sept 2 to Oct 16 open Thurs, Frid, Sats only 2-5.
Admission: £1.50, Chd 20p*In aid of National Gardens Scheme.*

EASTNOR CASTLE 🏛

nr Ledbury map G5
Telephone: (0531) 633160/632302
Fax: (0531) 631030

EASTNOR CASTLE

Nr. Ledbury   map G5
Telephone: Ledbury (0531) 2302/3160/2849 *(Administrator)*
Fax: (0531) 631030
(James Hervey-Bathurst, Esq)

Splendid Norman Revival Castle built in 1812 in a dramatic setting within the Malvern Hills, Eastnor Castle captures the spirit of medieval chivalry and romance. The lavish interiors, in Italianate, Norman and Gothic style, display a unique collection of armour, tapestries, fine furniture and pictures by Van Dyck, Kneller, Romney, Watts and others. Castellated terraces descend to a lake. There is a renowned arboretum in the pleasure grounds, and a 500 acre park with red deer.

Splendid Norman Revival Castle built in 1812 in a dramatic setting within the Malvern Hills, Eastnor Castle captures the spirit of medieval chivalry and romance. The lavish interiors, in Italianate, Norman and Gothic style, display a unique collection of armour, tapestries, fine furniture and pictures by Van Dyck, Kneller, Romney, Watts and others. Castellated terraces descend to a lake. There is a renowned arboretum in the pleasure grounds, and a 500 acre park with red deer.

Location: 5 m from M50 (exit 2) 2 m E of Ledbury on Hereford/Tewkesbury Road A438.
Station(s): Ledbury (2 m).
Open: Suns from Easter to end Sept, Bank Holiday Mons, Sun to Fri during August. 12-5pm. *Group bookings at other times throughout the year by appointment.*
Admission: £3.50, Chd £1.75. Reduced rates for parties.
Refreshments: Home-made cream teas.
Dogs on lead allowed.

GOODRICH CASTLE   English✠Heritage

map G5
Telephone: (0600) 890538

The castle was built to command the ancient crossing of the Wye by the Gloucester/Caerleon road. Among the extensive remains of the original castle the keep survives, which largely dates from the late 13th century. For almost 300 years from the mid-14th century it was held by the Earls of Shrewsbury.

Location: 3 m (4.8 km) south west of Ross-on-Wye.
Open: Good Friday or Apr 1 (whichever is earlier) to Sept 30: Open Daily 10-6. Oct 1 to Maundy Thursday or Mar 31 (whichever is earlier): Open Tues to Sun 10-4. *Closed* Dec 24-26, Jan 1.
Admission: £1.70, Concessions £1.30, Chd 85p.

THE GREYFRIARS   🌳 The National Trust

Worcester map G6 △
Telephone: (0905) 23571

A richly timber-framed house built c. 1480, was rescued from demolition at the time of World War II. Carefully restored and refurbished; interesting textiles and furnishings add character to panelled rooms; an archway leads through to a delightful garden.

Location: In Friar Street, Worcester.
Station(s): Worcester, Foregate Street (½ m).
Open: Apr to end Oct - Weds & Thurs and Bank Holiday Mons 2-5.30. (Last adm ½hr before closing). Other times adult parties by written application only.
Admission: £1.60, Chd 80p, Family ticket £4.40. Parties of children (inc schools) not admitted.
No dogs. Unsuitable for wheelchairs.

HANBURY HALL   🌳 The National Trust

nr Droitwich map G6 ♿
Telephone: (0527) 821214

William and Mary style red brick house built c. 1700 for a wealthy lawyer. Outstanding painted ceilings and staircase by Sir James Thornhill. The Watney Collection of porcelain; Orangery c. 1730.

Location: 4½ m E of Droitwich, 1 m N of B4090.
Open: Apr to end Oct, Sats, Suns and Mons 2-6. Last adm 30 mins before closing.
Admission: £3, Chd £1.50, Family ticket £8.30. *Parties by prior written arrangment only.*
Refreshments: Teas in the house.
Shop. No dogs. Wheelchair available.

HARTLEBURY CASTLE

nr Kidderminster map G6
Telephone: (0299) 250410
(The Church Commissioners)

Historic home of the Bishops of Worcester for over 1,000 years. Fortified in 13th century, rebuilt after sacking in the Civil War and Gothicised in 18th century. State Rooms include medieval Great Hall, Hurd Library and Saloon. Fine plaster-work and remarkable collection of episcopal portraits. Also County Museum in North Wing.

Location: In village of Hartlebury, 5 m S of Kidderminster, 10 m N of Worcester off A449.
Open: State Rooms Easter Mon to Sept 4 - First Sun in every month but please telephone to check. Every Wed Easter to end of August Bank Hol Sun & Mon 2-4. **County Museum** Mar to Nov - Mons to Thurs 10-5; Frid and Sun 2-5. *Closed* Sats and Good Friday. Open Bank Holidays 10-5.
Admission: State Rooms: 75p, chd 25p, OAPs 50p. Guided tours for parties of 30 or more on weekdays by arrangement. County Museum: £1.20, OAPs/Students/Chd 60p. Family tickets (2 adults and up to 3 chd) £3.20. School parties please telephone for information.
Refreshments: Available.
Picnic area.

HARVINGTON HALL

nr Kidderminster map G6
Telephone: (0562 777) 267
(The Roman Catholic Archdiocese of Birmingham)

Moated medieval and Elizabethan manor-house containing secret hiding-places and rare wall-paintings. Georgian Chapel in garden with 18th century altar, rails and organ. Harvington Festival July 16, 17 and 18 1993. Other events throughout the summer.

Location: 3 m SE of Kidderminster, ½ m from the junction of A448 and A450 at Mustow Green.
Open: Mar 1 to Oct 31 daily except Good Friday, 11.30-5.30. *Closed Nov to Feb except by appointment.*
Admission: £2.50, Chd £2, OAPs £1.50. (At time of going to press). Parties by arrangement with the custodian.
Refreshments: Licensed restaurant in the medieval wing overlooking the moat, open Apr 3 to Sept 30 daily (except Mons and Fris). Light refreshments on other afternoons. Bookings taken for Sunday lunch and evening functions.
Free car parking.

HELLEN'S

Much Marcle map G5 △
(The Pennington-Mellor-Munthe Trust)

Built as a stone fortress in 1292 by Mortimer, Earl of March, this manorial house has been lived in since then by descendants of original builder. Visited by Black Prince and Bloody Mary.

Location: In village of Much Marcle on Ledbury/Ross Road. Entrance opp church.
Open: Good Fri to Oct 2 - Weds, Sats, Suns and Bank Hol Mons 2-6 (guided tours 2-5). *Other times by written appointment with the Custodian).*
Admission: £2.50, chd (must be accompanied by an adult) £1.

HERGEST CROFT GARDENS

Kington map F5
Telephone: (0544) 230160
(W L & R A Banks, Esq)

The gardens of fifty acres contains one of the finest and most thriving collections of exotic trees in the British Isles. Many of the trees and shrubs brought back from China in the early 1900's have grown to great size and the scope of the collection continues to expand with many recently introduced species. The wide range of maples and birches have been named as National Collections of these two genera. The trees are under-planted with rhododendrons and azaleas which include many rare species, some now more than thirty feet tall. In addition to the woodland garden there is a traditional kitchen garden, conservatory and herbaceous borders which are at their best in the summer months. From spring bulbs to autumn colour in October the gardens have much to interest the visitor at any season.

Location: On outskirts W of Kington off Rhayader Road (A44) *(signposted to Hergest Croft at W end of bypass).*
Open: Daily -Apr 9 to Oct 31, 1.30-6.30.
Admission: £2.20, Chd under 15 free. Reduced rates for pre-booked parties of over 20 by appointment at any time.
Refreshments: Home-made teas daily and for parties of over 20 by arrangement.

THE SIGN OF A GREAT DAY OUT

HILL COURT GARDENS & GARDEN CENTRE

Hom Green, Ross on Wye map G5   ♿
Telephone: (0989) 763123
(Mr J C Rowley)

Set in the beautiful grounds of a William and Mary Mansion. An avenue of white limes line the drive up to the house, gardens, and garden centre. The two and a half acres of ornamental gardens include an 18th century Yew Walk, colourful herbaceous borders, water garden with gazebo, rose gardens and monthly shrub borders. Set in one of the walled gardens these borders are designed to assist the visitors in their choice of shrubs for their own gardens throughout the year. The garden centre offers the gardener excellent choice in plants and products, professional advice from horticulturally trained staff, a relaxing environment and the pleasure of strolling through the gardens too. There is a tea garden serving light lunches and afternoon teas within another of the lovely walled gardens.

Location: B4234 from Ross on Wye, fork right at the Prince of Wales public house, drive for 2½ miles.
Open: Open daily 9.30-5.30, open all Bank Holidays.
Admission: Free.
Refreshments: A delightful tea garden set in one of the walled gardens with indoor and patio seating. Open Spring & Summer season, weekends only during early Spring season. Light lunches and afternoon teas available, all cakes homemade. Special group bookings possible. The house is not open to the public.
Ample car parking. Suitable for disabled, although shingled ground does sometimes cause problems.

HOW CAPLE COURT GARDENS

How Caple map G5
Telephone: (098 986) 626
(Mr & Mrs P L Lee)

11 acres overlooking the river Wye. Formal terraced Edwardian gardens, extensive plantings of mature trees and shrubs, water features and a sunken Florentine garden undergoing restoration. Norman church with 16th century Diptych. Specialist nursery plants and old variety apple trees for sale.

Location: B4224, Ross on Wye (4½ m) to Hereford (9 m).
Open: Apr 1 to Oct 31 Mons to Sats 9.30-5. May to Sept 30 also Suns 10-5.
Admission: £2, Chd £1. Parties by appointment.
Fabric Shop. Car parking. Toilets.

KENTCHURCH COURT

Hereford map F5
Telephone: (0981) 240228
(J E S Lucas-Scudamore, Esq)

Fortified border manor house altered by Nash. Gateway and part of the original 14th century house still survives. Pictures and Grinling Gibbons carving. Owen Glendower's tower.

Location: Off B4347, 3 m SE of Pontrilas; 12 m Monmouth; 14 m Hereford; 14 m Abergavenny, on left bank River Monnow.
Open: May to Sept. *Parties only by appointment.*
Admission: £3, chd £1.50.
Refreshments: At Kentchurch Court by appointment.

KINNERSLEY CASTLE

Kinnersley map F5
Telephone: (05446) 407
(H Garratt-Adams)

Medieval Welsh border Castle, reconstructed about 1588. Little changed since then, retaining fine plasterwork and panelling, leaded glass and stone tiled roof. Yew hedges, walled garden and fine trees including probably the largest example of a Ginkgo tree in the United Kingdom. Art and other exhibitions. Still a family home, used out of season for courses and conferences. Early home of the De Kinnardsley and De le Bere families, remodelled by Roger Vaughan and later home of parliamentary General Sir Thomas Morgan.

Location: 4 m W of Weobley on A4112 (Black and White Village Trail).
Admission: £2, chd £1, OAPs £1.50, Groups £1.50 (by arrangment throughout the year). Gardens only £1.
Refreshments: Tea room.

LANGSTONE COURT

Llangarron map G5
(R.M.C. Jones Esq.)

Mostly late 17th century house with older parts. Interesting staircases, panelling and ceilings.

Location: Ross on Wye 5m, Llangarron 1m.
Open: By prior appointment, write to R.M.C. Jones at the above address.
Admission: Free.

LITTLE MALVERN COURT AND GARDENS

nr Great Malvern map G5
Telephone: (0684) 892988
(Mr and Mrs T M Berington)

14th century Prior's Hall once attached to 12th-century Benedictine Priory, and principal rooms in Victorian addition by Hansom. Family and European paintings and furniture. Collection of 18th and 19th century needlework. Home of the Berington family by descent since the Dissolution. 10 acres of former monastic grounds. Magnificent views, lake, garden rooms, terrace. Wide variety of spring bulbs, old fashioned roses, shrubs and trees.

Location: 3 m S of Great Malvern on Upton-on-Severn Road (A4104).
Open: Apr 21 to Jul 22 - Weds and Thurs 2.15-5. Parties by prior arrangement. Guided tours - last adm 4.30.
Admission: House and Garden: £3.50, chd (5-14) £2. Garden only: £2.50, chd (5-14) £1. No concessions for OAPs.
Refreshments: Home made teas only available for parties by arrangement.
Unsuitable for wheelchairs.

LOWER BROCKHAMPTON   🌿 The National Trust

Bromyard map G6   ♿
Telephone: (0885) 488099

Small half-timbered manor house c. 1400 with unusual detached 15th century gatehouse and ruins of 12th century chapel.

Location: 2 m E of Bromyard N of A44 Bromyard/Worcester Road. Hall reached by narrow road through 1½ m woods and farmland.
Open: PLEASE NOTE: Major building works will take place in 1993 which will cause some disruptions to opening arrangments. Please telephone before visiting. Medieval Hall and Parlour only: Apr to end of Sept - Weds, Thurs, Frids, Sats, Suns & Bank Hol Mons 10-5. *Closed* Good Friday. Oct - Wed to Sun 10-4.
Admission: £1.30, Chd 65p, Family ticket £3.50. Parties by prior written arrangement only. No dogs in Hall. Wheelchair access.

MOCCAS COURT

Moccas map F5
Telephone: (098 17) 381
(R T G Chester-Master, Esq)

'Built by Anthony Keck in 1775 overlooking the River Wye, decoration by Robert Adam including the round room and oval stair. Scene of famous 17th century romance and destination of epic night ride from London. Set in 'Capability' Brown parkland with an attractive walk to The Scar Rapids.'
Location: 10 m E of Hay on Wye and 13 m W of Hereford on the River Wye. 1 m off B4352.
Open: HOUSE & GARDENS. Apr to Sept - Suns 2-6.
Admission: £1.80.
Refreshments: Food and drink available at the Red Lion Hotel, Bredwardine, by prebooking only.
Picnics in garden allowed.

THE PRIORY

Kemerton map G5
(The Hon Mrs Peter Healing)

4 acre garden; main features are long herbaceous borders planned in colour groups; stream and sunken garden; many interesting and unusual plants and shrubs.
Location: NE of Tewkesbury, turn off A435 (Evesham/Cheltenham) at Beckford.
Open: GARDEN ONLY. Every Thurs May 27 to end Sept; also Suns May 23, Jun 13, Jul 11, Aug 8, 29; Sept 12: 2-7.
Admission: £1.50, chd over 7 yrs 50p. *In aid of National Gardens Scheme and other charities.*
Refreshments: Teas on Sundays only.
Plants for sale.

SPETCHLEY PARK

Worcester map G5
(Mr & Mrs R J Berkeley)

This lovely 30 acre garden is a plantsman's delight, with a large collection of trees, shrubs and plants, many of which are rare or unusual. There is colour and interest throughout the months that the garden is open to visitors. The park contains red and fallow deer.
Location: 3 m E of Worcester on Stratford-upon-Avon Road (A422).
Open: Gardens & Garden Centre: Apr 1 to Sept 30 - Tues, Wed, Thurs, Fri 11-5; Suns 2-5; Bank Hol Mons 11-5. *Closed* other Mons and all Sats.
Admission: £2, Chd £1. Reduced rates for pre-booked parties of 25 or more.
Refreshments: Tea in the garden.
Regret no dogs. Plants and shrubs for sale. House not open.

STONE HOUSE COTTAGE GARDENS

Kidderminster map G6
Telephone: (0562) 69902
(Major & The Hon Mrs Arbuthnott)

Sheltered wall garden with towers. Rare wall shrubs and climbers also interesting herbaceous plants, all labelled. Adjacent Nursery.
Location: 2 m SE of Kidderminster on A448 to Bromsgrove; next to Stone Church.
Station(s): Kidderminster (2 m).
Open: GARDEN & NURSERY ONLY. Mar to Oct: Weds, Thurs, Fris, Sats. (Now opwn Bank Hol Mons). Easter Mon Apr 12 and Bank Hol Mon May 3, 31 and Aug 30. (10-6). Suns, May and June. Also open Easter Mon Apr 12 and Bank Hol Mons May 3, 31 and Aug 30.
Admission: £1.50, accompanied chd free. Coaches by appointment only. *In aid of National Gardens Scheme and CRMF.*
Refreshments: Food & drink available at Harvington Hall.

THE WEIR   ❦   The National Trust

Swainshill, nr Hereford map F5

Delightful riverside garden, particularly spectacular in early spring. Fine views of the river Wye and Black Mountains.
Location: 5 m W of Hereford on A438.
Open: Feb 14 to end Oct - Wed to Sun & Bank Hol Mon 11-6. (incl Good Friday).
Admission: £1.50. No reductions for parties.
Unsuitable for coaches. No dogs. Unsuitable for wheelchairs or visually handicapped. No WC's.

WHITE COTTAGE

Earls Common Road, Stock Green map G6
Telephone: (0386) 792414
(Mr and Mrs S. M. Bates)

2 acre garden developed since 1981. Large herbaceous and shrub borders, many unusual varieties. Specialist collection of hardy geraniums. Stream and natural garden carpeted with primroses, cowslips and other wild flowers. Nursery featuring plants propagated from garden.

Location: Droitwich 5 m, Worcester 10 m. A422 Worcester/Alcester, turn L at Red Hart pub (Dormston), 1½ m to T junction. Turn L for 75 yards. Or Droitwich/Feckenham B4030, turn R through Bradley Green, R at first T junction, R at second T junction, continue ¼ m.
Open: GARDEN ONLY: Apr 4 to Oct 10 - Daily 10-5. (August by prior appointment only). *Closed* Thurs. Sun openings are Apr 4, 11, 18, May 2, 16, 30, June 13, 27, July 11, 25, Aug 29, Sept 12, 26, Oct 10 and all Bank Hol Mons. Nursery open daily Apr 4 to Oct 10. *Closed* Thurs. (Winter by appointment).
Admission: £1, chd free. OAP 75p. Parties by arrangement only.*In aid of National Gardens Scheme.*
Refreshments: Teas at Jinney Ring Craft Centre, Hanbury.
Car parking. Suitable for disabled persons. No dogs please.

WITLEY COURT English Heritage

map G6
Telephone: (0299) 896636

This is one of the most spectacular country house ruins. Cast in the Victorian Italian style of the 1860s, it is on a huge scale, with a glorious facade. Looking from the house to the gardens, a view enjoyed by Edward VII, who as Prince of Wales often stayed at the house, the scene is dominated by the immense Perseus Fountain.

Location: 10 m NW of Worcester on the A443.
Open: Good Fri or Apr 1 (whichever is earlier) to Sept 30, open daily 10-6. Oct 1 to Maundy Thurs or Mar 31 (whichever is earlier), open Tues to Sun 10-4. *Closed* Dec 24 to 26 and Jan 1.
Admission: £1.20, concessions 90p, chd 60p.

WORCESTER CATHEDRAL

Worcester map G6 △ ♿
Telephone: (0905) 28854
(The Dean and Chapter of Worcester)

Beside the River Severn opposite the Malvern Hills. Built between 1084 and 1375. Norman Crypt and Chapter House. Early English Quire, Perpendicular Tower. Monastic buildings include refectory (now College Hall and open on request during August), cloisters, remains of guesten hall and dormitories. Tombs of King John and Prince Arthur. Cloister herb garden, Elgar memorial window, misericords. Edgar Tower gatehouse.

Location: Centre of Worcester. Main roads Oxford and Stratford to Wales. 3 m junction 7 (M5).
Open: Every day 7.30-6. Choral Evensong daily (except Thurs and school hols).
Admission: No admission charge by donations of £1.50 accepted. Parties: suggested minimum donation of £2 (chd £1) per head for guided tours.
Refreshments: Light refreshment in Cloister Tea Room. Special arrangements made for parties.
No cathedral car parking - City centre parking. Disabled visitors most welcome - some steps, but help and wheelchair available. Information Desk, shop and toilets.

HERTFORDSHIRE

ASHRIDGE

Berkhamsted map J5
Telephone: (0442) 843491
(Governors of Ashridge Management College)

150 acres of both Parkland and intimate smaller gardens. The landscape influenced by Humphrey Repton. Mature trees combined with unique features e.g. Beech Houses with Windows and doors, in a Pink and Grey Garden, Grotto - Ferns planted between Herts Pudding Stone.

Location: 3½ m N of Berkhamsted (A41), 1 m S of Little Gaddesden.
Open: Gardens open Apr to Oct - Sats & Suns 2-6.
Admission: Gardens: £2, Chd/OAP £1.

KNEBWORTH·HOUSE
HERTFORDSHIRE
HISTORIC HOME OF THE LYTTON FAMILY SINCE 1490

For details see Hertfordshire section

BENINGTON LORDSHIP GARDENS

nr Stevenage map K5
Telephone: (0438) 869668
(Mr & Mrs C. H. A. Bott)

Laid out in 1906 around a Norman castle this hilltop garden has changed little and is very 'English'. Full of atmosphere the entrance is through a magnificent neo-Norman gate house. Sweeping lawns stretch downhill towards lakes and parkland. A broad terrace cuts across the lawn and leads to a Spring rock/water garden, double herbaceous borders which are a delight from May until Oct, kitchen garden and nursery. There are also masses of old and modern shrubs and many unusual plants of interest all the year.

Location: 4 m E of Stevenage in village of Benington between Walkern (B1037) & Watton-at-Stone. Tourist signs off A602 and A507.
Open: GARDENS ONLY: Snowdrops, Weds & Suns in Feb, 12-5 (weather permitting). Rest of the year. Easter, Spring and Summer Bank Hol Mons 12-5. Every Wed beginning of Apr to end Sept, 12-5. Every Sun beginning of Apr to end of Aug 2-5. Floral Festival with adjoining church June 26 & 27, 12-6. Nursery open by appointment on weekdays Apr to Sept. Garden open by appointment for parties (20 minimum). Coaches please book.
Admission: £2.20, Chd free. Free parking.
Refreshments: Teas every Sun and Bank Hols: Apr - Aug. Wed: June to end Aug.
Regret unsuitable for wheelchairs and disabled. No dogs.

CAPEL MANOR

nr Enfield map K5 △ ♿ Ⓔ
Telephone: (0992) 763849

A 100 acre estate used extensively by one of the country's leading Horticultural and Environmental Colleges. The 30 acres of historical and modern theme gardens are all richly planted and include the 17th Century garden, large Italian style maze, Rock and Water features, a 5 acre Demonstration and Theme garden run by Gardening from Which ? Walled garden with rose collection and display glasshouses, tree collection and woodland walks. The National Gardening Centre features more theme gardens including a new Japanese garden. The Gardens offer seasonal interest to all keen gardeners looking for inspiration or just a relaxing day out. Mostly level surface, disabled persons - 2 wheelchairs available. Unfortunately the House is not open to viewing. The educational farm is on a neighbouring site 1 mile from the gardens and shows a small range of livestock. Usually baby animals and milking demonstrations to see (cow permitting!)

Location: 3 min from M25 junction M25/A10 S and turn right at traffic lights. Nearest station Turkey Street/Liverpool Street line.
Open: GARDENS: Apr to Oct - Daily 10-5.30. (Last entry 4.30). Nov to Mar - Weekdays only 10-4.30. Please check for Public Hol Opening times. FARM: Apr to Oct - Weekends and most School Hols. 1-5.30. (Last entry 4.30). Please check for winter opening times and Public Hols.
Admission: £2, concessions £1.50, chd £1 (Repeated for farm visit). SPECIAL SHOWS; April, May, June, July, Sept (please check for dates and charges). Usually £4, concessions £2, Family ticket £10. (this price includes a visit to the Farm). Special rates for coaches, garden tours. All parking free.
Refreshments: Usually available
Further details from Capel Manor, Bullsmoor Lane, Enfield, Midx EN1 4RQ. Tel (0992) 763849.

CROMER WINDMILL

Ardeley, Stevenage, Hertfordshire map K5
Telephone: (0438) 861293
(Hertfordshire Building Preservation Trust)

Hertfordshire's unique 17th century Post Windmill, under restoration to working order. Static display, guided visits.

Location: Adjoins the B1037 between Walkern and Cottered, 4 m NE of Stevenage.
Open: Sun May 9 National Mill Day', and Suns to Sept 12, second and fourth Weds May 12 to Sept 1, 2.30-5.
Admission: 75p, chd 25p. Individual appointments possible with prior arrangments. Groups by prior appointment with Mr and Mrs Hughes (0438) 886 1293.
Refreshments: None, public houses with catering in Walkern (2m) and Cottered (2m).
Not suitable for disabled visitors.

THE GARDENS OF THE ROSE

Chiswell Green, St Albans map K5 ♿
Telephone: (0727) 50461
(Royal National Rose Society)

The Showgrounds of the R.N.R.S. containing some 30,000 roses of over 1,650 different varieties.

Location: Off B4630 (formerly A412) St Albans/Watford Road.
Station(s): St Alban's City (2 m).
Open: Jun 13 to Oct 18 - Mons to Sats 9-5; Sun & Bank Hols 10-6.
Refreshments: Facilities for the disabled.

GORHAMBURY

St Albans map K5 △
Telephone: (0727) 54051
Fax: 0727 43675
(The Earl of Verulam)

Mansion built 1777-84 in modified classical style by Sir Robert Taylor. 16th century enamelled glass and historic portraits.

Location: 2 m W of St Albans. Entrance off A4147 at St. Michael's by Roman Theatre.
Open: May to Sept - Thurs 2-5. Gardens open with the house.
Admission: £3, Chd £2, OAPs £1.50. Guided tours only. Parties by prior arrangement Thur, £2.50, other days £3.50. Just the gardens £1.

HATFIELD HOUSE

Hatfield map K5 △
Telephone: (0707) 262823
(The Marquess of Salisbury)

This celebrated Jacobean house, which stands in its own great park, was built between 1607 and 1611 by Robert Cecil, 1st Earl of Salisbury and Prime Minister to King James I. It has been the family home of the Cecils ever since. The Staterooms are rich in world-famous paintings, fine furniture, rare tapestries and historic armour. The beautiful stained glass in the chapel is original. Within the delightful gardens stands the surviving wing of the Royal Palace of Hatfield (1497) where Elizabeth I spent much of her girlhood and held her first Council of State in November 1558. She appointed William Cecil, Lord Burghley as her Chief Minister. Some of her relics can be seen in the house. 25 minutes by regular fast train service from Kings Cross to Hatfield (station faces Park gates). The Moorgate to Hatfield electric train service has direct Underground links; Victoria Line at Highbury, Circle Line at Moorgate, Piccadilly Line at Finsbury Park. Hatfield House Lodge is opposite the station. Further particulars from The Curator, Hatfield House.

Location: In Hatfield, close to A1(M), 7 m M25.
Station(s): Hatfield (opposite house).
Open: Mar 25-Oct 10, 1993. Hatfield House: Daily except Mon and Good Friday. Weekdays from 12. Guided tours only, last tour 4. Sun 1.30-5-no guided tours, guides in each room. Also open on Easter, May Day, Spring and Aug Bank Hol Mon, 11-5, no guided tours-guides in each room. Park: 10.30-8, daily except Good Friday. West Gardens: 11-6, daily except Good Friday. East Gardens: 2-5, Mon only (except Bank Hol Mons). Guided Tour (Tues-Sat) takes about 1 hour. LIVING CRAFTS EXHIBITION: May 6-9, 10-6; A FESTIVAL OF GARDENING: June 19-20, 10-6;10-6.
Admission: Reductions for pre-booked parties of 20 or more. Coach and car park free.
Refreshments: Available in adjacent restaurant - coffee shop. ELIZABETHAN BANQUETING IN THE OLD PALACE THROUGHOUT THE YEAR. Telephone: (0707) 262823 (Curator); Banqueting and Restaurant (0707) 262055/262030. Telex: 26527 OLD PAL G.
Dogs not admitted to House or garden.

KNEBWORTH HOUSE

Knebworth map K5
Telephone: (0438) 812661
Fax: (0438) 811908
(The Lord Cobbold)

Home of the Lytton family for over 500 years. The original Tudor Manor House was transformed 150 years ago by the spectacular high gothic decoration of Victorian novelist and statesman, Sir Edward Bulwer-Lytton. There are many beautiful rooms, important portraits and furniture, and a fine collection of manuscripts and letters associated with many famous visitors to the House. Charles Dickens acted here in private theatricals and Winston Churchill painted at his easel in the superb Jacobean Banqueting Hall. It was the home of Constance Lytton, the suffragette, and Robert Lytton, Viceroy of India. Lord Lytton's Viceroyalty and the great Delhi Durbar of 1877 are commemorated in a fascinating exhibition and audio-visual display. The Lutyens gardens include a Jekyll herb garden. The house is situated in a 250 acre country park with deer herds. Large Adventure Playground with Fort Knebworth and Miniature Railway.

Location: 28 m N of Central London. Own direct access off A1 (M) Junction 7 (Stevenage South A602). 12 m N of M25.
Station(s): Stevenage (2 m).
Open: HOUSE, GARDENS AND PARK: Weekends, Bank Hols and School Hols from Apr 3 to May 31; then daily (except Mons) Jun 1 to Sept 5, plus weekends only to Oct 3. *(Closed July 16 - 19 incl.)* Open Park; 11-5.30. House and Gardens; 12-5.
Admission: House, Gardens and Park;£4, Chd/OAPs £3.50. Park only £2.50 (no reductions for Chd/OAPs). Reductions for pre-booked parties of 20 or more (Apr 3 to Oct 3). Opening times and prices subject to special events. Coach and car park free.
Refreshments: Licensed Cafeteria in 16th Century Tithe Barns close to House & Gardens (Tel:(0438) 813825). Oakwood Restaurant in hotel at Park entrance. (Tel:(0438) 742299). Dogs admitted to Park only on leads. Telephone above number for further details.

MOOR PARK MANSION

nr Rickmansworth map J4
Telephone: (0923) 776611
(Three Rivers District Council)

Palladian house reconstucted in 1720 by Sir James Thornhill and Giacomo Leoni incorporating house built in 1678/79 for James, Duke of Monmouth. Magnificent interior decorations by Verrio, Sleker and others. Club House of Moor Park Golf Club. Being restored by the District Council.

Location: 1 m SE of Rickmansworth.
Station(s): Rickmansworth or Moor Park.
Open: All the year except Bank Hols - Mon to Frid, 10-12, 2-4. Sats 10-12 noon.*Restricted viewing may be necessary on occasions.*Visitors are requested to report to reception.
Admission: Free. Descriptive leaflet available. Guided tours during summer months. Telephone Council's Information Centre for more details.

SCOTT'S GROTTO

Ware map K5
Telephone: (0920) 464131/ (0992) 584322
(East Hertfordhire District Council)

Grotto, summerhouse and garden built 1760-73 by Quaker poet, John Scott. Described by English Heritage as 'one of the finest grottos in England.' Now extensively restored by The Ware Society.

Location: Scott's Road, Ware (off A119 Hertford Road)
Station(s): Ware/Liverpool Street line.
Open: New extended opening times. Every Sat beginning of Apr to Sept and Easter, Spring and Summer Bank Hol Mons 2-4.30.
Admission: Free but donation of £1 requested.
Please park in Amwell End car park by level crossing (300 yds away) and walk up Scott's Road. Advisable to wear flat shoes and bring a torch. Parties by prior arrangement.

HUMBERSIDE

BEVERLEY GUILDHALL

Beverley map J9
Telephone: (0482) 867430
(East Yorkshire Borough of Beverley Borough Council)

Beverley's heritage spans a period of 1300 years which is reflected in its fine old buildings and outstanding Market Square, in particular, in Register Square, is the Guildhall. Bought by the Council for use as a Town Hall in 1500 and extended in 1762, containing the Mayor's Parlour and the Tourist Information Centre. Doric portico leads to 18th century Courtroom and Magistrates' Room. Fine collection of civic regalia, charters, period furniture and other exhibits. Notable features - medieval wall and outstanding work of Italian stuccoist Cortese in beautiful ceiling depicting all-seeing figure of Justice.

Location: In Town Centre, off pedestrianised zone, Register Square.
Open: Easter to Oct and Oct to Easter. Various sections open/closed according to time of year
Admission: Free most dates but for full details enquire The Tourist Information Office, The Giuldhall, Register Square, Beverley HU17 9AU.
Refreshments: Facilities in near proximity.
Car parking very limited. Free car parks in near vicinity. Ground floor only suitable for disabled.

BLAYDES HOUSE

Hull map J9
Telephone: (0482) 26406
(The Georgian Society for East Yorkshire)

Mid-Georgian merchants house, fine staircase and panelled rooms. Restored by the Society in 1974-5.

Location: 6 High Street, Hull.
Station(s): Hull.
Open: Staircase, Blaydes and Partners' Rooms - all the year Mons to Frid (except Bank Hols) 10.30-1, 2-4. By appointment only with Blackmore Son & Co, Chartered Architects at Blaydes House.
Admission: 50p.

BURNBY HALL GARDENS

Pocklington map J9   ♿
Telephone: (0759 30) 2068
(Stewart's Burnby Hall Gardens & Museum Trust)

Large gardens with 2 lakes. Finest display of hardy water lilies in Europe - 70 varieties, **designated National Collection.** Museum housing Stewart Collection - sporting trophies, ethnic material. Picnic area, rose garden. Sales kiosk.

Location: 13 m E of York on A1079.
Open: Sat Apr 3 to mid Oct - daily 10-6.
Admission: £1.80, Party rate (over 20) £1.40. Chd (under 5) free, (5-16) 50p. OAPs £1.30, Party rate (over 20) £1.10 (1993 rates).
Refreshments: Teas in the garden.
Free coach and car park. Disabled facilities.

🌳 THE SIGN OF A GREAT DAY OUT

BURTON AGNES HALL

nr Bridlington map J10
Telephone: (0262) 490324
Fax: (0262) 490513
(Preservation Trust Ltd)

BURTON AGNES HALL
near BRIDLINGTON, Humberside
Described by 'Everybody's' as a Yorkshire Treasure House

Burton Agnes Hall, built AD 1598-1610, is filled with treasures collected during four centuries. Antique furniture. Elizabethan carved ceilings, oriental china and the largest private collection in the North of French Impressionist and Modern paintings—Renoir, Pissaro, Corot, Utrillo, Gauguin, Augustus John, etc.

Open to the public daily from 1st April – 31st October 1993. Admittance to Hall and Gardens £3, Senior Citizens £2.50, Children £2. Group rates on application. Gardens only – £1. Hours of opening 11am to 5pm. Licensed Cafeteria, Teas, light lunches and refreshments served. Guides and guide books are available and there is a free car park within a few yards of the Hall. Bus service 200 yards from Hall. Bridlington 6 miles, Scarborough 18 miles, York 34 miles. Toilets for Disabled.

For further particulars apply: Estate Office, Burton Agnes, Driffield, East Yorkshire. Tel: Burton Agnes (0262) 490324.

The Hall is a magnificent example of late Elizabethan architecture - still lived in by descendants of the family who built it in 1598. There are wonderful carvings, lovely furniture and fine collection of modern French and English paintings of the Impressionist Schools - Renoir, Pissaro, Corot, Utrillo, Gauguin, Augustus John, etc. The recently redeveloped walled garden contains a potager, maze, herbaceous borders, campanula collection, jungle garden and giant games set in coloured gardens. Also woodland gardens and walk, children's corner, Norman manor house, donkey wheel and gift shop.

Location: In village of Burton Agnes, 6 m SW of Bridlington on Driffield/Bridlington Road (A166).
Open: Apr 1 to Oct 31 - Daily 11-5.
Admission: £3, OAPs £2.50, Chd £2. Group rates on application. Garden only: £1.50. *The management reserves the right to close the house or part therof without prior notice; adm charges will be adjusted on such days.*
Refreshments: Licensed cafeteria. Teas, light lunches & refreshments.
Toilets for the disabled.

BURTON CONSTABLE

nr Hull map K9
Telephone: (0964) 562400
Fax: (0964) 563229
(Burton Constable Foundation)

Magnificent Elizabethan House, built c 1570. Outstanding collection of furniture, pictures, works of art, and eighteenth century scientific instruments. Eighteenth century decoration by Robert Adam and Thomas Lightoler. Unusual chapel converted from billiard room, and an outstanding eighteenth century Chinese room. Parkland by 'Capability' Brown.

Location: At Burton Constable; 1½ m N of Sproatley; 7½ m NE of Hull (A165); 10 m SE of Beverley (A1035).
Open: Easter to Sept 19. Suns - Weds incl.
Admission: Parties anytime by arrangement. Further details write to: the Director, Burton Constable Hall, Hull, HU11 4LN, or Tel: (0964) 562400.
Refreshments: Coffee shop.
Gift Shop.

THE CHARTERHOUSE

Hull map J9
Telephone: (0482) 20026
(Charterhouse Trustees)

Charterhouse, was founded in 1384 by Michael de la Pole, Earl of Suffolk. The Charterhouse is an almshouse which provides accommodation for the elderly, and visitors are requested not to enter areas other than the Chapel and Gardens.

Location: Charterhouse Lane, Hull.
Open: CHAPEL & GARDENS open daily during July and on Good Friday, Easter Day, Easter Monday, Spring and Summer Bank Holidays 10-8.
Admission: No charge but prior notice should be given for parties of 10 or more.
Refreshments: Facilities in nearby City centre.
Children should be accompanied by an adult. Dogs not permitted. Limited car parking available.

ELSHAM HALL COUNTRY AND WILDLIFE PARK

Brigg map J8 △ & Ⓔ
Telephone: (0652) 688698
(Capt J Elwes, DL)

Beautiful English park with lakes and wild gardens. Giant Carp. Domestic animals, Wild Butterfly walkway. Adventure playground, Arts and Craft Centre, Granary Tearooms, Animal farm, Wrawby Moor Art Gallery, Falconry Centre. Caravan site. Eight National Awards for Catering and Conservation. An excellent unspoilt venue for a good day out. Also excellent New Theatre and Conference Facility.

Location: Near Brigg. M180 Jct 5.
Open: Times and Prices on application.

EPWORTH

The Old Rectory map J8
Telephone: (0427) 872268
(Trustees of the World Methodist Council)

Built 1709. Restored 1957. Childhood home of John & Charles Wesley, oldest Methodist shrine.

Location: In Epworth, 3 m N of Haxey on A161, 18 m E of Doncaster M180 exit 2.
Open: Mar 1 to Oct 31- Weekdays 10-12, 2-4; Suns 2-4. Adm £1.50, Chd 75p. A/V presentation. Coaches by arrangement only. Accommodation by arrangement.
Refreshments: At the House *by arrangement only.*

MAISTER HOUSE   🏵 **The National Trust**

Hull map J9
Telephone: (0482) 24114
Rebuilt 1744 with a superb staircase-hall designed in the Palladian manner.

Location: 160 High Street, Hull.
Station(s): Hull (¾ m).
Open: Staircase and entrance hall only. All the year - Mons to Fris 10-4. *Closed Bank Hols.*

Admission: By Guide book 80p.
No dogs. Unsuitable for wheelchairs and parties.

SEWERBY HALL

Bridlington map K10
(Borough of East Yorkshire)

Built 1714-20 by John Greame with additions 1803. Sewerby Hall occupies a dramatic setting overlooking Bridlington Bay. The 50 acres of gardens of great beauty and botanical interest include fine old English walled garden and small zoo and aviary. There is also an art gallery and a museum which includes the Amy Johnson Trophy Room dedicated to the pioneer woman aviator.

Location: In Bridlington on the cliffs, 2 m NE from centre of town.
Station(s): Bridlington (2½ m); Bempton (2 m).
Open: Park open all year - Daily 9-dusk. Art Gallery open Easter to Oct - Suns to Frid 10-6; Sats 1.30-6. Open off Peak Months:- Feb, Mar, Nov, Christmas, 11-4, 7 days.
Admission: From May - Sept (New charges to be agreed).
Refreshments: Self-service snack bar in the Hall (summer season only).

SLEDMERE HOUSE

Driffield map J10
Telephone: (0377) 86028
(Sir Tatton Sykes, Bart)

A Georgian house begun in 1751 with important additions attributed to Samuel Wyatt in conjunction with Sir Christopher Sykes, containing superb library 100ft long. The entire building was burnt to the ground in 1911 and splendidly restored with an Edwardian feeling for space by York architect Walter Brierley during the first world war. The latter copied Joseph Rose's fine ceilings and inserted a magnificent Turkish room. The House contains much of its original furniture and paintings. An unusual feature is the great organ, which is played daily 2-4. Capability Brown Park. 18th century walled rose garden. Main garden under reconstruction.

Location: 24 m E of York on main York/Bridlington Road; 8 m NW of Driffield at junction of B1251 & B1253.
Open: Easter weekend, Apr 9 to Sept 26 - Daily (except Mons and Fris); open all Bank Hols; 1.30-5.30 (last adm 5).
Admission: £2.75, Chd £1.50, OAPs £2.30. Special rates for booked parties; Grounds only £1, Chd 60p. Private parties arranged by appointment on Wed evenings. Free car and coach parks.
Refreshments: Excellent self service licensed restaurant, Driffield (0377) 86208.
Illustrated brochure from The House Secretary, Sledmore House, Driffield, East Yorkshire.

WILBERFORCE HOUSE

Hull map J9 Ⓢ
Telephone: (0482) 593902
(Hull City Council)

17th century Merchant's house, now a local history museum with period furniture. Hull silver, costume, dolls, toys and adjoining chemists' shop. New displays were opened in 1983 to commemorate the 150th Anniversary of the Death of William Wilberforce, the slave emancipator, born in the house in 1759. Secluded gardens.

Location: 25 High Street, Hull.
Station(s): Hull.
Open: All the year - Weekdays 10-5; Suns 1.30-4.30. *Closed Good Friday, Christmas Day, Boxing Day & New Year's Day.*
Admission: Free.

ISLE OF WIGHT

THORNTON ABBEY   English ⌗ Heritage

map J9
Telephone: (0469) 40357

The great crenellated gatehouse demonstrates that Thornton was one of the richer monasteries of the Augustinian Order. It was founded about 1139 by William le Gros, Earl of Albemarle, who is buried here. The dissolution of the monastery in the 16th century gave rise to a macabre legend - that the remains of a monk had been found walled up in a room, seated at a table with a book, pen and ink.

Location: 2 m (3.2 km) north east of Thornton Curtis.
Open: Good Friday or Apr 1 (whichever is earlier) to Sept 30: Open Daily 10-6. Oct 1 to Maundy Thursday or Mar 31 (whichever is earlier): Open Weekends only 10-4. *Closed* Dec 24-26, Jan 1.
Admission: £1.20, Concessions 90p, Chd 60p.

APPULDURCOMBE HOUSE   English ⌗ Heritage

map J2
Telephone: (0983) 852484

The only house in the 'grand manner' on the Island, Appuldurcombe (pronounced 'Applercombe') was a status symbol and not a home. Sir Robert Worsley started the house in 1701 but ran out of money. The east faade, a beautiful example of English baroque, dates from this year. The house was not completed until the end of the century. The house is now an empty shell but still stands in its fine park, moulded by 'Capability' Brown.

Location: ½ m (0.8 km) west of Wroxall.
Open: Good Friday or Apr 1 (whichever is earlier) to Sept 30: Open Daily 10-6. Oct 1 to Maundy Thursday or Mar 31 (whichever is earlier): Open Tues to Sun 10-4. *Closed* Dec 24-26, Jan 1.
Admission: £1.20, Concessions 90p, Chd 60p.

CARISBROOKE CASTLE   English⌗Heritage

map H2
Telephone: (0983) 522107

Here are seven acres of castle and earthworks to explore. The oldest parts of the castle are 12th century, but the great mound - 71 steps high - bore a wooden castle before that, and there are fragments of Roman wall at its base. Fortified against the French, then the Spaniards, the castle is best known as the prison of Charles I in 1647/8. A bold escape plan failed when the King became wedged between the bars of the great chamber window. The castle contains the island's museum. A personal stereo guided tour is available.

Location: 1¼ m (2 km) south west of Newport.
Open: Good Friday or Apr 1 (whichever is earlier) to Sept 30: Open Daily 10-6. Oct 1 to Maundy Thursday or Mar 31 (whichever is earlier): Open Daily 10-4. *Closed* Dec 24 -26, Jan 1.
Admission: £3.20, Concessions £2.40, Chd £1.60.

THE NEEDLES OLD BATTERY   The National Trust

West Highdown, Totland Bay   map H2
Telephone: (0983) 754772

A former Palmerstonian fort built in 1862, 77m above sea level; 60m tunnel to spectacular view of the Needles. Exhibition on history of the Needles Headland.

Location: At Needles, Headland. W of Freshwater Bay and Alum Bay.
Open: Mar 28 to end Oct - Daily, except Frid & Sats but open Good Friday, Apr 4 to Apr 15, and daily from May 30 to end Sept. 10.30-5. (Last admission 4.30). Conducted school and special visits Mar 28 to end Oct (but not Aug) by written appointment.
Admission: £2.20, Chd half-price. No reductions for parties.
Refreshments: Tearoom open same days as Battery (but closed 3 - 14 Oct).

NEWTOWN OLD TOWN HALL   The National Trust

Newtown   map H2

18th century building of brick and stone. One of the buildings surviving from the island's former ancient borough.

Location: In Newtown, midway between Newport and Yarmouth.
Open: Apr 1 to end Sept: Mons, Weds & Suns 2-5; (also open Good Friday, Easter Sat and Sun, and Tues and Thurs in July and Aug), (last adm 4.45). *Closed Oct to end March.*
Admission: £1, Chd half-price. No reduction for parties.
No dogs. Unsuitable for wheelchairs.

NUNWELL HOUSE AND GARDENS 🏛

Brading   map J2
Telephone: (0983) 407240
(Colonel & Mrs J A Aylmer)

Nunwell with its historic connections with King Charles I is set in beautiful gardens and parkland with channel views. A finely furnished home with Jacobean and Georgian wings. Home Guard museum and family military collection.

Location: 1 m from Brading, turning off A3055; 3 m S of Ryde.
Station(s): Brading.
Open: HOUSE AND GARDENS: July 4 to Sept 30, Sun-Thurs, 10-5.*Closed* Fri and Sat.
Admission: £2.30, OAPs £1.80, accompanied Chd 60p, School parties £1.15.
Refreshments: Large parties may book catering in advance. Picnic areas.
Coach and School parties welcome at all times by appointment. No dogs.

OSBORNE HOUSE English ♯ Heritage

East Cowes map H3
Telephone: (0983) 200022

This was Queen Victoria's seaside residence built at her own expense, in 1845. The Prince Consort played a prominent part in the design of the house, it was his version of an Italian villa, and the work was carried out by Thomas Cubitt, the famous London builder. The Queen died here in 1901 and her private apartments have been preserved more or less unaltered. Crowded with furniture and bric-a-brac they epitomise the style we call 'Victorian'. Also see the Queen's bathing machine. There is a carriage drawn by horse running from House to the Swiss Cottage Gardens and Museum. This is included in the adm price, see below for details.

Location: 1 m SE of East Cowes.
Station(s): Ferry terminal East Cowes (1 m).
Open: Good Friday or Apr 1 (whichever is earlier) to Sept 30: daily 10-6, Oct 1 to 31 daily 10-5.
Admission: House and Grounds: £5.40, Concessions £4, Chd £2.70. Grounds only: £2.50, Concessions £1.90, Chd £1.20.

YARMOUTH CASTLE English ♯ Heritage

map H2
Telephone: (0983) 760678

Part of the coastal defences of Henry VIII, Yarmouth embodied the very latest fashion in military engineering. Completed in 1547, it is square in plan, and washed on two sides by the sea. During the Civil War the island was strongly royalist and throughout the Commonwealth Cromwell kept a large garrison here. When Sir Robert Holmes was appointed Captain of the Island in 1667, the castle was already outmoded and ineffective. He reduced it in size, filled in the moat and built himself a house - now the hotel - on the site. There is a site display and an exhibition of paintings.

Location: Yarmouth.
Open: Good Friday or Apr 1 (whichever is earlier) to Sept 30: Open Daily 10-6.
Admission: £1.70, Concessions £1.30, chd 85p.

KENT

BEDGEBURY NATIONAL PINETUM

nr Goudhurst map L3
Telephone: (0580) 211044
(Forest Enterprise)

Has the most comprehensive collection of conifers in Europe. Conifers from all continents are planted in generic groups within 160 acres. Landscaped with grass avenues, paths, stream valleys, ridges and a lake. Rhododendrons, azaleas, maples and uncommon oak species add colour in spring and autumn.

Location: On B2079, 1 m from A21 London to Hastings travelling towards Goudhurst.
Open: Daily 10 till dusk. Visitor centre: open daily Easter to end Sept 11-5.
Admission: £1.50, OAPs £1, Chd 75p.
Refreshments: In nearby villages, ice cream vendor in car park and light refreshments available in visitor centre.
Car parking, difficult for wheelchairs.

BELMONT

nr Faversham map L4 △ &
Telephone: (0795) 890202
(Harris (Belmont) Charity)

Belmont was built in the late 18th century to the design of Samuel Wyatt, in a splendid elevated position with commanding views over the attractive and unspoilt countryside. It has been the seat of the Harris family since it was acquired in 1801 by General George Harris, the victor of Seringapatam. The Mansion remains in its original state and contains interesting mementos of the family's connections with India and the finest collection of clocks in any English country house open to the public.

Location: 4 m SSW of Faversham. 1½ m W of A251 follow brown signs from Badlesmere.
Open: Easter Sun to end Sept - Sat, Sun and Bank Hol Mons. Guided tours 2-5. Last adm 4.30. Telephone (0795) 890202 to confirm availability. Groups (minimum 10) by prior arrangement only, Tues and Thurs.
Admission: Mansion, Grounds and Clock Museum £3.80, Chd £2.20.
Refreshments: Teas in the Stables Tearoom Sat, Sun and Bank Hol Mons June 1 to end Sept. Pre-booked parties by arrangement.
Car parking. Shop.

BLACK CHARLES

nr Sevenoaks map K4
Telephone: (0732) 833036
(Mr & Mrs Hugh Gamon)

Charming 14th century home of John de Blakecherl and his family. A hall house with beautiful panelling, fireplaces and many other interesting features.

Location: 3 m S of Sevenoaks off A21; 1 m E in the village of Underriver.
Open: Open to groups by appointment (minimum of 10).

BOUGHTON MONCHELSEA PLACE

nr Maidstone map L4 △
Telephone: (0622) 743120
(Charles W. Gooch)

Battlemented Elizabethan Manor of Kentish ragstone built in 1567, with interesting Regency alterations. Dramatically situated with breathtaking view over its own landscaped park, in which fallow deer have roamed for at least 300 years, and beyond, to the whole Weald of Kent. The beautiful interior is still that of an intimate and inhabited home to which successive generations have added new treasures. Dress display and early farm implements. Manor records. Walled flower gardens with interesting plants. Tudor kitchen tearoom. The House and Grounds are available for private hire, wedding receptions, lunches, suppers and dinners. Also clay shoots, ballooning, archery. Further land is available for other activities. Contact (0622) 743120,

Location: On B2163. In village of Boughton Monchelsea 5 m S of Maidstone. Turn off Maidstone/Hastings Road (A229) at Linton. Junction 8 off M20.
Open: Good Fri to early Oct - Suns & Bank Hols (also Weds during July & Aug) 2.15-6.
Admission: House and Grounds: £3,25, Chd (under 14) £2, Student/OAP/Disabled £2.75. Grounds Only: £2.25, Chd (under 14) £1.25, Student/OAP/Disabled £2. Group (20 or more) House and Grounds: £2.75, Chd (under 14) £1.75, Student/OAP/Disabled £2.75. Grounds only £2, Chd (under 14) Student/OAP/Disabled £2.*Parties by previous arrangement.*
Refreshments: Tea rooms at the House. For parties lunch or supper can be ordered in advance.

CHARTWELL - *SEE PAGE 89*

CHIDDINGSTONE CASTLE

nr Edenbridge map K4   ♿   Ⓔ
Telephone: (0892) 870347
(Trustees of the Denys Eyre Bower Bequest)

The dream-child of two romantics. Squire Henry Streatfeild, who c.1805 had his family seat transformed into a fantasy castle, and whose money ran out; and Denys Bower, eccentric and inspired art collector, who never had any money at all. Entranced with the (by then) semi-derelict Castle, he made it his home in 1955. He died in 1977 leaving the Castle and its fascinating contents to the Nation. Untouched by commercialism, lovingly restored and cherished, it remains a home, with its fine furnishings, personal collections of Japanese lacquer and swords, Egyptian antiquities, Stuart and Jacobite relics. Landscaped grounds in course of restoration.

Location: In Chiddingstone village, off the B2027 at Bough Beech about 10 m Sevenoaks, Tonbridge and Tunbridge Wells.
Station(s): Penshurst 2½ miles, Edenbridge 4 miles.
Open: Apr 1 to Oct 31. Apr, May and Oct: public holidays, Weds and Suns only. June to Sept: Tues to Suns and public holidays. Weekdays (inc. Sats) 2-5.30, Suns and public holidays 11.30-5.30. Last adm 5. Open all year round for booked parties of 20 or more, by special arrangement.
Admission: £3.50, chd (5-15) £1.50, (under 5 free). Parties of 20 or more (normal hours) £3. (At other times of the year; Special fee arranged with Administrator). Lake open in season for coarse fishing dawn till dusk £8. One onlooker per fisherman £3.50.
Refreshments: Tearoom serves tea and cakes. Cream teas and light meals for parties by arrangment.
Picnics allowed adjacent car park, not in grounds. Dogs on lead only. FUNCTIONS WITH CATERING: for details of facilities apply Administrator (0892) 870347. The Trustees reserve the right to close the Castle for special functions.

CHARTWELL 🌳 The National Trust

Westerham map K4 ♿
Telephone: (0732) 866368

The home for many years of Sir Winston Churchill.

Location: 2 m S of Westerham off B2026.
Open: House. Mar to end Nov: Mar & Nov - Sats, Suns & Weds only 11-4.30 ; Apr to end Oct - Tues, Weds, Thurs 12-5.30; Sats, Suns & Bank Hol Mons 11-5.30 (last adm 30 minutes before closing). Closed Good Fri and Tues following Bank Hol. All Tues mornings (except after Bank Hols) reserved for prebooked parties and guided tours. Garden & Studio: Apr to end Oct - Same times as house.
Admission: House & Garden £4.20, Chd £2.10, Garden only £2, Chd £1. Studio 50p extra (Chd no reduction). Pre-booked parties, Tues mornings only. Parties welcome on other days; no need to book, no reduction. Write to the Administrator, Chartwell, Westerham, Kent.
Refreshments: Restaurant open from Apr to end Oct - 10.30-5 (Mar & Nov: 10.30-4) on days when house is open. Self-service, licensed (no spirits).
Car park. Lavatory for disabled.

CHILHAM CASTLE GARDENS 🏛

nr Canterbury map L4
Telephone: (0227) 730319
(Viscount Massereene & Ferrard DL)

25 acre garden with formal terraces first made by Tradescant when the Jacobean house was built by the side of the old Norman Castle Keep. Informal lake garden. Magnificent views and many fine trees. Birds of Prey on display and flying free, afternoons daily except Mon and Fri. Gift shop. Medieval banquets, dinners, wedding receptions in Gothic Hall. Special events as advertised. House open by appointment only.

Location: In Chilham village, 6 m W of Canterbury (A252); 8 m NE of Ashford (A28); 22 m NW of Dover, Faversham turn off M2.
Station(s): Chilham (1 m).
Open: Apr to mid-Oct - Daily (inc Bank Hols). Open from 11 am.
Admission: Weekdays:£2.80, Chd half-price. Free parking. Special rates for parties on application.
Refreshments: Jacobean tea room.
Coaches welcome.

Sir Anthony Van Dyck
Portrait and religious painter
Born in Antwerp 1599, died in London 1641
First visited England in 1620, knighted by Charles I in 1633

His work can be seen in the following properties included in Historic Houses Castles and Gardens:

Alnwick Castle
Arundel Castle
Boughton House
Euston Hall
Goodwood House

Hinwick House
Sudeley Castle
Warwick Castle
Weston Park

COBHAM HALL

nr Rochester map L4
Telephone: (047 482) 3371
(Westwood Educational Trust Ltd)

Charming mixture of Gothic and Renaissance architecture. The 150 acres of grounds with giant cedars, other specimen trees and 100 year old lawns provide a good example of Repton's landscape gardening. Fine example of work of James Wyatt. Family gilded State Coach built in 1715, and gilt Banqueting Hall. Now an independent girls' school.

Location: 4 m W of Rochester on Watling Street & Rochester Way (B2009 off A2). 27 m from London.
Station(s): Sole Street (1½ m).
Open: Apr 4, 9, 11, 12, 14, 15, 18, 21 & 22. July 25, 28, 29; Aug 4, 5, 8, 11, 12, 15, 18, 19, 22, 25, 26 & 30, 2-5 (last tour 5).
Admission: £2, Chd/OAPs £1. No reduction for parties.
Refreshments: Teas and light refreshments, enquiries (0474 82) 3371.

CRITTENDEN HOUSE

Matfield map L3
(B P Tompsett, Esq)

Garden completely planned and planted since 1956 on labour-saving lines. Spring shrubs, roses, lilies, foliage, waterside planting of ponds in old iron workings. Of interest from the early Spring bulbs to Autumn colour. Garden featured in RHS Journal Feb 1960 and Apr 1990.

Location: 5 m SE of Tonbridge off B2160.
Open: GARDENS ONLY. Suns Mar 28, Apr 11, 25, May 16, June 6, 20, Mons Apr 12, May 3, 31 in aid of *National Gardens Scheme*. Sun, May 2; RSPCA; 2-6.
Admission: £1.25, chd (under 12) 25p. Cars free.
No dogs.

DEAL CASTLE   English⌗Heritage

map M4
Telephone: (0304) 372762

When Henry VIII divorced Catherine of Aragon he defied the Pope and broke with Catholic Europe. Deal and Walmer were built under the threat of a 'crusade' against Henry - an invasion which never came. Deal contains an exhibition on the coastal defences of Henry VIII. At Walmer the atmosphere is country house rather than martial, for this has long been the official residence of the Lords Warden of the Cinque Ports. One of the best remembered is the Duke of Wellington (the original 'Wellington boot' may be seen here), and one of the best loved, Queen Elizabeth the Queen Mother.

Location: Deal Castle is near the town centre.
Open: Deal: Good Friday or Apr 1 (whichever is earlier) to Sept 30: Open Daily 10-6. Oct 1 to Maundy Thursday or Mar 31 (whichever is earlier): Open Weds to Sun 10-4. *Closed* Dec 24-26, Jan 1.
Admission: £2, concessions £1.50, chd £1. Price includes a Personal Stereo Guided Tour.

DODDINGTON PLACE GARDENS

nr Sittingbourne map L4
Telephone: (079586) 385
(Mr Richard and The Hon. Mrs Oldfield)

Large landscaped gardens in the grounds of a Victorian country house with good views over surrounding countryside. Edwardian rock garden and formal garden, rhododendrons and azaleas in a woodland setting, fine trees and yew hedges.

Location: 4 m from A2 and A20. 5 m from Faversham. 6 m from Sittingbourne. 12 m from Canterbury.
Open: 11-6 every Wed and Bank Holiday Mon from Easter to end Sept. Also Suns in May only 11-6. (*In aid of the National Gardens Scheme*. Suns 2, 9, 16, 23 May.)
Admission: £1.50, chd 25p. Groups of 25 or more and coaches by prior arrangement only.
Refreshments: Restaurant serving morning coffee, lunches, afternoon teas. Present shop.

DOVER CASTLE   English ✜ Heritage

map M4
Telephone: (0304) 201628

Castle Hill dominates the shortest passage between Britain and the Continent, and has been the scene of military activity from the Iron Age to the present day. Here is extensive proof from every age of man's ingenuity in devising ways to repel invaders. Dover Castle had its narrowest escape in 1216 when in an heroic siege it just managed to hold out against the French. There is much to see, including the Roman lighthouse (now the bell tower of a fine Saxon church) and the great keep itself and a spectacular exhibition 'All the Queen's Men'. The secret war tunnels of the castle are now open to the public. The evacuation of the troops from Dunkirk was planned by Vice-Admiral Ramsay from this once secret base. Entry is by guided tours only; for full details of Hellfire Corner see below.

Location: East side of Dover.
Open: Good Friday or Apr 1 (whichever is earlier) to Sept 30 daily 10-6. Oct 1 to Maundy Thursday or Mar 31 (whichever is earlier) daily 10-6. *Closed* Dec 24-26, Jan 1.
Admission: £5, concessions £3.70, Chd £2.50.
Refreshments: in the Keep Yard.

EMMETTS GARDEN   🍂   The National Trust

nr Brasted   map K4   ♿
Telephone: (0732) 750367 or 750429

Hillside shrub garden of 5 acres. Lovely spring and autumn colours, rock garden, formal garden and roses. Further areas of garden being restored and re-planted.

Location: 1½ m S of A25 on Sundridge/Ide Hill Road.
Open: Garden only: Apr to end Oct - Wed to Sun, Good Fri, Bank Hol Mon 1-6. Last adm 5.
Admission: £2.50, Chd £1.30, Pre-booked parties £2, Chd £1 (15 or more).
Refreshments: Tearoom.2-5.(Oct, weekends only) Thur 11-1, reserved for pre-booked parties.
Dogs admitted on lead. Wheelchair access to level parts of garden only.

FINCHCOCKS

Goudhurst   map L3
Telephone: (0580) 211702
(Mr & Mrs Richard Burnett)

Finchcocks, dated 1725, is a fine example of Georgian baroque architecture, noted for its brickwork, with a front elevation attributed to Thomas Archer. It is set in beautiful gardens and parkland near the village of Goudhurst. The house contains a magnificent collection of historic keyboard instruments which are restored to full playing condition, and provides a unique setting where visitors can hear music performed on the instruments for which it was written. Demonstration tours and music whenever the house is open.

Location: 1½ m W of Goudhurst, 10 m E of Tunbridge Wells off A262.
Open: Easter to Sept 26 - Suns; also Bank Hol Mons & Weds to Suns in Aug: 2-6pm. Demonstrations & Music on instruments of the collection on Open Days.
Admission: £4.50, chd £3, Family ticket £11. Free parking.
Refreshments: Teas available.
Also private visits by appointment with music April to Christmas.

GAD'S HILL PLACE

Rochester   map L4
(Gads Hill School Ltd)

Grade 1 listed building, built in 1780. Home of Charles Dickens from 1857 to 1870.

Location: On A226; 3 m from Rochester, 4 m from Gravesend.
Station(s): Higham (1 m).
Open: By prior appointment only. Apply to the Headmistress, Gad's Hill School, Higham, Rochester. Tel. 047482 2366.
Admission: £1.50, Chd/OAPs £1, parties by arrangement. Proceeds to restoration fund.
Refreshments: Food & Drink available at Sir John Falstaff Inn opposite House.

GODINTON PARK

Ashford map L4 △
(Godinton House Preservation Trust, Alan Wyndham Green, Esq)

The existing house belongs mostly to Jacobean times though there are records of another house being here in the 15th century. The interior of Godinton contains a wealth of very fine panelling and carving, particularly in the Hall and on the Staircase. The house contains interesting portraits and much fine furniture and china. The gardens were originally laid out in the 18th century and were further extended by Sir Reginald Blomfield with topiary work and formal gardens giving a spacious setting to the house.

Location: 1½ m W of Ashford off Maidstone Road at Potter's Corner (A20).
Station(s): Ashford (2 m).
Open: Easter Sat, Sun & Mon; then June to Sept - Suns & Bank Hols only 2-5.
Admission: House & Gardens £2, Chd (under 16) 70p. Weekdays by appointment only. Parties of 20 or more £1.50.

GOODNESTONE PARK

nr Canterbury map M4
Telephone: (0304) 840107
(The Lord & Lady FitzWalter)

The garden is approximately 14 acres, with many fine trees, a woodland garden and the walled garden with a large collection of old roses and herbaceous plants. The house has a fine collection of family portraits and furniture. Jane Austen was a frequent visitor, her brother Edward having married a daughter of the house.

Location: 8 m SE of Canterbury; 4 m E of A2; 1/4 m SE of B2046; S of A257.
Station(s): Adisham (2 m).
Open: GARDEN ONLY. **Weekdays:** Mar 29 to Oct 29 (incl. Bank Holidays), Mon to Fri (NOT TUES OR SAT) 11-5. **Suns:** Apr 4 to Oct 3: 12-6.
Admission: £2, OAP £1.60, Chd (under 12) 20p. Wheelchairs £1. Parties (20 or more) £1.60, Guided tour (20 or more) £2.20. *House open by appointment for parties of not over 20 people.*
Refreshments: Teas, Sun & Wed only. May 23 to Aug 29. Pre-booked parties anyday.
Coach parties welcome but please book in advance. Rates on application. *No Dogs Allowed in the Garden.*

GREAT COMP GARDEN

nr Borough Green   map L4
Telephone: (0732) 882669/886154
(The Great Comp Charitable Trust)

This outstanding garden of seven acres has been expertly developed by Mr and Mrs Cameron since 1957 to provide interest throughout the year. In a setting of well maintained lawns the carefully designed layout and good use of plants allows the visitor to wander through areas of different character. Around the 17th century house are formal areas of paving, terraces, old brick walls and hedges. These are surrounded by less formal planting providing winding paths, vistas and woodland glades with occasional ornaments and constructed 'ruins' for additional interest. A wide variety of trees, shrubs, herbaceous plants and heathers offer inspiration and pleasure and include many which are rarely seen. Good Autumn colour. Nursery open daily with wide range of plants from garden for sale. Music festival and other events in July & September. S.A.E. to R. Burton, Great Comp, Borough Green, Sevenoaks, Kent TN15 8QS.

Location: 2 m E of Borough Green B2016 off A20. First right at Comp crossroads ½ m on left.
Station(s): Borough Green & Wrotham (1½ m).
Open: GARDEN AND NURSERY ONLY. Apr 1 to Oct 31 - Daily 11-6. Free parking. *Parties by prior arrangement (coaches welcome).* Guided tours and lectures by arrangement.
Admission: £2.50, Chd £1, Guide book available. Annual tickets £7.50, OAPs £5, annual ticket holders may visit any day Apr to Oct, and out of season in Nov, Feb and Mar.
Refreshments: Teas on Sun and Bank Hols and for parties by arrangement.
No dogs.

GREAT MAYTHAM HALL   - *SEE BELOW*

GROOMBRIDGE PLACE

Groombridge   map L4
Telephone: (0892) 863999

The authentic period setting for Peter Greenaway's Restoration Mystery film 'The Draughtsman's Contract', these magical and historic walled gardens surrounding possibly the most perfect 17th Century moated house in Britain, are planned to open to the public for the first time during 1993. The house, not open to the public, but forming a backdrop to this immaculate setting, in on the site of a much earlier medieval castle. Among the attractions for the visitor is a Drunken Topiary Garden, an Oriental Garden and Chaucer's wild English Garden. You can walk

in historic parkland and relax in a lakeside picnic area with a variety of interesting wildfowl. Close by is one of England's best preserved village greens with tile hung cottages, a pub and 17th Century church.

Location: Approx. 1hr and 15 mins from London. Groombridge is 4 m W of Tunbridge Wells. From Tunbridge Wells take A264 towards East Grinstead. After 2 m take B2110 south to Groombridge. Groombridge is on the left past Village Green and Church.
Station(s): Charing Cross to Tunbridge Wells (45 mins). Victoria to Eridge (Change at Oxted, 60 mins).
Open: Daily from Apr 9 - Oct 10 (please telephone to check 0892-863999). 11am-6pm.
Admission: Adult £3, Chd (under 17) £1.50. Reduced rates for groups.
Refreshments: Enjoy light refreshments and home made teas in the magnificent 17th Century Grade 1 listed barn.
There is wheelchair access. No dogs admitted in walled gardens. Dogs on leads elsewhere.

GREAT MAYTHAM HALL

Rolvenden   map L3
(Country Houses Association)

Built in 1910 by Sir Edwin Lutyens.

Location: ½ m E of Rolvenden village, on road to Rolvenden Layne.
Open: May to Sept - Weds & Thurs 2-5. Last entry 4.30.
Admission: £1.50, chd 50p. Free car park.
No dogs admitted.

HAXTED MILL & MUSEUM - *SEE PAGE 95*

HEVER CASTLE & GARDENS

nr Edenbridge map K4
Telephone: (0732) 865224; Fax (0732) 866796
(Broadland Properties Limited)

Enchanting 13th century double-moated castle, childhood home of Queen Anne Boleyn, set in magnificent gardens of 40 acres. The gardens feature fine topiary including a maze, the magnificent Italian garden with statuary and sculpture dating back 2000 years, and the 35 acre lake alongside which visitors can walk and picnic. The Castle was restored and filled with treasures by William Waldorf Astor in 1903. Exhibitions on the Astors of Hever and the life and times of Anne Boleyn. Regimental Museum. Open-air theatre season.

Location: Mid-way between London and S coast, between Sevenoaks and East Grinstead, 3 m SE Edenbridge off B2026. M25 - junction 5/6, 20 mins. M23 - junction 10, 20 mins. *Station(s): Hever (1 m walk, no taxis available), Edenbridge Town (3 m, taxis available).*
Open: CASTLE & GARDENS open daily - Mar 16-Nov 7. GARDENS: 11-6 (last entry 5pm). CASTLE: opens 12 noon. Dogs on leads gardens only. Adventure playground. Facilities for disabled visitors. Special pre-booked private tours available all year. Residential Conferences, private dining, day meetings and receptions available in the Tudor Village linked to the Moated Castle.
Admission: Special rate for groups.
Refreshments: Large self-service licensed restaurant. Picnics welcome.

HAXTED MILL & MUSEUM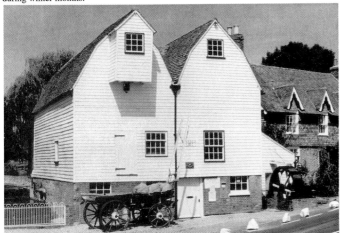

Haxted, nr Edenbridge map K4
Telephone: Curator, Summer months (0732) 865720. Mr. D.G. Neville. (0306) 887979 during winter months.

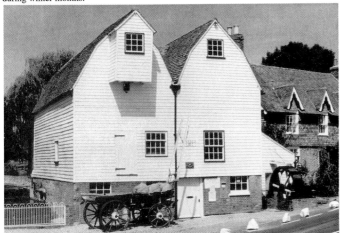

An ancient working watermill and dynamic museum of functioning mill machinery combining to provide a unique illustration of the history, development and uses of water power throughout the centuries. The galleries contains artefacts and working models relating to all aspects of milling. There are special attractions for children - including a den of lions and tigers with their cubs

Location: 1½ m W of Edenbridge beside road joining B2029 at Lingfield Common with B2026 at Edenbridge.
Open: April to Sept: Weds, Sat, Sun & Bank Hols, 1-5. Guided parties at any time by prior appointment.
Admission: £2.75, chd £1.75, OAPs £2, Reductions for parties booked in advance.
Refreshments: Licensed restaurant adjacent, open daily *except Mon.*

IGHTHAM MOTE   The National Trust

Ivy Hatch map K4
Telephone: (0732) 810378

One of the most complete remaining examples of a medieval moated manor house. Major exhibition of building conservation in action.

Location: 3 m S of Ightham, off A227, 4½ m E of Sevenoaks off A25.
Open: Apr to end Oct - Mons, Weds, Thurs, Fris 12-5.30; Suns and Bank Hol Mons 11-5.30 (last adm 5); pre-booked guided tours 11-12 weekdays, no reduction, open Good Friday.
Admission: £4, £3, for Pre-booked guided tours, (No reduction for pre-booked guided tour.)
Refreshments: Tea pavilion in car park. Open as house but closes at 5 and may close earlier in bad weather.

KNOLE   The National Trust

Sevenoaks map K4 △
Telephone: (0732) 450608

One of the largest private houses in England, dating mainly from 15th century, with splendid Jacobean interior and fine collection of 17th century furniture.

Location: At the Tonbridge end of Sevenoaks, just E of A225; 25 m from London.
Station(s): Sevenoaks (1½ m)
Open: Apr to end of Oct. Open Wed, Fri, Sat & Sun 11-5. Thur 2-5 last admission 4. Open Bank Hol Mon. Pre-booked guided tours 10-1 Thurs only, no reductions. Oct: all visitors guided. Garden - May to Sept: first Wed in each month only.
Admission: Car park £2.50 (NT members free). House: £4, Chd £2. Garden: 50p, chd 30p. Pre-booked parties Wed - Sat (Thurs pm only). £3.

LADHAM HOUSE

Goudhurst map L3
(Betty, Lady Jessel)

10 acres of rolling lawns, fine specimen trees, rhododendrons, azaleas, camellias, shrubs and magnolias. Newly planted arboretum. Spectacular twin mixed borders. Fountain garden and bog garden. Fine view.

Location: 11 m E of Tunbridge Wells off A262 on NE of village.
Open: Garden only. Easter Sun Apr 11, Suns May 2, 30, July 11: (11-6). *Open other times by appointment and for coaches:*
Admission: £2, Chd (under 12) 50p.*In aid of National Gardens Scheme.* Free parking.
Refreshments: Teas served on the 4 open days, but not on days arranged by appointment.

Gertrude Jekyll
writer and gardener
(1843–1932)

Her designs were used at the following properties included in Historic Houses Castles and Gardens:

Hestercombe House and Gardens
Knebworth
Vann

LEEDS CASTLE

nr Maidstone map L4
Telephone: (0622) 765400
Fax: (0622) 735616
(Leeds Castle Foundation)

Leeds Castle stands as one of the most beautiful and ancient Castles in the Kingdom, rising from its two small islands in the middle of a lake and surrounded by 500 acres of magnificent parkland and gardens. Dating back to the 9th century and rebuilt by the Normans in 1119, Leeds Castle was then a Royal Palace for over three centuries. It now contains a superb collection of mediaeval furnishings, French and English furniture, tapestries and paintings. You can wander down through the Duckery into the Wood Garden, where peacocks and swans roam free. Visit the aviaries with rare tropical birds and the Culpeper Garden full of old fashioned flowers and fragrance. See a fascinating underground grotto at the centre of the maze and visit the greenhouses and vineyard. There's also a museum of Medieval Dog Collars in the 13th century Gate Tower. Or, come and play our 9-hole golf course. Beautiful gifts available from the Castle Shop and Plant Shops. Now owned by the Leeds Castle Foundation, a private Charitable Trust, the Castle is also used as a high level residential conference centre. **Special Events: New Year's Day Treasure Trail:**Fri, Jan 1; **Spring Garden's Week:**Fri Mar 27 to Sun 4 Apr; **Easter Egg Hunt:**Sat Apr 10 to Mon Apr 12; **Wine Festival:**Sat May 15 to Sun May 16; **Balloon and Bentley Fiesta:**Sat June 5 to June 6; **Open Air Concerts:**(Advance ticket sales only) Sat June 26 and Sat July 3; **Flower Festival:**Fri Sept 17 to Mon Sept 20; **Grand Firework Display:**Sat Nov 6; **Kentish Evening Dinners:**Sats all year except Aug (by reservation); **Special Christmas Shop:**daily from Nov 1 to Dec 23.
Location: 4 m E of Maidstone; access on B2163 at junction 8 of the M20.
Station(s): Bearsted or Hollingbourne (2 m). Inclusive rail/admission tickets from British Rail, Victoria Station to Bearsted.
Open: Mar 15 to Oct 31 - Daily 11-5*. Nov to Mar - Sats & Suns only 11-4* (*last admission to grounds). Also daily in Christmas week (Dec 26 to Jan 1).*NB The Trustees reserve the right to close all or parts of the Castle for Government seminars. Closed June 26, July 3 & Nov 6 for Open Air Concerts & Fireworks Display.*
Admission: Reduced prices for Chd (under 16) Students & OAPs, Family tickets, also for Groups and School parties who are welcomed at any time all year round, by appointment.
Refreshments: Lunch and refreshments available in the Fairfax Hall licensed restaurant and fast food outlets in the Stable Courtyard.
Picnic area. Car park. Fully accessible minibus provides shuttle service to and from car and coach parks, for disabled and elderly visitors. Facilities for disabled. Regret no dogs. Castle shop and plant shop.

LULLINGSTONE CASTLE

Eynsford map K4
Telephone: (0322) 862114
(Guy Hart Dyke, Esq)

Family portraits, armour, Henry VII gateway. Church.
Location: In the Darenth valley via Eynsford on A225.
Station(s): Eynsford (½ m).
Open: CASTLE & GROUNDS. Apr to Oct, Sats, Suns, Bank Hols 2-6. Wed, Thur and Frid by arrangement, (2-6). Telephone for enquiries or bookings.
Admission: £3, chd £1, OAPs £2.50. Free car parking.
Refreshments: In the gatehouse tea rooms.
No dogs.

LULLINGSTONE ROMAN VILLA   English⌗Heritage

map K4
Telephone: (0322) 863467

(Closed for refurbishment in 1990.)The ancient Romans understood the art of gracious living. In this country villa they walked on mosaic floors, dined off fine tableware and commissioned elaborate wall paintings to decorate one of the earliest churches in Britain.

Location: ½ m (0.8 km) south west of Eynsford.
Open: Good Friday or Apr 1 (whichever is earlier) to Sept 30: Open Daily 10-6. Oct 1 to Maundy Thursday or Mar 31 (whichever is earlier): Open Tues to Sun 10-4. *Closed* Dec 24-26, Jan 1.
Admission: £1.70, concessions £1.30, chd 85p. Price includes a Personal Stereo Guided Tour.

LYMPNE CASTLE

nr Hythe map M3
Telephone: (0303) 267571
(Harry Margary, Esq)

This romantic medieval castle with an earlier Roman, Saxon and Norman history was once owned by the Archdeacons of Canterbury. It was rebuilt about 1360, and restored in 1905, 300 feet above the well known Roman Shore Fort - Stutfall Castle. Four miles from the ancient Cinque Port of Hythe, it commands a tremendous view across Romney Marshes to Fairlight over the great sweep of the coast from Dover to Dungeness and across the sea to France. Terraced gardens with magnificent views out to sea.

Location: 3 m NW of Hythe off B2067, 8m W of Folkestone.
Station(s): Sandling (2½ m).
Open: Easter to Sept 30 - Daily 10.30-6. *Parties by appointment. Closed, occasionally on Sats.*
Admission: £2, Chd 50p.

MOUNT EPHRAIM

Hernhill, nr Faversham map L4
Telephone: (0227) 751310 or 751496.
(Mrs M N Dawes & Mr & Mrs E S Dawes)

Mount Ephraim has been the Dawes home for 300 years but the present gardens were laid out around 1912. By the end of the Second World War they were badly overgrown and it has taken many years to reclaim them. With some simplifications their old beauty and serenity have been restored. The site is magnificent, with views over the Thames estuary and rose terraces sloping down to a small lake and woodland area. There are many fine trees, a topiary garden, a herbaceous border and an extensive Japanese rock garden with a series of pools and a diversity of plants and shrubs. A new vineyard and water garden are added attractions.

Location: 6 m W of Canterbury, 3 m E of Faversham; ½ m N of A2 at Boughton.
Open: GARDENS ONLY. End of Apr to end Sept 2-6.
Admission: £1.75, Chd 25p. Parties by arrangement.
Refreshments: Teas available daily.

NEW COLLEGE OF COBHAM

Cobham map L4 ♿
Telephone: (0474) 814280
(Presidents of the New College of Cobham)

Almshouses based on medieval chantry built 1362, part rebuilt 1598. Originally endowed by Sir John de Cobham and descendants.

Location: 4 m W of Rochester; 4 m SE of Gravesend; 1½ m from junction Shorne-Cobham (A2). In Cobham rear of Church of Mary Magdalene.
Station(s): Sole St (1 m).
Open: Apr to Sept - Daily (except Thurs) 10-7. Oct to Mar - Mons, Tues, Weds, Sats & Suns 10-4.
Refreshments: Afternoon teas by prior arrangement.

NORTHBOURNE COURT GARDENS

Deal map M4
Telephone: (0304) 611281
(The Hon C James, Esq)

Northbourne Court is on the site of a palace which belonged to Eadbald, son of Ethelbert Saxon King of Kent. In 618 he gave it to the monks of St Augustines Abbey who used the produce from the farms and fish ponds for the support of the poor. After the dissolution it reverted to the crown and finally King James I gave it to Sir Edwyn Sandys. Sir Edwyn built a large house facing three tiers of terraces, which were probably built by Edwin Saunders. These terraces and their high flanking walls are still standing and provide the principal architectural feature of the gardens. The terrace forms a mount which is a rarely surviving characteristic of Tudor Gardens. These gardens are planted with a wide range of old fashioned and grey foliage plants on chalk soil to provide interest and colour all year round.

Location: A256 (Dover to Sandwich). Turn right towards Deal/Mongeham for approx. 2 m.
Open: Suns May 2, 30, June 13, 27, July 11, 25, Aug 15, 29, Sept 12, 26: 2-6.
Admission: £2.50, OAP/Chd £1.50 in aid of *National Gardens Scheme.*
Refreshments: Pub in village serves good food.
Plenty of car/coach parking nearby. Limited access for disabled persons (no wheelchairs available.

OWL HOUSE GARDENS

Lamberhurst map L3
(Maureen, Marchioness of Dufferin & Ava)

13 acres of romantic gardens surround this 16th century timber framed wool smuggler's cottage. Spring flowers, roses, rare flowering shrubs and ornamental fruit trees. Expansive lawns lead to leafy woodland walks graced by English and Turkish oaks, elm, birch and beech trees. Rhododendrons, azaleas, camellias encircle peaceful informal sunken water gardens.

Location: 8 m SE of Tunbridge Wells; 1 m from Lamberhurst off A21.
Open: GARDENS ONLY. All the year - daily and weekends including all Bank Hol weekends 11-6.
Admission: £2, Chd £1. (Proceeds towards Lady Dufferin's charity, Maureen's Oast House for Arthritics). Free parking.
Dogs on lead. Coach parties welcome.

PENSHURST PLACE

Tunbridge Wells map K4 △
Telephone: (0892) 870307
(The Rt Hon Viscount De L'Isle, MBE)

One of England's finest family-owned statley homes with a history going back six and a half centuries. Unique mediaeval Baron's Hall with splendid 60 foot-high chestnut beamed roof, paintings, furniture, and tapestries from 15th, 16th and 17th centuries. Other highlights include Toy Museum, Venture Playground, Nature and Farm Trails, and magnificent gardens dating back to the 14th century, recently restored to their former glory.

Location: Penshurst, near Tonbridge. From M25, junction 5, follow A21 to Tonbridge, leaving Tonbridge (North) exit; the follow brown tourist signs to Penshurst Place. From M26 Junction 2A. Follow A25 (Sevenoaks) and the A21 for Tonbridge; further directions as above.
Station(s): Penshurst (2 m). Regular services operate from BR Charing Cross to Hildenborough (4 miles) or Tonbridge (6 miles); then taxi.
Open: Open seven days a week from 27 Mar to 4 Oct. House and Grounds; 1-5.30. (last entry 5). Grounds only; 11-dusk.
Admission: HOUSE & GROUNDS; £4.50, Chd £2.50, OAP/Student/UB40 £3.75. GROUNDS ONLY; £3, Chd £2, OAP/Student/UB40 £2.50. Adult groups £3.75 (minimum 20). Groups should book in advance.
Refreshments: Light luncheons and teas available in Restaurant.
No dogs admitted. Wheelchair visitors free. (Disabled access limited by age/architecture of House. For enquiries and group bookings, contact Penshurst Place, Penshurst, Tonbridge, Kent TN11 8DG. (0892) 870307

PORT LYMPNE ZOO PARK, MANSION & GARDENS

Lympne, Hythe map M3
Telephone: (0303) 264646/264647
(John Aspinall, Esq)

Built for Sir Philip Sassoon between 1911 and 1915, and described as the 'last historic house built this century', Port Lympne encompasses the essence of Roman villas and the English country house. Overlooking the Romney Marsh and Channel and set in 15 acres of terraced gardens around the Trojan Stairway of 125 steps, the interior of the Mansion features a Moorish Patio, marble columns, an intriguing mosaic hall floor, plus the rare Rex Whistler Tent Room, and the new Spencer Roberts Mural Room and other wildlife Exhibitions. The principal architect was Sir Herbert Baker who designed New Delhi. Bought and restored by Mr John Aspinall in 1973, it is now open to the public together with its 300 acre rare wildlife park. Gorillas, lions, tigers, rhinos and many more rare animals. Gift shop. Picnic areas. Safari trailer, check for service times.

Location: 3 m W of Hythe; 6 m W of Folkestone; 7 m SE of Ashford off A20.
Open: All the year - Daily. Summer 10-5*; Winter 10-one hour before dusk* (*last admissions). *Closed Christmas Day.*
Admission: Reduced prices for OAPs and Chd 4-14 (3 and under free). Special party rates. Free car park.
Refreshments: Licensed restaurant and kiosks in summer.
Some areas not suitable for disabled.

QUEBEC HOUSE   🌸 **The National Trust**

Westerham map K4
Telephone: (0959) 62206

Probably early 16th century in origin, now mainly 17th century. Mementos of General Wolfe, and colourful exhibition about the Battle of Quebec.

Location: At junction of Edenbridge & Sevenoaks Roads (A25 & B2026).
Open: Apr to end Oct - Daily (except Thurs & Sats), inc Good Fri and Bank Hol Mon 2-6. Last adm 5.30.
Admission: £2, chd £1. *Pre-booked parties £1.50, chd 80p.*
No dogs. Unsuitable for wheelchairs.

Sir Edwin Landseer Lutyens
Architect

His work can be seen at the following properties included in Historic Houses Castles and Gardens:

> *Castle Drogo*
> *Goddards*
> *Great Dixter*
> *Great Maytham Hall*
> *Hestercombe House and Gardens*
> *Knebworth*

QUEX HOUSE, QUEX PARK 🏛

Birchington map M4
Telephone: (0843) 42168
(Trustees of the Powell-Cotton Museum)

Wander through the period rooms of P.H.G. Powell-Cotton's mansion, Quex House, the only stately home in Thanet, with its superb woodcarving and panelling, beautiful plasterwork and an air of mellow maturity. The rooms are arranged much as they were in his lifetime and contain fine 17th and 18th century English furniture and many family treasures. The unique Chinese Imperial porcelain collection, however, has been moved into its own gallery in the Powell-Cotton Museum as have the English and Continental porcelain collections. This purpose-built museum, adjoining the Mansion, now extends to nine large galleries; here Powell-Cotton created huge dioramas showing 500 African and Asian animals, all mounted by Rowland Ward, in scenes re-creating their natural habitats. He assembled the world's finest collection of African ethnography gathered on his 28 expeditions, and displayed it at Quex, together with superb weapons collections, cannon, local archaeological material and outstanding fine arts from many countries of the Orient. Enjoy the Pleasure Gardens and see the Victorian Walled Kitchen Garden presently under restoration.

Location: In Birchington, ½ m S of Birchington Square (signposted). SW of Margate; 13 m E of Canterbury.
Station(s): Birchington (1 m).
Open: Easter to Sept 30 - Weds, Thurs & Suns (also Frid in Aug): 2.15-6. Open Bank Hols in summer. (last entry 5). Museum only open in winter, Sun afternoons, reduced rates. Parties on other days by arrangement.
Admission: £1.50, OAPs £1, Chd £1.
Refreshments: Tea-room, light refreshments, summer only.
Ground floor rooms and museums only, suitable for disabled. Free car and coach parking.
New museum shop in recently completed Visitor Centre. Registered Charity.

RICHBOROUGH CASTLE   English✠Heritage

map M4
Telephone: (0304) 612013

The sea has deserted Richborough, but as Rutupiae it was well-known in Roman times as a seaport. It was here that the conquering Roman army landed in AD 43. The massive stone walls were built in the 3rd century to combat the ferocious attacks of Saxon sea-raiders. A personal stereo guided tour is available.

Location: 1½ m (2.4 km) north of Sandwich.
Open: Good Friday or Apr 1 (whichever is earlier) to Sept 30: Open Daily 10-6. Oct 1 to Maundy Thursday or Mar 31 (whichever is earlier): Open Tues to Sun 10-4. *Closed* Dec 24-26, Jan 1.
Admission: £1.50, concessions £1.10, chd 75p.

RIVERHILL HOUSE

Sevenoaks map K4   △
Telephone: (0732) 452557/458802
(The Rogers Family)

Small Ragstone house built in 1714 and home of the Rogers family since 1840. Panelled rooms, portraits and interesting memorabilia. An historic garden with rare trees and shrubs. Sheltered terraces and rhododendrons and azaleas in woodland setting. Bluebells. Ancient trackway known as 'Harold's Road'.

Location: 2 m S of Sevenoaks on road to Tonbridge (A225).
Station(s): Sevenoaks (2 m).
Open: Garden: Apr 1 to June 30: every Sun and the Sat and Mon of all Bank Holiday weekends during this period, 12-6. Picnics allowed. **The HOUSE is now only open to party bookings** and for a limited period when the gardens are at their best. Any day in April, May or June except Sun and Bank Holidays.
Admission: Garden: £1.50, Chd 50p. House: Adults only £2.50 (minimum of 20).
Refreshments: Home made teas in the old stable from 2.30 on Suns. Special Catering for booked parties - Ploughman's Lunches, teas etc - by arrangement. All enquiries to Mrs Rogers (0732) 458802/452557.
No dogs.

ROCHESTER CASTLE   English✠Heritage

Rochester map L4
Telephone: (0634) 402276

Large 11th century castle partly founded on the Roman city wall, with a splendid keep of c. 1130, the tallest in England. A Personal, Stereo Guided Tour is available.

Location: By Rochester Bridge (A2).
Open: Good Friday or Apr 1 (whichever is earlier) to Sept 30 daily 10-6. Oct 1 to Maundy Thursday or Mar 31 (whichever is earlier) Tues to Sun 10-4. *Closed* Dec 24-26, Jan 1.
Admission: £1.70, Concessions £1.30, chd 85p.

ST. AUGUSTINE'S ABBEY   English✠Heritage

map M4
Telephone: (0227) 767345

This was founded in 598 by St Augustine, the first Archibishop of Canterbury. The excavated finds from this early building are rare memorials of the Anglo-Saxon church. The remains we see today are from the later Norman church, its well-preserved crypt, and the medieval monastery.

Location: Canterbury, near the Cathedral.
Open: Good Friday or Apr 1 (whichever is earlier) to Sept 30: Open Daily 10-6. Oct 1 to Maundy Thursday or Mar 31 (whichever is earlier): Open Tues to Sun 10-4. *Closed* Dec 24-26, Jan 1.
Admission: £1.20, Concessions 90p, chd 60p.

SCOTNEY CASTLE GARDEN   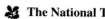 The National Trust

Lamberhurst map L3   &
Telephone: Lamberhurst (0892) 890651

Romantic landscape garden framing moated castle.

Location: 1½ m SE of Lamberhurst (A21).
Open: Garden: Apr to Nov 7 - Weds to Frid 11-6 or sunset if earlier *(closed Good Fri)*; Sats & Suns 2-6 or sunset if earlier. Bank Hols and Suns preceeding Bank Hol. 12-6. Old Castle: May to Sept 19 - days and times as for garden. Last adm one hour before closing.
Admission: £3.20 (pre-booked parties £2, weekdays only) Chd £1.60 and £1.
No dogs. Picnic area next to car park. Shop. Wheelchairs available. (Steep entrance to garden.).

SISSINGHURST GARDEN   The National Trust

Sissinghurst map L3
Telephone: (0580) 712850

The famous garden created by the late Vita Sackville-West and Sir Harold Nicolson between the surviving parts of an Elizabethan mansion. New exhibition and woodland walks.

Location: 2 m NE of Cranbrook; 1 m E of Sissinghurst village (A262).
Open: Apr to Oct 15 - Tues to Frid 1-6.30; Sats, Suns & Good Fri 10-5.30. (Last adm 5.) *Closed Mons, incl Bank Hol Mons.* Timed tickets in operation. Because of the limited capacity of the garden, visitors will often have to wait before admission.
Admission: £5, Chd £2.50. Parties by appointment only.
Refreshments: In the Granary Restaurant. Apr to Oct 15 - Tues to Fri 12-6, Sat & Sun 10-6, also Oct 28 to Dec 21 - Wed to Sat 11-4. Closed Mons.
No dogs. No picnics in garden. Admission to wheelchair visitors is restricted to 2 at any one time. Shop.

SMALLHYTHE PLACE   The National Trust

Tenterden map L3
Telephone: (058 06) 2334

The Ellen Terry Memorial Museum. Half-timbered 16th century yeoman's home. Mementoes of Dame Ellen Terry, Mrs Siddons, etc.

Location: 2½ m S of Tenterden on E side of Rye Road (B2082).
Open: Apr 3 to end of Oct - Daily (except Thurs & Frid) 2-6 or dusk if earlier. Open Good Fri. Last adm half-hour before closing. *Parties should give advance notice - no reduction. No parties in August. Can only take 25 at a time in house.*
Admission: £2.50, Chd £1.30 (Accompanied by an adult).
Refreshments: Tea available at The Spinning Wheel & the Tudor Rose, Tenterden.
No indoor photography. No dogs. Unsuitable for wheelchairs.

SOUTH FORELAND LIGHTHOUSE

map M4

On the cliff top between Dover and St. Margaret's Bay.

Location: 1½ m SW of St. Margaret's at Cliffe village. Visitors are advised to park in village car park (2 miles).
Open: Apr to end Oct. Sat, Sun & Bank Hol Mon, 2-5.30. Last adm 5.
Admission: £1.50, Chd 80p.

SQUERRYES COURT

Westerham map K4
Telephone: (0959) 562345 or 563118
(J St A Warde, Esq)

William and Mary manor house built in 1681. Home of the Warde family since 1731. Paintings, tapestries, furniture and porcelain collected and commissioned by the family in the 18th century. Memorabilia of General Wolfe of Quebec, a family friend. Landscaped grounds lovely all year round. Of special interest a recently restored formal garden.

Location: Western outskirts of Westerham signposted from A25.
Open: Mar: Suns only 2-6. Apr 1 to Sept 30: Weds, Sats, Suns and Bank Hol Mons 2-6 pm (last adm 5.30).
Admission: £3, Chd (under 14) £1.50, Grounds only £1.80, chd (under 14) 90p. Parties over 20 (any day except Suns) by arrangement at reduced rates.
Refreshments: Homemade teas at weekends & for booked parties.
Dogs on leads in grounds only. Free parking at house.

STONEACRE   The National Trust

Otham map L4

A half-timbered small manor house, c. 1480. Small garden.

Location: In Otham, 3 m SE of Maidstone; 1 m S of A20.
Station(s): Bearsted (2 m).
Open: Apr to end Oct - Weds & Sats 2-6 (last adm 5).
Admission: £2, Chd £1. No reduction for parties.
No dogs. Unsuitable for wheelchairs. Narrow access road.

TONBRIDGE CASTLE

Tonbridge map K4   △   Ⓔ
Telephone: (0732) 770929
(Owned and Managed by Tonbridge & Malling Borough Council)

Built by Richard de Fitzgilbert, remains of Norman Motte and Bailey Castle with 13th century Gatehouse overlooking River Medway. Reputedly England's finest example of the layout of a Norman Motte and Bailey Castle with 13th century Gatehouse set in landscaped gardens overlooking the River Medway. The site is clearly interpreted for your enjoyment. Superb exhibition in Castle Gatehouse depicting life at it was 700 years ago. Tours are available from the Tourist Information Centre.

Location: In town centre off High Street.
Open: Apr to Sept: Mon to Sat 9-5, Sun & Bank Hol 10.30-5. Oct to Mar: Mon to Fri 9-5, Sat 9-4. Sun 10.30-4. *Closed* Christmas Day and New Year's Day (last tours leave 1 hr before closing time). Guided tours by arrangement.

UPNOR CASTLE   English❖Heritage

map L4
Telephone: (0634) 718742

The Castle was built in 1559 on the orders of Elizabeth I, to protect her warships moored in the Medway alongside the new dockyards at Chatham. Within a century the castle was out of date, and was used as a magazine for gunpowder and munitions.

Location: At Upnor, on unclassified road off A228.
Open: Good Friday or Apr 1 (whichever is earlier) to Sept 30: Open Daily 10-6.
Admission: £1.80, concessions £1.30, Chd 85p.

WALMER CASTLE

Walmer map M4
Telephone: (0304) 364288

One of the coastal castles built by Henry VIII and the official residence of The Lords Warden of The Cinque Ports, including Queen Elizabeth, the Queen Mother and the Duke of Wellington who died at Walmer and whose furnished rooms have been preserved unaltered. (The original 'Wellington Boot' may be seen here).

Location: On coast at Walmer 2 m S of Deal off the Dover/Deal Road.
Station(s): Walmer (1½ m).
Open: Good Friday or Apr 1 (whichever is earlier) to Sept 30 daily 10-6. Oct 1 to Maundy Thursday or Mar 31 (whichever is earlier). Tues-Sun 10-4. *Closed* Dec 24-26, Jan 1 to Feb 28.
Admission: £2.70, concessions £2, chd £1.30. Price includes a Personal Stereo Guided Tour.

WILLESBOROUGH WINDMILL

Ashford map L4
(Willesborough Windmill Trust)

Willesborough Windmill, built in 1869, has now been restored as a working smock mill. Visitors can view the turn-of-the-century miller's cottage, enjoy guided tours of the mill and visit the mill's own tea room and shop.

Location: 2 m E of Ashford town centre, just off A292 and approx ¼ m from Junction 10 of the M20.
Open: Easter to Oct 31. Sat, Sun and Bank Hols. 2-5.
Admission: £1, Chd/OAP 50p. Group rates available on application.
Refreshments: Tea shop in restored barn adjacent to the mill. Light refreshments available -suitable for disabled.
Limited parking. Not suitable for disabled.

LANCASHIRE

ASTLEY HALL

off Hallgate, Astley Park, Chorley map G9
Telephone: (0257) 262166
Fax: (0257) 262166
(Chorley Borough Council)

A charming Tudor/Stuart building set in beautiful parkland, this lovely Hall retains a comfortable 'lived-in' atmosphere. There are pictures, glass-ware and pottery to see, as well as fine furniture and rare plasterwork ceilings.

Location: Lies ½ m NW of Town Centre. Footpath access from Town Centre (A6) through park. (½ m). By car: signposted from M61, slip road (Jct 8); from A581. (Southport to Chorley) and from Town Centre.
Open: Apr 1 to Oct 31. Daily (incl. Bank Hols). 11-12 and 1-5. (last entry 4.30) Nov 1 to Mar 31. Fri/Sat/Sun. 11-12 and 1-4. (last entry 3.30). Mon to Thur: Party Bookings only.
Admission: £2, Concessions £1, Family ticket £4. Evening party bookings and Suppers by arrangement.
Refreshments: Adjacent Cafe. (100 yds).
Large Free Car Park.

BROWSHOLME HALL

nr Clitheroe map G9
Telephone: (0254) 826719

Home of the Parker family, Bowbearers of the Forest of Bowland. Tudor with Elizabethan front, Queen Anne Wing and Regency additions. Portraits furniture and antiquities. Guided tours by members of the family.

Location: 5 m NW of Clitheroe; off B6243; Bashall Eaves - Whitewell signposted.
Open: Easter: Good Friday to Mon. Late May Bank Hol weekend. July: Every Sat; Aug: every Sat & Sun, and Aug Bank Hol weekend 2-5.
Admission: Reductions for booked parties at other times by appointment with A. Parker, Tel. as above.

GAWTHORPE HALL   ❧ The National Trust

Padiham map G9
Telephone: (0282) 778511

House built in 1600-1605, restored by Barry in 1850; Barry's designs newly re-created in principal rooms. Display of Rachel Kay-Shuttleworth textile collections; private study by arrangement. Major display of late 17th century portraits on loan from the National Portrait Gallery. Estate building, recently restored, houses a broad programme of craft and management courses.

Location: On E outskirts of Padiham (¾ m drive to house is on N of A671).
Station(s): Station: Rose Grove (2 m).
Open: Apr 1 to Oct 31. HALL: Tues, Weds, Thurs, Sats & Suns, 1-5, last adm 4.15. Open Good Fri & Bank Holiday Mons. GARDEN: Open daily all year 10-6. SHOP: Daily (except Mons & Fri) Apr 1 to Dec 21, 11-5.
Admission: House: £2.30, Chd £1. Reductions for pre-booked parties of 15 or more (except Bank Hols).
Refreshments: Refectory in Estate Building open as shop.
No dogs. Access for disabled: Ground floor of Hall, Shop. W/C.

HOGHTON TOWER

nr Preston map F9
Telephone: (0254) 852986
(Sir Bernard de Hoghton, Bt, D.L.)

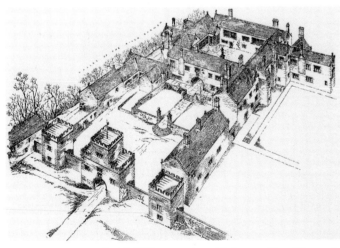

Dramatic 16th century fortified hilltop mansion with the magnificent Banqueting Hall where James I knighted the 'Sirloin' of Beef in 1617. The seat of Sir Bernard de Hoghton, Bt, D.L. Spend a few hours in this delightful historic mansion where there are permanent exhibitions, Chinese teapots, Dolls Houses and historic Hoghton documents. Underground passages, dungeons and Lancashire witches' kitchen. Gift shop. Walled gardens and Old English Rose Garden.

Location: 5 m E of Preston on A675.
Station(s): Preston (5 m).
Open: Easter Sat, Sun & Mon, then Suns to end of Oct. Jul and Aug, Tues, Wed and Thurs, also most Bank Holidays. Private visits welcome by arrangement both in and out of season. Available for private hire for receptions etc. Apply Administrator, Hoghton Tower, Preston PR5 0SH.
Refreshments: Tea room.
Gift Shop.

LEIGHTON HALL

Carnforth map F10
Telephone: (0524) 734474
(Mr & Mrs R. G. Reynolds)

Mid 12th century House rebuilt in the late 18th century with a neo Gothic facade added in 1822. Extensive grounds, garden and labyrinth. **Displays with trained eagles and falcons at 3.30 pm unless raining.**

Location: 2 m W of A6 through Yealand Conyers; signposted from M6, exit 35 junction with A6.
Station(s): Silverdale (1½ m, bridlepath only); Carnforth (2½ m).
Open: May to Sept - Suns, Bank Hol Mons & Tues to Frid 2-5. In August only 11.30-5. (last tour of House 4.30). Other times by appointment for parties of 25 or more. Special Educational Programme for Schools - mornings from 10 am.
Admission: House & Grounds £3, (OAPs/Parties £2.50), Chd £1.90, Chd party £1.50. Teachers with schools free. Inquiries: Mrs Reynolds at the Hall.
Refreshments: Teas at the Hall. Salad lunches/high teas for booked parties.

MARTHOLME

Great Harwood, Blackburn map G9

Screens passage and service wing of medieval manor house altered 1577 with 17th century additions. Gatehouse built 1561, restored 1969.

Open: Exterior: Fri & Sat. Interior: by appointment only.

RUFFORD OLD HALL   ❧ The National Trust

Rufford, nr Ormskirk map F9
Telephone: (0704) 821254

One of the finest 15th century buildings in Lancashire. The Great Hall is remarkable for its ornate hammer-beam roof and unique screen. There are fine collections of 17th century oak furniture, 16th century arms, armour and tapestries.

Location: 7 m N of Ormskirk at N end of Rufford village on E side of A59.
Station(s): Stations: Rufford (½ m) (not Suns); Burscough Bridge (2½ m).
Open: Apr 1 to Oct 31 - Daily (except Frid) 1-5. Last adm 4.30. Garden and shop: open 12-5.30 on same days, Suns 1-5. Refreshments same days 12-5, Sun 2-5.
Admission: £2.70, Chd £1.40. Reduced parties of 15 or more by arrangement.
Refreshments: At the Hall (parties should book).
Access for disabled garden only. Guide dogs.

STONYHURST COLLEGE

Hurst Green map G9
Telephone: (0254) 826345

The original house, (situated close to the picturesque village of Hurst Green in the beautiful Ribble Valley) dates from the late 16th century. Set in extensive grounds which include ornamental gardens. The College has an impressive approach down a long avenue flanked by man made rectangular ponds constructed in the 17th century. The Parish Church of St. Peters built in 1832, is linked to the main building which is a boys' Catholic boarding school, founded by the Society of Jesus in 1593.

Location: Just off the B6243 (Longridge - Clitheroe) on the outskirts of Hurst Green. 10 m from junction 31 on M6.
Open: House: weekly from Aug 3 to Sept 4, Tues to Sun only (plus Aug Bank Hol Mon) 1-5. Grounds & Gardens: weekly from July 10 to Sept 4, Tues to Sun only (plus Aug Bank Hol Mon) 1-5.
Admission: House and Grounds £3, Chd (4-14) £2, (under 4 free), OAPs £2, Grounds only £1.
Refreshments: Refreshments/Gift Shop: Limited facilities for disabled. Coach parties by prior arrangement.
No dogs permitted.

TOWNELEY HALL ART GALLERY & MUSEUM AND MUSEUM OF LOCAL CRAFTS & INDUSTRIES

Burnley map G9
Telephone: (0282) 24213
(Burnley Borough Council)

The House dates from the 14th century, with 17th and 19th century modifications. The furnished rooms include an Elizabethan Long Gallery, and a fine entrance hall with plasterwork by Vassali completed in 1729. Collections include oak furniture, 18th and 19th century paintings and Zoffany's painting of Charles Towneley. Loan exhibitions are held throughout the summer. There is a Museum of Local Crafts and Industries in the old Bew House, and the Natural History Centre, with an aquarium in the grounds.

Location: ½ m SE of Burnley on the Burnley/Todmorden Road (A671).
Station(s): Burnley Central (1¾ m).
Open: All the year - Mons to Fris 10-5, Suns 12-5. *Closed Sats throughout year. Closed Christmas-New Year.*
Admission: Free.
Refreshments: At cafe in grounds during the summer.

LEICESTERSHIRE

ASHBY DE LA ZOUCH CASTLE   English⌗Heritage

map H7
Telephone: (0530) 413343

In 1464 Edward IV granted the Norman manor house of Ashby to his Lord Chamberlain, Lord Hastings, who built the impressive four-storey tower. His enjoyment of it was short-lived, alas, for in 1483 he was beheaded by Richard III. His successors fared better and among royal visitors were Henry VII, Mary Queen of Scots, James I and Charles I. In 1649 the tower was partially destroyed by Parliamentary forces.

Location: In Ashby de la Zouch.
Open: Good Friday or Apr 1 (whichever is earlier) to Sept 30: Open Daily 10-6. Oct 1 to Maundy Thursday or Mar 31 (whichever is earlier): Open Tues to Sun 10-4. *Closed Dec 24-26, Jan 1.*
Admission: £1.20, concessions 90p, chd 60p.

BELGRAVE HALL

Belgrave map H7

Small Queen Anne house of 1709-13, with period room settings from late 17th to late 19th century. Coaches in stable block. Outstanding period and botanic gardens with over 6,500 species of plants.

Location: Church Road, Belgrave, off Thurcaston Road in Leicester.
Open: Open weekdays 10-5.30, Sun 2-5.30. *Closed Good Friday, Christmas Day and Boxing Day.* Access for disabled to all gardens, but ground floor only of 3-storey house. Unrestricted street parking outside.

BELVOIR CASTLE

nr Grantham   map J7
Telephone: (0476) 870262
(His Grace the Duke of Rutland)

Seat of the Dukes of Rutland since Henry VIII's time, and rebuilt by Wyatt in 1816. A castle in the grand style, commanding magnificent views over the Vale of Belvoir. The name dates back to the famous Norman Castle that stood on this site. Many notable art treasures, and interesting military relics. The Statue gardens contain many beautiful 17th century sculptures. Flowers in bloom throughout most of the season. Medieval Jousting Tournaments. Conference and filming facilities. Banquets, school visits, private parties.

Location: 7 m WSW of Grantham, between A607 (to Melton Mowbray) and A52 (to Nottingham).
Open: Apr 1 to Oct 1 1993, Tues Wed, Thurs, Sat - 11-5. Sun and Bank Hols - 11-6. Other times for groups by appointment.
Admission: £3.50, Chd/OAPs £2.50. All coach tours and excursions £2.75 (coach driver free). Parties of 20 or more adults £2.75 (organiser free). School parties £2 (teacher free). On Jousting Tournament days an extra charge of 50p per person will apply. Ticket office and catering facilities in the Castle close approximately 30 mins before the Castle. Guide books are on sale at the ticket office or inside the Castle, or by post (£2.50) incl. post and packing.
We regret that dogs are not permitted (except Guide dogs).

BOSWORTH BATTLEFIELD VISITOR CENTRE & COUNTRY PARK

Market Bosworth   map H6   ♿
Telephone: (0455) 290429
(Leicestershire County Council)

Site of the famous Battle of Bosworth Field (1485) with extensive Visitor Centre including exhibitions, models, film theatre, book and gift shops and cafeteria; and outdoor interpretation of the Battle. Series of special mediaeval attractions during summer months.

Location: 15 m W of Leicester; 2 m S of Market Bosworth (sign posted off M42, A5, A447, A444 and B585).
Open: BATTLEFIELD VISITOR CENTRE. Apr 1 to Oct 31 - Mons to Sats 1-5.30; Suns and Bank Hols 1-6. July 1 to Aug 31: open from 11a.m. COUNTRY PARK & BATTLE TRAILS: Open all year during daylight hours.
Admission: £1.50, Chd (under 16) and OAPs £1. Special charges apply on main Special Event days. Parties at any time by appointment at reduced rates. *All times/charges subject to review.*
Refreshments: Bosworth Buttery Cafeteria.

KIRBY MUXLOE CASTLE   English⌗Heritage

map H7
Telephone: (0533) 386886

William, Lord Hastings, was a very wealthy man, so he was able to indulge his passion for building. He developed his moated brick mansion from a fortified manor house, but it was never completed. A striking feature is the patterned brickwork, clearly visible on the gatehouse walls.

Location: 4 m (6.4 km) west of Leicester.
Open: Good Friday or Apr 1 (whichever is earlier) to Sept 30: Open Daily 10-6. Oct 1 to Maundy Thursday or Mar 31 (whichever is earlier): Open Tues to Sun 10-4. *Closed* Dec 24-26, Jan 1.
Admission: £1.20, concessions 90p, Chd 60p.

We've Travelled Back In Time

Travel back in time with a visit to one of Leicestershire's 14 museums

You'll find plenty to amaze and amuse you – from the Rutland Dinosaur at New Walk to the Rutland rural life exhibition at Oakham, and from the Roman remains at Jewry Wall to the Regency elegance of Belgrave Hall.

There's so much to enjoy that we think you'll keep coming back, time after time.

LEICESTERSHIRE MUSEUM AND ART GALLERY
New Walk, Leicester.

JEWRY WALL MUSEUM AND SITE
St. Nicholas Circle, Leicester.

NEWARKE HOUSES MUSEUM
The Newarke, Leicester.

HARBOROUGH MUSEUM
Council Offices, Adam and Eve Street, Market Harborough.

MUSEUM OF COSTUME, WYGSTON'S HOUSE
Applegate, St. Nicholas Circle, Leicester.

MELTON CARNEGIE MUSEUM
Thorpe End, Melton Mowbray.

MUSEUM OF TECHNOLOGY
Corporation Road, Abbey Lane, Leicester.

LEICESTERSHIRE RECORD OFFICE
Long Street, Wigston Magna, Leicester

RUTLAND COUNTY MUSEUM
Catmos Street, Oakham.

OAKHAM CASTLE
Market Place, Oakham.

MUSEUM OF THE ROYAL LEICESTERSHIRE REGIMENT
The Magazine, Oxford Street, Leicester.

BELGRAVE HALL
Church Road, Belgrave, Leicester.

THE MANOR HOUSE
Donington-le-Heath, Coalville.

SNIBSTON DISCOVERY PARK
Ashby Road, Coalville

You'll keep coming back to...

LEICESTERSHIRE
COUNTY COUNCIL
MUSEUMS, ARTS AND
RECORDS SERVICE

96 New Walk, Leicester LE1 6TD   Tel: (0533) 554100

LYDDINGTON BEDE HOUSE   English ⌗ Heritage

map J6
Telephone: (057 282) 2438

The building is the only surviving part of the medieval palace of the Bishops of Lincoln. After the Reformation it passed to Thomas, Lord Burghley, who turned it into an almshouse. It was used as such until the present century.

Location: In Lyddington 6m (9.6 km) north of Corby.
Open: Good Friday or Apr 1 (whichever is earlier) to Sept 30 - daily 10-6.
Admission: £1.20, Concessions 90p, Chd 60p.

THE MANOR HOUSE

Donington-le-Heath   map H7

Fine medieval manor house circa 1280 with 16th to 17th century alterations. Now restored as period house.

Location: In Donington-le-Heath, Hugglescote nr Coalville.
Open: Wed before Easter to Sept 30 inc: Wed to Sun 2-6, and all Bank Holidays: Mon and Tues except May Day Mon only. Access for disabled to ground floor only. Visitors' car park.
Refreshments: Cream teas in adjoining stone barn.

OAKHAM CASTLE

Market Place, Oakham   map J7
Telephone: (0572) 723654

12th century Great Hall of Norman castle in castle grounds with earlier motte. Unique collection of horseshoes presented by visiting Peers of the Realm.

Location: In Oakham.
Open: Castle Grounds: Apr to Oct - daily 10-5.30. Nov to Mar - daily 10-4. Sun 2-4. Great Hall: Apr to Oct - Tues to Sat and Bank Holiday Mon 10-1, 2-5.30. Sun 2-5.30. Nov to Mar - Tues to Sat 10-1, 2-4. *Closed* Good Friday, Christmas Day and Boxing Day. Access for disabled to Great Hall. Parking for disabled visitors **only** on request.

The National Trust
THE SIGN
OF A GREAT
DAY OUT

STANFORD HALL

Lutterworth map J6 △
Telephone: (0788) 860250
(The Lady Braye)

A William and Mary House built in the 1690's containing a fine collection of pictures (including the Stuart Collection), antique furniture and family costumes dating from Queen Elizabeth I's time. There is a full-size replica of the 1898 Flying Machine of Percy Pilcher who is officially recognised as England's Pioneer Aviator. He experimented at Stanford where he was killed whilst flying in 1899. The Motorcycle Museum contains an outstanding collection of Vintage and historic motorcycles. Walled Rose Garden leading to Old Forge. Nature Trail. Craft Centre most Sundays.

Location: 7½ m NE of Rugby; 3½ m from A5; 6 m from M1 at exit 18; 5 m from M1 at exit 20; 9 m from M6 at exit 1; 1¼ m from Swinford.
Open: Easter Sat to end of Sept - Sats & Suns also Bank Hol Mons & Tues following 2.30-6. (last adm 5.30). NB On Bank Hols and Event Days open 12 noon (House 2.30).
Admission: House and Grounds, etc; £2.90, chd £1.30; Grounds, Rose Garden, Flying Machine, Old Forge, Craft Centre (most Suns) £1.60, chd 70p. Parties of 20 or more (min £52) £2.60, chd £1.15. OAPs with a party of 20 or more £2.40. School parties of 20 or more (one teacher adm free) £2.60, chd £1.15. Prices are subject to increase on some Event Days. Motorcycle Museum 90p, chd 20p.
Refreshments: Home-made teas. Light lunches most Suns. Lunches, Teas, High Teas or Suppers for pre-booked parties any day during season.

WYGSTON'S HOUSE, MUSEUM OF COSTUME

Applegate, St Nicholas Circle, Leicester map J7 &
Telephone: (0533) 554100

Important late medieval building, with later additions housing costume from 1750 to present day. Reconstruction of draper's shop of 1920s.

Location: St Nicholas Circle, in Leicester
Open: Weekdays 10-5.30, Sun 2-5.30. Closed Good Friday, Christmas Day and Boxing Day. Access for disabled on ground floor only. Public car park adjacent.

LINCOLNSHIRE

AUBOURN HALL

nr Lincoln map J8
(Sir Henry Nevile)

Late 16th century house attributed to J. Smythson (Jnr). Important carved staircase and panelled rooms. New rose garden.

Location: In Aubourn village 7 m S of Lincoln
Open: July and Aug: Wed, 2-6. Also Sun June 6 and June 20, or by appointment.
Admission: £2, Chd/OAPs £1.50.

BELTON HOUSE   ❧   The National Trust

nr Grantham map J7 ⓢ
Telephone: (0476) 66116

The crowning achievement of Restoration country house architecture, built 1685-88 for Sir John Brownlow, heir to the fortunes of a successful Elizabethan lawyer; alterations by James Wyatt 1777, plasterwork ceilings by Edward Goudge, fine wood carvings of the Grinling Gibbons school. Family portraits, furniture, tapestries, Speaker Cust's silver and silver-gilt, Duke of Windsor memorabilia. Formal gardens, orangery by Jeffrey Wyattville, 17th century stables, magnificent landscape park. Extensive Adventure Playground for children.

Location: 3 m NE of Grantham on A607 Grantham/Lincoln Road; easily accessible from A1.
Open: Apr 1 to end of Oct - Weds to Suns & Bank Hol Mons 1-5.30. *Closed* Good Friday. Gardens open 11. Parkland opens daily with free access on foot (may be closed for special events). Last adm 5.
Admission: House: £4, School parties contact the Administrator for details. 1993 Events - details from the Administrator.
Refreshments: Counter service licensed restaurant open 12-5 for lunches and teas.

BELVOIR CASTLE

See under Leicestershire.

BISHOP'S PALACE   English⌗Heritage

map J8
Telephone: (0522) 27468

When James I visited Lincoln in 1617 the palace was a ruin. It was not until the 1880s that it was partially restored by Bishop King. Excavations have revealed most of the medieval layout which largely dates from the 12th, 13th and 15th centuries.

Location: South side of Lincoln cathedral.
Open: Good Friday or Apr 1 (whichever is earlier) to Sept 30: Open Thurs to Sun 10-6.
Admission: 80p, Concessions 60p, chd 40p.

BURGHLEY HOUSE

Stamford   map J7   △
Telephone: (0780) 52451
*(Burghley House Trustees)*K2

The finest example of later Elizabethan architecture in England. Eighteen State rooms open containing fine furniture, porcelain, silver and the largest private collection of Italian art. Also magnificent painted ceilings by Verrio and Laguerre. Much of the renowned Burghley collection of Oriental porcelain is on display within the State Rooms. There is also a Special Exhibition which changes annually. During 1993 this will feature a selection of early Royal charters and documents from the immense collection of records at Burghley. The period covered will be from the time of King Arthur to that of Queen Elizabeth 1. This Special Exhibition, the 11th of it's kind, follows the theme of showing of parts of the collection that are not normally available to visitors. The 'Capability' Brown Deer Park is open to visitors at no extra charge nor is there a charge for car parking.

Location: 1 m SE of Stamford clearly signposted from the A1.
Station(s): Stamford (1m).
Open: Apr 1 to Oct 3 - Daily 11-5. *Closed Sept 4.*
Admission: £4.80, OAPs £4.50. Accompanied Chd Free, (1 per adult, otherwise £2.50 per chd). Party rates available.
Refreshments: Snacks, lunches and teas in the Orangery. Enquiries for bookings, party rates & menus tel: (0780) 52451.

DODDINGTON HALL

Doddington   map J8   △   Ⓢ
Telephone: (0522) 694308
(Mr & Mrs A. G. Jarvis)

One of the Elizabethan gems of England. A romantic house set in 5 acres of superb gardens, with beautiful contents which reflect 400 years of unbroken family occupation. Fine furniture, porcelain, tapestries and pictures, and still very much a family home.

Location: 5 m W of Lincoln on the B1190 & signposted off the A46 Lincoln by-pass.
Open: Easter Mon then May to Sept - Weds, Suns & Bank Hol Mons 2-6.
Admission: £3.40, Chd £1.70. Gardens only: £1.70, Chd 80p. Minimum charge per booked party of 20 people £68.
Refreshments: The Littlehouse Restaurant opens from noon on open days, 'phone (0522) 690980 for bookings.

FULBECK HALL

Grantham   map J7   ᨔ
Telephone: (0400) 72205
(Mrs M. Fry)

Home of the Fane family since 1632, with alterations and additions by nearly every generation. This is a friendly, lived-in house where visitors receive a personal welcome from the owners. It is mainly 18th century with an older service wing and later additions to the main block. Links with Wellington, the Raj and Arnhem. In the eleven acre garden there has been much recent planting of unusual subjects within the Edwardian design. Planting plans may be borrowed. Plants for sale, nature trail with free leaflet, peacocks, Hebridean sheep, picnic area. Fulbeck Hall and Fulbeck Manor (see list at back) will open together for groups of more than 20 at any time by prior arrangement.

Location: On A607. Lincoln 14 m, Grantham 11 m. 1 m S of A17.
Open: House and Garden: Easter, May and Aug Bank Holiday Mons. Sun May 30 and daily from July 4 to Aug 1 incl, 2-5.
Admission: £3, OAPs £2.50, Chd £1. Garden only: £1.50, Chd £1. Car parking free.
Refreshments: Teas. Special catering of any kind available for groups - lunch, tea or dinner. Suitable for disabled persons (no wheelchairs available).

GRANTHAM HOUSE   ❧   The National Trust

Grantham   map J7

Dating from 1380 but extensively altered and added to throughout the centuries. Ground floor only open to the public. The grounds run down to the river.

Location: In Castlegate, immediately E of Grantham Church.
Station(s): Grantham (1 m).
Open: Apr to end of Sept, Weds only - 2-5 by written appointment only with Maj-Gen Sir Brian Wyldbore-Smith, Grantham House, Castlegate, Grantham NG1 6SS.
Admission: £1, Chd 50p. No reductions for parties.
No dogs. Unsuitable for wheelchairs. No lavatories.

GRIMSTHORPE CASTLE AND GARDENS

Bourne   map J7
(Grimsthorpe & Drummond Castle Trust)

The home of the Willoughby de Eresby family since 1516. Examples of early 13th century architecture, the Tudor period of the reign of Henry VIII and work by Sir John Vanbrugh. State Rooms and Picture Galleries open to the Public.

Location: 4 m NW of Bourne on A151 Colsterworth/Bourne Road, SE of Grantham.
Open: Park and Gardens: Easter Sun and Mon, Apr 11, 12. May 2 to Sept 12: every Thur, Sun, Bank Hol. 12-6, last entry 5. Castle: Easter Sun and Mon, Apr 11, 12. Suns and Bank Hols May 30 to Sept 12: 2-6, last entry 5. Guided tours by arrangement. Nature Trails Jul 12 to Sept 13. Open daily 12 noon to 6pm.
Admission: Garden £1, Chd (under 16)/OAPs 50p. PLUS Castle: £2, Chd (under 16)/OAPs £1, (under 5 free). Guided Tours £3.60 (min). Nature Trails 50p.
Refreshments: The Coach House cafeteria serves home made teas.
Conference room available.

Burghley House Stamford

THE LARGEST AND GRANDEST HOUSE OF THE ELIZABETHAN AGE

Home of the Cecils for over 400 years.

Built in 1587 by William Cecil, first Lord Burghley and Lord High Treasurer to Queen Elizabeth I and occupied by his descendants ever since. Eighteen treasure filled State Rooms are on view including the Heaven Room – the finest painted room in England. Of special interest are the silver fireplaces, needlework, painted ceilings, medieval kitchen with over 260 copper utensils, and one of the largest private art collections in Britain. The house is set in a Deer Park landscaped by 'Capability' Brown. Home of the famous Burghley Horse Trials.

Easily reached – just 1 mile from the Great North Road (A1) at Stamford.

Refreshments available in the Orangery.

Open daily from Good Friday to October 4 (not September 12) 11 am to 5 pm.

For further information and details of special party rates and menus contact: The Manager, telephone Stamford (0780) 52451.

GUNBY HALL   The National Trust

Burgh-le-Marsh map K8

Built by Sir William Massingberd in 1700. Reynolds' portraits, contemporary wainscoting. Ground floor only open to the public. Walled gardens full of flowers and roses.

Location: 2½ m NW of Burgh-le-Marsh; 7 m W of Skegness on S side of A158.
Open: House & Garden. Apr 1 to end of Sept - Weds 2-6; Tues, Thurs & Fris by prior written appointment only to J. D. Wrisdale, Esq., Gunby Hall, nr Spilsby, Lincs. Gardens only also on Thurs 2-6.
Admission: House & Gardens £2.50, Chd £1.20. Garden only £1.50, Chd 70p. No reduction for parties.
Dogs in garden only, on leads. Wheelchairs in garden only.

LINCOLN CASTLE

Castle Hill map J8
Telephone: (0522) 511068
(Recreational Services Dept, Lincolnshire County Council)

MARSTON HALL

Grantham map J7
Telephone: (0400) 50225
(The Rev Henry Thorold, FSA)

TATTERSHALL CASTLE   The National Trust

Lincoln map K8
Telephone: (0526) 342543

The Keep is one of the finest examples of a fortified brick dwelling, although built more for show than defence, c. 1440, for Ralph Cromwell. Museum and shop in Guardhouse.

Location: 12 m NE of Sleaford on Louth Road (A153); 3½ m SE of Woodhall Spa.
Open: Daily - Apr 1 to end of Oct, 10.30-6. Nov to end Mar 1993 12-4.30 *Closed Christmas Day & Boxing Day.*
Admission: £2, Chd £1. Parties of 15 or more - details from Custodian.
Refreshments: Fortescue Arms Hotel, Tattershall.
Dogs in grounds only, on leads. Wheelchair access.

WOOLSTHORPE MANOR   The National Trust

nr Grantham map J7
Telephone: (0476) 860338

17th century farm house, birthplace of Sir Isaac Newton. Traditionally it was under an apple tree in this garden that Newton was struck with the theory of gravity.

Location: 7 m S of Grantham, ½ m NW of Colsterworth; 1 m W of A1 (not to be confused with Woolsthorpe, nr Belvoir).
Open: Apr 1 to end of Oct - Wed-Sun 1-5.30, last adm 5. *Closed Thur & Fri. Closed Good Fri.*
Admission: £2.30, chd £1.10. No reduction for parties.
Wheelchair access to garden & ground floor only. Parking for coaches limited to one at a time - must book. *NB In the interests of preservation numbers admitted to rooms at any time must be limited; liable to affect peak weekends and Bank Hols.*

GREATER LONDON

APSLEY HOUSE

Wellington Museum map K4
Telephone: 071-499 5676
(Trustees of the Victoria & Albert Museum)

Closed 1993 for refurbishment.

ASHBURNHAM HOUSE

Westminster map K4
Telephone: 071-222 3116
(Westminster School)

THE BANQUETING HOUSE

Whitehall
(Historic Royal Palaces)

'A hidden Royal Treasure.' Step inside and enjoy peace and tranquility just yards away from the hustle and bustle of Whitehall. The Banqueting House is the only surviving part of the once great Palace of Whitehall. It was designed by Inigo Jones, for James I in 1619 and completed in 1622. The main hall is topped by a magnificent painted ceiling, installed in 1635, which Charles I commissioned from Sir Peter Paul Rubens. The Banqueting House was not always so tranquil. On 30 Jan 1649 Charles I walked through the Main Hall to his execution outside the building.

Location: Whitehall, London, SW1.
Station(s): Embankment, Westminster.
Open: Mon to Sat. 10-5pm. *Closed all public holidays and at short notice for government functions.*
Admission: £2.75, OAP/Student £2, Chd £1.80 (from 1/4/93).

THE BLEWCOAT SCHOOL
          The National Trust

Westminster map K4
Telephone: 071-222 2877

Built in 1709 at the expense of William Green, a local brewer, to provide an education for poor children; in use as a school until 1926, the building was bought by the Trust in 1954; it was restored in 1975 and now houses a National Trust shop and information centre.

Location: No 23 Caxton Street, Westminster, SW1.
Station(s): Victoria ¼ m; Underground St James's Park (Circle and District Lines) less than 100 yards.
Open: All year, Mon to Fri 10-5.30, (Dec 24, closes 4.30). Late night shopping Thurs until 7. Also Sats Dec 4, 11, 18, 11-4.30. *Closed Bank Holiday Mondays, Dec 25-31, Jan 3 and Good Friday.*
Admission: Free.

BOSTON MANOR

Brentford map K4
Telephone: 081-862 5805
(London Borough of Hounslow)

Jacobean house (1622) with elaborate plaster ceiling in the State Room which also contains a fireplace and mantelpiece dating from 1623. Original oak staircase. The house is set in a small park.

Location: In Boston Manor Road.
Open: May 30 to Sept 26 - Sun afternoons only 2-4.30.
Admission: Free.

BURGH HOUSE

Hampstead map K4
Telephone: 071-431 0144
(Burgh House Trust)

Built 1703. Used for art exhibitions, concerts. Hampstead Museum. Terrace Garden.

Location: New End Sq E of Hampstead Underground Station.
Station(s): Hampstead (Underground). Hampstead Heath (BR North London Link).
Open: Weds to Suns 12-5; Bank Hol Mons 2-5.
Admission: Free.
Refreshments: Coffee, lunches and Teas. Licensed Buttery (for reservations and enquiries about catering for functions at the House Tel: 071-431 2516).

CAREW MANOR AND DOVECOTE

Church Road, Beddington map K4
(London Borough of Sutton)

This building, formerly known as Beddington Park or Beddington Place, contains a late-medieval Great Hall, with an arch-braced hammer-beam roof, which is listed Grade I. The house is used as a school, but the Hall is now accessible every Sun and Bank Hol Mon from Easter until Nov, together with the restored early 18th century Dovecote, with its 1,288 nesting boxes and potence, which is a scheduled ancient monument. Guided tours available of the Dovecote, the Great Hall and the cellars of the house which contain medieval, Tudor, and later features (cellars accessible on guided tours only). Some tours take in the late 14th century Church of St Mary, Beddington, with its Norman font and its 15th century Carew Chapel containing important Carew memorials (the Carews of Beddington were lords of the manor for over four hundred years). Carew Manor and Beddington Church stand on the edge of Beddington Park, the landscaped home park of the Carews, through which a Heritage Trail has been established giving details of the history, historic buildings, garden features, and wildlife of this important conservation area. Guide book, trail leaflet and other publications and souvenirs available.

Location: Church Road, Beddington. Off A232 ¾ m E of junction with A237.
Open: Suns & Bank Hol Mons from Easter to Nov 1 (phone Sutton Heritage Service 081-773 4555).
Admission: Charge.

CARLYLE'S HOUSE   The National Trust

Chelsea map K4
Telephone: 071-352 7087

Home of Thomas and Jane Carlyle 1834-1881. *Note: Certain rooms have no electric light, visitors wishing to make a close study of the interior should avoid dull days.*

Location: At 24 Cheyne Row, Chelsea SW3 (off Cheyne Walk on Chelsea Embankment).
Station(s): Sloane Sq (Underground 1 m); Victoria (BR 1½ m).
Open: Apr to end of Oct - Weds to Suns & Bank Hol Mons 11-5. Last adm 4.30. *Closed Good Friday.*
Admission: £2.80, chd £1.40. No reductions for parties which should not exceed 20 and must book.
No dogs. Unsuitable for wheelchairs.

CARSHALTON HOUSE (Daughters of the Cross) St Philomena's School, Pound Street

Carshalton map K4

An important listed building, built by about 1707 around the core of an older house and with grounds laid out originally by Charles Bridgeman, Carshalton House is open on a limited number of occasions each year. Its garden buildings include the unique Water Tower, now in the care of the Carshalton Water Tower Trust. The house contains principal rooms with 18th century decoration, including the important Blue Room and the Painted Parlour (attributed to Robert Robinson). Openings are organised by Sutton Heritage Service in conjunction with the Water Tower Trust and the Daughters of the Cross. Tours of the house and grounds and a programme of short talks on the house and its people are given during the open days (included in entrance fee). Refreshments and publications are available. Carshalton House is close to Sutton's Heritage Centre at Honeywood, in the Carshalton conservation area.

Location: Pound Street, Carshalton, at junction with Carshalton Road, on A232.
Station(s): Carshalton (¼ m).
Open: 1993: Mon Apr 12 (Easter Monday), Sun Sept 12. 10-5 (last admission 4.15).
Admission: Charge. For further details telephone Sutton Heritage Service on 081-773 4555.
Refreshments: Available.

CHAPTER HOUSE AND PYX CHAMBER OF WESTMINSTER ABBEY
English ⌗ Heritage

map K4
Telephone: 071-222 5897

Described as 'incomparable' when it was finished in 1253, with some of the finest of English medieval sculpture, the chapter house was one of the largest in England and could seat 80 monks around its walls. It was converted to a record office in the 16th century, but by 1740 the roof had decayed and been removed. Restoration of the whole building took place in 1865 and again after it was bombed in 1941. The 11th century Pyx Chamber now houses the Abbey Treasures. A joint ticket admits to the Abbey Museum.

Location: East side of the abbey cloister.
Open: Good Friday or Apr 1 (whichever is earlier) to Sept 30: Open Daily 10-6. Oct 1 to Maundy Thursday or Mar 31 (whichever is earlier): Open Daily 10-4. *Closed* Dec 24 -26, Jan 1.
Admission: £2, concessions £1.50, Chd £1.
Liable to be closed at short notice on state occasions.

CHELSEA PHYSIC GARDEN

Chelsea map K4

The second oldest Botanic garden in the country, founded 1673 including notable collection of medicinal plants, comprises 4 acres densely packed with c. 5,000 plants, many rare and unusual.

Location: 66 Royal Hospital Road, Chelsea; nr junction of Royal Hospital Road & Chelsea Embankment.
Station(s): Sloane Square (Underground).
Open: Apr 4 to Oct 31 - Suns and Weds, 2-5. Also Mon 24 to Fri 28 May (Chelsea Flower Show Week) 12-5 and Mon 14 to Fri 18 Jun (Chelsea Festival Week). Open at other times for subscribing Friends and groups by appointment.
Admission: (1993 prices) £2.50, Chd/unemployed/students (with cards) £1.30. Garden accessible for disabled and wheelchairs via 66, Royal Hospital Road. Parking in street Suns, and other days across Albert Bridge in Battersea Park, free.
No dogs.

CHISWICK HOUSE   English🏛Heritage

Chiswick map K4
Telephone: 081-995 0508

Architect and patron of the arts, the third Earl of Burlington set a fashion with this Italian-style villa, built to house his library and art collections. The gardens were landscaped by William Kent.

Location: Burlington Lane (½ m) NE of Chiswick Station.
Open: Good Friday or Apr 1 (whichever is earlier) to Sept 30 daily 10-6. Oct 1 to Maundy Thursday or Mar 31 (whichever is earlier) daily 10-4. *Closed* Dec 24, 25.
Admission: £2.20, Concessions £1.60, Chd £1.10.

COLLEGE OF ARMS

City of London map K4 △
Telephone: 071-248 2762
(The Corporation of Kings, Heralds & Pursuivants of Arms)

Mansion built in 1670s to house the English Officers of Arms and their records, and the panelled Earl Marshal's Court.

Location: On N side of Queen Victoria Street; S of St Paul's Cathedral.
Open: EARL MARSHAL'S COURT ONLY. Open all the year (except Public holidays & on State & special occasions) Mons to Fris 10-4. Group visits (up to 10) by arrangement only. RECORD ROOM open for tours (groups of up to 20) by special arrangement in advance with the Officer in Waiting.
Admission: Free (parties by negotiation).
No coaches, parking, indoor photography or dogs. Shop - books, souvenirs.

DE MORGAN FOUNDATION

Old Battersea House map K4
Telephone: 081-788 1341
(De Morgan Foundation)

A substantial part of the De Morgan Foundation collection of ceramics by William De Morgan and paintings and drawings by Evelyn De Morgan (nee Pickering), her uncle Roddam Spencer Stanhope, J. M. Strudwick and Cadogan Cowper are displayed in the ground floor rooms of elegantly restored Old Battersea House - a Wren style building. The setting is that of a privately occupied house.

Location: 30 Vicarage Crescent, Battersea.
Open: Admission by appointment only - usually Weds afternoons. All visits are guided.
Admission: £1, optional catalogue £1.50. No special reductions. Parties - max 30. (split into two groups of 15).
Refreshments: No catering at house. Many facilities in Battersea/Wandsworth.
Car parking in Vicarage Crescent. Suitable for disabled, (no special facilities for wheelchairs) front steps are the only obstacle. Adm by writing in advance to De Morgan Foundation, 21 St Margaret's Crescent, London SW15 6HL.

THE DICKENS HOUSE MUSEUM

map K4
Telephone: 071-405 2127
(The Trustees of the Dickens House)

House occupied by Dickens and his family 1837-39. Relics displayed include manuscripts, furniture, autographs, portraits, letters and first editions.

Location: 48 Doughty Street, near Grays Inn Road/Guilford Street.
Open: All the year - Mons to Sats 10-5. *Closed Suns, Bank and Christmas week Holidays.*
Admission: £2, Students £1.50, Chd £1; Families £4 (subject to alteration). Parties by appointment. Ground floor only (2 rooms) suitable for disabled - reduced adm charge.

FENTON HOUSE   🍂   The National Trust

Hampstead map K4
Telephone: 071-435 3471

Collection of porcelain, pottery and Benton Fletcher collection of early keyboard musical instruments. Late 17th century house, walled garden.

Location: On W side of Hampstead Grove.
Station(s): Hampstead (Underground 300 yards); Hampstead Heath (BR 1 m).
Open: Mar - Sat & Sun only 2-6; Apr to end Oct - Sats, Suns and Hol Mons 11-6; Mon, Tues, and Wed 1-7. Last adm ½ hour before closing time. *Closed Good Friday.*
Admission: £3, Chd half-price. No reductions for parties, which must book. No dogs. Suitable for wheelchairs on ground floor only.

FULHAM PALACE

Fulham map K4   △   ᕋ   Ⓔ
Telephone: 071-736 5821; 071-736 3233 (Museum and tours only).
(London Borough of Hammersmith and Fulham)

Former residence of the Bishops of London since the 8th century. Buildings include a Tudor courtyard and fine Georgian additions. The gardens, which became famous in the 17th century when many American species were introduced to Europe through Fulham Palace, contain specimen trees and a knot garden of herbs. Museum of Fulham Palace now open with an historical exhibition, paintings, archaeology and stained glass.

Location: In Bishop's Ave, ½ m N of Putney Bridge underground station (District Line).
Open: Grounds, Botanic Garden and herb collection open daily, daylight hours. Museum: Mar to Oct, Wed to Sun 2-5 and BH Mons; Nov to Feb 1-4.
Admission: Grounds and Botanic Garden - Free. Museum - 50p, Concessions 25p, Chd free. Free tour of 3 rooms and gardens every second Sun throughout the year at 2. Private tours at other times by arrangement (£3.50 per head, incl. tea). Function rooms available for private hire incl. receptions and filming (071-736-7181).

GUNNERSBURY PARK MUSEUM

Gunnersbury Park map K4   ᕋ
Telephone: 081-992 1612
(London Boroughs of Ealing & Hounslow)

Large mansion built c.1802 by architect owner Alexander Copland. Fine rooms by Sydney Smirke and painted ceilings by E. T. Parris for N. M. Rothschild c.1836. Now a local history museum which includes Rothschild carriages. Original Victorian kitchens open summer. Large park with other buildings of interest, and sporting facilities.

Location: Mansion at NE corner of Park; alongside North Circular (A406); N of Great West Road & M4; Kew Bridge 1¼ m; Chiswick Roundabout ½ m. Bus: E3 (daily), 7 (Suns only).
Station(s): Acton Town (Underground ¼ m).
Open: House & Museum. Mar to Oct - Mons to Fris 1-5; Sats, Suns & Bank Hols 1-6. Nov to Feb - Mons to Fris 1-4; Sats, Suns & Bank Hols 1-4. *Closed Christmas Eve, Christmas Day, Boxing Day New Years Day & Good Friday.* Gardens. Daily dawn till dusk. Special facilities for school parties by arrangement with Interpretative Officer.
Admission: Free.
Refreshments: Cafeteria in Park (daily, winter weekends according to weather). Vehicle access Popes Lane. Pedestrians - many entries to Park.

HALL PLACE

Bexley map K4
(Bexley London Borough Council)

Historic mansion (1540). Outstanding Rose, Rock, Water, Herb, Peat gardens and Floral bedding displays, Conservatories, Parkland, Topiary designed in the form of the Queen's Beasts.

Location: Near the junction of A2 and A223.
Station(s): Station: Bexley (½ m).
Open: MANSION. Mon to Sat 10-5 (or dusk if earlier); Suns 2-6 (British Summertime only). Museum & other exhibitions. PARK & GROUNDS. Daily during daylight throughout the year.
Admission: Free.
Refreshments: At cafe.

HAM HOUSE   🌲 The National Trust

Ham, Richmond map K4   ᕋ
Telephone: 081-940 1950

Outstanding Stuart house, built about 1610, redecorated and furnished in 1670s in the most up to date style of the time by the Duke and Duchess of Lauderdale; restored 17th century garden.

Location: On South bank of the river Thames, W of A307 at Petersham.
Station(s): Richmond 2 m by road. Kingston 2 m. Bus: LT 65 Ealing Broadway-Kingston. 371 Richmond-Kingston (both passing BR Richmond and Kingston), 71 also passing BR Surbiton.
Open: House: Closed throughout 1993 for major restoration. Garden: all year: daily except Mon 10.30-6 (or dusk if earlier).*Closed Christmas, New Year and Good Friday.*
Admission: Garden free.
Refreshments: Teas - limited facilities only serving tea, coffee daily except Mon, (Bank Hol Mons excepted), Apr and Oct Weekends only, May to Sept daily. 1.30-5.30. Please check in advance (tel: 081-940 1950).
Disabled visitors may park near entrance. Lavatory for disabled in garden.

HAMPTON COURT PALACE

Hampton Court map K4
Telephone: 081- 977 8441
(Historic Royal Palaces)

The splendour of Cardinal Wolsey's country house, began in 1514, surpassed that of many a royal palace, so it was not surprising that Henry VIII at first coveted and then obtained it prior to Wolsey's fall from power. Henry enlaged it; Charles I lived in it as a prisoner; Charles II repaired it; William III and Mary II re-built the state apartments to a design by Sir Christopher Wren, and Queen Victoria opened it to the public. The beauty of Wren's building is combined with some of the finest Tudor architecture in Britain. Highlights include the Tudor kitchens and the newly restored King's Apartments.

Location: N side of the Thames by Hampton Court Bridge.
Station(s): Hampton Court (30 mins from Waterloo).
Open: PALACE & MAZE: Mid Mar to Mid Oct: Mon (10.15 - 6), Tues to Sun (9.30-6). Mid Oct to Mid Mar: Mon (10.30-4.30), Tues to Sun (9.30-4.30). Last ticket sold 45 mins before closing. *Closed.* Dec 24 - 26. Banqueting House and Tudor Tennis Courts summer only. GARDENS: Open free of charge throughout the year 7 until dusk or 9 at the latest.
Refreshments: Garden Cafe, Tiltyard Restaurant and Privy Kitchen. Coffee shop. Shops in palace and gardens.

HERITAGE CENTRE

Honeywood, Carshalton map K4
Telephone: 081-773 4555
(London Borough of Sutton)

K10Honeywood is a 17th century listed building, with later additions. Discover the fascinating history of the area and its people. (The London Borough of Sutton includes Beddington, Carshalton, Cheam, Sutton and Wallington.) A permanent exhibition and a/v, plus a changing programme of exhibitions, cover many aspects of local life. Honeywood stands at the head of Carshalton's picturesque town ponds, one of the sources of the River Wandle, and at the heart of a conservation area.

Location: Honeywood Walk, Carshalton. By Carshalton Ponds, opp. the Greyhound Inn. (off A232).
Station(s): Carshalton (¼ m).
Open: Tues to Sun and Bank Hol Mon 10-5.30. *Closed* Mons.
Admission: Charge. Further details: Phone Sutton Heritage Service 081-773 4555.
Refreshments: Access to Tea Room free.
Gift shop and tea room available.

HOGARTH'S HOUSE

Chiswick map K4 △
Telephone: 081-994 6757
(London Borough of Hounslow)

The artist's country house for 15 years containing many prints and some relics associated with the artist.

Location: In Hogarth Lane, Great West Road, Chiswick W4 2QN (200 yards Chiswick House).
Station(s): Chiswick (½ m) (Southern Region); Turnham Green (1 m) (District Line).
Open: Apr to Sept - Mons to Sats 11-6; Suns 2-6. Oct to Mar-Mons to Sats 11-4; Suns 2-4. *Closed Tues, Good Friday, first 2 full weeks in Sept, last 3 weeks in Dec & New Year's Day.*

KEATS HOUSE

Wentworth Place, Keats Grove, Hampstead map K4
Telephone: 071-435 2062
(London Borough of Camden)

Keats House was built in 1815-1816 as Wentworth Place, a pair of semi-detached houses. John Keats, the poet, lived here from 1818 to 1820; here he wrote 'Ode to a Nightingale', and met Fanny Brawne, to whom he became engaged. Keats' early death in Italy prevented the marriage. Keats House was completely restored in 1974-1975. It houses letters, books and other personal relics of the poet and his fiancee.

Location: S end of Hampstead Heath nr South End Green.
Station(s): (BR Hampstead Heath). Underground: Belsize Park or Hampstead. Bus: 24, 46, 168, C12 (alight South End Green). 268 (alight Downshire Hill).
Open: All the year - Apr 1 to Oct: Mon-Fri 10-1, 2-6, Sat 10-1, 2-5; Sun and Bank Holiday 2-5. Nov to Mar: Mon-Fri 1-5, Sat 10-1, 2-5; Sun 2-5. *Closed Christmas Eve, Christmas Day, Boxing Day, New Year's Day, Good Friday, Easter Eve & May 3. Please check times on 071-435 2062.*
Admission: charged.

KENSINGTON PALACE

Kensington map K4
Telephone: 071-937 9561
Fax: 071-376 0198
(Historic Royal Palaces)

In 1698 William III and Mary II bought Nottingham House in the village of Kensington. The principal London residence of the Monarch at the time was Whitehall Palace but the riverside location aggravated William's asthma. Sir Christopher Wren was commissioned to extend and convert Nottingham House to provide both State and Private Apartments for the King and Queen. Superb craftsmen including Grinling Gibbons and Jean Tijou provided decorations and fittings. In the 1720s George I had the artist William Kent embellish the walls and ceilings with magnificent paintings. The King's Gallery ceiling tells the story of Odysseus, the King's Staircase portrays courtiers and servants of the King, and Cupola Room ceiling is a masterpiece of illusion. The State Apartments on the first floor begin with Queen Mary II's Apartments with carvings by Grinling Gibbons. The King's Apartments were built for William III and were decorated by William Kent for George I. The ground floor of Kensington Palace is the home of The Court Dress Collection which is displayed in period room settings. This display spans the reigns of 12 monarchs since 1750. The State Apartments have been open to the public since 1899 and The Court Dress Collection since 1984. Kensington Palace also has its own fine gardens.

Location: On the Western side of Kensington Gardens, off the Broad Walk.
Open: Throughout the year except Dec 24-26, New Years Day and Good Friday.
Admission: Charged. Tel: 071-937 9561
Refreshments: The Orangery is open for Morning coffee, Light lunches and Afternoon tea from Easter to end of Sept.

KENWOOD, THE IVEAGH BEQUEST   English ⌗ Heritage

Hampstead map K4
Telephone: 081-348 1286

Location: Hampstead Lane, NW3.
Station(s): Archway or Golders Green Underground (Northern Line), then Bus 210.
Open: Good Friday or Apr 1 (whichever is earlier) to Sept 30 daily 10-6. Oct 1 to Maundy Thursday or Mar 31 (whichever is earlier) daily 10-4. *Closed* Dec 24, 25.
Admission: Free.
Refreshments: At the Coach House.

KEW GARDENS

Kew map K4   ♿
Telephone: 071-940 1171
(Royal Botanic Gardens)

KEW PALACE (DUTCH HOUSE)

Kew   map K4
Telephone: 081-940 3321
(Historic Royal Palaces)

The smallest of the Royal Palaces, Kew Palace was built in 1631 as a family home, known as the Dutch House. Between 1802 - 1818 George III, Queen Charlotte and their fifteen children lived there as their country retreat.

Location: In Kew Gardens on the south bank of the Thames.
Station(s): Kew Bridge ¾ m (Underground) Kew Gardens ¼ m.
Open: Apr to Sept. Daily 11-5.30.
Refreshments: In Kew Gardens.

Adam mansion, once the seat of Lord Mansfield. The Iveagh Bequest of Old Master and British paintings, including works by Rembrandt, Vermeer, Hals, Gainsborough, Turner and Reynolds. Fine collection of neo-classical furniture.

LEIGHTON HOUSE MUSEUM

12 Holland Park Road map K4
Telephone: 071-602 3316
(Royal Borough of Kensington and Chelsea)

Leighton House Museum from the Garden

LEIGHTON HOUSE MUSEUM

The Arab Hall

Royal Borough of Kensington Libraries and Arts Service

Adjacent to Holland Park in Kensington lies the Artists' Colony, a group of remarkable Studio Houses, built by some of the leading figures of the Victorian art world. Leighton House Museum was the first of these to be built, and is today a museum of high Victorian art. The opulent fantasy of Frederic Lord Leighton, President of the Royal Academy, the house was designed by George Aitchison. Leighton lived here from 1866 until his death in 1896. His unique collection of Islamic tiles is displayed in the walls of the Arab Hall, and the Victorian interiors, restored to their original splendour, are hung with paintings by Leighton, Millais, Watts, Burne-Jones and others. Fine 'New Sculpture' is displayed in the house and garden. The study collection of Leighton drawings may be seen by appointment. Temporary exhibitions of modern and historic art throughout the year.

Location: Kensington.
Open: All year. Mon-Sat 11-5.30. **Garden:** Apr-Sept *(Closed Bank Holidays)*. Parties by arrangement with the Curator. Chd under 16 must be accompanied by an adult.

LINLEY SAMBOURNE HOUSE

map K4
Telephone: 081-994 1019
(The Victorian Society)

The home of Linley Sambourne (1844-1910), chief political cartoonist at 'Punch'. A unique survival of a late Victorian town house. The original decorations and furnishings have been preserved together with many of Sambourne's own cartoons and photographs, as well as works by other artists of the period.

Location: 18 Stafford Terrace, W8 7BH.
Station(s): (Underground) Kensington High Street.
Open: 1 Mar to 31 Oct - Weds 10-4, Suns 2-5. Parties at other times by prior arrangement. Apply to The Victorian Society, 1 Priory Gardens, London W4. Telephone: 081-994 1019.
Admission: £3.

LITTLE HOLLAND HOUSE

Carshalton map K4
(London Borough of Sutton)

The home of Frank Dickinson (1874-1961), follower of the Arts and Crafts movement: artist, designer and craftsman in wood and metal who built the house himself to his own design and in pursuance of his philosophy and theories. Features his interior design, paintings, hand-made furniture and other craft objects.

Location: 40 Beeches Avenue, Carshalton. On B278 (off A232).
Station(s): Few minutes from Carshalton Beeches BR.
Open: Mar to Oct - first Sun in the month plus Bank Hol Suns & Mons 1-6. Further information from Sutton Heritage Service on 081-773 4555.

MARBLE HILL HOUSE   English⌗Heritage

Twickenham map K4
Telephone: 081-892 5115

A complete example of an English Palladian villa. Early Georgian paintings and furniture.

Location: Richmond Road.
Station(s): St Margaret's (½ m); Twickenham (1 m); Richmond (2 m).
Open: Good Friday or Apr 1 (whichever is earlier) to Sept 30 daily 10-6. Oct 1 to Maundy Thursday or Mar 31 (whichever is earlier) daily 10-4. *Closed* Dec 24, 25.
Admission: Free.
Refreshments: In Stable Block.

MUSEUM OF GARDEN HISTORY

Lambeth map K4
Telephone: 071-261 1891
Fax: 071 071 401 8869
(The Tradescant Trust) (Registered Charity No 273436)

Welcome to the Museum of Garden History - not just a fascinating exhibition but a flourishing fully recreated 17th century garden displaying authentic shrubs and flowers of the period, seeds from which may be purchased at our Garden Shop. Lectures, courses, concerts, fairs and art shows are held regularly throughout the year and you must visit our unique Gift Shop. With a cafe open all day serving a home-made selection of delicious meals and snacks, there really is something for everyone.

Location: Lambeth Palace Road.
Station(s): Waterloo or Victoria, then 507 Red Arrow bus, alight Lambeth Palace.
Open: Mons to Frid 11-3; Suns 10.30-5. *Closed Sat. Closed from second Sun in Dec to first Sun in Mar.*
Admission: Free. Donation requested.
Refreshments: Tea, coffee, light lunches; parties catered for but prior booking essential. Literature sent on request with SAE.

THE OCTAGON, ORLEANS HOUSE GALLERY

Riverside Twickenham map K4 &
Telephone: 081-892 0221
(London Borough of Richmond upon Thames)

The magnificent Octagon built by James Gibbs in c.1720 for James Johnston, Joint Secretary of State for Scotland under William III. An outstanding example of baroque architecture. The adjacent wing has been converted into an art gallery which shows temporary exhibitions and the whole is situated in an attractive woodland garden.

Location: Access from Richmond Road (A305).
Station(s): St Margaret's (½ m); Twickenham (½ m); Richmond (underground 2 m)
Open: Tues to Sats 1-5.30 (Oct to Mar, 1-4.30); Suns 2-5.30 (Oct to Mar, 2-4.30). Easter, Spring, Summer Bank Hols 2-5.30. *Closed Christmas.* Please telephone to check opening times.
Admission: Free. Parking also free.
Disabled access to Octagon:W

THE OLD PALACE

Old Palace Road, Croydon map K4 △
Telephone: 081-680 5877
(Old Palace School (Croydon) Ltd)

Seat of Archbishops of Canterbury since 871. 15th century Banqueting Hall and Guardroom, Tudor Chapel, Norman undercroft.

Location: In central Croydon. Adjacent to Parish Church.
Station(s): East Croydon or West Croydon (few mins walk).
Open: Conducted Tours only. Doors open 2pm. Last tour commences 2.30. Tues Apr 13 to Sat Apr 17, Mon May 31 to Fri Jun 4. Mon July 12 to Sat July 17, Mon July 19 to Sat July 24.
Admission: £3.50, Chd/OAPs £2.50, this includes home made tea served in the undercroft. Car park. Souvenir shop. Parties catered for,apply Burar. Unsuitable for wheelchairs.

OLD ROYAL OBSERVATORY

Greenwich map K4
Telephone: 081-858 4422
(National Maritime Museum)

Following a major restoration and reinterpretation the Old Royal Observatory re-opens in March 1993.It includes Flamsteed House, designed by Sir Christopher Wren, the Meridian Building and the Greenwich Planetarium.

Location: In Greenwich Park, N side of Blackheath.
Station(s): Maze Hill (short walk).
Open: Mon to Sat 10-6 (10-5 in winter); Sun 12-6 (2-5 in winter). *Closed* Dec 24/25/26.
Admission: Each site: £3.75, Chd/OAP/Student £2.75. Passports to four attraction including Cutty Sark £7.45, Chd/OAP/Student £5.45, Family £14½0.
Refreshments: In Park cafeteria and museum main buildings.

OSTERLEY PARK ![National Trust oak leaf logo] The National Trust

Isleworth, Middlesex map K4 △ &
Telephone: 081-560 3918

Elizabethan mansion transformed by Robert Adam 1760-80; with Adam decorations and furniture; 140 acres of parkland.

Location: ¼ m E of Osterley Underground station (Piccadilly Line) and ½ m W of Gillette Corner, access from Thornbury Road, N side of Great West Road (A4)
Station(s): Syon Lane (1¾ m); Underground: Osterley (¾ m). Bus: LT 91 Hounslow-Wandsworth (½ m.)
Open: House: Apr to end Oct: Wed to Sat 1-5; Sun and Bank Holiday Mon 11-5. House closed Good Friday. Last admission 4.30. Park: all year 9-7.30 or sunset if earlier. Car park closed Dec 25, 26.
Admission: £3.50, Family ticket £9. Parties must book, rates on application to Administrator. Park free. Car park 250 yds £1. Guided tours may be arranged in advance with the Administrator.
Refreshments: Teas and light lunches in stables, Tues to Sun and Bank Holiday Mon, Mar to end Oct 12-5. Also open Good Friday.
Park suitable for disabled. Lavatory for disabled. Dogs in park only; On leads except in certain areas as specified at the property.

PITSHANGER MANOR MUSEUM

Mattock Lane, Ealing map K4
Telephone: 081-567 1227 or 081-579 2424 ext 42683
(London Borough of Ealing)

Set in an attractive park, Pitshanger Manor was built 1800-04 by the architect Sir John Soane (1753-1837) as his family home. The house incorporates a wing of the late 1760s by George Dance. The interiors are being restored. A Victorian room holds a changing and extensive display of Martinware pottery including a unique chimney-piece of 1891. Exhibitions and cultural events are held regularly.

Location: one third m from Ealing Broadway Tube Station (Central and District Lines). On the A3001 (Ealing Green). No parking.
Open: Tues to Sat 10-5. *Closed Sun & Mon.* (but open Sun afternoons in July and Aug). *Also closed Christmas, Easter and New Year. All rooms are open to the public after 1pm. Please enquire in advance as to which rooms are open in the mornings.*
Admission: Free. Parties by arrangement in advance.
Refreshments: Tea and coffee vending machine.
Limited disabled access - further details available on request.

QUEEN CHARLOTTE'S COTTAGE

Kew map K4
Telephone: 081-940 3321
(Historic Royal Palaces)

Queen Charlotte's Cottage, in the south of Kew Gardens, was used by the family of George III for picnics, and the upper room has floral decorations painted by one of the young princesses.

Location: In Kew Gardens on the south bank of the Thames.
Station(s): Kew Bridge ¾ m. (Undrground): Kew Gardens ¼ m.
Open: Apr to Sept, weekends and Bank Hols 11-5.30.
Refreshments: In Kew Gardens.

THE QUEEN'S HOUSE

Greenwich map K4
Telephone: 081-858 4422
(National Maritime Museum)

THE QUEENS HOUSE

GREENWICH
A Royal Palace by the Thames

Visit the House of Delights designed by Inigo Jones for the wife of Charles I. Admire the sumptuous Royal Apartments that recreate the original seventeenth century splendour, and learn the fascinating history of the House in the special display in the vaulted brick basement.

A combined ticket allows you to visit the Old Royal Observatory, National Maritime Museum and *Cutty Sark* which are nearby

ADMISSION – SEE EDITORIAL REFERENCE

Royal Palace designed by Inigo Jones for Anne of Denmark, wife of James I, and Henrietta Maria, wife of Charles I. Now restored to its former 17th century glory, after a £5M refurbishment. Highlights include the sumptuous Royal Apartments and the Great Hall, a perfect 40ft cube. The vaulted brick basement houses a display on the history of the house, and the treasury, showing the NMM's richest trophies, swords and ornamental silver.
Location: Greenwich, London.
Station(s): Maze Hill (BR); Island Gardens (Docklands Light Railway); River Buses.
Open: Mon to Sats 10-6 (10-5 in winter), Suns 12-6 (2-5 in winter). *Closed* Christmas Eve, Christmas Day, Boxing Day.
Admission: Each site: £3.75, Chd/OAP/Student £2.75. Passport to all sites including Cutty Sark £7.45, Chd/OAP/Student £5.45. Family £14½0.
Refreshments: Licensed restaurant.
Wheelchair access to ground floor and basement. Wheelchairs available.

RANGER'S HOUSE   English Heritage

Blackheath map K4 Ⓢ
Telephone: 081-853 0035

A Gallery of English Portraits in the 4th Earl of Chesterfield's house, from the Elizabethan to the Georgian period. Dolmetsch Collection of musical instruments in period rooms on restored first floor.

Location: Chesterfield Walk, SE10.
Station(s): Greenwich or Blackheath (15 mins walk).
Open: Good Friday or Apr 1 (whichever is earlier) to Sept 30 daily 10-6. Oct 1 to Maundy Thursday or Mar 31 (whichever is earlier) daily 10-4. *Closed* Dec 24, 25.
Admission: £2. Concessions £1.50, Chd £1.

ROYAL INSTITUTE OF BRITISH ARCHITECTS: DRAWINGS COLLECTION AND HEINZ GALLERY

W1 map K4
Telephone: 071-580 5533
(Royal Institute of British Architects)

Changing architectural exhibitions throughout most of the year.

Location: 21 Portman Square W1H 9HF.
Open: Weekdays 11-5, Sats 10-1. Study room open 10-1pm weekdays, by appointment only for serious enquiries.
Admission: Free.
Unsuitable for disabled persons. No car parking.

RSA (The Royal Society for the Encouragement of Arts, Manufactures and Commerce)

8 John Adam Street map K4
Telephone: 071-930 5115

Founded in 1754, the RSA moved to its bespoke house, designed and built by Robert Adam, in 1774. The most interesting features of the Society's premises are its Great Room, a lecture hall, capacity 200, with murals by James Barry and the recently restored vaults.

Location: 8 John Adam Street, London WC2N 6EZ.
Open: Mon to Fri 10-1. Visitors who wish to see any of the Society's rooms are requested to telephone in advance in order to avoid disappointment if the rooms are in use and therefore inaccessible.
Admission: Free.

ST. JOHN'S GATE

Clerkenwell map K4 △ Ⓔ
Telephone: 071-253 6644, Ext 35
(The Order of St John)

Headquarters of the Order in England, the 16th century gatehouse contains the most comprehensive collection of items relating to the Order of St John outside Malta. Together with the nearby Priory Church and 12th century Crypt it now forms the headquarters of the modern Order of St. John, whose charitable foundations include St. John Ambulance and the Ophthalmic Hospital in Jerusalem. The collection includes Maltese silver, Italian furniture, paintings, coins and pharmacy jars.

Location: In St John's Lane, EC1M 4DA.
Station(s): (Underground) Farringdon, Barbican.
Open: Mon to Fr 10-5, Sats 10-4. Tours of the building, including the Grand Priory Church and Norman crypt on Tues, Fri and Sat 11 & 2.30.

SIR JOHN SOANE'S MUSEUM

13 Lincoln's Inn Fields   map K4
Telephone: 071-405 2107; Information line 071-430 0175

Built by Sir John Soane, RA, in 1812-13 as his private residence. Contains his collection of antiquities and works of art.

Open: Tues to Sat 10-5pm(lecture tours Sat 2.30pm, maximum 22 people, no groups): Groups welcome at other times, but must book in advance. Late evening opening on the first Tues of each month, 6-9pm. Also library and architectural drawings collection: access by appointment. *Closed* Bank Holidays.

SOUTHSIDE HOUSE

Wimbledon Common   map K4   △
Telephone: 081-947 2491 or 081-946 7643
(The Pennington-Mellor-Munthe Charity Trust

Built by Robert Pennington as a safe retreat for his family after his little son died in the London Plague in 1665. Still lived in by his descendants today. Much original furnishing remains. Family portraits by Van Dyke & Hogarth. Personal possessions of Ann Boleyn - whose sister married into this family - are shown. Also a bedroom prepared for the Prince of Wales in 1750 and gifts to John Pennington - the family 'Scarlet Pimpernel' - by those he helped to escape from the guillotine - including a pearl necklace which fell from Marie Antoinette when her head was cut off. Also the Dining Room where Admiral Lord Nelson dined with Sir William and Lady Hamilton and the Music Room where she performed her 'attitudes'. In 1907 the heiress of this house, Hilda Pennington Mellor married

Axel Munthe the Swedish Doctor and Philanthropist who wrote part of his 'Story of San Michele' here.

Location: On S side of Wimbledon Common (B281), opposite The Crooked Billet Inn. *Station(s): Wimbledon (British Rail & Underground) 1 m. Buses: No 93, alight Rose & Crown Inn, Wimbledon High Street - six minutes walk along Southside of Common to Crooked Billet Inn and Southside House.*
Open: From Oct 1 until May 31. Guided tours only on Tues, Thurs, Sat & Bank Holiday Mons (*Closed Christmas*) on the hour from 2-5 (last admission), lasting approximately 1 hr. Other times by special agreement with Administrator. Organised school groups accompanied by responsible teachers free by appointment in writing.
Admission: £5, (Chd accompanied by adult £2).

SPENCER HOUSE

27 St.James's Place   map K4
Telephone: 071-409 0526

Spencer House, built 1756-66 for the first Earl Spencer, an ancestor of HRH The Princess of Wales, is London's finest surviving 18th c townhouse. This magnificent private palace, overlooking Green Park, has regained the full splendour of its 18th c appearance after a painstaking five-year restoration. Nine state rooms are open to the public for viewing on Sundays and are available for private and corporate entertaining during the rest of the week.

Location: 27 St.James's Place, London SW1A 1NR
Station(s): Green Park.
Open: Every Sunday (except during Jan and Aug) from 11.30-4.45. Tours last approx. 1 hr. Tickets available at door from 10.30 on day. However, advance reservation recommended for both individuals and groups (Tel 071-499 8620) - Tues to Fri 10-1.
Admission: £5, Concessions £4 (OAPs/Students/NT Members/Friends of the V&A-all with cards;Chd 10-16), under 10 not admitted.*Prices valid until end March 1993.*
Accessible for wheelchair users.

❦ THE SIGN OF A GREAT DAY OUT

SYON HOUSE

Brentford map K4 △
Telephone: 081-560 0881/3
(His Grace the Duke of Northumberland)

Noted for its magnificent Adam interior and furnishings, famous picture collection, and historical associations dating back to 1415, 'Capability' Brown landscape.

Location: On N bank of Thames between Brentford & Isleworth.
Station(s): Gunnersbury (District line), Kew Bridge (BR). Buses 237, 267.
Open: Apr 1 to Sept 29. Wed to Suns incl. and Bank Hol Mons. 11-5pm (last adm 4.15pm) Also Suns in Oct 11-5pm.
Admission: Charges not available at time of going to press.

SYON PARK GARDENS

Brentford map K4
Telephone: 081-560 0881/3
(His Grace the Duke of Northumberland)

Includes the Great Conservatory by Dr Fowler. Within the Estate is the London Butterfly House and the British Heritage Motor Museum (telephone details below); also the Syon Art Centre.

Location: On N bank of Thames between Brentford & Isleworth.
Station(s): Waterloo to Kew Bridge, nearest tube Gunnersbury. Buses: 267 or 237 to Brentlea.
Open: All the year - Mar to Oct - Daily 10-6. Oct to Feb - Daily 10-dusk; Last adm 1 hour before closing. *Closed Christmas Day & Boxing Day.* Adm charges not available at time of going to press. Free car park. Telephone 081-560 0881/3. London Butterfly House - opening times & adm charges: Telephone 081-560 7272. British Heritage Motor Museum - opening times & adm charges: Telephone 081-560 1378.
Admission: For admission charges telephone 081-560 1378
Refreshments: Cafeteria and Restaurant. Telephone 081-568 0778/9. Enquiries to Administrator, Syon Park.

Sutton Heritage Service

A unique collection of Historic Houses.

HERITAGE CENTRE
HONEYWOOD, CARSHALTON

Opened in 1990, a 17th century listed building, with later additions. Permanent displays outline the history of the Borough and its people plus a changing programme of exhibitions on varied subjects. Features include magnificent Edwardian billiard room.
Tea room and gift shop

WHITEHALL
CHEAM, SURREY

This unique timber-framed, continuous jettied house dates back to about 1500. Originally built as a farm house. Whitehall with its many additions has associations with Henry VIII's Nonsuch Palace, the English Civil War and Cheam School. Whitehall features revealed sections of original fabric and displays including Medieval Cheam Pottery, Nonsuch Palace, timber-framed buildings and Cheam School.
Tea room and gift shop.

CAREW MANOR & DOVECOTE
CHURCH ROAD, BEDDINGTON

This building contains a late-medieval Great Hall, with an arch-braced hammer-beam roof, listed Grade 1. The Hall is open every Sunday from Easter until 1 November, together with the recently-restored early 18th century Dovecote, with its 1,288 nesting boxes and potence (circular ladder). Guided tours available which include the cellars of the house with their medieval, Tudor, and later features and the 15th century Carew Chapel in the nearby St Mary's Church.
A Heritage Trail around Beddington Park features the history, historic buildings, garden features, and wildlife of this important conservation area. Guide book, trail leaflet, books and souvenirs available.

CARSHALTON HOUSE
ST. PHILOMENA'S SCHOOL, CARSHALTON

Built about 1707 around the core of an older house, with grounds laid out originally by Charles Bridgeman, Carshalton House contains principal rooms with 18th century decoration. Garden buildings include the unique Water Tower. Tours of the grounds and a programme of short talks are included in entrance fee. Refreshments, publications and souvenirs available. **Open Days for 1993: Easter Bank Holiday Monday April 12; Sunday September 12.**
Carshalton House is close to the Heritage Centre, in the Carshalton conservation area.

LITTLE HOLLAND HOUSE
CARSHALTON BEECHES

The Living Room and part of the Sitting Room

The home of Frank Dickinson (1874-1961), follower of the Arts and Crafts movement: artist designer and craftsman in wood and metal who built the house himself to his own design and in pursuance of his philosophy and theories. Features his interior design, painting, hand-made furniture and other craft objects.
Guide Book and other publications available.

For information, call 081-773 4555

Sutton
Leisure Services

HM TOWER OF LONDON

Tower Hill map K4
Telephone: 071-709 0765
(Historic Royal Palaces)

Her Majesty's Royal Palace and Fortress begun by William the Conqueror in 1078, spans over 900 years of history. Home of the Crown Jewels, Yeoman Warders - 'Beefeaters', the Royal Armouries' national collection of arms and armour and the legendary Ravens.

Open: Mar to Oct, Mon - Sat 9.30-6. Sun 10-6. Nov to Feb, Mon - Sat only 9.30-5. Closed Sunday. Last adm 1 hour before closing. *Closed Jan 1, Good Friday, 24-26 Dec. (Jewel House closed Jan each year).*
Admission: for full details please telephone the above number.

THE TRAVELLERS' CLUB

Pall Mall map K4
Telephone: 071-930 8688 *(by prior appointment)*

Built in 1829-33 by Sir Charles Barry. (Roof restored in 1986).
Location: 106 Pall Mall.
Station(s): Piccadilly Circus Underground.
Open: By prior appointment Mon to Fri only from 10-12 and 3-5.30. Weekends by negotiation. *Closed Bank Hols, Aug and Christmas.*
Admission: £5.

WHITEHALL

1 Malden Road, Cheam map K4
Telephone: 081-643 1236
(London Borough of Sutton)

A unique timber-framed house built c 1500. A feature is the revealed sections of original fabric. Displays include medieval Cheam pottery; Nonsuch Palace; timber-framed buildings and Cheam School. Changing exhibitions throughout the year.

Location: On A2043 just N of junction with A232.
Station(s): Cheam (1/4 m).
Open: Apr to Sept - Tues to Fris, Sun 2-5.30. Sat 10-5.30. Oct to Mar - Wed, Thurs, Sun 2-5.30. Sat 10-5.30. Also open Bank Holiday Mons 2-5.30. *Closed Dec 24 to Jan 2 incl.* Further information from Sutton Heritage Service on 081-773 4555. Party bookings, guided tour facilities.
Admission: Charge.
Refreshments: Tea room available.
Gift Shop.

GREATER MANCHESTER

DUNHAM MASSEY

See under Cheshire.

HALL I' TH' WOOD

Bolton map G9
Telephone: (0204) 301159
(Bolton Metropolitan Borough)

Dating from latter half of the 15th century and furnished throughout in the appropriate period. The Hall, built in the post and plaster style, dates from 1483, a further extension was added in 1591, the last addition being made in 1648. Home of Samuel Crompton in 1779 when he invented the Spinning Mule. House contains Crompton relics.

Location: In Green Way, off Crompton Way; 2 m NE of town centre off A58 (Crompton Way); signposted. Hall i' th' Wood (1/2 m).
Station(s): Bolton (2 1/2 m); Bromley Cross (1 1/4 m). Hall i' th' Wood (1/2 m).
Open: Apr to Sept: Tues to Sat 11-5; Sun 2-5. *Closed* Mons except Bank Holidays. Oct to Mar: *Closed* to general public. Open to pre-booked parties and evening party tours.

SMITHILLS HALL

Bolton map G8
Telephone: (0204) 841265
(Bolton Metropolitan Borough)

One of the oldest manor houses in Lancashire, a house has stood on this site since the 14th century. The oldest part of Smithills, the Great Hall, has an open timber roof. Smithills has grown piece by piece over the centuries and such irregularly planned buildings, with the cluster of gables at the west end, gives the hall its present day picturesque effect. Furnished in the styles of the 16th and 17th centuries. With-drawing room contains linenfold panelling. Grounds contain a nature trail and trailside museum which is open to the public between Easter and October.

Location: Off Smithills Dean Road; 1 1/2 m NW of town centre off A58 (Moss Bank Way); signposted.
Station(s): Bolton.
Open: Apr to Sept: Tues to Sat 11-5, Sun 2-5. *Closed* Mons except Bank Holidays. Oct to Mar: *Closed* to general public. Open to pre-booked educational parties and to evening party tours.

MERSEYSIDE

BLUECOAT CHAMBERS

Liverpool map F8
Telephone: 051-709 5297
(Bluecoat Arts Centre)

CROXTETH HALL & COUNTRY PARK

Liverpool map F8   ♿   Ⓢ
Telephone: 051-228 5311

500 acre Country Park centred on the ancestral home of the Molyneux family, Earls of Sefton. Hall rooms with character figures on the theme of an Edwardian houseparty. Victorian Home Farm and Walled Garden both with quality interpretive displays; superb collection of farm animals (Approved Rare Breeds Centre). Miniature Railway. Special events and attractions most weekends. Picnic areas and adventure playground.

Location: 5 m NE of Liverpool City Centre; Signposted from A580 & A5088 (ring road).
Open: Parkland open daily throughout the year, adm free. Hall, Farm & Garden open 11-5 daily in main season, please telephone to check exact dates.
Admission: (Inclusive) Hall, Farm and Gardens £2, Chd/OAPs £1. (Provisional prices). Reduced rates for parties. Free car parking.
Refreshments: 'The Old Riding School' cafe during season.
Wheelchair access to Farm, Garden and Cafe but to ground floor only in Hall.

MEOLS HALL

Southport map F9
(R. F. Hesketh, Esq.)

A 17th century house, with subsequent additions, containing an interesting collection of pictures, furniture, china etc.

Location: 1 m N of Southport; 16 m SW of Preston; 20 m N of Liverpool; near A565 & A570.
Open: Mid July to mid Aug 2-5.
Admission: £2, Chd 75p. Chd under 10 accompanied by adult free.

SPEKE HALL   The National Trust

Liverpool map F8
Telephone: 051-427 7231

Richly half-timbered Elizabethan house around a courtyard; features include Great Hall, Priest holes; Jacobean plasterwork and Victorian restoration and decoration. Attractive gardens and extensive woodlands.

Location: On N bank of Mersey 8 m from City centre. 1 m off A561 on W side of Liverpool Airport. Follow airport signs from M62; M56 junction 12.
Station(s): Garston (2 m); Hunts Cross (2 m).
Open: Apr 1 to Oct 31 - daily except Mons, but open Bank Holiday Mons, 1-5.30. *(Closed Good Fri).* Nov 6 to Dec 12 - Sats & Suns 1-4.30. Garden; Open every day except Mon 12-5.30. (Please note garden is closed Good Fri, Dec 24, 25, 26, 31 and Jan 1 1994.
Admission: £3.20. Family ticket £8. Garden only 70p. Discount for parties. Guided tours and school visits by prior arrangement with Administrator.
Refreshments: Tea room and shop.

NORFOLK

BEESTON HALL 🏛

Beeston St Lawrence map M7
Telephone: (0692) 630771
(Sir Ronald & Lady Preston)

18th century 'Gothick' country house with Georgian interiors in picturesque setting.

Location: 2½ m NE of Wroxham on S side of A1151; 11 m NE of Norwich.
Station(s): Wroxham (2¾ m). Also accessible from Broads at Neatishead.
Open: Principal Rooms, Gardens, Wine Cellars and Woodland Walks. Apr 11 to Sept 19 - Fris & Suns, also Bank Hols 2-5.30, Aug also Weds.
Admission: £2.50, Chd (Accompanied by adult) £1. Garden only 60p. Parties by arrangement.
Refreshments: Teas and light refreshments in the Orangery.

BERNEY ARMS WINDMILL   English ♯ Heritage

map M7   ♿
Telephone: (0493) 700605

At one time the Norfolk and Suffolk marshes were drained entirely by wind-power, a function carried out by this 'tower' mill after it was no longer used for its original purpose of grinding cement clinker. The mill has seven floors, making it the highest marsh-mill in the area and a landmark for miles around.

Location: North bank of River Yare, 3½ m (5.6 km) north east of Reedham. Accessible only by boat, or ½ m walk.
Open: Good Friday or Apr 1 (whichever is earlier) to Sept 30: Open Daily 10-6.
Admission: 80p, concessions 60p, Chd 40p.

BLICKLING HALL   🍂   The National Trust

Aylsham   map M7   ♿
Telephone: (0263) 733084

Great Jacobean house, altered 1765-70. State rooms include Peter the Great Room with fine Russian tapestry, Long Gallery with exceptional ceiling and State bedroom. The Formal Garden design dates from 1729. Temple and Orangery, park and lake.

Location: 1½ m NW of Aylsham on N side of B1354 (which is 15 m N of Norwich on A140).
Open: Hall: Mar 27 to Oct 31 (*Closed* Good Friday): Tues, Wed, Fri, Sat, Sun and Bank Hol Mon 1-5. Garden: as Hall but open 12 noon.
Admission: House and Garden: £4.90, Chd (with adult) £2.40. Pre-booked parties £3.90. Garden only: £2.50, Chd £1.20. Free car park.
Refreshments: Teas, coffee and lunches 11-5. (*Parties by arrangement;* table license). Picnic area in walled orchard. Restaurant, shop and garden open daily in July & Aug. Plant centre in orchard open all year. Buckinghamshire Arms Inn open all year. NB Free access to the South Front, shop and restaurant when Hall is open.
Shop. Dogs in park and picnic area only, on leads. Wheelchair access - 2 provided. Lift to first floor.

BRESSINGHAM GARDENS

Bressingham, Diss   map L6
Telephone: (037988) 464/8133

Enjoy the six acres of Alan Blooms Dell Garden, one of the most respected gardens in the country. Trees, shrubs and thousands of hardy perennials and alpines, it is a mecca for gardeners from all over the world. One part of a totally enjoyable day, which included steam museum, train rides and plant centre.

Location: A1066 3 m from Diss on Thetford Road.
Open: All year, seven days a week 10-5.30.

CASTLE ACRE PRIORY

map L7
Telephone: (07605) 394

William de Warenne and his wife were so impressed with the great Abbey of Cluny in Burgundy that they determined to found the Order in England. This they did - at Lewes. The priory at Castle Acre was probably established by their son and it survived, not without friction, until 1537 when it was surrendered to Henry VIII. The gaunt ruins span seven centuries and include a 16th century gatehouse, a church of mixed origins and a prior's lodging almost fit to be lived in. The castle, at the other end of the village started as an undefended Norman manor house but later evolved into a conventional keep. Ruins of this keep and outer earthworks can be seen.

Location: 3½ m (5.6 km) north of Swaffham.
Open: Good Friday or Apr 1 (whichever is earlier) to Sept 30: Open Daily 10-6. Oct 1 to Maundy Thursday or Mar 31 (whichever is earlier): Open Tues to Sun 10-4. *Closed* Dec 24-26, Jan 1.
Admission: £2, concessions £1.50, Chd £1.

CASTLE RISING CASTLE

map K7
Telephone: (055387) 330

The long and distinguished history of Castle Rising began in 1138. It was then that William de Albini started to build a grand castle to mark the upturn in his fortunes which followed his marriage to Henry I's widow. Later owners were no less notable and included Isabella 'The She-Wolf of France', wife of Edward II, the Black Prince, Prince Hal and the Howard Dukes of Norfolk. The 12th century keep, reached through a handsome decorated doorway is the finest part of the castle. Outside, there is a gatehouse of the same date and the remains of a church.

Location: 4 m (6.4 km) north of King's Lynn.
Open: Good Friday or Apr 1 (whichever is earlier) to Sept 30: Open Daily 10-6. Oct 1 to Maundy Thursday or Mar 31 (whichever is earlier): Open Tues to Sun 10-4. *Closed* Dec 24-26, Jan 1.
Admission: £1.20, Concessions 90p, Chd 60p.

THE FAIRHAVEN GARDEN TRUST

Nr Norwich   map M7
Telephone: (060549) 449
(G. E. Debbage)

Unique woodland and water gardens with private broad. Primroses and bluebells in profusion. Many rare and unusual plants. Wild flowers and cultivated varieties grow happily together. Spectacular display of candelabra primulas in May and June and azaleas and rhododendrons. Giganteum lilies end of June, early July. 900 year old oak. Lots to interest naturalists and horticulturists in a lovely peaceful part of the Norfolk Broads.

Location: 9 m NE of Norwich on the B1140.
Open: 11am-6pm Except Sats 2-6pm. Apr 11 to May 3, Suns and Bank Hols. May 5 to Sept 26, Wed to Sun and Bank Hols. EASTER WEEK FOR PRIMROSES - Good Friday to Apr 18. CANDELABRA PRIMULA WEEKEND - May 29, 30, & 31. WALKS WITH THE WARDEN at 2.30 each Sun in Jul (up to 50 people). £4, OAPs £3.50 (Price includes gardens, bird sanctuary, tea and cream scone). To book Tel; (060549) 449. AUTUMN COLOURS Sun Oct 31, 10am to Dusk.
Admission: £2, OAPs £1.50, Chd £1, Bird Sanctuary £1, Season £7, Family Season £20.
Refreshments: Small tea room on car park. Cream teas, all cakes home-made. (South Walsham Hall Hotel & Country Club nearby).
Car parking for 450 on grass. Mainly suitable for disabled persons. Plants for sale grown in gardens.

FELBRIGG HALL   The National Trust

nr Cromer   map M7   ♿
Telephone: (0263) 837444 (Restaurant: (0263) 838237

17th century country house with Georgian interiors set in a fine wooded park. Important 18th century Library and Orangery, Traditional walled garden. Woodland and Lakeside walks.

Location: 2 m SW of Cromer on S side of A148.
Station(s): Cromer (2¼ m).
Open: Hall & Gardens - Mar 27 to Oct 31: Mons, Weds, Thurs, Sats and Suns, 1-5. Bank Hol Suns and Mons 11-5. Gardens 11-5.30.
Admission: £4.30, Chd (with adult) £2.15. Gardens only: £1.70. Pre-booked parties of 15 or more £3.30.
Refreshments: 11-5.15, coffee, lunches, teas in the Park restaurant. Note: Free access to restaurant, shop, park and picnic area.
Shop. No dogs. Wheelchair access, 2 provided. Picnic area.

GRIME'S GRAVES   English ♯ Heritage

map L6
Telephone: (0842) 810656

This is an intricate network of pits and shafts sunk by our neolithic ancestors some 4000 years ago. The purpose of all this industriousness was to find flints for the world's first farmers - flints to make axes to fell trees so that the cleared ground could be sown with seed. Between 700 and 800 pits were dug, some of them to a depth of 30 or 40ft (9-12m). Two of the 16 excavated shafts have been left open; they give an idea of those early miners' working conditions.

Location: 2¾ m (4.4 km) north east of Brandon.
Open: Good Friday or Apr 1 (whichever is earlier) to Sept 30: Open Daily 10-6. Oct 1 to Maundy Thursday or Mar 31 (whichever is earlier): Open Tues to Sun 10-4. *Closed* Dec 24-26, Jan 1.
Admission: £1.20, Concessions 90p, Chd 60p.

HOLKHAM HALL 🏛

Wells   map L7
Telephone: (0328) 710227

Fine Palladian mansion. Pictures, Tapestries, Statuary, Furnishings. Bygones Museum.

Location: 2m W of Wells; S of the Wells/Hunstanton Road (A149).
Open: Daily (except Frid/Sats) from May 30 to Sept 30: 1.30-5, also Easter, May, Spring and Summer Bank Holiday: Suns and Mons 11.30-5 (last adm 4.40).
Admission: £2.70, Chd (5-15) £1.20. Bygones and Park: £2.70, Chd £1.20. All inclusive: £4.70, Chd £2. 10% reduction on pre-paid parties of 20 or more.
Refreshments: Served in tea rooms.

🌳 THE SIGN OF A GREAT DAY OUT

HOUGHTON HALL

Kings Lynn map L7 &
Telephone: (0485) 528569
(The Marquess of Cholmondeley)

The Home of the Marquess of Cholmondeley, Houghton Hall was built in the 18th century for Sir Robert Walpole by Colen Campbell and Thomas Ripley, with interior decoration by William Kent, and is regarded as one of the finest examples of Palladian architecture in England. Houghton was later inherited by the 1st Marquess of Cholmondeley through his grandmother, Sir Robert's daughter. Situated in beautiful parkland, the house contains magnificent furniture, pictures and china. Pleasure grounds. Shetland ponies, heavy horses on show in the stables. A private collection of 20,000 model soldiers and militaria.

Location: 13 m E of King's Lynn; 10 m W of Fakenham off A148.
Open: Easter Sun (Apr 19) to Sept 27 - Suns, Thurs & Bank Hols. OPENING TIMES TO BE ANNOUNCED. Gates, Picnic Area. Children's Playground, stables and Model Soldier & Militaria Collection opens Suns, Thurs & Bank Hols TIMES TO BE ANNOUNCED.
Admission: £4, OAPs £3.50, Chd £2 (under 5 free). No additional charges except for special events which will be advertised. Reduction of 10% for pre-booked parties of 20 or more.
Refreshments: Tea room.
Car park near House, toilets and lift to State floor for the disabled. Free parking for coaches and cars.

MANNINGTON GARDENS AND COUNTRYSIDE

Saxthorpe, Norfolk map L7
Telephone: (026 387) 4175
(Lord and Lady Walpole)

15th century moated house and Saxon church ruin set in attractive gardens. Outstanding rose gardens. Extensive walks and trails around the estate.

Location: 2 m N of Saxthorpe, nr B1149; 18 m NW of Norwich. 9 m from coast.
Open: GARDEN. Apr to Oct: Suns 12-5. Also June to Aug: Weds, Thurs and Fris 11-5.
Admission: £2, chd (accompanied children under 16) free, OAPs/Students £1.50. House open by prior appointment only.
Refreshments: Coffee, salad lunches and home-made teas.

NORWICH CASTLE

Norwich map M7 &
Telephone: (0603) 222222
(Norwich City Council/Norfolk Museums Service)

OXBURGH HALL   The National Trust

Swaffham map L7 &
Telephone: (036 621) 258

Late 15th century moated house. Outstanding gatehouse tower. Needlework by Mary Queen of Scots. Unique French parterre laid out circa 1845. Woodland walk and traditional herbaceous garden. Chapel with fine altar piece.

Location: 7 m SW of Swaffham on S side of Stoke Ferry Road.
Open: House: Mar 27 to Oct 31 - Sat to Wed, 1.30-5.30. Garden: 12-5.30. Bank Hol Mons 11-5.30.
Admission: £3.60, Chd (with adult) £1.80. Pre-booked parties of 15 or more £2.60.
Refreshments: In Old Kitchen. Light lunches and teas 12-5.30.
Shop. No dogs. Wheelchair access, 2 provided.

RAINTHORPE HALL & GARDENS

Flordon, nr Norwich map M6 △ ⌖
(George Hastings, Esq.)

Rebuilt in 1503 after a fire, and modernised during the reign of Elizabeth, Rainthorpe Hall is one of the very few half-timbered houses of its period in East Anglia. Its chimney breasts are placed in the French manner, at either end of the Great Hall - a pattern rare in this country. It is set in large gardens, with a conservation lake. Rainthorpe Hall has appeared in several Television productions. In both 1982 and 1987 it was used for 'Tales of the Unexpected'. It served as the principal location for the six hour murder mystery 'Cover Her Face', which was shown in England in 1985 and in the United States in 1987. Its drive and gates were used in 'The Black Tower' in 1986, and it was the scene of the Hunt Ball in 'Menace Unseen', a three-hour drama shown in 1988. In 1989 and 1991, ITV used it for the live show 'Ghost Train', and the BBC for Omnibus.

Location: 1 m SSW of Newton Flotman (A140) on Flordon Road, 8 m S of Norwich.
Open: GARDENS. Easter to Oct: Weds, Sats, Suns & Bank Hol Mons 10-5. House open by appointment.
Admission: £1.50, Chd/OAPs 75p. Car park free.
Refreshments: Home-made teas.
Willimott's Plant Sales. Gardens only suitable for disabled.

RAVENINGHAM HALL GARDENS

Norwich map M6
Telephone: (050846) 222
(Sir Nicholas Bacon Bt.)

An extensive garden laid out at the turn of the century surrounding original Georgian house. In the last thirty years a large number of new areas have been designed and brought into cultivation, many in the traditional style, with plantings of unusual shrubs, herbaceous plants and roses. An Arboretum planted in March 1990 contains many unusual trees. In recent years an important and extensive Nursery and Plant Centre has developed, to include many rare and exotic plants that can be seen in the garden. (Catalogue 3 x first class stamps). Also Victorian Conservatory and walled vegetable garden. The house is not open to the public.

Location: 4 m from Beccles off the B1136 between Beccles and Loddon.
Open: Plant Centre: Mon to Fri 9-4 all year; Sats 9-4 and Suns 2-5. mid-Mar to mid-Sept. Garden: Suns and Bank Hol Mons 2-5, Weds 1-4, Mar 23 to Sept 12.
Admission: £2, Chd free, in aid of local charities. Free car park.
Refreshments: Home-made teas served on Sundays and Bank Hol Mons.

SANDRINGHAM HOUSE & GROUNDS

Sandringham map L7
Telephone: (0553) 772675
(Her Majesty The Queen)

A fine country residence, the private home of four generations of monarchs. All the principal rooms normally occupied by the Royal Family when in residence are open to the public during the times shown below. These include the Saloon, the Small Drawing Room (used by the Lady-in-Waiting in attendance), the Main Drawing Room, the Dining Room, the Lobby, the Ballroom Corridor and the Ballroom. Superb grounds laid out by W.B. Thomas in 1862, with two lakes and extensive woodland walks. The Grounds are particularly colourful during the rhododendron season (mid-May - end-June). The Museum contains exhibits of gifts presented to the Royal Family, part of the Royal Doll Collection, Big Game trophies, commemorative china and glass relating to royal events, local archaeological finds and vehicles used by members of the Royal Family. Outside the House and Grounds is Sandringham Country Park, a free attraction open all year round.

Location: 8 m NE of King's Lynn (off A149).
Open: House, Grounds and Museum open daily from Apr 11 to Oct 3 incl. (except the period stated below when H.M. The Queen or any member of the Royal Family is in residence). House *closed* from July 19 to Aug 7 inclusive. Grounds *closed* from July 23 to Aug 4 inclusive.
Admission: House, Grounds and Museum £3, OAPs £2, Chd £1.50. Grounds and Museum £2, OAPs £1.50, Chd £1. Free car and coach parks.
Refreshments: Available in Country Park in restaurant (capacity 60 people) serving teas and lunches. Self-service cafeteria also available.

TRINITY HOSPITAL

Castle Rising map L7
(Trustees)

Nine 17th century brick and tile Almhouses with court, chapel and treasury.

Location: 4 m NE of King's Lynn on A149.
Open: All the year - Tues, Thurs & Sats. Summer: 10-12, 2-6. Winter: 10-12, 2-4.
Admission: Free.

WOLTERTON PARK

Erpingham map M7
Telephone: (026 387) 4175
(Lord and Lady Walpole)

Extensive historic park with lake, Hawk and Owl Trust display.

Location: Nr Erpingham, signposted from A140 Norwich to Cromer road.
Open: Park open all year, daily 9-5 or dusk if earlier.
Admission: £2 per car. See local press for details of special events, and garden and Hall tours.

NORTHAMPTONSHIRE

AYNHOE PARK

Aynho map H5
(Country Houses Association)

17th century mansion. Alteration by Soane.

Location: 6 m SE of Banbury on A41.
Open: May to Sept - Weds & Thurs 2-5. Last entry 4.30.
Admission: £1.50, Chd 50p. Free car park.
No dogs admitted.

Lancelot 'Capability' Brown

Born 1716 in Northumberland, Capability Brown began work at the age of 16 in the vegetable gardens of Sir William and Lady Loraine at Kirharle Tower. He left Northumberland in 1739, and records show that he worked at Stowe until 1749. It was at Stowe that Brown began to study architecture, and to submit his own plans. It was also at Stowe that he devised a new method of moving and replanting mature trees.

Brown married Bridget Wayet in 1744 and began work on the estate at Warwick Castle in 1749. He was appointed Master Gardener at Hampton Court in 1764, and planted the Great Vine at Hampton Court in 1768. Blenheim Palace designs are considered amongst Brown's finest work, and the technical achievements were outstanding even for the present day.

Capability Brown died in February 1783 of a massive heart attack. A monument beside the lake at Croome Court was erected which reads "To the memory of Lancelot Brown, who by the powers of his inimitable and creative genius formed this garden scene out of a morass". There is also a portrait of Brown at Burghley.

Capability Brown was involved in the design of grounds at the following properties included in Historic Houses Castles and Gardens:

Luton Hoo	*Corsham Court*	*Stowe*	*Burton Constable*
Bowood	*Fawley Court*	*Weston Park*	*Sledmere House*
Burghley House	*Longleat*	*Wotton House*	*Syon House*
Chilham Castle (reputed)	*Moccas Court*	*Wrest Park*	*Warwick Castle.*
Claremont	*Nuneham Park*	*Broadlands*	
Chillington Hall	*Petworth*	*Berrington Hall*	

❧ THE SIGN OF A GREAT DAY OUT

BOUGHTON HOUSE 🏛

Kettering map J6 △ ♿ ⓢ
Telephone: (0536) 515731
(His Grace the Duke of Buccleuch & Queensberry KT and the Living Landscape Trust)

A 500 year old Tudor monastic building gradually enlarged around 7 courtyards until the French style addition of 1695. Outstanding collection of 17/18th century French and English furniture, tapestries, 16th century carpets, porcelain, painted ceilings - notable works by El Greco, Murillo, Caracci and 40 Van Dyck sketches - celebrated Armoury and Ceremonial Coach. Exhibition and lecture rooms in Stable block with audio/visual facilities. Beautiful parkland with avenues and lakes - picnic area - gift shop - exciting adventure woodland play area - garden centre. For details of our specialist one, three and five day Fine Art Courses run in conjunction with Sotheby's and our Schools Education Facilities (Sandford Award Winner), please telephone the Living Landscape Trust at Kettering (0536) 515731.

Location: 3 m N of Kettering on A43 at Geddington; 75 m N of London by A1 or M1.
Open: House and grounds: Aug 1 to Sept 1. Daily, grounds 1-5; House 2-5. Staterooms strictly by prior booking. Grounds: May 1 to Sept 30 - Daily except Frid, 1-5. **Facilities:** Garden Centre open daily throughout year. Adventure play area and tearooms open 1-5 at weekends and public holidays from May to Sept and daily throughout Aug, at other times by appointment. Museum and educational groups welcome by appointment at other times.
Refreshments: Tea rooms.

CANONS ASHBY HOUSE   🍂   The National Trust

Canons Ashby map H5
Telephone: (0327) 860044

The home of the Dryden family since the 16th century; a manor house c. 1580 and altered for the last time in 1710; Elizabethan wall paintings and outstanding Jacobean plasterwork; formal garden with terraces, walls and gatepiers of 1710: medieval Priory Church, privately owned since the Reformation. 70 acre park.

Location: Easy access from either M40 junction 11 or M1 junction 16. From M1 signposted from A5 2 m S of Weedon crossroads, along unclassified road (13 m) to Banbury. From M40 at Banbury take A422 exit, then left along unclassified road.
Open: Apr 1 to end of Oct - Weds to Suns & Bank Hol Mons 1-5.30. *Closed Good Friday.*
Admission: £3, Chd £1.50. Parking for cars and coaches which must pre-book (discount for parties).
Refreshments: Party bookings afternoon tea 2-5 in Brewhouse. Light lunches 12-2. Dogs on leads, in Home Paddock only. 1993 events - details from the Administrator.

COTON MANOR GARDENS

map J6   ♿
Telephone: (0604) 740219
(Ian Pasley-Tyler Esq)

An outstanding old English Garden exquisitely laid out on different levels. Old hedges, herbaceous borders, lawns and water gardens lend it a special charm and character enhanced by flamingoes, cranes and waterfowl roaming at large.

Location: 10 m N of Northampton & 11 m SE of Rugby. Follow tourist signs on A428 and A50.
Open: Easter to end of Sept: Weds, Suns and Bank Hol Mons (and Tues following), also Thurs in July & Aug, 2-6.
Admission: £2.50, OAPs £2, Chd 50p.
Refreshments: Home-made teas.
Unusual plants for sale.

COTTESBROOKE HALL AND GARDENS

nr Northampton map J6
Telephone: (060 124) 808
(Captain & Mrs John Macdonald-Buchanan)

Architecturally magnificent Queen Anne house commenced in 1702. Renowned picture collection, particularly of sporting and equestrian subjects. Fine English and Continental furniture and porcelain. Main vista aligned on celebrated 7th century Saxon church at Brixworth. House reputed to be the pattern for Jane Austen's 'Mansfield Park'. Notable gardens of great variety including fine old cedars and specimen trees, herbaceous borders, water and wild gardens.

Location: 10 m N of Northampton nr Creaton on A50, nr Brixworth on A508.
Open: Thurs from Apr 15 to Sept 30, Easter Mon, May day, Spring Bank Holiday, Aug Bank Holiday 2-5.30. Last adm 5.
Admission: £3.50. Gardens only £1.50. Chd half-price.
Refreshments: In the Old Laundry 2.30-5.
Parties accomodated by appointment, when possible. Car parking. Gardens but not house suitable for disabled. No dogs.

DEENE PARK

nr Corby map J6 △ &
Telephone: (078 085) 278 or 361 (office hours)
(Edmund Brudenell, Esq.)

Deene is a 16th and 17th century transformation of a mediaeval manor house with extensive 19th century additions and has belonged to the Brudenell family since 1514. It is still the 'elegant habitation of the Brudenells' as William Camden described it in the 16th century, and was the home of the Earl of Cardigan who led the Charge of the Light Brigade. Its special appeal lies in its indefinable atmosphere of a home cherished by the same family for over four centuries. The house which is of considerable architectural importance and historical interest, overlooks a large park and lake and has extensive gardens with old fashioned roses, rare trees and shrubs.

Location: 8 m NW of Oundle; 6 m NE of Corby on Kettering/Stamford Road (A43).
Open: Easter, May, Spring & Summer Bank Hol Suns & Mons, also every Sun in June, July & Aug 2-5. Upstairs rooms now on view. *Special guided tours to parties of 20 or more may be arranged throughout the year on application to the House Keeper.*
Admission: Charges not available at time of going to press.

DELAPRE ABBEY

nr Northampton map J6
(Northamptonshire Borough Council)

❧ THE SIGN OF A GREAT DAY OUT

HOLDENBY HOUSE GARDENS

Northampton map J6   ⓢ
Telephone: (0604) 770074
(Mr & Mrs James Lowther)

house with it's collection of rare pianos is open Bank Hol Mons and by appointment.

Location: 7 m NW of Northampton, off A428 & A50; approx 7 m from M1 exit 15a, 16 or 18.
Open: Apr to end Sept - GARDENS: Tues - Fri 1-5. Sun 2-6. HOUSE: Bank Hol Mons 1-6.*HOUSE. Open by arrangement to pre-booked parties Mons to Frid.*
Admission: GARDEN: £2.50, Chd £1.50. OAPs £2. HOUSE & GARDENS: £3.50, Chd £1.75. Enquire for special rates for school parties and business conferences throughout the year.
Refreshments: Home-made teas in Victorian Kitchen.
Plant and souvenir shop. Craf shops.

Once the largest house in Elizabethan England, Holdenby secured its place in history when it became the prison of Charles I during the Civil War. Today Holdenby's Falconry Centre and collection of rare farm animals complement the beauty and history of the grounds with their Elizabethan and fragrant borders. As buzzards and other birds of prey capture the attention in the sky above, train rides and a 'cuddle farm' ensure an enjoyable day for the children on the ground. The

KIRBY HALL   English⌗Heritage

map J6
Telephone: (0536) 203230

Richness and variety of architectural detail distinguish this Elizabethan country house from others. Begun by Sir Humphrey Stafford in 1570, it was completed by Sir Christopher Hatton, a talented courtier to Queen Elizabeth. The fourth Sir Christopher Hatton devoted his energies to the garden in the late 17th century. The gardens are currently undergoing a complete restoration.

Location: 2 m (3.2 km) north of Corby.
Open: Good Friday or Apr 1 (whichever is earlier) to Sept 30 daily 10-6. Oct 1 to Maundy Thursday or Mar 31 (whichever is earlier) Tues to Sun 10-4. *Closed* Dec 24-26, Jan 1.
Admission: £1.20, Concessions 90p, Chd 60p.

LAMPORT HALL AND GARDENS

Northampton map J6 ⓢ
Telephone: (060128) 272
(Lamport Hall Trust)

Lamport Hall was the home of the Isham family from 1560 to 1976. The South West front is a rare example of the work of John Webb, pupil and son-in-law of Inigo Jones and was built in 1655 (during the Commonwealth) with wings added in 1732 and 1740. High Room with plaster ceiling by John Woolston, an outstanding library, and thirteen other fine rooms containing the Ishams' collections of superb paintings, furniture and china. The Hall is set in spacious wooded parkland with tranquil gardens including a remarkable rock garden. Teas in Victorian dining room. Now run by the Lamport Hall Trust, school visits, group and private bookings are especially encouraged and a programme of fairs, music, art and craft events is put on throughout the season - details from the Director.

Location: 8 m N of Northampton on A508 to Market Harborough. M1 J15/16/18/20.
Open: House & Gardens. Easter to end of Sept - Suns & Bank Hol Mons 2.15-5.15. Also Thurs in July & Aug, 2.15-5.15. School & private parties any time by appointment.
Admission: £2.80, OAPs £2.20, Chd £1.20. Group rates on application. Coach parties welcome. Free car park and coach parking.
Refreshments: Home-made teas at the house.
Dogs on leads in picnic area only.

LYVEDEN NEW BIELD 🌿 The National Trust

Oundle map J6
Telephone: (083 25) 358

The shell of an unusual Renaissance building erected about 1600 by Sir Thomas Tresham to symbolize the Passion. He died before the building could be completed and his son was then imprisoned in connection with the Gunpowder Plot. A viewing platform allows visitors to look from the East Window.

Location: 4 m SW of Oundle via A427. 3 m E of Brigstock (A6116) (½ m walk from roadside parking).
Open: All the year - Daily. *Property approached via two fields. Parties by arrangement with Custodian, Lyveden New Bield Cottage, nr Oundle, Northants. No parking for coaches but they may drop & return to pick up passengers.*
Admission: £1, Chd 50p.
Dogs admitted on leads. Unsuitable for disabled or visually handicapped.

THE PREBENDAL MANOR HOUSE

Nassington map J6
Telephone: (0780) 782575

Probably the earliest surviving Manor in Northamptonshire, dating from the early 13th century. The present Manor overlays one of King Canute's Royal Manors and the site is of significant architectural and archaeological interest. The Manor forms the focus of a group of stone buildings which include a fine 16th century Dovecote. A historical exhibition is an added attraction.

Location: 6 m N of Oundle. A605-C14, 7 m S of Stamford. A1 to Wansford C14. 9 m E of Peterborough. A47-C14.
Open: Wed 2-6 from June to Aug 31. Easter Mon 2-6. Bank Hol Mons 2-6 and last Sun in June. Every Sun during Jul and Aug.
Admission: £3, OAP £2.50, Chd £2. Parties by arrangement. Free car parking.
Refreshments: Teas on Suns.
Not suitable for disabled.

PRIEST'S HOUSE 🌿 The National Trust

Easton-on-the-Hill map J7
Telephone: (0780) 62506

Pre-Reformation priest's house given to the National Trust by The Peterborough Society. Contains a small museum of village bygones.

Location: 2 m SW of Stamford off A43.
Station(s): Stamford (2 m).
Open: Access only by prior appointment with Mr. R. Chapman, Glebe Cottage, 45 West St., Easton-on-the-Hill, nr Stamford.
Admission: Free.
No dogs. Unsuitable for disabled or visually handicapped and coaches.

ROCKINGHAM CASTLE

nr Corby   map J6   △   ⑤
Telephone: (0536) 770240
(Commander Michael Saunders Watson)

A Royal Castle till 1530, since then the home of the Watson family. Rockingham Castle was built by William the Conqueror on the site of an earlier fortification and was used by the early Kings of England until the 16th century when it was granted by Henry VIII to Edward Watson whose family still live there today. The house itself is memorable not so much as representing any particular period, but rather a procession of periods. The dominant influence in the building is Tudor within the Norman walls, but practically every century since the 11th has left its mark in the form of architecture, furniture or works of art. There is a particularly fine collection of English 18th, 19th and 20th century paintings, and Charles Dickens, a frequent visitor, was so captivated by Rockingham that he used it as a model for Chesney Wold in Bleak House. The Castle stands in 12 acres of formal and wild garden and commands a splendid view of five counties. Particular features are the 400 year old elephant hedge and the rose garden marking the foundations of the old keep. See also the Special Exhibition: Castles in Northamptonshire.

Location: 2 m N of Corby; 9 m from Market Harborough; 14 m from Stamford on A427; 8 m from Kettering on A6003.
Open: Easter Sun to Sept 30 - Suns & Thurs also Bank Hol Mons & Tues following and Tues during Aug: 1.30-5.30. *Any other day by previous appointment for parties.*
Admission: £3.50, OAPs £2.80, Chd £2. Gardens only £2.
Refreshments: Teas: home-made at Castle.

RUSHTON HALL

Rushton, nr Kettering   map J6
(Royal National Institute for the Blind)

RUSHTON TRIANGULAR LODGE   English✠Heritage

map J6
Telephone: (0536) 710761

Three walls with three windows and three gables to each ...three storeys topped by a three-sided chimney. What is the reason for this triangular theme? The building is the brainchild of Sir Thomas Tresham and every detail is symbolical of the Holy Trinity and the Mass. Tresham's religious beliefs, unpopular in Elizabethan England, earned him many years' imprisonment. The lodge, begun on his return home in 1593, was finished four years later.

Location: ¾ m (1 km) west of Rushton; 4 m (6.4 km) north west of Kettering.
Open: Good Friday or Apr 1 (whichever is earlier) to Sept 30: Open Daily 10-6.
Admission: £1.20, Concessions 90p, Chd 60p.

SOUTHWICK HALL

nr Oundle   map J6
Telephone: (0832) 274064
(Christopher Capron, Esq.)

A family home since 1300, retaining medieval building dating from 1300, with Tudor re-building and 18th century additions. Exhibitions:- Victorian and Edwardian life; collections of agricultural and carpentry tools, named bricks and local archaeological finds and fossils.

Location: 3 m N of Oundle 4 m E of Bulwick.
Open: Bank Holidays, Sun & Mon (Apr 11, 12; May 2, 3, 30, 31; Aug 29, 30). Weds from May 6 to Aug 26: 2-5. Parties at other times by arrangement with Secretary at Southwick Hall, Peterborough PE8 5BL.
Admission: £2.50, OAPs £1.80, Chd £1.50.
Refreshments: Teas available.

STOKE PARK PAVILIONS

Towcester map J5
(A. S. Chancellor, Esq)

Two pavilions and colonnade. Built in 1630 by Inigo Jones.

Location: Stoke Bruerne village; 7 m S of Northampton just W of Stony/Northampton Road A508.
Open: June, July & Aug - Sats, Suns & Bank Hols 2-6. *Exterior only on view.*
Admission: £1. Car park free.

SULGRAVE MANOR

Banbury map H5 △
Telephone: (0295) 760205
(The Sulgrave Manor Board)

of a wealthy man's home and gardens in Elizabethan times, restored and refurbished with scholarly care and attention to detail which makes a visit both a delight and an education. Sulgrave Manor has been open to the public since 1921 when it was established as a 'Token of Friendship' between the people of Britain and the United States. It is now held in trust for the peoples of both nations, the trustees being the American Ambassador in London, the British Ambassador in Washington, and the Regent of Mount Vernon, Virginia. Endowed by the National Society of Colonial Dames of America.

Location: Sulgrave Village is off Banbury/Northampton Road (B4525); 5 m from Banbury junction of M40, 12 m from Northampton junction of M1. 7 m NE of Banbury; 28 m SE of Stratford-upon-Avon; 30 m N of Oxford; 70 m NW of London.
Open: Mar to Dec 31 - Daily (except Weds); Apr to Sept (inc) 10.30-1, 2-5.30. Other months 10.30-1, 2-4. *Closed Sat 17th July for private function. Closed Christmas Day, Boxing Day, and all January.* February: Groups only by appointment.
Admission: £3, Chd £1.50, Family ticket £9. Group rate for Pre-booked Parties of 12 or more.
Refreshments: At Thatched House Hotel opposite, Tel Sulgrave (029 576) 0232. Light refreshments in Brewhouse.

The Washington ownership dates from 1539 when Lawrence Washington purchased the land upon the Dissolution by Henry VIII, of St. Andrew's Priory, Northampton. The House was completed in 1558 (the year Elizabeth I came to the throne of England) and was lived in by descendants of the Washington family for 120 years. Today it is an excellent example of a small Manor House, typical

NORTHUMBERLAND

ALNWICK CASTLE

Alnwick map H12
Telephone: (0665) 510777
Fax: (0665) 510876
(His Grace the Duke of Northumberland)

Described by the Victorians as 'Windsor of the North', Alnwick Castle is the second largest inhabited Castle in England and has been in the possession of the Percys, Earls and Dukes of Northumberland since 1309. Once the most impenetrable of border strongholds, this mighty fortress now lies in a peaceful landscape designed by Capability Brown. The stark exterior belies its magnificent interior, refurbished in the 19th C in Italian Renaissance style. The Castle houses an exquisite collection of art treasures, including the finest examples of Italian paintings in the north of England with works by other great artists including Van Dyck and Turner, in addition to fine English and French furniture and ornately carved wooden ceilings. The Castle also houses one of the country's most important collections of early Meissen porcelain. Northumberland Fusiliers Museum, Museum of Stone, Bronze and Iron age antiquities.

Location: Just off the town centre on the northern side of Alnwick.
Open: Daily Maundy Thursday (8 Apr) to mid Oct 11-5 (last admission 4.30). *Guided Connoisseurs Tours by arrangement.*
Admission: CASTLE, MUSEUMS & GROUNDS: £3.60, Chd £2.20, OAPs/Students £3, Families *i.e. 2 adults and 2 chd under 16yrs.* £10. Reductions for groups of 12 or more people by arrangement with the Supervisor at the following address: Estate Office, Alnwick Castle, Alnwick, Northumberland NE66 1NQ. Free parking for cars and coaches.
Refreshments: Tea-room serving home-made food.
Large Gift Shop. To obtain a 1993 illustrated Guide Book prior to your visit send P.O/cheque for £2.25 to The Supervisor at the above address. Functions may be held in the magnificent Guest Hall, weddings, fairs, luncheons, dinners and seminars. Superb kitchen facilities. We can arrange guided tours in several foreign languages.

AYDON CASTLE   English Heritage

map G12
Telephone: (043 471) 2450

Built as a manor house at the end of the 13th century, Aydon Castle fortified almost immediately afterwards as a result of the insecurity of the borders with Scotland. Captured by the Scots in 1315, it was pillaged and burned, and seized again by English rebels two years later. It has survived as a result of its conversion to a farmhouse in the 17th century.

Location: 1 m (1.6 km) north east of Corbridge, on minor road off B6321 or A68.
Open: Good Friday or Apr 1 (whichever is earlier) to Sept 30: Open Daily 10-6.
Admission: £1.70, Concessions £1.30, Chd 85p.

BAMBURGH CASTLE

Bamburgh map H13
Telephone: (066 84) 208

BAMBURGH CASTLE

AND ARMSTRONG MUSEUM, The home of Lady Armstrong

The Norman Keep has stood for eight centuries and its setting upon The Crag, which is referred to as a Royal Centre by A.D. 547, is certainly one of the most dramatic of all Castles in Britain.

Featuring:
- Magnificent Seascapes including Holy Island and the Farne Islands, and Landscapes extending to the Cheviot Hills.
- Public Rooms with exhibition of porcelain, china, paintings, furniture and items of interest.
- The Armoury, including loan collections from H.M. Tower of London, The John George Joicey Museum, Newcastle-upon-Tyne, and others.
- Fine Paintings including some from the Duke of Cambridge's collection.

Open to the Public from Maundy Thursday to the last Sunday in October.
Concessionary Rates for parties in or out of Season – Restaurant – Tea Room in the Castle Clock Tower
Operators — All at one stop. Tour. Food. Cloakrooms. Free Coach Parking at Entrance to Walled Castle.

CUSTODIAN – TEL: BAMBURGH (066 84) 208

Fine 12th century Norman Keep with its setting upon The Crag, and referred to as a Royal Centre by AD 547, is certainly one of the most dramatic of all Castles in Britain. Remainder of the Castle considerably restored. Magnificent seascapes including Holy Island and the Farne Islands, the landscapes extending to the Cheviot Hills. Public rooms with exhibition of porcelain, china, paintings, furniture and items of interest. The Armoury includes loan collections from HM Tower of London, The John George Joicey Museum, Newcastle upon Tyne and others. Fine paintings, including some from the Duke of Cambridge's collection.

Location: Coastal - 16 m N of Alnwick 6 m from Belford; 3 m from Seahouses.
Open: Easter to last Sun of Oct - Daily (incl Suns) open at 1; *Parties may be booked out of normal hours.* For closing times enquire The Custodian.
Admission: £2.20, Chd £1.(1992 prices).
Refreshments: Clock Tower tea rooms.

The National Trust
THE SIGN OF A GREAT DAY OUT

BELSAY HALL CASTLE AND GARDENS

English ⌗ Heritage

map G12
Telephone: (066 181) 636

19th-century Neo-Classical mansion lies at the entrance to 30 acres of exciting gardens, which in turn lead on to the 14th-century castle and ruined manor. Important collections of rare and exotic flowering trees grow in the meandering, deep ravines of the 'picturesque' Quarry Gardens. Massed plantings of rhododendrons. Large heather garden. Spring bulbs. Exhibition of Belsay's architectural and landscape history in stable block.

Location: 14 m (22.4 km) north west of Newcastle upon Tyne.
Open: Good Friday or Apr 1 (whichever is earlier) to Sept 30 daily 10-6. Oct 1 to Maundy Thursday or Mar 31 (whichever is earlier) Tues to Sun 10-4. *Closed* Dec 24-26, Jan 1.
Admission: £2.20, Concessions £1.60, Chd £1.10.

BERWICK UPON TWEED BARRACKS   English ⌗ Heritage

map G13
Telephone: (0289) 304493

The barracks were designed in 1717 to accommodate 36 officers and 600 men, first being occupied in 1721. The buildings consist of three blocks of accommodation around a square, the fourth side having a splendidly decorated gatehouse. The barracks' new exhibition, the award winning 'Beat of Drum' traces the history of the British infantryman from 1660 to the end of the 19th century. The regimental museum of the King's Own Scottish Borderers and Borough Museum of Berwick on Tweed are also housed here.

Location: On the Parade, off Church St, Berwick town centre.
Open: Good Friday or Apr 1 (whichever is earlier) to Sept 30: Open Daily 10-6. Oct 1 to Maundy Thursday or Mar 31 (whichever is earlier): Open Tues to Sun 10-4. *Closed* Dec 24-26, Jan 1.
Admission: £2, Concessions £1.50, Chd £1.

BRINKBURN PRIORY   English#Heritage

map G12
Telephone: (066 570) 628

The priory church stands within a loop of the River Coquet, in beautiful surroundings. Founded about 1130, the priory suffered badly from Scottish raids. In the last century the church was carefully restored by the Newcastle architect, Thomas Austin, and is still in occasional use. It is a fine example of early Gothic architecture.

Location: 5 m (8 km) east of Rothbury.
Open: Good Friday or Apr 1 (whichever is earlier) to Sept 30: Open Daily 10-6.
Admission: £1.20, Concessions 90p, Chd 60p.

CHERRYBURN   The National Trust

Mickley map G11
Telephone: (0661) 843276

Birthplace of Northumbria's greatest artist, wood engraver and naturalist, Thomas Bewick, in 1753. His family cottage is restored. The museum explores his famous works and life and in the Printing House demonstrations of hand printing from wood blocks can be seen. Farmyard Animals; Picnic Area.

Location: 11 m W of Newcastle on A695 (200 yards signed from Mickley Square).
Open: Apr 1 to Oct 31 - daily except Tues 1-5.30. Last adm 5.
Admission: £2.50, No party rate.
Wheelchair access and WC.

CHESTER'S ROMAN FORT AND MUSEUM

English#Heritage

map G12
Telephone: (043481) 379

An impressive bath-house, buildings of great interest inside the fort, the remains of the bridge carrying Hadrian's Wall across the Tyne, a museum full of Roman inscriptions and sculptures, all set in one of the most beautiful valleys in Northumberland - these are among the attractions of Chesters, once garrisoned by a regiment of Roman cavalry.

Location: ½ m (0.8 km) south west of Chollerford.
Open: Good Friday or Apr 1 (whichever is earlier) to Sept 30: Open Daily 10-6. Oct 1 to Maundy Thursday or Mar 31 (whichever is earlier): Open Daily 10-4. *Closed* Dec 24-26, Jan 1.
Admission: £2, Concessions £1.50, Chd £1.

CHILLINGHAM CASTLE AND GARDENS

Alnwick map G13
Telephone: (06685) 359
(Sir Humphry Wakefield Bt)

This medieval family fortress has been home since the 1200's to the Earls Grey and their relations. Complete with jousting course, alarming dungeon and even a torture chamber, the Castle displays many remarkable restoration techniques in action, alongside antique furnishings, paintings, tapestries, arms and armour. The Italian ornamental garden, landscaped avenues and gate lodges were created by Sir Jeffrey Wyatville, fresh from his triumphs at Windsor Castle. There are attractive woodland walks and a lake, tea room, gift shop and antique shop.

Location: 12 m N of Alnwick, signposted from the A1 and A697.
Open: Good Friday to Easter Mon; May 1 to Sept 30: 1.30-5 (*closed* Tues).
Admission: £3, OAPs £2.50, Chd (Over 5) £2, Parties (Over 20) £2 per head. Unlimited free car parking.
Refreshments: Tea room serving light refreshments available within the Castle during opening hours. Nearest restaurant - Percy Arms, Chatton (2 m). Restaurant facilities available by arrangement.
Access for disabled difficult due to number of stairs. Wheelchairs available only by arrangement. Holiday apartments available withing Castle. Fishing and Clay pigeon shooting by arrangement. Musical and Theatrical events regularly planned.

CORBRIDGE ROMAN SITE   English ✛ Heritage

map G11
Telephone: (043471) 2349

For nearly a century this was the site of a sequence of Roman forts, since Corbridge was an important junction of roads to Scotland, York and Carlisle. It developed into a prosperous town and supply base for Hadrian's Wall, with shops, temples, houses, granaries and an elaborate fountain. Among the rich collection of finds in the museum is a remarkable fountainhead - the Corbridge Lion.

Location: ½ m (0.8 km) north west of Corbridge.
Open: Good Friday or Apr 1 (whichever is earlier) to Sept 30: Open Daily 10-6. Oct 1 to Maundy Thursday or Mar 31 (whichever is earlier): Open Tues to Sun 10-4. *Closed* Dec 24-26, Jan 1.
Admission: £2, Concessions £1.50, Chd £1.

CRAGSIDE HOUSE, GARDEN AND GROUNDS

🌿 The National Trust

Rothbury map G12   ♿
Telephone: (0669) 20333/20266

The House was designed by Richard Norman Shaw for the first Lord Armstrong and built between 1864-95. It contains much of its original furniture and Pre-Raphaelite paintings. It was the first house in the world to be lit by electricity generated by water power. The Grounds are famous for their rhododendrons, magnificent trees and the beauty of the lakes. The Armstrong Energy Centre displays the past and future stories of 'energy' and the 'Power Circuit Walk' includes restored hydraulic and hydroelectric machinery. Formal garden with Orchard House, Rose loggia, Ferneries opened in 1992.

Location: ½ m E of Rothbury; 30 m N of Newcastle-upon-Tyne. Entrance off Rothbury/Alnwick Road B6341; 1 m N of Rothbury at Debdon Burn Gate.
Open: House and Garden: Apr 1 to Oct 31 - daily except Mon (open Bank Holiday Mons), 1-5.30. Last adm 5. Grounds: Apr 1 to Oct 31 - daily except Mon (open Bank Holiday Mon) 10.30-7. Nov and Dec: Tues, Sat & Sun 10.30-4.
Admission: House, Garden, Grounds, Museum and Power circuit: £5.40, Parties £5; Garden and Grounds: £3.30, Parties £3. *Parties are by prior arrangement only with the Administrator.* Family ticket: (House, Gardens and Grounds - 2 adults and 2 chd) £14.
Refreshments: Restaurant in Visitor Centre. Telephone Rothbury (0669) 20134.
Armstrong Energy Centre & Shop in visitor centre. Dogs in Grounds only. Wheelchair access to House - lift available (wheelchairs provided). Toilets for disabled. Fishing.

DUNSTANBURGH CASTLE   English ✛ Heritage

map H13
Telephone: (066576) 231

Isolated and unspoilt, the ruins stand on a large, rocky cliff top rising steeply from the sea. Begun by Thomas, Earl of Lancaster, in 1313, the castle was attacked by the Scots and besieged during the Wars of the Roses. The keep gatehouse is still impressive and the south wall an enduring memorial to the workmanship of Earl Thomas's masons.

Location: 8 m (13 km) north east of Alnwick.
Open: Good Friday or Apr 1 (whichever is earlier) to Sept 30: Open Daily 10-6. Oct 1 to Maundy Thursday or Mar 31 (whichever is earlier): Open Tues to Sun 10-4. *Closed* Dec 24-26, Jan 1.
Admission: £1.20, Concessions 90p, Chd 60p.

HADRIAN'S ROMAN WALL IN NORTHUMBERLAND AND TYNE AND WEAR
English ✛ Heritage

map G12

The wall runs from Bowness to Wallsend-on-Tyne, a distance of 73 miles (117 km). Although parts of the wall have been lost over the centuries, fine sections remain at Walltown Crags, Cawfields, Sewingshields and Heddon-on-the-Wall. At Denton, near Newcastle, there is a well-preserved turret, and there are others at Brunton, where the wall is still 7ft (2m) high, at Sewingshields and Black Carts. These turrets, or observation towers, punctuated the wall at every third of a Roman mile between milecastles, good examples of which may be seen at Cawfields and Sewingshields. At Benwell and Carrawburgh there are Roman temples; at Chesterholm a milestone and the great fort Vindolanda, for which there is an admission fee. Other sites may be visited free of charge.

Location: Locations: OS map references. Heddon-on-the-Wall NZ136669; Planetrees Farm, Chollerford NY928696; Brunton Turret, Chollerford NY921698; Chesters Bridge Abutment, Chollerford NY913701; Black Carts NY884713; Carrawburgh, Temple of Mithras NY869713; Sewingshields, Haydon Bridge NY813702; Chesterholm, Vindolanda Roman Fort and Milestone NY771664; Winshields Milecastle, Bardon Mill NY745676; Cawfields Milecastle NY726669; Walltown Crags, Greenhead NY674664; Benwell Condercum NZ215646; Benwell Roman Temple NZ217646; Denton Hall Turret NZ198655 and West Denton NZ195656.

HOUSESTEADS ROMAN FORT   English ✛ Heritage

map G12
Telephone: (04984) 363

This is the best-preserved Roman troop-base on Hadrian's Wall. In the museum, a model shows the layout of barracks, headquarters buildings, commandant's house and granaries. Also displayed are relics from the fort and the settlement that grew up outside the walls in the 3rd and 4th centuries.

Location: 2¾ m (4.4 km) north east of Bardon Mill.
Open: Good Friday or Apr 1 (whichever is earlier) to Sept 30: Open Daily 10-6. Oct 1 to Maundy Thursday or Mar 31 (whichever is earlier): Open Daily 10-4. *Closed* Dec 24-26, Jan 1.
Admission: £2, Concessions £1.50, Chd £1.

HOWICK HALL GARDENS

Alnwick map H12
(Howick Trustees Ltd)

Extensive grounds including a natural woodland garden in addition to the formal gardens surrounding the Hall.

Location: 6 m NE of Alnwick, nr Howick village.
Open: Apr to Oct - Daily 1-6.
Admission: £1.50 (OAPs 75p).

KIRKLEY HALL GARDENS

Ponteland map H12
Telephone: (0661) 860808
(Dr R. McParlin)

Prestigious gardens, Greenhouses, Plantsman's paradise, All plants labelled, Plant sales, Sculptures, Conducted tours (prior arrangement).

Location: 3 m N of Ponteland off A696.
Open: Every day throughout the year. 10 till dusk.
Admission: £1.50 per person. £3 per family, Parties of 20 or more (prior notice) £1.20 per person. Group guided tours (min no 13, prior notice) £2.50 per person. Free parking.
Refreshments: Available.
No dogs.

LINDISFARNE CASTLE   🌿 The National Trust

Holy Island map G13
Telephone: (0289) 89244

Built about 1550. Sympathetically restored as a comfortable house by Lutyens in 1903.

Location: 5 m E of Beal across causeway.
Open: Apr 1 to Oct 31 - Daily (closed Frid, open Good Frid) 1-5.30; Last adm 5.
Admission: £3.20. No party rate.
No dogs in Castle. Unsuitable for wheelchairs.

LINDISFARNE PRIORY English⌗Heritage

map G13
Telephone: (028989) 200

Roofless and ruined, the priory is still supremely beautiful, its graceful arches and decorated doorways commemorating the craftsmanship of their Norman builders. This has been sacred soil since 634 when the missionary Bishop Aidan was sent from Iona, to spread Christianity through northern England. New visitor centre with atmospheric exhibition and shop.

Location: On Holy Island, which can be reached at low tide across a causeway. Tide tables are posted at each end of the causeway.
Open: Good Friday or Apr 1 (whichever is earlier) to Sept 30: Open Daily 10-6 subject to tides. Oct 1 to Maundy Thursday or Mar 31 (whichever is earlier): Open Tues to Sun 10-4 subject to tides. *Closed* Dec 24-26, Jan 1.
Admission: £2, Concessions £1.50, chd £1.

NORHAM CASTLE English⌗Heritage

map G13
Telephone: (028982) 329

Built in the 12th century by the Bishop of Durham, this massive castle stands on a site of great natural strength. It withstood repeated attacks in the 13th and 14th centuries and was thought to be impregnable. But in 1513 it was stormed by the forces of James IV and partially destroyed. Although later rebuilt, the castle lost its importance as a defensive stronghold by the end of the 16th century.

Location: 8 m (13 km) south west of Berwick.
Open: Good Friday or Apr 1 (whichever is earlier) to Sept 30: Open Daily 10-6. Oct 1 to Maundy Thursday or Mar 31 (whichever is earlier): Open Tues to Sun 10-4. *Closed* Dec 24-26, Jan 1.
Admission: Free.

William Kent (1685–1748)
Painter, architect, garden designer

His work can be seen in the following properties included in Historic Houses Castles and Gardens:

> *Chiswick House*
> *Ditchley Park (decoration of Great Hall)*
> *Euston Hall*
> *Rousham House*
> *Stowe*

PRESTON TOWER 

Chathill map H13
(Major T. H. Baker-Cresswell)

One of the few survivors of 78 Pele Towers listed in 1415. The tunnel vaulted rooms remain unaltered and provide a realistic picture of the grim way of life under the constant threat of 'Border Reivers'. Two rooms are furnished in contemporary style and there are displays of historic and local information.

Location: 7 m N of Alnwick; 1 m E from A1. Follow Historic Property signs.
Station(s): Chathill (1 m).
Open: All year - Daily during daylight hours.
Admission: £1, chd/OAPs 50p. Free car park.
No dogs (except those left in car).

PRUDHOE CASTLE English ♯ Heritage

map G11
Telephone: (0661) 33459

Extensive remains of 12th century castle with gatehouse, curtain wall and keep enclosed within surrounding earthworks. In the 19th century a gothick house was built within the ruins, now containing an exhibition on the history of the castle and video about Northumberland Castles.

Location: In Prudhoe, on minor road off A695.
Open: Good Friday or Apr 1 (whichever is earlier) to Sept 30: Open Daily 10-6. Oct 1 to Maundy Thursday or Mar 31 (whichever is earlier): Open Tues to Sun 10-4. *Closed* Dec 24-26, Jan 1.
Admission: £1.70, Concessions £1.30, Chd 85p.

The National Trust
THE SIGN
OF A GREAT
DAY OUT

SEATON DELAVAL HALL

Whitley Bay map H12
Telephone: 091-2373040/2371493
(The Lord Hastings)

The house was designed by Sir John Vanbrugh in his most theatrical manner for Admiral George Delaval and built between 1718-1728. Regarded by many as Sir John Vanbrugh's masterpiece. Built on a small budget it is ducal magnificence in miniature. Relatively small, the house gives the impression of being vast, which is of course what was intended. It is the theatre again - Vanbrugh the playwright using stones, columns and pediments instead of words. It comprises a centre block between two arcaded and pedimented wings, the centre block being gutted by fire in 1822 and for many years stood a gaunt ruin, but it was partially restored in 1862-63 and again in 1959-62. The East Wing contains very fine stables and in the grounds are extensive gardens and statues.

Location: ½ m from coast at Seaton Sluice, and between Blyth and Whitley Bay (A190). (Northumbria Bus from Newcastle 363, 364.)
Open: May 1-Sept 30: Wed, Sun, and Bank Holidays 2-6.
Admission: £1.50, chd (accompanied by adult) 50p.
Refreshments: Tea room.

WALLINGTON HOUSE, WALLED GARDEN AND GROUNDS

The National Trust

Cambo map G12 &
Telephone: (067 074) 283 (House)

Built 1688, altered 18th century. Central Hall added in 19th century, decorated by William Bell Scott, Ruskin and others. Fine porcelain, furniture and pictures in series of rooms including a late Victorian nursery and dolls' houses. Museum. Coach display in West Coach House. Woodlands, lakes, walled terraced garden and conservatory with magnificent fuchsias.

Location: Access from N, 12 m W of Morpeth on B6343. Access from S, A696 from Newcastle; 6 m NW of Belsay B6342 to Cambo.
Open: HOUSE: Apr 1 to Oct 31, daily 1-5.30. Last adm 5. *Closed* Tues. WALLED GARDEN: Open all year daily. Apr 1 to Sept 10.30-7, Oct 10.30-6, Nov to Mar 10.30-4 (or dusk if earlier). GROUNDS: All year during daylight hours.
Admission: House and Grounds: £4, Grounds only: £2, Party rate - House and Grounds: £3.50, Grounds only: £1.50.
Refreshments: Available at Clock Tower Restaurant. Telephone (067 074) 274.
No dogs in house; on leads in walled garden. Shop and Information Centre. Wheelchairs provided. *Parties by prior arrangement with the administrators.*

WARKWORTH CASTLE AND HERMITAGE

English ♯ Heritage

map H12
Telephone: (0665) 711423

From 1332 the history of Warkworth was the history of the Percy family. In 1399 this became the history of England, when the third Percy lord of Warkworth and his son Harry Hotspur put Henry IV on the throne. Three scenes from Shakespeare's Henry IV Part 1 are set at Warkworth. Norman in origin, the castle has some very fine medieval masonry. Part of the keep was restored and made habitable in the 19th century. The hermitage and chapel of Holy Trinity is situated in a peaceful, retired place, overshadowed and surrounded by trees upon the left bank of the River Coquet half a mile above the castle.

Location: 7½ m (12 km) south of Alnwick.
Open: Good Friday or Apr 1 (whichever is earlier) to Sept 30: Open Daily 10-6. Oct 1 to Maundy Thursday or Mar 31 (whichever is earlier): Open Tues to Sun 10-4. *Closed* Dec 24-26, Jan 1.
Admission: £1.70, Concessions £1.30, chd 85p.

NOTTINGHAMSHIRE

CARLTON HALL

Carlton-on-Trent map J8 △
(Trustees of G H Vere-Laurie dec'd)

George III house built c.1765 by Joseph Pocklington of Newark, banker, 1736-1817. Beautiful drawing room. Magnificent ancient cedar in grounds. Stables attributed to Carr of York.

Location: 7 m N of Newark just off A1.
Open: Any day, telephone (0636) 821421 to be certain of being shown round.
Admission: House and Garden: £1.50.

CLUMBER PARK   The National Trust

nr Worksop map J8
Telephone: (0909) 476592

4,000 acre landscaped park with lake and woods. Classical bridge, temples, lawned Lincoln Terrace and pleasure grounds. Walled kitchen garden and tools exhibition.

Location: Clumber Park 4½ m SE of Worksop; 6½ m SW of East Retford.
Open: Open daily all year. The Estate Office, Gardens Cottage, Clumber Park, Worksop, Notts S80 3AZ. **1993 Events:** July 10,'All That Jazz'.
Admission: Vehicle parking charges.
Refreshments: Cafeteria open all year daily. Licensed restaurant for lunches daily, evening meals available for pre-booked parties. Telephone: (0909) 484122.
Dogs admitted. Shop. Cycle hire. Fishing bank. Wheelchairs and special fishing platform for disabled.

HOLME PIERREPONT HALL

Radcliffe-on-Trent, nr Nottingham map J7 △
Telephone: (0602) 332371
(Mr & Mrs Robin Brackenbury)

Medieval brick manor house. Historic Courtyard garden with box parterre, 1875. Regional 17th, 18th, 19th and 20th century furniture, china and pictures. Quiet and free from crowds. Jacob sheep. Shop with Jacob wool products.

Location: 5 m SE from centre of Nottingham by following all signs to the National Water Sports Centre and continue for 1½ m.
Open: June - Suns 2-5.30. July - Thurs and Suns 2-5.30. Aug - Tues, Thurs, Frid, Suns 2-5.30. Easter, Spring and Summer Bank Hol Suns, Mons and Tues 2-6. Groups by appointment throughout the year, including evenings.
Admission: £2.75, Chd £1, subject to alteration.
Refreshments: Home-made teas. Other refreshments by arrangement.

THE SIGN OF A GREAT DAY OUT

HODSOCK PRIORY GARDENS

Blyth, nr Worksop. map J8
Telephone: (0909) 591204
(Sir Andrew and Lady Buchanan)

Enjoy a very special afternoon out in these romantic gardens on the historic site mentioned in Domesday Book. Five acres of beauty and peace bounded by dry moat. Grade I listed gatehouse c.1500. Mature trees include huge cornus, catalpas, tulip tree, swamp cypress. Small lake, bog garden, spring bulbs, mixed borders, roses old and new, established holly hedges. Featured in 'The Rose Gardens of England', 'The Shell Guide to the Gardens of England and Wales', 'Country Life' and the 'Good Gardens Guide'.

Location: 1 m from A1 at Blyth. Off B6045 Blyth to Worksop road.
Open: Mar - Sun 21 (Mothering Sunday). Apr - Sun 11 (Easter) & Wed 21. May - Suns 16 & 23, and Wed 12 & 19 (includes Bluebell walks). June - Suns 13 & 27 and every Wed. July - Sun 11 & Wed 7 & 14. Aug - Sun 15 and Wed 11 & 18. All 1-5 (last entry 4.30).
Admission: £1.80. Accompanied chd and visitors in wheelchairs free. Discount for pre-booked groups. *Coaches must book.*
Refreshments: Teas.
Annual Snowdrop Spectacular 10 to dusk -£1.50. Gardens and woodland walk in Feb/Mar depends on weather so SEE LOCAL PRESS or telephone. All enqiries to Lady Buchanan as above or telephone (0909) 591204. *Dogs on leads are welcome in the park only and not in the gardens of Snowdrop/Bluebell wood (Guide Dogs excepted).* 1 & 2 day Gardening Courses run by qualified horticulturalist/teacher now booking for 1993 and 1994.

George Stubbs
Portrait, animal and rural painter
(1724–1806)
Produced his engraved work,
The Anatomy of a Horse, in 1766

His work can be seen in the following properties included in Historic Houses Castles and Gardens:

St Osyth Priory
Upton House

NEWARK TOWN HALL

Newark map J7
Telephone: (0636) 640100
(Newark Town Council)

One of the finest Georgian Town Halls in the country, the building has recently been refurbished in sympathy with John Carr's original concept. On display is the Town's collection of Civic Plate, silver dating generally from the 17th and 18th century, including the 'Newark Monteith' and the Newark Siege Pieces. Other items of interest are some early historical records and various paintings including a collection by the artist Joseph Paul.

Location: Market Place, Newark; located on A1 and A46.
Station(s): Newark Castle; Northgate (½ m).
Open: All the year - Mons to Frid 10-12, 2-4. Open at other times for groups by appointment. *Closed* Sats, Suns, Bank Holiday Mons and Tues following and Christmas week.
Admission: Free.

NEWSTEAD ABBEY HOUSE AND GROUNDS

Linby map H7
Telephone: (0623) 793557
(Nottingham City Council)

Newstead Abbey is best known as the home of the poet Lord Byron who made the house and its ghostly legends famous. Visitors can see Byrons apartments and mementos of the poet including letters, manuscripts and first editions. Splendid 19th century rooms bring the lives of later Victorian residents of the house to life. The early history of Newstead as a religious building can be seen in the remains of the medieval priory. The cloisters of the priory surround a secret garden, in the centre is an ancient stone foundation carved with fantastic beasts. The grounds at Newstead Abbey are magnificent in all seasons and include waterfalls, lakes and ponds. There are delightful rose, iris and Japanese gardens to explore.

Location: 12 m N of Nottingham on A60 (Mansfield Rd). Close to junction 27 of the M1. By Bus: (Trent no's 63 and x2) from Nottingham Victoria Coach Station, drops off at Abbey gates (1 m from house).
Open: HOUSE: Easter to Oct, daily 12-6. GARDENS: all year daily 10-dusk (except last Fri in Nov).
Admission: House and Gardens: £3.50, Reductions £2, Gardens only: £1.50, Reductions £1.
Refreshments: Tea room and licensed restaurant in grounds, tel (0623) 797392.

NORWOOD PARK

nr Southwell map J7

1760, Carr of York House, with lovely lived in feeling, set in mediaeval Episcopalial deer-park. Glorious views and walks; Temple, Avenue, ponds, ice-house, etc. Apple orchards increase the interest. (Original Bramley apple came from Southwell) Strawberries. Civil War connections. Costumes, bygones, children's interests, I Spy, Nature Exhibition. Cricket and Lawn Tennis. An experience of Magic and Charm.

Location: W of Southwell on Halam Road. 8 m from Newark (A1). 15 m from Nottingham (M1).
Open: May to end Aug, Suns and Bank Hol Mons, 2-6. Specialist and Guided Tours, Historical, Technical and Social welcomed. Tel (0636) 812762 for arrangements.
Admission: Car park £1 per car (refundable if visiting house), Garden £1 each, House and Garden £2.50.
Refreshments: Strawberry Cream Teas. Home pressed Apple Juice.

PAPPLEWICK HALL

Near Nottingham map H7
Telephone: (0602) 633491
(Dr R. B. Godwin-Austen)

Fine Adam house built 1784 with lovely plasterwork ceilings.Park and woodland garden, particularly known for its rhododendrons.

Location: 6m N Nottingham off A60. 2m from exit 27 M1.
Open: By appointment only, all year.

THRUMPTON HALL

Nottingham map H7 △
Telephone: (0602) 830333
(George FitzRoy Seymour, Esq)

Fine Jacobean house, built 1607, incorporating earlier manor house. Priest's hiding hole, magnificent Charles II carved staircase carved and panelled saloon and other fine rooms containing beautiful 17th and 18th century furniture and many fine portraits. Large lawns separated from landscaped park by ha-ha and by lake. This house retains the atmosphere of a home, being lived in by owners who will show parties around.

Location: 7 m S of Nottingham; 3 m E of M1 at junction 24; 1 m from A453.
Open: By appointment for parties of 20 or more persons. Open all year including evenings.
Admission: House and Gardens: £3, Chd £1.50. Minimum charge of £60.
Refreshments: By prior arrangement.

WOLLATON HALL

Nottingham map H7
Telephone: (0602) 281333 or 281130
(City of Nottingham)

Fine example of late Elizabethan Renaissance architecture. Natural History Museum - one of the finest in the country.

Location: 2½ m W of City centre.
Station(s): Nottingham (2¾ m).
Open: All the year. Apr to Sept: weekdays 10-7, Suns 2-5; Oct to Mar: weekdays 10-dusk, Suns 1.30-4.30.*Closed Christmas Day.*
Admission: Free (Small charge Suns and Bank Hols). Conducted tours by arrangement £1, Chd 50p (Subject to alteration).
Refreshments: Tea at refreshment pavilion all year.

OXFORDSHIRE

ARDINGTON HOUSE

nr Wantage map H4
Telephone: (0235) 833244
(Mrs Desmond Baring)

Early 18th century of grey brick with red brick facings. Hall with Imperial staircase, panelled dining room with painted ceiling. Attractive Stable Yard.

Location: 12 m S of Oxford; 12 m N of Newbury; 2½ m E of Wantage.
Station(s): Didcot (8 m).
Open: May to Sept - Mons & all Bank Hols 2.30-4.30. Parties of 10 or more welcomed any day by appointment.
Admission: House & Grounds £2.
Refreshments: Coffee & Teas by arrangement.

ASHDOWN HOUSE   ❧ **The National Trust**

nr Lambourn map H4 △

17th century house built by 1st Lord Craven and by him 'consecrated' to Elizabeth, Queen of Bohemia; great staircase rising from hall to attic; portraits of the Winter Queen's family; access to roof, fine views; box parterre and lawns. Avenues and woodland walks.

Location: 2¼ m S of Ashbury; 3½ m N of Lambourn on W side of B4000.
Open: Hall, stairway & roof only (fine views). Apr to end Oct - Weds & Sats 2-6. Guided tours only: at 2.15, 3.15, 4.15 and 5.15, from front door. *Closed* Easter and Bank Holidays. **Woodlands** open all year - Sats to Thurs, dawn to dusk.
Admission: Grounds, hall, stairway & roof: £2, Chd half-price. Woodlands - free. No reduction for parties (which should pre-book in writing).
Refreshments: None available.
No dogs allowed in house or grounds. Wheelchair access to garden only. No WCs.

BLENHEIM PALACE

Woodstock map H5 △ ⑤
Telephone: (0993) 811325 (24 hr information)
(His Grace the Duke of Marlborough)

The Long Library

Masterpiece of Sir John Vanbrugh in the classical style. Fine collection of pictures and tapestries. Gardens and park designed by Vanbrugh and Queen Anne's gardener, Henry Wise. Later construction was carried out by 'Capability' Brown, who also created the famous Blenheim lake. Exhibition of Churchilliana and Sir Winston Churchill's birth room. Churchill paintings on exhibition. A visit to Blenheim Palace is a wonderful way to spend a day. An inclusive ticket covers the Palace Tour, Park and Gardens, Butterfly House, Motor Launch, Train, Adventure Play Area and Nature Trail. Optional are the new Marlborough Maze and Boat Hire on Queen Pool. Events planned for 1993 include the Annual Grand Charity Cricket Match, in aid of the Oxfordshire Association of Young Peoples' Celebrity XI and Oxford University XI on 30th May. The Blenheim Audi International Horse Trials take place on 16th, 17th, 18th and 19th September. Further details from The Administrator, Blenheim Palace, Woodstock, Oxon OX20 1PX. Telephone: (0993) 811091.

Location: SW end of Woodstock which lies 8 m N of Oxford (A44).
Open: mid-Mar to Oct 31 - Daily 10.30-5.30 (last adm 4.45). Different prices apply on Spring Bank Holiday Sunday when the Charity Cricket Match takes place. *Reduced rates for parties.* Educational service for school parties - Palace, Farm, Forestry, Horticulture & Nature Trail. Blenheim Audi International Horse Trials Sept 16, 17, 18 & 19. The right to close the Palace or Park without notice is reserved.
Admission: Charges not available at time of going to press.
Refreshments: Licensed Restaurant & self service cafeteria at the Palace. Self Service Cafeteria at Pleasure Gardens.

BOTANIC GARDENS

Oxford map H5
(University of Oxford)

BROOK COTTAGE

Well Lane, Alkerton map H5
Telephone: (029 587) 303 or 590
(Mr & Mrs David Hodges)

4-acre hillside garden, formed since 1964, surrounding 17th century house. Wide variety of trees, shrubs and plants of all kinds in areas of differing character; water garden; alpine scree; one-colour borders; over 200 shrub and climbing roses; many clematis. Interesting throughout season.

Location: 6 m NW of Banbury; ½ m A422 (Banbury/Stratford-upon-Avon). In Alkerton take Well Lane (opposite war memorial) then right fork.
Open: GARDEN ONLY. Apr 1-Oct 31, Mon-Fri 9-6. Evenings, weekends and all group visits by appointment.
Admission: £1.50, OAPs £1, Chd free.*In aid of National Gardens Scheme.*
Refreshments: For parties by prior arrangement; otherwise DIY coffee/tea.
Unusual plants for sale.

BROUGHTON CASTLE

Banbury map H5
Telephone: (0295) 262624
(The Lord Saye & Sele)

The home of Lord and Lady Saye and Sele and owned by the family for 600 years. A moated medieval Castle greatly enlarged in 1550. Fine panelling and fireplaces, splendid plaster ceilings and good period furniture. Interesting Civil War connections including the secret meeting room of the parliamentary leaders.

Location: 2 m SW of Banbury on the Shipston-on-Stour Road (B4035).
Open: May 19 to Sept 12 - Weds & Suns 2-5; also Thurs in July & Aug 2-5; Bank Hol Suns & Bank Hol Mons including Easter 2-5.
Admission: £3, Chd £1.50, OAPs/Students £2.30. Groups on other days throughout the year by appointment (reduced rates).
Refreshments: Buffet teas on open days; by arrangement for groups.

BUSCOT OLD PARSONAGE   The National Trust

Buscot, Faringdon map H4 △

Built in 1703 of Cotswold stone and stone tiles. On the banks of the Thames. Small garden.

Location: 2 m SE of Lechlade; 4 m NW of Faringdon on A417.
Open: Apr to end Oct - Weds 2-6, by appointment in writing with the tenant.
Admission: £1.*No parties.*
No dogs,no WCs. Unsuitable for wheelchairs.

BUSCOT PARK   ❧   The National Trust

nr Faringdon   map H4   △
Telephone: (0367) 242094 (not weekends)

Built 1780. Fine paintings and furniture. Burne-Jones room. Attractive garden walks, lake. Administered for the National Trust by Lord Faringdon.

Location: 3 m NW Faringdon on Lechlade/Faringdon road (A417).
Open: Apr to end Sept (incl Good Friday, Easter Sat & Sun) - Weds, Thurs, Fris and every 2nd and 4th Sat, and immediately following Sun, 2-6, i.e. Apr 10, 11, 24, 25; May 8, 9, 22 & 23; June 12, 13, 26, 27; July 10, 11, 24, 25; Aug 14, 15, 28, 29; Sept 11, 12, 25, 26. Timed entry to house if crowding occurs.
Admission: House and Grounds: £3.80, Chd £1.90. Grounds only £2.80, Chd £1.40.
Refreshments: Tea room.
No dogs. No indoor photography. Unsuitable for wheelchairs.

DITCHLEY PARK

Enstone   map H5
Telephone: (0608) 677346
(Ditchley Foundation)

Third in size and date of the great 18th century houses of Oxfordshire, Ditchley is famous for its splendid interior decorations (William Kent and Henry Flitcroft). For three and half centuries the home of the Lee family and their descendants - with whom Robert E. Lee was thought to be connected - Ditchley was frequently visited at weekends by Sir Winston Churchill during World War II. It has now been restored, furnished and equipped as a conference centre devoted to the study of issues of concern to the people on both sides of the Atlantic.

Location: 1½ m W of A44 at Kiddington; 2 m from Charlbury (B4437).
Station(s): Charlbury (2 m).
Open: Visits by arrangement with The Bursar, afternoons only. *Closed* mid-July to mid-Sept.

FAWLEY COURT - MARIAN FATHERS HISTORIC HOUSE & MUSEUM   🏛

Henley-on-Thames   map J4
(Marian Fathers)

Designed by Sir Christopher Wren, Fawley Court was built in 1684 for Colonel William Freeman as a family residence. The Mansion House, decorated by Grinling Gibbons and later by James Wyatt, is situated in a beautiful park designed by Lancelot 'Capability' Brown. The Museum consists of a library, various documents of the Polish kings, a very rare and well preserved collection of historical sabres and many memorable military objects of the Polish Army. There are classical sculptures, and paintings from Renaissance and later times. Fawley Court also serves nowadays as a seat of religious community, and from 1953 has been cared for, maintained and restored by the Congregation of Marian Fathers.

Location: 1 m N of Henley-on-Thames via A4155 to Marlow.
Station(s): Henley-on-Thames (1½ m).
Open: Mar to Oct: Weds, Thurs, Suns 2-5. *Closed Easter and Whitsuntide weeks.* Nov, Feb: open to groups by pre-booked appointment.
Admission: £2, Chd £1, OAPs £1.50.
Refreshments: Tea, coffee & home-made cakes available July & Aug.
Car park. No dogs.

THE GREAT BARN  The National Trust

Great Coxwell map H4

13th century, stone built, stone tiled roof, exceptionally interesting timber roof construction. Magnificent proportions.

Location: 2 m SW of Faringdon between A420 & B4019.
Open: All year daily at reasonable hours. Dogs on leads admitted. Wheelchair access.
Admission: 50p.

GREYS COURT  The National Trust

Henley-on-Thames map J4
Telephone: (0491) 628529

Jacobean house with Georgian additions set amid the remains of the courtyard walls and towers of a 14th century fortified house; beautiful gardens; Tudor donkey wheel well-house; Archbishop's Maze.

Location: At Rotherfield Greys 3 m W of Henley-on-Thames E of B481.
Open: House: Apr to end Sept - Mons, Weds, Fris 2-6. Garden: Apr to end of Sept - Mon to Wed, Fri and Sat 2-6. *Closed* Good Friday. Last admissions half-hour before closing.
Admission: House and Garden: £3.80, Garden only: £2.80, Chd half-price. Parties must book in advance. No reduction for parties.
Refreshments: Teas, Apr to end Sept - Mons, Weds, Fris & Sats 2.30-5.15, also for booked parties at other times by arrangement.
Dogs in car park only. No picnicking in grounds.

KINGSTON BAGPUIZE HOUSE

Kingston Bagpuize map H4 △ &
Telephone: (0865) 820259
(Lady Tweedsmuir)

A superb Charles II manor house surrounded by parkland, a large garden and attractive 17th century stable buildings. The house has a magnificent cantilevered staircase and well-proportioned panelled rooms with fine furniture and pictures. The large and interesting garden contains beautiful trees, lawns, a woodland garden, herbaceous and shrub borders and many lovely bulbs.

Location: 5½ m W of Abingdon near junction of A415 & A420.
Open: Apr 1 to Sept 30, Suns and Bank Holiday Mons 2.30-5.30 (last adm 5).
Admission: House and Gardens: £2.50, OAPs £2, Chd £1.50. Garden only: 50p. (Chd under 5 free adm to Gardens, not admitted to House). Groups welcome by appointment. Group rates on request.
Refreshments: Teas.
Wheelchairs garden only. No dogs. Gifts, books, plants for sale. Car parking.

MAPLEDURHAM HOUSE AND WATERMILL - *SEE PAGE 150*

MILTON MANOR HOUSE

nr Abingdon map H4   △   ♿
Telephone: (0235) 831287 or 831871
(Anthony Mockler-Barrett Esq)

Mellow restoration house, with Georgian wings, traditionally designed by Inigo Jones. Very much a family home, seat of the Barret family for six generations. Exquisite Roman Catholic chapel where Mass is still celebrated. 'Like all the best things in England', wrote the late Poet Laurete John Betjeman (a family friend) 'This is hidden. Milton village street is true Berkshire. The Manor House is splendid. Inside are handsome rooms and an exciting contrast - a Chapel and Library in Strawberry Hill Gothick. Do go and see it.' Walled garden (fruit, veg and flowers for sale), Stables, Dovecoat, Doves, Pygmy goats, Shetland ponies, Rare-breed pigs and other animals to see. Fine mature trees and a (rather overgrown) woodland walk. Headquarters of the 'Back to Berkshire Campaign,' and host to the annual 'Authors' Book Fair.' 'A perfect gem of an historic house - the interior is a delight,' says Elisabeth de Stroumillo, writing in the Daily Telegraph. 'Milton Manor is not to be missed.'

Location: 9 m S of Oxford. A34 leading S towards Newbury and the M4. Turning off signposted Milton. Village ½ m. Entrance gates by church. 3 m S of Abingdon. 1 m from Sutton Courteney on B4016. 1½ hrs from London via M4 or M40.
Station(s): Didcot (2 m).
Open: Easter Weekend & Bank Hol. *Then closed.* Open: Whitsun Weekend & Bank Hol. Thereafter Open Tues to Fri only, from Tues June 1 till Tues Aug 31. CLOSED every weekend in the summer except for Aug Bank Hol Weekend & Mon. On days open: Open 2-5. Guided tours 2.30, 3.30, 4.30.*Dogs not admitted (except in picnic/parking area).*
Admission: House and gardens: £3, Gardens only £1.50. chd half-price. Groups: (min 20) always welcome by appointment at any time. £2.50 each in summer months, £3 each the rest of the year.
Refreshments: Home-made teas in the old kitchens, where the famous teapot collection of Mrs Marjorie Mockler, the present owner's late mother, is on show. Light suppers and lunches can be arranged for groups. *Weddings and other special events can be booked.*
Specialist Attraction A century-old Ryder 1/2 horsepower water-pump in the cellars has been restored to working order and can be demonstrated (by appointment only) to enthusiasts.

MAPLEDURHAM HOUSE AND WATERMILL

nr Reading map J4
Telephone: (0734) 723350
(J J Eyston and Lady Anne Eyston)

MAPLEDURHAM HOUSE

MAPLEDURHAM WATERMILL

Late 16th century Elizabethan home of the Blount family. Original moulded ceilings, great oak staircase, fine collection of paintings and private chapel in Strawberry Hill Gothic added in 1797. Interesting literary connections with Alexander Pope, John Galsworthy's Forsyte Saga and Kenneth Graham's Wind in the Willows. Unique setting in grounds running down to the Thames. The 15th century Watermill is fully restored and producing flour and bran which are sold in the gift shop. Walkman audio tours included in the entry to Mill.

Location: 4 m NW of Reading on North Bank of Thames. Signposted off Caversham/Woodcote Road on A4074. Boats from Caversham Bridge 2pm on open days. (Caversham Bridge is ½ m from Reading Station).
Open: Easter to end of Sept - Sats, Suns & Bank Hols. Country Park/Picnic Area: 12.30-7(*last adm 5*) Watermill: 1-5. House: 2.30-5. Winter Suns: Watermill only open 2-4. Midweek party visits by prior arrangement include guided tours.
Refreshments: Tea room serving home made cream teas, cakes, and ice cream in original old manor built in 1390.

MINSTER LOVELL HALL AND DOVECOTE

English⌗Heritage

map H5
Telephone: (0993) 75315

Originally a 15th century manor house, the Hall was built around a courtyard. The medieval dovecote, complete with nesting boxes, has recently been restored. When the hall was dismantled in the 18th century, a skeleton was found in the cellars. This is thought to have been the Yorkist Lord Lovell who disappeared after the Battle of Bosworth 1485, where he fought on the losing side.

Location: 2½ m (4 km) north west of Witney.
Open: Good Friday or Apr 1 (whichever is earlier) to Sept 30 Thurs to Sun and Bank Hols 10-6.
Admission: £1, Concessions 75p, Chd 50p.

NUFFIELD PLACE

Nettlebed map J4
Telephone: (0491) 641224
(Nuffield College, Friends of Nuffield Place)

The home from 1933-1963 of Lord Nuffield, founder of Morris Motors, Nuffield Place is a rare survival of a complete upper-middle class home of the 1930s. Built in 1914, the house was enlarged in 1933 for Lord Nuffield. Several rooms are still decorated in the '30s style, and all rooms contain furnishings acquired by Lord and Lady Nuffield when they took up residence. Clocks, rugs and some tapestries are of fine quality. Some of the furniture is antique but much was custom made by Cecil A. Halliday of Oxford, and is of skilled craftsmanship. The gardens, with mature trees, stone walls and rockery, were laid out during and just after the First World War. Lady Nuffield's Wolseley car is also on display.

Location: Approximately 7 m from Henley-on-Thames, just off A423 to Oxford.
Open: May to Sept, every 2nd and 4th Sun 2-5.
Admission: £2, Concessions £1.50, Chd 50p. Parties by arrangement. Tel: (0491) 39422.
Refreshments: Teas.
Ground floor and garden suitable for disabled.

ROUSHAM HOUSE

Steeple Aston   map H5   △
Telephone: (0869) 47110 or (0860) 360407
(C Cottrell-Dormer, Esq)

Rousham House was built by Sir Robert Dormer in 1635 and the shooting holes were put in the doors while it was a Royalist garrison in the Civil War. Sir Robert's successors were Masters of Ceremonies at Court during eight reigns and employed Court artists and architects to embellish Rousham. The house stands above the River Cherwell one mile from Hopcrofts Holt, near the road from Chipping Norton to Bicester. It contains 150 portraits and other pictures and much fine contemporary furniture. Rooms were decorated by William Kent (1738) and Roberts of Oxford (1765). The garden is Kent's only surviving landscape design with classic buildings, cascades, statues and vistas in thirty acres of hanging woods above the Cherwell. Wonderful herbaceous borders, pigeon house and small parterre. Fine herd of rare Long-Horn cattle in the park. Wear sensible shoes and bring a picnic, and Rousham is yours for the day.

Location: 12 m N of Oxford off Banbury Road (A4260) at Hopcrofts Holt Hotel (1 m).
Station(s): Heyford (1 m).
Open: Apr to Sept inclusive: Weds, Suns & Bank Hols 2-4.30. Gardens only, every day all year, 10-4.30. No children under 15. No dogs. *Groups by arrangement on other days*

STANTON HARCOURT MANOR

Stanton Harcourt   map H5   ♿
(Mr Crispin & The Hon Mrs Gascoigne)

Unique medieval buildings in tranquil surroundings - Old Kitchen, Pope's Tower and Domestic Chapel. House maintained as family home, contains fine collection of pictures, furniture, silver and porcelain. 12 acres of Garden with Great Fish Pond and Stew Ponds.

Location: 9 m W of Oxford; 5 m SE of Witney; on B4449, between Eynsham & Standlake.
Open: House & Gardens. Apr 11, 12, 22, 25, 29; May 2, 3, 13, 16, 27, 30, 31; June 10, 13, 24, 27; July 8, 11, 22, 25; Aug 5, 8, 19, 22, 26, 29, 30; Sept 9, 12, 23, 26; **2-6**.
Admission: House and Garden: £3, Chd (12 and under) and OAPs £2. Coaches by prior arrangement. Gardens only £1.50. Chd (12 and under)/OAPs £1.
Refreshments: Teas on Suns and Bank Hols in aid of Parish Church.
Disabled visitors welcome. Home container-grown shrubs and pot plants for sale.

STONOR PARK

nr Henley-on-Thames map J4
Telephone: (0491) 638587
(Lord & Lady Camoys)

Ancient home of Lord and Lady Camoys and the Stonor family for over eight hundred years, and centre of Catholicism throughout the Recusancy Period, with its own medieval Chapel where mass is still celebrated today. Sanctuary for St. Edmund Campion in 1581. An exhibition features his life and work. The house is of considerable architectural interest, built over many centuries from c.1190, and the site of prehistoric stone circle, now recreated within the grounds. A family home containing fine family portraits and rare items of furniture, paintings, drawings, tapestries, sculptures and bronzes from Britain, Europe and America. Peaceful hillside gardens with magnificent roses and ornamental ponds. Souvenir gift shop and afternoon tearoom serving home-made cakes. Parties welcome, lunches available by prior arrangement.

Location: On B480; 5 m N of Henley-on-Thames, 5 m S of Watlington.

Open: Apr: Suns and Bank Hol Mons only; May, June and Sept: Weds, Suns and Bank Hol Mons; Jul: Weds, Thurs, Suns; Aug: Weds, Thurs, Sats, Suns and Bank Hol Mons 2-5.30 (Bank Hol Mons 12.30-5.30). Last adm 5. Parties by prior arrangement any Tues, Wed or Thur (morning, afternoon or evening with supper) and Sun (afternoon only).

Admission: (1993) £3.30, Chd (under 14 with adult) free, Gardens and Chapel only £1.20. Party rates on application. Discount for NT and English Heritage members, HHA members free on production of card.

WALLINGFORD CASTLE GARDENS

Castle Street, Wallingford

These Gardens are situated on part of the site of Wallingford Castle, which was built by William the Conqueror and demolished by Oliver Cromwell in 1652. The remains of St Nicholas Priory are a feature of the Gardens, which is a haven of beauty and tranquillity.

Open: 1st March - 31st October 10a.m - 6p.m.
Admission: Free.

WATERPERRY GARDENS

nr Wheatley map J5
Telephone: (0844) 339226 and 339254

WATERPERRY GARDENS
Nr. WHEATLEY, OXFORDSHIRE

The peaceful gardens at Waterperry feature a magnificent herbaceous border, shrub and heather borders, alpine and rock gardens, and a new formal garden. Together with stately trees, a river to walk by and a quiet Saxon Church to visit – all set in 83 acres of unspoilt Oxfordshire – the long established herbaceous and alpine nurseries provide year round interest. For the experienced gardener, the novice, or those who have no garden of their own, here is a chance to share, enjoy and admire the order and beauty of careful cultivation.

Garden Shop and Plant Centre with exceptionally wide range of plants, shrubs and fruit produced in the nurseries for sale. Expert care and training is shown in all stages of development. Pots, tubs and sundries also available.

The Teashop provides a delicious selection of home-made food, tea, coffee, fruit juices, etc. Light lunches, morning coffee, teas with scones and cream, cakes, etc. Wine licence.

Open all year from 10 am. Closed for Christmas and New Year Holidays. Open only to visitors to ART IN ACTION between 15th and 18th July.

Enquiries Telephone: (0844) 339226/339254

ADMISSION SEE EDITORIAL REFERENCE

Spacious and peaceful ornamental gardens of 6 acres. Church of Saxon origin and historical interest in grounds with famous old glass, brasses and woodwork. Many interesting plants. Shrub, Herbaceous and Alpine Nurseries.

Location: 2½ m from A40, turn off at Wheatley. 50 m from London, 9 m from Oxford. 62 m Birmingham M40, junction 8. Well signposted locally with Tourist Board Rose' symbol.
Open: All the year. Daily - Mar to Oct 10-5.30 (weekdays); 10-6 (weekends); Nov to Feb 10-5 *(Teashop closes 30 mins earlier). Closed* for Christmas and New Year Hols. Open only to visitors to ART IN ACTION (enquiries 071-381 3192) July 15-18. Parties and coaches at all times by appointment only. High quality Plant Centre and Garden Shop, telephone: (0844) 339226. *In aid of National Gardens' Scheme & Gardeners' Sun, June 6 & Aug 8.*
Admission: Ornamental Gardens & Nurseries - Mar to Oct £1.95, Nov to Feb 75p.
Refreshments: Teashop for morning coffee, light lunches and teas. Wine licence.

SHROPSHIRE

ACTON ROUND HALL

Bridgnorth map G6
(H L Kennedy, Esq)

Built in 1714 for Sir Whitmore Acton by the Smith Brothers of Warwick and abandoned from 1717-1918, the house remains altered from its original state.

Location: 6 m W of Bridgnorth; 15 m SE of Shrewsbury.
Open: May, Jun, Jul, Aug - Thurs 2.30-5.30. Opening hours and catering for organised parties by arrangement.
Admission: £2.

ADCOTE

Little Ness, nr Shrewsbury map F7
Telephone: (0939) 260202
(Adcote School Educational Trust Ltd)

'Adcote is the most controlled, coherent and masterly of the big country houses designed by Norman Shaw' (Mark Girouard, 'Country Life' Oct 1970).

Location: 7 m NW of Shrewsbury off A5.
Open: Apr 19 to July 15 (except May 28-Jun 1 inclusive); 2-5. Re-open Sept 13-Oct 22. All other times by appointment.
Admission: Free but the Governors reserve the right to make a charge.

ATTINGHAM PARK   The National Trust

nr Shrewsbury map G7
Telephone: (0743 77) 203

Designed in 1785 by George Steuart for the 1st Lord Berwick. Elegant classical interior decoration. Famous painted boudoir. Nash Picture Gallery. Fine collection of Regency Silver. Park landscape designed by Humphry Repton, 1797. Extensive deer park.

Location: At Atcham; 4 m SE of Shrewsbury, on N side of Telford Road B4380 (formerly A5).
Open: Apr 3 to Sept 29: Sats to Weds 1.30-5, (Bank Hol Mons 11-5). Oct: Sat & Sun 1.30-5. Last adm 4.30. Shop open as house. Pre-booked parties, including evening opening, by arrangement. Deer park and grounds open daily (except Christmas Day) dawn to dusk.
Admission: House & Grounds: £3.20, Chd £1.60, Family ticket £8. Deer Park & Grounds £1.20.
Refreshments: Home-made lunches and refreshments in tearoom 12.30-5, Bank Holiday Mon 11-5. Licensed. Lunches and suppers at other times for pre-booked parties.
Dogs in grounds only (Not in deer park). Wheelchairs available. Shop. Mother and Baby room.

BENTHALL HALL   The National Trust

Broseley map G6
Telephone: (0952) 882159

16th century stone house with mullioned windows. Interior improved in 17th century. Fine oak staircase and plaster ceilings. Plantsman's garden.

Location: 1 m NW of Broseley; 4 m NE of Much Wenlock; 6 m S of Wellington, (B4375).
Open: Apr 4 to end Sept - Weds, Suns and Bank Hol Mons 1.30-5.30 (last adm 5). House visits and garden visits at other times for groups by appointment.
Admission: £2.50, Chd £1. Garden only: £1.50.
No dogs. Wheelchair access.

BOSCOBEL HOUSE   English ⌗ Heritage

Shifnal map G6
Telephone: (0902) 850244K2

When John Giffard built his hunting lodge in the 17th century, he little knew that it would become a refuge for the future King Charles II after his defeat at the battle of Worcester in 1651. It is now fully re-furnished with historic tapestries, paintings and antique furniture as the Victorians thought it would have appeared when Charles II hid in the priest's hole and took refuge in the oak tree in the grounds. Exhibition and shop.

Location: 8 m NW of Wolverhampton; 3¾ m N of Albrighton.
Open: Good Friday or Apr 1 (whichever is earlier) to Sept 30, daily 10-6. Oct 1 to Maundy Thursday or Mar 31 (whichever is earlier), Tues to Sun 10-4. *Closed* Dec 24-26, Jan 1 to 31.
Admission: £3, Concessions £2.20, Chd £1.50.
Refreshments: Tea room.

BUILDWAS ABBEY   English ⌗ Heritage

map G7
Telephone: (095 245) 3274

Founded in 1135 as an offshoot of Furness Abbey in Cumbria, the abbey belonged briefly to the Savignac Order, then to the Cistercians. Building continued throughout the 12th century and, once completed, the abbey changed little until the Dissolution. The almost complete church typifies the austere style favoured by the Cistercians.

Location: 3¼ m (5.2 km) north east of Much Wenlock.
Open: Good Friday or Apr 1 (whichever is earlier) to Sept 30: Open Daily 10-6. Oct 1 to Maundy Thursday or Mar 31 (whichever is earlier): Open Tues to Sun 10-4. *Closed* Dec 24-26, Jan 1.
Admission: £1.20, Concessions 90p, Chd 60p.

CARDING MILL VALLEY & LONG MYND

🍂 The National Trust

Church Stretton map F6
Telephone: (0694) 722631

Chalet Pavilion in the magnificent scenery of Carding Mill Valley.

Location: 15 m S of Shrewsbury; W of Church Stretton Valley & A49.
Station(s): Church Stretton (1 m).
Open: Moorland open all year. Chalet Pavilion Information Centre, Shop & Cafe. Apr 1 to end June and Sept: Tues to Sun and Bank Hol Mons 11-5, (Shop 12-5). July to end Aug: Daily 11-5 (Shop 12-5). Oct: Sat and Sun 12-4. (Shop 1-4). Booked parties at other times by arrangement.
Admission: Per vehicle: £1.30. Coaches free.
Refreshments: Snacks, light lunches, teas, etc at Chalet Pavilion.
Dogs allowed if kept under control on moorland; not admitted to Chalet Pavilion.

CASTLE GATES LIBRARY

Shrewsbury map F7
Telephone: (0743) 241487

Former premises of Shrewsbury Grammar School, from 16th and 17th centuries. Now used as a public library. Also houses Shropshire's Local Studies Library. Granted a Civic Trust award for a recent restoration scheme.

Open: Public part of the building Mon - Frid 9-5, Sat 9-4. Private areas by prior appointment only.

CONDOVER HALL

nr Shrewsbury map F6
(Royal National Institute for the Blind)

DUDMASTON   🍂 The National Trust

Quatt, Bridgnorth map G6 &
Telephone: (0746) 780866

Late 17th century house; collections of Dutch flower paintings, modern art, botanical paintings and family history. Extensive grounds, woodlands and lakeside garden.

Location: 4 m SE of Bridgnorth on A442.
Open: Apr 4 to end of Sept - Weds & Suns 2.30-6 (last adm 5.30). Special opening for pre-booked parties Thur 2.30-6.
Admission: House and Garden: £3, Family £7.50. Garden only £2. Parties must book in advance.
Refreshments: Home-made teas 2.30-5.30.
Dogs in Dingle and Park only, on leads. Shop.

HAUGHMOND ABBEY   English ⌗ Heritage

map F7
Telephone: (074 377) 661

William FitzAlan re-established this house for Augustinian canons in 1135. It was rebuilt when FitzAlan became abbot, and further changes and additions were made over the centuries. In 1539 the church was demolished and the abbot's lodging, great hall and kitchens were converted into a private house. Some fine Norman doorways and 14th century statues repay a visit.

Location: 3½ m (5.6 km) north east of Shrewsbury.
Open: Good Friday or Apr 1 (whichever is earlier) to Sept 30: Open Daily 10-6. Oct 1 to Maundy Thursday or Mar 31 (whichever is earlier): Open Tues to Sun 10-4. *Closed* Dec 24-26, Jan 1.
Admission: £1.20, Concessions 90p, Chd 60p.

🍂 THE SIGN OF A GREAT DAY OUT

HODNET HALL GARDENS

nr Market Drayton map G7 &
Telephone: (063 084) 202
(Mr & the Hon Mrs Heber Percy)

LUDLOW CASTLE

Castle Square, Ludlow map F6
Telephone: (0584) 873947
(The Trustees of the Powis Castle Estate)

From the glorious daffodils of Spring to the magnificent roses of Summer, each season brings fresh delights to these award winning gardens. Over 60 acres of magnificent forest trees, sweeping lawns and tranquil pools ensure plentiful wildlife and brilliant natural colour within this beautiful setting.

Location: 12 m NE of Shrewsbury; 5½ m SW of Market Drayton, at junction of A53 to A442; M6 18½ m (junction 15) leading to A53 or M54 (junction 3).
Open: Apr 1 to Sept 30, Mon to Sat 2-5; Suns & Bank Hols 12-5.30.
Admission: £2.50, OAPs £2, Chd £1.*Reduced rates for organised parties of 25 or over.*Seson tickets on application. Free car and coach park.
Refreshments: Tearooms open daily 2-5. Suns and Bank Holidays 12-5.30. *Parties to pre-book (menu on request). Gift shop, kitchen garden sales.*
Dogs allowed but must be kept on leads.

Originally a Norman Castle of which the remains include the round nave of a Chapel with fine Norman doorways. Then a fortified Royal Palace and headquarters of the Council of the Marches. An unusually complete range of medieval buildings still stands. Visitors can enjoy the large open space of the outer bailey.

Location: Castle Square, Ludlow.
Open: Daily Feb 1 to Apr 30, 10.30-4. May 1 to Sept 30, 10.30-5. Oct 1 to Nov 30, 10.30-4. *Closed* Dec and Jan.
Admission: £2, Chd £1, OAPs £1.50. Family ticket £6. Discounts for school parties by arrangement with the Custodian.
Refreshments: In Castle Square.
Public car park off Castle Square. Suitable for disabled.

LUDFORD HOUSE

Ludlow map F6
(Mr D. F. A. Nicholson)

House dating back to 12th century.

Location: ½ m S of Ludlow, B4361 road.
Open: Grounds and exterior by written permission, with limited inspection of interior.
Admission: £2.50.
Refreshments: Hotels and Restaurants in Ludlow available.
Unsuitable for disabled.

MAWLEY HALL

Cleobury Mortimer map G6

18th century house.

Location: 1 m S of Cleobury Mortimer (A4117); 7 m W of Bewdley.
Open: By written appointment to Mrs R. Sharp, 43 Dover Street, London W1X 3RE.
Admission: £3.

MOAT HOUSE

Longnor, nr Shrewsbury map F4
Telephone: (0743) 718434
(Mr & Mrs C. P. Richards)

Fine example of a timber framed manor house of c1463. The hall exhibiting unique timber work and wooden masks, Surrounded by its moat of c1250.

Location: 8 m S of Shrewsbury E off A49 through village left into lane.
Open: Apr to Sept. Thurs & Spring & Summer Bank Hols 2.30-5, other times by arrangement for parties of 20 plus.
Admission: £1.50.
Accommodation for six, dinner if pre booked, licensed, brochure available. No dogs. Not suitable for disabled.

PREEN MANOR GARDENS

Church Preen, nr Church Stretton map F6
Telephone: (0694) 771207
(Mr and Mrs P. Trevor-Jones).

Extensive gardens on site of C12 Cluniac Priory later Norman Shaw mansion (now demolished). Gardens restored and replanned over last 14 years; Woodland walks, fine trees in park, C13 Monastic Church with oldest Yew tree in Europe. House not open.

Location: 5 m W Much Wenlock. B4371 to Church Stretton 3 m turn R to Church Preen and Hughley. 1½ m L to Church Preen, over Xrds, ½ m drive on R.
Open: Jun 3, 17. Jul 1, 15 & 29. (Thurs). Sun Jul 18. 2-7. Sun Sept 26. 2-5. *In aid of National Gardens Scheme and other charities.* Parties: Jun/Jul Pre-booked. (min of 10 persons).
Admission: £1.50, Chd 50p.
Refreshments: Home made teas. Not Sept 26.
Car parking. Not suitable for disabled. Plants for sale.

SHIPTON HALL

Much Wenlock map G6
Telephone: (074 636) 225
(J N R N Bishop, Esq)

Delightful Elizabethan stone manor c. 1587 with Georgian additions. Interesting Roccoco and Gothic plasterwork by T. F. Pritchard. Georgian stable block containing working pottery. Stone walled garden, medieval dovecote and Parish Church, dating from late Saxon period.

Location: In Shipton; 6 m SW of Much Wenlock junction B4376 & B4368.
Open: Easter to end Sept: Thurs, Bank Holiday Suns and Mons (except Christmas and New Year) 2.30-5.30. Also by appointment for parties of 20 or more any time of year.
Admission: House and Garden: £2, Chd £1. Special rate for parties.
Refreshments: Teas/buffets by prior arrangement.

STOKESAY CASTLE   English✄Heritage

Craven Arms map F6
Telephone: (0588) 672544

Finest example of a moated and fortified manor house, dating from the 13th century.

Location: 8m from Ludlow; ¾m S of Craven Arms on 3rd class Road off A49.
Station(s): Craven Arms (1m).
Open: Good Friday or Apr (whichever is earlier) to Sept 30 daily 10-6. Oct 1 to Mar 31 Wed - Sun 10-4. *Closed 24-26 Dec and Jan 1.*
Admission: £2.20, concessions £1.60, chd £1.10. Party bookings in advance.

UPTON CRESSETT HALL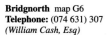

Bridgnorth map G6
Telephone: (074 631) 307
(William Cash, Esq)

Elizabethan Manor House and magnificent Gatehouse in beautiful countryside by Norman church. Unusually fine medieval timber work and interesting brick and plaster work; 14th century Great Hall.

Location: 4 m W of Bridgnorth; 18 m SE of Shrewsbury off A458.
Open: May to Sept - Thurs 2.30-5. *Parties at other times throughout the year by appointment.*
Admission: £2, Chd £1.

WALCOT HALL

Lydbury North map F6
Telephone: 071-581 2782
(C.R.W. Parish)

Built by Sir William Chambers for Lord Clive of India. This Georgian House possesses a free-standing and recently restored ballroom, stable yard with matching clock towers, extensive walled garden, in addition to its icehouse, meat safe and dovecote. There is a fine arboretum, noted for its rhododendrons and azaleas and specimen trees.

Location: 3 m E of Bishop's Castle, on B4385, ½ m outside Lydbury North.
Open: Bank Hols: Sun & Mon (excl. Christmas and New Year). May: Sun, Wed, Fri. Jun: Wed, Fri. Jul & Aug: Sun. Sept: Wed. 2.15-4.30. Groups of 10 or more and other times, by appointment.
Admission: £2.50. Chd (under 15) free.
Refreshments: Powis Arms; teas when available.
Suitable for disabled.

WENLOCK PRIORY   English✄Heritage

Much Wenlock map G6
Telephone: (0952) 727466

The long history of Wenlock stretches back to the 7th century, although nothing visible remains of the religious house founded by St Milburge. After the Norman Conquest, a Cluniac priory was established, which came to be regarded as alien during the Hundred Years' War with France. Decorative arcading from the 12th century chapter house survives and some unusual features in the later, rebuilt church.

Location: In Much Wenlock.
Open: Good Friday or Apr 1 (whichever is earlier) to Sept 30 daily 10-6. Oct 1 to Maundy Thursday or Mar 31 (whichever is earlier) Tues to Sun 10-4. *Closed* Dec 24-26, Jan 1.
Admission: £1.70, Concessions £1.30, Chd 85p. Price includes a Personal Stereo Guided Tour.

WESTON PARK

nr Shifnal map G7
Telephone: (095276) 207
(Weston Park Foundation)

Built 1671 and designed by Lady Wilbraham, contains a superb collection of antiques and paintings including works by Van Dyck, Lely and Gainsborough. Set in 1000 acres of classic 'Capability' Brown Parkland and formal gardens including recently restored Rose Garden, Italian Broderie. Fine Arboretum. Miniature Railway, Woodland Adventure Playground, Museum and Pets Corner. Horse Trials, Classical Concerts and other special events throughout the Summer.

Location: Entrance from A5 at Weston-under-Lizard, 6 m W of Junction 12, M6 (Gailey); 3 m N of Junction 3, M54 (Tong).
Open: Easter to Sept. (Please enquire for dates and times. Daily in Aug. Park: 11-7 (last adm 5). House: 1-5 (last adm 4.30).
Admission: House, Park and Gardens: £4, Chd/OAPs £2.75. Park and Gardens: £3, Chd/OAPs £2. Special rates for pre-booked parties and school visits. Entry charges may be adjusted on certain days for special events. Free coach/car parking.
Refreshments: Traditional country cooking in The Old Stables. Tearooms and licensed bar. Restaurant service for pre-booked parties. Gourmet Dinners in the House on selected dates. Private functions incl. residential dinners and wedding receptions by arrangement.
Dogs (on leads) welcome in Park.

WILDERHOPE MANOR 🌿 The National Trust

Wenlock Edge map G6 &
Telephone: (06943) 363

Elizabethan manor house with 17th century plaster ceilings. House now run as a Youth Hostel.

Location: 7 m SW of Much Wenlock; ½ m S of B4371.
Open: Apr 1 to end of Sept - Weds & Sats 2-4.30; Oct to Mar - Sats only 2-4.30.
Admission: £1, Chd 50p. *No reduction for parties.*
Dogs around Manor on leads.

WROXETER (VIROCONIUM) ROMAN CITY

English ♯ Heritage

map G6
Telephone: (0743) 761330

Viroconium was the fourth largest city in Roman Britain and the largest to escape modern development. Deep beneath the exposed walls of the market-hall excavations are revealing a legionary fortress of the first century; while nearby the timber buildings of later settlers are being examined. The most impressive feature is the huge wall dividing the exercise yard from the baths.

Location: 5½ m (8.8 km) south east of Shrewsbury.
Open: Good Friday or Apr 1 (whichever is earlier) to Sept 30: Open Daily 10-6. Oct 1 to Maundy Thursday or Mar 31 (whichever is earlier): Open Tues to Sun 10-4. *Closed* Dec 24-26, Jan 1.
Admission: £1.70, Concessions £1.30, Chd 85p.

BARRINGTON COURT 🌿 The National Trust

Nr Ilminster map F3

Beautiful garden influenced by Gertrude Jekyll and laid out in a series of rooms. Tudor manor house restored in 1920s by the Lyle family. Now sub-let to Stuart Interiors, the furniture reproducers.

Location: In Barrington village, 5 m NE of Ilminster off A303, 6 m S of Curry Rivel on A378 between Taunton and Langport (193: ST397182).
Open: Barrington Court Garden, Apr 1 to Oct 1, Daily except Thur and Frid, 11-5.30; Court House, Apr 1 to Oct 1, Weds only, 1.30-5.
Admission: Garden: £3, Chd £1.50; Parties £2.50, Chd party £1.20. Court House 50p. (Guided tours only).
Refreshments: Licensed restaurant open same days as Garden.
Garden suitable for wheelchairs.

SOMERSET

BARFORD PARK

Enmore map F3
Telephone: (0278) 671269
(Mr & Mrs Michael Stancomb)

Set in a large garden and looking out across a ha-ha to a park dotted with fine trees, it presents a scene of peaceful domesticity, a miniature country seat on a scale appropriate today. The well proportioned rooms, with contemporary furniture, are all in daily family use. The walled flower garden is in full view from the house, and the woodland and water gardens and archery glade with their handsome trees form a perfect setting for the stone and red-brick Queen Anne building.

Location: 5 m W of Bridgwater.
Open: By appointment only. Please telephone above number.
Admission: Charges not available at the time of going to press.

THE BISHOP'S PALACE

Wells map G3
Telephone: (0749) 78691
(The Church Commissioners)

The fortified and moated Palace comprises Jocelin's Hall (early 13th century), the Bishop's Chapel and the ruins of the Banqueting Hall (both late 13th century) and the Bishop's Residence (15th century). The grounds which include the wells from which Wells derives its name, provide a beautiful setting for gardens of herbaceous plants, roses, shrubs, mature trees and the Jubilee Arboretum. On the Moat are waterfowl and swans.

Location: City of Wells, at end of Market Place (enter through Bishop's Eye).
Open: Palace, Chapel and Grounds and Wells. Easter to end of Oct - Bank Holiday Mons, Thurs & Suns; Aug - Daily: 2-6. Special exhibitions are announced from time to time in the press, when different admission charges may apply. Last admission 5.30.
Admission: £1.50, Chd 50p. Party rates by appointment.
Refreshments: Available in Undercroft.

THE CHURCH HOUSE

Crowcombe map F3
(The Charity Commissioners)

CLAPTON COURT GARDENS AND PLANT CENTRE

Crewkerne map F3 &
Telephone: (0460) 73220/72200
(Capt S J Loder)

One of the West Country's most beautiful and interesting 10 acre gardens in lovely park-like setting. Immaculate formal gardens with terraces, rockery, rose and water gardens. Fascinating woodland garden with natural streams and glades. Fine collection of rare and unusual plants, shrubs and trees of botanical interest. Largest and oldest Ash in Great Britain, an original Metasequoia now over 80 feet. Dazzling display of spring bulbs, glorious autumn colours, worth visiting at all seasons. Featured in BBC Gardeners World, Country Life and House and Garden. PLANT CENTRE selling high quality, rare and choice plants, shrubs and trees.

Location: 3 m S of Crewkerne on B3165 to Lyme Regis.
Open: GARDENS AND PLANT CENTRE ONLY. Mar to Oct inclusive - Mons to Frid 10.30 -5; Suns 2-5. *Closed* Sats (except Easter Sat 2-5).
Admission: Parties must be pre-booked. Free car parking.
Refreshments: Home-made lunches and teas, licensed Apr to Sept, times as garden. Meals by arrangement for parties.
No dogs.

CLEEVE ABBEY English Heritage

map F3
Telephone: (0984) 40377

Although little remains of the church, most of the buildings surrounding the cloister of this Cistercian abbey are remarkably complete. A timber roof of outstanding workmanship survives in the 15th century dining hall; also preserved are fragments of pavements, tiles and wall paintings of earlier date.

Location: Washford.
Open: Good Friday or Apr 1 (whichever is earlier) to Sept 30: Open Daily 10-6. Oct 1 to Maundy Thursday or Mar 31 (whichever is earlier): Open Tues to Sun 10-4. *Closed* Dec 24-26, Jan 1.
Admission: £1.70, Concessions £1.30, chd 85p.

COLERIDGE COTTAGE The National Trust

Nether Stowey, nr Bridgwater map F3
Telephone: (0278) 732662

Home of S T Coleridge from 1797-1800, where he wrote 'The Ancient Mariner'.

Location: At W end of village on S side of A39; 8 m W of Bridgwater.
Open: Parlour and Reading Room only. Apr 1 to Oct 3: Tues to Thurs and Suns 2 -5.
Admission: £1.50, Chd 75p. No reduction for parties. Parties must book beforehand. *Adm in winter by written application to the tenant.*
Refreshments: In village.
No dogs. Unsuitable for wheelchairs and coaches.

COMBE SYDENHAM COUNTRY PARK

Monksilver, Taunton map F3 (s)
Telephone: (0984) 56284
(Mr and Mrs W. Theed)

Built in 1580 on the site of a monastic settlement and home of Elizabeth Sydenham, wife of Sir Francis Drake. Beautifully restored Courtroom and working Cornmill. Elizabethan style gardens, Deer Park, Children's play area. Woodland Walks with Alice Trail and The Ancient Trail of Trees. Trout Farm, Fly fishing for beginners.

Location: 5 m N of Wiveliscombe; 3 m S of Watchet on B3188.
Open: Mar to Oct. Sun - Frid, 10-5. (Country Park only Sun). Farm Shop open Sat 9.30-12. Evening Tours of Private Rooms and Supper by arrangement.
Admission: Free car/coach parking.
Refreshments: Tea-room/Gift Shop selling our speciality Smoked Trout/Pate.

CROWE HALL

Widcombe, Bath map F11
Telephone: (0225) 310322
(Mr John Barratt)

Elegant George V classical Bath villa, retaining grandiose mid-Victorian portico and great hall. Fine 18th century and Regency furniture; interesting old paintings and china. 10 acres of romantic gardens cascading down hillside. Terraces, Victorian grotto, ancient trees.

Location: 3/10 m on right up Widcombe Hill.
Open: Gardens only, Suns Apr 18 and Jun 6 *for NGS*, Also Suns May 9, 23 and Aug 15. House and Gardens by appointment (closed in July). Groups welcome.
Admission: Gardens only £1, House and Gardens £2.
Refreshments: Teas on opening days and by appointment.

DODINGTON HALL

nr. Nether Stowey, Bridgwater map F3
Telephone: (0278 74) 400
(Lady Gass, occupiers Mr and Mrs P Quinn).

Small Tudor Manor House on the lower slopes of the Quantock Hills. Great hall with oak roof. Carved stone fireplace. Semi-formal garden with roses and shrubs.

Location: ½ m from A39. 11 m from Bridgwater; 7 m from Williton.
Open: Suns May 23 to Jul 25 (inclusive) 2-5. Donations for Charity.
Refreshments: Parking for 15 cars. Regret unsuitable for disabled.

DUNSTER CASTLE   The National Trust

Dunster, nr.Minehead map F3
Telephone: (0643) 821314

Castle dating from 13th century, remodelled by Anthony Salvin in 19th century. Fine 17th century staircase and plaster ceilings. Terraced Gardens.

Location: In Dunster, 3 m SE of Minehead on A396.
Station(s): Dunster (West Somerset Railway) (1½ m).
Open: Castle: Apr 3 to Oct 3 - Sat to Wed 11-5. Oct 4 to Nov 1: Sat to Wed - 11-4. Garden and Park: Feb 1 to Dec 13: daily. Feb, Mar, Oct, Nov, Dec 11-4; Apr to Sept 11-5.
Admission: Castle, garden and park: £4.50, Chd (under 16) £2.20. Parties £4 by prior arrangement. Garden and park only £2.50, Chd (under 16) £1.20.
Refreshments: In village (not N.T.). National Trust Shop.
Shop. Ten minute steep climb from NT car park. No dogs in garden, in park area on leads. Lift available from car park. Areas of the house can be visited by wheelchair, and assistance given if needed.

FARLEIGH HUNGERFORD CASTLE   English ♯ Heritage

map G4
Telephone: (0225) 754026

Sir Thomas de Hungerford, Speaker of the House of Commons, fortified the original manor house without permission; he was later pardoned. His mailed effigy, surrounded by the tombs of other Hungerfords, lies in the chapel, a place to stir the imagination.

Location: Farleigh Hungerford 3½ m (5.6 km) west of Trowbridge.
Open: Good Friday or Apr 1 (whichever is earlier) to Sept 30: Open Daily 10-6. Oct 1 to Maundy Thursday or Mar 31 (whichever is earlier): Open Tues to Sun 10-4. *Closed Dec 24-26, Jan 1.*
Admission: £1.20, Concessions 90p, Chd 60p.

GAULDEN MANOR

Tolland, nr Taunton map F3 △
Telephone: (09847) 213
(Mr & Mrs James LeGendre Starkie)

Small historic red sandstone Manor House of great charm. A real lived-in home. Past Somerset seat of the Turberville family, immortalised by Thomas Hardy. Great Hall has magnificent plaster ceiling and oak screen to room known as the Chapel. Fine antique furniture. Interesting grounds include bog garden with primulas and other moisture loving plants. Herb garden.

Location: 9 m NW of Taunton; 1 m E of Tolland Church. Gaulden Manor signposted from A358 Taunton/Williton Rd just N of Bishops Lydeard and from B3188 Wivelscombe/Watchet Rd (cars only). Nearest village Lydeard St Lawrence (1½ m).
Open: May 2 to Sept 5 - Suns & Thurs; also Easter Sun and Mon and all Bank Hols: 2-5.30 (last adm 5).
Admission: House and Garden: £2.80, Chd (under 14) £1.25. Garden only: £1.25. *Parties on other days by prior arrangement. Mornings, afternoons or evenings & out of season.*
Refreshments: Teas in Garden Tearoom.
Shop-books, rare and unusual plants.

HADSPEN GARDEN & NURSERY

Castle Cary map G3
Telephone: (0963) 50939

An eight acre Edwardian Garden in a sheltered situation with a unique walled garden of colourist borders, ponds and a woodland area including an ancient meadow. The many unusual plants that grow have been developed in the garden are available in the nursery.

Location: 2 m E of Castle Cary on the A371.
Open: Mar 1 to Oct 1: Thurs, Fri, Sat, Sun and Bank Holiday Mon.
Admission: £2, Chd 50p. Wheelchairs free.
Refreshments: Sunday afternoons.
Car parking.

THE SIGN OF A GREAT DAY OUT

HATCH COURT

Hatch Beauchamp map F3 △
Telephone: (0823) 480120
(Dr and Mrs Robin Odgers)

A fine Bath stone mansion in the Palladian style, designed in 1755 by Thomas Prowse of Axbridge. Curved wings, magnificent stone staircase and much of the internal decoration carried out around 1800. The house has a good collection of pictures, 17th and 18th century furniture and unusual semicircular china room. Small Canadian Military Museum. Gardens undergoing extensive redevelopment with a fine restored walled kitchen garden, parkland and deer park. The medieval parish church of St. John the Baptist is situated nearby.

Location: 6 m SE of Taunton midway between Taunton & Ilminster off A358.
Open: House and Garden: Jun 17 to Sept 16 - Thurs and Aug Bank Holiday Mon 2.30-5.30. Garden only: Jun 4 to Sept 24 - Fri 2.30-5.30.
Admission: £2.80. Garden only: £1.50.
Refreshments: Full catering by arrangement. Teas available Thurs.
No coaches. Organised parties by prior appointment at all times (unless open as above).

KELWAYS NURSERIES LTD

Langport
Telephone: (0458) 250521
(0458) 250521

The Royal Nurseries of Langport - special open fields in May and June during the Paeony Festival.

Location: On Somerton Road from Langport (B3153) just 200 yards from A372.
Open: Nursery: all year. Please telephone for dates of Paeony Festival.
Refreshments: during June.

KENTSFORD HOUSE

Watchet map F3
(Mrs Wyndham. Occupier: Mr H Dibble)

House open **only** by written appointment with Mr H. Dibble.

Open: Gardens: Tues and Bank Hols Apr 16 to Aug 31.
Admission: Donations towards renovation of fabric.

LYTES CARY MANOR   🌿 The National Trust

nr Ilchester map G3

Mediaeval manor house with chapel; fine furnishings; formal garden.

Location: On W side of Fosse Way (A37); 2½ m NE of Ilchester signposted on bypass (A303).
Open: Apr 3 to Oct 30 - Mons, Weds & Sats 2-6 or dusk if earlier (last adm 5.30).
Admission: £3.50, Chd £1.70.
Refreshments: Refreshments and National Trust Shop at Montacute.
No dogs, no lavatories. NB Coaches by appointment only, large coaches cannot pass gate piers, so must stop in narrow road, ¼ m walk.

MAUNSEL HOUSE

North Newton, nr Bridgwater map F3
Telephone: (0278) 663398
(Maggie Lennie)

MIDELNEY MANOR

Drayton, nr Langport map F3 △
(Mr John Cely Trevilian)

16th to 18th century Manor House. Originally island manor of Abbots of Muchelney and property of Trevilian family since 1500. 17th century Falcons Mews. Gardens; Woodland walks; Heronry.

Location: Signposted from A378 at Bell Hotel; Curry Rivel & from B3168 Hambridge/Curry Rivel Road & in Drayton.
Open: Every Thurs, Apr 29 to Sept 30 and all Bank Holiday Mons 2.30-5.30 (last tour 4.30).
Admission: £2.50, Chd £1.
Refreshments: Teas and Private Functions by appointment.
Coach parties.

MILTON LODGE GARDENS

Wells map G4
Telephone: (0749) 672168
(Mr & Mrs David Tudway Quilter)

'The great glory of the gardens of Milton Lodge is their position high up on the slopes of the Mendip Hills to the north of Wells ...with broad panoramas of Wells Cathedral and the Vale of Avalon.' *Lanning Roper.* Mature alkaline terraced garden of great charm dating from 1909. Replanned 1962 with mixed shrubs and herbaceous plants, old fashioned roses and ground cover; numerous climbers; old established yew hedges. Fine trees in garden and in separate 7 acre arboretum on opposite side of Old Bristol Road.

Location: ½ m N of Wells. From A39 Bristol-Wells turn N up Old Bristol Road; free car park first gate on left.
Open: GARDEN AND ARBORETUM ONLY: Easter to end Oct: daily (except Sat) 2-6. Parties and coaches by prior arrangement.
Admission: £2, Chd (under 14) free. *Open on certain Suns in aid of National Gardens Scheme.*
Refreshments: Teas available Suns and Bank Hols. Apr to Sept.
No dogs.

MONTACUTE HOUSE   The National Trust

Yeovil map G3
Telephone: (0935) 823289

Magnificent Elizabethan house of Ham Hill stone begun in the 1590s by Sir Edward Phelips. Fine heraldic glass, tapestries, panelling and furniture. National Portrait Gallery Exhibitions of Elizabethan and Jacobean portraits. Fine formal garden and park.

Location: In Montacute village 4 m W of Yeovil on E side of A3088; 3 m E of A303 nr Ilchester.
Open: House: Apr 1 to Oct 31: Daily (except Tues) 12-5.30. *Closed* Good Friday. Last adm 5 (or sunset if earlier). *Parties by written appointment with the Administrator.* Garden & Park: Apr 1 to Apr 1994 - Daily (except Tues) 11.30-5.30 or dusk if earlier.
Admission: House, Garden and Park: £4.60, Chd £2.30; Parties £4.30, Chd £2.10. Garden and Park only: Apr 1 to Nov 1 £2.50, Chd £1.20. Nov 2 to Apr 1994 £1.20, Chd 50p.
Refreshments: Light lunches & teas. *Parties catered for by arrangement with the Restaurant Manager.*
National Trust Shop.

ORCHARD WYNDHAM

Williton, nr Taunton map F3
(Mrs Wyndham)

Modest English Manor House. Family home for 700 years encapsulating continuous building and alteration between 14th and 20th centuries.

Location: 1 m from A39 at Williton.
Open: House and Gardens: Guided tours only - Aug 1993 - Mon & Tues 2-4.30. Last tour begins at 4. *(Property undergoing restoration, please telephone 0984 32309 before planning a visit.)* Limited parking, no coaches - narrow access road. Maximum of 15 people in house at any one time. No dogs. Not suitable for the disabled.
Admission: £2.50, Chd under 12 £1.
Refreshments: Available in Williton.

STOKE-SUB-HAMDON PRIORY   ⚜   The National Trust

nr Montacute map G3 ♿

Complex of buildings begun in 14th century for the priests of the chantry chapel of St Nicholas (destroyed).

Location: Between A303 & A3088; 2 m W of Montacute between Yeovil & Ilminster.
Open: All the year - Daily 10-6 (or sunset if earlier). *Great Hall only open to the public.*
Admission: Free.
No dogs.

TINTINHULL HOUSE GARDEN   ⚜   The National Trust

nr. Yeovil map G3 △ ♿

20th century formal garden surrounding 17th century house (house not open).

Location: 5 m NW of Yeovil; ½ m S of A303 on outskirts Tintinhull village.
Open: Apr 1 to Sept 30 - Weds, Thurs & Sats, also Bank Hol Mons 2-6 (last adm 5.30).
Admission: £3.20. *No reductions for parties or children.*
Coach parties by written arrangement with the tenant. No dogs. Wheelchairs provided.

STAFFORDSHIRE

ANCIENT HIGH HOUSE

Stafford map G7

The Ancient High House is the largest timber-framed town house in England, and was built in 1595 by John Dorrington from local oak. It has been in the hands of several famous Staffordshire families, inlcuding the Sneyds and Dyotts, and has enjoyed a long and varied history. It has recently been restored to its Elizabethan splendour and houses a permanent collection of furniture, costume, paintings and ceramics, all in period room settings. A special feature of interest is the collection of rare 18th and 19th century wallpapers, found during the restoration. The house also has an exhibition area, along with a video theatre, heritage shop selling traditional gifts made by local craftsmen, and a children's costume wardrobe. Heritage Exhibition and Tourist Information Centre.

Location: M6 Off junction 13 - A449 to Stafford and M6 junction 14 - A5013 to Stafford.
Open: House and Exhibition Centre: Mon to Fri 9-5; Sat Apr to Oct: 10-4. Nov to Mar: 10-3.
Admission: £1.20, Chd/OAPs 60p, reduced rate for parties.
Tourist Information Centre: Mon to Fri 9-5; Oct to Mar: Sat 10-3. Apr to Sept: 10-4. Contact: The Heritage Manager (0785) 223181 ext 352, or (0785) 40204. No car park.

BIDDULPH GRANGE GARDEN  The National Trust

Biddulph, Stoke-on-Trent map G7
Telephone: (0782) 517999

An exciting and rare survival of a high Victorian garden, acquired by the National Trust in 1988. The garden has undergone an extensive restoration project, which will continue for a number of years. Conceived by James Bateman, the 15 acres are divided into a number of smaller gardens which were designed to house specimens from his extensive and wide-ranging plant collection. An Egyptian Court, Chinese Pagoda, Bridge, Joss House and Pinetum, together with many other settings, all combine to make the garden a miniature tour of the world.

Location: ½ m N of Biddulph, 5 m SE of Congleton, 7 m N of Stoke-on-Trent. Access from A527 (Tunstall/Congleton). Entrance on Grange Road.
Station(s): Kidsgrove or Congleton, both 4 m. Stoke-on-Trent 7m.
Open: Apr 1 to end Oct - Wed to Fri 12-6 (last adm 5.30 or dusk if earlier). Sat, Sun and Bank Holiday Mon 11-6. *Closed Good Friday.* Pre-booked guided tours at 10, Wed, Thurs, Fri £5 (inc NT members); Nov 6 to Dec 19 - Sat and Sun 12-4.
Admission: £3.70, Chd half-price, Family ticket £9.25. Free parking (car park 50 yds).
Refreshments: Coffee, light refreshments including teas. Tea room and shop open same time as garden.
Access for disabled visitors is extremely difficult, unsuitable for wheelchairs, please contact Head Gardener for details.

CHILLINGTON HALL

nr Wolverhampton map G7 △
Telephone: (0902) 850236
(Mr & Mrs Peter Giffard)

Georgian house. Part 1724 (Francis Smith); part 1785 (Sir John Soane). Fine saloon. The lake in the Park is believed to be the largest ever created by 'Capability' Brown. The bridges by Brown and Paine, and the Grecian and Roman Temples, together with the eyecatching Sham House, as well as many fine trees and plantations add great interest to the four mile walk around the lake. Dogs welcome in grounds if kept on lead.

Location: 4 m SW of A5 at Gailey; 2 m Brewood; 8 m NW of Wolverhampton; 14 m S of Stafford. Best approach is from A449 (Junction 12, M6, Junction 2, M54) through Coven and follow signposts towards Codsall (no entry at Codsall Wood).
Open: May to Sept 14 - Thurs (also Suns in Aug) 2.30-5.30. Open Easter Sun & Suns preceding May and late Spring Bank Holidays 2.30-5.30.*Parties of at least 15 other days by arrangement.*
Admission: £2; Grounds only £1. Chd half-price.

DOROTHY CLIVE GARDEN

Willoughbridge map G7 &
(Willoughbridge Garden Trust)

8 acre woodland and rhododendron garden; shrub roses, water garden and a large scree in a fine landscape setting. Good herbaceous plantings are a summer feature: autumn colour. Spectacular waterfall, many interesting and less usual plants. Fine views.

Location: 9 m SW Newcastle-under-Lyme. On A51 between junctions with A525 & A53, 1 m E of Woore.
Open: Garden only. Apr to Oct: daily 10-5.30.
Admission: £2, Chd 50p.
Refreshments: Attractive tea-room and lawn open daily. Home baking.
Large car park.

HANCH HALL

Lichfield map H7
Telephone: (0543) 490308
(Mr Douglas Milton-Haynes and Mrs Mary Milton-Haynes)

Original mansion built in the reign of Edward I. Seat of the Aston family until the end of the 16th c, then the Ormes, staunch supporters of Charles 1st. Home of General William Dyott from 1817, then Sir Charles Forster in the 19th c. The present house which is lived in as a family home, exhibits Tudor, Jacobean, Queen Anne and Georgian architecture. Wealth of oak panelling; Observation Tower, interesting collections. Pleasant gardens, trout pool, waterfowl. Tiny Chapel in grounds.

Location: 4 m NW of Lichfield on Uttoxeter Road (B5014).
Open: Apr 11 to Sept 26 1993. Suns only and Bank Hol Mons 2-6. (Last tour of House 5). Parties of 20 or more, daily, mornings, afternoons or evenings by arrangement.
Admission: House & Gardens: £3, Chd £1.50. Reductions for parties of 20 or more. Free car park.
Refreshments: Teas and home baking in the 17th c Stable Block. Hot or cold meals by arrangement.
Gifts and Bric-a-brac shop. Lengthy tour of House not suitable for small children. Candlelight evenings first week in Dec. Regret no dogs. *No stiletto heels please in the house.* For further information contact Mrs Mary Milton-Haynes. NB HANCH HALL ESTATE *reserves the right to change days and hours of opening and to close all or parts of the Hall without prior notice.*

MOSELEY OLD HALL    The National Trust

Wolverhampton map G6 △ ♿ ⑤
Telephone: (0902) 782808

A 17th century formal garden surrounds this mainly Elizabethan house where Charles II hid after the battle of Worcester.

Location: 4 m N of Wolverhampton mid-way between A449 & A460 Roads. Off M6 at Shareshill then via A460. Traffic from S via. M6 and M54 take junction 1 to Wolverhampton and Moseley is signposted after ½ m. Coaches via. A460 to avoid low bridge.
Open: Apr 3 to Oct 31, Wed, Sat, Sun & Bank Hol Mons (and Tues in July & Aug) 2-5.30. Bank Hol Mon 11-5. Pre-booked parties at other times including evening tours. Shop as Hall; also open Nov 7 to Dec 19. Sun only 2-4.30.
Admission: £3, Chd half-price. Family ticket £7.50.
Refreshments: Tearoom in 18th century barn. Teas as house 2-5.30; Light lunches Sun and Bank Hol Mons, May to Sept from 12.30. Christmas Shop and Tea-room open Nov 7 to Dec 19, Sun only 2-4.30. Other times for parties by prior arrangement. Licensed.
Educational facilities. Wheelchair access ground floor only.

RODE HALL

Scholar Green, Stoke-on-Trent map G7
Telephone: (0270) 873237
(Sir Richard Baker Wilbraham Bt.)

18th century country house with Georgian stable block. Later alterations by L. Wyatt and Darcy Braddell.

Location: 5 m SW of Congleton between A34 & A50.
Station(s): Alsager (2¼ m).
Open: Apr 7 to Sept 29: Weds and Bank Hols 2-5.
Admission: £2.50.
Refreshments: Bleeding Wolf Restaurant, Scholar Green.

SHUGBOROUGH   🌳   The National Trust

Stafford map G7   △   ♿   Ⓔ   Ⓢ
Telephone: (0889) 881388
(Administered by Staffordshire County Council)

Seat of the Earls of Lichfield. Architecture by James Stuart and Samuel Wyatt. Rococo plasterwork by Vassalli. Extensive parkland with neo-classical monuments. Beautiful formal gardens. Victorian terraces and rose-garden. Guided garden and woodland walks. Working rare breeds farm. Restored Mill. Working Brewhouse, kitchen and laundry.

Location: 6 m E of Stafford on A513, entrance at Milford common 10 mins drive from M6, junction 13.
Open: House, Museum, Farm, Working Brewhouse and Mill. Grade I Historic Garden: Mar 27 to Oct 31 - daily inc. Bank Holiday Mons 11-5. Site open all year round to pre-booked parties only from 10.30. (Mansion House open for 'Good Housekeeping' Tours from Jan to Mar. Booked parties only).
Admission: House £3 (reduced rate £2). Museum £3 (reduced rate £2). Farm £3 (reduced rate £2). All-in ticket (House, Museum and Farm) £7.50 (reduced rate £5). Family All-in ticket (2 adults and 2 reduced rates) £15. Coach parties All-in ticket £5 or £2 per site (prices subject to change). Reduced rates available for Chd, OAPs and registered unemployed. Chd (under 5) free. *NT members free entry to house, reduced rate to Museum and Farm.* Party bookings for guided tours. Specialist tours and demonstrations available. (A Servant's Place). School parties guided tour £1.50 per head, per site (all 3 sites inc. of guide - £4). Working School demonstrations Oct to Easter £2.50 per head, per demo. When Special Events are held charges may vary.
Refreshments: Tea-rooms restaurant.

Guide Dogs admitted to House and Museum. Site access for parking, picnic area, gardens, monuments and woodland trails £1 per vehicle. Coaches free. National Trust shop and toilets.

TAMWORTH CASTLE

Tamworth map H7
Telephone: (0827) 63563
(Tamworth Borough Council)

Tamworth's sandstone Castle is one of the few remaining shell-keeps in the Country. Occupied at various periods between Norman and Victoran times, the Castle's room settings include the Tudor Chapel & Great Hall. Jacobean state apartments and the Victorian Suite. Norman exhibition, dungeon, haunted bedroom plus local history collections and audio visual.

Location: In Tamworth; 15 m NE of Birmingham.
Station(s): Tamworth (³⁄₄ m).
Open: All the year - Weekdays 10-5.30, Suns 2-5.30. Last adm 4.30. Open Bank Hols. *Closed Christmas Day & Boxing Day.*
Admission: £2.75, OAPs £1.50, Chd (up to 16 years) £1, Family ticket £6.50.

WALL (LETOCETUM) ROMAN SITE   English✠Heritage

map H7
Telephone: (0543) 480768

Much of the business of Imperial Rome depended on official couriers who travelled the comprehensive road network. Posting stations were built for them at regular intervals. At Wall, on Watling Street, traces of the hostel and a large part of the bath-house survive.

Location: 2 m (3.2 km) south west of Lichfield.
Open: Good Friday or Apr 1 (whichever is earlier) to Sept 30: Open Daily 10-6. Oct 1 to Maundy Thursday or Mar 31 (whichever is earlier): Open Tues to Sun 10-4. *Closed* Dec 24-26, Jan 1.
Admission: £1.20, Concessions 90p, Chd 60p.

WHITMORE HALL

Whitmore, nr Newcastle-under-Lyme map G7
Telephone: (0782) 680478
(Mr G. Cavenagh-Mainwaring)

Carolinian Manor House, owner's family home for over 800 years. Family portraits dating back to 1624. Outstanding Tudor Stable Block.

Location: Four miles from Newcastle-under-Lyme on the A53 Road to Market Drayton.
Open: Open 2-5.30 every Tues & Weds, May to Aug inclusive (last tour 5).
Admission: £2,*No reduction for parties.* Free car parking.
Refreshments: Mainwaring Arms Inn, Whitmore & also at Whitmore Art Gallery & Tea rooms, Whitmore.
Not suitable for disabled. No wheelchairs available.

SUFFOLK

AKENFIELD

Charsfield Woodbridge map M6
Telephone: (047337) 402

BELCHAMP HALL

Belchamp Walter, Sudbury map L5
Telephone: (0787) 72744
(M. M. J. Raymond, Esq)

Queen Anne period house with period furniture and 17th and 18th century family portraits. Gardens.

Location: 5 m SW of Sudbury.
Open: By appointment only. May to Sept - Tues & Thurs and Easter, Spring & Summer Bank Hol Mons 2.30-6.
Admission: £2.75, Chd £1.50. Reduction for parties.
Refreshments: Ploughman's lunches, teas, by arrangement.

BLAKENHAM WOODLAND GARDEN

Little Blakenham, nr Ipswich map L6
(Lord Blakenham)

5 acre wood with many rare trees and shrubs. Lovely throughout the year, with bluebells, camellias and magnolias followed by azaleas, rhododendrons, roses, hydrangeas and fine autumn colouring.

Location: 4 m NW of Ipswich. The garden is signposted from Little Blakenham which is 1 m off the old A1100 now called B1113.
Open: Apr 1 to Sept 30 - Weds, Thurs, Suns and Bank Hols 1-5.
Admission: £1. Free car park.
No dogs.

✿ THE SIGN OF A GREAT DAY OUT

CHRISTCHURCH MANSION

Christchurch Park, Ipswich   map M5
Telephone: (0473) 253246/213761
(The Borough of Ipswich)

A fine Tudor house set in beautiful parkland. Period rooms furnished in styles from 16th to 19th century; outstanding collections of china, clocks and glass. Paintings by Gainsborough, Constable and other Suffolk artists. Attached Wolsey Art Gallery shows lively temporary exhibition programme.

Location: In Christchurch Park, near centre of Ipswich.
Station(s): Ipswich (1¼ m).
Open: All the year - Tues to Sats 10-5 (dusk in winter); Suns 2.30-4.30. (dusk in winter). Open Bank Hol Mons.*Closed* Dec 24, 25, 26, Jan 1 and Good Friday.
Admission: Free.

EUSTON HALL

Thetford   map L6
Telephone: (0842) 766366
(The Duke and Duchess of Grafton)

Euston Hall - Home of the Duke and Duchess of Grafton. The 18th century house contains a famous collection of paintings including works by Stubbs, Van Dyck, Lely and Kneller. The pleasure grounds were laid out by John Evelyn and William Kent. The garden and nearby 17th century parish church in Wren style. Teas and Craft Shop in Old Kitchen. Picnic area.

Location: A1088; 3 m S Thetford.
Open: June 3 to Sept 30 - Thurs only 2.30-5. Also Sun June 27 & Sept 5, 2.30-5.
Admission: £2.25, Chd 50p, OAPs £1.50. Parties of 12 or more £1.50 per head.
Refreshments: Teas in Old Kitchen. Craft shop. Picnic area.

FRAMLINGHAM CASTLE   English # Heritage

map M6
Telephone: (0728) 723330

The present massive walls and their 13 towers were built by Roger Bigod, second Earl of Norfolk, on a site given to his father by Henry I. The ornamental brick chimneys were added in Tudor times when the arch of the entrance gateway was rebuilt. In 1636 the castle passed to Pembroke College, Cambridge, and in later years the great hall was converted to a poor-house and many of the buildings inside the walls were demolished. It was here, in 1553, that Mary Tudor learned she had become Queen of England.

Location: North side of Framlingham.
Open: Good Friday or Apr 1 (whichever is earlier) to Sept 30 daily 10-6. Oct 1 to Maundy Thursday or Mar 31 (whichever is earlier) Tues to Sun 10-4. *Closed* Dec 24-26, Jan 1.
Admission: £1.70, Concessions £1.30, Chd 85p.

GAINSBOROUGH'S HOUSE

Sudbury map L5
Telephone: (0787) 372958
(Gainsborough's House Society)

Thomas Gainsborough's birthplace. Large collection of his work in 18th century setting. Temporary exhibitions of historic and contemporary art and craft throughout the year. Print workshop, charming town garden containing mulberry tree planted in 1600s.

Location: 46 Gainsborough Street, Sudbury.
Station(s): Sudbury (¼ m).
Open: Open all the year. Easter to Oct - Tues to Sats 10-5; Sun & Bank Hol Mons 2-5; Nov to Maundy Thursday - Tues to Sats 10-4; Sun and Bank Hol Mons 2-4. *Closed Mons, Good Fri & between Christmas & New Year.*
Admission: £2, OAPs £1.50, Students/Chd £1.

GUILDHALL OF CORPUS CHRISTI

🍂 The National Trust

Lavenham map L6

Early 16th century timber-framed Tudor building; originally hall of Guild of Corpus Christi. Display of local history, industry and farming including a unique exhibition of 700 years of the woollen cloth trade. Delightful walled garden.

Location: Market Place Lavenham, Sudbury.
Open: Mar 27 to Oct 31 - Daily 11-5. *Closed* Good Friday.
Admission: £2.30, Chd *first two free, then* 60p. Parties £1.90. Please book with sae to Administrator. School parties 50p by prior arrangement.
Refreshments: Coffee, light lunches and teas.

HAUGHLEY PARK

nr Stowmarket map L6
(Mr & Mrs A J Williams)

Jacobean manor house. Gardens and woods, fine trees and shrubs.

Location: 4 m W of Stowmarket signed on A45 nr Wetherden (not Haughley).
Open: May to Sept - Tues 3-6.
Admission: £2, Chd £1.

HELMINGHAM HALL GARDENS

Ipswich map M6
Telephone: (0473) 890363
(The Lord & Lady Tollemache)

ICKWORTH 🍂 The National Trust

nr Bury St Edmunds map L6   ♿
Telephone: (0284) 735270

The house, begun c. 1794, was not completed until 1830. Contents of this architectural curiosity include late Regency and 18th century French furniture, magnificent silver, pictures. Formal gardens, herbaceous borders, orangery. Extensive waymarked park walks.

Location: 3 m SW of Bury St Edmunds on W side of A143.
Open: House & Garden. Mar 27 to Apr 30: Sats and Suns. May 1 to Sept 30: Tues, Weds, Frid, Sats and Suns 1.30-5.30. Oct: Sats and Suns 1.30-5.30. Open Bank Hol Mons: 1.30-5.30. Park open daily 7-7.
Admission: £4.30, Chd £2. Access to Park, Garden, Restaurant and Shop £1.50, Chd 50p. Parties £3.50.
Refreshments: Lunch & tea in old Servants' Hall. Table license, restaurant opens 12 noon on House open days.
Dogs in park only, on leads. Wheelchair access, one provided. Shop.

The Hall, which was completed in 1510, has been the home of the Tollemache family from that date to the present day. It is one of the finest houses of the Tudor period, surrounded by a wide moat with drawbridges raised every night. There are two superb gardens which extend to several acres all set in 400 acres of ancient park containing herds of Red and Fallow deer and Highland Cattle. The main garden is surrounded by its own moat and 1740 wall, with wide herbaceous borders and planted tunnels intersecting an immaculate kitchen garden; the second is a very special rose garden enclosed within high yew hedges with a herb and Knot garden containing plants grown in England before 1750. English Heritage Grade I Garden.

Location: 9 m N of Ipswich on B1077.
Open: GARDENS ONLY. May 2 to Sept 12 - Suns only 2-6. *House not open to the public.*
Admission: £2.20, Chd (15 and under) £1.20, OAPs £2.
Refreshments: In the Coach House Tea Rooms. Cream teas. Home-grown plants and produce for sale.
Safari rides. Gift shop.

IPSWICH MUSEUM

Ipswich map M6
Telephone: (0473) 213761/2
(Ipswich Borough Council)

Geology and natural history of Suffolk; Mankind galleries covering Africa, Asia, America and the Pacific. 'Romans in Suffolk' gallery showing local archaeology. Temporary exhibitions in attached gallery.

Location: High Street, in town centre.
Station(s): Ipswich.
Open: Tues to Sats 10-5. Temporary exhibition programme.
Admission: Free.

KENTWELL HALL

Long Melford map L6
(J. Patrick Phillips, QC)

KENTWELL
Spend an hour or a day & share the magic of its spell

THE HALL	*Magnificent mellow redbrick moated Tudor manor still a family home*
MOAT HOUSE	*Remnant of 15th C. house, equipped as then*
GARDENS	*Ancient Walled Garden, Moats & Herb Garden*
MAZE	*Unique brick-paved mosaic Tudor Rose*
TUDOR FARM	*Working Farm - traditional buildings, rare breeds, early tools & equipment*

FOR ADMISSION AND STANDARD OPENING TIMES SEE EDITORIAL ENTRY

DIARY OF MAIN SPECIAL EVENTS FOR 1993

Easter: Fri 9-Mon 12 Apr	Great Easter Egg Quiz; Tudor Bakery & Dairy
May Day: Sat 1-Mon 3	Tudor May Day Celebrations
Spring BH: Sat 29-Mon 31	Re-Creation of Tudor Life
June 20-July 18 (Sats, Suns & Fri 16 Jul only)	Main Re-Creation - 250 'Tudors' take the Manor back to a year in the 16th Century
Aug BH: Fri 27-Mon 30 Aug	Re-Creation of Tudor Life
September 25-26	Miichaelmas Re-Creation of Tudor Life

KENTWELL HALL, LONG MELFORD, SUFFOLK. TEL 0787 310207

Romantic mellow red brick moated Tudor manor, in lovely setting. Still a family home. Moat House: unaltered 15th c house, furnished and equipped as then. Walled garden and large Herb garden. Mosaic brick maze and separate 'Tudor' farm.

Location: Entrance on W of A134, N of Green in Long Melford; 3 m N of Sudbury.
Open: Mar 28 to Jun 13 - Suns only. Plus Apr 13 - 16 and Jun 1 to 4 daily, 12noon-5pm. *Bank Hols and other W/E with Re-creations of Tudor Life:* Easter (Apr 9 - 12), May Day W/E (May 1-3), Spring BH W/E (May 29-31) - all daily from 11-6. **Main Re-creation** Jun 20 to Jul 18 - Sats, Suns and Frid Jul 16 only (11-5). Aug BH W/E (Aug 27-30) 11-6. Michelmas (Sept 25/26) 12-5. Jul 21 to Sept 26, daily, 12-5.
Admission: Prices not available at time of going to press.
Refreshments: Light lunches and afternoon teas available.
No dogs.

LITTLE HALL

Lavenham map L6
(Suffolk Preservation Society)

15th century 'hall' house, rooms furnished with Gayer Anderson collection of furniture, pictures, china, books, etc.

Location: E side Lavenham Market Place.
Open: Good Friday to mid-Oct - Weds, Thurs, Sats, Suns & Bank Hols 2.30-5.30 *Groups by appointment tel: (0787) 247179.*
Admission: £1, Chd 50p.

MELFORD HALL   The National Trust

nr Sudbury map L5

Built between 1554 and 1578 by Sir William Cordell, contains fine pictures, furniture and Chinese porcelain. Interesting garden and gazebo. Beatrix Potter display.

Location: In Long Melford on E side of A134; 3 m N of Sudbury.
Open: Principal Rooms & Gardens. Mar 27 to Apr 30: Sats and Suns. May 1 to Sept 30: Weds, Thurs, Sats, Suns and all Bank Holiday Mons 2-5.30. Oct: Sats and Suns 2-5.30.
Admission: £2.60, Chd (with adult) £1.30. Pre-booked parties of 15 or more £2.20, Weds & Thurs only.
Refreshments: In Long Melford.
No dogs. Wheelchair access, one provided.

NETHER HALL

Cavendish, nr Sudbury map L5
(B. T. Ambrose, Esq)

15th century Manor House with gallery museum and vineyard. Wines for sale.

Location: 12 m S of Bury St Edmunds; beside A1092. N of church.
Open: Daily 11-4.
Admission: £2.50. Parties by appointment.

ORFORD CASTLE   English Heritage

map M6
Telephone: (039 44) 50472

No sooner had Henry II built this castle on the Suffolk coast than rebellion broke out (in 1173). The castle's powerful presence helped to uphold the King's authority and it continued to be an important royal residence for more than 100 years. In 1280 it was granted to the Earl of Norfolk for his lifetime, and from then on it remained in private hands. The design was very advanced for its time, and the keep, much of which remains, is unique in England. The outer wall of the castle, the last section of which collapsed in 1841, was punctuated by rectangular towers, an innovation that provided excellent cover for the defenders.

Location: In Orford.
Open: Good Friday or Apr 1 (whichever is earlier) to Sept 30: Open Daily 10-6. Oct 1 to Maundy Thursday or Mar 31 (whichever is earlier): Open Tues to Sun 10-4. *Closed* Dec 24-26, Jan 1.
Admission: £1.70, Concessions £1.30, Chd 85p.

OTLEY HALL

Otley, nr Ipswich map M6
Telephone: (0473) 890264
Fax: (0473) 890803
(Mr J G Mosesson)

THE PRIORY

Lavenham map L6
Telephone: (0787) 247417
(Mr & Mrs A Casey)

Through the ages the home of Benedictine monks, medieval clothiers, an Elizabethan rector, and now of the Casey family, who rescued the house from a derelict ruin. Beautiful timber-framed building (Grade 1) with stimulating interior design blending old and new, enhanced by paintings, drawings and stained glass by Ervin Bossanyi (1891-1975). Lovely herb garden of unique design. Work still continues on parts of the building. On display is an exhibition of photographs illustrating the restoration.

Location: In Water Street, Lavenham; 10 m S of Bury St Edmunds.
Open: Apr to end Oct - Daily 10.30-5.30.
Admission: £2.50, Chd £1. Open by appointment for groups, morning, afternoon or evening, please telephone above number.
Refreshments: Coffee, lunches and teas served in the Refectory. Gift shop. Selection of unusual gifts and woven tapestries.
Guided tours can emphasise timber framed buildings and their restoration, history of the house and the area, the Bossanyi collection, interior decor - according to your interests.

SAXTEAD GREEN POST MILL   English ⊞ Heritage

map M6
Telephone: (0728) 82789

In the 13th century Framlingham was a thriving farming community, whose wealth derived from cereals, particularly wheat. This corn-mill, one of the finest in the world, probably dates from 1287 and produced flour until the First World War. The upper part of the mill, containing the machinery, was rotated by a track-mounted fantail. This ensured that the sails always faced square into the wind.

Location: 2 m (3.2 km) west of Framlingham.
Open: Good Friday or Apr 1 (whichever is earlier) to Sept 30: Mon-Sat 10-6.
Admission: £1.20, Concessions 90p, Chd 60p.

SOMERLEYTON HALL 🏛

nr Lowestoft map M6
(The Lord & Lady Somerleyton)

Somerleyton Hall is an extravagantly splendid early Victorian mansion built around a Tudor and Jacobean shell, epitomising an era of self confident expansion. No expense was spared in the building or the fittings. Stone was brought from Caen and Aubigny and the magnificent carved stonework created by John Thomas (who worked on the Houses of Parliament) has been recently fully restored. In the State rooms there are paintings by Landseer, Wright of Derby and Stanfield, together with fine wood carving by Willcox of Warwick and from the earlier house, Grinling Gibbons. Twelve acres of gardens surround the Hall with magnificent specimen trees, azaleas, rhododendrons and splendid statuary. There are handsome glass houses designed by Paxton. The most notable feature is the MAZE, planted in 1846, which ranks amongst the finest in the country. The stable tower clock by Vulliamy made in 1847 is the original model for a great clock to serve as the Tower Clock in the new Houses of Parliament, now world famous as Big Ben. A quarter mile long MINIATURE RAILWAY carries passengers at the edge of the park on most days. No dogs allowed.

Location: 5 m NW Lowestoft off B1074; 7 m Yarmouth (A143).
Station(s): Somerleyton (1½ m).
Open: House, Maze and Gardens open - Easter Sun to end of Sept, Thurs, Suns and Bank Holidays. Also Tues & Wed in July & Aug. House open 2-5pm. Gardens 12.30-5.30pm.
Admission: £3.50, Chd £1.60, OAPs £2.70. Free car parking.
Refreshments: Luncheon and Teas in the loggia from 12.30.

WINGFIELD COLLEGE 🏛

Nr Eye map M6 △
Telephone: (0379) 384505
(Ian Chance, Esq)

Founded in 1362 on the 13th century site of the Manor House by Sir John de Wingfield, a close friend of the Black Prince. Magnificent Medieval Great Hall. Surrendered to Henry VIII in 1542 and seized by Cromwell's Parliament in 1649. Mixed period interiors with 18th century neo-classical facade. Walled gardens and Topiary. Teas. Celebrated Arts and Music Season. Adjacent church with tombs of College founder and Benefactors, The Earls and Dukes of Suffolk.

Location: Signposted off B1118; 7 m SE of Diss.
Open: Easter Sat to Sept 26 - Sats, Suns & Bank Hols 2-6.
Admission: £2, Concessions £1.
Refreshments: Home-made teas.

SURREY

ALBURY PARK

Albury, Guildford map J4
(Country Houses Association)

Country mansion by Pugin.

Location: 1½ m E of Albury off A25 Guildford to Dorking road.
Station(s): Stations: Chilworth (2 m); Gomshall (2 m); Clandon (2 m). Bus Route: Tillingbourne No 25 Guildford-Cranleigh
Open: May to Sept - Weds & Thurs 2-5. Last entry 4.30.
Admission: £1.50, Chd 50p. Free car park.
No dogs admitted.

ASGILL HOUSE

Richmond map K4
(Asgill House Trust Ltd)

CHILWORTH MANOR

nr Guildford map J4
(Lady Heald)

Garden laid out in C17 on site of C11 monastery, C18 walled garden, spring flowers, flowering shrubs, herbaceous border.

Location: 3¾ m SE of Guildford off A248 in Chilworth Village turn at Blacksmith Lane.
Station(s): Chilworth (¾ m).
Open: GARDEN ONLY: Sat to Wed Apr 3-7; May 8-12; June 12-16; July 17-21; Aug 7-11. Other times by appointment. Car park open 12.30 for picnics.
Admission: Garden: £1.50. House with floral arrangements £1 extra (on the above Sats & Suns only) £1, accompanied Chd free. Cars free. *In aid of National Gardens Scheme.*
Refreshments: Tea at the house, **Sat & Sun openings only.**

CLANDON PARK  The National Trust

nr Guildford map J4 &
Telephone: (0483) 222482

A Palladian house built 1731-35 by Giacomo Leoni. Fine plasterwork. Collection of furniture, pictures and porcelain. Museum of the Queen's Royal Surrey Regiment. Garden with parterre, grotto and Maori house.

Location: At West Clandon 3 m E Guildford on A247; S of A3 & N of A246.
Station(s): Clandon (1 m).
Open: Apr 3 to end Oct: daily (except Thurs and Frid) 1.30-5.30 (last adm 5). Open Bank Hol Mons 11-5.30; open Good Friday. Parties & guided tours by arrangement with the Administrator *(no reduced rate at weekends and Bank Hols).*
Admission: £3.60, Chd half-price. Parties (Mons, Tues, Weds only) £3.
Refreshments: Licensed Restaurant in house lunches 12.30-2 & teas 3.15-5.30. Prior booking advisable for luncheon, Tel Guildford (0483) 222502.
Shop. Picnic area. Dogs in car park and picnic area only. Wheelchairs provided.

CLAREMONT

Esher map K4
Telephone: (0372) 467841
(The Claremont Fan Court Foundation Ltd)

Excellent example of Palladian style; built 1772 by 'Capability' Brown for Clive of India; Henry Holland and John Soane responsible for the interior decoration. It is now a co-educational school run by Christian Scientists.

Location: ½ m SW from Esher on Esher/Cobham Road A307.
Open: Feb to Nov: first complete weekend (Sats and Suns) in each month 2-5.
Admission: £2, Chd/OAPs £1. Reduced rates for parties.
Refreshments: Not available.
Souvenirs.

CLAREMONT LANDSCAPE GARDEN

 The National Trust

Esher map K4 &

One of the earliest surviving English landscape gardens, restored by the NT. *House not National Trust property.*

Location: ½ m SE of Esher on E side of A307. NB: no access from A3 by-pass.
Station(s): Esher (2 m) (not Suns); Hersham (2 m); Hinchley Wood (2½ m).
Open: Mar: daily 10-5. Apr to end Oct, Mon to Fri 10-6; Sat, Sun & Bank Hol Mon 10-7. (14-18 Jul garden closes 4). Nov to end Mar 1994: daily (except Mon) 10-5 or sunset if earlier. Last adm ½hr before closing. *Closed Christmas Day and New Year's Day.* No coaches on Sunday.
Admission: Sun and Bank Hols £2.50; Mons to Sats £1.70 (Chd half-price). Guided tours (minimum 15 persons) £1.20 plus adm price by prior booking. Tel (0372) 469421. No reduction for parties.
Refreshments: Tea room open Jan 16 to end Mar: Sats and Suns 11-4.30; Apr to end Oct: daily (except Mons) 11-5.30 (open Bank Hol Mon); Nov to Dec 12: daily (except Mons) 11-4. Wheelchairs provided. Dogs allowed Nov to Mar but **not** admitted Apr to end Oct.

COVERWOOD LAKES

Peaslake Road, Ewhurst map K4
Telephone: (0306) 731103
(Mr & Mrs C G Metson)

Landscaped water and cottage gardens in lovely setting between Holmbury Hill to the north and Pitch Hill to the south. Rhododendrons, azaleas, primulas, fine mature trees. New 3½ acre arboretum, planted 1990. Four small lakes and bog garden. Herd of pedigree Poll Hereford cattle and flock of sheep in the adjoining farm (Mr and Mrs Nigel Metson).

Location: ½ m from Peaslake village. 8 m from Guildford. 8 m from Dorking (A25). 3 m from A25.
Open: GARDEN ONLY: Suns May 9, 16 for *National Gardens Scheme* Suns May 23 and 30. (2-6.30) GARDEN AND FARM: Sun Apr 25, May 2, 23, 30. Wed May 26. (2-6.30) Sun Oct 24, (11-4.30).
Admission: Garden: £1.50, Chd £1. Garden & Farm: £2, Chd £1, (under 5) free.
Refreshments: Teas and home-made cakes available, plus hot soup and sandwiches on Oct 24. Nearest hotel is the Hurtwood, (THF) at Peaslake village (½ m away from garden).

CROSSWATER FARM

Churt, Farnham map J4
Telephone: (0252) 792698
(Mr & Mrs E. G. Millais)

6-acre woodland garden surrounded by acres of National Trust property. Plantsman's collection of Rhododendrons and Azaleas including many rare species collected in the Himalayas, and hybrids raised by the owners. Pond, stream and companion plant ings. Plants for sale from adjoining Rhododendron nursery. (See Millais Nurseries entry in Garden Specialists section).

Location: Farnham/Haslemere 6 miles. From A287 turn East into Jumps Road ½ m north of Churt village centre. After ¼ m, turn left into Crosswater Lane, and follow Nursery signs.
Open: May 1 to June 13 daily 10-5. In aid of the *National Gardens Scheme* on May 29, 30, 31.
Admission: £1.50, Chd free.
Refreshments: Teas available on NGS days.
No dogs.

FARNHAM CASTLE

Farnham map J4 △
(The Church Commissioners)

Bishop's Palace built in Norman times by Henry of Blois, with Tudor and Jacobean additions. Formerly the seat of the Bishops of Winchester. Fine Great Hall re-modelled at the Restoration. Features include the Renaissance brickwork of Waynefleter's tower, and the 17th century chapel.

Location: ½ m N of Town Centre on A287.
Station(s): Farnham.
Admission: £1, OAP/Chd/Students 50p. Reductions for parties.
Refreshments: Castle - All year Weds 2-4. Parties at other times by arrangement. All visitors are given guided tours.
Centrally heated in winter.

FARNHAM CASTLE KEEP   English ♯ Heritage

Farnham map J4
Telephone: (0252) 713393

Farnham formed part of the estate of the Bishops of Winchester long before the Norman Conquest. And there was still a bishop in residence until 1955 - an impressive tenancy. But why should the massive keep be built *around* the mound of earth, and not on top of it? Your guess is as good as the archaeologists'!

Location: ½ m N of Farnham town centre on A287.
Open: Good Friday or Apr 1 (whichever is earlier) to Sept 30: Open Daily 10-6.
Admission: £1.50, Concessions £1.10, Chd 75p. Price includes a Personal Stereo Guided Tour.

GODDARDS

Abinger Common, Dorking map K4
Telephone: (0306) 730487
(The Lutyens Trust)

Edwardian country house by Sir Edwin Lutyens, with Gertrude Jekyll garden, in beautiful setting on slopes of Leith Hill. Given in 1991 to The Lutyens Trust by the family whose home it was for 38 years.

Location: 4½ m SW of Dorking in Abinger Common.
Open: By appointment Apr to Oct. Please telephone for details.
Refreshments: Group teas by arrangement.

GREATHED MANOR

Lingfield map K4
(Country Houses Association)
Victorian Manor house.

Location: 2½ m SE of Lingfield on B2028 Edenbridge road, take Ford Manor road beside Plough Inn, Dormansland for final 1 m.
Station(s): Dormans (1½ m); Lingfield (1½ m). Bus Route: No. 429 to Plough Inn, Dormansland.
Open: May to Sept - Weds & Thurs 2-5. Last entry 4.30.
Admission: £1.50, Chd 50p. Free car park.
No dogs admitted.

HATCHLANDS PARK   🍂 The National Trust

East Clandon map K4
Telephone: (0483) 222482

Built by Admiral Boscawen in 18th century, interior by Robert Adam, with later modifications. Contains Cobbe collection of keyboard instruments, paintings and furniture. Garden.

Location: E of East Clandon on N side of Leatherhead/Guildford Road (A246).
Station(s): Clandon (2½m).
Open: Apr 1 to Oct 31: Tues, Weds, Thurs, Suns and Bank Hol Mons, but also open Sats in Aug, 2-5.30 (no admission after 5). Pre-booked parties (Tues, Weds and Thurs only).
Admission: £3.50, Chd half-price. Pre-booked parties £3.
Refreshments: Licensed restaurant 12.30-2pm and home-made teas 3-5pm, same days as house.
No dogs. Wheelchair access to ground floor and part of the garden. Shop. Batricar available for transport to house.

LITTLE HOLLAND HOUSE

Cheam - See under Greater London.

🍂 THE SIGN OF A GREAT DAY OUT

LOSELEY HOUSE

Guildford map J4 △ &
Telephone: (0483) 304440
(Mr and Mrs James More-Molyneux)

The Elizabethan country house with the friendly atmosphere. Built of stone from Waverley Abbey in a glorious parkland setting by an ancestor of the present owner and occupier. Queen Elizabeth I stayed here three times, James I twice. Queen Mary visited in 1932. Panelling from Henry VIII's Nonsuch Palace. Fine ceilings, unique carved chalk chimney piece, inlaid cabinets, tapestries, needlework, but Loseley is a home, not a museum. Moat walk. Farm tours. Restaurant and farm shop housed in the 17th century Tithe Barn. Wholefood lunches, teas and organic wine. Farm Shop selling Loseley ice cream, yoghurt and cream as well as Loseley organic bakery products and organic vegetables.

Location: 2½ m SW of Guildford (take B3000 off A3 through Compton); 1½ m N of Godalming (off A3100).
Station(s): Farncombe (2 m).
Open: May 31 to Oct 2: Weds, Thurs, Frid and Sats 2-5; also Summer Bank Hol Mon Aug 30 2-5. Farm Tours when house is open; at other times, booked parties only.
Admission: £3.50, Chd £2. Parties of 20 and over £2.75 per person. School parties £2 per person. Gardens and grounds £1.50, Chd 50p. Parties of 20 or more £1.20 per person.
Refreshments: Home produce, morning coffee, home made lunches and teas in Tithe Barn. Open May 31 to Oct 2: Wed, Thurs, Fri & Sat; also Bank Hol Mon (Aug 30).
Tithe Barn Restaurant and Farm Shop open same days as House 11-5. Tithe Ban available for hire for weddings and other functions.

PAINSHILL PARK

Portsmouth Road, Cobham map K4
Telephone: (0932) 868113
(Painshill Park Trust)

Painshill, contemporary with Stourhead & Stowe, is one of Europe's finest eighteenth century landscape gardens. It was created by The Hon Charles Hamilton, plantsman, painter and brilliantly gifted designer, between 1738 and 1773. He transformed barren heathland into ornamental pleasure grounds and parkland of dramatic beauty and contrasting scenery, dominated by a 14 acre meandering lake fed from the river by an immense waterwheel. Garden buildings and features adorned the Park, including a magnificent Grotto, Temple, ruined Abbey, Chinese Bridge, castellated Tower, and a Mausoleum. Well maintained for 200 years in private ownership, the Park was neglected after 1948 and sank into dereliction. In 1981 the Painshill Park Trust, a registered charity, was formed to restore the gardens to their original splendour, raising the extensive funds

needed for such an ambitious project. The Trust has made enormous progress, and this masterpiece is re-emerging from the wilderness.

Location: W of Cobham on A245. 200 yards E of A3/A245 roundabout.
Open: Apr 11 to Oct 17: (Suns only) 11-5 (gates close 6pm). Pre-booked parties (min. 10) any day except Suns. Please ring (0932) 864674 for more information. Wide ranging Education programme. School parties welcomed, holiday activities organised and childrens parties catered for by arrangement with Painshill Park Education Trust, (0932) 866743. No evening events after 7pm.
Admission: £3, OAPs/Students/UB40's £2.50. Accompanied chd (under 14) free *max 3 per adult.*
Refreshments: Light refreshments available.
Much of park accessible for disabled (wheelchairs available). Limited facilities and parking. No dogs please.

POLESDEN LACEY   The National Trust

nr Dorking map K4 &
Telephone: (0372) 458203 or 452048

Originally a Regency villa altered in Edwardian period. Greville collection of pictures, tapestries, furniture. 18th century garden extended 1906, with herbaceous borders, rose garden, clipped hedges, lawns, beeches. Views.

Location: 5 m NW of Dorking, reached via Great Bookham (A246) & then road leading S (1½ m).
Station(s): Boxhill or Bookham (both 2½ m).
Open: Mar and Nov: Sats and Suns 1.30-4.30; Apr 1 to end of Oct: Weds to Suns (including Good Friday) 1.30-5.30. Last adm half hour before closing. Open Bank Hol Mons and preceding Suns 11-5.30. Garden open daily all year, 11-6.
Admission: GARDEN ONLY: (Apr 1 to end Oct) £2.50. (Nov to end Mar 1994) £2. HOUSE: (Sun and Bank Hol Mons) £3.50 extra. Other open days £2.50 extra. Chd half-price. *Party reductions on Weds, Thurs and Frid only by prior arrangement with the Administrator.* £4.
Refreshments: Licensed Restaurant in courtyard. Jan 16 to end Mar: (light refreshments). Sats and Suns only 11-4.30. Apr 1 to end Oct: Weds to Suns and Bank Hol Mons 11-5.30. (Closed 2-2.30). Nov to Dec 19: Wed - Sun 11-4.30. Special times before Christmas. Tel (0372) 456190.
Wheelchairs admitted and provided. Shop open: Jan, Feb, Mar: Sat & Sun only from Jan 16, 11-4.30. Apr to end Oct: Wed to Sun 11-5.30. Nov to Dec 19: Wed to Sun, 11-4.30. (Tel (0372) 457230).

PYRFORD COURT

Pyrford Common Road, nr Woking map J4
Telephone: (0483) 765880

Twenty acres of wild and formal gardens, azaleas, wisteria, rhododendrons, pink marble fountain, venetian bridge, and views to North Downs.

Location: 2 m E of Woking, M25 (exit 10) on to A3 towards Guildford, off to Ripley, turn right in centre of Ripley to B367 - Newark Lane, signposted Pyrford. 1¾ m on left Jct Pyrford Common Road and Upshott Lane.
Open: Sat & Sun: May 15 and 16. 2-6.30. Sun: Oct 17. 12-4 and by appointment. Open in aid of *National Gardens Scheme and Cancer Research Campaign*. For details of operas, concerts and other events in the house please phone.
Admission: £2, Chd 70p.
Refreshments: Teas.
Parking, suitable for wheelchairs, dogs on lead. Toilet facilities.

RAMSTER

Chiddingfold map J3
Telephone: (0428) 644422
(Mr & Mrs Paul Gunn)

Mature 20 acre woodland garden of exceptional interest. Laid out by Gauntlett Nurseries of Chiddingfold in early 1900's. Fine rhododendrons, azaleas, camellias, magnolias, trees and shrubs in lovely setting.

Location: On A283 1½ m S of Chiddingfold.
Open: GARDEN ONLY. Apr 24 to June 6 - Daily 2-6. *Embroidery for Gardeners Exhibition May 16 to 31 (2-6).*
Admission: £1.50, Chd free. Parties by arrangement. *Share to National Gardens Scheme.* Exhibition: £1.50.
Refreshments: Teas Sats, Suns & Bank Hol Mons in May only.

THE ROYAL HORTICULTURAL SOCIETY'S GARDEN, WISLEY

Wisley map K4

British gardening at its best in all aspects. 250 acres of glorious garden. The wooded slopes with massed rhododendrons and azaleas, the wild daffodils of the alpine meadow, the calm of the pinetum, the gaiety of the herbaceous border, the banked mounds of heathers, the new alpine house, the panorama of the rock garden, the model fruit and vegetable gardens and the range of greenhouse displays are there waiting for you to enjoy and to learn from.

Location: In Wisley just off M25 Junction 10, on A3. London 22 m, Guildford 7 m.
Open: The garden is open to the public Mon to Sat throughout the year (except Christmas Day) from 10-sunset (or 10-7 during the summer). ON SUNDAYS THE GARDEN IS OPEN ONLY TO MEMBERS of RHS.
Admission: £4.20, Chd (6-14) £1.75, Chd (up to 5) Free. Parties of more than 20; (Mon to Sat) £3.50, (Fri) £3.20. Tickets must be obtained 14 days in advance of visit. *RHS Members: Free.*
Dogs not admitted other than guide dogs. Information centre. Shop and Plant sales centre.

VANN

Hambledon map J3
Telephone: (0428) 683413
(Mr & Mrs M. B. Caroe)

16th to 20th century house surrounded by 5 acre 'paradise' garden. Water garden by Gertrude Jekyll 1911.

Location: 6 m S of Godalming; A283 to Wormley, turn left at Hambledon cross roads and follow signs along Vann Lane for 2 m.
Station(s): Witley (2 m).
Open: GARDENS ONLY: Easter Mon Apr 12, Bank Holiday Mon May 3, Sun June 6, 2-7. Tues to Sun, Apr 13-18, Tues to Sun May 4-9, Mon to Sat June 7-12, 10-6. Easter to Sept: by prior appointment. Plant and vegetable stall. Party bookings and guided tours with morning coffee, lunches or home made teas in house or garden by arrangement.
Admission: £1.50, Chd 30p. *In aid of National Gardens Scheme and Hambledon Village Hall.*
Refreshments: Home made teas in house, Apr 12, May 3, June 6 only.

WHITEHALL

Cheam - See under Greater London.

WINKWORTH ARBORETUM 🌿 The National Trust

nr Godalming map J3 &

99 acres of trees and shrubs planted mainly for Spring and Autumn colour. Two lakes, fine views.

Location: 2 m SE of Godalming on E side of B2130.
Station(s): Godalming (2 m).
Open: All year during daylight hours.
Admission: £2, Chd half-price. No reduction for parties. *Coach parties by prior appointment in writing.* Bookings Tearoom Concessionaire, Winkworth Arboretum, nr Godalming, Surrey. (048 632 265) When tea room open.
Refreshments: Apr 1 to Nov 14: daily 11-5.30 (weather permitting) for light lunches and teas. Also open weekends in Mar and Mid Nov - Xmas.
Dogs must be kept under control. Wheelchair access.

EAST SUSSEX

ALFRISTON CLERGY HOUSE 🌿 The National Trust

Alfriston, nr Seaford map K3
Telephone: (0323) 870001

Bought in 1896, the first building acquired by the Trust. Wealden hall-house, possibly a parish priest's house, c. 1350.

Location: 4 m NE of Seaford just E of B2108; adjoining The Tye & St Andrew's Church.
Station(s): Berwick (2½ m).
Open: Exhibition Room, Medieval Hall, two other rooms & Garden. Apr to end Oct - Daily 11-6 (or sunset if earlier). Last adm half-hour before closing.
Admission: £2, Chd £1, Pre-booked parties £1.50, Chd 80p.
Shop (open until Christmas). No dogs. Unsuitable for wheelchairs.

BATEMAN'S 🌿 The National Trust

Burwash map L3 △
Telephone: (0435) 882302

Built 1634. Rudyard Kipling lived here. Water-mill restored by the National Trust. Attractive garden, yew hedges, lawns, daffodils and wild garden.

Location: ½ m S of Burwash on the Lewes/Etchingham Road (A265).
Open: Apr 3 to end of Oct - Daily (except Thurs & Frid but open Good Fri) 11-5.30. Last adm 4.30.
Admission: House, Mill & Garden: £3.50, Chd £1.80, Sun & Bank Hols £4, Chd £2. Pre-booked parties £3, Chd £1.50.
Refreshments: Tea room: coffees, light lunches and teas, open as House.
No dogs. Shop.

BATTLE ABBEY English✠Heritage

Battle map L3
Telephone: (04246) 773792

BENTLEY HOUSE & GARDENS

Halland map K3

The Battle of Hastings, 1066 - the best-known date in English history. Battle Abbey was built by William the Conqueror as a thanksgiving for his victory, with the high altar on the spot where King Harold died. The church has yet to be fully excavated, but visitors may walk over the battlefield, and see the remains of many of the domestic buildings of the monastery and see an audio-visual show. An exhibition is open in the newly restored 14th century gatehouse re-creating the history of this famous monument. A Personal Stereo Guided Tour is available.

Location: Battle.
Open: Good Friday or Apr 1 (whichever is earlier) to Sept 30, daily 10-6. Oct 1 to Maundy Thursday or Mar 31 (whichever is earlier), daily 10-4. *Closed* Dec 24-26, Jan 1.
Admission: £2.70, Concessions £2, Chd £1.30.

BAYHAM ABBEY English✠Heritage

map L3
Telephone: (0892) 890381

Built by monks in the 13th century, the abbey owes its survival not to historical or archaeological interest, but to its being a picturesque ruin. By the 18th century the building was in a desperate condition, but then came the Gothic revival and the structure was repaired and landscaped to provide a romantic vista for the nearby Dower House.

Location: 1¾ m (2.8 km) west of Lamberhurst.
Open: Good Friday or Apr 1 (whichever is earlier) to Sept 30: Open Daily 10-6.
Admission: £1.70, Concessions £1.30, Chd 85p.

Bentley House dates back to Tudor times and was built on land granted to James Gage by the Archbishop of Canterbury with the permission of Henry VIII. The family of Lord Gage was linked with Bentley from that time until 1904. The estate was purchased by Gerald Askew in 1937, and during the 1960's he and his wife, Mary, added two large double height Palladian rooms to the original farmhouse. The architect who advised them was Raymond Erith, who had previously worked on 10 Downing Street. The drawing room in the East wing contains mid 18th century Chinese wallpaper and gilt furniture, and the Bird room in the West wing contains a collection of wildfowl paintings by Philip Rickman. The Gardens at Bentley have been created as a series of 'rooms' divided by Yew hedges, one room leading into the next, specialising in many old fashioned roses including the Bourbons, the Gallicas and the Damask. Nearby six stone sphinxes stand along a broad grass walk where daffodils bloom in spring.

Location: 7 m NE of Lewes signposted on A22, A26 & B2192.
Open: Apr 1 to Oct 31 daily. HOUSE: 12-5. ESTATE: 10.30-5.
Admission: £3.40, OAPs £2.60, Chd (4-15) £1.70, Family ticket (2 adults, 4 chd) £9. Special rates for disabled (wheelchiars available). Parties of 11 or more - 10% discount. Adm price allows entry to: House, Garden and Grounds, Wildfowl reserve, Motor Museum, Woodland Walk, Animal section, Children's adventure play area, Picnic area, Tea room, Gift Shop and Education Centre with audio/visual.
Refreshments: Tea Rooms on site (licensed).
Ample free parking. Dogs allowed in this area only. Special arrangements can be for parties outside normal hours. Please contact the Manager for details. (0825) 840573.

BODIAM CASTLE  The National Trust

nr Robertsbridge map L3   &
Telephone: (0580) 830436

Built 1385-9, one of the best preserved examples of medieval moated military architecture.

Location: 3 m S of Hawkhurst; 1 m E of A229.
Open: Apr to Oct 31 incl. Good Fri. Daily 10-6 (or sunset if earlier). Nov to end Mar - Tues to Sats only. 10-sunset. Last adm half-hour before closing. *Closed Dec 25 to 29.*
Admission: £2.50, Chd £1.30. *Parties of 15 or more by prior arrangement.* £2, Chd 50p. Car park - 50p.
Refreshments: Restaurant, Apr to Dec 24.
Museum. Audio visual. Shop. Dogs admitted except in shop and museum. Wheelchair access.

The National Trust
THE SIGN OF A GREAT DAY OUT

BRICKWALL HOUSE   ·

Northiam, Rye map L3
Telephone: (0797) 252494 or Curator (0797) 223329
(Frewen Educational Trust)

Home of the Frewen family since 1666. 17th century drawing room with superb 17th century plaster ceilings, and family portraits spanning 400 years of history. Grand staircase. Chess garden and arboretum.

Location: 7 m NW of Rye on B2088.
Open: Apr to end Sept - Sats and Bank Holiday Mons 2-5; Open at other times by prior arrangement with the curator.
Admission: £1.50

CHARLESTON FARMHOUSE

Firle, nr Lewes map K3
Telephone: (0323) 811265 (Visitor information), (0323) 811626 (Administration)
(The Charleston Trust)

COBBLERS GARDEN

Crowborough map K3
Telephone: (0892) 655969
(Mr & Mrs Martin Furniss)

17/18th century farmhouse, the home of Vanessa and Clive Bell and Duncan Grant from 1916 until Grant's death in 1978. Virginia and Leonard Woolf 'discovered' Charleston in 1916, when her sister Vanessa was looking for a house in the country, 'If you lived there, you could make it absolutely divine' Virginia wrote prophetically. Here over the decades Maynard and Lydia Keynes, David Garnett, Roger Fry, Lytton Strachey, Raymond Mortimer, Desmond MacCarthy, T.S. Eliot and E.M. Forster were residents or constant visitors. Others included G.E. Moore, Bertrand Russell, Georges Duthuit, Charles Mauron, Andre Dunoyer de Segonzac, Matthew Smith, Ernest Ansermet, Kenneth Clark, Benjamin Britten, Peter Pears and Frederick Ashton. As a habitation of genius and talent, a theatre of intellectual activity for over half a century, it would be remarkable. But Charleston is far more: from the start Vanessa Bell and Duncan Grant, her children, and other artists, adorned the house and garden. The place was enriched by an accumulation of decorative achievements; a particular style, now a part of art history, is found here, in its finest and most characteristic form.

Location: 6 m E of Lewes, on A27, between Firle and Selmeston.
Station(s): Lewes 6 m; Berwick 3 m.
Open: Apr 1 to Oct 31 - Weds, Thurs, Sats (Guided Tours) and Suns and Bank Hol Mons (unguided), 2-6 (last adm 5). *Also open Frids Jul 23 to Sept 3 incl. - Guided tours, 2-6 (last adm 5).* Kitchen open Thurs only.
Admission: £3.75, Car park 50p (no parking charge midweek Apr, May, Oct). Student/OAP/UB40 concessions midweek throughout the season, also W/E Apr, May, Oct. Numbers in the House will be limited. No dogs. Coaches by prior appointment only. Contact Charleston Office at Farmhouse.

Designed by architect Martin Furniss and described as a 'work of art' by Anita Periere, this superb 2 acre garden on a sloping site was created for all season interest, and has all the intimacy and character of an English cottage garden. Large range of herbaceous and shrub species; natural pool with waterside plants chosen to give a long season of colour and variety. Featured in RHS Journal 1978 and two BBC television programmes, August 1978 'Country Life' and 'Homes and Gardens' 1981 and TVS 'That's Gardening' 1991.

Location: At Crowborough Cross (A26) turn on to B2100 (signposted Crowborough station & Rotherfield); at 2nd crossroads turn right into Tollwood Road.
Station(s): Crowborough (1 m).
Open: GARDEN ONLY - Mon May 31, Suns May 23; June 6, 20, 27; July 11, 25; Aug 1, 15. Coaches by appointment. Open 2.30-5.30.
Admission: £2.50, Chd £1 (including home made tea).*In aid of National Gardens Scheme and The National Trust.*
Refreshments: Home-made teas.
No dogs please. Excellent range of plants for sale. Car park.

FIRLE PLACE

nr Lewes map K3 △
Telephone: (0273) 858335
(Viscount Gage)

Home of the Gage family since the 15th century, the original Tudor house was largely altered about 1730. The House contains an important collection of European and British Old Masters. The pictures are further enhanced with French and English furniture by famous craftsmen. There is also a quantity of S vres porcelain of the finest quality. These are largely derived from the Cowper collection, and can be seen in a spacious family setting. A Connoisseurs house there are items of particular interest to visitors from the USA through General Gage, Commander-in-Chief of the British Forces at the beginning of the War of Independence, and his wife Margaret Kemble of New Jersey. The House is set in parkland under the South Downs, 55 miles from London by road. Hourly rail service Victoria to Lewes, takes 65 minutes, thence by taxi (5 miles).

Location: 5 m SE of Lewes on the Lewes/Eastbourne Road (A27).
Station(s): Lewes (5 m, taxis available).
Open: May, June, July, Aug & Sept - Wed, Thurs & Suns. Also Easter, May, Spring & Summer Bank Hol Suns & Mons: 2pm, last tickets at 5pm. First Wed in month longer unguided Connoisseurs' tour of House.
Admission: Pre-booked group parties of 25 on Open Days (except first Wed in month) at reduced rate. Special exclusive viewings at other times of year for private parties over 25 by arrangement.*Party bookings in writing to Showing Secretary, Firle Place, nr Lewes; East Sussex BN8 6LP (0273) 858335.*
Refreshments: Cold buffet luncheon 12.30-2 daily *except Sat.* Sussex cream teas from 3, only on house open days. (Bookings (0273) 858307).
Shop and contemporary pictures exhibition. Car park adjacent to house.

GLYNDE PLACE

nr Lewes map K3 △
Telephone: (0273) 858337
(Viscount Hampden)

Set below an escarpment of the ancient hill-fort of Mount Caburn, Glynde Place is a magnificent example of Elizabethan architect and is the manor house of an estate which has been in the same family since the 12th century. Built in 1579 of Sussex flint and Caen stone around a courtyard the house commands fine views towards Pevensey marshes and the South Downs. Amongst the collections of four hundred years of family living can be seen a fine collection of 17th century portraits of the Trevors, an early 18th century set of embroidery and a Victorian silver garniture given to Mr Speaker Brand. The house is still the family home of the Brands and can be enjoyed as such.

Location: In Glynde village 4 m SE of Lewes on A27.
Station(s): Within easy walking distance of Glynde Station with hourly services to Eastbourne and Brighton with connecting services from London at Lewes.
Open: June to Sept - Weds & Thurs and first and last Sun of each month. Open Easter Day and Easter Mon and Bank Hols. Guided tours for parties (25 or more) can be booked either on a regular open day (£2.50 per person) or a non-open day (£5 per person) by telephoning Lord Hampden on 0273 858 224 (daytime) or by writing to him.
Admission: to house: £3, Chd £1.50. Free parking.
Refreshments: Teas in Georgian Stable Block. Parties to book in advance (as above).

GREAT DIXTER

Northiam map L3 △
Telephone: (0797) 253160
(Quentin Lloyd, Esq)

A beautiful example of a 15th century half-timbered manor house with a Great Hall of unique construction in a truly 'English' garden setting. Restorations and the addition of a smaller 16th century hall house were carried out by Sir Edwin Lutyens who also designed the gardens. Yew hedges, topiary and garden buildings create a delightful setting for flower borders. These contain a rich diversity of plants of horticultural interest. Naturalised daffodils and fritillaries; paeonies; primulas, fuchsias, rose garden, clematis, herbaceous and bedding plants informally arranged.

Location: ½ m N of Northiam; 8 m NW of Rye; 12 m N of Hastings. Just off A28.
Open: Apr 1 to Oct 10 - Daily except Mons (but open all Bank Hol Mons) also weekends Oct 16, 17, 23, 24; open 2 until last adm at 5. Gardens open at 11 on May 29, 30, 31. Suns in July & Aug, also Aug 30.
Admission: House and Gardens: £3.30, Chd 50p. Gardens only £2.20, Chd 25p. Concessions to OAPs and NT members on Frid - House and Gardens ask for details.
No dogs.

HASTINGS CASTLE AND 1066 STORY

Hastings map L3
Telephone: (0424) 717963
(Hastings Heritage Ltd)

Majestic ruins of England's first Norman castle, with panoramic views of the coastline. William of Normandy's original mound - or motte - of earth and sand, with a deep ditch to the east side, was the site of the pre-fabricated wooden fort originally erected here, and can still be seen today. Also remaining are the walls of the collegiate Church of St. Mary, within the grounds, and the north and east curtain walls incorporating the magnificent eastern gateway. The famous 'whispering' dungeons beneath the mound also open for viewing. Within the grounds is an 11th Century 'siege tent', home of the '1066 Story' - a hi-tec audio/visual experience, incorporating surround sound and scenic effects, and depicting the story of the Battle of Hastings, and the 900 year dramatic history of the castle.

Location: On West Hill Cliff, adjacent Hastings Town Centre ½m from A259 and A21.
Open: Apr 3 to Sept 26 1993 - Daily 10-last adm 5. Open during winter by arrangement - Tel. (0424) 422964.
Admission: £2.30, Chd £1.60, Student/OAPs £1.85, Parties £1.20, (minimum of 10).
Refreshments: Numerous seafront and town centre restaurants nearby. West Hill Cafe 200m from entrance, on cliff top.
Seafront car park, access via cliff railway (West Hill). Unsuitable for disabled persons.

KIDBROOKE PARK WITH REPTON GROUNDS

Forest Row map K3
(The Council of Michael Hall School)

Sandstone house and stables built in 1730s with later alterations.

Location: 1 m SW of Forest Row, off A22, 4 m S of East Grinstead.
Open: Spring Bank Hol Mon (May 30) then Aug - Daily (inc Bank Hol Mon), 11- 6.
Admission: Apply for admission to the Bursar.

LAMB HOUSE   🍀   The National Trust

Rye map L3

Georgian house with garden. Home of Henry James from 1898 to 1916.

Location: In West Street facing W end of church.
Station(s): Rye (½ m).
Open: House (Hall & 3 rooms only) & Garden. Apr to end of Oct - Weds & Sats 2- 6 (last admission 5.30).
Admission: £2. No reduction for children or parties.
No dogs. Unsuitable for wheelchairs. No lavatories.

MICHELHAM PRIORY

nr Hailsham map L3 △ &
(Sussex Archaeological Society)

Founded in 1229 this Augustinian Priory is surrounded by one of the largest moats in England. Elizabethan wing and 14th century gatehouse. Special exhibitions and events. Tudor barn. Working Watermill restored, grinding wholemeal flour.

Location: ½ m E of Upper Dicker just off London/Eastbourne Road (A22); 10 m N of Eastbourne.
Open: Mar 25 to Oct 31 - Daily 11-5.30; Nov and Mar - Sun only, 11-4.
Admission: (inc Watermill) £3.30, Chd (5-16) £1.90. Family ticket (2 adult, 2 chd) £9. Booked parties (20 or more) £2.80 per person. OAPs £2.90.
Refreshments: Morning coffees, farmhouse lunches and Sussex teas at licensed restaurants in Grounds.
No dogs. Sussex Crafts & Small Industries Aug 4-8 (incl.) and many other events incl. 6 art exhibitions.

MONKS HOUSE   🦋 The National Trust

Rodmell map K3

A small village house and garden. The home of Virginia and Leonard Woolf from 1919 until his death in 1969. House administered and largely maintained by tenants.

Location: 3 m SE of Lewes, off C7 in Rodmell village.
Station(s): Southease (1 m).
Open: Apr to end Oct - Weds & Sats 2-5.30 (last adm ½ hour before closing time).
Admission: £2. No reduction for chd or parties.
No dogs. Unsuitable for wheelchairs. Max. of 15 people in house at any one time. Narrow access road. Car park 50 yds.

MOORLANDS

Crowborough map K3
Telephone: (0892) 652474
(Dr and Mrs Steven Smith)

Three acres set in lush valley adjoining Ashdown Forest; water garden with ponds and streams; herbaceous border, primulas, rhododendrons, azaleas and many unusual trees and shrubs; good autumn colour.

Location: Friar's Gate. 2m N of Crowborough. Approach via B2188 at Friar's Gate - take L fork signposted Crowborough Narrow Road', entrance 100 yards on left. From Crowborough crossroads take St Johns Road to Friar's Gate.
Open: Suns May 16 and 30. 2-6. Also by appointment only; Apr 1 to Oct 31. *In aid of National Gardens Scheme.*
Admission: £1.50, Chd 30p. Limited free car parking.
Refreshments: Teas in garden on open days; and for parties by prior arrangement. Unsuitable for disabled persons.

PASHLEY MANOR

Ticehurst, Wadhurst map L3
Telephone: (0580) 200692
(Mr & Mrs J.A. Sellick)

Pashley Manor is a Grade 1 Tudor timber-framed ironmaster's house dating from 1550 with a Queen Anne rear elevation of 1720. Standing in a well timbered park with magnificent views across to Brightling Beacon. The 8 acres of formal garden, dating from the 18th c, were created in true English romantic style and are planted with many ancient trees and fine shrubs, new plantings over the past decade give additional interest and subtle colouring throughout the year. All is enhanced by waterfalls, ponds and a moat which encircled the original house built in 1262. The delightful view, peaceful environment and the sound of running water makes this garden very worthwhile visiting.

Location: Between Ticehurst and A21 on B2099. Wadhurst 5 m.
Open: GARDENS ONLY: Apr 10 to Oct 16 - Tues, Wed, Thurs, Sat and all Bank Hols. 11-5.
Admission: £2.50, OAPs £2. Coaches by appointment only.
Refreshments: Teas on terrace in fine weather.
Car park. Unsuitable for wheelchairs. No dogs. Plants for sale.

PEVENSEY CASTLE English⌗Heritage

Pevensey map L3
Telephone: (0323) 762604

The walls that enclose this 10-acre site are from the 4th century Roman fort, Anderida. The inner castle, with its great keep, is medieval. With the fall of France in 1940, Pevensey was put into service again, after centuries of neglect. A Personal Stereo Guided Tour is available.

Location: Pevensey.
Open: Good Friday or Apr 1 (whichever is earlier) to Sept 30: Open Daily 10-6. Oct 1 to Maundy Thursday or Mar 31 (whichever is earlier): Open Tues to Sun 10-4. *Closed* Dec 24-26, Jan 1.
Admission: £1.70, Concessions £1.30, Chd 85p.

PRESTON MANOR

Brighton map K3
Telephone: (0273) 603005
(Borough of Brighton)

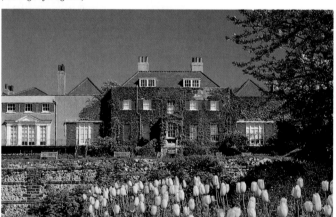

A Georgian house built in 1738 and added to in 1905; the house of the Stanford family for nearly 150 years. The house is fully furnished and illustrates the way of life of a rich gentry family and their servants. Delightful grounds with walled garden and pets' cemetery.

Location: On main Brighton to London Road at Preston Park.
Station(s): Preston Park.
Open: All the year - Tues-Sat 10-5. Sun 2-5. Closed Mons (except Bank Hols) Good Fri, Christmas & Boxing Day.
Admission: Charged. *Reduced rates for parties, families, Chd and OAPs.* Garden free. Parties by arrangement.

ROYAL PAVILION

Brighton map K3 &
Telephone: (0273) 603005

Spectacular seaside palace of the Prince Regent, transformed by John Nash (1815-1822) into one of the most dazzlingly exotic buildings in the British Isles. Interiors furnished in the Chinese style. The ten years structural restoration programme is now complete. NEW - Queen Victoria's apartments. Pavilion shop.

Location: In centre of Brighton (Old Steine).
Station(s): Brighton (¾ m).
Open: All the year - Daily 10-5 (June to Sept 10-6). *Closed Christmas Day & Boxing Day.*
Admission: Charged. *Reduced rates for parties, families, Chd and OAPs.*
Refreshments: Tearoom with balcony overlooking the gardens.
Ground floor accessible for the disabled.

SHEFFIELD PARK GARDEN 🌿 The National Trust

nr Uckfield map K3
Telephone: (0825) 790655

Large garden with series of lakes linked by cascades; great variety of unusual shrubs.

Location: Midway between East Grinstead & Lewes on E side of A275; 5 m NW of Uckfield.
Open: Apr to Nov 7 - Tues to Sats (closed Good Fri) 11-6 or sunset if earlier; Suns and Bank Hol Mons 2-6 or sunset if earlier. Suns during Oct & Nov: 1-sunset. Last adm one hour before closing. *Closed Tues following Bank Hol Mons.*
Admission: May, Oct & Nov: £4, Chd £2. Apr & Jun to Sept: £3.50, Chd £1.80. Pre-booked parties £3. *No reduction for parties on Sats, Suns & Bank Hols.*
No dogs. Shop. Wheelchairs available.

THE ROYAL PAVILION
BRIGHTON

£10 MILLION
STRUCTURAL RESTORATION
NOW COMPLETE

OPEN DAILY (except Dec 25 and 26)

For further information on guided tours, room hire and special events telephone Public Services (0273) 603005.

WEST SUSSEX

ARUNDEL CASTLE

Arundel map J3   ♿
Telephone: (0903) 883136
(Arundel Castle Trustees Ltd.)

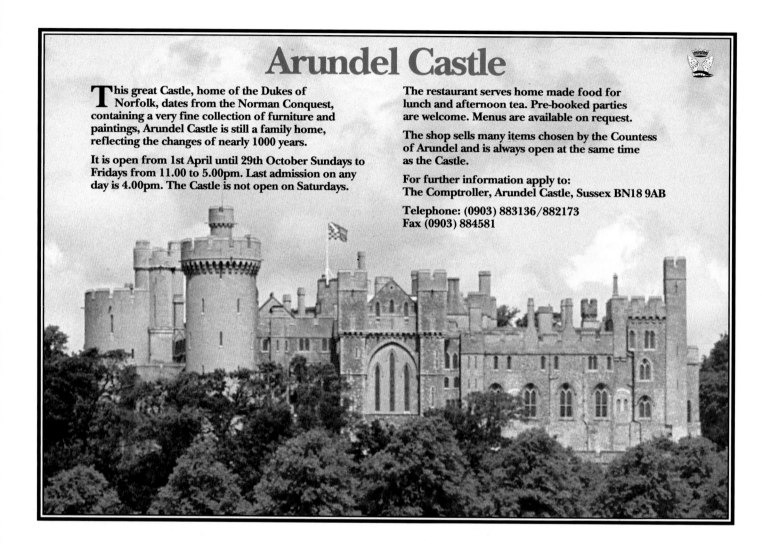

Arundel Castle

This great Castle, home of the Dukes of Norfolk, dates from the Norman Conquest, containing a very fine collection of furniture and paintings, Arundel Castle is still a family home, reflecting the changes of nearly 1000 years.

It is open from 1st April until 29th October Sundays to Fridays from 11.00 to 5.00pm. Last admission on any day is 4.00pm. The Castle is not open on Saturdays.

The restaurant serves home made food for lunch and afternoon tea. Pre-booked parties are welcome. Menus are available on request.

The shop sells many items chosen by the Countess of Arundel and is always open at the same time as the Castle.

For further information apply to:
The Comptroller, Arundel Castle, Sussex BN18 9AB

Telephone: (0903) 883136/882173
Fax (0903) 884581

BERRI COURT

Yapton map J3
Telephone: (0243) 551 663
(Mr & Mrs J. C. Turner)

BORDE HILL GARDEN

Haywards Heath   map K3
Telephone: (0444) 450326

Large garden with woods and parkland of exceptional beauty. Rare trees and shrubs, herbaceous borders and fine views. Woodland Walk, water feature, picnic area by lake.

Location: 1½ m N of Haywards Heath on Balcombe Road. Brighton 17 m; Gatwick 10 m.
Open: Open Suns only: Mar 7 to Apr 4 then daily from Apr 9 to Oct 31. 10-6. (8pm May/June).
Admission: £3, OAPs £2.50, Chd £1, Parties (20 and over) £2.50. Bank Hol W/E in Apr/May: £3.50, OAPs £3, Chd £1, Parties (20 and over) £3. Parkland admission: 50p per person (not available during special events).
Refreshments: Licensed - morning coffee, light lunches, cream teas; parties by arrangement.

CHAMPS HILL

Coldwaltham, nr Pulborough   map J3
(Mr & Mrs David Bowerman)

27 acres of formal garden and woodland walks around old sandpits. Conifers and acid-loving plants. Many species labelled. Superb views across Arun Valley. Special features:- March - Winter heathers and Spring flowers. May - Rhododendrons, Azaleas, Wild Flowers. Aug - Heaths and other specialities.

Location: S of Pulborough on A29 in Coldwaltham turn Right to Fittleworth; 800 yds on R.
Open: 11-5. (Suns 1-5). Mar 21, 27, 28. May 15, 16, 22, 23, 30. Aug 7, 8, 21, 22.
Admission: £1.50, Chd free. *In aid of National Gardens Scheme.*
Refreshments: Coffees, Teas (Not March).
No dogs.

CHICHESTER CATHEDRAL

West Street   map J3
Telephone: (0243) 782595
(The Dean & Chapter of Chichester)

In the heart of the city, this fine Cathedral has been a centre of Christian worship and community life for 900 years. Site of Shrine of St Richard of Chichester; Romanesque stone carvings; works by Sutherland, Feibusch, Procktor, Chagall, Skelton, Piper, and Ursula Benker-Schirmer. Treasury. Cloister. Refectory. Shops in Bell Tower and South Street. Schools should contact the Education Adviser. Vicars' Close and Hall.

Location: Centre of city; British Rail; A27, A286.
Open: All year 7.40-7 (5 in winter except for those attending Evensong). Choral Evensong daily (except Weds) during term time; occasionally visiting choirs at other times. Ministry of welcome operates. Guided tours must be booked.
Admission: Free: suggested donations Adults £1, Chd 20p.
Refreshments: Refectory off Cathedral Cloisters with lavatory facilities (including those for the disabled).
No dogs except guide dogs. Wheelchair access (one wheelchair available on application to Vergers). Loop system for the hard of hearing. Touch and hearing Centre for the blind. Parking in city car parks.

COKE'S BARN

West Burton, nr Pulborough   map J3
(Mr & Mrs Nigel Azis)

¾ acre garden surrounding C17 barn. Intensely planted courtyard with brick paving, gravel and grass leading to main garden of herbaceous, roses, shrubs and water areas planted with a wide variety of unusual plants. Long views of South Down Hills. South facing conservatory.

Location: West Burton 5 m SW of Pulborough/Petworth. At foot of Bury Hill turn W off A29 to W. Burton for 1 m then follow signs.
Open: Suns and Mons, Apr 25, 26. May 2, 3. June 6, 7. Aug 15, 16. 2-6.
Admission: £1, Chd 25p. *In aid of National Gardens Scheme.*
Refreshments: Tea on Suns only.
No dogs. Plants for sale.

DANNY

Hurstpierpoint   map K3
(Country Houses Association)

Elizabethan E-shaped house, dating from 1593.

Location: Between Hassocks and Hurstpierpoint (B2116) - off New Way Lane.
Station(s): Hassocks (1 m).
Open: May to Sept - Weds & Thurs 2-5. Last entry 4.30.
Admission: £1.50, Chd 50p. Free car park.
No dogs admitted.

DENMANS

Fontwell   map J3
Telephone: (0243) 542808
(Mrs J. H. Robinson)

Unique 20th century walled garden extravagantly planted for overall, all-year interest in form, colour and texture; areas of glass for tender species. John Brookes School of Garden Design at Clock House, short courses throughout the season.

Location: Between Arundel and Chichester; turn off A27 into Denmans Lane (W of Fontwell racecourse).
Station(s): Barnham (2 m).
Open: Open daily throughout the year including all Bank Holidays except Christmas Day and Boxing Day 9-5. Coaches by appointment.
Admission: £2.25, Chd £1.25, OAPs £1.85. Groups of 15 or more £1.65.
Refreshments: Restaurant and shop open 10-5.
Plant centre. The Country Shop. No dogs. National Gardens Scheme

GOODWOOD HOUSE

Chichester   map J3
Telephone: (0243) 774107
(Duke of Richmond)

Bought by the first Duke of Richmond (son of King Charles II and a French female spy!) and home of the Dukes of Richmond ever since, Goodwood House is filled with the treasures collected by all ten Dukes. They include Canaletto's first London paintings, snuff boxes, tapestries, family portraits by Van Dyck, Kneller, Lely, Reynolds, etc; French commodes(!) and a collection of S vres porcelain bought by the Third Duke when (a very bad) British Ambassador at Versailles. There are royal relics, Napoleonic booty and the bits and pieces inevitable after a family has stayed put for 300 years. Chambers, then Wyatt, enlarged the House to hold these Collections. Country Park near the Racecourse on crest of South Downs. Pleasure flights available from the Goodwood Aerodrome together with flying instruction to top standards. Dressage Championships (National & International) and other events in Goodwood Park. Glorious Goodwood Racecourse.

Location: 3½ m NE of Chichester, approach roads A283 & A286, A27. Aerodrome 1 m from House.

Open: Easter Sun & Mon then May 9 to Sept 27 - Suns & Mons (except June 13, and event days, prospective visitors should check these dates before setting out); also Tues, Weds & Thurs in Aug, 2-5pm.

Admission: Large free car park for visitors to House during open hours; For all information and group rates contact the House Secretary. Goodwood House, Chichester, West Sussex PO18 0PX.

Refreshments: Teas in one of the State Rooms for pre-booked parties (min 15); unbooked teas for individuals and families on days when no evening function, or tea and biscuits at The Goodwood Park Hotel Golf and Country Club at the Park Gate (east). Weddings and Functions throughout the year.

House suitable for wheelchairs (no steps); a wheelchair available. Goodwood souvenirs and prints for sale.

HAMMERWOOD PARK

nr East Grinstead map K3
Telephone: (0342) 850594
Fax: (0342) 850864
(David Pinnegar, Esq)

HAMMERWOOD PARK is said by visitors to be the most interesting house in Sussex. Built in 1792, the house was the first work of **Latrobe**, the architect of **The White House and The Capitol, Washington D.C., U.S.A.** Set in Reptonesque parkland on the edge of the Ashdown Forest, the house is an early example of Greek Revival. In 1982 David Pinnegar purchased the house as a near ruin from the pop-group Led Zeppelin. A decade of award winning restoration works has been completed and one of the most ambitious *trompe-l'oeil* decoration schemes of this century was finished last year in the staircase hall. Just one room remains spectacularly derelict. Various collections include photographica, musical instruments, nurseries, and a copy of the **Elgin Marbles.** Guided tours by the owner and his family, luscious cream teas and musical evenings bring the house to life.

Location: 3½ m E of East Grinstead on A264 Tunbridge Wells; 1 m W of Holtye.

Open: Easter Mon to end Sept - Weds, Sats & Bank Holiday Mons 2-5.30. Guided tour starts just after 2. Coaches (21 seats or more) by appointment. School groups welcome.

Admission: £3.50, Chd £1.50, OAPs £3.

Refreshments: Luscious cream teas in the Elgin Room.

Sir Christopher Wren – architect (1632–1723)

*Fawley Court
Hampton Court Palace
Kensington Palace (alterations and additions)
Old Royal Observatory
Winslow Hall*

HIGH BEECHES GARDENS

Handcross map K3
Telephone: (0444) 400589
(High Beeches Gardens Conservation Trust)

Twenty acres of enchanting woodland valley gardens, planted with Magnolias, Camellias, Rhododendrons, and Azaleas, for Spring. In Autumn, this is one of the most brilliant gardens for leaf colour, superbly landscaped with Maples, Liquid-ambers, Amelanchiers and Nyssas. Gentians, Primulas, and Iris are naturalised, with Royal Fern and Gunnera in the Water Gardens. There are four acres of Wildflower Meadows, with cowslips and many Orchids.

Location: 1 m E of A23 at Handcross, on B2110.

Open: GARDENS ONLY. Easter Mon to June 26, and Sept 4 to Oct 30, daily 1-5 except Weds & Suns. EVENTS: Daffodil day (in the gardens) & Water Colour Portraits - Mon Apr 12, 10-5. Bluebell Day, Plant Sale & Wine Tasting, Mon May 3, 10-5. Azalea Day, Mon May 31 & Plant Sale 10-5. Traditional Haymaking Aug 22, 11-6. Autumn Event, Plant Sale & Bazaar, for Motor Neurone Disease Ass. Sun Oct 24.

Admission: £2.50, Accompanied Chd free, £3.50 for guided groups (by appointment) at any time.

Refreshments: Homemade lunches and teas on Event Days only, or by appointment for Groups.

LEONARDSLEE GARDENS

Horsham map K3
(The Loder Family)

One of the most beautiful gardens in the country. Fantastic setting of natural valley with 6 lakes. Famous for camellias & magnolias in April, glorious rhododendrons and azaleas in May, tranquil Summer foliage; brilliant Autumn tints. Rock garden, Bonsai exhibition, Alpine house. Wallabies, Deer parks. Souvenirs & plants for sale.

Location: In Lower Beeding at junction of A279 & A281: 5 m SE of Horsham or 3 m SW of Handcross at bottom of M23.

Open: Apr 9 to Oct 31: every day 10-6. (In May 10-8).

Admission: May £3.50 (May Suns & Hol Mons £4). Chd £2. Apr,Jun & Oct £3. July to Sept £2.50, Chd £1.

Refreshments: Licensed Restaurant and Tea Room.

No dogs please.

MALT HOUSE

Chithurst, nr Midhurst map J3
Telephone: (0730) 821433
(Mr & Mrs Graham Ferguson)

Approximately 5 acres; flowering shrubs including exceptional rhododendrons and azaleas, leading to 60 acres of lovely woodland walks.

Location: 3½ m W of Midhurst via A272, turn N to Chithurst cont 1½ m; or via A3, 2 m S of Liphook turn SE to Milland and Chithurst.
Open: GARDEN ONLY. Suns - Apr 25 to May 30; Bank Hol Mons; May 3 & 31, 2-6.
Admission: £1.50, Chd 50p. *In aid of National Gardens Sheme.* Also open by appointment for parties.
Refreshments: Tea and biscuits.
Plants for sale.

NEWTIMBER PLACE

Newtimber map K3
Telephone: (0273) 833104
(His Honour & Mrs John Clay)

Moated house - Etruscan style wall paintings.

Location: Off A281 between Poynings and Pyecombe.
Open: May to Aug - Thurs 2-5.
Admission: £2.

NYMANS GARDEN The National Trust

Handcross map K3   &
Telephone: (0444) 400321 or 400002

One of the great gardens of the Sussex Weald; rare and beautiful plants, shrubs and trees from all over the world; azaleas, rhododendrons, eucyphias, hydrangeas, magnolias, camellias and roses; walled garden, hidden sunken garden, pinetum, laurel walk; romantic ruins.

Location: At Handcross just off London/Brighton M23/A23.
Open: Mar: Sat & Sun only, Apr 1 to end Oct - Daily (except Mons & Fris) and open B.H. Mon and Good Friday 11-7 or sunset if earlier. Last adm 1 hour before closing.
Admission: £3.30, Chd half-price. Parties of 15 or more £2.80 by prior arrangement with Head Gardener.
Refreshments: Teas.
No dogs (In car park only). Wheelchair provided. Batricar on request. Shop and exhibition, same days as garden 12-6.

PARHAM HOUSE AND GARDENS 🏛

Pulborough map J3
Telephone: (0903) 742021

Beautiful Elizabethan House with important collection of Elizabethan and Stuart portraits, fine furniture, carpets, tapestries and a profusion of rare needlework. Fresh flowers in each room. Eleven acres of gardens (including a 4 acre walled garden) with lake, fine statuary, brick and turf maze, a vegetable garden.

Location: A283 Storrington/Pulborough road.
Open: Weds, Thurs, Sun and Bank Hol. Mon afternoons from Easter Sun to first Sun in Oct. Gardens 1-6, House 2-6 (last adm 5pm).
Admission: £3.50, OAPs £3, Chd £2 (House and Gardens); Adult/OAPs £2.50, Chd £1 (Gardens only). Group rates for both guided (Wed & Thurs mornings by arrangement) and unguided visits available on application.
Refreshments: Self service teas in Big Kitchen. Some outside seating.
Church, shop. Picnic area close to house. Large car park. Access for disabled to garden only, 1 wheelchair available. Bookings and all enquiries to Administrator.

PETWORTH HOUSE The National Trust

Petworth map J3   &
Telephone: (0798) 42207

Magnificent late 17th c house in beautiful deer park; important collection of pictures (many by Turner and Van Dyck), sculpture and furniture; carving by Grinling Gibbons; archive room.

Location: In centre of Petworth 5½ m E of Midhurst.
Open: Apr 1 to end Oct daily (except Mon and Fri) (open Good Friday and Bank Hol Mons, *closed* Tues following) 1-5.30 (last adm 5). Gardens and Car park 12.30-6. Deer Park open daily all year - 8- sunset, (*closed* June 25 - 27 from 12 noon). Car park for visitors to House during open hours, 800 yds. Car park for Park only on A283, 1½ m N of Petworth.
Admission: £4, Chd half-price. Pre-booked parties of 15 or more welcome on Weds, Thurs and Sats only, £3.50. Deer park free.
Refreshments: Light lunches 12.30-2.30, and teas 3-5 (last orders 4.30) in House on open days. Shop 1-5.
No dogs in House or Pleasure grounds and must be kept under control in Deer Park. Shop. Wheelchairs provided. No prams or pushchairs in showrooms.

SACKVILLE COLLEGE

East Grinstead map K4
Telephone: (0342) 323279/326561
(Patron Earl De La Warr)

Jacobean Almshouses founded in 1609. Common Room, Dining Hall, Chapel and Study. Original furniture.

Location: High Street, East Grinstead off A22.
Open: June 1 to Aug 31 daily 2-5.
Admission: £1.25, Chd 65p. Parties by arrangement Apr to Oct.
Refreshments: Teas to order for parties.

ST. MARY'S HOUSE AND GARDENS

Bramber map K3
Telephone: (0903) 816205
(Peter Thorogood Esq)

ST. MARY'S HOUSE

Bramber

c. 1470

Magnificent Grade I medieval house, classified as "the best late 15th century timber-framing in Sussex". Rare 16th century painted wall-leather. Fine panelled rooms, including the unique trompe l'oeil 'Painted Room', decorated for the visit of Queen Elizabeth I. Furniture, marquetry, books manuscripts. Charming gardens with Topiary. Teas.

Tourist Board "Warmest Welcome" commendation.

ADMISSION–SEE EDITORIAL REFERENCE

The foundations of St Mary's go back to the 12 century when land at Bramber was granted to the Knights Templar. The present house (c.1470) was re-fashioned by William Waynflete, Bishop of Winchester, founder of Magdalen College, Oxford, and is classified as 'the best late 15th century timber-framing in Sussex'. Fine panelled rooms, including unique 'Painted Room' decorated for Elizabeth I's visit. The 'King's Room' has connections with Charles II's escape to France in 1651. Also other Royal and historic associations. Rare 16th century painted wall-leather, splendid carved oak fireplaces, massive 'dragon-beam' in the 'Monks Parlour', superb marquetry decoration and strapwork doors. Furniture, pictures, manuscripts. Library contains largest private collection of first editions and illustrated books by celebrated 19th century comic poet and artist, Thomas Hood. Victorian Music room, with elaborate medieval Gothic stone fireplaces, added in 1896 by Hon. Algernon Bourke, son of the Earl of Mayo. Sherlock Holmes connection during ownership (1903-13) of Alfred Musgrave. Ring for details of concerts and other events, May to December.

Location: 10 m NW of Brighton in village of Bramber off A283.
Station(s): Shoreham-by-Sea (4 m). Trains from London (Victoria).
Open: Easter Sun to last Sun in Sept - Suns & Thurs 2-6. Bank Hol Mons 2-6. Also Mons in July, Aug & Sept 2-6. **Coach party bookings** daily morning or afternoon by prior arrangement from Apr to Oct.
Admission: £3.30, OAPs £3, Chd £2. Reduced rates for parties £3 (25 or over). Free coach and car parking in grounds.
Refreshments: Homemade afternoon tea in the Music Room. Catering for parties by arrangement. Seating for 60.

STANDEN 🌿 The National Trust

East Grinstead map K3
Telephone: (0342) 323029

A family house of the 1890s, designed by Philip Webb. William Morris wallpapers and textiles. Period furniture, paintings. Hillside garden with fine views across Medway Valley.

Location: 2 m S of East Grinstead signposted from the Turners Hill road (B2110).
Station(s): East Grinstead (2 m).
Open: Apr 1 to end Oct, Wed to Sun (incl Good Friday) 1.30-5.30 (last adm 5). Open Bank Holiday Mon (*closed* Tues following). Access may be restricted at busy times. Pre-booked parties Weds, Thurs & Frid only; telephone Administrator.
Admission: House and Garden: £3.80; Sat, Sun, Good Frid & Bank Hol Mon £4.50. Garden only £2.30, Chd half price, Parties of over 15 people £3.
Refreshments: Light lunches and teas served from 12.30-5.30, last admission 5.
Dogs admitted to car park & woodland walks only. Wheelchairs provided; disabled drivers may park near house with prior permission from administrator. Shop.No pushchairs or back-packs in house.

WAKEHURST PLACE GARDEN 🌿 The National Trust

nr Ardingly map K3 ♿
Telephone: (0444) 892701
(Administered by Royal Botanic Gardens, Kew)

A wealth of exotic plant species including many fine specimens of trees and shrubs. Picturesque watercourse linking several ponds and lakes. Heath garden and rock walk.

Location: 1½ m NW of Ardingly on B2028.
Open: All the year - Daily Nov to end Jan, 10-4; Feb & Oct, 10-5; Mar, 10-6; Apr to end of Sept, 10-7. Last adm ½ hour before closing. *Closed Christmas Day & New Year's Day. Opening times may be subject to alteration.*
Admission: £3.30, Chd (16 and under) £1.10. Reduced rates for Students/OAPs/Pre-booked parties but prices may be subject to alteration. *Visitors should check with Wakehurst place for 1994 prices.*
Refreshments: Light refreshments.
No dogs. Wheelchairs provided. Exhibition in Mansion. Book shop open, not NT.

THE WEALD AND DOWNLAND OPEN AIR MUSEUM

Singleton, nr Chichester map J3
Telephone: (024 363) 348

The Museum is rescuing and re-erecting historic Buildings from South-East England. The Collection illustrates the history of vernacular architecture in the Weald and Downland area. Exhibits include a Medieval Farmstead, Garden and History of Farming Exhibition centred on Bayleaf Farmhouse (above) Timber-framed Houses, a Tudor Market Hall, a 16th century Treadwheel. Farm Buildings include two 18th century Barns and a Granary, a Blacksmith's Forge, Plumber's and Carpenter's Workshops, a Charcoal Burner's Camp, a Village School and a History of Brickwork Exhibition.

Location: 6 m N of Chichester on A286 just S of Singleton.
Open: Mar 1 to Oct 31 - Daily 11-5. Nov 1 to Feb 28 - Weds, Suns and Bank Hols only 11-4.
Admission: Charged. Parties by arrangement. (Group rates available).
Refreshments: Light refreshments during main season.

WEST DEAN GARDENS   🏛

nr Chichester map J3
Telephone: (0243 63) 301
(The Edward James Foundation)

Extensive garden in a downland setting with specimen trees, 300ft pergola, summerhouses, herbaceous borders, wild garden, extensive walled garden under restoration and Mower museum. Circuit walk (2¼ miles) through parkland and the 45 acre St. Roches Arboretum. House not open to visitors.

Location: 6 m N of Chichester on A286, nr Weald & Downland Open Air Museum.
Open: Mar to Oct incl. - Daily 11-6 (last adm 5). Parties by arrangement.
Admission: £2.25, OAPs £2, Parties £1.70 per person.
Refreshments: Available.
Coach and car parking. Sorry no dogs.

TYNE & WEAR

GIBSIDE CHAPEL & GROUNDS   🌿 The National Trust

Gibside map H11
Telephone: (0207) 542255

Built to James Paine's design soon after 1760. Outstanding example of Georgian architecture approached along a terrace with an oak avenue. Seven mile walk with views of River Derwent.

Location: 6 m SW of Gateshead; 20 m NW of Durham between Rowlands Gill and Burnopfield.
Open: Apr 1 to Oct 31 daily except Mons (open Bank Hol Mons) 11-5.
Admission: Chapel & Grounds £2.20, Chd half-price.
Refreshments: Tea room.
Shop, picnic area, circular walk.

SOUTER LIGHTHOUSE   🌿 The National Trust

Whitburn map H11
Telephone: (091) 529 3161

Shore based lighthouse and associated buildings, built in 1871 - the first to be powered by an alternative electric current.

Location: 2½m S of South Shields on A183, 5m N of Sunderland.
Open: Apr 1 to Oct 31 - Daily except Mon (open Bank Holiday Monday) 11-5. Last adm 4.30.
Admission: £2.20, Chd half-price. Pre-booked parties £1.60.
Refreshments: Restaurant.
Shop, picnic area.

TYNEMOUTH CASTLE AND PRIORY   English ⌗ Heritage

map H12
Telephone: 091-257 1090

Two saints were buried within the walls of this Benedictine priory, established in the 11th century on the site of an earlier abandoned monastery. Two walls of the presbytery still tower to their full height and the 15th century chantry chapel has a splendid collection of roof bosses. A fortified gatehouse was added during the Border wars, which persuaded Henry VIII to retain the priory as a royal castle after the Dissolution. The headland remained in use for coastal defence until 1956, one restored battery is open to the public.

Location: Tynemouth.
Open: Good Friday or Apr 1 (whichever is earlier) to Sept 30: Open Daily 10-6. Oct 1 to Maundy Thursday or Mar 31 (whichever is earlier): Open Tues to Sun 10-4. *Closed* Dec 24-26, Jan 1.
Admission: £1.20, Concessions 90p, Chd 60p.

WASHINGTON OLD HALL   🌿 The National Trust

Washington map H11   ♿
Telephone: 091-416 6879

Jacobean manor house incorporating portions of 12th century house of the Washington family.

Location: In Washington on E side of Ave; 5 m W of Sunderland (2 m from A1); S of Tyne Tunnel, follow signs for Washington New Town District 4 & then village.
Open: Apr 1 to Oct 31 - Daily (except Fri, but open Good Friday) 11-5; (last adm 4.30).
Admission: £2, Chd half-price. *Parties of 15 or more £1.50 each, by prior arrangement only with Administrator.*
Shop. Dogs in garden only, on leads. Wheelchair access.

WARWICKSHIRE

ARBURY HALL

Nuneaton map H6 △
Telephone: (0203) 382804
(The Rt Hon the Viscount Daventry)

16th century Elizabethan House, gothicized late 18th century, pictures, period furniture etc. Park and landscape gardens. Arbury has been the home of the Newdegate family since the 16th century. For a country house the Gothic architecture is unique, the original Elizabethan house being Gothicised by Sir Roger Newdigate between 1750 and 1800, under the direction of Sanderson Miller, Henry Keene, and Couchman of Warwick. Beautiful plaster ceilings, pictures and fine specimens of period furniture, china and glass. Fine stable block with central doorway by Wren. Arbury Hall is situated in very large grounds and is about 1½ miles from any main road. Excellent carriage drives lined with trees. George Eliot's 'Cheveral Manor'.

Location: 2 m SW of Nuneaton off B4102.
Open: Suns from Easter Sun to end of Sept. Bank Hol Mons. Gardens 2-6, Hall 2-5.30 (last adm 5). The Arbury dining room can also be available for exclusive luncheons and dinner functions.
Admission: Hall and Gardens £3, Chd £1.60, Gardens and Park £1.60, Chd 80p. Organised parties most days 25 or over) special terms by prior arrangement with Administrator. School parties also welcome. Free car park.
Refreshments: Available on all open days. Set meals arranged for parties.

BADDESLEY CLINTON ♣ The National Trust

Solihull map H6 &
Telephone: (0564) 783294

A romantically sited medieval moated manor house, with 120 acres, dating back to the 14th century and little changed since 1634.

Location: ¾ m W of A4141 Warwick to Birmingham Road, nr Chadwick End; 7½ m NW of Warwick; 15 m SE of Birmingham.
Station(s): Lapworth (2 m) (not Suns).
Open: Mar 3 to end of Sept-Weds to Suns & Bank Hol Mons 2-6.*Closed Good Frid.* Grounds and shop open from 12.30. Oct - Weds to Suns 12.30- 4.30. Mar '94: Wed to Sun 2-6. Last admissions 30 mins before closing. Coach parties (weekdays only) by prior arrangement.
Admission: £3.80, Chd £1.90, grounds only £2. Family tickets £10.40.
Refreshments: Lunches and teas in licensed restaurant from 12.30-5.30. (Oct 4.30). Also open Nov 3 to Dec 19, Wed to Sun 12.30-4.30.
No prams or pushchairs in the house. No dogs. Wheelchair available. Shop.

Geoffrey Alan Jellicoe –
contemporary garden architect
and designer

His work can be seen in the following properties included in Historic Houses Castles and Gardens:

Hever Castle
Wisley

CHARLECOTE PARK ♣ The National Trust

Warwick map H6 △ &
Telephone: (0789) 470277

Originally built by the Lucy family, 1550s. Refurbished 1830s in Elizabethan Revival style. 'Capability' Brown Deer park.

Location: 5 m E of Stratford-upon-Avon on the N side of B4086.
Open: Apr to end Oct - Daily (except Mon & Thurs) House: 11-1 & 2-5.30, Park 11-6 (*Closed* Good Friday, open Bank Hol Mons). Last adm to house 5 (*closed* 1-2). Parties (including schools) by prior arrangement only. Evening guided tours for pre-booked parties Tues, May to Sept 7.30-9.30.
Admission: £3.50, Chd £1.75, Family ticket £9.70. Full price for evening visits (incl. NT members).
Refreshments: Morning coffee, lunches, afternoon teas in the Orangery Restaurant (Licensed) 11-5.30. Also Nov 6 to Dec 12: Sat & Sun 12-4.
No dogs. Wheelchairs provided. Shop.

COUGHTON COURT   The National Trust

Alcester   map H6
Telephone: (0789) 762435

Impressive central gatehouse dating from 1530. Two mid-Elizabethan half-timbered wings. Jacobite relics. Family portraits and memorabilia. The home of the Throckmorton family since 1409. Tranquil lake and riverside walk.

Location: 2 m N of Alcester on A435.
Open: Apr - Sats, Suns 1.30-5.30, Easter Sat to Wed 1.30-5.30. All B H Mons incl. Easter Mon 12.30-5.30), Closed Good Fri. May to end Sept - Daily except Thur & Fri, 1.30-5.30. Oct - Sats, Suns 1.30-5. Last admissions to house 30 mins before closing. Evening Guided tours for pre-booked parties Mons to Weds. Garden tours by appointment. Grounds open same days as house but 12-6 (5 in Oct).
Admission: £3.50, Chd £1.75, Family ticket £9.50, Grounds £1.50. Parties by prior written arrangement. No party rate or membership concessions for out-of-hour visits.
Refreshments: Restaurant open 12.30-5.30 for lunches and teas (licensed).
Shop. Limited access for wheelchairs in house. Riveride walk and new garden suitable for wheelchairs. Dogs on leads in car park only. House, grounds and restaurant managed by the family.

FARNBOROUGH HALL The National Trust

nr Banbury map H5

Mid 18th century house incorporates fine plasterwork and ancient sculpture. ¾ mile terrace walk feature temples and obelisk.

Location: 6 m N of Banbury; ½ m W of A423.
Open: House, grounds and terrace walk: April to end of Sept - Weds and Sats 2-6. Also May 2 & 3, 2-6. Terrace Walk only: Thurs & Fris 2-6. Last adm 5.30.
Admission: House, grounds and terrace walk £2.60, Garden and terrace walk £1.50. Terrace walk £1. Chd half-price. *No reductions for parties. Parties by prior written arrangement only. Dogs in grounds only, on leads. No indoor photography. NB: The tenants are responsible for the showing arrangements.*

HALL'S CROFT

Stratford-upon-Avon map H6 △ &

A fine Tudor house complete with period furniture and walled garden where Shakespeare's daughter Susanna and Dr John Hall lived.

Location: Old Town.
Open: Jan 1 to Feb 29 and Nov 1 to Dec 31: Mon - Sat 10-4. Suns 1.30-4. Mar 1 to Oct 31: Mon - Sat 9.30-5, Suns 10.30-5. The property closes 30 mins later than the last entry times shown. Dec 24/25 amd 26 *Closed.* Jan 1 *Open* 1.30-4.30.
Admission: £1.70, Chd 70p.

ANNE HATHAWAY'S COTTAGE

Stratford-upon-Avon map H6 △

The picturesque thatched home of Anne Hathaway before her marriage to Shakespeare. Attractive garden and Shakespeare Tree Garden.

Location: Shottery (1¼ m).
Open: Jan 1 to Feb 29 and Nov 1 to Dec 31: Mon - Sat 9.30-4, Suns 10.30-4. Mar 1 to Oct 31: Mon - Sat 9-5.30, Suns 10-5.30. The property will close 30 mins after the last entry times shown. Dec 24/25 and 26 *Closed.* Jan 1 *Open* 1.30-4.30.
Admission: £2.10, Chd £1. Free coach park.
Refreshments: All year.

HONINGTON HALL

Shipston-on-Stour map M5
Telephone: (0608) 661434
(B. Wiggin Esq.,)

Originally built by the Parker family in 1680. Contains fine 18th century plasterwork.

Location: 10 m S of Stratford-on-Avon; ½ m E of A3400.
Open: June, July, Aug - Weds & Bank Hol Mons 2.30-5. Parties at other times by appointment.
Admission: £2, Chd 50p.

KENILWORTH CASTLE English Heritage

map H6
Telephone: (0926) 52078

One of the grandest ruins in England, this castle was made famous by Sir Walter Scott. Gone now is the great lake that once surrounded it, but still standing is the huge Noman keep with walls nearly 20ft (6m) thick in places. Inside the encircling walls built by King John are the remains of John of Gaunt's chapel and great hall, the Earl of Leicester's stables and gatehouse. The most splendid royal occasion took place in 1575 when Queen Elizabeth I was entertained lavishly by the Earl with music and dancing, fireworks and hunting, for 19 days.

Location: West side of Kenilworth.
Open: Good Friday or Apr 1 (whichever is earlier) to Sept 30 daily 10-6. Oct 1 to Maundy Thursday or Mar 31 (whichever is earlier) Tues-Sun 10-4. *Closed* Dec 24-26, Jan 1.
Admission: £1.70, Concessions £1.30, Chd 85p.

LORD LEYCESTER HOSPITAL

Warwick map H6 △
Telephone: (0926) 492797
(The Governors of Lord Leycester Hospital)

In 1100 the chapel of St. James was built over the West Gate of Warwick and became the centre for the Guilds established by Royal Charter in 1383. In 1571 Robert Dudley, Earl of Leycester, founded his Hospital for twelve 'poor' persons in the buildings of the Guilds, which had been dispersed in 1546. The Hospital has been run ever since for retired or disabled ex-Servicemen and their wives. The buildings have been recently restored to their original condition including the Great Hall of King James the Guildhall (museum), the Chaplain's Hall (Queen's Own Hussars Regimental Museum) and the Brethren's Kitchen.

Location: W gate of Warwick (A46).
Station(s): Warwick (¾ m).
Open: All the year - Tues to Suns 10-5.30 (summer) 10-4 (winter). Last admission 15 mins earlier. *Closed Mons, Good Fri & Christmas Day.*
Admission: £2, Chd (under 14) £1, OAPs/Students £1.50. Free car park.
Refreshments: (Easter to Oct) morning coffee, light lunches, afternoon teas.

NEW PLACE/NASH'S HOUSE

Stratford-upon-Avon map H6 △ &

Foundations of Shakespeare's last home, preserved in an Elizabethan garden setting with Nash's House adjoining which is furnished in period style.

Location: Chapel Street.
Open: Jan 1 to Feb 29 and Nov 1 to Dec 31: Mon - Sat 10-4, Suns 1.30-4. Mar 1 to Oct 31: Mon - Sat 9.30-5, Suns 10.30-5. The properties will close 30 mins later than the last entry times shown. Dec 24/25 and 26 *Closed*. Jan 1 *Open* 1.30-4.30.
Admission: £1.70, Chd 70p.

The National Trust
THE SIGN
OF A GREAT
DAY OUT

PACKWOOD HOUSE   The National Trust

Hockley Heath map H6
Telephone: (0564) 782024

Elizabethan house with mid-17th century additions. Tapestry, needlework, Carolean formal garden, and yew garden of c. 1650 representing the Sermon on the Mount.

Location: 2 m E of Hockley Heath (which is on A3400) 11 m SE of Birmingham.
Station(s): Lapworth (1½ m); Dorridge (2 m).
Open: Apr to end of Sept - Weds to Suns & Bank Hol Mons 2-6. *Closed* Good Friday. Oct - Wed to Suns 12.30-4.30. Last adm ½hr before closing.
Admission: £3, Chd £1.50, Family tickets £8.20. Gardens only £2. Parties by prior written arrangement only.
Shop. No dogs. No prams in House. Wheelchair access to part of garden and ground floor.

RAGLEY HALL

Alcester   map H6
Telephone: (0789) 762090
(The Earl and Countess of Yarmouth)

Built in 1680. Superb baroque plasterwork, fine paintings, china, furniture and works of art including the mural 'The Temptation'. Gardens, park and lake. Woodland trails, lakeside picnic areas. Superb Adventure Wood playground and maze for children.

Location: 2 m SW of Alcester on Birmingham/Alcester/Evesham Road (A435); 8 m from Stratford-upon-Avon; 20 m from Birmingham.
Open: Apr 10 to Sept 26. PARK & GARDENS: Open daily 10-6 (except Mon & Fri, but open Bank Holiday Mons). HOUSE: Open daily except Mon and Fri 12-5 (open Bank Holiday Monday).
Admission: (1993 prices):- HOUSE, GARDENS & PARK: (includes Adventure Wood and Woodland Trails) £4.50, Chd/OAPs/Group Rate Adults £3.50. GARDEN & PARK ONLY: Adult/OAPs £3.50, Chd £2.50. Free car park.
Refreshments: Licensed Cafeteria open daily except Mon and Fri. Please telephone for group reservation of Restaurant. Refreshments available in park. **Advance Bookings:** (at any time of the year). Coach parties welcome by arrangement. Lunches and teas - parties please write for menus. Private dinner parties for any number up to 150 can be arranged. For further information please contact: The Business Manager, Ragley Hall, Alcester, Warwickshire B49 5NJ. Telephone: Alcester (0789) 762090.
Dogs welcome on leads in Park and on Woodland Trails, not in House, Gardens or Adventure Wood.

❦THE SIGN OF A GREAT DAY OUT

THE SHAKESPEARE BIRTHPLACE TRUST PROPERTIES

THE SHAKESPEARIAN PROPERTIES

STRATFORD-UPON-AVON

5 historic houses associated with **William Shakespeare** and his family **open all year round.**

Besides the world famous attractions of **Shakespeare's Birthplace** and **Anne Hathaway's Cottage** there are also **The Shakespeare Countryside Museum at Mary Arden's House,** Wilmcote. Tudor farmstead home of Shakespeare's mother plus turn-of-the-century Glebe Farmhouse. Exhibits illustrating country life over 400 years. Gipsy caravans, dovecote, duck pond, field walk, and daily displays of falconry. Refreshments and picnic area. Ideally allow 2 hours.

Hall's Croft. A delightful Elizabethan town house, once the home of Dr. Hall, Shakespeare's physician son-in-law. Exceptional furniture and paintings. 17th century-style doctor's consulting room and exhibition about medical life in Shakespeare's time. Lovely secluded garden. Refreshments.

Shakespeare's Birthplace

New Place. Site and grounds of Shakespeare's last home, with colourful Elizabethan-style knott garden, provides quiet oasis in the heart of Stratford.
Nash's House adjoining contains fine Tudor furniture.

Single admission fees available but particularly good value offered by **3 Property Town Heritage Trail** or **5 Property Inclusive Tickets**

See editorial for opening times and admission fees

Anne Hathaway's Cottage

All the properties are open daily except on Good Friday morning, Christmas Eve, Christmas Day, Boxing Day and the morning of Jan 1st. For those needing transport there is a regular guided bus tour service all the year round connecting the town properties with Anne Hathaway's Cottage and Mary Arden's House.

THE SHAKESPEARE COUNTRYSIDE MUSEUM AT MARY ARDEN'S HOUSE

Stratford-upon-Avon map H6 △ &

The Tudor farmhouse where Shakespeare's mother lived, with a farming and Shakespeare countryside museum now extended to include the adjoining Glebe Farm. Interesting dovecote. Rural Crafts. Daily falconry displays. Light refreshments all year.

Location: Wilmcote (3½ m).
Open: Jan 1 to Feb 29 and Nov 1 to Dec 31: Mon - Sat, 10-4. Suns 1.30-4. Mar 1 to Oct 31: Mon - Sat, 9.30-5. Suns 10.30-5. The properties close 30 mins later than the last entry times shown. Dec 24/25 and 26 *Closed*. Jan 1 *Open* 1.30-4.30.
Admission: £3, Chd £1.20. Also, at this property only: Family ticket £7, admitting 2 adults and 2/3 children.Inclusive ticket admitting to all five properties: £7.50, Chd £3,25, OAP £7.**Shakespeare's Town Heritage Trail**: Ticket includes combined admission to the three town Properties (Birthplace, New Place and Hall's Croft) and a self-guiding Town Heritage Trail leaflet £5, Chd £2, OAP £4.50.**Educational Groups:** For admission to single properties all organised school (primary and secondary) parties will be admitted at the normal children's rates and all university/college groups will be admitted at the normal adult rates. *The Trust also offers special inclusive visit permits as follows:*Inclusive admission permit for accompanied school parties £3 per pupil. Inclusive admission permit for organised college and university student parties £4.50 per student. One member of staff to each 10 pupils/students is admitted free, with all school/college/university parties. Large groups may wish to divide into parties of 10 or more but all groups must be accompanied by staff throughout.*Groups visiting any property except Shakespeare's Birthplace can claim a discount of 10% if 20 or more are paying admission.*Free coach park.

SHAKESPEARE'S BIRTHPLACE

Stratford-upon-Avon   map H6   △   ♿

The half-timbered house where Shakespeare was born, containing many rare Shakespearian exhibits, also BBC Television Shakespeare Costume Exhibition.

Location: Henley Street.
Open: Jan 1 to Feb 29 and Nov 1 to Dec 31: Mon - Sat 9.30-4. Suns 10.30-4. Mar 1 to Oct 31: Mon - Sat 9-5.30. Suns 10-5.30. The property will *close* 30 mins later than last entry times shown. Dec 24/25 and 26 *Closed*. Jan 1 *Open* 1.30-4.30.
Admission: (1993 prices) incl. Exhibition £2.50, Chd £1.10. Free Coach park.

UPTON HOUSE   🌳   The National Trust

Edge Hill   map H5   ♿
Telephone: (0295 87) 266

17th century house containing one of the National Trust's finest collections of paintings and porcelain. Tapestries and 18th century furniture. Beautiful terraced garden descending to lakes and bog garden in deep valley.

Location: 1 m S of Edge Hill; 7 m NW of Banbury on the Stratford Road (A422).
Open: Due to works being carried out to improve environmental conditions, the house, tea room and shop will re-open on Sat Jun 12 until Sept 29: daily (except Thurs & Fri) 2-6. Last adm 5.30. Garden only: open Apr and Oct: Sat, Sun & Bank Hol Mon 2-6 and May 1 to Jun 9: daily (except Thur & Fri) 2-6. *Note: Entry to the House, Tea room and shop is by timed tickets at peak times on Suns in July, Aug and Bank Hols, therefore delays are possible.* Motorized buggy with driver available for access to/from lower garden, manned by volunteers of the Banbury NT Association.
Admission: £4, Chd £2, Family ticket £11, Garden only £2.
Refreshments: Tearoom in House.
No indoor photography. Wheelchair available. Wheelchair access ground floor only.

WARWICK CASTLE

Warwick   map H6   △
Telephone: (0926) 408000

WARWICK CASTLE
The finest mediaeval castle in England

Rising majestically from the banks of the River Avon, Warwick Castle spans one thousand years of history. The site was selected and fortified by William the Conqueror in 1068 and to this day Warwick Castle remains the finest mediaeval castle in England with commanding Battlements and Towers, Dungeon and Torture Chamber.

The magnificently appointed State Rooms contain a wealth of historic treasures and in the former Private Apartments there is a unique award-winning exhibition by Madame Tussaud's entitled 'A Royal Weekend Party 1898'.

The castle is set in 100 acres of parkland landscaped by 'Capability' Brown, and is a delight in all seasons. The magnificently restored Conservatory with views across the Pageant Field and River Avon, plus the faithfully recreated Victorian Rose Garden – one of many evocative attractions.

Warwick Castle offers an unforgettable day out for all the family.

Open every day
except Christmas Day

Tel: (0926) 495421

One of the finest medieval castles, standing on a steep rock cliff beside the River Avon, 8 miles from Stratford. The present castle is a fine example of 14th century fortification with towers and dungeons open to visitors all the year round. The State Rooms contain a magnificent collection of pictures by Rubens, Van Dyck and other Masters. Surrounded by acres of parkland landscaped by 'Capability' Brown, gardens where peacocks roam freely.

Location: In the centre of Warwick.
Station(s): Warwick (½ m); Leamington Spa (2 m).
Open: Daily (except Christmas Day) all year. Mar 1 to Sept 31 - Daily 10-5.30. Oct 1 to Feb 29 - Daily 10-4.30.
Admission: (From Mar 1 1993) £6.75, Chd (4-16 yrs incl.) £4.25, OAPs £4.75, Students £5. Free Car Park.

WEST MIDLANDS

ASTON HALL

Birmingham map H6 △
Telephone: 021-327 0062
(Birmingham City Council)

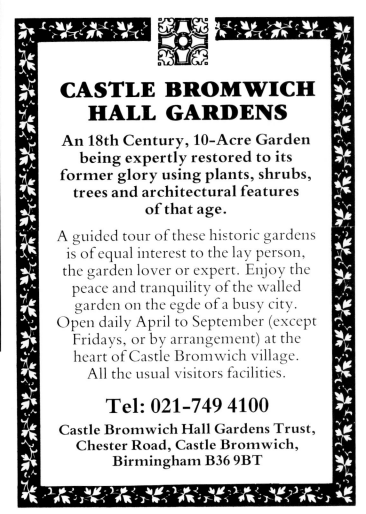

ASTON HALL

ONE OF THE LAST GREAT JACOBEAN COUNTRY HOUSES
ADMISSION FREE

Jacobean kitchen & nursery. 20 period rooms.
Rare Long Gallery. Jacobean woodcarving
& plasterwork. Paintings, furniture, glass, ceramics.
Special events. Shop, parking, park.

Open daily from Mar 27 - Oct 31 1993
from 2-5pm.

Near A38(M) Expressway & Aston Villa Football Ground
Contact: 021-327 0062 or 021-235 2834

Birmingham Museums & Art Gallery

Birmingham City Council

A fine Jacobean house built 1615-35, with many rooms furnished as period settings. Home of the Holte family for 200 years, with outstanding Jacobean plasterwork, panelling and great staircase. Long Gallery, paintings, tapestry and furniture of 17-19th centuries. James Watt the Younger lived here. Summer events, bi-ennial Candlelight evenings. Pre-booked parties by arrangement. A branch of Birmingham Museums and Art Galleries.

Location: 2½ m from centre of city. Entrance for coaches at Frederick Road; entrance for cars at Witton Lane.
Station(s): Aston (¾ m).
Open: Late Mar to end Oct 1993 - Daily 2-5.
Admission: Free. School parties can arrange to visit throughout the year.

BLAKESLEY HALL

Birmingham map M6
Telephone: 021-783 2193
(Birmingham City Council)

A timber-framed yeoman's farmhouse c.1590 carefully furnished to an inventory of the period. Built for Richard Smallbroke, a leading merchant in late 16th century Birmingham, with original wall paintings and diminutive Long Gallery. Also contains displays of building methods and 17th century pottery from a single excavation. In walking distance of Yardley Village (medieval church, trust school,

Georgian cottages). Pre-booked parties by arrangement. Summer events. Admission is free. A branch of Birmingham Museums and Art Gallery.

Location: 3 m from city centre; entrance in Blakesley Road.
Station(s): Stechford (¾ m); Birmingham New Street. Buses: 16 & 17, 11 on Outer Circle.
Open: Late Mar to end Oct 1993 - Daily 2-5.
Admission: Free. School parties can arrange to visit throughout the year.

CASTLE BROMWICH HALL GARDENS

Birmingham map H6 ♿
Telephone: 021-749 4100

CASTLE BROMWICH HALL GARDENS

An 18th Century, 10-Acre Garden being expertly restored to its former glory using plants, shrubs, trees and architectural features of that age.

A guided tour of these historic gardens is of equal interest to the lay person, the garden lover or expert. Enjoy the peace and tranquility of the walled garden on the egde of a busy city.
Open daily April to September (except Fridays, or by arrangement) at the heart of Castle Bromwich village.
All the usual visitors facilities.

Tel: 021-749 4100

Castle Bromwich Hall Gardens Trust, Chester Road, Castle Bromwich, Birmingham B36 9BT

A vision of England more than 250 years ago. The ongoing restoration, started six years ago, now provides visitors, academics and horticulturists the opportunity of seeing a unique collection of historic plants, shrubs, medicinal and culinary herbs and a fascinating plant collection. The Gardens are a cultural gem and an example of the Formal English Garden of the 18th century.

Location: 4 m E of Birmingham, 1 m from exit 5 of the M6 (exit Northbound only).
Open: Mainly Apr to Sept (others by arrangement), Mon to Thur 1.30-4.30 (*closed* Friday). Sat, Sun, Public Holidays 2-6. Guided tours Wed, Sat, Sun.
Admission: £2, Concessions for seniors and chd.
Refreshments: Coffee shop, but also light meals by arrangement. Gift shop.

HAGLEY HALL

nr Stourbridge map G6
Telephone: (0562) 882408
(The Viscount & Viscountess Cobham)

The last of the great Palladian Houses, designed by Sanderson Miller and completed in 1760. The House contains the finest example of Rococo plasterwork by Francesco Vassali, and a unique collection of 18th century furniture and family portraits including works by Van Dyck, Reynolds and Lely. Teas in the House. Receptions and private dinner parties by arrangement throughout the year.

Location: Just off A456 Birmingham to Kidderminster; 12 m from Birmingham within easy reach M5 (exit 3 or 4), M6 or M42.
Station(s): Hagley (1 m) (not Suns); Stourbridge Junction (2 m).
Open: From Jan 4 to Mar 3 daily except Sats. Thereafter only Apr 11, 12, 13, May 30, 31, Jun 1, Aug 29, 30, 31, 2-5.
Admission: Open for pre-booked parties by arrangement. For further details, please telephone (0562) 882408.
Refreshments: Tea available in the House.

PERROTT'S FOLLY

Edgbaston map G6
(The Perrott's Folly Company - a registered charity)

Perrott's Folly, 'Birmingham's most eccentric building' is a striking 96ft high Tudor style tower with seven floors, built 1758.

Location: Waterworks Road, Edgbaston. Situated 2m W of Birmingham city centre at the junction of Waterworks Road and Monument Road (which leads off the A456).
Open: Easter to Sept: Suns, Bank Hol Mons 2-5.
Admission: £1.50, Chd free.

RYTON ORGANIC GARDENS

Ryton-on-Dunsmore, Coventry map H6
(Henry Doubleday Research Association)

WIGHTWICK MANOR  The National Trust

Wolverhampton map G6 △ &
Telephone: (0902) 761108

Strongly influenced by William Morris the interiors of this late 19th century house include Morris wallpapers and fabrics, Kempe glass, de Morgan ware and a connoisseurs' collection of pre-Raphaelite paintings. Victorian/Edwardian gardens, terraces & pools.

Location: 3 m W of Wolverhampton, up Wightwick Bank (A454).
Open: House: Mar 4 to Sept 30: Thur and Sat 2.30-5. Also open Bank Holiday Sat, Sun and Mon 2.30-5.30 (Ground floor only, no guided tours). Garden open same days as house 2-6. Also open for pre-booked parties Weds & Thurs, also special evening tours. School visits on Wed & Thurs, contact Administrator for details. Owing to the fragile nature of their contents and the requirements of conservation, some rooms cannot always be shown. Tours of the house will vary, therefore, during the year. *Note: Due to essential building and conservation work the property will be closed from beginning of Oct 1993 to end of Mar 1994.*
Admission: £4, Chd half price. Students £2. Gardens only £1.50. *Parties must book in advance (no reductions).*
Dogs in garden only, on leads.

WILTSHIRE

AVEBURY MANOR & GARDEN   The National Trust

Nr Marlborough   map H4

Open: Parts of the house are open subject to restoration work, please telephone 06723 388 (answer phone) to check opening times. Garden: Apr 2 to Nov 2 daily except Mon & Thurs 11-5.30. Last adm 5.
Admission: Garden: £2, Chd £1.30. Parties £1.80, Chd £1.10.

AVEBURY MUSEUM   English Heritage

map H4
Telephone: (06723) 250

No one knows quite why our ancient ancestors built Silbury Hill or the Sanctuary. But fortunately some of their tools, pottery and weapons have survived and are housed in the museum, which lies at the heart of Britain's earliest beginnings.

Location: In Avebury, 7 m (11.2 km) west of Marlborough.
Open: Good Friday or Apr 1 (whichever is earlier) to Sept 30: Open Daily 10-6. Oct 1 to Maundy Thursday or Mar 31 (whichever is earlier): Open Daily 10-4. *Closed* Dec 24 -26, Jan 1.
Admission: £1.30, Concessions £1, Chd 65p.

BOWOOD HOUSE & GARDENS

Calne   map G4   &
Telephone: (0249) 812102
(The Earl and Countess of Shelburne)

Outstanding example of 18th century architecture, set in one of the most beautiful parks in the country, landscaped by 'Capability' Brown and not altered since his time. On display in the House is a remarkable collection of family heirlooms built up over 250 years, including Victoriana, Indiana, silver, porcelain, fine paintings and watercolours. Interesting rooms include Robert Adam's famous Library, Dr. Joseph Priestley's Laboratory where he discovered oxygen gas, and the Chapel. The 100 acre park contains many exotic trees, a 40 acre lake, Cascade, Grotto, caves and a Doric Temple, arboretum, pinetum, rose garden and Italian garden. For children, a massive Adventure Playground. For six weeks during May and June a separate garden of 50 acres features spectacular rhododendron walks.

Location: 2½ m W of Calne; 5 m SE of Chippenham. Immediately off A4 at Derry Hill village between Calne and Chippenham.
Open: House, Gardens & Grounds. Apr 1 to Oct 31 - Daily incl Bank Hols 11-6. Rhododendron Walks (entrance off A342 at Kennels Lodge) six weeks during May and June (depending on season) 11-6.
Admission: Free car park. £4.50, OAPs £3.80, Chd £2.25. Party rates (20 and over) £4.15, OAPs £3,25, Chd £2.
Refreshments: Licensed restaurant & Garden Tearoom. **Advance Bookings:** Coach parties welcome by arrangement. Lunches and Teas - please write for party menus and further information: The Estate Office, Bowood Estate, Calne, Wiltshire SN11 0LZ.
No dogs.

BROADLEAS GARDENS (CHARITABLE TRUST)

Devizes map G4
Telephone: (0380) 722035
(Lady Anne Cowdray)

A delightful garden with rare and unusual plants and trees, many Rhododendrons, Azaleas and Magnolias with interesting perennials and ground cover.

Location: 1½ m SW of Devizes on A360
Open: Apr 1 to Oct 31 - Suns, Weds & Thurs 2-6.
Admission: £1.50, chd (under 12) 50p. Discount for parties.
Refreshments: Home-made teas on Sundays - also by prior arrangement.
Plants propagated for sale.

CHARLTON PARK HOUSE

Malmesbury map G4
(The Earl of Suffolk and Berkshire)

Jacobean/Georgian mansion, built for the Earls of Suffolk, 1607, altered by Matthew Brettingham the Younger, c. 1770.

Location: 1½ m NE Malmesbury. Entry only by signed entrance on A429, Malmesbury/Cirencester Road. No access from Charlton village.
Open: May to Oct, Mon & Thurs 2-4. Viewing of Great Hall, Staircase and saloon.
Admission: £1, Chd/OAPs 50p.
Car parking limited. Unsuitable for wheelchairs. No dogs. No picnicking

CORSHAM COURT

Chippenham map G4 &
Telephone: (0249) 712214
(The Lord Methuen)

Elizabethan (1582) and Georgian (1760-70) house, fine 18th century furniture. British, Spanish, Italian and Flemish Old Masters. Park and gardens laid out by 'Capability' Brown and Humphrey Repton. Contains one of the oldest and most distinguished collections of Old Masters and furniture.

Location: In Corsham 4 m W of Chippenham off the Bath Road (A4).
Open: Staterooms. Jan 1 to Nov 30 - Daily except Mons and Frid 2-4.30. (From Good Friday to Sept 30, 2-6 (including Fri and Bank Hols); *Closed* Dec. Last adm 30 minutes before closing time. Other times by appointment. Parties welcome.
Admission: (incl gardens) £3, Chd £1.50; Parties of 20 or more by arrangement. Gardens only £1.50, Chd £1.
Refreshments: Audrey's Tea Room Tel: (0249) 714931.

THE COURTS GARDEN   🌱   The National Trust

Holt map G4 &
Telephone: (0225) 782340

7 acre garden of mystery - of interest to amateur and botanist. Borders, lily pond and arboretum carpeted with wild flowers.

Location: 2½ m E of Bradford-on-Avon on S side of B3107; 3 m N of Trowbridge.
Station(s): Bradford-on-Avon (2½ m).
Open: GARDEN ONLY. Apr 1 to Nov 1 - Daily (except Sat), 2-5. House not open.
Admission: £2.50, Chd £1.50. Other times by appointment: please telephone the Head Gardener.
No dogs. Wheelchair access. No lavatory.

FITZ HOUSE GARDEN

Teffont Magna, nr Salisbury map H3
Telephone: (0722) 716257
(Major & Mrs Mordaunt-Hare)

Lovely hillside terraced gardens frame a listed group of beautiful ancient stone buildings in one of Wiltshire's prettiest villages. 16th/17th century House (not shown) admired by Nikolaus Pevsner in his Wiltshire Guide. One time home of Edith Olivier the authoress, and of Siegfried Sassoon, the author. The gardens, bordered by yew and beech hedges and a stream, are a haven of tranquillity, planted with spring bulbs and blossom, azaleas, roses and clematis of all types, honeysuckles, vines and mixed borders. Something of interest throughout the season including much new planting during the last three years. Many scented plants. Featured in *English Private Gardens* by Judy Johnson and Susan Berry published May 1991, *Country Life* July 1990 and featured on Southern Television May 1992.

Location: On B3089 Barford St Martin (A30) to Mere Road (A303) in the village; 10 m W of Salisbury on direct route Wilton House-Stourhead.
Open: GARDEN ONLY: May 1 to Sept 26: Sats and Suns 2-5.30. Parties by appointment only Mons to Fridays.
No dogs. No lavatories. Unsuitable for disabled.

GREAT CHALFIELD MANOR   🌱   The National Trust

nr. Melksham map G4

15th century moated manor house restored in the 20th century. Set across a moat between Parish Church and stables.

Location: 2½ m NE Bradford-on-Avon via B3109, signposted in Holt village.
Open: Apr 1 to Oct 28 - Tues to Thurs. Guided tours only starting at 12.15, 2.15, 3, 3.45 & 4.30.
Admission: £3.50. *Closed* Public Hols. *Historical & other Societies by written arrangement. No reductions for parties or children.*
Refreshments: Bradford-on-Avon; Melksham.
No dogs. Unsuitable for wheelchairs. No lavatory.

HAMPTWORTH LODGE

Landford, Salisbury map H3
Telephone: (0794) 390215
(Mr N. Anderson)

Reproduction Jacobean Manor.

Location: 10 m SE of Salisbury on the C44 road between Redlynch and Landford, which is a link road joining the A36 Salisbury-Southampton and the A338 Salisbury-Bournemouth.
Open: House and garden open daily, except Suns, Mar 29 to Apr 29, 2.15-5. Conducted parties only 2.30 and 3.45.
Admission: £3, under 11 free. No special arrangements for parties, but about 15 is the maximum.
Refreshments: Nearest Hotel is in Salisbury. No refreshments at house.
Car parking. Suitable for disabled ground floor only. Coaches only by arrangement.

HAZELBURY MANOR GARDENS

nr Box map G4
Telephone: (0225) 812113

8 acres of Grade II landscaped formal gardens surrounding a charming 15th C fortified Manor House. An impressive topiary display and clipped beeches surround the large lawn; herbaceous and mixed borders blaze in summer; laburnums and limes form splendid walkways. Other notable features include rose garden, stone ring, ponds, an enchanting fountain and rockery. Beyond the Manor House is a new plantation of specimen trees, mostly conifers.

Location: 5 m SW of Chippenham; 5 m NE of Bath; 3 m N of Bradford-upon-Avon. From A4 at Box, take A365 to Melksham, turn left onto B3109, left at Chapel Plaister, drive immediately on right.
Open: Gardens only: May 1 to Sept 30 daily 10-6. Apr & Oct Suns only.
Admission: £2.80, OAPs £2, Chd £1. Coach parties welcome by appointment.
Refreshments: Teas.
Wheelchairs. No dogs.

HEALE GARDENS AND PLANT CENTRE

Woodford, Salisbury map H3   &
Telephone: (072 273) 504
(Mr. Guy & Lady Anne Rasch)

Winner of Christie's/HHA Garden of the Year award 1984. Early Carolean manor house where King Charles II hid during his escape. The garden provides a wonderfully varied collection of plants, shrub, musk and other roses, growing in the formal setting of clipped hedges and mellow stonework, at their best in June and July. Particularly lovely in Spring and Autumn is the water garden, planted with magnificent Magnolia and Acers, surrounding an authentic Japanese Tea House and Nikko Bridge which create an exciting focus in this part of the garden.

Location: 4 m N of Salisbury on the Woodford Valley road between A345 and A360. Midway between Salisbury, Wilton and Stonehenge.
Open: Garden Plant Centre and Shop open throughout the year, 10-5. Tours of the house for parties of over 20 by arrangement.
Refreshments: Lunches & Teas in the House for parties over 20 by arrangement.
Plant Centre and Shop. Unusual trees, shrubs, climbers and herbaceous plants, including many of those growing in the garden, can be found in the Plant Centre, together with presents for all ages in the shop, with particular emphasis on the garden enthusiast.

IFORD MANOR GARDENS

Bradford-on-Avon map G4
Telephone: (0225) 863146
(Mrs Cartwright-Hignett)

Iford Manor, a Tudor house with an 18th century facade, stands beside the medieval bridge over the River Frome. Once a busy centre of the woollen trade, it is now surrounded by a peaceful terraced garden of unique character. Designed in the Italian style, it was the creation of Harold Peto, the Edwardian landscape architect and desiquer who lived at Iford from 1899-1933. There are pools, statues, a colonnade, antique carvings, cloisters and many plants of the period.

Location: 7 m SE of Bath on A36, signpost Iford 1 m; or from Bradford-on-Avon and Trowbridge via Lower Westwood.
Open: GARDENS ONLY: 2-5 Tues, Weds, Thurs, Sats and Suns in May, June, July, Aug and Sept and Summer Bank Holidays. Also Apr and Oct Suns and Easter Mon.
Admission: £2, Chd/OAPs £1.50, Parties and coaches by arrangement at other times. Free car parking.
Refreshments: On the premises. Sun and Bank Holiday Mons May-Sept.
Dogs on leads.

LACOCK ABBEY   🏵   The National Trust

nr Chippenham map G4
Telephone: (0249) 730227

13th century abbey converted into a house in 1540, with 18th century Gothick alterations for the Talbot family whose home it still is. The medieval cloisters, the brewery and the house are also open to the public. Fine trees.

Location: In the village of Lacock; 3 m N of Melksham; 3 m S of Chippenham just E of A350.
Open: House: Apr 1 to Oct 31 daily (except Tues) 1-5.30. Cloisters and Grounds: Daily 12-5.30 (last adm 5). *Closed* Good Friday.
Admission: House, Grounds and Cloisters: £4, Chd £2. Parties (15 or more) £3.50, Chd party £1.70 per person. Cloisters and Grounds only: £2, Chd £1/

LONGLEAT HOUSE

Warminster map G3 △
Telephone: Longleat House: (0985) 844551 Safari Park: (0985) 844328 Caravan Club site: (0985) 844663
(The Marquess of Bath)

LUCKINGTON COURT

Luckington map G4
Telephone: (0666) 840205
(The Hon Mrs Trevor Horn)

Mainly Queen Anne with magnificent group of ancient buildings. Beautiful mainly formal garden with fine collection of ornamental trees and shrubs.

Location: 6 m W of Malmesbury on B4040 Bristol Road.
Open: All the Year - Weds 2-6. Open Sun, May 16, 2.30-6.*Collection box for National Gardens' Scheme.* Inside view by appointment 3 weeks in advance.
Admission: Outside only 50p. Inside £1.
Refreshments: Teas in garden or house (in aid of Luckington Parish Church). May 16 1993 only.

LYDIARD HOUSE

Lydiard Park, Lydiard Tregoze, Swindon map H4 △ ♿ Ⓔ
(Borough of Thamesdown)

Once delapidated and now fully restored ancestral home of the St.John family, remodelled in the Georgian classical style in 1743 and set in attractive country parkland. Fine furniture, family portraits (16th - 19th century), beautiful plasterwork, original wallpaper, fascinating painted glass window and room devoted to artistic works of Lady Diana Spencer, 2nd Viscountess Bolingbroke incl large scale decorative panels. Adjacent church of St.Mary's houses exceptional St.John family monuments.

Location: 5 m W of Swindon just N of Junction 16 M4; signpost Lydiard Country Park.
Open: Weekdays and Sat 10-1, 2-5.30; Suns 2-5.30. (Early closing 4pm, Nov to Feb incl.). *Slight alterations to daily opening hours may occur as from Apr 1.*
Admission: £1.40, Concessions 70p.
Coach parking. Wheelchair access. Gift shop. Teachers resource pack, adventure playgrounds. Visitors centre in grounds houses cafe and toilet facilites.

Longleat House, built by Sir John Thynne in 1580, and still owned and lived in by the same family, was the first truly magnificent Elizabethan House to be built in the Italian Renaissance style. Longleat was also the first Stately Home to be opened to the public in 1949. Throughout its existence, ancestors have commissioned alterations within the House; ceilings by Italian craftsmen, rooms and corridors by Wyatville, additional libraries to house the vast collection of rare books and of course, the beautiful parkland landscaped by Lancelot 'Capability' Brown. In 1966, Lord Bath, in conjunction with Jimmy Chipperfield established the first drive through wild animals reserve outside Africa and it remains the model for Safari Parks throughout the world. Many other attractions have since been opened, making Longleat a full day's entertainment for all the family. Attractions include, Victorian Kitchens, Lord Bath's Bygones, Dolls Houses, Dr. Who Exhibition, Butterfly Garden, Railway, World's Largest Maze, Pets Corner, Safari Boat Ride, Lord Bath's V.I.P. Vehicle Exhibition. 'Adventure Castle' for children. 1:25 scale model of Longleat House.

Open: Longleat House open all year - Daily (Except Christmas Day) incl. Suns Easter to Sept 10-6, remainder of year 10-4. Safari Park every day from Mid Mar to end Oct, 10-6. (Last cars admitted 5.30 or sunset if earlier). All other attractions every day from Easter to Oct 30, 11-6 - for Maze, Railway & Adventure Castle last entry 5.30.
Admission: School Parties welcome at all times of the year - reduced rates for Parties booking in advance. Helicopter landing facilities provided advance notice given.
Refreshments: At the Old Cellar Restaurant at the House and in the Restaurant Complex.

MOMPESSON HOUSE   ✿ The National Trust

Salisbury map H3
Telephone: (0722) 335659

Fine Queen Anne town house, furnished as the home of a Georgian gentleman; walled garden.

Location: In Cathedral Close on N side of Choristers' Green.
Station(s): Salisbury (½ m).
Open: Apr 3 to Oct 31 daily except Thurs & Fri 12-5.30. Last adm 5.
Admission: £3, Chd £1.50, parties £2.70.
Refreshments: Garden tea room.
No dogs. Visitors sitting room.

NEWHOUSE 🏛

Redlynch map H3
Telephone: (0725) 20055
(Mr & Mrs George Jeffreys)

Brick Jacobean 'Trinity' house, c. 1619, with two Georgian wings. Contents include costume collection, and 'Hare' picture. - Documents.

Location: 9 m S of Salisbury; 3 m from Downton, off B3080.
Open: Aug 1 to Aug 31, excluding Sun, 2-5.30. Open by arrangement at other times between May and Sept for groups of 25 plus. Telephone (0725) 20055.
Admission: £2, chd (under 15) £1.
Refreshments: Available.

OLD SARUM   English ⌗ Heritage

map H3
Telephone: (0722) 335398

On the summit of a hill north of Salisbury, huge ramparts and earth mounds are silhouetted against the skyline. Ancient Britons fortified the hill-top which was later inhabited by Romans, Saxons and Normans. Parts of an 11th century castle remain and the foundations of two successive cathedrals are marked on the grass.

Location: 2 m (3.2 km) north of Salisbury.
Open: Good Friday or Apr 1 (whichever is earlier) to Sept 30: Open Daily 10-6. Oct 1 to Maundy Thursday or Mar 31 (whichever is earlier): Open daily 10-4. *Closed* Dec 24-26, Jan 1.
Admission: £1.30, Concessions £1, Chd 65p.

OLD WARDOUR CASTLE   English ⌗ Heritage

map G3
Telephone: (0747) 870487

The ruins stand in a romantic lakeside setting as a result of landscaping and planting in the 18th century. French in style and designed more for living than defence, the castle was built in 1393 by the fifth Lord Lovel, a campaigner in France. It was badly damaged in the Civil War and never repaired. The 18th century Banqueting House contains a small display about the 'Capability' Brown landscape.

Location: 2 m (3.2 km) south of Tisbury.
Open: Good Friday or Apr 1 (whichever is earlier) to Sept 30: Open Daily 10-6. Oct 1 to Maundy Thursday or Mar 31 (whichever is earlier): Open Weekends only 10-4. *Closed* Dec 24-26, Jan 1.
Admission: £1.30, Concessions £1, Chd 65p.

PHILIPPS HOUSE   ✿ The National Trust

Dinton map G3
Telephone: (072 276) 208

Classical house completed in 1816 by Sir Jeffry Wyattville for the Wyndham family.

Location: 9 m W of Salisbury; on N side of B3089.
Open: By prior written appointment only with the Warden.
Admission: £1.50. *No reduction for parties or children.* House leased to YWCA for residential conferences.
No dogs.

PYTHOUSE

Tisbury map G3
(Country Houses Association)

Palladian style Georgian mansion.

Location: 2½ m W of Tisbury; 4½ m N of Shaftesbury.
Station(s): Tisbury (2½ m).
Open: May to Sept - Weds & Thurs 2-5. Last entry 4.30.
Admission: £1.50, Chd 50p. Free car park.
No dogs admitted.

✿ THE SIGN OF A GREAT DAY OUT

SHELDON MANOR

Chippenham   map G4   △   ♿
Telephone: (0249) 653120
(Major Martin Gibbs, DL, JP)

Plantagenet Manor House, lived in as a family home for 700 years. There has been a house here since early Plantagenet times. The present Great Porch and Parvise above, dating from 1282, were built by Sir Geoffrey Gascelyn, Lord of the Manor and Hundred of Chippenham and were 700 years old in 1982. Sheldon is the sole survivor of a vanished medieval village. Succeeding generations and other families, notably the Hungerfords, have added to the beautiful house, its forecourt and surrounding buildings. All the house is lived in and it is shown by the family. There are good collections of early oak furniture, Nailsea glass, porcelain and Persian saddlebags. There are beautiful informal terraced gardens with ancient yew trees, water, interesting trees and shrubs and a connoisseur collection of old fashioned roses. Home-made lunches and cream teas served in the Barn or on the lawn. Visitors to Sheldon will find the food 'a major consideration'. 'In nominating an eating place with an intimate atmosphere, I could do no better than to recommend Sheldon'. Hugh Montgomery-Massingberd, Weekend Telegraph, July 11th, 1987. 'It was worth the whole trip for this.' - American visitor 1992.

Location: 1½ m W of Chippenham, signposted from A420; eastbound traffic also signposted from A4, E of Corsham (2½ m). M4 exit 17 4 m.
Station(s): Chippenham (2½ m).
Open: Open Easter Sun and Easter Mon then every Sun, Thurs and Bank Hol to Oct 3 12.30-6. House opens 2.
Refreshments: Home-made lunches & cream teas. Coaches welcome by appointment.
Most of the property suitable for wheelchairs.

STONEHENGE   English ⚑ Heritage

map H3

Built between 3100 and 1100 BC, this is Britain's most famous ancient monument and one of the world's most astonishing engineering feats. Many of the stones, some weighing 4 tons each, were brought from the Preseli Mountains in Wales to Salisbury Plain, there to be erected by human muscle power. Refreshments are available.

Location: 2 m (3.2 km) west of Amesbury.
Open: Good Friday or Apr 1 (whichever is earlier) to Sept 30 daily 10-6. Oct 1 to Maundy Thursday or Mar 31 (whichever is earlier) Daily 10-4. *Closed* Dec 24-26, Jan 1.
Admission: £2.70, Concessions £2, Chd £1.30.

Sir Peter Paul Rubens (1577–1640)
Knighted by Charles I in 1630

His work can be seen in the following properties included in Historic Houses Castles and Gardens:

Sudeley Castle
Warwick Castle

STOURHEAD   🌳   The National Trust

Stourton, nr Mere   map G3   △   ♿
Telephone: (0747) 840348

The world famous garden was laid out 1741-80; its lakes, temples and rare trees forming a landscape of breath-taking beauty throughout the year. Palladian House designed in 1722 by Colen Campbell. Furniture by Thomas Chippendale the Younger.

Location: 3 m NW of Mere (A303) in the village of Stourton off the Frome/Mere Road (B3092).
Open: Garden all year daily 8-7 or sunset if earlier (except July 21-24, when garden closes at 5). House Apr 3 to Oct 31 daily except Thur & Fri, 12-5.30 or dusk if earlier. Last adm 5. Other times by written arrangement with the Administrator.
Admission: House: £4, Chd £2, Parties by prior written appointment only. Garden: Mar to Oct £4, Chd £2, Parties £3.40. Nov to end Feb £3, Chd £1.50.
Refreshments: Accommodation, Spread Eagle Inn at Garden entrance, (0747) 840587. National Trust Shop.
Wheelchair provided - access to gardens only. No dogs in garden except on leads from Nov to end Feb only. In woods throughout the year.

TOTTENHAM HOUSE

Savernake Forest, Marlborough map H4
Telephone: (0672) 870331
(The Trustees of the Savernake Estate)

Tottenham House, built by the Marquess of Ailesbury, was originally designed by Burlington and built in the early 18th century. About one hundred years later the house was completely rebuilt by Thomas Cundy although some evidence of Burlington's work still remains. The house is let to Hawtreys Preparatory School.

Location: 3 m A4; 6 m Marlborough.
Open: HOUSE ONLY. Open in School holidays - 10.30-1.30, Jan 5-9; Mar 27-31; Apr 20-24; July 4-8; Aug 30; Sept 1-4; Dec 12-16
Admission: £1, Chd (under 14) 50p. No reductions.
Refreshments: Savernake Forest Hotel ½ m.
There are steps to the front door (although there is assistance permanently available), thereafter every room open to the public is on one floor. The property could not be strictly described as unsuitable for the disabled. Car park.

WESTWOOD MANOR  The National Trust

nr. Bradford-on-Avon map G4 △

15th c stone manor house altered in the late 16th c. Fine furnishings, Gardens of clipped yew. Administered for the National Trust by a tenant.

Station(s): Avoncliff (1 m); Bradford-on-Avon.
Open: Apr 4 to Sept 29: Suns, Tues, Wed 2-5.*Other times parties of up to 20 by written application to the tenant.*
Admission: £3.20. No reduction for parties or children.
No photography. No dogs. Unsuitable for wheelchairs. No lavatory.

WILTON HOUSE

Salisbury map H3 △
Telephone: (0722) 743115
(The Earl of Pembroke)

Superb 17th Century State Rooms including magnificent Double and Single Cube Rooms. World famous collection of paintings and other treasures. The New Earls Time theatre incorporating the latest technology to present an exciting and entertaining documentary drama film on The Lives & Times of the Earls of Pembroke. Superb exhibition of toy soldiers and other fascinating displays. A true-to-life reconstruction of a Tudor Kitchen with all the utensils and equipment. Superb gardens and grounds with notable cedar trees and the Palladian Bridge. Adventure playground.

Location: In town of Wilton - 2½ m W of Salisbury on A30. Trains from Waterloo and many other southern and western region stations to Salisbury. Buses from Salisbury Centre.
Station(s): Salisbury 2 miles.
Open: HOUSE, GROUNDS, EXHIBITIONS AND ADVENTURE PLAYGROUND: Apr 5 to Oct 17 1993. Mon to Sun inclusive 11-6. Sun 12-6. Last admission 4.45.
Admission: Ticket options: £5, OAPs/Students (with student card) £4.50, Chd (over 5 and under 16) £3.50, Parties (min of 15 persons) all adults £4.20, Chd £3.50. Family ticket - two adults and two chd £15. Grounds only: £2, Chd £1.50. Guided Tours by appointment only. Over 15 people £8, fewer than 15 people £10, fewer than 10 people £15. Pre-booked school parties (Mon only) £2.90 per pupil, 1 teacher free for every 10 children.
Refreshments: Licensed self-service restaurant and Gift shop, Garden Centre and nearby Pembroke Arms Hotel.

NORTH YORKSHIRE

ALDBOROUGH ROMAN TOWN   English⚏Heritage

map H10
Telephone: (0423) 322768

The little village of Aldborough lies within the bounds of what was once the rich Roman city Isurium Brigantum, Aldborough has even retained part of the Roman street plan - a regular grid with a central open space, once the forum. Part of the Roman town walls survive, and two mosaic pavements may be seen in their original positions. A remarkable collection of Roman objects is on display in the Museum.

Location: ¾ m (1 km) east of Boroughbridge.
Open: Good Friday or Apr 1 (whichever is earlier) to Sept 30: Open Daily 10-6. Oct 1 to Maundy Thursday or Mar 31 (whichever is earlier): *Closed* Dec 24-26, Jan 1.
Admission: £1.20, Concessions 90p, Chd 60p.

ALLERTON PARK   🏛

nr. Knaresborough   map H9
Telephone: (0423) 330927
(The Gerald Arthur Rolph Foundation for Historic Preservation and Education)

The grandest of the surviving Gothic revival stately homes. Its Great Hall and Dining Room are considered amongst the finest carved wood rooms in England. Allerton Park is the ancestral home of Lord Mowbray (c. 1283), Segrave (c. 1283) and Stourton (c. 1448), the premier Baron in England. House designed by George Martin, some interior rooms by Benjamin Baud. Temple of Victory built by Frederick, Duke of York (brother to King George IV) in 18th century. The setting for Sherlock Holmes film 'The Sign of Four'. Private collection of mechanical music machines and luxury antique motor cars. World War II museum dedicated to Number 6 Group (RCAF).

Location: 14½ m W of York; ¼ m E of A1 on York Road (A59); 4½ m W of Knaresborough, 6 m N of Wetherby; 7 m S of Boroughbridge; 14 m N of Leeds.
Open: Easter Sun to end Sept - Suns and Bank Holiday Mons 1-6: last house tour 5. Other days by appointment for parties of 25 or more and events. Enquiries to: Mr. Farr, Administrator, Allerton Park, nr. Knaresborough, N. Yorkshire HG5 0SE. Tel: (0423) 330927.
Admission: House, Grounds and Car Museum: £3, Students/OAPs/accompanied Chd (under 16) £2. Parties (25 and over) £2.50. School groups £2. Free car parking.
No dogs, except guide dogs for the blind.

THE BAR CONVENT

York   map H9
Telephone: (0904) 643238
(The Bar Convent Museum Trust)

Impressive Georgian town house (1787) enclosing neo-classical Chapel (1769), both by Thomas Atkinson. 19th century covered courtyard with Coalbrookdale floor tiles and cast iron furniture. Museum tells story of the Convent. Exhibition programme.

Location: At Micklegate Bar on the A1036 from A64 which links to A1.
Open: Feb 2 to Dec 23, Tues to Sat 10-5. *Closed* Good Friday.
Admission: £1.75, Concessions £1.50, Chd £1, Family ticket £3.50.
Refreshments: Cafe; home made fare.
Disabled access. Nearby public parking. Shop.

BENINGBROUGH HALL   🦋 The National Trust

nr York   map H9   △   ♿
Telephone: (0904) 470666

This handsome Georgian house has been completely restored and in the principal rooms are 100 famous portraits on loan from the National Portrait Gallery. Victorian laundry, potting shed and exhibitions. Garden and wilderness play area.

Location: 8 m NW of York; 3 m W of Shipton (A19); 2 m SE Linton-on-Ouse; follow signposted route.
Open: Apr 3 to Sept 30: Mon, Tues, Wed, Sat, Sun & Good Friday. Also Frids in July and Aug. House 11-5 (last adm 4.30); Grounds, shop and restaurant 11-5.30. (last adm 5). Closed in Oct for essential building work.
Admission: HOUSE, GARDENS & EXHIBITION: £4.40, Chd £2.20, Family £11, Parties £3.40, Chd party £1.70. GARDEN & EXHIBITION: £2.80, Chd £1.40, Family £7. (Family ticket - 2 adults, 2 chd).
Refreshments: The Restaurant serves homemade hot & cold lunches, teas, special suppers. Wheelchair access. Picnic area. Kiosk. Special functions catered for, details from the Administrator.
No dogs, Wheelchairs provided. Baby changing facilities.

BYLAND ABBEY   English⚏Heritage

map H10
Telephone: (03476) 614

Built in the shadow of the Hambleton Hills, this 12th century Cistercian monastery is still magnificent, both in size and workmanship. The area of the cloister, for example, is larger than either Fountains or Rievaulx Abbeys. Some of the carved stone details are particularly fine, and sections of medieval green and yellow glazed tile floor may be seen.

Location: 1 m (1.6 km) north east of Coxwold.
Open: Good Friday or Apr 1 (whichever is earlier) to Sept 30: Open Daily 10-6. Oct 1 to Maundy Thursday or Mar 31 (whichever is earlier): Open Tues to Sun 10-4. *Closed* Dec 24-26, Jan 1.
Admission: £1.20, Concessions 90p, Chd 60p.

CASTLE HOWARD

York map J10
Telephone: (065 384) 333
(The Hon. Simon Howard)

Designed by Vanbrugh 1699-1726 for the 3rd Earl of Carlisle, assisted by Hawksmoor, who designed the Mausoleum. Has been open to the public since the day it was built. Impressive Great Hall and many other magnificent rooms filled with fine collections of pictures, statuary and furniture. Interesting rooms include The Castle Howard Bedroom, Lady Georgiana's Bedroom and Dressing Room, The Antique Passage, The Music Room, The Tapestry Room, The Museum Room, The Long Gallery, and the Chapel. Costume Gallery features tableaux of authentic historical costumes which are changed annually. Beautiful park and grounds with nature walks, rose gardens in season, superb Atlas fountain, Temple of The Four Winds. Lakeside Adventure Playground for children. Plant Centre. Boat trips on the lake in Victorian style launch in season, (weather permitting).

Location: 15 m NE of York; 3 m off A64; 6 m W of Malton; 38 m Leeds; 36 m Harrogate; 22 m Scarborough; 50 m Hull.
Open: Daily Mar 19 to Oct 31. House and Costume Galleries open from 11. Plant centre, rose gardens, grounds and cafeteria open from 10. Last admissions: 4.30.
Admission: £5.50, Chd £3, OAPs £5, Special terms for booked parties.
Refreshments: Cafeteria. Licensed restaurant available for families and booked parties.

CLIFFORD'S TOWER   English ⌗ Heritage

York map H9
Telephone: (0904) 646940

York Castle, like the city itself, has had a long and turbulent history. Clifford's Tower was built on an earlier motte (or mound) in the 13th century. The tower is named after a Lancastrian leader from the Wars of the Roses, Sir Robert Clifford, who was defeated in 1322, and his body hung in chains from the tower.

Location: Near Castle Museum.
Open: Good Friday or Apr 1 (whichever is earlier) to Sept 30 daily 10-6. Oct 1 to Maundy Thursday or Mar 31 (whichever is earlier) daily 10-4. *Closed* Dec 24-26, Jan 1.
Admission: £1.20, Concessions 90p, Chd 60p.

CONSTABLE BURTON HALL

Leyburn   map H10
Telephone: (0677) 50428
(M. C. A. Wyvill, Esq.)

Extensive borders, interesting alpines, large informal garden. John Carr house completed in 1768.

Location: On A684, between Leyburn (3 m) & Bedale; A1 (7 m).
Open: Gardens. May 1 to Sept 1 - Daily 9-6. House: opening dates not available at time of going to press.
Admission: Garden: £1, collecting box. House: Charges not available at time of going to press. Party rates by arrangement.

DUNCOMBE PARK

Helmsley   map H10
(The Rt Hon Lord Feversham)

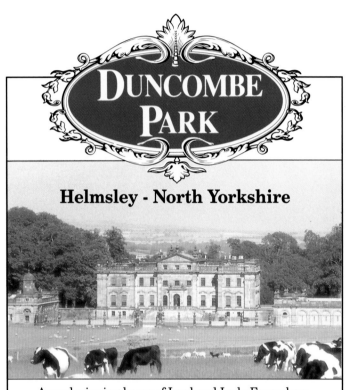

Home of the Duncombes for 300 years; 60 years a school, now restored to family home and opened to public for first time in 1990. Fine 19th century interiors, family pictures, English and Continental furniture. Unique early 18th century landscape garden with lawns, temples, tree-lined terraces, woodland and riverside walks. Visitor Centre, gift shop, children's playground, car park. Winner BTA Come to Britain Award.

Location: 3 mins from Helmsley market square.
Open: Apr: Suns 11-6, Easter weekend (Apr 9-13) 11-6; May 1 to Oct 24: Sun to Thurs 11-6; Bank Hol Sats and all events Sats.
Refreshments: Tea room.

EBBERSTON HALL

Scarborough   map J10
(W. de Wend Fenton, Esq.)

Palladian Villa of 1718 designed by the architect Colin Campbell. Water gardens attributed to William Benson and Switzer. Elaborate woodwork and cornices comparable to Castle Howard and Beningbrough.

Location: 11 m W of Scarborough on A170 Scarborough/Pickering Road.
Open: Easter to Oct 1 - Daily 2-6.
Admission: £2.50.

FAIRFAX HOUSE

Castlegate, York map H9
Telephone: (0904) 655543
(York Civic Trust)

An 18th century house designed by John Carr of York and described as a classic architectural masterpiece of its age. Certainly one of the finest townhouses in England and saved from near collapse by the York Civic Trust who restored it to its former glory during 1982/84. In addition to the superbly decorated plasterwork, wood and wrought iron, the house is now home for an outstanding collection of 18th century Furniture, and Clocks, formed by the late Noel Terry. Described by Christie's as one of the finest private collections of this century, it enhances and complements the house and helps to create a very special 'lived in' feeling. The gift of the entire collection by Noel Terry's Trustees to the Civic Trust has enabled it to fill the house with appropriate pieces of the period and has provided the basis for what can now be considered a fully furnished Georgian Townhouse.

Location: Centre of York, follow signs for Castle Area and Jorvik Centre.
Open: Mar 1 to Dec 31: Mon to Thurs and Sat 11-5; Sun 1.30-5 (last admission 4.30). *Closed* on Fridays except during August. Special evening tours, connoisseur visits and receptions welcomed by arrangement with the Director.
Admission: £3, OAP/Student £2.50, Chd £1.50. Parties, Adult (pre-booked 15 or more) £2.50, Chd £1.
Public car park within 50 yds. Suitable for disabled persons only with assistance (by telephoning beforehand staff can be available to help). A small gift shop offers selected antiques, publications and gifts. Opening times are the same as the house.

FOUNTAINS ABBEY & STUDLEY ROYAL

🍂 The National Trust

Ripon map H10   ♿
Telephone: (0765) 608888

Extensive ruins of Cistercian monastery. Ornamental gardens laid out by John Aislabie, 1720. 400 acre deer park with fine Burges church. Awarded World Heritage status.

Location: 2 m W of Ripon; 9 m W of Harrogate; NW of A61.
Open: Deer Park open all year during daylight hours. Fountains Hall: Apr to Sept 11-6, Oct to Mar 11-4. Abbey & Gardens open daily except 24 & 25 Dec and Frid in Jan, Nov & Dec. Jan to Mar, Oct to Dec 10-5 or dusk if earlier. Apr to Sept 10-7.
Admission: Deer Park: Free. Fountains Hall: Free. Abbey & Gardens: Nov '92 - Mar '93 £3, Chd £1.50, Family £7.50, Group (min of 15) £2.50, Chd £1.30. Apr - Oct £3.80, Chd £1.90, Family £9, Group (min of 15) £3.40, Chd £1.70. Nov - Mar '94 £3.30, Chd £1.60, Family £8, Group (min of 15) £2.80, Chd £1.40. Free car parking at Visitor Centre Car Park. Studley Park - £1.70.
Refreshments: Light lunches, sandwiches, soup and cakes etc. Visitor Centre Restaurant: Daily Jan - Mar, Oct - Dec, 10-5. Apr - Sept, 10-6. Studley Royal Tearoom Weekends Jan - Mar and Oct - Dec, 10-5. Daily Apr - Sept, 10-6.
Wheelchair access. Picnics can be taken anywhere on Estate. Dogs on leads only. Visitor Centre shop: open daily.

GEORGIAN THEATRE ROYAL

Richmond map H10
Telephone: (0748) 823710
(The Georgian Theatre (Richmond) Trust Ltd.)

HARLOW CARR BOTANICAL GARDENS

Harrogate map H9
(The Northern Horticultural Society)

HELMSLEY CASTLE   English⌗Heritage

map H10
Telephone: (0439) 70442

Even in its ruined state, Helmsley Castle is spectacular. Begun by Walter Espec shortly after the Norman Conquest, the huge earthworks - now softened to green valleys - are all that remain of this early castle. The oldest stonework is 12th century. Like many English castles, Helmsley rendered indefensible during the Civil War, when it belonged to the notorious George Villiers, Duke of Buckingham. It was abandoned as a great house when its owners built nearby Duncombe Park. The 17th century domestic buildings contains an exhibition about the castle.

Location: Helmsley.
Open: Good Friday or Apr 1 (whichever is earlier) to Sept 30: Open Daily 10-6. Oct 1 to Maundy Thursday or Mar 31 (whichever is earlier): Open Tues to Sun 10-4. *Closed* Dec 24-26, Jan 1.
Admission: £1.70, Concessions £1.30, Chd 85p.

HOVINGHAM HALL

York map J10
(Sir Marcus & Lady Worsley)

Palladian house designed c. 1760 by Thomas Worsley. Unique Riding School, magnificent yew hedges, dovecot, private cricket ground. Family portraits.

Location: 20 m N of York on Malton/Helmsley Road (B1257).
Open: Open for parties of 15 or more **by written appointment only** - Apr 13 to Sept 30, 1993, Tues, Weds & Thurs 11-7.
Admission: £2.50, Chd £1.25.
Refreshments: At the Hall by arrangement. Meals at The Worsley Arms, Hovingham.

KIRKHAM PRIORY   English⌗Heritage

map J10
Telephone: (065381) 768

The patrons of this monastery, the Lords of Helmsley, are still much in evidence. Their coats of arms adorn the gatehouse, and four family graves have survived amid the ruins of the Church. Built for the monks the Augustinian Order, or Black Canons, Kirkham was founded early in the 12th century by Walter Espec, who also founded Rievaulx Abbey.

Location: 5 m (8 km) south west of Malton.
Open: Good Friday or Apr 1 (whichever is earlier) to Sept 30: Open Daily 10-6. Oct 1 to Maundy Thursday or Mar 31 (whichever is earlier): Open Tues to Sun 10-4. *Closed* Dec 24-26, Jan 1.
Admission: £1.20, Concessions 90p, Chd 60p.

MARKENFIELD HALL

Ripon map H10
(The Lord Grantley, MC)

Fine example of English manor house 14th, 15th & 16th century buildings surrounded by moat.

Location: 3 m S of Ripon off the Ripon/Harrogate Road (A61). Access is up a road marked Public Bridleway Hell Wath Lane'.
Open: Apr to Oct - Mons 10-12.30, 2.15-5. Exterior only outside courtyard and moat all other days in May - times as above.
Admission: £1, Chd (accompanied by adult) free. Exterior and outside courtyard: Free.

MIDDLEHAM CASTLE   English⌗Heritage

map H10
Telephone: (0969) 23899

The great days of Middleham were in the 14th and 15th centuries, when it was the stronghold of the mighty Neville family. After the death of Richard Neville - 'Warwick the Kingmaker' - in 1471, the castle was forfeited to the Crown and was the childhood home of Richard III. The dominant feature of the castle is the great keep, one of the largest in England. A replica of the famous Middleham jewel is on display.

Location: 2 m (3.2 km) south of Leyburn.
Open: Good Friday or Apr 1 (whichever is earlier) to Sept 30: Open Daily 10-6. Oct 1 to Maundy Thursday or Mar 31 (whichever is earlier): Open Tues to Sun 10-4. *Closed* Dec 24-26, Jan 1.
Admission: £1.20, Concessions 90p, Chd 60p.

MOUNT GRACE PRIORY   English⌗Heritage

map H10
Telephone: (0609) 83249

These 14th century ruins provide a rare opportunity to study the plan of a Carthusian monastery, or 'charterhouse'. The Carthusian monks lived like hermits - in seclusion not only from the world, but from each other. They met together only in chapel, and for religious feasts. Every monk had his own cell - 21 in all - a tiny two-storey house with its own garden and workshop. And each cell had running water - a remarkable luxury in the Middle Ages. A fully restored cell with hand-carved furniture and exhibition gives a fascinating insight into the lives of the monks.

Location: 7 miles (11.3 km) north east of Northallerton.
Open: Good Friday or Apr 1 (whichever is earlier) to Sept 30: Open Daily 10-6. Oct 1 to Maundy Thursday or Mar 31 (whichever is earlier): Open Tues to Sun 10-4. *Closed* Dec 24-26, Jan 1.
Admission: £2, Concessions £1.50, Chd £1.

NEWBURGH PRIORY

Coxwold map H10
Telephone: (034 76) 435
(Sir George Wombwell Bt)

One of the North's most interesting Historic Houses. Originally built in 1145 with alterations in 1568 and 1720-1760, the Priory has been the home of one family and its descendants since 1538. The house contains the tomb of Oliver Cromwell (his third daughter, Mary, was married to Viscount Fauconberg - owner 1647-1700). In the grounds there is a really beautiful Water Garden full of rare alpines, plants and rhododendrons. Afternoon tea is served in the original kitchen.

Location: 5 m from Easingwold off A19, 9 m from Thirsk.
Open: GROUNDS AND HOUSE: Apr 4 to July 1, (GROUNDS ONLY: July 5 to Aug 30), Suns and Weds, Easter Mon and Bank Hol Mons. HOUSE OPEN: 2.30-4.45. GROUNDS: 2-6. *Other days for parties of 25 or more by appointment with the Administrator.*
Admission: House and Grounds £3, Chd £1.20, Grounds only £1.50, Chd free.
Refreshments: In the Old Priory Kitchens.

The National Trust
THE SIGN
OF A GREAT
DAY OUT

NEWBY HALL & GARDENS

Ripon map H10 &
Telephone: (0423) 322583
(R. E. J. Compton, Esq.)

The family home of Mr and Mrs Robin Compton is one of Yorkshire's renowned Adam houses. It is set amidst 25 acres of award-winning gardens full of rare and beautiful plants. The contents of the house are superb and include an unique Gobelins Tapestry Room, a gallery of classical statuary and some of Chippendale's finest furniture. Other attractions are railway rides beside the river, adventure gardens for children, a woodland discovery walk, Newby shop and plants stall, and picnic area. Coach and car park free.

Location: 4m SE of Ripon on Boroughbridge Road (B6265). 3m W of A1; 14m Harrogate; 20m York; 35m Leeds; 32m Skipton.
Open: Apr 1 to Sept 30 - Daily except Mons (but open Bank Holidays) from 11am. Full visitor information from the Administrator, The Estate Office, Newby Hall, Ripon HG4 5AE. See colour photograph in preliminary section.
Refreshments: Lunches & teas in the licensed Garden Restaurant.

NORTON CONYERS

Ripon map H10 △ &

Telephone: House:(0765) 640333, Garden:(0765) 640601
(Sir James Graham, Bt)

Late medieval house with Stuart and Georgian additions. Family pictures, furniture and wedding dresses. Friendly atmosphere, noticed by many visitors, resulting from over 360 years of occupation by the same family. Visited by Charlotte Brontë in 1839; the house is one of the originals of Thornfield Hall in 'Jane Eyre', and a family legend was reputedly the inspiration for the mad Mrs Rochester. 18th century walled garden in full cultivation, with Orangery and herbaceous borders, small Garden Centre specialising in unusual hardy plants. Pick Your Own Fruit in June - August. Intending pickers in June are advised to check beforehand.

Location: 3½ m NW of Ripon nr Wath. 3 m from A1; turn off at the Baldersby Flyover, take A61 to Ripon, turn right to Melmerby.
Open: Suns from May 9 to Sept 12, also all Bank Holiday Suns & Mons, and daily from July 26 to 31, 2-5.30. Any time for booked parties; inquiries to Lady Graham at above address. Guided tours by previous arrangement only. The garden is open all year Mon-Fri 9-5, Sat & Sun Mar 6 to Sept 5, 2-5.30pm.
Admission: £2.30, Chd (4-16) £1, OAPs £1.50, parties of 20 or more £1.50. Free parking. Garden - free.
Refreshments: Teas served Bank Holidays and Charity openings. Teas, light refreshments and buffet lunches for booked parties by request.
Dogs on grounds and garden only, and must be on a lead. Visitors are requested not to wear high-heeled shoes in the house.

NUNNINGTON HALL   🍂 **The National Trust**

nr Helmsley map J10
Telephone: (043 95) 283

Sixteenth century manor house with fine panelled hall and staircase. Carlisle Collection of Miniature Rooms on display.

Location: In Ryedale; 4½ m SE of Helmsley; 1½ m N of B1257.
Open: Apr 1 to Oct 31, Tues, Wed, Thurs, Sat & Good Friday 2-6. Suns, Bank Hols 12-6. Also Frid in July & Aug 2-6. Last adm 5. Shop and tearoom open as house. School Parties on weekdays by arrangement with the administrator.
Admission: HOUSE & GARDEN: £3.30, Chd £1.50, Parties £2.80, Chd party £1.20, GARDEN: £1.60, Chd 80p.
Refreshments: Afternoon teas available at all times when house is open 2-5.30 in indoor tearooms or tea garden. Lunches July & Aug.
Shop. Access to Ground floor and tearoom only for Wheelchairs. Lavatory for disabled at rear of house. Access to main gardens via ramp. Guide dogs permitted. Dogs in car park only. Baby changing facilities.

PICKERING CASTLE   English⌗Heritage

map J10
Telephone: (0751) 74989

Most of the medieval kings visited Pickering Castle. They came to hunt deer and wild boar in the neighbouring forest. It was a sport of which they were inordinately fond, and the royal forests were zealously guarded. Romantics may like to speculate as to why Rosamund's Tower has been linked with 'Fair Rosamund', mistress of Henry II. They should, however, be aware that the tower was built in 1323, a century after the lady died.

Location: Pickering.
Open: Good Friday or Apr 1 (whichever is earlier) to Sept 30: Open Daily 10-6. Oct 1 to Maundy Thursday or Mar 31 (whichever is earlier): Open Tues to Sun 10-4. *Closed* Dec 24-26, Jan 1.
Admission: £1.70, Concessions £1.30, Chd 85p.

RICHMOND CASTLE   English⌗Heritage

map H10
Telephone: (0748) 822493

Surrounded on three sides by high moorland, Richmond Castle is in a strongly defensible position. However, the castle has seen little active service, which accounts for the remarkable amount of early Norman stonework that has survived. Built by Alan the Red, shortly after 1066, the castle went with the title 'Duke of Richmond' and has had many royal and powerful owners. The 100 foot high keep provides fine views over the ruins and surrounding countryside.

Location: Richmond.
Open: Good Friday or Apr 1 (whichever is earlier) to Sept 30: Open Daily 10-6. Oct 1 to Maundy Thursday or Mar 31 (whichever is earlier): Open Tues to Sun 10-4. *Closed* Dec 24-26, Jan 1.
Admission: £1.70, Concessions £1.30, Chd 85p.

RIEVAULX ABBEY   English ⌗ Heritage

map H10
Telephone: (043 96) 228

RIEVAULX TERRACE   🌿 The National Trust

Helmsley   map H10   ♿
Telephone: (04396) 340

Beautiful half mile long grass terrace with views of Rievaulx Abbey. Two 18th century Temples and permanent exhibition.

Location: 2½ m NW of Helmsley on Stokesley Road (B1257).
Open: Apr 1 to Oct 31 - Daily 10.30-6 (or dusk if earlier). Ionic Temple closed 1-2. Last adm 5.
Admission: £2.10, Chd 90p, Parties £1,70, chd party 80p.
Refreshments: Teas available at Nunnington Hall, 7m E.
All dogs on a lead. Battery operated 'Runabout' available.

The fluctuating fortunes of the abbey may be read from the ruins. Within two decades of its foundation in 1131, Rievaulx - the first Cistercian monastery in the north - was vast, with 140 monks and 500 lay brothers. A costly building programme followed, and it is little wonder that by the 13th century the monastery was heavily in debt, and buildings were being reduced in size. By the Dissolution in the 16th century, there were only 22 monks. The church is a beautiful example of early English Gothic. New visitor centre with exhibition and shop.

Location: 3 miles (4.8 km) north west of Helmsley.
Open: Good Friday or Apr 1 (whichever is earlier) to Sept 30: Open Daily 10-6. Oct 1 to Maundy Thursday or Mar 31 (whichever is earlier): Open daily 10-4. *Closed* Dec 24-26, Jan 1.
Admission: £2, Concessions £1.50, Chd £1.

RIPLEY CASTLE

Ripley map H9
Telephone: (0423) 770152
(Sir Thomas Ingilby Bt)

Ripley Castle and Gardens

Home of the Ingilby Family for over 650 years, the castle is situated ten minutes north of Harrogate, in the centre of one of England's most beautiful and historic estate villages. The castle itself overlooks a seventeen acre lake and deer park; the setting is wonderful. The rooms are packed with anecdote, humour and items of fascination, and the knight's chamber in the 1555 tower remains one of the most startlingly complete medieval rooms in the country, complete with waggon roof ceiling, ancient panelling, Royal Greenwich armour and secret priest's hiding hole.

The extensive walled gardens contain the national hyacinth collection and a magnificent assortment of tropical and semi tropical plants in the greenhouse.

The village is quite unique and well worth a visit, and the four star **Boar's Head Hotel** with its first class restaurant and bar makes an excellent base for touring Yorkshire's stately homes, almost all of which are within one hour's drive.

OPENING TIMES: April and October: Sats & Suns 11.30-4.30. **May:** Tues, Weds, Thurs 11.30-3.30, Sats & Suns 11.30-4.30. **June to Sept** (incl.) Daily except Mons & Fri, 11.30-4.30; Good Friday and all Bank Holidays in season 11.00-4.30. **Booked Parties:** Groups of 15+ can visit the Castle on any day throughout the year, by prior appointment, 10.00-7.00. **Gardens:** Daily April 1st to Oct.

Has been the home of the Ingilby family since early 14th century. Priests secret hiding place and Civil War armour. Main gateway dates from reign of Edward IV. Extensive gardens. National Hyacinth and tropical plant collections.

Location: In Ripley 3½ m N Harrogate; 7½ m from Ripon.
Open: Apr and Oct - Sats & Suns, 11.30-4.30; May - Tues, Weds, Thurs 11.30-3.30. Sats and Suns 11.30-4.30. June to Sept (incl.) Daily except Mons and Frid 11.30-4.30. Good Friday and all Bank Hols in season 11-4.30. Booked parties: Groups (15 plus) can visit the castle on any day during the year, by prior appointment 10-7. Gardens: Daily Apr 1 to Oct.
Refreshments: Licensed restaurant and public bar (The Boar's Head Hotel) in village: Tearoom in castle courtyard, serving teas and refreshments.

SCARBOROUGH CASTLE   English⌗Heritage

Scarborough map J10
Telephone: (0723) 372451

Standing on the massive headland between the North and South Bays, the castle commands magnificent views. There was a prehistoric settlement here, and a Roman signal station, but the first mention of the castle is in the 12th century, when it was seized by Henry II. During the Civil War the castle was besieged and changed hands several times. A hundred years later it was still in use to detain political prisoners - notably George Fox, founder of the Society of Friends (Quakers).

Location: East of town centre.
Open: Good Friday or Apr 1 (whichever is earlier) to Sept 30: Open Daily 10-6. Oct 1 to Maundy Thursday or Mar 31 (whichever is earlier): Open Tues to Sun 10-4. *Closed Dec 24-26, Jan 1.*
Admission: £1.70, Concessions £1.30, Chd 85p.

SHANDY HALL

Coxwold map H10 △
Telephone: (034 76) 465
(The Laurence Sterne Trust)

Here in 1760-67 the witty and eccentric parson Laurence Sterne wrote *Tristram Shandy* and *A Sentimental Journey,* 'novels that jump clean out of the 18th century into the 20th', influencing Dickens, Goethe, Tolstoy, Balzac, Proust, Melville, Joyce, Virginia Woolf, and other great writers. Shandy Hall was built as a timber-framed open-hall in the mid-15th century, modernised in the 17th, curiously added to by Sterne in the 18th. It survives much as he knew it, almost as full of surprises and odd digressions as his novels, most of which he wrote in his little book-lined study. Not a museum but a lived-in house where you are sure of a personal welcome. Surrounded by a walled garden full of old-fashioned roses and cottage-garden plants. Also one acre wild garden in old quarry.

Location: 20 m from York via A19; 6 m from A19 at Easingwold; 8 m from Thirsk; 13 m from A1 at Dishforth.
Open: June to Sept - Weds 2-4.30. Suns 2.30-4.30. *Any other day or time all year by appointment with Hon Curators.* Gardens open when fine.
Admission: £2, Chd (accompanied) half-price. Garden only £1.
Refreshments: Close by in village.
Book and handicrafts shop. Unusual plants for sale.

SION HILL HALL

Kirby Wiske, nr Thirsk map H10 △
Telephone: (0845) 587206
(The H W Mawer Trust)

Charming neo-Georgian country house designed by the York Architect Walter H. Brierley in the Lutyens style, one of the last country mansions. Now houses the beautiful Mawer bequest of fine furniture, paintings, porcelain, clocks etc. The house also contains collections of specialised interest more recently acquired. R.I.B.A. Award Winner for outstanding architectural merit.

Location: 6 m S of Northallerton, 4 m W of Thirsk, ½ m off A167 signpost Kirby Wiske.
Open: First Sun in each month, May to Oct 2-5 (last adm 4.30). By arrangement with the Curator at any reasonable time. Feb to Nov. Ring now on (0845) 587206.
Admission: £3, Concessions £2.50, Chd free if accompanied.
Refreshments: Teas served in our Granary Tearoom.

SKIPTON CASTLE

Skipton map G9 △
Telephone: (0756) 792442

This is one of the best preserved mediaeval castles in England, Over 900 years old and fully roofed. Explore this massive fortress and discover Lady Anne Clifford's famous yew in the beautiful Conduit Court.

Location: Head of High Street.
Station(s): (½ m). Bus Station: (town centre).
Open: Every day from 10 (Sunday 2). Last admission 6 (Oct-Feb 4pm). *Closed* Christmas Day.
Admission: With illustrated Tour Sheet £2.60; under 18's with Tour Sheet and new 1993 Castle Explorer's badge, half price; under 5's free with badge! Party visits welcomed: school parties £1.30 per head, supervising teachers free; adult parties of 15 or more, less 10%. Complimentary guided tour for pre-booked parties, otherwise illustrated Tour Sheets are provided in a choice of 8 languages; English, French, German, Dutch, Italian, Spanish, Japanese or Esperanto.
Large coach and car park off nearby High Street.**SEE BACK COVER**

STOCKELD PARK

Wetherby map H9
Telephone: (0937) 586101
(Mr and Mrs P. G. F. Grant)

This small country mansion is set amidst an extensive rural estate of farms, wood and parklands on the edge of the Vale of York and is one of the finest examples of the work of the celebrated architect James Paine and a splendid example of the Palladian style. Stockeld Park was built for the Middleton family during the period 1758-63 and purchased in 1885 by Robert John Foster. Mr Foster was the great grandson of John Foster who founded John Foster & Son based at the Black Dyke Mills. Visitors have an opportunity to see the house as it is lived in at present, together with furniture and pictures collected by the Foster family over many years.

Location: 2 m N of Wetherby; 7 m SE of Harrogate on A661.
Open: Thursdays only from Apr 1 to Oct 7 1993 incl. 2-5. (other times by appointment in writing to the Estate Office or tel: (0937) 586101).
Admission: £1.50, Chd 75p, OAPs £1.

THORP PERROW ARBORETUM

nr Snape map H10
(Sir John Ropner)

Thorp Perrow, the country home of Sir John Ropner, contains a magnificent arboretum - a collection of over 1,000 varieties of trees and shrubs, including some of the largest and rarest in England. It has rapidly become a popular attraction in the area and can be enjoyed by all members of the family, who may wander amidst these 85 acres of landscaped grounds. Lake, grassy glades, tree trails and woodland walks. Masses of daffodils in Spring, summer wild flowers and glorious autumn colour. Nature trail, children's mystery trail. Tea room and information centre. Plant centre.

Location: on Well to Ripon Road, south of Bedale. O.S. map ref. SE258851. 4 m from Leeming Bar on A1.
Open: All year, dawn to dusk. Guided tours available. Tel:0677 425323
Admission: £2.20, Chd (under 16)/OAPs £1.10 Free car and coach park.
Picnic area. Toilets. Dogs permitted on leads.

TREASURER'S HOUSE   The National Trust

York map H9
Telephone: (0904) 624247

Large 17th century house of great interest. Fine furniture and paintings. Exhibition.

Location: Behind York Minster.
Station(s): York (½ m).
Open: Apr 1 to Oct 31 - Daily 10.30-5. Last adm 4.30. Guided tours by arrangement.
Admission: £2.80, Chd £1.40, Parties £2.40, Chd party £1.20.
Refreshments: Available in licensed tea rooms serving morning coffee, light lunches, teas. Open for pre-booked parties during and outside normal opening hours and for private functions. Tel: York 646757.
Wheelchair access - part of ground floor only. No car parking facilities. Dogs not allowed, except for guide dogs. Baby changing facilities. Shop and tearoom open as house.

WHITBY ABBEY   English ⌗ Heritage

map J10
Telephone: (0947) 603568

Founded in 657 and presided over by the Abbess Hilda, Whitby was a double monastery for both men and women - a feature of the Anglo-Saxon church. This early history has been chronicled by the Venerable Bede, who tells us that here the poet Caedmon lived and worked. Destroyed by invading Danes in 867, the monastery was refounded after the Norman Conquest, but its exposed cliff-top site continued to invite attack by sea pirates. The building remains are from the later Benedictine monastery.

Location: Whitby.
Open: Good Friday or Apr 1 (whichever is earlier) to Sept 30: Open Daily 10-6. Oct 1 to Maundy Thursday or Mar 31 (whichever is earlier): Open Tues to Sun 10-4. *Closed* Dec 24-26, Jan 1.
Admission: £1.20, Concessions 90p, Chd 60p.

SOUTH YORKSHIRE

CANNON HALL

Cawthorne map H8
Telephone: (0226) 790270
(Barnsley Metropolitan Borough Council)

18th century house by Carr of York. Collections of fine furniture, paintings, glassware, pewter and pottery. Also the Regimental Museum of the 13th/18th Royal Hussars. 70 acres of parkland.

Location: 5 m W of Barnsley on A635; 1 m NW of Cawthorne.
Open: All the year - Tues to Sat 10.30-5; *Closed Mon.* (Open Bank Hol Mons). Suns 2.30-5. *Closed Dec 25 to Jan 1 (incl.) Also closed Good Friday.*
Admission: Free.

CONISBROUGH CASTLE   English ⌗ Heritage

map H8
Telephone: (0709) 863329

Sir Walter Scott's novel 'Ivanhoe' made Conisbrough Castle famous. The magnificent keep - still largely intact - is one of the finest examples of 12th century building in England. Sited by the River Don, the castle we see today was probably the work of Hamelin Plantagenet, illegitimate half-brother of Henry II.

Location: 4½ m (7.2 km) south west of Doncaster.
Open: Good Friday or Apr 1 (whichever is earlier) to Sept 30: Open Daily 10-6. Oct 1 to Maundy Thursday or Mar 31 (whichever is earlier): Open Tues to Sun 10-4. *Closed* Dec 24-26, Jan 1.
Admission: £1.70, Concessions £1.30, Chd 85p.

MONK BRETTON PRIORY   English ⌗ Heritage

map H8
Telephone: (0226) 204089

The monastery was founded about 1153, initially for monks of the Cluniac Order. The priory was involved in violent arguments with another Cluniac monastery at Pontefract, and more than once an armed force was sent to occupy Monk Bretton. Their differences were only resolved by Monk Bretton leaving the Order to become a Benedictine house. The remains show the layout of the monastery. One of the best preserved buildings is the 14th century prior's lodging, which stands three storeys high.

Location: 2 m (3.2 km) north east of Barnsley.
Open: Good Friday or Apr 1 (whichever is earlier) to Sept 30: Open Daily 10-6. Oct 1 to Maundy Thursday or Mar 31 (whichever is earlier): Open Tues to Sun 10-4. *Closed* Dec 24-26, Jan 1.
Admission: 80p, Concessions 60p, Chd 40p.

ROCHE ABBEY   English ⌗ Heritage

map H8
Telephone: (0709) 812739

Most medieval monasteries are near running water, since the monks were more fastidious about sanitation than their contemporaries. The two founders of Roche gave land on either side of a stream, and parts of the building bridge the water. Founded in 1147 for monks of the Cistercian Order, the name 'Roche' derives from its rocky site. Sadly, the only part of the abbey's history of which we know any detail, is the Dissolution. When the monks left, the monastery was plundered and the carved wood from the church burnt in order to melt the lead taken from the roof.

Location: 1½ m (2.4 km) south of Maltby.
Open: Good Friday or Apr 1 (whichever is earlier) to Sept 30: Open Daily 10-6. Oct 1 to Maundy Thursday or Mar 31 (whichever is earlier): Open Weekends only 10-4. *Closed* Dec 24-26, Jan 1.
Admission: £1.20, Concessions 90p, Chd 60p.

THE SUE RYDER HOME, HICKLETON HALL

nr Doncaster map H8
(The Sue Ryder Foundation)

This Home cares for 50 physically handicapped and others who are homeless and unable to cope on their own.

Location: 6 m NW of Doncaster; on A635 Doncaster/Barnsley Road (behind Hickleton Church).
Open: Individuals wishing to visit the Home may do so, Mons to Fris 2-4 without prior appointment. Please report your arrival to the Office in the main entrance.
Refreshments: Hotels & Restaurants in Doncaster.

SHEFFIELD BOTANIC GARDENS

Clarkehouse Rd, Sheffield   map H8
(Sheffield City Council)

WEST YORKSHIRE

BAGSHAW MUSEUM

Wilton Park, Batley
Telephone: (0924) 472514
(Kirklees Metro Council)

BRAMHAM PARK

Wetherby   map H9
Telephone: (0937) 844265
(Mr & Mrs George Lane Fox)

The house was created during the first half of the 18th century and affords a rare opportunity to enjoy a beautiful Queen Anne mansion containing fine furniture, pictures and porcelain - set in magnificent grounds with ornamental ponds, cascades, tall beech hedges and loggias of various shapes - unique in the British Isles for its grand vistas design stretching out into woodlands of cedar, copper beech, lime and Spanish chestnut interspersed with wild rhododendron thickets.

Location: 5 m S of Wetherby on the Great North Road (A1).
Open: GROUNDS ONLY. Easter weekend, May Day Weekend, Spring Bank Hol weekend. HOUSE & GROUNDS. June 20 to Sept 5 (incl. Bank Holiday Mon) - Suns, Tues, Weds & Thurs also Bank Hol Mon 1.15-5.30. Last adm 5 pm. 'BRAMHAM HORSE TRIALS' - June 10 - 13 1993.
Admission: For charges and concessionary rates contact The Estate Office, Bramham Park, Wetherby, W. Yorks LS23 6ND Tel: (0937) 844265.

EAST RIDDLESDEN HALL   The National Trust

Keighley   map H9
Telephone: (0535) 607075

17th century manor house. Magnificent tithe barn. Small formal garden.

Location: 1 m NE of Keighley on S side of A650, on N bank of Aire.
Station(s): Keighley (1½ m).
Open: Apr 3 to Oct 31, Sat - Wed also Good Frid. and Thurs in July and Aug 12-5. Last adm 4.30.
Admission: £2.80, Chd £1.40, Parties £2.20, Chd party £1.10.
Refreshments: Afternoon teas and refreshments in Bothy Tearoom, adjacent to house (on first floor), special arrangements for disabled visitors contact Administrator.
Dogs with the exception of guide dogs, allowed in grounds only and must be on a lead. Only ground floor and garden accessible for disabled visitors. Braille guide. Baby changing facilities. Shop and tearoom open as house.

THE SIGN OF A GREAT DAY OUT

HAREWOOD HOUSE AND BIRD GARDEN

Leeds map H9   Ⓢ
Telephone: (0532) 886331
(The Earl of Harewood)

18th century house designed by John Carr and Robert Adam and still the home of the Lascelles family. As well as superb ceilings, plasterwork and Chippendale furniture it contains fine English and Italian paintings and Sevres and Chinese porcelain. In the grounds, landscaped by 'Capability' Brown, are lakeside and woodland walks, displays of roses and rhododendrons and a herbaceous border running the length of the Terrace.

Location: 7 m S of Harrogate; 8 m N of Leeds on Leeds/Harrogate road; Junction A61/659 at Harewood village; 5 m from A1 at Wetherby 22m from York.
Open: HOUSE, GROUNDS, BIRD GARDEN AND ALL FACILITIES - Apr 3 to Oct 31 daily. Gates open 10 House open 11. Concession rates for Coach parties, school parties welcome at all times.
Admission: Charges and details of Summer and Weekend - including Car Rallies and Leeds Championship Dog Show available from Adrian Wiley, Visitors Information, Estate Office, Harewood, Leeds LS17 9LQ. State Dining Room (max 48 available).
Refreshments: Cafeteria; Restaurant; also Courtyard Functions Suite for Conference/Product launches throughout the year.

LEDSTON HALL

nr Castleford map H9
(G. H. H. Wheler, Esq.)

17th century mansion with some earlier work.

Location: 2 m N of Castleford off A656.
Station(s): Castleford (2¾ m).
Open: Exterior only. May, June, July and Aug - Mon to Fri 9-4. Other days by appointment.
Refreshments: Chequers Inn, Ledsham (1 m).

LOTHERTON HALL

Aberford   map H9
(Leeds Metro District Council)

Lotherton Hall was built round an earlier house dating from the mid-eighteenth century. The extensions to the east were completed in 1896 and those to the west in 1903. The Hall, with its art collection, park and gardens, was given to the City of Leeds by Sir Alvary and Lady Gascoigne in 1968 and opened as a country house museum in 1969. The Gascoigne collection, which contains pictures, furniture, silver and porcelain of the 17th and 18th centuries, as well as works of a later period, includes a magnificent portrait of Sir Thomas Gascoigne by Pompeo Batoni and an impressive group of silver race cups ranging in date from 1776 to 1842. The first floor and costume galleries were opened in 1970 and the oriental gallery in 1975. There is also a Museum shop and audio visual room.

Location: 1 m E of A1 at Aberford on the Towton Road (B1217).
Open: All the year - Tues to Sun 10.30-5.30 (or dusk if earlier); *Closed Mons except Bank Hol Mons.*
Admission: £1.10, Chd/OAPs/Students 50p, Season Ticket £4.50 (includes Temple Newsam, see below). Tel: (0532) 813259.

NOSTELL PRIORY   🌳   The National Trust

Wakefield   map H9   ♿
Telephone: (0924) 863892

Built for Sir Rowland Winn by Paine; a wing added in 1766 by Robert Adam. State rooms contain pictures and famous Chippendale furniture made especially for the house.

Location: 6 m SE of Wakefield, on N side of A638.
Station(s): Fitzwilliam (1½ m).
Open: Apr 3 to Oct 31: Apr, May, June, Sept & Oct - Sats 12-5, Suns 11-5; July & Aug - Daily (except Frid) 12-5, Sun 11-5. Bank Hol Openings: Good Friday, Easter Mon & Tues; May Day Mon; Spring Bank Hol Mon & Tues; Aug Bank Hol Mon - Mons 11-5, Tues 12-5. Guided tours on weekdays only (last tour 4).
Admission: HOUSE & GROUNDS: £3.50, Chd £1.80, Parties £3, Chd party £1.50. GROUNDS: £2.20, Chd £1.10. Free parking. Pre-booked parties welcome outside normal published opening times. However, on these occasions, a charge will be made to National Trust members.
Refreshments: Lunches and afternoon teas available in stable tea rooms (not NT).
Dogs in grounds on leads, not in house (except guide dogs). Lift available for disabled.

OAKWELL HALL

Birstall

RED HOUSE

Gomersal, Cleckheaton   map H9
Telephone: (0274) 872165
(Kirklees Metropolitan Council)

🌳 THE SIGN OF A GREAT DAY OUT

SHIBDEN HALL

Halifax map G9 △ Ⓔ
Telephone: (0422) 352246 or (0422) 321455
(Calderdale Metropolitan Borough Council)

An early 15th century half-timbered house with later additions, furnished with 17th and 18th century material. The 17th century barn and outbuildings are equipped with early agricultural implements and craft workshops. The museum is set in a large park and surrounded by terrace gardens. Cafe facilities.

Location: ¼ m SE of Halifax on the Halifax/Hipperholme Road (A58).
Open: Mar to Nov - Mons to Sats 10-5, Suns 12-5. Feb - Suns only 2-5. *Closed December to January.*
Admission: £1.50, Chd/OAPs 75p.*Conducted tours after normal hours.*(Fee payable).
Refreshments: At the Hall.

TEMPLE NEWSAM

Leeds map H9
(Leeds Metro District Council)

The Temple Newsam estate belonged to the Knights Templar and later passed to the D'Arcy family who retained it until 1537. The house was the birthplace of Lord Darnley and a centre of English and Scottish intrique during the reign of Elizabeth I. It was later acquired by Sir Arthur Ingram, whose descendants became Viscounts Irwin. It was eventually inherited by the late Lord Halifax who sold it to Leeds Corporation in 1922. The house has many fine features of 16th and 17th century date, as well as a magnificent suite of Georgian rooms, and contains some superb furniture, silver, ceramics and a fine collection of pictures. There is also a Museum shop in the house.

Location: 5 m E of Leeds; 1 m S of A63 (nr junction with A642).
Station(s): Cross Gates (1¾ m).
Open: All the year - Tues to Sun 10.30-5.30 (or dusk if earlier); *Closed Mons except Bank Hol Mons.*
Admission: £1.10, Chd/OAPs/Students 50p. Season tickets £4.50 (includes Lotherton Hall, see above). Tel: (0532) 647321.

TOLSON MEMORIAL MUSEUM

Ravensknowle Park, Huddersfield map H9
Telephone: (0484) 530591

WALES

CLWYD

BODELWYDDAN CASTLE

Bodelwyddan, St Asaph map E8
Telephone: (0745) 583539
(Clwyd County Council)

Bodelwyddan Castle has been authentically restored as a Victorian Country House and contains a major collection of portraits and photography on permanent loan from the National Portrait Gallery. The collection includes works by many eminent Victorian Portraitists such as G. F. Watts, William Holman Hunt, John Singer Sargeant, Sir Edwin Landseer and Sir Thomas Lawrence. The portraits are complemented by furniture from the Victoria & Albert Museum and sculptures from the Royal Academy. The castle is set in beautiful countryside and is a member of the National Garden Scheme. The extensive formal gardens have been restored to their former glory and provide a magnificent display of flowering plants, water features, maze, aviary and woodland walks. For children there is an adventure woodland and play area.

Location: Just off the A55 near St. Asaph (opposite the Marble Church).
Open: Easter to July 1 and Aug 26 to Nov 1: Daily except Fri July 2 to Aug 27: open daily 10-5. Williams Hall opens 10.30. Last admission one hour before closing. For details of winter openings please ring.
Admission: Fee charged. Discount rates available for groups of 20 or more.
Refreshments: Victorian Tea Room, Pavilion Restaurant, Cafeteria.
Suitable for disabled persons (wheelchair available). Giftshop. Picnic Area. Woodland Walk. Maze and Aviary.

CHIRK CASTLE The National Trust

nr Wrexham map F7
Telephone: (0691) 777701
Built 1310; a unique example of a border castle of Edward I's time, inhabited continuously for 660 years. Interesting portraits, tapestries etc. Gardens.

Location: ½ m from Chirk (on A5 trunk road) then 1½ m private driveway; 20 m NW of Shrewsbury 7 m SE of Llangollen.
Station(s): Chirk (2 m).
Open: Apr 1 to Sept 26 - Daily except Mons & Sats but open Bank Holiday Mon. Oct 2 to Oct 31, Sat & Sun only. Castle: 12-5. (Last adm to Castle 4.30.) Grounds: 12-6.
Admission: £3.80, Chd £1.90, Family £9.50, Group £3.
Refreshments: Tea rooms (light lunches & teas).
No dogs. Very limited access for wheelchairs.

ERDDIG The National Trust

nr Wrexham map F7 Ⓔ
Telephone: (0978) 355314
Late 17th century house with 18th century additions and containing much of the original furniture, set in a garden restored to 18th century formal design and containing varieties of fruit known to have been grown there during that period. Range of domestic outbuildings include laundry, bakehouse, sawmill and smithy, all in working order; the extensive restoration work on house and garden is now complete. Visitor Centre containing early farm implements.

Location: 2 m S of Wrexham off A525.
Station(s): Wrexham Central (1¾ m); Wrexham General (2½ m), includes 1 m driveway to House.
Open: Apr 3 to Oct 3 Daily except Thurs and Fris (open Good Friday), House 12-5. Last adm 4. Garden 11-6. *NB: Certain rooms have no electric light; visitors wishing to make a close study of pictures & textiles should avoid dull days early & late in season. Due to extreme fragility the Tapestry & Chinese Rooms will be open only on Weds & Sats.*
Admission: Servants Tour: £3, Chd £1.50, Family £7.50, Group £2.40. Family Rooms: £5, Chd £2.50, Group £4.
Refreshments: Light lunches & teas.

EWLOE CASTLE

nr Hawarden map F8
(Cadw: Welsh Historic Monuments)

Native Welsh castle with typical round and aspidal towers.

Location: 1 m NW of Ewloe on A55.
Admission: Free.

GYRN CASTLE

Llanasa, Holywell map F8
Telephone: (0745) 853500
(Sir Geoffrey Bates, BT, MC)

Dating, in part, from 1700; castellated 1820. Large picture gallery, panelled entrance hall. Pleasant woodland walks and fantastic views to Mersey and Lake District.

Location: 26 m W of Chester (off A55); 4 m SE of Prestatyn.
Open: All the year - by appointment.
Admission: £3, parties welcome.
Refreshments: By arrangement.

VALLE CRUCIS ABBEY

Llangollen map F7
(Cadw: Welsh Historic Monuments)

The lovely ruins of this 13th century Abbey are set beside the Eglwyseg stream in a narrow valley.

Location: B5103 from the A5, west of Llangollen, or A542 from Ruthin.
Open: Mar 29 to Oct 25, daily 9.30-6.30. Oct 26 to Mar 28, weekdays 9.30-4; Sun 2-4.

DYFED

CARREG CENNEN CASTLE

Trapp map E5
(Cadw: Welsh Historic Monuments)

A 13th century castle dramatically perched on a limestone precipice.

Location: Minor roads from A483 (T) to Trapp Village, near Llandeilo.
Open: Mar 29 to Oct 25 daily 9.30-6.30; Oct 26 to Mar 28 weekdays 9.30-4, Sun 2-4.

CILGERRAN CASTLE

Cilgerran map E5
(Cadw: Welsh Historic Monuments)

Picturesque remains that date essentially from the time of William Marshall the Younger, chiefly early 13th century.

Location: 3 m S of Cilgerran off A478.
Open: Mar 29 to Oct 25 daily 9.30-6.30; Oct 26 to Mar 28 weekdays 9.30-4, Sun 2-4.

COLBY WOODLAND GARDEN The National Trust

Amroth map D5
Telephone: (0558) 822800,(0834) 811885

Formal and woodland gardens; walks through a secluded valley along open and wooded pathways with rhododendrons and azaleas. Mr and Mrs A. Scourfield Lewis kindly allow access to the Walled Garden during normal visiting hours.

Location: NE of Tenby off A477; E of junction A477/A478.
Station(s): Kilgetty (2½ m).
Open: Apr 1 to Oct 30 daily 10-5.
Admission: £2.50, Chd £1.

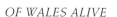
SOME OF THE FINEST HISTORIC ATTRACTIONS IN THE WORLD

he beautiful Welsh landscape embraces so much history, everything from prehistoric tombs, Roman forts and manor houses to monasteries, ironworks and magnificent castles. Many of these historic places are in the care of Cadw: Welsh Historic Monuments.

It's not simply their splendid architecture or dramatic settings that make them so interesting, but also that they tell the story of a nation and give you the opportunity to steep yourself in the atmosphere of Wales' often turbulent past.

As well as the world-famous fortresses of Caernarfon, Harlech, Conwy and Caerphilly, there are 120 more Cadw sites waiting to be explored.

CASTELL COCH

Strongholds of the native Welsh princes like Dolbadarn deep in the mountains of North Wales. Peaceful abbeys like the lovely Valle Crucis Abbey, near Llangollen and Tintern Abbey in the Wye Valley. The grand manor house Tretower Court in Powys, where a medieval pleasure garden has been created. Castell Coch, a Victorian fantasy castle, the inside of which is a decorative extravaganza.

THE GREAT SEAL OF KING EDWARD I

HERITAGE IN WALES

At no other time has the conservation of our heritage and environment been so important. If you cherish our country's historic buildings become a member of Heritage in Wales. You will enjoy free admission to all Cadw attractions and half price entry to around 900 sites in England and Scotland.

For more information about castles and historic places in Wales and Cadw's 'Heritage in Wales' membership scheme, please write or fill in the coupon and send it to:

Cadw, Welsh Historic Monuments, Marketing Dept, Brunel House, 2 Fitzalan Road, Cardiff CF2 1UY.

TINTERN ABBEY

Name_____ (Please print clearly)

Address_____

_____

_____

_____ Postcode_____

HHC&G/92

HARLECH CASTLE

Cadw
WELSH HISTORIC MONUMENTS

KIDWELLY CASTLE

Kidwelly map D5
(Cadw: Welsh Historic Monuments)

One of the finest castles in west Wales, an outstanding example of late 13th century castle design, with its 'walls within walls' defensive system.

Location: Kidwelly via A484 (between Carmarthen & Burry Port).
Open: Mar 29 to Oct 25, daily 9.30-6.30. Oct 26 to Mar 28, weekdays 9.30- 4; Sun 2-4.

LAMPHEY BISHOP'S PALACE

Lamphey map D4
(Cadw: Welsh Historic Monuments)

Substantial remains of the medieval Bishops of St David's country residence.

Location: 2½ m E of Pembroke on A4139.
Open: Mar 29 to Oct 25, 9.30-6.30 daily; Oct 26 to Mar 28 weekdays 9.30-4, Sun 2-4.

LLAWHADEN CASTLE

Llawhaden map D5
(Cadw: Welsh Historic Monuments)

A fortified palace at the centre of a manorial estate belonging to the Bishops of St Davids.

Location: Llawhaden, off A40(T) 3m NW of Narberth.
Open: Mar 29 to Oct 25, 9.30-6.30 daily; Oct 26 to Mar 28 weekdays 9.30-4, Sun 2-4.

PICTON CASTLE

Haverfordwest map D5
(The Picton Castle Trust)

A scheduled ancient monument, but also a beautiful home, occupied continuously since the 15th century by the Philipps family who are still in residence.

Location: 4 m SE of Haverfordwest S of A40 via the Rhos.
Open: CASTLE: Easter Sun & Mon, and following Bank Hols. Also every Sun & Thurs from mid-July to mid-Sept: 2-5. GROUNDS: Apr 1 to Sept 30 - Daily 10.30-5, except Mon. GRAHAM SUTHERLAND GALLERY (tel: (0437) 751296): Apr 1 to Sept 30 daily 10.30-12.30, 1.30-5 *except Mon*, but open Bank Hol Mons. Dates and times of opening under review.
Admission: Grounds £1, Castle and Grounds £2, Chd half-price. (Subject to review). Free car park.
Refreshments: Restaurant.*Closed* Mon.
Craft Shop.

ST. DAVIDS BISHOP'S PALACE

St Davids map C5
(Cadw: Welsh Historic Monuments)

A most impressive medieval Bishop's Palace within the Cathedral Close.

Location: A487 to St Davids, minor road past cathedral.
Open: Mar 29 to Oct 25 daily 9.30-6.30; Oct 26 to Mar 28, weekdays 9.30-4, Sun 2-4.

STRATA FLORIDA ABBEY

Strata Florida map E6
(Cadw: Welsh Historic Monuments)

Founded in 1164, the ruins of this Cistercian abbey stand in a lovely valley once known as 'The Vale of Flowers.'

Location: 1¼ m SE of Pontrhydfendigaid reached from B4340 or B4343.
Open: Mar 29 to Oct 25 daily 9.30-6.30; Oct 26 to Mar 28, weekdays 9.30-4, Sun 2-4.

TALLEY ABBEY

Talley map E5
(Cadw: Welsh Historic Monuments)

A small early 13th century monastic site founded for the Premonstratensian Order.
Location: Talley on B4302 6m N of Llandeilo.
Open: Mar 29 to Oct 25 daily 9.30-6.30; Oct 26 to Mar 28, weekdays 9.30-4, Sun 2-4.

TUDOR MERCHANT'S HOUSE The National Trust

Tenby map D4
Telephone: (0834) 2279

An example of a merchant's house of the 15th century.

Location: Quay Hill, Tenby.
Station(s): Tenby (8 mins walk) (not Suns, except June-Aug).
Open: Apr 1 Oct 29, Mon-Fri 11-6. Sun 2-6. *Closed Sat.*
Admission: £1.60, Chd 80p. Group discount 20%.

MID GLAMORGAN

CAERPHILLY CASTLE

Caerphilly map F4
(Cadw: Welsh Historic Monuments)

Caerphilly Castle is one of the largest surviving castles of the medieval western world, with extensive water defences covering over 30 acres.

Location: A468 (from Newport), A470/A469 (from Cardiff).
Open: Mar 29 to Oct 25, daily 9.30-6.30. Oct 26 to Mar 28, weekdays 9.30-4; Suns 2-4.

COITY CASTLE

Coity map E4
(Cadw: Welsh Historic Monuments)

An early Norman stronghold. In the Owain Glyndwr uprising, the castle withstood a long siege by the Welsh.

Location: M4 (Jct 36), A473, A4061 minor roads to Coity village 2 m NE of Bridgend.
Open: Mar 29 to Oct 25, daily 9.30-6.30. Oct 26 to Mar 28, weekdays 9.30-4; Suns 2-4.

LLANCAIACH FAWR

Treharris map F4
Telephone: (0443) 412248
(Rhymney Valley District Council)

Llancaiach Fawr is an award-winning Living History Museum set in this beautifully restored semi-fortified Manor House. Built in the 1530's by the Prichard family the house came to the centre of public interest during the Civil War period when the master of Llancaiach Fawr dramatically changed his allegiance from Royalist to Parliamentarian. Today the house is furnished as it was when King Charles visited in 1645. Costumed stewards, taking on the roles of servants from the gentry household of Colonel Prichard, guide visitors around with fascinating tales of 17th century life. Visitors can try out the furniture, dress in period costume or even take a turn in the stocks! The period gardens have also been recreated whilst an excellent Visitor Centre provides an insight into the history of the house through exhibition and audio visual displays. Other visitor centre facilities include gift shop, restaurant, teaching room. There is disabled access to all Visitor Centre facilites, the garden and ground floor of the house itself. Wales Tourist Board 'Best New Tourist Attraction 1992.' British Tourist Authority 'Come To Britain Special Award Winner 1991.'

Location: Thirty minutes north of Cardiff (M4 Jtn 32) just off the A470 at Nelson on the B4254.
Open: All year except Dec 25, 26, Jan 1. Mon to Fri 10-3.30, Sat and Sun 10-4.30.
Admission: Charged. Ample free car and coach parking.
Refreshments: In Conservatory Cafe. Serves 17th century 'dish of the day' as well as more contemporary cuisine. Period Banquets, Murder Mysteries and 17th Century Evenings in the manor.

SOUTH GLAMORGAN

CARDIFF CASTLE

Cardiff map F4 △
(Cardiff City Council)

Begun 1090 on remains of Roman Fort. Rich interior decorations.
Location: In centre of Cardiff city.
Station(s): Cardiff Centre (½ m).

CASTELL COCH

Tongwynlais, nr Cardiff map F4
(Cadw: Welsh Historic Monuments)

This late 19th century castle - a combination of Victorian Gothic fantasy and timeless fairytale - peeps unexpectedly through the trees on the north hills of Cardiff.
Location: M4 (Junction 32), A470 and signposted.
Open: Mar 29 to Oct 25, daily 9.30-6.30. Oct 26 to Mar 28, weekdays 9.30-4; Suns 2-4.

WEST GLAMORGAN

MARGAM PARK

nr Port Talbot map E4 ⓢ
Telephone: (0639) 881635
Fax: (0639) 895897
(West Glamorgan County Council)

This 850 acre country park has historic buildings including the famous Orangery, a deer herd, one of Europe's largest hedge mazes, and outdoor sculpture park, audio visual theatre, putting, gift shop, and cafeteria plus Fairy Tale Land - a nursery rhyme village for the under 8s. Large coach and car park.

Location: Easy access on A48 ¼ m from Exit 38 off M4 near Port Talbot.
Open: Apr to Sept: daily 10-6 (last adm 4); Oct to Mar: Wed to Sun 10-6 (last adm 3).
Admission: Apr to Sept - entry and use of certain facilities - Adults £3, Chd/OAPs £2, Under 3's free. Special rates for families and pre-booked parties. Adm charge Oct to Mar, Country Park only therefore £2 per car.
Refreshments: Charlotte's Pantry. The magnificent Orangery can be hired. Please telephone for details.

NEATH ABBEY

Neath map E4
(Cadw: Welsh Historic Monuments)

Originally founded as a daughter house of Savigny by Richard de Granville in 1130, the abbey was absorbed into the Cistercian order in 1147.
Location: M4 (Jct 44), A48 (T), A483, A4109, A474 all leading to A465, Neath.
Open: Mar 29 to Oct 25 daily 9.30-6.30. Oct 26 to Mar 28 weekdays 9.30-4; Sun 2-4.

WEOBLEY CASTLE

Weobley map E4
(Cadw: Welsh Historic Monuments)

Picturesque fortified late medieval manor house combining domestic comfort with security.
Location: B4271 or B4295 to Llanrhidian village, then minor road.
Refreshments: Mar 29 to Oct 25 daily 9.30-6.30. Oct 26 to Mar 28 weekdays 9.30-4; Sun 2-4.

GWENT

CAERLEON ROMAN FORTRESS

Caerleon map F4
(Cadw: Welsh Historic Monuments)

Impressive remains of the fortress baths, amphitheatre, barracks and fortress wall. Videos, models, reconstructions, lighting effects and information panels.
Location: B4236 to Caerleon, from M4 (junction 25).
Open: Mar 29 to Oct 25 daily 9.30-6.30. Oct 26 to Mar 28 weekdays 9.30-4; Sun 2-4.

CHEPSTOW CASTLE

Chepstow map G4
(Cadw: Welsh Historic Monuments)

This strategic fortress - one of the earliest stone built castles in Britain - guards one of the main crossings from England to Wales.
Location: Chepstow via A466, B4235, A48 or M4 (Junction 22).
Open: Mar 29 to Oct 25, daily 9.30-6.30. Oct 26 to Mar 28, weekdays 9.30-4; Suns 2-4.

PENHOW CASTLE

Nr Newport map F4 △ Ⓔ Ⓢ
Telephone: (0633) 400800
(Stephen Weeks Esq.,)

Two Sandford Awards. Penhow Castle is Wales' Oldest Lived-in Castle, and was the first home in Britain of the illustrious Seymour family, ancestors of Queen Jane Seymour, King Edward VI and the Dukes of Somerset. This most enchanting Knight's Border Castle has been substantially restored since 1973 by the present owner. Visitors explore the many period rooms guided by the acclaimed 'Time Machine' Walkman Tours included in the admission price. Visitors discover at their own pace the only restored Norman Bedchamber in Wales, the splendid view from atop the Keep Tower's battlements, 15th century Great Hall with its minstrels' gallery, Tudor Moat Room and excavated moat, elegant Charles II panelled Dining Room, 18th century kitchen, cosy Victorian Housekeeper's room and more. The Castle holds several awards for its fine restoration, entertaining Tours and imaginative educational activities. Guests can also stay in the Castle's Dower House adjoining, and sometimes in the Castle itself.

Location: On A48, midway between Chepstow and Newport. M4 junctions 22 or 24.
Open: Good Fri to end of Sept - Weds to Suns inclusive and Bank Holidays; Aug: open daily 10-6 (last adm 5.15). Winter opening: Wed only, 10-5 & selected Sunday afternoons.
Admission: £2.95, Chd £1.65, Family (2+2) £7.55. *Price includes TIME MACHINE Walkman Tour.* Open all year round for group bookings, Evening Candlelit Tours and educational visits. Christmas Candlelit tours Nov 15 - Jan 5.*Special rates on all Tours for groups by arrangement.*
Refreshments: At tour point.
*Accommodation:*at the Castle's Dower House all year round. *Special events:*Evening Candlelit Tours of the Castle may be arranged for groups of 10 or more at any time of year, also Christmas Candlelit Tours with mince pies and hot punch.

RAGLAN CASTLE

Raglan map F5
(Cadw: Welsh Historic Monuments)

This 15th century castle with its Great Tower or 'Yellow Tower of Gwent', was as much a product of social grandeur as it was military necessity.

Location: Via the A40 (between Monmouth and Abergavenny).
Open: Mar 29 to Oct 25, daily 9.30-6.30. Oct 26 to Mar 28, weekdays 9.30-4; Suns 2-4.

TINTERN ABBEY

Tintern map G4
(Cadw: Welsh Historic Monuments)

Impressive ruins of Cistercian abbey, founded in 1131, set in the picturesque Wye valley. Exhibition and self-guided audio-cassette tours.

Location: Tintern via A466 (between Chepstow and Monmouth), from the M4 (Junction 22).
Open: Mar 29 to Oct 25, daily 9.30-6.30. Oct 26 to Mar 28, weekdays 9.30-4; Suns 2-4.

TREDEGAR HOUSE

Newport map F4 △ ♿
Telephone: (0633) 815880
(Newport Borough Council)

One wing of the 16th century house survives, but Tredegar House owes its character to lavish 17th century rebuilding in brick. Ancestral home of the Morgan family, Lords of Tredegar. The 90 acre park includes gardens, lake adventure play farm, carriage rides and craft workshops.
Location: SW of Newport; signposted from M4 junction 28, A48.
Station(s): Newport (2¾ m).
Open: PARK. Daily 6.15-Sunset. HOUSE AND ATTRACTIONS. Good Fri to Sept. Weds to Suns and Public Hols and Tues, school hols and weekends in Oct. House Tours every ½ hour from 11.30-4. House open at other times by appointment.
Admission: House and Walled Gardens: £3.40, Chd/OAPs £2.60, Family £9. Coach and school parties welcome if booked in advance.
Refreshments: Lunch and teas at the Old Brewhouse Bar and Tea Room.

WHITE CASTLE

Llantilio Crossenny map F5
(Cadw: Welsh Historic Monuments)

Imposing moated remains of 12th century castle, probably the work of Henry II.

Location: 6 m E of Abergavenny, off B4233.
Open: Mar 29 to Oct 25 daily 9.30-6.30. Oct 26 to Mar 28 weekdays 9.30-4; Sun 2-4.

GWYNEDD

ABERCONWY HOUSE The National Trust

Conwy map E8
Telephone: (0492) 592246

Town house that dates from 14th century. Furnished rooms and an audio-visual presentation show daily life from different periods in its history.

Location: In the town at junction of Castle Street & High Street.
Station(s): Conwy 300 yds.
Open: Apr 1 to Oct 31 - Daily (except Tues) 11-5.30 (last admission 5);
Admission: £1.80, Chd 90p, Family £4.50, Pre-booked parties £1.60.
Shop.

BEAUMARIS CASTLE (World Heritage Listed Site)

Beaumaris, Anglesey map E8
(Cadw: Welsh Historic Monuments)

The last and largest of the castles built by King Edward I, Beaumaris is the most perfect example of a concentrically planned castle in Britain.

Location: A545 (Menai Bridge), A5 (Bangor).
Open: Mar 29 to Oct 25, daily 9.30-6.30. Oct 26 to Mar 28, weekdays 9.30- 4; Suns 2-4.

BODNANT GARDEN The National Trust

Tal-y-Cafn map E8
Telephone: (0492) 650460

Begun in 1875 by Henry Pochin. Amongst the finest gardens in the country. Magnificent collections of rhododendrons, camellias, magnolias and conifers.

Location: 8 m S of Llandudno & Colwyn Bay on A470; Entrance along Eglwysbach Road.
Station(s): Tal-y-Cafn (1½ m).
Open: Mar 13 to Oct 31 - Daily 10-5 (last adm 4.30).
Admission: £3.30, Chd £1.65, Group £2.90 (for groups over 20 adults) Free car park.
Refreshments: Pavilion in car park.
No dogs (except guide dogs for the blind) Wheelchairs provided but garden is steep and difficult. Braille guide.

BRYN BRAS CASTLE

Llanrug map E8
Telephone: (0286) 870210
(Mr & Mrs N E Gray-Parry)

The Castle, Grade II* listed, was built in c.1830 in the Romanesque style on an earlier structure built before 1750. There are fine examples of stained glass, panelling, interesting ceilings and richly carved furniture in this romantic castle, which was built by a Welshman, and is still a Welsh family home. The extensive and tranquil landscaped gardens of natural beauty, with much wild life, gradually merge into the foothills of Snowdon. They include peaceful lawns, herbaceous borders, roses, walled Knot Garden, stream and pools, woodland walks and a ¼ mile mountain walk with magnificent panoramic views of Snowdon, Anglesey and the sea.

Location: 4½ m E of Caernarfon; 3½ m NW of Llanberis; ½ m off A4086.
Open: Spring Bank Hol to mid-July & Sept - Daily (except Sats) 1-5. Mid-July to end Aug - Daily (except Sats) 10.30-5.
Admission: £2.80, Chd £1.40 (1992 rates). *10% reduction for parties.* Free car park. No dogs.
Refreshments: Home made Welsh teas (including Bara Brith) in charming tea room & the tea garden. Picnic area.
Castle Apartments for holidays available all year.

CAERNARFON CASTLE (World Heritage Listed Site)

Caernarfon map D7
(Cadw: Welsh Historic Monuments)

This mighty medieval fortress, built by King Edward I was planned as both a royal residence and seat of government for North Wales. The castle earned itself a place in modern history on July 1, 1969 as the setting for the Investiture of HRH Prince Charles as Prince of Wales. Exhibitions, audio-visual programme and Royal Welsh Fusiliers Regimental Museum.

Location: A4085, A487(T), A4086 and B4366.
Open: Mar 29 to Oct 25, daily 9.30-6.30. Oct 26 to Mar 28, weekdays 9.30- 4; Suns 2-4.

COCHWILLAN OLD HALL

Talybont, Bangor map E8
Telephone: (0248) 364608
(R. C. H. Douglas Pennant, Esq)

Fine example of medieval architecture (restored 1971).

Location: 3½ m Bangor; 1 m Talybont village off A55.
Open: Open by appointment.

CONWY CASTLE (World Heritage Listed Site)

Conwy map E8
(Cadw: Welsh Historic Monuments)

Imposing fortress built between 1283 and 1289. Conwy castle remains a masterpiece of medieval architecture. Exhibition and scale model of castle and town.

Location: Conwy via A55 or B5106.
Open: Mar 29 to Oct 25, daily 9.30-6.30. Oct 26 to Mar 28, weekdays 9.30- 4; Suns 2-4.

CRICCIETH CASTLE

Criccieth map D7
(Cadw: Welsh Historic Monuments)

Perched in a commanding position above Tremadog Bay, the castle was established in around 1230 by the Welsh prince Llywelyn the Great. Two exhibitions.

Location: A497 to Criccieth from Porthmadog or from Pwllheli.
Open: Mar 29 to Oct 25, daily 9.30-6.30. Oct 26 to Mar 28, weekdays 9.30- 4; Suns 2-4.

CYMER ABBEY

Cymer map E7
(Cadw: Welsh Historic Monuments)

Substantial remains of Cistercian abbey founded in a peaceful and remote spot at the head of the Mawddach estuary in 1199.

Location: 2 m N of Dolgellau off A494.
Open: Mar 29 to Oct 25 daily 9.30-6.30. Oct 25 to Mar 28 weekdays 9.30-4; Sun 2-4.

GWYDIR UCHAF CHAPEL

Llanrwst map E7
(Cadw: Welsh Historic Monuments)

A 17th century chapel with elaborately painted ceilings and walls.

Location: On Forestry Commission land ½ m SW of Llanrwst. B5106, then minor road, then forest road.
Open: Mar 29 to Oct 25 daily 9.30-6.30. Oct 26 to Mar 28 weekdays 9.30-4; Sun 2-4.

HARLECH CASTLE (World Heritage Listed Site)

Harlech map D7
(Cadw: Welsh Historic Monuments)

The powerful walls and towers of this magnificent castle were built by King Edward I, during his conquest of Wales in 1283 and were mainly complete by 1289.

Location: A496 from Blaenau Ffestiniog or from Barmouth.
Open: Mar 29 to Oct 25, daily 9.30-6.30. Oct 26 to Mar 28, weekdays 9.30- 4; Suns 2-4.

PENRHYN CASTLE   The National Trust

Bangor map E8 ©
Telephone: (0248) 353084

The 19th century Castle is a unique and outstanding example of neo-Norman architecture. The garden and grounds have exotic and rare trees and shrubs. There is an Industrial Railway Museum. Victorian formal garden. Superb views of mountains and Menai Strait.

Location: 1 m E of Bangor, on A5122.
Station(s): Bangor (3 m).
Open: Apr 1 to Oct 31 - Daily except Tues. Castle: Daily except Tues 12-5, July & Aug 11-5. Last adm 4.30.(last audio tour 4). Grounds: 11-6.
Admission: £4.20, Chd £2.10, Family £10.50. Group £3.40. Grounds only: £2, Chd £1.
Refreshments: Light lunches & teas at Castle.

PLAS BRONDANW GARDENS

Nr Penrhyndeudraeth map E7
Telephone: (0766) 771136

Created by Sir Clough Williams-Ellis, architect of Portmeirion, below his ancestral home. Italian inspired gardens with spectacular mountain views, topiary and folly tower.

Location: 2 m N of Penrhyndeudraeth. ¼ m off the A4085 on Croesor Road.
Open: Open all year, daily 9-5.
Admission: £1.50, Chd 25p.

PLAS MAWR

Conwy map E8
(Royal Cambrian Academy of Art)

PLAS NEWYDD   The National Trust

Isle of Anglesey map D8
Telephone: Llanfairpwll (0248) 714795

18th century house by James Wyatt in unspoilt position adjacent to Menai Strait. Magnificent views to Snowdonia. Fine spring garden. Rex Whistler exhibition and mural painting. Military museum.

Location: 1 m SW of Llanfairpwll on A4080 to Brynsiencyn; turn off A5 to Llanfairpwll at W end of Britannia Bridge.
Station(s): Llanfairpwll (1¾ m).
Open: Apr 1 to Sept 26 - Daily except Sats 12-5. Garden 11-5 in July and Aug, daily except Sat. Oct 1 to 31 - Fri and Sun only 12-5. Last adm 4.30.
Admission: £3.50, Chd £1.75, Family £8.80. Groups £2.80.
Refreshments: Tea rooms (light lunches & teas).

TŶ MAWR WYBRNANT   The National Trust

nr. Penmachno map E7
Telephone: (069 03) 213

The birthplace of Bishop William Morgan. (c. 1545-1604), the first translator of the Bible into Welsh.

Location: At the head of the little valley of Wybrnant, 3½ m SW of Betws-y-Coed; 2 m W of Penmachno.
Open: Apr 1 to Sept 26 - Weds, Thurs, Frid, Suns 12-5. Oct 1 to 31: Fri and Sun 12-4. Last adm 30 mins before closing. Open Bank Hol Mons.
Admission: £1.30, Chd 65p, Family £3.20, Group £1.10.

POWYS

GREGYNOG

Newtown map F6
Telephone: (0686) 650224
(The University of Wales)

A Victorian mansion, in 750 acres of wooded parkland with extensive gardens, including one of the most striking displays of rhododendrons in Wales; the Western red cedar 'Zebrina' is probably the biggest tree of this variety in the U.K. Many walks in the grounds. The Hall has an exceptionally fine carved parlour of 1636, retained when the old hall was rebuilt in the 1840s. The works of art still remaining from the collections of the Davies sisters include two Rodin bronzes. On show also are books by the Gregynog Press, one of the best-known private presses of the 1920s and 30s, and by the present Gwasg Gregynog, where fine printing is still carried on. This is a working Press and visitors can only be accepted occasionally by prior appointment. Accommodation is sometimes available in the Hall, depending on the nature and size of the resident conference. Since 1963, The Hall has operated as an intercollegiate course and conference centre for the various colleges and institutions of the University of Wales. During the last week in June, an important annual Music Festival is held here.

Location: Near the village of Tregynon, 5 m N of Newtown, off B4389.
Open: Gardens always open. Hall: Jun 1-Sept 30, Mon to Sat. Guided tours only at 11 and 3. Hall and Gardens may very exceptionally have to be closed for a day.
Admission: £2 - Guided tour to include morning coffee or afternoon tea. Chd (under 15) half-price. Parties by arrangement. Free car parking.
Suitable for disabled persons (no wheelchairs provided).

POWIS CASTLE  The National Trust

Welshpool map F6   &
Telephone: (0938) 554336

The medieval stronghold of the Welsh princes of Upper Powys, the home of the Herbert family since 1587. Clive of India Museum. Fine plaster work, murals, furniture, paintings and tapestry. Historic terraced garden; herbaceous borders, rare trees and shrubs.

Location: 1 m S of Welshpool on A483; Pedestrian access from High Street (A490); Cars enter road to Newtown (A483); 1 m.
Station(s): Welshpool (1¼ m); Welshpool Raven Square (1¼ m); BR service Aug only.
Open: Apr 1 to end of June and Sept to Oct 31: daily except Mons and Tues. July and Aug: daily except Mons (But open Bank Hol Mons). Castle: 12-5. Museum & Garden 11-6. Last adm 30 mins prior to closing.
Admission: All-in: £5.80, Chd £2.90, Group £5.40. Museum/Garden: £3.60, Chd £1.80, Family £9, Group £2.80.
Refreshments: Tea rooms (light lunches & teas).

TRETOWER COURT & CASTLE

Crickhowell map F5
(Cadw: Welsh Historic Monuments)

One of the finest medieval houses in Wales. The castle is located across an open meadow to the rear. Audio-cassette tour and 'medieval' garden.

Location: 3 m NW Crickhowell off A479, and A470.
Open: Mar 29 to Oct 25 daily 9.30-6.30. Oct 26 to Mar 28 weekdays 9.30-4; Sun 2-4.

IRELAND

ANNES GROVE GARDENS

Castletownroche map (i)X
Telephone: (022) 26145
(Mr and Mrs Patrick Grove Annesley)

Extensive Robinsonian woodland and riverside gardens with notable collection of rhododendrons and other exotica. Edwardian flower garden.

AYESHA CASTLE

Killiney, Co. Dublin map (iii)Z
(Mr & Mrs Aylmer)

A romantic 19th century Victorian Castle of ashlar with a round tower and various turrets affording the finest views of Killiney Bay and Sugar Loaf. Built in 1840 by Robert Warren who named it Victoria Castle, commemorating Queen Victoria's accession to the throne. The Castle was damaged by fire in 1924, purchased in 1928 by Sir Thomas Power who restored and renamed it 'Ayesha' after the goddess in Ryder Haggard's Book 'She' - purchased by Colonel Aylmer in 1947 and has remained in that family to present day. Notable features include the fine oak panelling in the entrance hall and dining room coupled with the magnificent oak spiral staircase. Ayesha is situated in 4½ acres of garden and woodland containing most unusual and exotic plants, flowers and shrubs. Exhibitions include family lace (English and Irish), Military Exhibition and Historical/Pictorial Record of Killiney/Dalkey and its environs.

BANTRY HOUSE

Bantry, Co. Cork map (i)X
Telephone: (027) 50047
(Mr & Mrs Egerton Shelswell-White)

Partly-Georgian mansion standing at edge of Bantry Bay, with beautiful views. Seat of family of White, formerly Earls of Bantry. Unique collection of tapestries, furniture etc. Terraces and Statuary in the Italian style in grounds.

Location: In outskirts of Bantry (½ m); 56 m SW of Cork.
Open: Open all year-Daily 9-6 *(open until 8 on most summer evenings).*
Admission: House & Grounds £2.50, Chd (up to 14) accompanied by parents, free, OAPs/Students £1.50. Parties (20 or more) £2.
Refreshments: Tea room. Bed and Breakfast.
Craft shop.

BIRR CASTLE DEMESNE

Co. Offaly map (iii)Y
Telephone: (509) 20056

Over 100 acres of gardens, rivers with waterfalls, lake and lake walks, terraces and parkland, scenically laid out and planted with most important collection of plants, many introduced directly from the wild. The Park contains the nineteenth century's largest telescope. Facilities include exhibition gallery, educationally explained tree trail, picnic and play area, coffee shop, tourist office and Bureau de Change.

Open: Jan to Mar and Nov to Dec: Daily 9-1 and 2-5. Apr to Oct: Daily 9-6 (or dusk when earlier). *Expo 93:* Sugar and Spice, featuring castle cooking over the last three centuries, open May 1 to Sept 30, 2.30-5.30.
Admission: Jan to Mar and Nov to Dec: £2, chd £1. Apr to Oct: £3, chd £1.50; group rate £2, chd £1. *Expo 93: No extra charge.*
Refreshments: Morning coffee, lunch, afternoon tea from St. Patrick's Day to Oct.

Irish Heritage Properties

Historic Irish Tourist Houses & Gardens Association Ltd. (H.I.T.H.A.)
Under the auspices of Bord Failte (Irish Tourist Board) to promote
Houses, Castles and Gardens open to the public
3a Castle Street, Dalkey, Co. Dublin.   Tel: 2859323
More than 50 properties in Ireland including those listed on these pages.

 BIRR CASTLE

 MALAHIDE

 DUNKATHEL

 MOUNT USHER GARDENS

 JAPANESE GARDENS

 NEWBRIDGE HOUSE

 LISMORE

 POWERSCOURT GARDENS

BLARNEY CASTLE AND BLARNEY HOUSE

Blarney, Co. Cork map (i)X   &
(Sir Richard Colthurst, Bart)

Blarney Castle and Rock Close. Situated 5 miles from Cork City, the Castle is famous for its Stone which has the traditional power of conferring eloquence on all who kiss it. The word 'Blarney' has found its way into the English language and has been described as conferring upon anyone who kisses it 'a cajoling tongue and the art of flattery, or of telling lies with unblushing effrontery'. The battlements crowning the fine intact keep are typically Irish in form and set in the walls below the battlements is the Stone. To kiss it one has to lean backwards out from the parapet walk. Adjacent to the Castle is the Rock Close, said to have Druidic connections and containing the gardens laid out by the Jefferies family in 1759 and now containing many old specimens and much new planting of shrubs, trees and beds, amongst the fine old limestone rocks scattered in 25 acres. **Blarney House & Gardens:** 200 yards from the Castle is Blarney House and Gardens, a fine Scottish Baronial type house, with distinguished corner turrets and bartizans with conical roofs and now restored inside with fine rooms and stairwell. Outside, the formal gardens and fine view of Blarney Lake together with the walk down to it and between the House and the Castle a large area of new planting, with shrubs, trees, beds and walks.

Location: 7 m from Cork City. 9 m from Cork Airport; 9 m from Ringaskiddy Port.
Open: Blarney Castle & Rock Close: Mon to Sat, May, 9-6. June, July, Aug 9-7; Sept 9-6; Oct to Apr 9-5 (or sunset). Sun, Summer 9.30-5.30. Winter 9.30-5.30 (or sunset). **Blarney House & Gardens:** June-mid Sept Mons to Sat only 12-6. (Last adm 30 mins before stated closing times.)
Admission: Blarney Castle and Rock Close: IR £3, Chd IR £1, OAPs/Students IR £2. **Blarney House & Gardens:** IR £2.50, Chd IR £1, OAPs/Students IR £2.
Refreshments: Sweet and soft drink kiosk; three hotels, three public houses; tea houses. Car and coach parking.

BUNRATTY CASTLE & FOLK PARK

Bunratty, Co. Clare map (ii)X
(Shannon Free Airport Development Company)

Bunratty Castle, built in 1469, is the most complete and authentic example of a Medieval Castle in Ireland. Its furniture, tapestries and works of art are displayed to give the visitor an idea of the furnishings and arrangement of a Castle of the late 16th or early 17th century. The Folk Park, in the grounds of the Castle, contains typical rural dwellings recreated and furnished to reflect life in Ireland at the turn of the century. The Park also features the complete reconstruction of a 19th century Irish village street, including craft shops, post office and general stores. **Bunratty House** (1805) has also been restored and furnished.

CARRIGGLAS MANOR

Longford map (iv)Y
Telephone: (043) 45165
Fax: (043) 45875
(Mr & Mrs Lefroy)

Tudor Gothic Revival House with beautifully furnished interiors. Fine Georgian stableyard by James Gandon with costume museum. Tea room & shop. Woodland Garden.

Location: 3 m from Longford on T15/R194 Ballinalee/Granard Road. 2 m N of main N4 Route on signed turn-off avoiding Longford Town congestion.
Open: House, Stableyard, Costume Museum, Tea Room & Shop. June 5 to Sept 5, daily except Tues & Weds 12.30-5pm (Aug 6pm). Pre-booked parties at other times by arrangement. Hourly House Tours - Last Tour 4pm (Aug 5pm).
Admission: IR £3, Chd IR £2, Adult Group rate IR £2, Chd Group rate IR £1.
Refreshments: Tea room, light lunches & afternoon teas. Hotels, pubs etc. in Longford (3m). Dinner, Bed & Breakfast available. Pre-booking absolutely essential. Self catering apartments in Gandon Stableyard. For all details contact Mrs Lefroy: Tel. Longford (043) 45165. International code (010 353 43) 45165. Fax: 043 45875.

CASTLETOWN HOUSE

Celbridge, Co. Kildaire map (iii)Z
Telephone: (01) 628 8252
(Castletown Foundation)

Begun c.1722, Ireland's largest and finest Georgian country house.

Location: 12 m W of Dublin. Bus 67/67A to the gates.
Open: Open throughout the year. Summer every day, winter Suns and Bank Hols. Telephone for times.
Refreshments: Coffee shop and West Wing restaurant.

CLOGHAN CASTLE

Banagher, Co Offaly, Ireland
Telephone: (0509) 51650
Brian and Elyse Thompson

One of the oldest inhabited castles in Ireland (circa 1180 with later editions) lovely contents. Superb parkland settings grazed by Jacob Sheep in a 42,000 winter bird sanctuary.

Location: 8m west of Burr Castle, 3m south of Banagher near the Shannon River.
Open: Daily from 2-6.00pm except Mondays and Tuesdays, June, July, August, September (and other times by appointment).
Admission: Adults £3.00, children £1.50, OAPs £2.00.
Refreshments: Teas also available.

CLONALIS HOUSE

Castlerea, Co. Roscommon map (iv)X
Telephone: (0907) 20014

Clonalis is the ancestral home of the O'Conor's of Connaught, descendants of the last High Kings of Ireland and traditional kings of Connaught. The Gaelic history of the family is recorded through the collection of archives, documentation and portraits in the house.

CRAGGAUNOWEN - THE LIVING PAST

Kilmurry, Sixmilebridge, Co. Clare map (ii)X
(The Hunt Museums Trust)

The Craggaunowen project is pleasantly situated in the wooded farmland of County Clare. The site consists of a mediaeval Tower House containing a display of furniture and art objects, including some rare Irish pieces. There are two iron-age dwellings - a lake dwelling and a ring fort - and the leather boat 'Brendan' sailed by Tim Severin from Ireland to Newfoundland. In the summer months displays and experiments are conducted on the techniques associated with milling, pottery making and weaving in the iron age.

Location: 6 km E of Quin, 9 km N of Sixmilebridge. 24 km NW of Limerick.

CRATLOE WOODS HOUSE

Cratloe, Co. Clare map (ii)X
Telephone: (061) 327028.
Fax: (061) 327031
(Mr & Mrs J.G. Brickenden)

One of the few roofed examples of an Irish Longhouse, this is a home of special architectural and historical interest. Displays of antiquities, decorative arts, memorabilia and period farm machinery. Guided tours, farm animals and rare breeds, craft shop.

DUNGUAIRE CASTLE

Kinvara, Co. Galway map (iii)X

Dunguaire was the stronghold of Guaire, King of Connaught in the 7th century. The 15th century Dunguaire Castle, now beautifully restored overlooks Galway Bay and gives an insight into the lifestyles of those that lived there. Dunguaire features mediaeval banquets nightly, May to September.

DUNKATHEL

Dunkathel, Glanmire map (x)I
Telephone: (021) 821014

DUNKATHEL is a fine example of late Georgian architecture in the style of Davis Ducart. Situated 3 m to the East of Cork City, it commands an outstanding situation overlooking Lough Mahon, with far-reaching views to Passage West and Blackrock Castle. It is easily acessible from both main Cork/Dublin and Cork/Waterford roads. The house's well-proportioned rooms have simple friezes and centrepieces, and there are fine Adam fireplaces in the front Drawing Room and Dining Room. The focal point of the house is its magnificent staircase built of Bath stone with graceful balustrades. The front hall keeps its early 19th century Italian painted decoration, representing marble, and the ceiling is painted as a blue sky with clouds.

Location: 3 m E of Cork.
Open: May 1 to Oct 15. Wed - Sun 2-6.
Refreshments: By arrangement.

DUNLOE CASTLE HOTEL GARDENS

Beaufort, Killarney, Co. Kerry map (i)W
Telephone: (064) 44111 or (064) 31900
Fax: (064) 44583

The gardens at Dunloe Castle contain an extensive and interesting collection of plants, several of which are rarely, if at all, found elsewhere in Ireland. Each season brings its own specialities, camelias and rhododendron in spring, magnolias and sun roses in summer, Irish heaths and richly tinted leaves in autumn, are just a few of the many attractions. This combination of wild grandeur and garden exotica is situated in a setting of incomparable views of mountains and lakes.

Location: Situated adjacent to the Deluxe 140 bedroomed Hotel Dunloe Castle, off the main Killarney/Killorglin road, on the route to the Gap of Dunloe, approximately 8 km from Killarney.
Open: May 1 to end Sept.
Admission: Free. Catalogue of plants and trees available at hotel reception for £1.
Refreshments: Available at Hotel Dunloe Castle.

EMO COURT

Portlaoise, Co. Leix map (iii)Y
Telephone: (0502) 26110
(C.D. Cholmeley-Harrison)

Outstanding neo-classical house by James Gandon completed in 1792. Extensive gardens containing a wealth of specimen trees & flowering shrubs, spectacular in spring and autumn.

FERNHILL GARDEN

Sandyford map (iii)Z
Telephone: (01) 956000
(Mrs Sally Walker)

A Garden for all seasons, 200 years old in Robinsonian style with over 4,000 species and varieties of trees, shrubs and plants. Dogs not allowed.

FOTA

Fota Island, Carrigtwohill, Co. Cork map (i)Y
(Richard Wood)

Regency mansion with fine neo-classical and French Revival rooms, contains an important collection of Irish period landscapes. Furnished with Irish 18th and 19th century pieces. Also world famous arboretum and 70 acre wildlife park. **European Museum of the Year Award Winner.**

GLIN CASTLE

Glin map (ii)X
Telephone: (068) 34173/34112
Fax: (068) 34364
(The Knight of Glin and Madam Fitz-Gerald)

A Georgian Gothic castle with a series of battlemented folly lodges on lands held by the Knights of Glin for over 700 years. The interiors possess elaborate neo-classical plaster ceilings, a flying grand staircase and a notable collection of 18th century Irish mahogany furniture, family portraits and Irish landscapes. Formal gardens.

GPA-BOLTON LIBRARY

John St, Cashel, Co. Tipperary map (ii)Y
Telephone: (062) 61944
(The Very Revd the Dean of Cashel, Custodian)

Founded by Archbishop Theophilus Bolton in 1744, his Library of 12,000 titles is today housed in an early 19th century building, situated beside the small Georgian Cathedral. This was recently extensively renovated due to the generosity of the Irish aircraft leasing firm, Guinness Peat Aviation. The collection covers printed books from 1473, and includes examples from the houses of Caxton and Pynson (London); and from the great continental houses of Koberger, Froschover, Estienne (Stephanus), Aldus, Plantin, Elzevir and others. There are many very rare books, some 800 not recorded elsewhere in Ireland and about 50 believed to be unique to Cashel. A selection from these can be seen daily, in two displays. One is representative of the whole collection, the other covers a special topic. These are announced in the press, and include Mathematics, Eastern Europe, Medicine, Rare Books, Conservation, and Bindings. Authors include Berkeley, Swift, Euclid, Archimedes, the writers of Greek and Latin antiquity, Drayton, Trussel, Sidney, Burton, More, Raleigh, Donne, Milton, Dante, Cervantes, and Macchiavelli. There is also a small but fine collection of Silver on display, dating from 16th century to 19th century. A genealogical service is available on request.

Location: The Library is 300 yards up John Street, immediately opposite the Cashel Palace Hotel.
Open: Sat 9.30-5.30, Sun 2.30-5.30 - March-October inclusive (excepting Good Friday) (Closed Nov,Dec,Jan,Feb)
Admission: £1, OAPs/Students 70p, chd 50p. Group rates on application. Groups and students welcome.
Ample parking. (*G - *E)

JAPANESE GARDENS

Tully map (iii)Y
Telephone: (045) 21617
(Irish National Stud)

Created between 1906-1910, the Japanese Gardens symbolise the Life of Man from the Cave of Birth to the Gateway to Eternity. Special features include the Tea House, Bridge of Life and some very old bonsai trees.

Location: Co. Kildare 1 m from Kildare Town and 5 m from Newbridge.
Open: Easter to Oct 31 - Mon to Fri 10-5, Suns 2-6, Sat and Bank Holidays 10-6.
Admission: £2.50, Students/OAPs £2, Chd £1.50, Family (2 adults and 2 chd under 12) £6.
Refreshments: Tea, coffee, soup, salads, sandwiches etc. Groups can be catered for with some notice.
Unsuitable for the disabled. Entrance to The Irish National Stud is at the same gate. (Suitable for disabled).

JOHNSTOWN CASTLE DEMESNE

Wexford map (ii)Z △
Teagasc (Soils and Environment Centre)

Grounds and gardens only. 50 acres of well laid out grounds, with artificial lakes and fine collection of ornamental trees and shrubs. Agricultural museum.

Location: 5 m SW of Wexford.
Open: All the year - Daily 9-5. Guidebook available at Castle. Although the grounds will continue to be open throughout the year, an adm charge will apply only from May 1 to Oct 4 1993.
Admission: Car (and passengers) £2.50; coach (large) £16, coach (small) £8. Adults (pedestrians/cyclists) 60p. Wedding parties for photography £16.
Refreshments: Coffee shop during July & Aug at museum.

THE JAMES JOYCE TOWER

Sandycove map (iii)Z
Telephone: (01) 2809265/2808571
(Dublin Tourism)

KNAPPOGUE CASTLE

Quin, Co. Clare map (ii)X
Telephone: (061) 71103
(Mr and Mrs M E Andrews)

Knappogue Castle is one of the forty-two Castles built by the great McNamara Tribe which ruled over the territory of Clancullen from the 5th to the mid-15th centuries. The Castle has undergone extensive restoration work with its furnishings giving an authentic 15th century atmosphere. Craftshop.

KYLEMORE ABBEY

Kylemore, Connemara map (iii)W
Telephone: (095) 41146, or shops (095) 41113.
Fax: (095) 41123.

The only home of the Benedictine Nuns in Ireland. The Castle was acquired by the Nuns in 1920, and a precious heirloom was preserved, both for and on behalf of the people of Ireland, and visitors from all over the world. Built by Mr Mitchell Henry, MP for County Galway, and a native of Manchester. The Abbey is set amidst the lakes and mountains of Connemara in an area of outstanding beauty.

LISMORE CASTLE

Lismore, Co. Waterford map (i)Y
Telephone: (058) 54424
(Trustees of the Lismore Estates)

Beautifully situated walled and woodland gardens, containing a fine collection of camellias, magnolias and other shrubs. There is a remarkable yew walk.

Location: In town of Lismore; 45 m W of Waterford; 35 m NE of Cork.
Open: GARDENS ONLY. May 10 to Sept 10 - Daily (except Sats) 1.45-4.45.
Admission: £2, Chd (under 16) £1. Reduced rates for parties.

LISSADELL

Sligo map (iv)X
(Josslyn Gore-Booth, Esq)

The finest Greek-revival country house in Ireland. Splendid views of the surrounding countryside. The home of Countess Markiewicz.

Location: 8 m NW of Sligo overlooking Sligo Bay.
Open: June 1 mid-Sept - Weekdays 10.30-12.15, 2-4.15. *Closed Suns.*
Admission: £2, Chd 50p.

LOUGH GUR VISITOR CENTRE

Lough Gur map (ii)X

Lough Gur Visitor Centre is modelled on Neolithic circular and rectangular houses and illustrates the story of man and his landscape through audio-visuals, artifacts and replicas of materials found in this historic place.

LOUGH RYNN ESTATE & GARDENS

Mohill, Co. Leitrim map (iv)Y

Formerly the home of the Earls of Leitrim, Lough Rynn makes for a wonderful stopping off point when travelling to or from the North West. Terraced 19th century gardens, extensive walks and nature trails, interesting Victorian rock garden and fernery, many 19th century buildings, castle ruins from 17th century, dolmen and crannog site. Craft shop, picnic area, plant sales, guided tours.

Open: May 1 to Sept 1, 10-7.
Admission: £1.25, Chd 75p, Group rates on request.
Refreshments: Full restaurant facilities, fast food.

MALAHIDE CASTLE

Malahide map (iii)Z
Telephone: 452655/452371
(Ann Chambers, Administrator)

One of Ireland's oldest and most historic castles containing a unique collection of Irish period furniture and Irish historical portraits, most of which are on permanent loan from the National Gallery of Ireland. In the adjacent gardens there are in excess of 5000 species and varieties of shrubs.

Location: 8 m from centre of Dublin.
Open: Jan to Dec: Mon to Fri 10-5; Nov to Mar: Sat, Sun and Public Holidays 2-5; Apr to Oct: Sat 11-6, Sun and Public Holidays 2-6. Closed for tours 12.45-2 weekdays.
Admission: £2.50, OAPs/Students (12-17 yrs) £1.90, chd (3-11 yrs) £1.25. Family ticket (2 adults, 3/4 chd) £7.50. Group rates: £2.15, OAPs/Students (12-17 yrs) £1.70, Chd £1.15.
Refreshments: Restaurant.

MOUNT USHER GARDENS

Ashford map (iii)Z
Telephone: (0404) 40205/40116
(Mrs Madelaine Jay)

The Gardens (20 acres) extend along the Vartry river in beautiful County Wicklow. They are laid out in the informal 'Robinsonian' style comprising rare plants, shrubs and trees, collected from many parts of the world.

Location: Ashford, 1 m from Wicklow on Dublin-Bray-Wexford Road.
Open: Mar 17 to Oct 31, open daily including Suns and Bank Holidays 10.30-6.
Admission: IR £2.20, OAPs/Students/Chd IR £1.50. Groups (20 +) IR £1.70, OAPs/Students/Chd IR £1.20.
Refreshments: Tea room at entrance, snacks, light lunches.
Car parking. Suitable for disabled. No wheelchairs provided. Shopping courtyard.

MUCKROSS HOUSE AND GARDENS

Killarney, Co. Kerry map (i)X
Telephone: (064) 31440
Fax: (064) 33926

Muckross House is a 19th century manor house, beautifully situated close to Muckross Lake, second largest of Killarney's three lakes. The house has many items of historic interest including locally carved period furniture, prints, maps and items which illustrate a traditional way of life of the people of Kerry. Skilled craftworkers at Muckross House carry on some of the traditional crafts of Kerry as their predecessors did in bygone days. The gardens, informal in design, are noted for their fine collection of rhododendrons and azaleas, extensive water gardens and an outstanding rock garden on natural limestone. New in 1992 a 70 acre outdoor portrayal of rural life in Kerry in the 1930's complete with working period farms and crafts.

Location: 6 km (3½ m) from Killarney on the Kenmare road.
Open: Daily all year. 9-5.30pm. During July and Aug 9-7pm.
Admission: IR £2.50, Chd IR £1, group rates for 20 plus IR £1.75, Family ticket IR £6. Free adm to gardens. Free car park, suitable for buses.
Refreshments: Restaurant located in the old coach-house, serving teas, coffees, soup, sandwiches, pastries, hot and cold lunches. Wine licence.

NATIONAL BOTANIC GARDENS

Glasnevin, Dublin 9 map (iii)Z
(Office of Public Works)

Founded 1795. 47 acres in extent containing 25,000 different living plant species and varieties. Flowering shrubs. Dwarf conifers. Orchids. Herbarium, 500,000 specimens.

Location: 2 m from city centre.
Open: All the year - Daily (except Christmas Day); Weekdays 9-6 (summer); 10-4.30 (winter). Sundays 11-6 (summer); 11-4.30 (winter). Conservatories. Mons to Fris 9-12.45, 2.15-5 (summer); 10-12.45, 2.15-4.15 (winter). Sats 9-12.15, 2.15-5.45 (summer); 10-12.15, 2.15-4.15 (winter). Suns 2-5.45 (summer); 2-4.15 (winter).
Admission: Free.

NEWBRIDGE HOUSE

Donabate map (iii)Z
Telephone: (1) 436534/5
(Ann Chambers, Administrator)

Newbridge House is an 18th century mansion in its own magnificent parkland of 300 acres. The Great Drawing room, in its original state, is one of the finest Georgian interiors in Ireland. Kitchen and laundry capture the 'below stairs' atmosphere of the big house, and the courtyard, with its coach house and various workshops, connect the past with the present.

Location: 12 m from the centre of Dublin.
Open: Apr to Oct - Tues-Fri 10-5. Sats 11-6. Suns & Bank Holidays 2-6. *Closed* for lunch weekdays 1-2, restaurant remains open. Nov to Mar - Sat, Suns & Bank Holidays 2-5. Open on request outside these hours for groups of 20 or more. Traditional farm open during above hours.
Admission: £2.25, OAPs/Students £1.90, Chd £1.20, Family ticket £6.50 (2 adults & 3/4 Chd); Parties £2, OAPs/Students £1.70, Chd £1.10.
Refreshments: Coffee Shop serving teas, coffees, cakes, sandwiches.
Bus and public car parks. Unsuitable for the disabled.

POWERSCOURT GARDENS & WATERFALL

Enniskerry, Co. Wicklow map (iii)Z
Telephone: (1) 2867676/7/8
Fax: (1) 2863561

Powerscourt is owned by the Slazenger family and has been welcoming visitors for more than 50 years. Powerscourt is a magnificent example of an aristocratic garden laid out with taste and imagination. The breathtaking location nestling under the Great Sugar Loaf, the beauty of its Italian and Japanese Gardens, the splendid statuary and the incomparable iron work make it a fairytale demesne. The Waterfall is 398 feet high, which makes it the highest in Ireland. Restaurant, souvenir gift and craft shop and children's play areas, garden centre and house-plant shop.

Location: ¼ mile Enniskerry, 12 miles S of Dublin.
Open: Gardens: Mar 1 to Oct 31 - Daily 9.30-5.30. Garden Centre open all year. Waterfall open all year 9.30-7. 10.30 to dusk in winter. Guided tours for specialist groups on request.
Admission: Gardens: £2.50, Student/OAPs £2, Chd £1; Waterfall £1.50, Student/OAPs £1, Chd 80p. Group reductions, season tickets.
Refreshments: Gardens: small restaurant (50 people) serving lunches, teas etc. Waterfall: Teas, light lunches available in high season.
Wheelchair available.

POWERSCOURT TOWNHOUSE CENTRE

59 South William Street, Dublin 2 map (iii)Z
Telephone: (1) 687477

Built in 1771 for Richard Wingfield - Third Viscount Lord Powerscourt. Designed by Robert Mack and contains fine plasterwork by James McCullagh and Michael Stapleton.

Location: 59 South William Street, Dublin 2.
Open: Open daily 9.30-5.30. *Closed* Bank Holidays. Wheelchair access to three floors.
Admission: Free.

THE ROYAL HOSPITAL KILMAINHAM/THE IRISH MUSEUM OF MODERN ART

Kilmainham map (iii)Z
Telephone: (01) 718666
Fax: (01) 718695

Founded in 1680 by the Duke of Ormond as a hospice for pensioner soldiers, the Royal Hospital Kilmainham is the earliest surviving public building in the country. Now the new Irish Museum of Modern Art, it comprises an important collection of Irish and international art.

RUSSBOROUGH

Blessington, Co. Wicklow map (iii)Z
Telephone: (045) 65239
(Alfred Beit Foundation)

Palladian house in romantic setting in the Wicklow mountains, built 1740-50 and housing the Beit Art Collection.

SLANE CASTLE

Slane map (iv)Z
Telephone: (041) 24207
Fax: (041) 24401
(The Earl of Mount Charles)

Dramatic 18th century Castle on river Boyne, featuring work of James Wyatt, Francis Johnston, James Gandon and Capability Brown, with fine pictures and furniture.

STROKESTOWN PARK HOUSE

Strokestown, Co. Roscommon map (iii)X
Telephone: (078) 33013

Ancestral home of the Pakenham Mahon family from 1660s to 1979. The house, built in the Palladian style, is complete with its original contents and has fine examples of 17th, 18th and 19th century interiors including extensive staff quarters. Incorporated into the tour is a display of documents relating to the Great Famine of the 1840s.

THOOR BALLYLEE

Gort map (iii)X
Telephone: (091) 31436

16th Century Norman Tower with thatched cottage attached. Summer home of W.B. Yeats for 12 years 1917-1929. Location of inspiration of the 'Tower' and 'Winding Stair' poems.

Location: 4 m from Gort Town. 1 m from N18 Galway/Gort road. 1 m from N66 Gort/Loughrea road.
Open: Open daily Apr-Sept 10-6. Large car park suitable for buses. Unsuitable for the disabled. Audio visual presentation on Yeats and the Tower. Bookshop specialising in Anglo-Irish literature. Gift shop.
Refreshments: Tea room in cottages attached to Tower supplying tea, coffee, soup, sandwiches, cakes, pastries, biscuits etc. Ample toilet facilities.

TIMOLEAGUE CASTLE GARDENS

Bandon map (i)X
Telephone: (023) 46116 or (021) 831512
(Mr N.R.E. Travers)

Seven acres of old fashioned gardens in a beautiful and historic setting. Palm trees and other frost-tender shrubs flourish in the mild climate of this beautiful part of West Cork.

Location: Adjoining Timoleague village, Bandon 8 m.
Open: GARDEN ONLY Easter Weekend, then daily mid May to mid Sept 12-6.
Admission: IR £2, Chd IR £1.
Refreshments: At local hotels.
Parties by arrangement. Car park. Suitable for the disabled.

TULLYNALLY CASTLE

Castlepollard, Co. Westmeath map (iii)Y
Telephone: (044) 61159 or (044) 61289

Home of the Pakenhams (later Earls of Longford) since the 17th century; the original house is now incorporated in a huge rambling Gothick castle. Approximately 30 acres of woodland and walled gardens are also open to the public.

NORTHERN IRELAND

ARDRESS HOUSE   The National Trust

Co Armagh map (v)Z   △   ⬦
Telephone: (0762) 851236

17th century country house with fine plasterwork. Small garden, agricultural display in farmyard. Woodland play area.

Location: 7 m W of Portadown on Portadown/Moy Road (B28); 2 m from Loughgall intersection on M1.
Open: Apr: weekends and Good Friday to Easter Tues (Apr 9-13); May, June: weekends and Bank Hols only; July and Aug: daily except Tues; Sept: weekends only 2-6. (Picnic area available from 12 noon.) Farmyard open May, June & Sept weekdays 12-4.
Admission: House, Grounds and Farmyard: £2, Chd £1, groups £1.50 (after hours £2.60). Grounds and Farmyard only: £1.30, Chd 65p, groups £1.10 (after hours £2.10).
Refreshments: Picnickers welcome.
Wheelchairs admitted. Picnic areas.

THE ARGORY   The National Trust

Co Armagh map (v)Y   △   ⬦
Telephone: (086 87) 84753

295 acre estate with neo-classical house, built c. 1820.

Location: 4 m from Moy on Derrycaw Road; 3 m from Coalisland intersection.
Open: Easter (Apr 9-13); Apr, May, June weekends and Bank Hols only; July and Aug: daily exc Thurs 2-6 (open from 1 on Bank Hols). Last adm 5.15. Wheelchairs provided - access to ground floor only.
Admission: House and grounds: £2, Chd £1, groups £1.50 (after hours) £2.60. Car park 50p.
Refreshments: Shop/Tea Room open as house 2-6; Bank Holidays 1-6; weekdays July & Aug 3-5.
Dogs in grounds only on leads.

CASTLE COOLE   The National Trust

Co Fermanagh map (iv)Y
Telephone: (0365) 322690

Magnificent 18th century mansion by James Wyatt with plasterwork by Joseph Rose.

Location: 1½ m SE of Enniskillen on Belfast/Clogher/Enniskillen Road (A4).
Open: The estate is open from dawn to dusk from Apr 1 to Sept 30. House: Easter (Apr 9-13); Apr, May: weekends and Bank Hols; June, July & Aug: daily exc Thurs Sept: weekends only, 2-6.
Admission: House and Grounds: £2.30, Chd £1.15, groups £1.80 (after hours £2.90).

CASTLE WARD 🌿 The National Trust

Co Down   map (v)Z   △   🔥   ⓢ
Telephone: (039 686) 204

Built by the first Lord Bangor in 1765 in a beautiful setting. Laundry museum. Wildfowl collection on lake. Strangford Lough Information Centre in converted barn on edge of shore.

Location: 7 m NE of Downpatrick; 1½ m W of Strangford village (A25).
Open: Apr: weekends and Good Friday to Sun after Easter (apr 9-18); May to Aug: daily (including Bank Hols) except Thurs 1-6. Sept, Oct: weekends only. Estate and grounds open all year dawn to dusk daily. Shop and Restaurant: open as house: weekends and Bank Holidays 1-6, weekdays 1-5. Strangford Lough Barn: weekends and Good Friday - Sun after Easter; Apr, May, June, Sept: weekends and Bank Holidays only; July and Aug, daily except Thurs 2-6.
Admission: House: £2.50, Chd £1.25, Groups £2 (after hours £3). Estate £3 per car (Nov to end Mar £1.50 per car). Coaches: Booked groups to house, no charge: others £10. Horses (using bridlepath £5 per single horsebox.
Refreshments: Shop & Tearoom open same days as house weekends and Bank Hols 1-6, weekdays 1-5.

DOWNHILL 🌿 The National Trust

Londonderry   map (v)Y   🔥

Built by the Earl of Bristol, Bishop of Derry, in 1783 with Mussenden Temple, the Bishop's Gate, the Black Glen and the Bishop's Fish Pond.

Location: 5 m W of Coleraine on Coleraine/Downhill Road (A2).
Station(s): Castlerock.
Open: Temple: Apr: weekends and Good Friday to Easter Tues (Apr 9-13); May, June: Sats, Suns and Bank Hols only; July and Aug: daily. Sept: weekends only: 12-6.
Admission: Grounds: free, Glen open, free at all times.
Dogs admitted. Wheelchair access.

FLORENCE COURT 🌿 The National Trust

Co Fermanagh   map (iv)Y   △   🔥
Telephone: (0365) 249

Important 18th century house built by John Cole. Excellent rococo plasterwork. Pleasure Gardens with working sawmill, ice house, waymarked walks.

Location: 8 m SW of Enniskillen via A4 and A32; 1 m W of Florence Court village.
Open: House: Apr: weekends and Good Friday to Easter Tues (Apr 9-13); May: weekends and Bank Hols; June, July and Aug: daily except Tues; Sept: weekends only, 1-6. Grounds open all year round 10 am to one hour before dusk.
Admission: House: £2.30, Chd £1.15, Groups £1.80. After hours £2.90. Estate parking £1.
Refreshments: Tearoom and shop open as house but open from 12 noon June to Aug.
Dogs in pleasure gardens only on leads. Wheelchair access - ground floor only.

GRAY'S PRINTING PRESS 🌿 The National Trust

Strabane, Co. Tyrone   map (v)Y
Telephone: (0504) 884094

The shop was in existence in 18th century. It has close links with Scots-Irish tradition in America. Audio visual show tells story of printing.

Location: In Main Street, Strabane.
Open: Apr to Sept daily 2-5.30 except Thurs, Suns and Bank Hols. At other times by prior arrangement. Shop (not N.T.): all year daily except Thurs, Suns and public hols, 9-1 and 2-5.30.
Admission: £1.30, Chd 65p. Groups £1 (after hours £1.80).

HEZLETT HOUSE 🌿 The National Trust

Co Londonderry   map (v)Y   △
Telephone: (0265) 848567

Thatched cottage of particular importance because of the unusual cruck/truss construction of the roof.

Location: 4 m W of Coleraine on Coleraine/Downhill Coast Road (A2).
Open: Apr: weekends and Good Friday to Easter Tues (Apr 9-13); May, June: weekends and Bank Hols only; July and Aug: daily except Tues. Sept weekends only: 1-5.
Admission: £1.30, Chd 65p, Groups £1 (after hours £1.80).
Unsuitable for wheelchairs. No dogs.

MOUNT STEWART HOUSE, GARDEN AND TEMPLE
🌿 The National Trust

Co Down   map (v)Z   △   🔥
Telephone: (024 774) 387

Interesting house with important associations with Lord Castlereagh. Gardens designed by Lady Edith, Marchioness of Londonderry. Fine topiary work, flowering shrubs and rhododendrons. Temple of the Winds, modelled on that at Athens, built 1783.

Location: On E shore of Strangford Lough; 5 m SE of Newtownards; 15 m E of Belfast (A20).
Open: Apr: weekends and Good Friday to Sun after Easter (Apr 9-18). May to Aug: daily except Tues 1-6. Sept and Oct: weekends only 1-6. Garden: Apr 1 to end Sept: daily. Oct: weekends only, 10.30-6. Temple of the Winds: Days open as House, but from 2-5. Shop and Tea Room: Apr: weekends and Apr 9-18. May: weekends and Bank Hols June, July and Aug: daily except Tues. Sept: weekends only 1.30-5.30. Bank Hols and Suns 1.30-5.30.
Admission: House, Garden and Temple: £3.30, Chd £1.65, groups £2.60 (after hours £4.30). Garden and Temple: £2.70, Chd £1.35, groups £2 (after hours £3.70; Temple only; 90p.
Refreshments: Tea room.
Wheelchairs provided. Booked parties by arrangement throughout the season.

ROWALLANE GARDEN 🌿 The National Trust

Saintfield, Co Down map (v)Z ♿
Telephone: (0238) 510131

Beautiful gardens containing large collection of plants, chiefly trees and shrubs. Of particular interest in spring and autumn.

Location: 11 m SE of Belfast; 1 m S of Saintfield on the W of the Downpatrick Road (A7).
Open: Apr 1 to end Oct: Mons-Fris, 10.30-6. Sats and Suns 2-6. Nov to end Mar 10.30-5 Mons-Fris. *Closed* Dec 25 and 26, Jan 1.
Admission: Easter to end Oct: £2.50, Chd £1.25. Parties £1.70 (after hours £3). Nov to end Mar: £1.30, Groups 80p.
Refreshments: Shop and Tearoom: Apr: weekends and Good Friday to Easter Tues (Apr 9-13); May to Aug: daily 2-6. Sept: weekends only.
Dogs admitted on leads, to indicated areas. Wheelchair access (1 provided).

SPRINGHILL 🌿 The National Trust

Moneymore, Co Londonderry map (v)Y △ ♿
Telephone: (064 87) 48210

House dating from 17th century. Magnificent oak staircase and interesting furniture & paintings. Costume museum. Cottar's kitchen.

Location: On Moneymore/Coagh Road (1 m from Moneymore).
Open: Apr: weekends and Good Friday to Easter Tues (Apr 9-13); May, June: weekends and Bank Hols only; July and Aug: daily except Thurs. Sept: weekends only 2-6.
Admission: House £2, Chd £1, Groups £1.50 (after hours £2.60).

WELLBROOK BEETLING MILL 🌿 The National Trust

Cookstown, Co. Tyrone map (v)Y
Telephone: (064 87) 51735

A water-powered mill built in 18th century with 19th century modifications. Final process in the manufacture of linen.

Location: 3 m from Cookstown on Cookstown/Omagh Road.
Open: Apr: weekends and Good Friday to Easter Tues (Apr 9-13); May, June: weekends and Bank Holidays. July and Aug: daily except Tues 2-6. Sept: weekends only.
Admission: £1.30, Chd 65p, Groups £1 (after hours £1.80).
Unsuitable for wheelchairs.

SCOTLAND

BORDERS

National Trust For Scotland

Last admissions to most NTS properties are 45 minutes before the advertised closing times. Other than guide-dogs for the blind and deaf, dogs are not generally permitted inside Trust buildings, walled and enclosed gardens or in the immediate area beside buildings which are open to the public. At a number of properties special "dog walks" are signposted.

ABBOTSFORD HOUSE

Melrose map 13F ♿
Telephone: (0896) 2043
(Mrs P. Maxwell-Scott)

The home of Sir Walter Scott, containing many historical relics collected by him.

Location: 3 m W of Melrose just S of A72; 5 m E of Selkirk.
Open: 3rd Mon of Mar to Oct 31 - Daily 10-5; Suns 2-5.
Refreshments: Teashop.
Cars with wheelchairs or disabled enter by private entrance. Gift Shop.

AYTON CASTLE

Eyemouth map G13
Telephone: (089 07) 81212

Victorian castle in red sandstone.

Location: 7 m N of Berwick-upon-Tweed on A1.
Open: May to Sept - Suns 2-5 or by appointment.
Admission: £2, Chd (under 15) free.

BOWHILL

nr Selkirk map F13 △ ♿
Telephone: (0750) 20732
(His Grace the Duke of Buccleuch & Queensberry KT)

Border home of the Scotts of Buccleuch. Famous paintings include 8 Guardis, Canaletto's Whitehall, Claudes, Gainsboroughs, Reynolds, Raeburns and the world famous Buccleuch collection of portrait miniatures. Superb French furniture and porcelain. Monmouth, Sir Walter Scott and Queen Victoria relics. For details of our specialist art courses, please tel: Buccleuch Heritage Trust Selkirk (0750) 20732. Restored Victorian kitchen. Audio-Visual programme. Lecture Theatre. Exciting Adventure Woodland Play Area. Walks to historic Newark Castle and by lochs and rivers along nature trails.

Location: 3 m W of Selkirk on A708 Moffat-St. Mary's Loch road. Edinburgh, Carlisle, Newcastle approx 1½ hours by road.
Open: House open July 1 to July 31 - Daily 1-4.30. Country Park (includes Adventure Woodland Play Area, Nature Trails) - First Sat in May to late summer, Bank Hols inclusive - Daily except Fri 12-5. Last entry 45 mins before closing time. Open by appointment at additional times for museums and specialist or educational groups. Riding Centre and Pony Trekking (0750) 20192 open all day all year. Mountain bike hire (0721) 20336.
Admission: House and Grounds:£3. Parties over 20 £2.50. OAPs £2. Grounds only £1. (Wheelchair users and Chd under 5 free). Free car and coach parking.
Refreshments: Gift shop and licensed tea room open daily during 'House open' period. Tea room open weekends during 'Country Park open' period. Mini shop in playground all seasons.

DAWYCK BOTANIC GARDEN

nr Peebles map 13F
(Royal Botanic Garden, Edinburgh)

DRYBURGH ABBEY

Dryburgh map 13F
(Historic Scotland)

Sir Walter Scott and Field Marshal Earl Haig are buried in this 12th century Abbey.

FLOORS CASTLE

Kelso map G13
Telephone: (0573) 223333
(The Duke of Roxburghe)

Built in 1721 by William Adam and later added to by Playfair. Magnificent tapestries, fine French and English furniture, paintings, porcelain.
Location: N of Kelso.
Open: Easter weekend from Apr 9 - 12 and from Apr 25 to end of Oct 1993. 10.30-5.30 (last admission to House 4.45). Sun to Thurs inclusive except during Jul and Aug when it opens daily. Oct: Open Sun and Wed 10.30-4.30.
Admission: £3.20, OAPs £2.50, OAPs pre-booked parties £2.30, pre-booked parties £2.50, chd (8 and over) £1.60, Family ticket £8. Chd party rates £1.30. Grounds: £1.50.
Refreshments: Licensed restaurant, gift shop and coffee shop.
Pipe Bands May 2, 30; June 13; July 11. Massed Pipe Bands Aug 29. Garden Centre and Coffee Shop open 7 days.
Location: 5 m SE of Melrose, nr St Boswells.

HERMITAGE CASTLE

Liddlesdale map F12
(Historic Scotland)

Here in 1566. Queen Mary visited her wounded lover Bothwell.
Location: In Liddlesdale; 5½ m NE of Newcastleton.

THE HIRSEL GROUNDS & DUNDOCK WOOD

Coldstream map G13
Telephone: (0890) 882834; 882965

Snowdrops, aconites and daffodils in Spring in grounds. Fantastic rhododendrons and azaleas May/June Dundock wood and grounds. Herbaceous borders and roses in summer. Marvellous Autumn colouring. Picnic areas. Parking. Playground. Homestead museum, Craft Centre and workshops.

Open: All reasonable daylight hours throughout the year.
Admission: Parking charge.
Refreshments: In main season.

JEDBURGH ABBEY

Jedburgh map F13
(Historic Scotland)

Founded by David I this Augustinian Abbey is remarkably complete. Recent excavations are now open to the public. New Visitor Centre.
Location: In Jedburgh.

OPEN HOUSE TO A SPLENDID HERITAGE

*H*ere, in the beautiful Scottish Borders, stand some of the finest homes and gardens you could wish to see. Many still in private, and proud, family hands. And all within no more than a 50-mile radius.

Abbotsford

Bowhill

Floors

The Hirsel

Manderston

Mellerstain

Paxton

Thirlestane

Traquair

Experience the eloquence of *Abbotsford* – where the walls echo with the words of one of Scotland's celebrated authors. Picture yourself at *Bowhill* – taking in the delights of one of the finest private art collections. Feast your eyes on *Floors* – where you'll see furniture that is genuine 17th-18th century French. Walk into a haven at *The Hirsel* – where beautifully stocked and maintained grounds extend to fully 3,000 acres. Marvel at *Manderston* – with the splendid sweep of its celebrated silver staircase. Delight in the magnificence of *Mellerstain* – with its masterly ceilings and decorations by Robert Adam. Soak up the history of *Paxton* – a Palladian mansion built for a daughter of Frederick the Great. Treat yourself to *Thirlestane* – and the glorious sight of its sumptuous state rooms. Take in centuries-old *Traquair* – where you follow in the footsteps of 27 kings and queens.

Step inside the coupon and send for the leaflet that opens all the doors invitingly wider.

SAVE 10% ON ADMISSION CHARGES - send for details of the NEW Scotland's Border Heritage Pass

- -

SCOTLAND'S BORDER HERITAGE

PLEASE SEND ME MORE INFORMATION ON

RETURN TO:–

SCOTLAND'S BORDER HERITAGE

c/o SBTB, HIGH STREET, SELKIRK TD7 4JX

NAME _____

ADDRESS _____

_____

_____ POST CODE _____

MANDERSTON

Duns map G13
Telephone: (0361) 83450
(Lord and Lady Palmer)

The swan-song of the great classical house. Georgian in its taste but with all the elaborate domestic arrangements designed for Edwardian convenience and comfort. Superb classical yet luxurious rooms and the only silver staircase in the world, in a house on which the architect was ordered to spare no expense. The extensive 'downstairs' domestic quarters are equally some of the grandest of their type. Biscuit Tin Museum. Outside, the grandeur is continued. See the most splendid stables and picturesque marble dairy. 56 acres of formal woodland garden and lakeside walks.

Location: 2 m E of Duns on A6105; 14 m W of Berwick upon Tweed.
Open: May 6 to Sept 30 - Thurs and Suns, also Bank Hol Mons May 31 and Aug 30 2-5.30.
Admission: Charges not available at time of going to press. Parties at any time.
Refreshments: Cream Teas.
Gift Shop.

MELLERSTAIN

Gordon map G13
Telephone: (057 381) 225
(The Mellerstain Trust)

Scotland's famous Adam mansion. Beautifully decorated and furnished interiors. Terraced gardens and lake. Gift shop.

Location: 9 m NE of Melrose; 7 m NW of Kelso; 37 m SE of Edinburgh.
Open: Easter weekend (Apr 9 to Apr 12) then May 1 to Sept 30 - Daily (except Sats) 12.30-5. Last adm to House 4.30.
Admission: Charges not available at time of going to press. Free parking. *Special terms for organised parties by appointment, apply Curator.*
Refreshments: Tea rooms.

MELROSE ABBEY

Melrose map F13
(Historic Scotland)

Beautiful Cistercian Abbey founded by David Ist.

Location: In Melrose.

MERTOUN GARDENS

St Boswells, Roxburghshire map F13
Telephone: (0835) 23236
(His Grace the Duke of Sutherland)

20 acres of beautiful grounds with delightful walks and river views. Fine trees, herbaceous plants and flowering shrubs. Walled garden and well-preserved circular dovecot.

Location: 2 m NE of St Boswells on the B6404.
Open: Garden only. Sats and Suns, and Mons on Public Holidays only - Apr to Sept 2-6 (last entry 5.30). Parties by arrangement.
Admission: £1, Chd/OAPs 50p.
Refreshments: Dryburgh Abbey Hotel, Buccleuch Arms Hotel, St Boswells.
No dogs. Car parking.

NEIDPATH CASTLE

Peebles map F13
Telephone: (0721) 720333

Medieval castle updated in the 17th century, situated on a bluff above the River Tweed. Pit prison and well hewn out of solid rock. Fine views.

Location: 1 m W of Peebles on A72.
Open: Thurs before Easter to Sept 30 - Mons to Sats 11-5; Suns 1-5 and Tues in Oct 11-4.
Admission: £1.50, Chd 75p, OAPs £1. Parties at reduced rates - enquiries to The Custodian, Neidpath Castle, Peebles (0721) 720333.
Refreshments: Hotels in Peebles.

PAXTON HOUSE

Paxton, nr Berwick-upon-Tweed map G13 &
Telephone: (0289) 86291
(The Paxton Trust)

Scotland's most perfect Palladian country mansion. Built for a daughter of Frederick The Great. Designed by the Adam family and furnished by Chippendale and Trotter. Restored Regency picture gallery (outstation of National Galleries of Scotland). Gardens. Riverside Walks. Adventure Playground. Tearoom.

Location: 5 m from Berwick-upon-Tweed on B6461.
Open: Daily - Good Fri to Oct 31. House: noon-5. Grounds: 10-5. Last tour of house 4.15.
Admission: £3.50, grounds only £1.50, Family ticket £10. Parties catered for.
Refreshments: Morning coffee, light lunches, afternoon teas, Licensed.
Car parking. Suitable for disabled persons. No wheelchairs available.

PRIORWOOD GARDEN

Melrose map F13
Telephone: (089 682) 2965
(The National Trust for Scotland)

Garden featuring flowers suitable for drying. Shop and Trust visitor centre.

Location: In Melrose.
Open: Apr 1 to Apr 30 and Nov 1 to Dec 24: Mons to Sats 10-5.30. May 1 to Oct 31: Mon to Sats 10-5.30, Sun 2-5.30.

SMAILHOLM TOWER

nr Smailholm map F13
(Historic Scotland)

Simple tower house displaying a collection of costume figures and tapestries relating to Sir Walter Scott's 'Minstrelsy of the Scottish Borders.'

Location: nr Smailholm Village 6 m NW of Kelso.

What's ours is yours - to visit and enjoy

*F*ROM BROADSWORDS TO BATTLEFIELDS, CASTLES
TO COTTAGES, MOUNTAINS TO MILLSTONES,
PICNIC SITES TO PAINTINGS, FERNS TO FURNITURE,
GIFT SHOPS TO GARDENS, THERE ARE THOUSANDS
OF EXCITING THINGS TO ENJOY AT OVER A
HUNDRED PROPERTIES OF THE
NATIONAL TRUST FOR SCOTLAND.
*V*ISIT THEM - BRING THE FAMILY AND HAVE A REALLY
GOOD DAY OUT. BETTER STILL SAVE YOURSELF
MONEY BY BECOMING A MEMBER OF THE TRUST
AND ENJOY FREE ENTRY TO ALL OUR PROPERTIES -
AND LOTS MORE BESIDES.

For full details contact:
Membership Services,
National Trust for Scotland
Freepost
Edinburgh EH2 0DF
Telephone: 031-226 5922

 National Trust for Scotland

ROBERT SMAIL'S PRINTING WORKS

Tweeddale   map F13
Telephone: (0896) 830206
(The National Trust for Scotland)

The buildings contain vintage working machinery, including a 100-year-old printing press which was originally driven by water wheels. The Victorian office is on display complete with its acid-etched plate-glass windows and examples of historic items printed in the works.

Location: In Innerleithen High Street, 30 m S of Edinburgh.
Open: Shop and Printworks: Apr 1 to Oct 31: Mons to Sats 10-1, 2-5, Suns 2-5. Last adm 45 mins before closing am & pm.
Admission: £2, chd £1, adult parties £1.60, schools 80p.

THIRLESTANE CASTLE

Lauder, Berwickshire   map F13
Telephone: (0578) 722430

Described as one of the oldest and finest Castles in Scotland, Thirlestane has its roots in an original 13th century fort overlooking the Leader Valley. The main keep was built in 1590 by the Maitland family who have lived in the Castle for over 400 years; it was extended in 1670 and again in 1840. The Restoration Period plasterwork ceilings are considered to be the finest in existence. The family nurseries now house a large collection of historic toys and children are encouraged to dress up. Visitors see the old kitchens, pantries and laundries as well as the Country Life Exhibitions portraying day to day life in the Borders through the centuries. Grounds, picnic tables, woodland walk, gift shop and tea room.

Location: 28 m S of Edinburgh off A68 - follow signs on all main approach roads.
Open: Easter (Apr 7 to 14 inclusive), May, June and Sept: Weds, Thurs and Suns only. July and Aug: daily except Sats. Castle 2-5 (last adm 4.30). Grounds 12-6.
Admission: £3, party rate £2.50, Family ticket (parents and own children only) £8. Booked party tours at other times by arrangement. Free car park.
Refreshments: Tea room.

TRAQUAIR

Innerleithen   map F13   △
Telephone: (0896) 830323
(C. Maxwell Stuart of Traquair)

A house full of beauty, romance and mystery. Rich in associations with Mary Queen of Scots, the Jacobites and Catholic persecution. Priest's room with secret stairs. The world-famous Traquair House Ale is brewed in the 18th-century brewhouse. Extensive grounds, craft workshops and maze.

Location: 1 m from Innerleithen; 6 m from Peebles; 29 m from Edinburgh at junction of B709 & B7062 (40 minutes by road from Edinburgh Turnhouse Airport, 1½ hours from Glasgow).
Open: Easter week Apr 10-18. Daily from May 1 to Sept 30, 1.30-5.30; (July and Aug only 10.30-5.30). Last adm 5. Grounds: May to Sept: 10.30-5.30.
Refreshments: Home cooking at the 1745 Cottage Tea Room from 12.30.
Gits Shop, Antique Shop. Traquair Fair 7th +

CENTRAL

CASTLE CAMPBELL

Dollar   map E14
(Historic Scotland)

15th century oblong tower with later additions, set in a steep sided glen. Sometimes known as 'Castle Gloom.'

Location: 1 m N of Dollar; on N slope of Ochil Hills at head of Dollar Glen.
Open:

LINLITHGOW PALACE

Linlithgow   map E14
(Historic Scotland)

Birthplace of Mary Queen of Scots.

Location: In Linlithgow.
Station(s): Linlithgow (½ m).

STIRLING CASTLE

Stirling   map E14
(Historic Scotland)

Royal Castle on a great basalt rock dominating the surrounding countryside.

Location: In Stirling.
Station(s): Stirling (¾ m).

Sir Joshua Reynolds
Portrait painter (1723–1792)
First President of the Royal Academy, knighted in 1769

His work can be seen in the following properties included in Historic Houses Castles and Gardens:

Arundel Castle   *Kenwood*
Dalmeny House (Roseberry Collection of Political Portraits)   *Shalom Hall*
Goodwood House   *Weston Park*

DUMFRIES & GALLOWAY

ARBIGLAND GARDENS

Kirkbean map E11
(Captain and Mrs J. B. Blackett)

Built in the 18th century, the house is set amongst woodland, formal and water gardens arranged round a secluded bay in the Solway Firth. The garden in which John Paul Jones, regarded by history as the father of the United States Navy, worked as a boy, adjacent to The John Paul Jones Birthplace Museum. Birthplace of Dr James Craik, Washington's Physician.

Location: 15 m SW of Dumfries on A710.
Open: Gardens: May to Sept incl - Tues - Sun and Bank Hol Mons 2-6. House and Gardens: Sat May 22 to Mon May 31 1993 inclusive 2-6.
Admission: £2, Chd 50p. Toddlers free. Car park free.
Refreshments: Tea room. Hotels in Dumfries, Southerness (2 m) or New Abbey.
Picnic area on sandy beach. Dogs on lead please.

CAERLAVEROCK CASTLE

nr Dumfries map E11
(Historic Scotland)

One of the finest examples of early classical Renaissance building in Scotland and chief seat of the Maxwell family.

Location: 8 m SSE of Dumfries on the Glencaple Road (B725).

CARLYLE'S BIRTHPLACE

Ecclefechan map F12
Telephone: (057 63) 666
(The National Trust for Scotland)

Thomas Carlyle was born here in 1795. Mementoes and MSS.

Location: 5 m SE of Lockerbie on the Lockerbie/Carlisle Road (A74).
Open: Apr 1 to Oct 31: daily 12-5. Other times by appointment.
Admission: £1.50, Chd 80p (under 5) free. OAPs/Students (on production of their cards) half-price. Adult parties £1.20 school parties 60p.
Refreshments: Ecclefechan Hotel.

CASTLE KENNEDY GARDENS

Stranraer map D11
Telephone: Stranraer (0776) 2024
(The Earl and Countess of Stair)

World famous gardens, set in 75 acres of landscaped terraces and mounds between two lochs. Outstanding displays of Rhododendrons, Azaleas, Embothriums, Eucryphia. Surrounded by breathtaking scenery. Many original specimens from Hooker expeditions. Also only known Monkey Puzzle avenue. Plant Centre selling plants produced from garden stock.

Location: 5 m E of Stranraer on A75 opposite Castle Kennedy village.
Open: Easter to Sept - Daily 10-5.
Admission: Charged. Disabled free. Reduction for groups over 30.
Refreshments: Light refreshments only. Hotels Eynhallow, Castle Kennedy & Stranraer.

DRUMLANRIG CASTLE AND COUNTRY PARK

nr Thornhill map E12 △ ♿ Ⓢ
Telephone: (0848) 31682 (24 hr answering service). Country Park: (0848) 31555.
(Home of the Duke of Buccleuch & Queensberry KT)

Magnificent pink sandstone castle with outstanding art treasures - Leonardo, Rembrandt, Holbein - beautiful silverware, superb furniture and porcelain, Bonnie Prince Charlie's relics. Extensive grounds and woodland includes gardens, exciting adventure woodland play area, nature trails and picnic sites. Tearoom and giftshop. Working craft studios, lecture room and cycle hire. Bird of Prey Centre.

Location: 18 m N of Dumfries; 3 m N of Thornhill off A76; 16 m from A74 at Elvanfoot; approx 1½ hrs by road from Edinburgh, Glasgow & Carlisle.
Open: Castle and Country Park are both open early May to late Aug. Daily *(except Thurs)* 11-5. Suns 1-5. Times subject to change; please telephone to check.
Admission: Charges not available at time of going to press. Discounts for groups of 20 or over, OAPs and Students.
Refreshments: Lunches, Afternoon Teas and snacks at above times.

LOGAN BOTANIC GARDEN

Port Logan map D11
(Royal Botanic Garden, Edinburgh)

MAXWELTON HOUSE

Thornhill map E12 ♿
Telephone: (084 82) 385
(M. R. L. Stenhouse)

A stronghold of the Earls of Glencairn in the 13th/14th century, later the birthplace of Annie Laurie of the famous Scottish ballard. House, Chapel, Museum of Agricultural and Early Domestic Life, gardens, tea room and small shop.

Location: 3 m S of Moniaive, 13 m N of Dumfries on B729.
Open: Wed to Sun, Easter to end Sept, 11-5.
Admission: Car parking free.
Refreshments: Morning coffe, lunch and afternoon tea for 50 people.
Suitable for disabled. No wheelchairs available.

RAMMERSCALES

Lockerbie map E12
Telephone: (038 781) 0229
(M. Bell Macdonald, Esq)

Georgian manor house dated 1760 set on high ground with fine views over Annandale. Pleasant policies and a typical walled garden of the period. There are Jacobite relics and links with Flora Macdonald retained in the family. There is also a collection of works by modern artists.

Location: 5 m W of Lockerbie (M6/A74); 2½ m S of Lochmaben on B7020.
Open: 2-5 every day in Aug except Sats.

SWEETHEART ABBEY

New Abbey map E11
(Historic Scotland)

Cistercian monastery famous for the touching and romantic circumstances of its foundation by Lady Dervorgilla.

Location: 7 m S of Dumfries on coast road (A710).

THREAVE GARDEN

nr Castle Douglas map E11 ♿
Telephone: Castle Douglas (0556) 2575
(The National Trust for Scotland)

The Trust's School of Horticulture. Gardens now among the major tourist attractions of SW Scotland. Visitor centre. Magnificent springtime display of some 200 varieties of daffodil, Trust shop, Restaurant, Exhibition. Ramp into garden for wheelchairs.

Location: 1 m W of Castle Douglas off A75.
Open: GARDENS: All year, daily 9-sunset. WALLED GARDEN AND GLASSHOUSES: All year, daily 9-5. Visitor Centre, Exhibition and Shop: Apr 1 to Oct 31 daily 9-5.30.
Admission: £2.80, Chd £1.40. Adult parties £2.20, Schools £1.10, Chd (under 5 years) free. OAPs/Students (on production of their cards) half-price.
Refreshments: Restaurant: daily 10-5.

FIFE

ABERDOUR CASTLE

Aberdour map F14
(Historic Scotland)

A 14th century tower with the remains of a terraced garden and bowling green. There is also a splendid dovecot and panoramic views across the Firth of Forth.

Location: At Aberdour.

BALCARRES

Colinsburgh map F14
Telephone: (033334) 206
(Balcarres Trust)

16th century house with 19th century additions by Burn and Bryce. Woodland and terraced garden.

Location: ½ m N of Colinsburgh.
Open: WOODLANDS AND LOWER GARDEN: Feb 15 to Mar 3; Apr 5 to June 26 (daily except Suns). WEST GARDEN: June 10 to 16 (Daily except Suns) 2-5. *House not open except by written appointment* and Apr 26 to May 12 (except Suns).
Admission: £1.50, OAPs/Chd £1. House: £2.
Car park. Suitable for disabled persons, no wheelchairs provided.

BALCASKIE

Pittenweem map F14
Telephone: (0333) 311202
(Balcaskie Estate Trust)

An important 16th Century tower house expanded into a Classical Mansion in the late 17th Century. One of the first houses to be built by Sir William Bruce. Terraced gardens.

Location: 1 m NNW of Pittenweem.
Open: Jun 1 to Aug 31. Sat to Wed, 2-5pm.
Admission: £2.50, Chd £1.50, OAPs/Students £1.50. Gardens only £1.50.

FALKLAND PALACE & GARDEN

Fife map F14
Telephone: (0337) 57397
(Her Majesty the Queen. Hereditary Constable, Capt & Keeper: Ninian Crichton Stuart. Deputy Keeper: The National Trust for Scotland)

Attractive 16th century royal palace, favourite retreat of Stuart kings and queens. Gardens now laid out to the original Royal plans. Town Hall, Visitor Centre, Exhibition and Shop. Original royal tennis court built in 1539. Ramp into garden for wheelchairs.

Location: In Falkland, 11 m N of Kirkcaldy on A912.
Open: Apr 1 to Sept 30: Mon to Sat 10-6, Sun 2-6. (last adm 5). Oct 1 to 31: Mon to Sat 10-5, Sun 2-5.
Admission: Palace: £3.50, Chd £1.80. Adult parties £2.80, School parties £1.40. Gardens only £2, Chd (under 5) free. OAPs/Students (on production of their cards) half-price.
Refreshments: Bruce Arms, Falkland.
Visitor centre and Trust shop. Display in Town Hall: Apr 1 - Oct 31, 11-5. Sun 2-5 (last adm 4.30).

HILL OF TARVIT

nr Cupar map F14
Telephone: (0334) 53127
(The National Trust for Scotland)

Mansion house remodelled 1906. Collection of furniture, tapestries, porcelain and paintings. Gardens.

Location: 2½ m SW of Cupar A916.
Station(s): Cupar (2½ m).
Open: Apr 3 to Apr 25; Sats and Suns 2-6; Apr 9 to 12 and May 1 to Oct 31 daily 2-6, (last adm 5.30). Gardens and grounds: all year 10 - sunset.
Admission: House and Gardens £2.80, Chd £1.40. Adult arties (20 or more) £2.20. School parties £1.10. Gardens only £1 Chd 50p. Chd (under 5) free, OAPs/Students (on production of their cards) half-price.

KELLIE CASTLE AND GARDEN

Fife map F14   ♿
Telephone: (033 38) 271
(The National Trust for Scotland)

Fine example of 16th-17th century domestic architecture of Lowland Scotland. Victorian walled garden with wheelchair access. Nursery, video, adventure playground, picnic area, shop.

Location: 3 m NNW of Pittenweem on B9171.
Open: CASTLE: Apr 3 to Apr 25; Sats and Suns 2-6. Apr 9 to 12 and May 1 to Sept 30 daily 2-6. Oct 1 to 31 daily 2-5 (last adm 45 mins before closing). GARDEN AND GROUNDS open all the year, daily 10-sunset.
Admission: Castle and Gardens £2.80, Chd £1.40. Adult parties (20 or more) £2.20. School parties £1.10. Gardens only £1, Chd (accompanied by adult) 50p, (under 5) free. OAPs/Students (on production of their cards) half-price.
Refreshments: Tea room.
Gardens only suitable for the disabled. A/V presentation with induction loop for the hard of hearing.

THE TOWN HOUSE & THE STUDY

Culross map E14
Telephone: (0383) 880359
(The National Trust for Scotland)

Outstanding survival of Scottish 17th century burgh architecture carefully restored to 20th century living standards. Induction loop for the hard of hearing.

Location: 12 m W of Forth Road Bridge, off A985.
Open: Town House (with exhibition and visual presentation) open Apr 9 to 12 and May 1 to Sept 30 daily 11-1, 2-5. The Study open Apr 9 to 12 and May 1 to Sept 30, Sats and Suns 2-4. Adm other times by appointment.
Admission: Town House and Study: £2, Chd £1. Students (on production of their cards) half-price.

GRAMPIAN

BALMORAL CASTLE

nr Ballater map F16
(Her Majesty the Queen)

BALVENIE CASTLE

Dufftown map F17
(Historic Scotland)

A 13th century castle visited by Mary Queen of Scots in 1562.
Location: At Dufftown.

BRAEMAR CASTLE

Braemar map E16 △
Telephone: (03397) 41219 - *out of season* (03397) 41224
(Captain A A C Farquharson of Invercauld Trusts)

BRODIE CASTLE

nr Nairn Moray map E17 &
Telephone: (030 94) 371
(The National Trust for Scotland)

Ancient seat of the Brodies, burned in 1645 and largely rebuilt, with 17th/19th century additions. Fine furniture, porcelain and paintings. Audio-taped guide for the blind.

Location: Off A96 between Nairn & Foress.
Open: Apr 1 to Sept 26: Mons to Sats 11-6, Suns 2-6. Oct 2 to Oct 17: Sats 11-5, Suns 2-5. Grounds open all year 9.30-sunset.
Admission: £3.30, Chd £1.70 (under 5 free). Adult parties £2.60. School parties £1.30. OAPs/Students (on production of their cards) half-price. Grounds by donation.

CASTLE FRASER

Sauchen map G16
Telephone: (033 03) 463
(The National Trust for Scotland)

One of the most spectacular of the Castles of Mar. Z-plan castle begun in 1575 and completed in 1636. Formal garden.

Location: 3 m S of Kemnay off B993; 16 m W of Aberdeen.
Open: April: Weekends 2-5. May 1 to June 30, and Sept 1 to 30: daily 2-6. July 1 to Aug 31: daily 11-6. Oct: Weekends 2-5. Garden & Grounds open all year, 9.30 - sunset.
Admission: £3.30, Chd £1.70. Adult parties £2.60. School parties £1.30. Chd (under 5) free. OAPs/Students (on production of their cards) half-price. Garden and grounds:By donation. Tea-room, picnic area, childrens' adventure playground.

Built in 1628 by the Earl of Mar. Attacked and burned by the celebrated Black Colonel (John Farquharson of Inverey) in 1689. Repaired by the government and garrisoned with English troops after the rising of 1745. Later transformed by the Farquharsons of Invercauld, who had purchased it in 1732, into a fully furnished private residence of unusual charm. L-plan castle of fairy tale proportions, with round central tower and spiral stair. Barrel-vaulted ceilings, massive iron 'Yett', and underground pit (prison). Remarkable star-shaped defensive curtain wall. Much valuable furniture, paintings and items of Scottish historical interest.

Location: ½ m NE of Braemar on A93.
Open: May to mid Oct - Daily 10-6. Except Fridays.
Admission: £1.70, Chd 90p. Special rates for groups and OAPs. Free car and bus park.

CRATHES CASTLE & GARDEN

Banchory map G16 △ &
Telephone: (033 044) 525
(The National Trust for Scotland)

Fine 16th century baronial castle. Remarkable early painted ceilings. Beautiful gardens provide a wonderful display all year. Great yew hedges from 1702. Children's adventure playground.

Location: 3 m E of Banchory on A93; 15 m W of Aberdeen.
Open: CASTLE, VISITOR CENTRE, SHOP, LICENSED RESTAURANT AND PLANT SALES. Apr 1 to Oct 31: daily 11-6,other times by prior appointment only. GARDENS AND GROUNDS. All the year - Daily 9.30 - sunset.
Admission: Grounds only: 1½0, Chd 80p. Combined ticket (Castle, Garden & Grounds): £3.50, Chd £1.80, Adult parties £2.80, School parties £1.40. Garden & Grounds: Chd (under 5) free. OAPs/Students (on production of their cards) half-price.
Refreshments: Shop and licensed Restaurant.

DRUM CASTLE

nr Aberdeen map G16
Telephone: (033 08) 204
(The National Trust for Scotland)

The oldest part of the historic Castle, the great square tower - one of the three oldest tower houses in Scotland - dates from the late 13th century. Charming mansion added in 1619. Garden of historic roses.

Location: 10 m W of Aberdeen, off A93.
Open: CASTLE: April: Weekends 2-5. May 1 to Sept 30: daily 2-6. Oct: Weekends 2-5. WALLED GARDEN OF HISTORIC ROSES: May 1 to Oct 31, daily 10-6. Grounds open all year 9.30-sunset.
Admission: £3.30, Chd £1.70. Adult parties £2.60, School parties £1.30. Chd (under 5) free. OAPs/Students (on production of their cards) half-price. Grounds: By donation.

ELGIN CATHEDRAL

Elgin map F17
(Historic Scotland)

Probably Scotland's most beautiful cathedral with certainly the finest chapter house.
Location: In Elgin.

FASQUE

Fettercairn map G16
Telephone: (05614) 569 or 202
(The Gladstone Family)

1809 Home of the Gladstone family with a full complement of furnishings and domestic articles little changed for 160 years. A wonderful example of 'Upstairs-Downstairs' family life.

Location: 1 m N of Fettercairn on the B974 Cairn O Mount pass road; 34 m Aberdeen and Dundee; 17 m Stonehaven; 12 m Montrose; 18 m Banchory. Part of The Victorian Heritage Trail.
Open: House open May 1 to Sept 30 every day except Frid. 1.30-5.30 with last entry at 5 pm.
Admission: £2, OAPs £1.50, Chd £1. Parties £1.50 each (over 25 pre-booked). Morning and evening opening for parties by arrangement.

FYVIE CASTLE

Fyvie map G17
Telephone: (0651) 891266
(The National Trust of Scotland)

The oldest part of the castle dates from the 13th century and its five great towers are the monuments to the five families who owned the castle. The building contains the finest wheel stair in Scotland and a magnificent collection of paintings.

Location: Off A947, 8 m SE of Turriff.
Open: Weekends in Apr and Oct 2-5. May 1 to 31 and Sept 1 to 30, daily 2-6. June 1 to Aug 31, daily 11-6.
Admission: £3.30, Chd £1.70. Adult parties £2.60, School parties £1.30. Parkland free. Chd (under 5) free). OAPs/Students (on producton of their cards) half-price.
Permanent exhibition - Castles of Mar.

HADDO HOUSE

nr Methlick map G17 △ &
Telephone: (0651) 851440
(The National Trust for Scotland)

Georgian house designed in 1731 by William Adam. Home of the Gordons of Haddo for over 500 years. Terraced gardens.

Location: 4 m N of Pitmedden; 19 m N of Aberdeen (A981 & B999).
Open: House, permanent exhibition, shop and restaurant open. Apr: Weekends 2-5. May 1 to 31: daily 2-6. Jun 1 to Aug 31: daily 11-6. Sept 1 to 31: daily 2-6. Oct: Weekends 2-5. Garden and Grounds open all year 9.30-sunset.
Admission: £3.30, Chd £1.70 (under 5) free. Adult parties £2.60, School parties £1.30. OAPs/Students (on prouction of their cards) half-price. Gardens & grounds: By donation.
Refreshments: Restaurant open from Apr 1 daily 11-6.
Wheelchair access.

HUNTLY CASTLE

Huntly map F17
(Historic Scotland)

A magnificent ruin of an architectural and heraldic house built in the 16th and 17th centuries.
Location: In Huntly.

KILDRUMMY CASTLE GARDEN

Donside map F16 &
Telephone: (09755) 71277 or 71203
(Kildrummy Castle Garden Trust)

Approximately 10 acres of garden with shrubs, heaths, gentians, rhododendrons, lilies etc. Alpine and water garden dominated by ruins of 13th century castle. Museum (on request) interesting old stones. Coaches by arrangement. Write or telephone: Kildrummy Castle Garden Trust, by Alford, Aberdeenshire AB33 8RA.
Location: On A97 off A944 10 m W of Alford; 15 m S of Huntly; 35 m W of Aberdeen.
Open: GARDENS ONLY. Apr to Oct - Daily 10-5.
Admission: £1.70, Chd (6 to 16 yrs) 50p.
Refreshments: At Kildrummy Castle Hotel in the grounds (please make reservations) Kildrummy (09755) 71288. The Kildrummy Inn, Kildrummy (09755) 71227.
Plants for sale. Wheelchairs. **Play area. Video Room.** Walks.

LEITH HALL AND GARDEN

Kennethmont map F17 &
Telephone: (046 43) 216
(The National Trust for Scotland)

Home of the Leith family from 1650. Jacobite relics, and major exhibition of family's military collection. Charming garden.
Location: 1 m W of Kennethmont on B9002; 34 m NW of Aberdeen.
Open: May 1 to Sept 30: daily 2-6. Oct: Sats and Suns, daily 2-5. Gardens and Grounds: all the year, daily 9.30-sunset.
Admission: House and garden: £3.30, Chd £1.70 (under 5) free. Adult parties £2.60, School parties £1.30. OAPs/Students (on production of their cards) half-price. Gardens and grounds: By donation.
Picnic area.

PITMEDDEN GARDEN

Udny map G16 &
Telephone: (065 13) 2352
(The National Trust for Scotland)

Reconstructed 17th century garden with floral designs, fountains and sundials. Display on the evolution of the formal garden. Museum of Farming Life.
Location: 14 m N of Aberdeen on A920.
Open: Garden, Grounds Museum, Visitor Centre & other facilities - May 1 to Sept 30: daily 10-6.
Admission: Garden and Museum £2.80, Chd £1.40 (under 5) free. Adult parties £2.20, School parties £1.10. Grounds only £1, Chd 50p. OAPs/Students (on production of their cards) half-price.*House not open.*
No dogs in garden please.

PROVOST ROSS'S HOUSE

Aberdeen map G16
Telephone: (0224) 572215
(The National Trust for Scotland)

Built in 1593, this is the third oldest house in Aberdeen. It now contains Aberdeen Maritime Museum operated by the City of Aberdeen District Council. Trust Information Centre including a presentation on NTS Grampian properties. Members' Centre shop. Video 'Castle Country'.

Location: City centre.
Open: Open all year Mon to Sat 10-5 (except Christmas and New Year Holidays). Trust Visitor Centre and Shop May 1 to Sept 30, Mon to Sat 10-4.
Admission: Free.

HIGHLANDS

CAWDOR CASTLE

nr Inverness map E17
Telephone: Cawdor (06677) 615 Fax: (06677) 674
(The Earl of Cawdor)

The 14th century Keep, fortified in the 15th century and impressive additions, mainly 17th century, form a massive fortress. Gardens, nature trails and splendid grounds. Shakespearian memories of Macbeth. The most romantic castle in the Highlands.

Location: S of Nairn on B9090 between Inverness and Nairn.
Open: May 1 to Oct 3: daily 10-5.30 (last adm 5).
Admission: £3.50 Chd. (aged 5-15) £1.90, OAPs and disabled £2.80. Parties of 20 or more adults £3.30; 20 or more children (aged 5-15) £1.50. Family ticket (2 adults and up to 5 children) £10. Gardens, grounds and nature trail only £1.80. Blind people, no charge.
Refreshments: Licensed restaurant (self-service); Snack bar.
Gift shop. Book shop. Wool shop. Picnic area.9-hole Pitch and Putt. Nature Trails. No dogs allowed in Castle or Grounds.

DOCHFOUR GARDENS

Inverness map G16
Telephone: (0463 86) 218
(Lord and Lady Burton)

Fifteen acres of Victorian terraced garden at the north end of the Great Glen, with panoramic views over Loch Dochfour. Magnificent specimen trees, naturalised daffodils, rhododendrons, water garden, extensive yew topiary. Integral nursery selling shrubs, alpines and herbaceous plants. Pick-your-own soft fruit in season.

Location: 6 m SW of Inverness on A82 to Fort William.
Open: All year, Mon to Fri 10-5. Apr to Oct, Sat and Sun 2-5.
Admission: £1 (collection box) Chd (under 16) free. Parties by arrangement only. Parking free.
No dogs. HOUSE NOT OPEN.

DUNROBIN CASTLE

Golspie map E16
Telephone: (0408) 633177/633268 Fax: (0408) 633800
(The Countess of Sutherland)

One of Scotland's oldest inhabited houses. Historic home of the Sutherland family. Furniture, paintings and china. Exhibits of local and general interest. Victorian Museum in grounds.

Location: ½ m NE of Golspie on A9.
Station(s): Golspie (2 m).
Open: May: Mons to Thurs 10.30-12.30. June 1 to Sept 30: Mons to Sats 10.30-5.30, Suns 1-5.30. Last admission 5pm. Oct 1 to 15: Mon to Sat 10.30-4.30. Sun 1-4.30. Last adm 4pm. Open all year round for pre-booked groups.
Admission: £3.20, party rates £3, OAPs £2.10, Chd £1.60, party rates £1.50. Family tickets £8.
Refreshments: Tearoom.

DUNVEGAN CASTLE

Isle of Skye map B17 △
(John MacLeod of MacLeod)

Dating from the 13th century and continuously inhabited by the Chiefs of MacLeod. Fairy flag. Licensed restaurant; two craft and souvenir shops; castle water garden; audio-visual theatre; clan exhibition; items belonging to Bonnie Prince Charlie; loch boat trips; famous seal colony; pedigree highland cattle fold.

Location: Dunvegan village (1 m); 23 m W of Portree on the Isle of Skye.
Open: Mar 22 to Oct 31: Mon to Sat 10-5.30. Last adm 5. Sun: gardens, craft shop and restaurant open all day 10-5.30. Castle open 1-5.30. Last adm 5.
Admission: £3.80, Chd £2.10, Groups/OAPs/Students £3.40. Gardens only £2.20, Chd £1.40.

EILEAN DONAN CASTLE

Wester Ross map C16 △
Telephone: (059 985) 202
(Conchra Charitable Trust)

13th century Castle. Jacobite relics - mostly with Clan connections.

Location: In Dornie, Kyle of Lochalsh; 8 m E of Kyle on A87.
Open: Easter to Sept 30: daily (inc Suns) 10-6.
Admission: £1.50.

FORT GEORGE

Ardersier map E17
(Historic Scotland)

One of the most outstanding military fortifications virtually unaltered from the 18th century. Re-creations of 18th & 19th century barrack rooms. Seafield collection of arms.

Location: At Ardersier. 11 m NE of Inverness.

INVEREWE GARDEN

Poolewe, Wester Ross map C17 &
Telephone: (044 586) 229 (Information Centre)
(The National Trust for Scotland)

Remarkable garden created by the late Osgood Mackenzie. Rare and sub-tropical plants.

Location: 7 m from Gairloch; 85 m W of Inverness, A832.
Open: Garden open all the year: daily 9.30-sunset. Visitor Centre: Apr 1 to May 21, Sept 6 to Oct 17: Mons-Sats 10-5.30, Suns 2-5.30, May 22 to Sept 5, Mons to Sats 9.30-5.30, Suns 12-5.30.
Admission: £2.80, Chd £1.40, Adult parties £2.20, School parties £1.10, Chd (under 5) free. OAPs/Students (on production of their cards) half-price.
Refreshments: (Licensed) restaurant in garden open during same period, *open at 11 and closes at 4.30.*
Ranger Naturalist Service. For disabled: Half garden, greenhouse, toilets, wheelchair available. Guided walks with gardener Apr 1 to Oct 17. Mon - Frid at 1.30pm.

HUGH MILLER'S COTTAGE

Cromarty map E17
Telephone: (038 17) 245
(The National Trust for Scotland)

Birthplace (10 Oct 1802) of Hugh Miller, stonemason, eminent geologist, editor and writer. Furnished thatched cottage built c 1711 for his grandfather contains an interesting exhibition on his life and work. Captioned video programme. Cottage garden.

Location: In Cromarty 22m from Invernes A832.
Open: Apr 1 to Sept 26: Mons to Sats 10-1, 2-5; Suns 2-5.
Admission: £1.50, Chd 80p (under 5) free. Adult parties £1.20, School parties 60p. OAPs/Students (on production of their cards) half-price.

URQUHART CASTLE

Loch Ness map D16
(Historic Scotland)

Remains of one of the largest Castles in Scotland

Location: On W shore of Loch Ness 1½ m SE of Drumnadrochit.
Open: Apr 1 to Sept 30 - All week 9.30-6.30. Oct 1 to Mar 31 - Mon to Sat 9.30-4.30, Suns 11.30-4. *Closed Dec 25, 26; Jan 1, 2.*
Admission: £1.50, Chd/OAPs 80p. Family ticket £4.50. Prices subject to change 1993 season.

LOTHIAN

AMISFIELD MAINS

nr Haddington map F14
Telephone: (08757) 201
(Lord Wemyss' Trust)

Georgian farmhouse with 'Gothick' Barn and Cottage.

Location: Between Haddington & East Linton on A1 Edinburgh/Dunbar Road.
Open: Exteriors only. By appointment, Wemyss & March Estates, Estate Office, Longniddry, East Lothian 32 0PY.

BEANSTON

nr Haddington map F14
Telephone: (08757) 201
(Lord Wemyss' Trust)

Georgian farmhouse with Georgian Orangery.

Location: Between Haddington & East Linton on A1 Edinburgh/Dunbar Road.
Open: Exteriors only. By appointment, Wemyss & March Estates, Estate Office, Longniddry, East Lothian 32 0PY.

DALMENY HOUSE

South Queensferry map F14 △ &
Telephone: 031-331 1888
(The Earl of Rosebery)

Family home of the Earls of Rosebery, magnificently set in beautiful parkland on the shores of the Firth of Forth, 7m from the centre of Edinburgh. Scotland's first Gothic Revival house, designed in 1814 by William Wilkins. Rothschild Collection of French furniture and decorative art. Portraits by Reynolds, Gainsborough, Raeburn and Lawrence. Goya tapestries. Napleonic Collection assembled by Prime Minister, the 5th Earl. Woodland garden with superb rhododendrons and azaleas.

Location: 3 m E of South Queensferry; 7 m W of Edinburgh off A90.
Open: May to Sept incl - Sun 1-5.30, Mon 12-5.30, Tues 12-5.30. Special parties also welcome at other times by arrangement with Administrator.
Refreshments: Light lunches and home-made teas.
Public Transport: From St. Andrew Sq Bus Station to Chapel Gate (1 m from house).

DIRLETON CASTLE & GARDEN

Dirleton map F14
(Historic Scotland)

Well preserved 13th century castle, attractive gardens.

Location: In the village of Dirleton on Edinburgh/North Berwick Road (A198).
Station(s): North Berwick (2 m).
Open: Apr 1 to Sept 30 - Mon to Sat 9.30-6.30, Suns 2-6.30. Oct 1 to Mar 31 - Mon to Sat 9.30-4.30, Suns 2-4.30.
Admission: £1.50, Chd/OAPs 80p. Prices subject to change 1993 season.

Murder, LOOTING, TREASON, ARSON, *Burning*, PILLAGE.

Consider an old building without any history. Dull stuff indeed.

What is it then that makes the historic buildings of Scotland so interesting? It's not just the beauty of the buildings and stones themselves but the fact that they were witness to a history crammed with heroism and betrayal, loyalty and deceit. A dastardly deed here. A conspiracy there.

And with a Historic Scotland Explorer Ticket you

Skara Brae, on Orkney, is one of the best-preserved stone-age villages in Europe and provides a wonderful illustration of life 5,000 years ago.

Fort George, eleven miles N.E. of Inverness. One of the most outstanding artillery fortifications in Europe. Visitor centre and reconstructions of period barrack rooms.

Edinburgh Castle, Scotland's most famous castle. Many attractions, including the Crown Jewels (Honours) of Scotland, the Great Hall and the famous 15th century gun Mons Meg.

Stirling Castle, without doubt, Scotland's grandest castle, both in its situation on a commanding rock outcrop and its architecture. Visitor Centre with audio-visual display.

The Border Abbeys, illustrated here is Jedburgh Abbey, founded in 1138 by David I. It is one of the four great border abbeys with Melrose, Kelso and Dryburgh. They lie within a 12 mile triangle.

New Abbey Cornmill, near Dumfries, is a fully renovated, water-powered oatmeal mill in working order which is regularly demonstrated for visitors.

can steep yourself in Scotland's turbulent past by visiting over 70 historic sites, all of which are open seven days a week from April to September. [Information on Winter opening times is easily available by telephoning 031-244 3101 (Mon-Fri 9am-5pm).]

If you have an appetite for romance and intrigue you'll find Historic Scotland has more than enough to feed your imagination.

THE PERFECT *Ingredients* FOR A *Wonderful* DAY OUT.

HISTORIC SCOTLAND

Thousands of years of history. Minutes from your door.

Historic Scotland, 20 Brandon Street, Edinburgh EH3 5RA. Tel: 031-244 3101 (Monday-Friday 9am-5pm)

Explorer Tickets give reduced cost entry for 7 or 14 days. Ask at Tourist Information Centres, Travel Agents and Historic Scotland properties.

EDINBURGH CASTLE

Edinburgh map F14
(Historic Scotland)

Ancient fortress of great importance. St Margaret's Chapel has Norman features.

Location: Castlehill, Edinburgh.

Location: In Edinburgh city centre.
Open: Apr 1 to Oct 31: Mons to Sats 10-5, Suns 2-5.
Admission: £2.80, Chd £1.40 (under 5) free. Adult parties £2.20, School parties £1.10. OAPs/Students (on production of their cards) half-price.**COMBINED TICKET FOR THE GEORGIAN HOUSE AND GLADSTONE'S LAND**: £5, Chd £2.50, Adult parties £4, School parties £2.

THE GEORGIAN HOUSE

No. 7 Charlotte Square, Edinburgh map F14 Ⓢ
Telephone: 031-225 2160
(The National Trust for Scotland)

The north side of Charlotte Square is classed as Robert Adam's masterpiece of urban architecture. The main floors of No. 7 are open as a typical Georgian House. Audio-visual shows. Shop.

GLADSTONE'S LAND

Edinburgh map F14
Telephone: 031-226 5856
(The National Trust for Scotland)

Built 1620 and shortly afterwards occupied by Thomas Gledstanes. Remarkable painted wooden ceilings; furnished as a typical 'Old Town' house of the period. Shop.

Location: 477B Lawnmarket, Edinburgh.
Open: Apr 1 to Oct 31: Mons to Sats 10-5, Suns 2-5.
Admission: £2.40, Chd £1.20 (under 5) free. Adult parties £1.90, School parties £1. OAPs/Students (on production of their cards) half-price.
For combined ticket with The Georgian House see above.

GOSFORD HOUSE

East Lothian map F14
Telephone: (08757) 201
(Lord Wemyss' Trust)

Robert Adam Mansion, central block surviving; striking maritime situation. Original wings replaced 1890; South wing contains celebrated Marble Hall, fine collection of paintings etc. Part of Adam block burnt 1940, re-roofed 1987. Policies laid out with ornamental water. Grey Lag Geese and other wildfowl breeding.

Location: On A198 between Aberlady & Longniddry; NW of Haddington.
Station(s): Longniddry (2 m).
Open: May 20 to July 20. Weds, Sats and Suns 2-5.*Special openings during Scottish Game Fair, between July 22-24, to be announced later.*
Admission: £1, Chd 50p, OAPs 75p.
Refreshments: Hotels in Aberlady.
Wemyss & March Estates, Longniddry, East Lothian EH32 0PY.

HARELAW FARMHOUSE

nr Longniddry   map F14
Telephone: (08757) 201
(Lord Wemyss' Trust)

Harelaw Farmhouse. An early 19th century 2-storey farmhouse built in the old fashioned way, as an integral part of the steading, which is also distinguished by a dovecote over the entrance arch surmounted by a windvane.

Location: Between Longniddry and Drem on the B1377.
Open: Exteriors only. By appointment. Wemyss and March Estates, Estate Office, Longniddry, East Lothian EH32 OPY.

HOPETOUN HOUSE

South Queensferry, nr Edinburgh   map E14   Ⓢ
Telephone: 031-331 2451
(Hopetoun House Preservation Trust)

Home of the Marquess of Linlithgow. Fine example of 18th century Adam architecture. Magnificent reception rooms, pictures, antiques.

Location: 2 m from Forth Road Bridge nr South Queensferry off A904.
Open: Daily 10-5.30 from Apr 9 to Oct 3 inclusive. (Last admission 4.45).The house is also available for private evening functions throughout the year. Enquiries to Administrator's Office 031-331 2451.
Admission: £3.50, party rates £2.90, OAPs £2.90, Chd 5-16 yrs £1.70, Chd party rates £1.50. Grounds only: £1.80, Chd 50p. Family tickets £9.50, grounds only £4.20. Free parking.
Refreshments: Licensed restaurant and snack bar in Tapestry Room.
Gift shop. Deer park. Picnic areas. Free Ranger service. Roof top viewing platform with magnificent views of the Forth and the Bridges.

THE HOUSE OF THE BINNS

by Linlithgow   map E14   △
Telephone: (050 683) 4255
(The National Trust for Scotland)

Historic home of the Dalyells. Fine plaster ceilings. Interesting pictures. Panoramic viewpoint.

Location: 3½ m E of Linlithgow off A904.
Open: Apr 10 to 12 and May 1 to Sept 30: daily Sat to Thurs 2-5 *(Closed Frid)*. Parkland open Apr 10 to Sept 30, 10-7.
Admission: £2.80, Chd £1.40 (under 5) free. Adult parties £2.20, School parties £1.10, OAPs/Students (on production of their cards) half-price. *Members of the Royal Scots Dragoon Guards (in uniform) admitted free.*

INVERESK LODGE GARDEN

Inveresk   map F13
(The National Trust for Scotland)

New garden, with large selection of plants.

Location: In Inveresk village; 6 m E of Edinburgh off A1.
Open: GARDEN. All year - Mons to Frid 10-4.30; Suns 2-5. Apr 9 to Sept 30 - Mon to Frid 10-4.30; Sat/Sun 2-5. Lodge open for temporary exhibitions only, as advertised.
Admission: 50p. Honesty Box.

LAMB'S HOUSE

Leith   map F13
Telephone: 031-554 3131
(The National Trust for Scotland)

Residence and warehouse of prosperous merchant of late 16th or early 17th century. Renovated 18th century and later in 1979. Now old people's day centre.

Location: In Leith.
Open: Mons to Frid - Daily 9-5. *(Except Christmas/New Year.)*
Admission: Visits by prior arrangement.

LAURISTON CASTLE

Edinburgh map F14 △
(City of Edinburgh District Council)

A late 16th century tower - house with extensive 19th century additions. It has a fine Edwardian interior containing 18th and 19th century furniture, impressive collections of Derbyshire Blue John, Crossley wool mosaics and objets d'art. Visitors are taken on a guided tour lasting approximately 40 minutes. There is a free car park. Opening hours - April to October, Daily (except Friday) 11am - 1pm, 2 - 5pm, last tour starts at approximately 3.20pm. Telephone 031 336 2060.

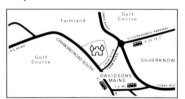

Admission Charges

Adults: £2.00 Children, UB40's, Benefit recipients and Leisure Access card holders: £1.00. Free admission to the Castle grounds.

THE CITY OF EDINBURGH DISTRICT COUNCIL
EDINBURGH
IMPROVING SERVICES - CREATING JOBS

Bus no 41 from George Street to Lauriston Castle gates, and Bus no 40 from the Mound, Princes Street to Davidson Mains.

A beautifully furnished Edwardian home, associated with John Law (1671-1729), founder of first bank in France.

Location: Cramond Road South, Davidsons Mains, 4½ m from GPO, Edinburgh.
Open: Castle. All year. Apr to Oct: daily (except Fris) 11-1, 2-5. Nov to Mar: Sats and Suns only 2-4. Guided tours only (last tour 40 mins before closing time). Grounds: daily 9-dusk.
Admission: £2, Chd £1.

LENNOXLOVE

Haddington map F13
Telephone: (062 082) 3720
(His Grace the Duke of Hamilton)

Lennoxlove, home of the Duke of Hamilton, is a house with a three-fold interest; its historic architecture, the association of its proprietors with the Royal House of Stewart and the famous Hamilton Palace collection of works of art, including the Casket, ring and Death Mask of Mary Queen of Scots. Formerly Lethington Tower, ancient home of the Maitlands. The Lime Avenue, known as Politician's Walk, was laid out by William Maitland, Secretary to Mary Queen of Scots.

Location: 1½ m S of Haddington on B6369; 18 m E of Edinburgh off A1.
Open: Easter weekend, then May to Sept - Weds, Sats & Suns 2-5. At other times by appointment (minimum of 10 people); apply to Estate Office, Lennoxlove, Haddington.
Admission: £2.50, Chd £1.25. Pre-booked parties (10 or more) £1.80, Chd 75p. Price includes guided tour of House, entry to gardens and parking.

LUFFNESS

Aberlady map F14
(Luffness Ltd)

16th century castle with 13th century keep - dry moat and old fortifications. Built on the site of a Norse raiders camp.

Location: 18 m E of Edinburgh.
Open: By request during summer months.

MALLENY GARDEN

Balerno map F13
(The National Trust for Scotland)

A delightfully personal garden with a particularly good collection of shrub roses. National Bonsai Collection for Scotland.

Location: In Balerno, off A70.
Open: GARDEN ONLY. All the year - Daily 10-sunset.
Admission: £1, Chd 50p (under 5) free. OAPs/Students (on production of their cards) half-price.
No dogs in garden please.

Sir Anthony Van Dyck
Portrait and religious painter
Born in Antwerp 1599, died in London 1641
First visited England in 1620, knighted by Charles I in 1633

His work can be seen in the following properties included in Historic Houses Castles and Gardens:

Alnwick Castle	*Hinwick House*
Arundel Castle	*Sudeley Castle*
Boughton House	*Warwick Castle*
Euston Hall	*Weston Park*
Goodwood House	

PALACE OF HOLYROODHOUSE

Edinburgh map E14
Telephone: 031-556 7371
(The official residence of HM The Queen in Scotland)

Palace of Holyroodhouse

See entry for details

The ridge, known as the Royal Mile, that slopes downwards from Edinburgh Castle, comes to a majestic conclusion at Holyroodhouse, where Palace and Abbey stand against the spectacular backdrop of Salisbury Crag. Throughout history, Holyrood has been the scene of turbulent and extraordinary events, yet the Palace retains a modern appeal appropriate to a Royal residence still in regular use.

Location: Central Edinburgh.
Open: Open all year (except when Her Majesty The Queen is in residence). Summer: Mon to Sat 9.30-5.15; Sun 10.30-4.30. Winter: Mon to Sat 9.30-3.45; Sun *Closed. The Palace and Abbey may sometimes be closed at short notice.* **Enquiries:** Telephone (031 556) 1096.
Admission: charge. Group rates available.
Refreshments: Tea room outside Main Gate.

PRESTON MILL

East Linton map F14
Telephone: (0620) 860426
(The National Trust for Scotland)

The oldest mill (16th century) of its kind still working and only survivor of many on the banks of the Tyne. Popular with artists. Renovated machinery.

Location: 5½ m W of Dunbar, off A1.
Open: Preston Mill and Phantassie Doo'cot: Apr 1 to Sept 30: Mons to Sats 11-1, 2-5; Suns 2-5. Oct: Weekends 11-1, 2-4, Suns 2-4.
Admission: £1.50, Chd 80p (under 5) free. OAPs/Students (on production of their cards) half-price. Adult parties £1.20, School parties 60p.

ROYAL BOTANIC GARDEN

Edinburgh map F14

STEVENSON HOUSE

Haddington map F13
Telephone: (062 082) 3376 Mrs. J. C. H. Dunlop
(Trustees of the Brown Dunlop Country Houses Trust)

KA family home for four centuries, of charm and interest and dating from the 13th century when it belonged to the Cistercian Nunnery at Haddington, but partially destroyed on several occasions, and finally made uninhabitable in 1544. Restored about 1560 and the present house dates mainly from this period, with later additions in the 18th century. Fine furniture, pictures etc.

Location: 20 m approx from Edinburgh; 1½ m approx from A1; 2 m approx from Haddington. (See Historic House direction signs on A1 in Haddington.)
Open: July to mid-Aug - Thurs, Sats & Suns 2-5. Guided tours take at least 1-1½ hours 3 pm. Other times by arrangement only. GARDENS (House and Walled Kitchen Garden) are open daily (Apr to Oct).
Admission: £2, OAPs £1.50, Chd (under 14) £1. Special arrangement parties welcome. GARDENS: 50p only (payable into Box on House Garden entrance gate).
Refreshments: Appointment parties morning coffee etc at Stevenson. Nearest hotels and restaurants are in Haddington, i.e. 2 m from Stevenson.
Car parking. Suitable for wheelchairs in garden only.

TANTALLON CASTLE

nr North Berwick map F14
(Historic Scotland)

Famous 14th century stronghold of the Douglases occupies a magnificent situation on the rocky coast of the Firth of Forth.

Location: On the coast approx 3 m E of North Berwick.

WINTON HOUSE

Pencaitland map F13 △
Telephone: (0875) 340 222; Housekeeper: (0875) 340357
(Sir David Ogilvy's 1968 Trustees)

Built 1620. Famous twisted stone chimneys and beautiful plaster ceilings in honour of Charles I's visit. Enlarged 1800. Fine pictures and furniture. Terraced gardens.

Location: Drive entrances with wrought-iron gates and lodges in Pencaitland (A6093) and towards New Winton village on B6355. Tranent (A1) 3 m, by B6355; Haddington (A1) by A6093 6 m; Pathhead (A68) 6 m by A6093.
Open: Restricted to groups of 10 or more (and others very specially interested) at any time by prior arrangement with the owner.
Admission: Party rate: House,*(personally conducted tour)* grounds and car park. £2.
Refreshments: Tea and biscuits can be arranged in the house, or Old Smiddy Inn, Pencaitland (1 m).

STRATHCLYDE

ARDUAINE GARDEN

Argyll map D12
Telephone: (08522) 287
(The National Trust for Scotland)

Outstanding 18 acre garden on a promontory bounded by Loch Melfort and the Sound of Jura. Nationally noted for rhododendrons and azalea specied, magnolias and other rare trees and shrubs.

Location: A816, 20 m S of Oban and 17 m N of Lochgilphead.
Open: All year 9.30-sunset.
Admission: £2, Chd £1 (under 5) free. Adult parties £1.60. School parties 80p.

BACHELORS' CLUB

Tarbolton map D13
Telephone: (0292) 541940
(The National Trust for Scotland)

17th century thatched house where Burns and his friends formed their club in 1780. Period furnishings.

Location: In Tarbolton village 7½ m NE of Ayr (off A758).
Open: Apr 1 to Oct 31: daily 12-5, other times by appointment.
Admission: £1.50, Chd 80p (under 5) free, OAPs/Students (on production of their cards) half-price. Adult parties £1.20, School parties 60p. *Other times by appointment.*

BALLOCH CASTLE COUNTRY PARK

Balloch map D14
Telephone: (0389) 58216
(Dumbarton District Council)

BELLAHOUSTON PARK

Glasgow map D13
(City of Glasgow District Council)

BENMORE YOUNGER BOTANIC GARDEN

nr Dunoon map D14
(Royal Botanic Garden, Edinburgh)

BLAIRQUHAN CASTLE AND GARDENS

Straiton, Maybole, Ayrshire map D12
Telephone: (065 57) 239
(James Hunter Blair)

Magnificent Regency castellated mansion approached by a 3 m private drive beside the river Girvan. Walled gardens and pinetum. Plants for sale. Picture gallery.

Location: 14 m S of Ayr; off A77. Entrance Lodge is on B7045 ½ m S of Kirkmichael.
Open: July 12 to Aug 9 *(not Mons).*
Admission: £3, Chd £2, OAPs £2. Parties by arrangement at any time of year.
Refreshments: Tea in castle.
Car parking. Wheelchairs - around gardens and principal floor of the castle.

BOTANIC GARDENS

Glasgow map D13
(City of Glasgow District Council)

BOTHWELL CASTLE

Bothwell map E13
(Historic Scotland)

The largest and finest 13th century Stone Castle in Scotland.

Location: At Bothwell but approached from Uddingston.

BRODICK CASTLE, GARDEN AND COUNTRY PARK

Isle of Arran map C13
Telephone: (0770) 2202
(The National Trust for Scotland)

Historic home of the Dukes of Hamilton. The castle dates in part from the 13th century. Paintings, furniture, objet d'art. Formal and woodland gardens, noted for rhododendrons. Country park.

Location: 1½ m N of Brodick pierhead on the Isle of Arran.
Station(s): Ardrossan Harbour and Claonaig in Kintyre (& hence by Caledonian MacBrayne ferry). Ferry enquiries to Caledonian MacBrayne. Tel. Gourock (0475) 33755.
Open: CASTLE. Apr 1 to 18 and May 2 to Sept 30: daily 1-5. Apr 19 to May 1 and Oct 2 to 23: Mon, Wed and Sat 1-5. COUNTRY PARK AND GARDEN (Cunninghame District Council and NTS). All the year: daily 9.30-sunset. VISITOR CENTRE AND SHOP. Dates as Castle daily 10-5.
Admission: Castle and Gardens: £3.50, Chd £1.80. Adult parties £2.80, School parties £1.40. Gardens only: £2, Chd £1 (under 5) free, OAPs/Students (on production of their cards) half-price. Free car park.
Refreshments: RESTAURANT. (Self-service in Castle). Dates as Castle, Mons to Sats 10-5, Suns 12-5.
Shop.

BURNS COTTAGE

Alloway map D12
(Trustees of Burns Monument)

CULZEAN CASTLE, GARDEN AND COUNTRY PARK

Maybole map D12   △   ⅚   ⑤
Telephone: (065 56) 274
(The National Trust for Scotland)

One of the finest Adam houses in Scotland. Spacious policies and gardens. Adventure playground.

Location: 12 m SW of Ayr just off A719.
Open: CASTLE, VISITOR CENTRE, LICENSED RESTAURANT AND SHOPS Apr 1 to Oct 31: daily 10.30-5.30. At other times by appointment. CULZEAN COUNTRY PARK *(NTS and Kyle & Carrick; Cummock & Doon Valley District Councils & Strathclyde Region)* - Open all year, daily 9-sunset.
Admission: Castle, Visitor Centre, Licensed Restaurant and Shops: £3.30, Chd £1.70 (under 5) free. Adult parties £4, School parties £2. OAPs/Students (on production of their cards) half-price. (Includes coach entry to Country Park). Culsean Country Park: Free to members and pedestrians. Cars £6, mini-buses/caravans £8, Coaches £28. School coaches £20, motorcycles £1.50 *Apr to Oct 31 only.* vehicles (except school coaches) free at other times.

DUMBARTON CASTLE

Dumbarton map D13
(Historic Scotland)

Sited on a volcanic rock overlooking the Firth of Clyde.
Location: At Dumbarton.

FINLAYSTONE HOUSE AND GARDENS

Langbank map D13
Telephone: (047 554) 285/505
(Mrs G MacMillan)

Formerly home of fifteen Earls of Glencairn; now the home of the chief of Clan MacMillan. Exhibitions of international dolls, flower books and Victoriana, and Celtic art. Beautiful Gardens, Woodlands, with picnic/play areas. Ranger service. Visitor centre. Clan Centre. Celtic Exhibition.

Location: On A8 between Langbank & Port Glasgow; 20 minutes W of Glasgow on S bank of the Clyde.
Station(s): Longbank (1¼ m).
Open: Beautiful gardens and woods open ALL THE YEAR. (House: Apr to Aug - Suns 2.30-4.30, **and** by appointment any time).
Admission: £1.50, Chd 80p. Pre-booked groups welcome. House: £1.50, Chd 80p.
Refreshments: Summer 11-5 and Winter weekends in walled garden.

GREENBANK GARDEN

Glasgow map D13   ⅚
Telephone: 041-639 3281
(The National Trust for Scotland)

Walled garden, woodland walk and policies. Wide range of plants, flowers and shrubs. Regular garden walks and events. Best seen Apr-Oct. Attractive series of gardens, extending to 2½ acres, surrounding Georgian house (not open to the public). Special garden and greenhouse for the disabled, together with special gardening tools.

Location: Flenders Road, near Clarkston Toll.
Station(s): Clarkston (1¼ m).
Open: Garden. All the year: daily 9.30-sunset.
Admission: £2, Chd (accompanied by adult) £1. Adult parties £1.60, School parties 80p. Chd (under 5) free. OAPs/Students (on production of their cards) half-price.

THE HILL HOUSE

Helensburgh map D14
Telephone: (0436) 73900
(The National Trust for Scotland)

Overlooking the estuary of the River Clyde the house is considered to be the finest example of the domestic architecture of Charles Rennie Mackintosh. Commissioned in 1902 and completed in 1904 for the Glasgow publisher Walter W Blackie. Special display about Charles Rennie Mackintosh.

Location: In Upper Colquhoun Street, Helensburgh; NW of Glasgow via A814.
Open: Apr 1 to Dec 23, and Dec 28 to 30: daily 1-5 (last adm 4.30). *CLOSED for restoration Dec 31 1993 to Mar 31 1994.*
Admission: £2.80, Chd £1.40. Adult parties £2.20, School parties £1.10.

HUTCHESONS' HALL

Glasgow map E13
Telephone: 041-552 8391
(The National Trust for Scotland)

Described as one of the most elegant buildings in Glasgow's city centre, the Hall was built in 1802-5 to a design by David Hamilton.

Location: 158 Ingram Street, nr SE corner of George Square.
Open: Hall viewing subject to functions. Visitor Centre and Function Hall: open all year (*except public holidays and Jan 1 to Jan 5*). Mons to Frid 9-5, Sats 10-4.
Admission: Free.
Shop: Mons to Sats 10-4.

INVERARAY CASTLE

Inveraray map D14
Telephone: (0499) 2203.
(The Trustees of the 10th Duke of Argyll)

Since the early 15th century Inveraray has been the Headquarters of the Clan Campbell. The present Castle was built in the third quarter of the 18th century by Roger Morris and Robert Mylne. The Great Hall and Armoury, the State Rooms, Tapestries, Pictures and 18th century Furniture and old kitchen are shown.

Location: ¾ m NE of Inveraray on Loch Fyne 58 m NW of Glasgow.
Open: First Sat in Apr to second Sun in Oct. Apr, May, June, Sept & Oct: daily (except Fri) 10-1, 2-6. Sun 1-6. July & Aug: daily 10-6, Sun 1-6. Last admission 12.30 & 5.30.. Gardens open by appointment, woodland walk open all year. Craft shop. *Enquiries:* The Factor, Dept HH, Cherry Park, Inveraray, Argyll. Telephone: (0499) 2203.
Refreshments: Tearoom.

KELBURN COUNTRY CENTRE AND KELBURN CASTLE

Largs map D13
Telephone: (0475) 568685
(The Home and Park of the Earls of Glasgow on the Firth of Clyde.)

Kelburn has been the home of the Earls of Glasgow since the creation of the title in 1703, but has been the seat of the Boyle family for over 800 years. The Kelburn Glen is one of the most romantic in Scotland, dropping 700 ft by way of many waterfalls and deep gorges. There is a Walled Garden full of unusual shrubs peculiar to the West Coast of Scotland, a New Zealand Garden created by the 7th Countess in 1898, a small formal Garden designed by the 3rd Earl in the 1760s for his four children, and two unique sundials. There are some very remarkable trees, including the largest Monterey Pine in Scotland, the thousand-year-old Yews, and the amazing Weeping Larch. Kelburn Castle is fully lived in, and open July and August only, but it makes an impressive background to many walks and views. The grounds and the riding school, however, are open all the year round and Kelburn Country Centre, open from Easter till mid-Oct, contains an Adventure course, Commando Assault course, pet's corner, children's stockade, pony trekking. Shop, exhibitions, craft workshop, museum, cartoon exhibition, display room.

Location: On the A78 between Largs and Fairlie in Ayrshire.
Station(s): Largs (2 m).
Open: Kelburn Country Centre: Open with all facilities daily 10-6 from Apr 4 to mid-Oct.
Winter opening: Grounds only mid Oct to Mar 30. **Kelburn Castle:** Open to visitors in the afternoons in July and Aug only. Closed at all other times except to special parties by prior arrangement.
Admission: Kelburn Country Centre: £3, Chd (accompanied) £1.50, OAPs/UB40 £1.50; Groups (12 +) £1.50 per person. Winter: £1, Chd 60p. Kelburn Castle: £1.50 excluding admission to Kelburn Country Centre.
Refreshments: Licensed cafe, lunches, snacks, home baking, ice cream parlour, picnic areas. Fully open from Apr 3 to Oct 24.
Country Centre: Dogs admitted on leads.

LINN PARK

Glasgow map D13
(City of Glasgow District Council)

POLLOK HOUSE & PARK

Glasgow map D13   ♿
Telephone: 041-632 0274
(City of Glasgow District Council)

Built 1747-52, additions by Sir Rowand Anderson 1890-1908. Contains Stirling Maxwell collection of Spanish and other European paintings; displays of furniture, ceramics, glass and silver. Nearby in Pollok Park is the Burrell Collection. Opening times as Pollok House.

Location: 3½ m from City Centre.
Station(s): Pollokshaws West (1 m).
Open: All the year: Mons to Sats 10-5, Suns 11-5. *Closed Christmas Day & New Year's Day.*
Admission: Free.
Refreshments: Tea room (reservations Tel 041-649 7547).

ROSS HALL PARK

Glasgow map D13
(City of Glasgow District Council)

SORN CASTLE

Sorn
Telephone: (0292) 268181 (Cluttons)

Dating from the 14th century in impressive setting on sandstone cliff over the River Ayr with attractive woodland walks.

Location: 4 m E of Mauchline on B743.
Open: Jul 24 to Aug 21, 2-5pm, or by appointment. Grounds - Apr 1 to Oct 30.
Admission: £3.50

SOUTER JOHNNIE'S COTTAGE

Kirkoswald map D12
Telephone: (065 56) 603
(The National Trust for Scotland)

Thatched home of the original Souter in Burns', 'Tam o' Shanter', Burns' relics. Life-sized stone figures of the Souter, Tam, the Innkeeper and his wife, in restored ale house in the cottage garden.

Location: In Kirkoswald village 4 m W of Maybole on A77.
Open: Apr 1 to Oct 31: daily 12-5 (or by appointment).
Admission: £1.50, Chd 80p. Adult parties £1.20, School parties 60p (under 5) free. OAPs/Students (on production of their cards) half-price.

THE TENEMENT HOUSE

Glasgow map D13
Telephone: (041) 333 0183
(The National Trust of Scotland)

A restored first floor flat in a Victorian tenement building, built 1892, presents a picture of social significance. A second flat on the ground floor provides reception, interpretative and educational facilities.

Location: No 145 Buccleuch Street, Garnethill (N of Charing Cross).
Open: Until Mar 28 1993: Sats & Suns 2-4. Apr 1 to Oct 31 daily 2-5. Nov 6 to Mar 27 1994: Sat & Sun 2-4. Weekday morning visits by educational & other groups (no more than 15) to be arranged by advance booking only.
Admission: £2, Chd £1. Adult parties £1.60, School parties 80p.

TOROSAY CASTLE AND GARDENS

Craignure, Isle of Mull map C15
Telephone: (068 02) 421
(Mr Christopher James)

Early Victorian house by David Bryce, still a family home, surrounded by 12 acres of terraced and contrasting informal gardens, all offset by dramatic West Highland scenery.

Location: 1½ m SE of Craignure by A849, by Forest Walk or by N.G. Steam Railway.
Open: Castle - Easter to mid-Oct, 10.30-5.30 (last adm 5). Gardens - Summer, 9 -7. Winter - sunrise to sunset. Parties at other times to Castle by appointment only.
Admission: Castle: £3.50, also concession rates. Garden only: £1.50, Chd (5-16), OAPs/Students £1 (honesty box when castle closed). Free car park.
Refreshments: Home baked teas in Castle.
Dogs on lead in Gardens only. Gardens and tearoom only suitable for wheelchairs. Local Craft Shop.

VICTORIA PARK

Glasgow map D13
(City of Glasgow District Council)

WEAVER'S COTTAGE

Kilbarchan map D13
(The National Trust for Scotland)

Typical cottage of 18th century handloom weaver: looms, weaving equipment, domestic utensils. (Weaving demonstrations check for times).

Location: In Kilbarchan village; 12 m SW of Glasgow off A737.
Station(s): Johnstone (2½ m).
Open: Apr 1 to May 30, and Sept 2 to Oct 31: Tues, Thurs, Sats and Suns 1-5. May 31 to Aug 31: daily 1-5 (last tour 4.30).
Admission: £1.50, Chd 80p (under 5) free. Adult parties £1.20, Chd parties 60p. OAPs/Students (on production of their cards) half-price.
Video programme.

TAYSIDE

ANGUS FOLK MUSEUM

Glamis map F15
Telephone: (030 784) 288
(The National Trust for Scotland)

Row of 19th century cottages with stone-slabbed roofs, restored by the Trust. Adapted to display the Angus Folk Collection, one of the finest in the country. In agricultural annexe are farming implements and the Bothy Exhibition incl. taped recordings.

Location: In Glamis village; 12 m N of Dundee A94.
Open: Apr 9 to 12 and May 1 to Sept 30: daily 11-5.
Admission: £1.50, Chd 80p (under 5) free. Adult parties £1.20, School parties 60p. OAPs/Students (on production of their cards) half-price.

BARRIE'S BIRTHPLACE

Kirriemuir map F15
Telephone: (0575) 72646
(The National Trust for Scotland)

Contains mementoes of Sir James Barrie. New exhibition features Peter Pan and other works of Barrie.

Location: No 9 Brechin Road, in Kirriemuir.
Open: Apr 9 to 12; May 1 to Sept 30: Mons to Sats 11-5.30, Suns 2-5.30.
Admission: £1.50, Chd 80p (under 5) free. OAPs/Students (on production of their cards) half-price. Adult parties £1.20, School parties 60p.
Refreshments: Airlie Arms Hotel.

BARRY MILL

Carnoustie
Telephone: (0241) 56761
(The National Trust for Scotland)

This 18th century meal mill works on a demonstration basis. Displays highlight the important place the mill held in the community.

Location: 2 m NW of Carnoustie.
Open: Apr 9 to 12 and May 1 to Oct 17, daily 11-1 and 2-5.
Admission: £1.50, Chd 80p, adult parties £1.20, schools 60p.

BRANKLYN GARDEN

Perth map E14
Telephone: (0738) 25535
(The National Trust for Scotland)

One of the finest gardens of its size in Britain (2 acres).

Location: In Perth on Dundee Road (A85).
Open: Mar 1 to Oct 31: daily 9.30-sunset.
Admission: £2, Chd £1 (under 5) free. OAPs/Students (on production of their cards) half-price. Adult parties £1.20, School parties 60p.

CASTLE MENZIES

Weem map E15
(Menzies Clan Society)

Magnificent example of a 16th century fortified house, seat of the Chiefs of Clan Menzies, situated in the beautiful valley of the Tay. It was involved in the turbulent history of the Central Highlands and here 'Bonnie Prince Charlie' rested on his way to Culloden in 1746.

Location: 1½ m from Aberfeldy on B846.
Open: Apr to mid-Oct - Weekdays 10.30-5, Suns 2-5.
Admission: £2, Chd 50p, OAPs £1. Reductions for parties by prior arrangement.

EDZELL CASTLE & GARDENS

Edzell map F15
(Historic Scotland)

16th century castle. Unique renaissance garden. New Visitor Centre.

Location: 1 m W of Edzell; 6 m N of Brechin off B996.

GLAMIS CASTLE

Glamis map F15
(The Earl of Strathmore and Kinghorne)

Family home of the Earls of Strathmore and Kinghorne and a royal residence since 1372. Childhood home of H.M. Queen Elizabeth The Queen Mother and birthplace of H.R.H. The Princess Margaret. Legendary setting of Shakespeare's play 'Macbeth'. Five-storey L shaped tower block dating from 15th century, remodelled 1606, containing magnificent rooms with wide range of historic pictures, furniture, porcelain etc.

Location: Glamis.
Open: Apr 4 to Oct 11: daily 10.30-5.30 (last tour 4.45)
Admission: £4, party rates £3.70. OAPs £3.10, party rates £2.80. Chd 5-16 £2.20, party rates £1.90. Grounds only: £2, Chd £1. Family tickets £12.
Refreshments: Licensed Restaurant at the Castle.
Ample bus and car parking. Picnic area, Shops, Garden and Nature Trail. Further details available from The Administrator, Tel: (030 784) 242. Fax: (030 784) 257

HOUSE OF DUN

Nr Montrose map G15
Telephone: (067481) 264
(The National Trust for Scotland)

Palladian house overlooking the Montrose Basin, built in 1730 for David Erskine, Lord Dun, to designs by William Adam. Exuberant plasterwork in the saloon.

Location: 4 m W of Montrose.
Open: House, Courtyard and Tearoom: Apr 9 to 12, then May 1 to Oct 17: daily 11-5.30. Garden and grounds open all year.
Admission: House: £3.30, Chd £1.70, Adult parties £2.60, School parties £1.30. Garden and grounds: Free.

HUNTINGTOWER CASTLE

nr Perth map E14
(Historic Scotland)

Two fine and complete towers in which are excellent painted ceilings.

Location: 2 m W of Perth.

SCONE PALACE

Perth map E15
Telephone: (0738) 52300
(Rt Hon the Earl of Mansfield)

This medieval palace was Gothicised for the third Earl of Mansfield in the early 19th century. Superb collections of French furniture, china, ivories, clocks, Vernis Martin vases and objets d'art.

Location: 2 m NE of Perth on the Braemer Road (A93).
Station(s): Perth (2½ m).
Open: Good Friday till mid Oct. Mon to Sat 9.30-5pm. Sun 1.30pm (Jul & Aug 10am) - 5pm.
Admission: Palace and Grounds: £4, party rate £3.50., OAPs £3.20, party rate £2.90.Chd £2.20, party rate £2. Family ticket £12. Grounds only: £2, Chd £1.10. Special rates for pre-booked parties. Free car park.
Refreshments: Coffee shop. Old Kitchen Restaurant (licensed). Home baking. State Room dinners.
Shops. Picnic park. Playground.

The Garden Specialists
in Great Britain and Ireland

A selection of nurseries specialising in rare or uncommon plants

♿ Denotes the major part of the property is suitable for wheelchairs

APPLE COURT

Hordle Lane, Hordle, Lymington
Telephone: (0590) 642130
(Mrs Diana Grenfell)

Specialists in hostas, daylilies, ferns, grasses and unusual perennials and foliage plants for flower arrangers. Good selection of plants for a white garden, as featured in THE WHITE GARDEN, Grenfell & Grounds (Crowood Press, 1990). Wide variety of plants displayed in formal garden being created by the designer-owners within the walls of a former Victorian kitchen garden. Five National Reference Collections including small leafed Hostas.

Location: 4 m equidistant Lymington and New Milton, 1/4 m off A337 travelling north at Downtown crossroads.

APULDRAM ROSES

Apuldram Lane, Dell Quay, Chichester, West Sussex ♿
Telephone: (0243) 785769
(Mrs D. R. Sawday)

Specialist Rose Nursery growing over 300 varieties of Hybrid Teas, Floribundas, Climbers, Ramblers, Ground Cover, Miniature and Patio Roses. Also a large selection of shrub roses both old and new. Mature Rose Garden to view. Field open during summer months. Suitable for disabled but no special toilet. One wheelchair available.

Location: 1 m SW of Chichester. A286 Birdham-Wittering road from Chichester. Turn right into Dell Quay Road and then right again into Apuldram Lane.
Open: Every day Jan 7 to Dec 23. Mon to Sat 9-5, Suns and Bank Hols 10.30-4.30. Parties can be taken around by prior arrangement with guided tour of roses June to Sept.
Admission: Charity box in garden.
One wheelchair available. Ample car parking.

ARCHITECTURAL PLANTS

Cooks Farm, Nuthurst, Horsham, West Sussex
Telephone: (0403) 891772
(Angus White)

Hardy Exotics - evergreen trees and shrubs with big, spiky and frondy leaves, including conservatory plants. Many extremely rare. Please send for free list.
Location: Behind Black Horse pub in Nuthurst, 5 m S of Horsham, West Sussex.
Open: Mons to Sats 9-5.

AYLETT NURSERIES LTD

North Orbital Road (A414),, St. Albans, Hertfordshire ♿
Telephone: (0727) 822255
(Mr R.S. Aylett)

Aylett Nurseries of St. Albans is a well known family business with a reputation of high quality plants and service. Famous for its dahlias - having been awarded a Gold Medal by the Royal Horticultural Society every year since 1961. Spacious planteria contains a profusion of trees, shrubs, herbaceous plants and many more! In the spring our greenhouses are full of geraniums, fuchsias, hanging baskets and many other types of bedding plants. Facilities also include garden shop, coffee and gift shop, houseplants, florist, garden furniture.

Location: 2 m out of St. Albans, 1 m from M10 and M1, M25 and A1.
Open: Mon to Fri 8.30-5.30, Sats 8.30-5, Suns and Bank Hols 9-5. *Closed* Christmas Day and Boxing Day. Parties with pre advice please.
Admission: Free.
Refreshments: Dahlia coffee shop serves light lunches, homemade cakes, creamy gateaux. Coffee, tea and soft drinks.
Suitable for disabled visitors. Five wheelchairs available.

BLACKTHORN NURSERY

Kilmeston, Alresford
Telephone: (0962) 771796
(Mr & Mrs A.R. White)

Specialist nursery growing a wide range of alpines and rock plants with a choice selection of perennials, shrubs, climbers and ferns. Daphnes, hellebores and epimediums a speciality.

Location: 1 m S of Cheriton just off A272 Winchester to Petersfield road. Five minutes from Hinton Ampner House & Gardens (NT).

BLAKENEY HOUSE NURSERIES LTD

Osier Grounds, Denton, Canterbury
Telephone: (0227) 831800
Fax: (0227) 831883

Conifer specialists, wholesalers and distributors of hardy nursery stock. As wholesalers, we can help with almost any enquiry.
Location: A260 towards Folkestone. Take first right after Jackdaw Public House then left at T junction.

BODIAM NURSERY

Ockham House, Bodiam, Robertsbridge, East Sussex
Telephone: (0580) 830811/830649
(Richard Biggs)

Set beside fine old oasthouse and Queen Anne house in unspoilt countryside. Spectacular view of Bodiam Castle just across the River Rother. Enormous selection of heathers (over 200), shrubs (over 700), climbers, conifers, alpine and herbaceous plants, many unusual, propagated and grown here. Sizes from tinies for the economy minded to specimens for instant gardening'. Acres of plants in pots.

Location: 11 m from Hastings, 3 m from Hurst Green which is on the A21. Follow signs for Bodiam Castle. Nursery is just across the river valley from the Castle.
Station(s): Etchingham (5 m).
Open: Every day: 9-7 (sunset in winter).

BODNANT GARDEN NURSERY LTD

Tal Y Cafn, Nr. Colwyn Bay, Clwyd &
Telephone: (0492) 650460

Bodnant Garden Nursery is famous for its rare trees and shrubs. We propagate over 800 species and varieties of flowering and foliage shrubs, including rhododendrons, azaleas, magnolias and camellias. The many thousands of plants produced in our own propagation units by experienced staff are available to purchase, either by personal selection or our efficient mail order service.

Location: 8 m S of Llandudno and Colwyn Bay on the A470, just off the A55 Coastal Expressway.
Open: Daily (excl. Christmas Day) 9.30-5.
Refreshments: Morning coffee, light lunches and afternoon teas are available from Apr to Sept.
Car parking. Ramps for disabled. Wheelchairs available.

BOSVIGO PLANTS

Bosvigo Lane, Truro, Cornwall map C1
Telephone: (0872) 75774
(Mrs Wendy Perry)

Small specialist nursery. Rare and unusual herbaceous plants. 3-acre display gardens. Catalogue available - send 4 x 2nd class stamps. N.B. No mail order.

Location: ¾ m from city centre. Take A390 towards Redruth. At Highertown turn right by Shell garage and drive 400 yds down Dobbs Lane.
Open: Mar to end Oct daily 11-dusk.

J.W. BOYCE

Bush Pasture, Fordham, Ely, Cambridgeshire
Telephone: (0638) 721158

Specialists in garden seeds for over 80 years. Specialising in the production of pansy seed and plants. Also over 1000 items of seed which includes a wide range of separate colours for cut flowers, bedding and drying. Also old and unusual vegetables. Seed list free on request: Telephone above number, or write to J. W. Boyce, Bush Pasture, Carter Street, Ely, Cambs CB7 5JU.

BRACKENWOOD GARDEN CENTRE

131 Nore Road, Portishead, Bristol, Avon
Telephone: (0275) 843484

Woodland Garden (6 acres), Camellias, Rhododendrons, Acers and Pieris plus Rare Trees and Shrubs. Superb views across the Bristol Channel.

Location: 1½ m from Portishead on Nore Road (Coast road); M5 junction 19, 4 m.
Open: Apr to Sept.
Refreshments: New Tea room/Cafe.

BRESSINGHAM PLANT CENTRE

Bressingham, Diss, Norfolk
Telephone: (037 988) 464/8133

Our customers and our plants are our lifeblood - we have neither room, time nor inclination for furniture and lawnmowers! We have built our reputation on our plants and our service. We pride ourselves on giving our customers a horticultural experience they will not forget. Friendly expert staff will help you browse through the thousands of superb varieties on display. As avid gardeners, our staff have particular specialities and can offer advice on almost every aspect of gardening. We specialise in perennials, alpines, conifers and shrubs, together with climbers, fruit, herbs, bedding, trees, roses and indoor pot plants, on our extensive site beside Bressingham Gardens. The Bressingham Gardens mail order colour catalogue is available from this address for £2 (refundable with first order, min order value £15). Variety, quality, service and value are the principles you can depend on us for.

Location: 2½ m W of Diss, on the A1066 Thetford to Diss road.
Open: 10-5.30 daily.*Except Christmas and Boxing Day.*
Refreshments: Available at the 'Garden Seat' - our comfortable coffee room where customers can relax and browse through our reference library.

BRIDGEMERE GARDEN WORLD

Nr. Nantwich, Cheshire
Telephone: (09365) 381 or 239

The Greatest Gardening Day Out in Britain. Bridgemere rolls out acre upon acre of gardens, plants, glasshouses and shop with an Egon Ronay recommended coffee house. Visit the Garden Kingdom, five acres and more than 20 styles of garden - the romance of a French rose garden, the music of waterfalls and pools, the quiet charm of shade loving plants and recreated Chelsea Flower Show gold medal winning gardens, all to give you ideas for your own garden. With seasonal displays indoors and out, we are Europe's largest garden centre. We grow more plants in more varieties than anyone else, and are constantly expanding. With events all year, Bridgemere is a garden lover's paradise.

Location: Bridgemere is on A51 between Woore and Nantwich on the Cheshire/Staffordshire/Shropshire borders. Signposted from M6 junctions 15 and 16.
Open: Daily until dusk - 8 summer, 5 winter (*Closed* Christmas Day and Boxing Day).
Admission: Free. Small admission charge into Garden Kingdom (£1, OAPs 50p). Car and coach parking.

BRITISH WILD FLOWER PLANTS

23 Yarmouth Road, Ormesby St. Margaret, Gt. Yarmouth, Norfolk
Telephone: (0493) 730244
(*Linda Laxton*)

200 plus species of British Wild Flower Plants. Nursery grown, not collected from the wild.

Location: 5 m NW of Gt. Yarmouth on main A149.

BROMAGES BONSAI CENTRE

St. Mary's Gardens, Worplesdon   &
Telephone: (0483) 232893
(*D.N. Bromage*)

Established 1922. Gold medalists at all major shows including Chelsea. We stock indoor bonsai from China, Israel and Hawaii and outdoor bonsai from Japan, together with pre-bonsai material. We also stock a large variety of sundries covering this fascinating art.

Location: On A322 Bagshot Road next to White Lyon.

BURNCOOSE NURSERIES AND GARDEN

Gwennap, Redruth, Cornwall
Telephone: (0209) 861112
(*C H Williams*)

The Nurseries are set in the 30-acre woodland gardens of Burncoose. Some 12 acres are laid out for nursery stock production of over 2000 varieties of ornamental trees, shrubs and herbaceous plants. Specialities include camellias, azaleas, magnolias, rhododendrons and conservatory plants. The nurseries are widely known for rarities, and for unusual plants. Full mail order catalogue £1 (posted).

Location: 2 m SE of Redruth on the main A393 Redruth to Falmouth road between the villages of Lanner and Ponsanooth.
Open: Mons to Sats 9-5. Suns 11-5. Gardens and tea rooms open all year.
Admission: Nurseries free. Gardens £1.

THE COTTAGE GARDEN

Langham Road, Boxted, Colchester, Essex   &
Telephone: (0206) 272269

Over 400 varieties of hardy perennials, alpines, herbs, trees, shrubs, conifers and hedging. All home grown. Connoiseurs' corner, climbers, conservatory plants. Garden antiques, statuary, terracotta, stone troughs, dovecotes, weather vanes.

Location: 3 m N of Colchester.
Open: Thurs, Fris, Sats 8-6. Suns 9.30-6.

THE COTTAGE HERBERY

Mill House, Boraston, Nr. Tenbury Wells
Telephone: (058 479) 575
(*Mrs Kim Hurst*)

Large collection of herbs, aromatics, scented foliage and cottage garden plants, a mixture of old favourites and the more unusual are for sale at the garden. All plants are organically grown. Artemisias, Menthas, Rosmarinus, Salvias, Thymus.

Location: 1 m E of Tenbury Wells on A456, turn for Boraston at Peacock Inn.

CRUCK COTTAGE CACTI

Cliff Road, Wrelton, Pickering
Telephone: (0751) 72042
(*Ronald J.A. Wood and Dorothy Wood*)

The Nursery is in a garden setting with a display area of mature cacti. On sale is an extensive selection of cacti and succulents for beginners to advanced collectors. Small to specimen plants on sale.

Location: On A170 between Pickering and Kirbymoorside.

DEACONS NURSERY (H.H.)

Moor View, Godshill, Isle of Wight
Telephone: (0983) 840750/(0983) 522243
(*Grahame and Brian Deacon - Partners*)

Specialist fruit tree growers. Over 220 varieties of apples on various types of rootstocks from M27 (4ft), M26 (8ft), to M25 (18ft). Plus Pears, Peaches, Nectarines, Plums, Gages, Cherry, soft fruits and an unusual selection of Family Trees. Many special offers. Catalogue always available, 30p stamp please.

Location: Godshill - a picturesque village visited by all. Deacons Nursery is in Moor View off School Crescent (behind the only school).
Open: Summer - Mon to Fri 8-4; winter - Mon to Fri 8-5, Sat 8-1.

FRUIT FOR THE CONNOISSEUR

PO Box 3, Botley, Hampshire
Telephone: (0329) 834812

A wide variety of fruit trees; also ornamental trees and old roses. Trained fruit tree specialists. Free mail order catalogues (and nursery location) from Family Trees, PO Box 3, Botley, Hampshire SO3 2EA.

G. REUTHE LTD

Crown Point Nursery, Sevenoaks Rd,, Ightam, Nr. Sevenoaks
Telephone: Reg. Office: Starborough Nursery (0732) 865614
(*C. Tomlin & Mrs P. Kindley*)

Rhododendron and Azalea Specialists including many unusual and specie rhododendrons. Chelsea Gold Medals and the Rothschild Challenge Cup winners. We also offer a wide range of rare and unusual shrubs including Acers, Magnolias, Eucryphias etc. Mail order our speciality. Descriptive catalogue available.

Location: On A25 between Seal and Ightham, Kent.
Open: Mon to Sat 9.30-4.30. During Apr and May we also open Suns and Public Hols 10-4.

THE GARDENS OF THE ROSE

Chiswell Green, St Albans map K5 &
Telephone: (0727) 50461
(Royal National Rose Society)

The Showgrounds of the R.N.R.S. containing some 30,000 roses of over 1,650 different varieties.
Location: Off B4630 (formerly A412) St Albans/Watford Road.
Station(s): St Alban's City (2 m).
Open: Jun 13 to Oct 18 - Mons to Sats 9-5; Sun & Bank Hols 10-6.
Refreshments: Facilities for the disabled.

HADSPEN GARDEN

Hadspen House, Castle Cary
Telephone: (0963) 50939
(Nori and Sandra Pope)

Specialising in choice garden plants - herbaceous, old fashioned and modern shrub roses, clematis, damp land plants. Very old hosta collection and National Collection of Rodgersias. All to be viewed in the 8 acre adjoining garden.
Location: Castle Cary
Open: Mar 1 to Oct 1, Thurs, Fri, Sat, Sun and Bank Hol Mons 9-6.

THE HAMPSHIRE HYDROPONICUM

Houghton Lodge, Stockbridge, Hampshire
Telephone: (0264) 810177

A Garden of the Future in a Garden of the Past. A living exhibition of horticulture without soil. No digging, no weeding, no soil borne pests. Learn about the many applications of hydroponic gardening from window sill to space capsule. Plants, produce, publications and equipment for sale.
Location: 1½ m S of Stockbridge on minor road to Houghton.
Open: Mar to Sept inclusive, Sats and Suns 10-4. Mon, Tues, and Fri 2-5, and by appointment.

HEALE GARDENS, PLANT CENTRE AND SHOP

Middle Woodford, Salisbury, Wiltshire
Telephone: (0722) 73504
(Maureen Taylor)

THE HERB AND HEATHER CENTRE

West Haddlesey, Nr. Selby
Telephone: (0757) 228279

The nursery has herb, heather and conifer display gardens, and specialises in herbs and heathers. Dried herbs for flower arranging. Pick your own soft fruit, everything organically grown.
Location: 6 m S of Selby off A19.
Open: Daily (except Weds) 10-6.
Refreshments: Herb shop and tea room.
New garden centre shop. Parking, WC.

JUNGLE GIANTS BAMBOO NURSERY

Plough Farm, Wigmore, Nr. Leominster, Herefordshire &
Telephone: (0568) 86708
(Michael John Brisbane)

KAYES GARDEN NURSERY

1700 Melton Rd, Rearsby, Leicester, Leics
Telephone: (0664) 424578
(Mrs Hazel Kaye)

Hardy herbaceous perennials and good selection of climbers and shrubs. The garden and nursery are in Rearsby, in the Wreake-Valley countryside of Leicestershire. Once an orchard, the one acre garden houses an extensive selection of hardy herbaceous plants. Mixed borders and a fine pergola provide year-round interest, while the nursery offers an excellent range of interesting plants.

Location: Just inside Rearsby village, N of Leicester on A607, on L.H. side approaching from Leicester.
Open: Mar to Oct inclusive: Weds to Sats 10-5.30, Suns 10-12. Nov to Feb inclusive: Fris and Sats 10-5.30. *Closed* Dec 22 to Jan 31 inclusive.

KELWAYS NURSERIES LTD

Langport, Somerset
Telephone: (0458) 250521

The Royal Nurseries of Langport, established in 1851, have been growers and breeders of Paeonies, Irises, Bulb and Hardy Herbaceous plants for 140 years.

Location: On Somerton Road from Langport (B31530 just 200 yards from A372).
Open: Daily 10-4 and special open fields in May and June during our Paeony Festival.

LANGLEY BOXWOOD NURSERY

Rake, Nr Liss, Hampshire
Telephone: (0730) 894467
Fax: (0730) 894703
(Mrs Elizabeth Braimbridge)

This small nursery in a beautiful setting specialises in box-growing, offering a chance to see together a unique range of old and new varieties, hedging, topiary, specimens and rarities. Some taxus also. Descriptive list available (4 x 1st class stamps).

Location: Off A3, 3 m S of Liphook.
Open: Notify by telephone first.

LEA GARDENS

Lea, Matlock, Derbyshire &
Telephone: (0629 534) 380 or 260
(Mr & Mrs J. Tye)

We specialise in, and grow, a wide variety of Rhododendrons, Azaleas and Kalmias. Approximately 60 varieties of Dwarf Rhodos, 120 varieties of larger growing Rhodos, 20 varieties of Yak Hybrid Rhodos, 12 varieties of Kalmias, 15 varieties of Decid Azaleas, 30 varieties of Evergreen Azaleas. These are grown outside at 600ft in Derbyshire, so are hardy and relatively compact. During our garden season we also have a large collection of Lewisias for sale.

Location: 3 m SE of Matlock between A6 and A615.
Open: Mar 20 to July 31, daily 10-7; Oct, Nov: Wed, Thurs and Sun, 2-5. Also always available for plant sales by appointment.
Admission: No charge for nursery.
Refreshments: During spring season.
Car parking immediately by nursery. Suitable for disabled visitors. No wheelchairs available.

MACPENNYS OF BRANSGORE

154 Burley Road, Bransgore, Nr. Christchurch, Dorset
Telephone: (0425) 72348
(T. Lowndes)

A four-acre mature woodland garden created from gravel pits in the 1950s to explore at leisure. Admission free but donations to the National Gardens Scheme welcomed. Also a large traditional nursery where many of the plants seen growing in the woodland gardens may be purchased. Many unusual plants, large herbaceous selection, camellias, rhododendrons, azaleas, heathers, conifers and general shrubs.

Location: Halfway between Christchurch and Burley on the Burley road at Bransgore. (Off A35 at Cat and Fiddle pub signed Bransgore. Turn right at Crown pub crossroads.
Open: Open all year Mons to Sats 9-5, Sun 2-5. *Closed* Christmas and New Year holidays.

MEADS END BONSAI

Forewood Lane, Crowhurst, Battle
Telephone: (0424) 83388
(Cordelia Silva)

We stock a wide variety of Bonsai trees ranging from pre-Bonsai material to mature specimens. The trees are either home-grown or imported from Japan. We also stock pots, tools, books and accesories. A 'Holiday Caring' service is offered. Kent County Show Gold Medal award winners.

Location: 1¾ m S of Battle on A2100, turn into Telham Lane, Nursery is 1.3 m from A2100 turn off.

MEARE CLOSE NURSERIES LTD

Tadworth Street, Tadworth, Surrey
Telephone: (0737) 812449
(Mr D B Easton)

Herbaceous perennials including hemerocallis selections (speciality), alpines, water lilies and aquatics (speciality), shrubs, conifers, fruit trees, roses, climbing plants. Established under same ownership 1938.

Location: ¼ m from A217 at Tadworth.
Open: Mons to Sats 9-5. *Closed* 1-2.15 (lunch break). Suns & Bank Holidays 10.30-1.

MILLAIS NURSERIES

Crosswater Lane, Churt, Farnham, Surrey
Telephone: (0252) 792698
Fax: (0252) 792526
(David Millais)

MILLAIS NURSERIES
RHODODENDRONS
AZALEAS
CROSSWATER LANE, CHURT, FARNHAM, SURREY GU10 2JN
FRENSHAM (0252) 792698

Growers of one of the finest ranges of Rhododendrons and Azaleas in the country, including many rare species from the Himalayas, and a good selection of new American hybrids. Specialist advice. Mail Order Catalogue available £1. Display garden also open (see Crosswater Farm).

Location: Farnham/Haslemere 6 m. From A287 turn E into Jumps Road ½ m N of Churt village centre. After ¼ m, turn into Crosswater Lane, and follow Nursery signs.
Open: Tues to Sats 10-1, 2-5. Also daily in May and early June.

PERHILL NURSERIES

Worcester Road, Great Witley, Worcestershire   &
Telephone: (0299) 896329
(Baker Straw Partnership)

Specialist growers of 1,900 varieties of alpines, herbs and border perennials. Many rare and unusual. Specialities include penstemons, salvias, osteospermums, dianthus, alpine phlox, alliums, campanulas, thymes, helianthemums, diascias, lavenders, artemesias, digitals and scented geraniums.

Location: 10 m NW of Worcester on main Tenbury Wells Road (A443).
Open: Every day except Christmas and Boxing Day and New Year's Day, Mon to Sat 9-6, Sun 9-5. Car parking. Suitable for disabled visitors.

PERRY'S PLANTS, RIVER GARDENS

Sleights, Nr. Whitby

Beautiful riverside tea gardens where all the plants for sale can be seen growing. Specialising in lavatera, malvacea, anthemis, euphorbias, osteospermum, uncommon hardy and conservatory plants.

Location: 2 m W of Whitby on the B1410 just off the A169.
Open: Easter to end of Oct: Daily 10-5.
Refreshments: Licensed cafe.

PERRYHILL NURSERIES

Hartfield, East Sussex
Telephone: (0892) 770377
Fax: (0892) 770929
(Mrs S M Gemmell)

The Plant Centre for the discerning gardener, with the widest range of plants in the South East of England. Old fashioned and shrub roses a speciality, also herbaceous plants. Trees, shrubs, rhododendrons, alpines, fruit trees and bushes, bedding plants in season. No mail order. Catalogues £1.40 inc. postage.

Location: 1 m N of Hartfield on B2026.
Open: Mar to Oct: 9-5. Nov to Feb: 9-4.30. Seven days a week.

PLANTS FROM A COUNTRY GARDEN

Wotton Road, Ludgershall, Aylesbury, Buckinghamshire
Telephone: (0844) 237415
(Mr and Mrs D. A. Tolman)

A pleasantly secluded nursery situated in unspoilt countryside and offering one of the widest ranges of traditional cottage garden plants in the country. Over 1,200 different varieties including a huge range of old fashioned pinks and violets, rare geraniums, asters, foxgloves, native wildflowers and herbs and many other uncommon hardy perennials and shrubs. Plants can be seen growing in display beds. The owners' nearby enchanting cottage garden is open several times a year - see Garden entry for The Thatched Cottage, Duck Lane, Ludgershall, Bucks. A descriptive catalogue is available from this address for £1 or 4 x 1st class stamps.

Location: 2 m S of A41 between Bicester and Aylesbury, leaving A41 at Kingswood or ¾ m from Ludgershall in the direction of Wotton.
Open: Mar 1 to Oct 31, Wed to Sun inclusive 10-6. Also open 10-6 on Bank Hols.
Refreshments: Teas are available on days when the Garden at the Thatched Cottage, Duck Lane, Ludgershall is open.
Car parking at nursery. Partially suitable for disabled visitors.

THE ROGER PLANT CENTRE

Malton Road, Pickering, North Yorkshire

A wide range of hardy garden plants, shrubs, fruit and ornamental trees grown on own farm. Six acres of roses in bloom from July to October. Co-holders of the National Erodium Collection. 60 page descriptive mail order catalogue 75p.

Location: Malton Road A169.
Open: Mons to Sats 9-5. Suns 1-5. Bank Holidays 10.30-5. *Closed* Christmas Day to Jan 2. Ample parking.

RYTON ORGANIC GARDENS

Coventry
Telephone: (0203) 303517, Fax: (0203) 639229

Demonstration gardens cultivated naturally, without the use of pesticides and artificial fertilisers. Speciality vegetables, fruit, herbs, flowers, shrubs, trees, lake, wildlife, bees, play area, picnic benches. Home of Channel 4's 'All Muck and Magic?'. Organic Wholefood café in Good Food Guide.

Location: We are on the B4029 which leads north from the A45 to Wolston, 5 m SE of Coventry. Look for the brown signposts to Ryton Gardens.

SAMARÈS HERBS-A-PLENTY

Samarès Manor, St. Clement, Jersey
Telephone: (0534) 70551
(Richard Adams, Lyn Le Boutillier)

Specialist Herb and Hardy Perennial Nursery situated in the grounds of Samar s Manor. Extensive range of culinary, fragrant and medicinal herbs including many variegated and ornamental forms. Specialist range of hardy perennials including plants for shade, ground cover and wet conditions. Availability list on request. Herb shop, craft centre, farm animals, herb gardens, tours of Manor.

Location: 2 m E of St. Helier on the St. Clements Inner Road.
Open: Daily 10-5 Apr to Oct.
Admission: Charge for gardens. No charge for Nursery.
Refreshments: Tea garden and restaurant.

SEAFORDE NURSERY AND BUTTERFLY HOUSE

Seaforde, Downpatrick, Down
Telephone: (039687) 225
Fax: (039687) 370
(Patrick Forde)

Over 600 trees and shrubs, container grown. Many Camellias and Rhododendrons. National collections of E. ucryphius. Tropical Butterfly House with hundreds of free flying butterflies. Also open beautiful gardens and maze.

Location: On A24 Ballynahinch to Newcastle Road.
Open: Easter to end Sept: Mon to Sat 10-5; Sun 2-6. Nursery only: Sept to Easter, 10-5.
Refreshments: Tea rooms.

SPINNERS

Boldre, Lymington
Telephone: (0590) 673347
(P. Chappell)

As wide a selection here (excluding conifers, heathers and roses) of rare and less common hardy plants, trees and shrubs for immediate sale as anywhere in the U.K. Just one example: 90 different Magnolias.

Location: 1½ m N of Lymington, 1 m off A337.

STAPELEY WATER GARDENS

Stapeley, Nantwich
Telephone: (0270) 628628

Stapeley is the Largest Water Garden centre in Europe. In its Palms Tropical Oasis - a 1 1/3 acre heated glasshouse - a tropical atmosphere is created with palms, giant Amazonian water lilies; a huge aquaria with sharks, piranhas, parrots and exotic flowers. There are two covered acres of garden plants, tools, furniture, gifts and seeds. See our National Collection of water lilies with over 100 varieties.

Location: 1 m S of Nantwich on the A51 to Stone, signposted from Jct 16 on the M6.
Open: Open every day.
Admission: SPECIAL GROUP RATES.
Refreshments: An excellent restaurant and cafeteria available.
Disabled catered for. No dogs please.

Why not visit other people's private gardens?

The owners of over 3,000 private gardens, not normally open to the public, invite you to visit them, on dates chosen when they expect their gardens to be looking their best.

Full details of when the gardens will be open, what is in each garden, how to get there, and where you can get tea, is given in the following yellow book published in March:-

GARDENS OF ENGLAND AND WALES

£2.50 from booksellers and newsagents or £3.00 (inc UK postage) from the National Gardens Scheme, Hatchlands Park, East Clandon, Guildford, Surrey GU4 7RT

Telephone: (0483) 211535

All proceeds to nominated Charities

STARBOROUGH NURSERY

Starborough Road, Marsh Green, Edenbridge, Kent
Telephone: (0732) 865614
(C. Tomlin & Mrs P. Kindley)

We have a wide selection of rare and unusual shrubs and trees including rhododendrons and azaleas, Acers, Magnolias, Camellias, Hamamelis etc. Mail Order a speciality. Descriptive catalogue available.

Location: On B2028 Lingfield Road.
Open: 10-4.30pm. Thurs to Mon. Occasional Bank Holidays.

TREHANE CAMELLIA NURSERY

Stapehill Road, Hampreston, Nr. Wimborne, Dorset
Telephone: (0202) 873490
(Miss Jennifer Trehane)

Britain's leading Specialists. Scented Sasanquas, rare Species from China and Japan, huge Reticulatas, extra hardy Williamsii varieties, specially selected free-flowering Japonicas. Also Evergreen Azaleas, Pieris, Magnolias, Blueberries. All sizes. Visitors most welcome. Mail Order and Export. Catalogue/Handbook £2.**Open:** All year: weekdays 9-4 and weekends from Mar to Oct. *Closed over the Christmas/New Year.*

WEBBS OF WYCHBOLD

Wychbold, Droitwich
Telephone: (0527) 861777
Fax: (0527) 861284

Our aim at Webbs is to provide a vast selection of all that's best in gardening. Browse at your leisure amongst thousands of plants from Azaleas to Yucca's grown in our 50-acre nursery, then perhaps relax in the popular Thatch Restaurant that specialises in good, wholesome, appetising food. Houseplants, Seeds, Bulbs, Aquatics, Garden Furniture, Books, Cards, Gifts, Greenhouses, Conservatories, Fencing, Paving and Sundries galore, it's all here for dedicated and occasional gardeners alike. Winners of the first ever Garden Centre Association award for Overall Excellence' in 1990 and runners-up as Garden Centre of 1991' by the magazine Retail Horticulture. Customers matter at Webbs where our emphasis is on quality and friendly service and where expert advice is always available.

Location: On A38 between Bromsgrove and Droitwich, 1 m from junction 5 of the M5 motorway and opposite the well-known landmark of the BBC radio masts.
Open: Mar to Nov, Mon to Sat 9-5.45; Dec to Feb, Mon to Sat 9-5. Mar to Nov, Wed 9.30-5.45; Dec to Feb, Wed 9.30-5. Mar to Nov, Sun 10-5; Dec to Feb, Sun 10-5. Bank Hols 10-5. Late night opening from late Mar until early autumn until 8 on Weds, Thurs and Fris. Parking for 400 cars, play area and disabled facilities.

WYCHWOOD CARP FARM

Farnham Road, Odiham, Basingstoke, Hampshire
Telephone: (0256) 702800
(Reg, Ann and Clair Henley)

The specialist producers of naturally grown water lilies, water iris, marginal plants, marsh plants, bog primulas and ensata irises. The only commercial producers of hardy water lily seed plus holders of a National Collection of Hardy Water Lilies. Free Mail Order Catalogue available on request with s.a.e.

Location: 3 m from M3 intersection 5 or 4 m from A30. 1½ m E of Odiham Village on A287.
Open: Every day 10-6, open Bank Hols. *Closed* Thursdays.
Admission: Free.
Car parking available on premises. Unsuitable for disabled.

UNIVERSITY OF CAMBRIDGE

NOTE: Admission to *Colleges* means to the Courts, not to the staircases and students' rooms. All opening times are subject to closing for College functions, etc., on occasional days. *Halls* normally close for lunch (12–2) and many are not open during the afternoon. *Chapels* are closed during services. *Libraries* are not usually open, special arrangements are noted. *Gardens* do not usually include the Fellows' garden. *Figures* denote the date of foundation, and existing buildings are often of later date. *Daylight hours*—some Colleges may not open until 9.30 am or later and usually close before 6 pm — many as early as 4.30 pm.

All parties exceeding 10 persons wishing to tour the colleges between Easter and October are required to be escorted by a Cambridge registered Guide. All enquiries should be made to the Tourist Information Centre, Wheeler Street, Cambridge CB2 3QB.

Terms: *Lent:* Mid-January to Mid-March. *Easter:* April to June. *Michaelmas:* 2nd week October to 1st week December. Examination Period closures which differ from one college to another, now begin in early April and extend to late June. Notices are usually displayed. Important: Before entering any college, please call at the Porter's Lodge. This applies both to individual visitors and guided parties.

Address of College and Entrance Gate	*Opening Arrangements*
Christ's College (1505). St. Andrew's Street (Porter's Lodge)	The College is closed to all visitors from May 1 to mid-June. At most other times it is open as follows:– *College:* Daily, all day. *Chapel:* Daily during Term. *Hall:* Weekdays 10–1. *Library:* By appointment with Librarian. *Fellows' Garden:* Mons to Fris 10.30–12.30, 2–4. (Closed Bank Hols, Easter week and weekends).
Clare College (1326). Trinity Lane CB2 1TL	*Hall:* Mons to Fris 9–12 during term time except Apr 17 to June 25. *Chapel:* Daily during term time except Apr 17 to June 25. Otherwise by prior arrangement with the Dean. *Gardens:* Mons to Fris 2–4 (usually). (Closed Bank Hols and weekends).
Corpus Christi College (1352). Trumpington Street (Porter's Lodge)	Opening times shown at Porter's Lodge.
Downing College (1800). Regent Street (Porter's Lodge)	*College & Gardens:* Daily, daylight hours. *Chapel:* Term—Daily, all day. Vacation—By appointment. *Hall:* Closed to the public. *Library:* By arrangement only.
Emmanuel College (1584). St. Andrew's Street (Porter's Lodge)	*College:* Daily 9–6. *Hall:* 2.30–5. *Chapel:* 9–6 both daily, except when in use. *Library:* Only by prior application to Librarian. *Gardens & Paddock:* Daily 9–6 or dusk if earlier. *Fellows' Garden:* Not open to visitors. (Closed for annual holidays, variable).
Gonville & Caius College (1348). Trinity Street (Porter's Lodge)	*College & Chapel:* Daily, daylight hours. *Library:* By appointment with Librarian. (Closed to all guided parties and parties of more than 6 persons) Closed during exams from early May to mid-June and for short periods each day: times shown at Porter's Lodge.
Jesus College (1496). Jesus Lane (Porter's Lodge)	*College:* Daily 9–5.30. *Chapel:* Apply Porter's Lodge. *Hall:* Closed to the public.
King's College (1441). King's Parade (Porter's Lodge)	*College:* Daily until 6. Limited access mid-Apr to mid-June. *Library:* Scholars, on application to librarian. *Chapel:* Term—Weekdays 9.30–3.45. Suns 2–3, 4.45–5.45. Summer Vacation—Weekdays 9.30–5.45. Suns 10.30–5.45 and subject to closure at other times for rehearsals etc. *Dining Hall:* Closed to the public.
Magdalene College (1542). Magdalene Street (Porters' Lodge)	*College & Chapel:* Daily 9–6.30 (except during exams). *Hall:* Daily 9.30–12.30 (except during exams). *Gardens:* Daily 1–6.30 (except during exams). *Pepys:* Jan 12 to Mar 13: weekdays 2.30–3.30. Apr 20 to Aug 31 1993: weekdays 11.30–12.30, 2.30–3.30 (not Suns).
Newnham College (1871). Sidgwick Avenue	*College & Gardens:* Daily during daylight hours. Apply Porter's Lodge. (College and gardens closed May 1–mid-June and last week in August and first week in September.
Pembroke College (1347). Trumpington Street	Opening times shown at Porter's Lodge. *Library:* By appointment with Librarian.
Peterhouse (1284). Trumpington Street (Porter's Lodge)	Guided parties of not more than 12. *Chapel:* Daily. *Hall:* Mornings only, during term. *Gardens:* Daily 10–5 (no dogs).
Queens' College (1448). Silver Street (Porter's Lodge). Visitor's entrance, Queen's Lane	Open daily 1.45–4.30 & also 10.15–12.45 during July, Aug & Sept & for guided parties of not more than 20. Adm charge.
St. Catharine's College (1473). Trumpington Street (Porter's Lodge)	*College & Chapel:* Daily, during daylight hours. (Closed May & June). *Hall:* Closed to the public.
St. John's College (1511). St. John's Street (Porter's Lodge)	*College:* Daily 10.30 until 5.30. (Closed May & June). *Chapel:* Apply Porter's Lodge. *Hall:* Closed to the public.
Sidney Sussex College (1596). Sidney Street (Porter's Lodge)	*College:* Daily, during daylight hours. *Hall & Chapel:* Apply Porter's Lodge.
Trinity College (1546). Trinity Street (Porter's Lodge)	Opening times shown at Great Gate Porter's Lodge.
Trinity Hall (1350). Trinity Lane	*College, Chapel & Gardens:* Daily, during daylight hours except during examination period (end April to mid-June). *Library:* Apply beforehand to College Librarian.

CONDUCTED TOURS IN CAMBRIDGE Qualified, badged, local guides may be obtained from: Tourist Information Centre, Wheeler Street, Cambridge CB2 3QB. Tel: (0223) 322640 or Cambridge Guide Service, 2 Montague Road, Cambridge CB4 1BX. Tel: (0223) 356735 (Principals: John Mellanby MA., and Mrs E. Garner). We normally obtain the Passes and make all negotiations regarding these with the Tourist Office, so separate application is not needed.

We have been providing guides for English, Foreign language and special interest groups since 1950. We supply couriers for coach tours of East Anglia, visiting stately homes etc. As an alternative to the 2 hour walking tour, we can now offer ½ hour panoramic tour in clients' coach (provided there is an effective public address system) followed by 1½ hours on foot or 1 hour panoramic only, special flat rate up to 55 people.

UNIVERSITY OF OXFORD

NOTE: Admission to *Colleges* means to the quadrangles, not to the staircases and students' rooms. All opening times are subject to closing for College functions, etc., on occasional days. *Halls* normally close for lunch during term (12–2). *Chapel* usually closed during services. *Libraries* are not usually open, special arrangements are noted. *Gardens* do not usually include the Fellows' garden. *Figures* denote the date of foundation, and existing buildings are often of later date.

Terms: *Hilary:* Mid-January to Mid-March. *Trinity:* 3rd week April to late June. *Michaelmas:* Mid-October to 1st week December.

Address of College and Entrance Gate	Opening Arrangements
All Souls College (1438). High Street (Porter's Lodge)	*College:* Daily 2–4.30. Closed in August.
Balliol College (1263). Broad Street (Porter's Lodge)	*Hall, Chapel & Gardens:* Daily 2–5 (summer), 2–5 (winter). Parties limited to 25.
Brasenose College (1509). Radcliffe Square (Porter on duty)	*Hall, Chapel & Gardens:* Tour parties: Daily 10–5 (summer), 10–dusk (winter). Individuals 2–5. *Hall:* 11.45–2.
Christ Church (1546). St. Aldate's (Meadow Gate)	*Cathedral:* Daily 9–4.30 (winter), 9–5.30 (summer). *Hall:* Oct to Mar: Daily 9.30–12, 2–4.30. Apr to Sept: Daily 9.30–12, 2–6. Adm £1.50, Chd 50p. *Picture Gallery:* Weekdays 10.30–1, 2–4.30. Adm 50p. *Meadow:* Daily 7–dusk. Hall published hours occasionally curtailed for College or Cathedral events.
Corpus Christi College (1517). Merton Street (Porter's Lodge)	*College, Chapel & Gardens:* Terms and vacations – Daily 2–4.
Exeter College (1314). Turl Street (Porter's Lodge)	*College & Chapel, Fellows' Garden:* Term and vacations – Daily 2–5.
Hertford College (1284, 1740 & 1874). Catte Street (Porter's Lodge)	*College, Hall & Chapel:* Daily 10–6. (Closed for a week at Christmas and Easter).
Jesus College (1571). Turl Street (Gate in Turl Street)	*College, Hall & Chapel:* Daily 2.30–4.30. *Library:* Special permission of Librarian. (Closed Christmas and Easter holidays).
Keble College (1868). Parks Road (Porter's Lodge)	*College & Chapel:* Daily 2–5.
Lady Margaret Hall (1878). Norham Gardens. (All visitors are requested to call at the Porter's Lodge)	*College Gardens:* Daily 2–6 (or dusk if earlier).
Lincoln College (1427). Turl Street (Porter's Lodge)	*College & Hall:* Weekdays 2–5. Suns 11–5. *Wesley Room:* On application to Porter's Lodge. *All Saints Library:* Tues & Thurs 2–4.
Magdalen College (1458). High Street (Front Lodge)	*College, Chapel, Deer Park & Water Walks:* Daily 2–6.15. Parties limited to 25.
Mansfield College (1886). Mansfield Road (Porter's Lodge)	*College:* Open May, June & July, Mon to Sat 9–5. Interior of Chapel and Library may be viewed by prior appointment, please enquire at Porter's Lodge.
Merton (1264). Merton Street (Porter's Lodge)	*Chapel & Quadrangles:* Mons to Fris 2–4 (closes at 5). Sats & Suns 10–4 (closes at 5). *Old Library and Max Beerbohm Room:* Mons to Sats 2–4. Adm £1. Apply Verger's Office (closed 1 week Christmas & 1 week Easter). Groups of 10 only.
New College (1379). New College Lane	*College, Hall, Chapel & Gardens:* Term – Daily 2–5. Vacation – Daily 11–5.
Nuffield College (1937). New Road (Porter's Lodge)	*College only:* Daily 9–5.
Oriel College (1326). Oriel Square (Main Gate)	*College:* Daily 2–5. (Closed Christmas & Easter holidays & mid-Aug to mid-Sept).
Pembroke College (1624). St. Aldate's (Porter's Lodge)	*College, Hall, Chapel & Gardens:* Term – Daily on application to the Porter's Lodge. (Closed Christmas and Easter holidays & occasionally in Aug).
The Queen's College (1340). High Street (Porter's Lodge)	*Hall, Chapel, Quadrangles & Garden:* Daily 2–5.
St. Edmund Hall (1270). Queen's Lane (at the Lodge)	*College, Old Hall, Chapel & Garden:* Daily, daylight hours. *Crypt of St. Peter in the East:* On application to Porter.
St. John's College (1555). St. Giles' (Porter's Lodge)	*College & Garden:* Term & Vacation – Daily 1–5 (or dusk if earlier). Guided parties must obtain permission from the Lodge). *Hall & Chapel:* Summer – 2.30–4.30 (Apply Porter). (Closed during conferences & College functions).
Trinity College (1554). Broad Street (Main Gate)	*Hall, Chapel & Garden:* Daily 2–5 (summer). 2–dusk (winter). (Opening hrs may vary – visitors should check in advance.)
University College (1249). High Street (Porter's Lodge)	*College, Hall & Chapel:* Term – 2–4. Apply Porter.
Wadham College (1610). Parks Road (Porter's Lodge)	*College, Hall, Chapel & Gardens:* Daily 1–4.30. Hall: Apply Lodge.
Worcester College (1714). Worcester Street (Porter's Lodge) (0865) 278300	*College & Gardens:* Term – Daily 2–6. Vacation – Daily 9–12, 2–6. *Hall & Chapel:* Apply Lodge.

Visitors and especially guided parties should always call at the Porter's Lodge before entering any College.

GUIDED WALKING TOURS OF THE COLLEGES AND CITY OF OXFORD Tours, conducted by the Oxford Guild of Guides Lecturers, are offered by the Oxford Information Centre, morning for much of the year, afternoon tours daily. For tour times please ring (0865) 726871.

Tours are offered for groups in English, French, German, Spanish, Russian, Japanese, Polish and Serbo-Croat. Chinese by appointment.

The most popular tour for groups, Oxford Past and Present, can be arranged at any time. The following special interest tours are available in the afternoon only: Alice in Oxford; Literary Figures in Oxford; American Roots in Oxford; Oxford Gardens; Modern Architecture in Oxford; Architecture in Oxford (medieval, 17th century and modern); Oxford in the Civil War and 17th century.

Further details are available from The Tours Assistant tel (0865) 726871.

Supplementary List of Properties
Open by Appointment Only

The list of Houses in England, Wales and Scotland printed here are those which are usually open 'by appointment only' with the Owner, or open infrequently during the summer months. These are in addition to the Houses and Gardens which are open regularly and are fully classified. Where it is necessary to write for an appointment to view, see code *(WA)*. *Indicates that these Houses are also classified and more details are shown under the respective 'County' headings.

The majority of these properties have received a grant for conservation from the Government, given on the advice of the Historic Buildings Councils. Public buildings, almshouses, tithe barns, business premises in receipt of grants are not usually included, neither are properties where the architectural features can be viewed from the street.

ENGLAND

House	Owner (with address if different from first column)

AVON

House	Owner (with address if different from first column)
The Refectory, The Vicarage, nr Bristol	Rev R. Salmon *Yatton* (0934) 833126
Eastwood Manor Farm, East Harptree	Mr A. J. Gay
Partis College, Bath	The Bursar *Bath* (0225) 421532
Woodspring Priory, Kewstoke	The Landmark Trust, Shottesbrooke, nr Maidenhead, Berks SL6 3SW *Open daily (still undergoing repair)*

BEDFORDSHIRE

The Temple, Southill Park, Biggleswade	The Estate Office *(WA)*
Warden Abbey, nr Biggleswade	The Landmark Trust, Shottesbrooke, nr Maidenhead, Berks SL6 3SW *(WA)*

BERKSHIRE

High Chimneys, Hurst, Reading	Mr & Mrs S. Cheetham Reading 345117 *(WA)*
St Gabriel's School, Sandleford Priory, Newbury	**The Headmaster** *Newbury* 40663

BUCKINGHAMSHIRE

Bisham Abbey, nr Marlow	*Viewing by appointment only.* The Director, Bisham Abbey *Marlow* (062 84) 76911
Brudenell House, Quainton, Aylesbury, Bucks HP22 4AW	Dr H. Beric Wright *(WA) 1 week's notice*
Church of the Assumption, Hardmead, Newport Pagnell	Friends of Friendless Churches *For key apply to* H. Tranter, Manor Cottage, Hardmead, by letter or telephone *North Crawley* 257
Iver Grove, Shreding Green, Iver	Mr & Mrs T. Stoppard *(WA)*
Remnantz, West St. Marlow *(WA)* to	A. Wethered Esq., Brampton House, 100 High St. Marlow SL7 1AQ
Repton's Subway Facade, Digby's Walk, Gayhurst	Mr J. H. Beverly, The Bath House, Gayhurst. *(WA)* or *Stoke Goldington* 564

CAMBRIDGE

Chantry (The), Ely	Mrs T. A. N. Bristol *(WA)*
Church of St John The Baptist, Papworth St Agnes	Friends of Friendless Churches *For key apply to* Mrs P. Honeybane, Passhouse Cottage, Papworth St. Agnes, Cambs by letter or telephone *Huntingdon* (0480) 830631
The King's School, Ely Canonry and Priory Boarding Houses, Monastic Barn	Bursar's Office, The King's School, Ely. *(WA)* (0353) 662837
Leverington Hall, Wisbech	Professor A. Barton *(WA)*
The Lynch Lodge, Alwalton, nr Peterborough	The Landmark Trust, Shottesbrooke, nr. Maidenhead, Berks SL6 3SW *(WA)*

CHESHIRE

Bewsey Old Hall, Warrington	The Administrator *(WA)*
Charles Roe House, Chestergate, Macclesfield	McMillan Martin Ltd *(WA)*
Crown Hotel, Nantwich	Prop P. J. Martin
Shotwick Hall, Shotwick	Mr R. B. Gardner, 'Wychen', 17 St Mary's Rd, Leatherhead, Surrey *By appointment only with the tenants:* Mr & Mrs G. A. T. Holland (0244) 881717 *Chester* 20095
Tudor House, Lower Bridge St, Chester	
Watergate House, Chester	Ferry Homes Ltd, Barclays Bank Chambers, 48 High St, Holywell, Clwyd *(WA)* (0352) 713353

CLEVELAND

St Cuthbert's Church & Turner Mausoleum, Kirkleatham	Kirkleatham Parochial Church Council Mr R. S. Ramsdale (0642) 475198 Mrs D. Cook, Church Warden (0642) 485395

CORNWALL

College (The), Week St Mary	The Landmark Trust, Shottesbrooke, nr Maidenhead, Berks SL6 3SW *(WA)*
Town Hall, Camelford	Camelford Town Trust
Trecarrel Manor, Trebullett, Launceston *(Hall & Chapel restored)*	Telephone application only to Mr N. H. Burden *Coads Green* 82286

CUMBRIA

Isle Hall, Cockermouth	The Administrator *(WA)*
Preston Patrick Hall, Milnthorpe	Mrs J. D. Armitage *Crooklands* 67200
Whitehall, Mealsgate, Carlisle	Mrs S. Parkin-Moore, 40 Woodsome Rd, London NW5 *(WA)*

DERBYSHIRE

Elvaston Castle, nr Derby	Derbyshire County Council *prior appt only Derby* 571342
The Mansion Church St, Ashbourne	Garden, Hall and Drawing Room by appointment only with the Headmaster (0335) 43685
10 North Street, Cromford	The Landmark Trust, Shottesbrooke, nr Maidenhead, Berks SL6 3SW *(WA)*
The Pavilion, Swarkestone, nr Ticknall	The Landmark Trust *(WA)*

DEVON

House	Owner (with address if different from first column)
Bindon Manor, Axmouth	Sir John and Lady Loveridge *(WA)*
Bowringsleigh, Kingbridge	Mr & Mrs M. C. Manisty *(WA)*
Endsleigh House, Milton Abbot, nr Tavistock	Endsleigh Fishing Club Ltd, Apr to Sept *Milton Abbot* (082 287) 248
Hareston House, Brixton	Mrs K. M. Basset *Mons, May to Sept Plymouth* 880 426
Library (The), Stevenstone, nr Torrington	The Landmark Trust, Shottesbrooke, nr Maidenhead, Berks SL6 3SW *(WA)*
Sanders, Lettaford	The Landmark Trust, Shottesbrooke, nr Maidenhead, Berks SL6 3SW *(WA)*
Shell House (The), Endsleigh Milton Abbot, nr Tavistock	Endsleigh Fishing Club Ltd *April to Sept Milton Abbot* 248
Shute Gatehouse, Shute Barton, nr Axminster	The Landmark Trust, Shottesbrooke, nr Maidenhead, Berks SL6 3SW *(WA)*
Town House, Gittisham, nr Honiton	Mr & Mrs R. J. T. Marker (tenant Mr & Mrs R. A. L. Hill) *(WA)*
Ugbrooke Park, Chudleigh	Captain The Lord Clifford *Chudleigh* 852179
Wortham Manor, Lifton	The Landmark Trust, Shottesbrooke, nr Maidenhead, Berks SL6 3SW *(WA)*

DORSET

Bloxworth House, Bloxworth	Mr T. A. Dulake *(WA)*
Clenston Manor, Winterborne Clenston, Blandford Forum	Mr & Mrs John Procter (0258) 880681
Higher Melcombe, Dorchester	Mr M. C. Woodhouse *(WA)*
Moignes Court, Owermoigne	Mr A. M. Cree *(WA)*
Woodsford Castle, Woodsford	The Landmark Trust, Shottesbrooke, nr Maidenhead, Berks SL6 3SW *(WA)*

DURHAM

The Buildings in The Square	Lady Gilbertson, 1 The Square, Greta Bridge, Barnard Castle *(WA)*
The College, Durham (on the south side of the Cathedral with access from the Bailey)	The Deanery, No. 6 The College. No. 9 The College. No. 10 The College. No. 11 The College. No. 15 The College. 28A North Bailey. The Dean and Chapter of Durham: All enquiries to the Chapter Steward, The Chapter Office. Durham DH1 3EH. Office hours Mon to Fri (091 386) 4266
Crook Hall, Sidegate, Durham DH1 5SZ.	Dr and Mrs J. Hawgood *(WA)*

ESSEX

Blake Hall Battle of Britain Museum and Gardens, Chipping Ongar	Mr R. Capel Cure *Parties catered for. Telephone the Administrator: Chipping Ongar* 362502
Church of St Andrews and Monks Tithe Barn, Netteswellbury	Now the Harlow Study and Visitor Centre. Sun–Thurs 9.30–4.30. Tel: (0279) 446745
Colville Hall, White Roding, Essex	Mr C. A. Webster *(WA)*
Great Priory Farm, Panfield, Braintree	Group of 10 separately listed buildings. *(Listed Grade II *Barn only)* Miss Lucy Tabor, anytime by telephoned appointment *Braintree* 550944
Grange Farm, Little Dunmow, Dunmow CM6 3HY 14th C Granary	Mr J. Kirby Tel: (0371) 820205
Guildhall (The), Great Waltham	Mr J. J. Tufnell
Old All Saints, Langdon Hills	Mr R. Mill *Basildon* 414146
Rainham Hall, Rainham	The National Trust (tenant Mr Ian Botes) *(WA)*
Rayne Hall, Rayne, Braintree	Mr and Mrs R. J. Pertwee *(WA)*
Round House (The), Havering-atte-Bower, Romford	Mr M. E. W. Heap *Romford* 728136

GLOUCESTERSHIRE

Abbey Gatehouse, Tewkesbury	The Landmark Trust, Shottesbrooke, Maidenhead, Berks SL6 3SW *(WA)*
Ashleworth Court, nr Gloucester	Mr H. J. Chamberlayne *Parties only* (0452) 700241
Ashleworth Manor, Ashleworth	Dr and Mrs Jeremy Barnes *(WA)*
Bearland House, Gloucester	The Administrator *(WA)*
Castle Godwyn, Painswick	Mr & Mrs John Milne *(WA)*
Chaceley Hall, nr Tewkesbury	Mr W. H. Lane *Tirley* 205
Thirlestaine House, Cheltenham College (Cheltenham Boys College), Cheltenham	The Bursar, The College, Bath Road, Cheltenham GL5 7LD *Cheltenham* 513540
Cottage (The), Stanley Pontlarge, Winchcombe	Mrs S. M. Rolt *(WA)*
Daneway House, Sapperton	Sir Anthony Denny, Bt *(WA)*
East Banqueting House, Chipping Campden	The Landmark Trust, Shottesbrooke, Maidenhead, Berks SL6 35W *(WA)*
Frampton Court & Gothic Orangery, Frampton-on-Severn, Gloucester	Frampton Court Estate *Apply to Mrs Clifford Gloucester* (0452) 740267 home *Gloucester* (0452) 740698 office
Frampton Manor, Frampton-on-Severn, Gloucestershire	Mr & Mrs R. Clifford *(WA)* (0452) 740698
Matson House, Gloucester	The Bursar, Selwyn School *During School holidays only Gloucester* 305663
Minchinhampton Market House, Stroud	Mr B. E. Lucas *Brimscombe* 883241
Old Vicarage (The), Church Stanway	'Lord Weymyss' Trust: Apply to Stanway House. Stanway, Cheltenham *Stanton* 469
St Margaret's Church, London Rd, Gloucester	Gloucester Municipal Charities *Services Suns 3 pm. Other times by appointment with Warden Gloucester* 23316
Stroud Subscription Rooms, George Street, Stroud	Stroud District Council, Subscription Rooms Manages. Old Town Hall, The Shambles, High St. Stroud (0453) 764999
Tyndale Monument North Nibley	Tyndale Monument Charity, 26 Long St, Dursley R. E. W. Derby *Dursley* 542357 Key available as per notice at foot of Wood Lane.

Where it is necessary to write for an appointment to view. see code *(WA)*

House	Owner (with address if different from first column)

GREATER MANCHESTER

Chetham's Hospital & Library, Manchester M3 1SB — The Feoffees of Chetham's Hospital & Library 061-834 9644
Slade Hall, Slade Lane. Manchester M13 0QP — Manchester and District Housing Assn. *(WA)*

HAMPSHIRE

Chesil Theatre (formerly St Peter Chesil Church) — Winchester Dramatic Society (0962) 867086
The Deanery, The Close. Winchester — The Cathedral Secretary, 5 The Close *Winchester 853137*
Houghton Lodge, Stockbridge — *(WA)* Captain and Mrs M. W. Busk 0264 810 177
Manor Farm House, Hambledon — Mr S. B. Mason (0705) 632433
Moyles Court, Ringwood — Headmaster, Moyles Court School *Ringwood 472856*

HEREFORD & WORCESTER

Britannia House, The Tything. Worcester — The Alice Ottley School *(WA) Apply to The Headmistress*
Church House, Evesham — The Trustees of the Walker Hall & Church House. Market Square
Grafton Manor, Bromsgrove — Mr J. W. Morris *Bromsgrove 31525*
Huddington Court, nr Droitwich — Professor Hugh D. Edmondson *(WA)*
Newhouse Farm, Goodrich, Ross-on-Wye — The Administrator *(WA)*
Old Palace (The), Worcester — The Dean & Chapter of Worcester *(WA) Apply to Diocesan Secretary, Old Palace. Deansway, Worcester WR1 2JE*
Shelwick Court, nr Hereford — The Landmark Trust. Shottesbrooke. nr Maidenhead. Berks SL6 3SW *(WA)*

HERTFORDSHIRE

Homewood, Park Lane. Knebworth — Mr & Mrs Pollock-Hill (WA)
Northaw Place, Northaw — Mural can be viewed by appt only (0707) 44059
Heath Mount School, Woodhall Park. Watton-at-Stone. Hertford — The Abel Smith Trustees *Estate Office,* Ware 0920 830286

KENT

Barming Place, Maidstone — Mr J. Peter & Dr Rosalind Bearcroft *Maidstone 27844*
Foord Almshouses, Rochester — *(WA)* The Clerk to the Trustees. Easter to Sept 30 2–5 except Mon & Thurs. Adm £1. Chd 50p
The Old Pharmacy, 6 Market Place. Faversham — Mr J. B. Kerr *(WA)*
Mersham-le-Hatch, nr Ashford — Lord Brabourne *Apply to tenant – The Directors, Caldecott Community* Ashford (Kent) 623954
Nurstead Court, Meopham — Mrs S. M. H. Edmeades-Stearns *Meopham 812121*
Prospect Tower, Belmont Park. Faversham — The Landmark Trust. Shottesbrooke. nr Maidenhead. Berks SL6 3SW *Open daily, times displayed*
Old College of All Saints, Kent Music Centre. Maidstone — *Apply to Area Director* Maidstone 690404
Yaldham Manor, Wrotham — Mr & Mrs John Mourier Lade. Yaldham Manor. Kemsing. Sevenoaks. Kent TN15 6NN (postal address) *(WA)*

LANCASHIRE

Music Room (The), Lancaster — The Landmark Trust. Shottesbrooke. nr Maidenhead. Berks SL6 3SW *Open daily, times displayed*
Parrox Hall, Preesall. Lancashire FY6 0JU — *(WA)* Mr & Mrs H. D. H. Elletson (0253) 810245

LEICESTERSHIRE

Launde Abbey, East Norton (Chapel only) — Warden: The Rev Canon Henry Evans MA. Open Easter Mon. May Bank Hol Mons. all Mons in June. July. Aug: all Sats in Aug. Other times by appointment only.
Moat House (The), Appleby Magna — Mr H. S. Hall (0530) 27031
Old Grammar School, Market Harborough — The Market Harborough Exhibition Foundation. 12 Hillcrest Avenue. Market Harborough (0858) 463201
Staunton Harold Hall, nr. Ashby de la Zouch — Ryder-Cheshire Foundation for the Relief of Suffering. Exhibition. Coffee shop and beautiful grounds open to the public. *Tours available by prior appt.* Melbourne 862798

LINCOLNSHIRE

Bede Houses, Tattershall — *Access for exterior viewing noon to sunset daily*
The Chateau, Gate Burton. nr Gainsborough — The Landmark Trust. Shottesbrooke. nr Maidenhead. Berks SL6 3SW *(WA)*
East Lighthouse, Sutton Bridge. Spalding PE12 9YT. Sir Peter Scott's Lighthouse Home 1933–39 — Exterior viewing of House and wildfowl ponds year round. Cdr. M. D. Joel RN. *(WA)* for interior
Fulbeck Manor, Grantham. Lincs NG32 3JN — Mr J. F. Fane *(WA)*
Harlaxton Manor, Grantham — University of Evansville *(WA)*
House of Correction, Folkingham — The Landmark Trust. Shottesbrooke. Maidenhead. Berks SL6 3SW *(WA)*
The Norman Manor House, Boothby Pagnell — Lady Netherthorpe *(WA)*
Pelham Mausoleum, Limber. Grimsby — The Earl of Yarborough. Brocklesby Park. Habrough. Lincs
Scrivelsby Court, nr Horncastle — Lt Col J. L. M. Dymoke. M.B.E.. D.L. *(WA)*

LONDON

All Hallows Vicarage, Tottenham. N17 — Rev R. Pearson 01-808 2470
69 Brick Lane, E1 — *(WA)*
24 The Butts, Brentford — Mrs Sally Mills *(WA)*
192, 194, 196, 198, 202, 204–224 Cable Street, E1 — *(WA)*
11–13 Cavendish Square, W1 — Heythrop College *(WA)*
Celia and Phillip, Blairman Houses, Elder St. E1 — *(WA)*

Charlton House, Charlton. SE7 — London Borough of Greenwich *Apply to Manager* 081-856 3951
Charterhouse, Charterhouse Square. EC1 — The Governors of Sutton's Hospital in Charterhouse *(WA)* April 1 to July 31 – every Wed 2.15 pm *(WA)*
88/190 The Crescent, Hertford Rd, N9 — *(WA)*
17/27 Folgate Street, E1 — *(WA)*
36 Hanbury Street, E1 — *(WA)*
Heathgate House, 66 Crooms Hill. Greenwich. SE10 8HN — Rev Mother Prioress, Ursuline Convent 081-858 0779
House of St Barnabas-in-Soho, 1 Greek St, W1V 6NQ — The Warden of the House *(WA)* 071-437 1894
140, 142, 166, 168 Homerton High Street, E5 — *(WA)*
Kensal Green Cemetery, Harrow Rd. W10 — General Cemetery Company 081-969 0152
69/83 Paragon Road, E5 — *(WA)*
Permanent Exhibition of Judicial & Legal Costume, Law Courts. Strand, WC2 — The Administrator *Adm free Mon–Fri 10–4.30*
Red House, Red House Lane. Bexleyheath — Mr & Mrs Hollamby *(WA only, with SAE)* First Sat & Sun in month 2.30–4.30 pm
Vale Mascal Bath House, Bexley — Mrs F. Chu (0322) 554894
Wesley's House, 47 City Rd, EC1 — The Trustees of Wesley's Chapel *Open weekdays 10 am–4 pm* 071-253 2262

MERSEYSIDE

The Turner Home, Dingle Head. Liverpool L8 9RN — *By appointment only with the Officer in Charge* Mr R. A. Waring. RGN. CGN 051-727 4177

NORFOLK

All Saints' Church, Bagthorpe — Norfolk Churches Trust – always open
All Saints' Church, Barmer — Norfolk Churches Trust Ltd – Keyholder – No 5 The Cottages on main road near the church.
All Saints' Church, Cockthorpe — Norfolk Churches Trust Ltd – Keyholder – Mrs Case at the farmhouse opposite the church.
All Saints' Church, Dunton — Norfolk Churches Trust – Always open – Key of Tower at Hall Farm
All Saints' Church, Frenze — Mrs Alston at Farmhouse opposite or adjacent cottage.
All Saints' Church, Hargham — Norfolk Churches Trust Ltd – Keyholder – Mrs Clifford Amos. Station Road. Attleborough
All Saints' Church, Moreton on the Hill — Lady Prince Smith at the Hall
All Saints' Church, Rackheath — Norfolk Churches Trust Ltd – Open
All Saints' Church, Snetterton — Norfolk Churches Trust Ltd – Keyholder – Col. R. Felton, Hall Farm next to Church.
All Saints' Church, West Binley — Key Mrs Eyre at Church Farm
All Saints' Church, West Rudham — Lord & Lady Romney, Wensum Farm or Mrs Walker; Pockthorpe Cottage
19-21 Bedford St, Norwich. — *Open times as restaurant and shops. Norwich City Council*
Billingford Mill, nr Scole — Norfolk County Council *Norwich 222709*
6 The Close, Norwich — The Dean & Chapter of Norwich Cathedral *(WA)* *Apply to Tenant in Residence Subud Norwich*
Erpingham Gate
3 The Close, Norwich
4 The Close, Norwich
27 The Close, Norwich
31 The Close, Norwich
32 The Close, Norwich
34 The Close, Norwich
35 The Close, Norwich
40 The Close, Norwich
41 The Close, Norwich — Cathedral Steward's Office, Messrs Percy Howes & Co. 3 The Close, Norwich *(WA)*
43 The Close, Norwich
44 The Close, Norwich
56a, b and c The Close, Norwich
67 The Close, Norwich
73 The Close, Norwich
The Deanery Norwich
Denver Mill, off A10 — Norfolk Windmills Trust. County Hall, Martineau Lane. Norwich NR1 2DH *Norwich 6222706*
Ditchingham Hall, Ditchingham. Bungay — The Rt Hon Earl Ferrers
Earlham Hall, University of East Anglia. Norwich. — *By appointment with the Senior Admin Assistant, School of Law, University of East Anglia.* (0603) 56161
Fishermen's Hospital, Great Yarmouth — J. E. C. Lamb, FIH. Clerk to the Trustees *Great Yarmouth 856609*
Gowthorpe Manor, Swardeston — Mrs Watkinson by appointment only *Mulbarton 70216*
Hales Hall, Loddon — Mr & Mrs T. Read *(WA) Open Tues to Sat 10–1, 2–5.* (050 846) 395
Hoveton House, Wroxham — Mr J. C. C. Blofeld *Open only to parties booked by prior appointment in writing. and not individuals.*
Lattice House, King's Lynn — Mr and Mrs T. Duckett *(WA)* Kings Lynn (0553) 777292
Little Cressingham Mill, Watton — Norfolk Windmill Trust. Mr Apling (0953) 850567
Little Hautbois Hall, — Mrs Duffield (0603) 279333
Manor House (The), Great Cressingham — Mrs F. Chapman *(WA)*
Manor House (The), 54 Bracondale. Norwich — Mr P.B. Macqueen. Small parties welcome *(WA)*
Music House (The) at Wensum Lodge. King Street. Norwich — The Warden Norwich 666021/2
The Old Princes Inn Restaurant, 20 Princes St. Norwich — *Open times as restaurant* (0603) 621043
Old Vicarage (The), Methwold. Thetford IP26 4NR — Mr & Mrs H. C. Dance (WA)
St Andrew's Church, Frenze — Norfolk Churches Trust Ltd – Keyholder – Mrs Alston at the farmhouse opposite or ask at adjacent cottage
St Margaret's Church, Morton-on-the-Hill — Norfolk Churches Trust Ltd – Keyholder – Lady Prince-Smith at The Hall. NE of church
St Mary's Church, Bagthorpe — Norfolk Churches Trust Ltd – Open
St Mary's Church, Dunton — Norfolk Churches Trust Ltd – Open
St Peter's Church, West Rudham — Norfolk Churches Trust Ltd – Keyholder – Lord & Lady Romney. Wensum Farm or Mrs Walker. Pockthorpe Cottages. West Rudham
Stracey Arms Mill, nr Acle (A47) — Norfolk County Council *Norwich 611122. Ext 5224*
The Strangers' Club, 22. 24 Elm Hill. Norwich — *By appointment with the Steward* (0603) 623814
Thoresby College, Queen Street. King's Lynn — King's Lynn Preservation Trust *(WA)*

Where it is necessary to write for an appointment to view, see code *(WA)*

House	Owner (with address if different from first column)
Wilby Hall, Quidenham	Mr & Mrs C. Warner *(WA)*
Wiveton Hall, Holt	D. MacCarthy *(WA)*

NORTHAMPTONSHIRE

House	Owner
Courteenhall, Northampton	Sir Hereward Wake. Bt. M.C. *(WA)*
Drayton House, Lowick. Kettering NN14 3BG	L. G. Stopford Sackville *(WA)*
Menagerie (The), Horton. Northampton	Mr Gervase Jackson-Stops *(WA)*
Monastery (The), Shutlanger	Mr & Mrs R. G. Wigley *(WA)*
Paine's Cottage, Oundle	Mr R. O. Barber *(WA)*
Weston Hall, Towcester	Mr & Mrs Francis Sitwell *(WA)*

NORTHUMBERLAND

House	Owner
Brinkburn Mill, Rothbury	The Landmark Trust. Shottesbrooke. Maidenhead. Berks SL6 3SW *(WA)*
Capheaton Hall, Newcastle upon Tyne	Exterior only. Mr J. Browne-Swinburne *(WA)*
Causeway House, Bardon Mill	The Landmark Trust. Shottesbrooke. Maidenhead. Berks SL6 3SW *(WA)*
Craster Tower, Alnwick	Col J. M. Craster, Miss M. D. Cra'ster. Mr F. Sharratt *(WA)*
Elsdon Tower, Elsdon	Mr K. Maddison, Hillview Cottage. Elsdon *Otterburn* 20538
Harnham Hall, Belsay	Mr J. Wake
Morpeth Castle, Morpeth	The Landmark Trust. Shottesbrooke. Maidenhead. Berks SL6 3SW *(WA)*
Netherwitton Hall, Morpeth	Mr J. C. R. Trevelyon *(WA)*

NOTTINGHAMSHIRE

House	Owner
Flintham Hall, nr Newark	Mr M. T. Hildyard *(WA)*
Winkburn Hall, nr Southwell	Mr R. Craven-Smith-Milnes (0636) 86465
Worksop Priory Church and Gatehouse, Cheapside	The Vicarage *Worksop* 472180

OXFORDSHIRE

House	Owner
39/43 The Causeway, Steventon	Mr & Mrs H. C. Dance. The Old Vicarage. Methwold. Thetford. Norfolk IP26 4NR *(WA)*
26/7 Cornmarket Street, and 26 Ship Street, Oxford	Shop on ground and first floors open during normal trading hours shop basement by written appt. Laura Ashley Ltd., 150 Bath Rd. Maidenhead. Berks SL6 4YS 2nd floor by written appt. Home Bursar. Jesus College. Oxford OX1 3DW.
Cote House, nr. Bampton	Mrs David Anderson *(WA)*
Hope House, Woodstock	Mrs J. Hageman
Manor (The), Chalgrove	Mr & Mrs Paul L. Jacques *(WA)*
Monarch's Court House, Benson	Mr R. S. Hine *(WA)*
Ripon College, Cuddesdon	The Principal *(WA)*

SHROPSHIRE

House	Owner
Clive House, College Hill, Shrewsbury	Shrewsbury and Atcham Borough Council. Open Mon to Sat (0743) 354811
Cronkhill House, nr. Crosshouses. Shrewsbury.	The National Trust. House designed c.1803 by John Nash *(WA)* Mrs L. Motley (tenant)
Guildhall, The, Dogpole. Shrewsbury	Shrewsbury & Atcham Borough Council
Halston, Oswestry	Mrs J. L. Harvey *(WA)*
Hatton Grange, Shifnal	Mrs P. Afia, Mon and Fri only May 1–Aug 10 *(WA)*
Moat House, The, Longnor. Shrewsbury SY5 7PP	Mr C.P. Richards (0743) 718434
Morville Hall, nr Bridgnorth	The National Trust (tenant Mrs J. K. Norbury) *(WA)*
Rowleys House and Mansion, Barker St. Shrewsbury	Shrewsbury & Atcham Borough Council *Open daily except winter Suns* (0743) 361196
Stanwardine Hall, Cockshutt. Ellesmere	P. J. Bridge (0939) 270212
St. Winifred's Well, Woolston. Oswestry	The Landmark Trust. Shottesbrooke. Maidenhead. Berks SL6 3SW *(WA)*

SOMERSET

House	Owner
Cothelstone Manor and Gatehouse, Cothelstone. Taunton	Mrs E. Warmington. Cothelstone House Estate. Cothelstone Manor. Taunton *(WA)*
Manor Farm, Meare. Wells	Mrs I. M. Bull (tenant Mr C. J. Look)
Old Drug Store (The), Axbridge	Mr & Mrs K. E. J. D. Schofield *(WA)*
Old Hall (The), Croscombe	The Landmark Trust. Shottesbrooke. nr Maidenhead. Berks SL6 3SW *(WA)*
Manor House (Elizabethan), Crowcombe	The Manager *(WA)*
The Priest's House, Holcombe Rogus. nr Wellington	The Landmark Trust. Shottesbrooke. nr Maidenhead. Berks SL6 3SW *(WA)*
Stogursey Castle, Stogursey. nr Bridgwater	The Landmark Trust. Shottesbrooke. nr Maidenhead. Berks SL6 3SW *(WA)*
West Coker Manor, West Coker BA22 9BJ	Mr & Mrs Derek Maclaren. Open on appointment Easter to October. (093 586) 2646
Whitelackington Manor, Ilminster	Dillington Estate Office. Ilminster *(WA)*

STAFFORDSHIRE

House	Owner
Broughton Hall, Eccleshall	The Administrator *(WA)*
The Great Hall in Keele Hall, Keele	Registrar. University of Keele *(WA)*
Ingestre Pavilion, nr. Stafford	The Landmark Trust. Shottesbrooke. Maidenhead. Berks SL6 3SW *(WA)*
Old Hall Gatehouse (The), Mavesyn Ridware	Mr R. M. Eades *Armitage* 490312
The Orangery, Heath House. Tean. Stoke-on-Trent	Mrs M. Phillips (0538) 722212
Park Hall, Leigh	Mr E. J. Knobbs *(WA)*
Tixall Gatehouse, Tixall	The Landmark Trust. Shottesbrooke. nr Maidenhead. Berks SL6 3SW *(WA)*

SUFFOLK

House	Owner
Deanery (The), Hadleigh	The Dean of Bocking *Hadleigh* 822218
Hall (The), Great Bricett. nr Ipswich	Mr & Mrs R. B. Cooper *(WA)*
Hengrave Hall, Bury St Edmunds	The Warden. Hengrave Hall Centre. Bury St Edmunds *(WA)* *Bury St. Edmunds* 701561

House	Owner (with address if different from first column)
Martello Tower, Aldeburgh	The Landmark Trust. Shottesbrooke. Maidenhead. Berks SL6 3SW *(WA)*
Moat Hall, Parham. nr Woodbridge	Mr J. W. Gray *Wickham Market* 746317
Newbourne Hall, nr Woodbridge	John Somerville Esq *(WA)*
New Inn (The), Peasenhall	The Landmark Trust. Shottesbrooke. nr Maidenhead. Berks SL6 3SW *Great Hall open daily*
Worlingham Hall, Beccles	Viscount Colville of Culross *(WA)*

SURREY

House	Owner
Crossways Farm, Abinger Hammer	Mr C. T. Hughes (tenant) *(WA)*
Great Fosters Hotel, Egham	Mr J. E. Baumann (Manager) (0784) 433822
St. Mary's Homes Chapel, Church Lane. Godstone	Open Oct to Mar 10–4; Apr to Sept 10–6 (0883) 742385
Sunbury Court, Sunbury-on-Thames. Middx	The Salvation Army *Sunbury* 782196

EAST SUSSEX

House	Owner
Ashdown House, nr Forest Row	The Headmaster. Ashdown House School (0342) 822574
Laughton Tower, nr Lewes	The Landmark Trust. Shottesbrooke. nr Maidenhead. Berks SL6 3SW *(WA)*

WEST SUSSEX

House	Owner
Chantry Green House, Steyning	Mr & Mrs G. H. Recknell *Steyning* 81-2239
Chapel (The), Bishop's Palace, Chichester	Church Commissioners. *(WA) only to* The Palace. Chichester *The Chaplain*
Christ's Hospital, Horsham	School buildings open by appointment with School Office (0403) 52547

TYNE & WEAR

House	Owner
Gibside Banqueting House, nr Newcastle	The Landmark Trust. Shottesbrooke. nr Maidenhead. Berks SL6 3SW *(WA)*

WARWICKSHIRE

House	Owner
Bath House, Walton. nr Stratford-on-Avon	The Landmark Trust. Shottesbrooke. nr Maidenhead. Berks SL6 3SW *(WA)*
Binswood Hall, Binswood Ave. Leamington Spa	North Leamington School *(WA) to Head of Hall* (0926) 423686
Foxcote, Shipston-on-Stour	Mr C. B. Holman *(WA)*
Nicholas Chamberlain's Almshouses, Bedworth	The Warden (0203) 312225
Northgate, Warwick	Mr R. E. Phillips *(WA)*
St Leonard's Church, Wroxall	Mrs I. D. M. Iles, Principal. Wroxall Abbey School. Warwick CV35 7NB *(WA)*
War Memorial Town Hall, Alcester	The Secretary, Mr J. W. Roberts, 10 Haselor Close. Alcester B49 6QD *Alcester* (0789) 762101 or Mr J. Adams (762648)

WILTSHIRE

House	Owner
*Abbey House (The), Malmesbury	Malmesbury Preservation Trust, 48 High St. Malmesbury SN16 9AT (066 82) 2212
Chinese Summerhouse, Amesbury Abbey. Amesbury	Visitors are requested to keep to the paths indicated. For open days Tel: (0980) 622957
Farley Hospital, Farley	The Warden (072 272) 231
Grove (The), Corsham	Trustees of Corsham Estate *(WA)*
Milton Manor, Pewsey	Mrs Rupert Gentle (0672) 63344
Old Bishop's Palace, 1 The Close. Salisbury	The Bursar. The Cathedral School *Salisbury* 322652
Old Manor House (The), 2 Whitehead Lane. Bradford on Avon	Mr John Teed *(WA)*
Orpins House, Church Street. Bradford-on-Avon	Mr J. Vernon Burchell *(WA)*
Porch House (The), Potterne. nr Devizes	*(WA)*

NORTH YORKSHIRE

House	Owner
Allerton Park, nr Knaresborough	Michael Farr, Administrator (0423) 330632
Beamsley Hospital, nr Skipton	The Landmark Trust. Shottesbrooke. Maidenhead. Berks SL6 3SW *(WA)*
Broughton Hall, Skipton	H. R. Tempest Esq. Open without appointment. Summer Bank Holidays and June weekdays (0756) 792267
Busby Hall, Carlton-in-Cleveland	Mr G. A. Marwood *(WA)*
Calverley Old Hall, Selby	The Landmark Trust. Shottesbrooke. nr Maidenhead. Berks SL6 3SW *(WA)*
Cawood Castle, nr Selby	The Landmark Trust. Shottesbrooke. Maidenhead. Berks SL6 3SW *(WA)*
Chapel and Coach House, Aske. Richmond	*Open daily during August 11 am–6 pm* Exterior **only**
The Church of Our Lady and Saint Everilda, Everingham	*View by appointment. Donations. Key at Riding Cottage.* Everingham (0430) 860531
Culloden Tower (The), Richmond	The Landmark Trust. Shottesbrooke. nr Maidenhead. Berks SL6 3SW *(WA)*
The Dovecote, Forcett Hall. Forcett. nr Richmond	External viewing from road through Forcett (B6274) Internal viewing – apply Mrs P. E. Heathcote. Forcett Hall. Forcett. Richmond (0325) 718226
Home Farm House, Old Scriven. Knaresborough	Mr G. T. Reece *(WA)*
Moulton Hall, nr Richmond	The National Trust (tenant the Hon. J. D. Eccles) *(WA)*
Old Rectory (The), Foston, nr York	Mrs R. F. Wormald *(WA)*
The Pigsty, Robin Hood's Bay	The Landmark Trust. Shottesbrooke. nr Maidenhead. Berks SL6 3SW *(WA)*

WEST YORKSHIRE

House	Owner
Fulneck Boys' School, Pudsey	I. D. Cleland, B.A.. M.Phil., Headmaster *(WA) Open during school holidays only*
Grand Theatre & Opera House (The), Leeds	Warren Smith, General Manager (0532) 456014
Horbury Hall, Horbury, nr Wakefield	D. J. H. Michelmore Esq (0924) 277552
Old Hall (The), Calverley. nr Pudsey. Leeds	The Landmark Trust. Shottesbrooke. nr Maidenhead. Berks SL6 3SW *(WA)*
Town Hall, Leeds	Leeds City Council *Leeds* 477989
Weston Hall, nr Otley	Lt Col H. V. Dawson *(WA)*

WALES

House	Owner (with address if different from first column)
CLWYD	
Fferm, Pontblyddyn, Mold	Dr M. C. Jones-Mortimer *Apply to tenant*
Gatehouse at Gilar Farm, Pentrefoclas	Mr P. J. Warbourton-Lee *(WA)*
Halghton Hall, Bangor-on-Dee, Wrexham	Mr J. D. Lewis *(WA)*
Lindisfarne College, Wynnstay Hall, Ruabon	The Headmaster *(0978) 810407*
Nerquis Hall, Mold	Mr A. W. Furse *(WA)*
Pen Isa'r Glascoed, Bodelwyddan	Mr M. E. Harrop *St Asaph 583501*
Plas Uchaf, Llangar	The Landmark Trust, Shottesbrooke, nr Maidenhead, Berks *(WA)*
DYFED	
French Mill, Carew	Mr Anthony Trollope-Bellew *April to Sept*
Monkton Old Hall, Pembroke	The Landmark Trust, Shottesbrooke, Maidenhead, Berks SL6 3SW *(WA)*
St David's University College, Lampeter	Principal: Professor Keith Robbins *Lampeter 422-351*
Taliaris Park, Llandeilo	Mr J. H. Spencer-Williams *(WA)*
West Blockhouse, Dale, Haverfordwest	The Landmark Trust, Shottesbrooke, Maidenhead, Berks SL6 3SW *(WA)*
MID GLAMORGAN	
Llancaiach Fawr, Nelson	Rhymney Valley District Council *Apply to Museums Officer* *Hengoed 815588 Ext 221*
GWENT	
Blackbrook Manor, Skenfrith	Mr & Mrs A. C. de Morgan *Skenfrith 453*
Castle Hill House, Monmouth	Mr T. Baxter-Wright *(WA)*
Clytha Castle, nr Abergavenny	The Landmark Trust, Shottesbrooke, nr Maidenhead, Berks SL6 3SW *(WA)*
Cwrt Porth Hir, Llanover	Coldbrook & Llanover Estate *(WA)*
Great Cil-Lwch, Llantilio Crossenny	Mr J. F. Ingledew *(WA)*
Kemys House, Kemys Inferior, Caerleon	Mr I. S. Burge *(WA)*

House	Owner (with address if different from first column)
Llanrihangel Court, Abergavenny	Mr D. Johnson *(WA)*
Overmonnow House (formerly Vicarage), Monmouth	Mr J. R. Pangbourne *(WA)*
3/4 Priory Street, Monmouth	Mr H. R. Ludwig *(WA)*
St James House, Monmouth	The Governors of Monmouth School; The Haberdashers Co *(WA)*
Treowen, Wonastow, Monmouth	Emma Wheelock *Dingestow 412*
GWYNEDD	
Bath Tower (The), Caernarfon	The Landmark Trust, Shottesbrooke, nr Maidenhead, Berks SL6 3SW *(WA)*
Cymryd, Conwy	Miss D. E. Glynne *(WA)*
Dolaugwyn, Towyn	Mrs S. Tudor *(WA)*
Nannau, Llanfachreth, nr Dolgellau	Mr P. Vernon *(WA)*
Penmynydd, Alms Houses, Llanfairpwll	The Rector of Llanfairpwll *(Hon Secretary)* *(WA)*
Plas Coch, Llanedwen, Llanfairpwll	Mrs N. Donald *Llanfairpwll (0248) 714272*
POWYS	
Abercamlais, Brecon	Mrs J. C. R. Ballance *(WA)*
Abercynrig, Llanfrynach	Mr W. R. Lloyd, Abercynrig, Brecon, Powys LD3 7AQ *(WA)*
1 Buckingham Place, Brecon	Mrs Meeres *(WA)*
3 Buckingham Place, Brecon	Mr & Mrs A. Whiley *(WA)*
Maesmawr Hall Hotel, Caersws	Mrs M. Pemberton, Mrs I. Hunt *(0686) 688255*
Newton Farm, Brecon	Mrs Ballance *(WA)* to Mr D. L. Evans, tenant
Pen-Y-Lan, Meifod	Mr S. R. J. Meade *Meifod 202*
Plasau Duon, Clatter	Mr E. S. Breese
Poultry House, Leighton	The Landmark Trust, Shottesbrooke, Maidenhead, Berks SL6 3SW *(WA)*
Rhydycarw, Trefeglwys, Caersws	Mr M. Breese-Davies *Trefeglwys 363*
Ydderw, Llyswen	Mr D. P. Eckley *(WA)*
SOUTH GLAMORGAN	
Fonmon Castle, Barry	Sir Brooke Boothby, Bt *Rhoose (0446) 710206*

SCOTLAND

House	Owner (with address if different from first column)
BORDERS REGION	
Darnick Tower, Melrose	Mrs T. H. Wilson *Melrose 2735*
Old Gala House, Galashiels	Ettrick & Lauderdale District Council *Open Apr to Oct daily. Other times by appointment* *Selkirk 20096*
Sir Walter Scott's Courtroom, Selkirk	Ettrick & Lauderdale District Council *Open weekdays 2–4 in July & Aug. Other times by appt.* *Selkirk 20096*
Wedderlie House, Gordon TD3 6NW	Mrs J. R. L. Campbell *By appointment* *Westruther 223*
CENTRAL REGION	
Castlecary Castle, by Bonnybridge, Stirlingshire	Mr Hugo B. Millar *(WA)* *Banknock 840031*
Church of the Holy Rude, Broad Street, Stirling	
Erskine Marykirk, St. John Street, Stirling	Now a Youth Hostel *(0786) 79000*
Gargunnock House, by Stirling	Gargunnock Estate Trust *(WA)*
Guildhall, Stirling District Council, Municipal Buildings, Stirling	*(0786) 79000*
John Cowane's House, Stirling District Council, Municipal Buildings, Stirling	*(0786) 79000*
Mars Wark and Argyll Lodgings, Stirling District Council	*(0786) 79000*
Old Tolbooth Building, Stirling	Stirling District Council, Municipal Buildings, Corn Exchange Rd *Stirling 79000*
Pineapple (The), Dunmore, Airth	The Landmark Trust, Shottesbrooke, nr Maidenhead, Berks SL6 3SW *(WA)*
Stirling Castle, Historic Scotland	*Area Office (0786) 50000*
Touch House, by Stirling	Mr P. B. Buchanan *(WA)*
DUMFRIES & GALLOWAY REGION	
Bonshaw Tower, Kirtlebridge, nr Annan	Dr J. B. Irving *View by appointment* *Kirtlebridge 256*
Carnsalloch House, Kirkton, nr Dumfries	The Leonard Cheshire Foundation *Dumfries 54924*
Craigdarroch House, Moniaive	Major and Mrs H. F. Stanley *Moniaive 202*
Kirkconnell House, New Abbey, nr Dumfries	Mr F. Maxwell Witham *New Abbey 276*
Tolbooth, Broad St., Stirling	Stirling District Council *Stirling 79400*
FIFE REGION	
Bath Castle, Bogside, nr Oakley	Mr Angus Mitchell, 20 Regent Terrace, Edinburgh EH7 5BS *031-556 7671*
Castle (The), Elie	Mr J. Bevan *(WA)*
Castle of Park, Glenluce	The Landmark Trust, Shottesbrooke, nr Maidenhead, Berks SL6 3SW *(WA)*
Charleton House, Colinsburgh	Baron St. Clair Bonde *(033 334) 249*
GRAMPIAN REGION	
Balbithan House, Kintore	Mr John McMurtrie *Kintore 32282*
Balfluig Castle	Mr Mark Tennant, 30 Abbey Gardens, London NW8 9AT *(WA)*
Barra Castle, Old Meldrum	Dr & Mrs Andrew Bogdan *(WA)*
Castle of Fiddes, Stonehaven	Dr M. Weir *Drumlithie 213*
Corsindae House, Sauchen By Inverurie, Aberdeenshire AB51 7PP	Mr Richard Fyffe *(WA)* *(03303) 295*
Craigston Castle, Turriff	Bruce Urquhart of Craigston *King Edward (08885) 228*
Drumminor Castle, Rhynie	Mr A. D. Forbes *(WA)*

House	Owner (with address if different from first column)
Gordonstoun School, Elgin (Round Square only)	The Headmaster, Gordonstoun School, Elgin Moray IV30 2RF *(WA)*
Grandhome House, nr Aberdeen	D. R. Paton Esq *Aberdeen 722202*
Kintore Town House, Kintore	Gordon District Council *Inverurie 20981*
Phesdo House, Laurencekirk	Mr J. M. Thomson *(WA)*
HIGHLAND REGION	
Embo House, Dornoch	Mr John G. Mackintosh *Dornoch 810260*
LOTHIAN REGION	
Arniston House, Gorebridge	Mrs A. R. Dundas-Bekker. June to mid-Sept, each Tues & first Sun of month 2–5 for guided tours
Cakemuir, Tynehead	Mr M. M. Scott *(WA)*
Castle Gogar, Edinburgh	Lady Steel-Maitland *Corstorphine 1234*
Ford House, Ford	F. P. Tindall, O.B.E. *(WA)*
Forth Road Bridge, South Queensferry	The Bridgemaster *031-319 1699*
Linnhouse, nr Livingston	Mr H. J. Spurway *(WA)*
Newbattle Abbey College, Dalkeith	The Principal *031-663 1921*
Northfield House, Prestonpans	Mr W. Schomberg Scott *(WA)*
Peffermill House, Peffermill Rd, Edinburgh EH16 5UX	Nicholas Groves-Raines, Architects *031-661 7172/3*
Penicuik House, Penicuik	Sir John Clerk, Bt *(WA)*
Prestonhall, Pathhead	Major J. H. Callander *(WA)*
Rosebery House, Murrayfield	Esq. M. E. Sturgeon *(WA)*
Town House, Haddington	East Lothian District Council *By arrangement with Reception Unit, Council Buildings, Haddington on Hand* *4161*
SHETLAND ISLANDS AREA	
Lodberrie (The), Lerwick	Mr Thomas Moncrieff
STRATHCLYDE REGION	
Ascog House, Isle of Bute	The Landmark Trust, Shottesbrooke, Maidenhead, Berks SL6 3SW *(WA)*
Barcaldine Castle, Benderloch	Morton, Fraser Milligan, W. S., 19 York Place, Edinburgh EH1 3EL (Trustees of Sir A. W. D. Campbell) *(WA)*
Craufurdland Castle, Kilmarnock	J. P. Houison Craufurd Esq *(056 06) 402*
Duntrune Castle, Lochgilphead	Robin Malcolm of Poltalloch *(WA)*
Kelburn Castle, Fairlie	The Earl of Glasgow *(WA)*
New Lanark, Lanark	New Lanark Conservation Trust, Mill No. 3, New Lanark Mills, Lanark ML11 9DB *(0555) 661345*
Place of Paisley (The), Paisley	Paisley Abbey, Kirk Session *(WA) Apply to Minister* *041-889 7654*
Saddell Castle, nr Campbeltown	The Landmark Trust, Shottesbrooke, nr Maidenhead, Berks SL6 3SW *(WA)*
Tangy Mill, nr Campbeltown	The Landmark Trust, Shottesbrooke, nr Maidenhead, Berks SL6 3SW *(WA)*
Tannahil Cottage, Queen St, Paisley	Secretary, Paisley Burns Club *041-887 7500*
TAYSIDE REGION	
Ardblair Castle, Blairgowrie	Laurence P. K. Blair Oliphant *Blairgowrie 873155*
Craig House, Montrose	Charles F. R. Hoste *Montrose 72239*
Kinross House, Kinross (Garden only)	Sir David Montgomery, Bt *(WA)*
Michael Bruce Cottage Museum, Kinnesswood	Michael Bruce Trust
The Pavilion, Gleneagles, Auchterarder PH3 1PJ	J. Martin Haldane Esq. *(WA)*
Tulliebole Castle, Crook of Devon	The Lord Moncreiff *By appointment only* *Fossoway 236*

Index to Houses, Castles and Gardens

A

A La Ronde, *Devon*   37
Abberley Hall, *Hereford & Worcester*   70
Abbot Hall Art Gallery & Museum of Lakeland Life & Industry, *Cumbria*   26
Abbotsford House, *Borders*   237
Aberconwy House, *Gwynedd*   226
Aberdour Castle, *Fife*   244
Acorn Bank Garden, *Cumbria*   26
Acton Round Hall, *Shropshire*   153
Adcote, *Shropshire*   153
Adlington Hall, *Cheshire*   14
Akenfield, *Suffolk*   165
Albury Park, *Surrey*   171
Aldborough Roman Town, *North Yorkshire*   206
Alfriston Clergy House, *East Sussex*   175
Allerton Park, *North Yorkshire*   206
Alnwick Castle, *Northumberland*   137
Amisfield Mains, *Lothian*   250
Ancient High House, *Staffordshire*   161
Anglesey Abbey and Garden, *Cambridgeshire*   11
Angus Folk Museum, *Tayside*   260
Annes Grove Gardens, *Ireland*   229
Antony, *Cornwall*   20
Antony Woodland Garden, *Cornwall*   20
Apple Court, *Hampshire*   263
Appuldurcombe House, *Isle of Wight*   84
Apsley House, *Greater London*   110
Apuldram Roses, *West Sussex*   263
Arbigland Gardens, *Dumfries & Galloway*   243
Arbury Hall, *Warwickshire*   190
Architectural Plants, *West Sussex*   263
Ardington House, *Oxfordshire*   145
Ardress House, *Northern Ireland*   235
Arduaine Garden, *Strathclyde*   256
The Argory, *Northern Ireland*   235
Arley Hall and Gardens, *Cheshire*   14
Arlington Court, *Devon*   37
Arundel Castle, *West Sussex*   184
Ascott, *Buckinghamshire*   7
Asgill House, *Surrey*   171
Ashburnham House, *Greater London*   110
Ashby de la Zouch Castle, *Leicestershire*   104
Ashdown House, *Oxfordshire*   145
Ashridge, *Hertfordshire*   77
Astley Hall, *Lancashire*   102
Aston Hall, *West Midlands*   197
Athelhampton, *Dorset*   43
Attingham Park, *Shropshire*   153
Aubourn Hall, *Lincolnshire*   107
Auckland Castle, *County Durham*   49
Audley End House and Park, *Essex*   51
Jane Austen's House, *Hampshire*   60
Avebury Manor & Garden, *Wiltshire*   199
Avebury Museum, *Wiltshire*   199
Avenue Cottage Gardens, *Devon*   37
Avington Park, *Hampshire*   61
Avoncroft Museum of Buildings, *Hereford & Worcester*   70
Aydon Castle, *Northumberland*   137
Ayesha Castle, *Ireland*   229
Aylett Nurseries Ltd, *Hertfordshire*   263
Aynhoe Park, *Northamptonshire*   129
Ayton Castle, *Borders*   237

B

Bachelors' Club, *Strathclyde*   256
Baddesley Clinton, *Warwickshire*   190
Bagshaw Museum, *West Yorkshire*   217
Balcarres, *Fife*   245
Balcaskie, *Fife*   245
Balloch Castle Country Park, *Strathclyde*   256
Balmoral Castle, *Grampian*   245
Balvenie Castle, *Grampian*   245
Bamburgh Castle, *Northumberland*   138
The Banqueting House, *Greater London*   110
Bantry House, *Ireland*   229
The Bar Convent, *North Yorkshire*   206
Barford Park, *Somerset*   157
Barnard Castle, *County Durham*   49
Barnsley House Garden, *Gloucestershire*   55
Barrie's Birthplace, *Tayside*   260
Barrington Court, *Somerset*   157
Barry Mill, *Tayside*   260
Barstaple House (Trinity Almshouses), *Avon*   1
Basildon Park, *Berkshire*   5
Basing House, *Hampshire*   61
Bateman's, *East Sussex*   175
Batsford Arboretum, *Gloucestershire*   55
Battle Abbey, *East Sussex*   176
Bayham Abbey, *East Sussex*   176
Beanston, *Lothian*   250
Beaulieu, *Hampshire*   62
Beaumaris Castle (World Heritage Listed Site), *Gwynedd*   226
Beckford's Tower, *Avon*   1
Bedgebury National Pinetum, *Kent*   86
Beeston Castle, *Cheshire*   14
Beeston Hall, *Norfolk*   124
Belchamp Hall, *Suffolk*   165
Belgrave Hall, *Leicestershire*   104
Bellahouston Park, *Strathclyde*   256
Belmont, *Kent*   87
Belsay Hall Castle and Gardens, *Northumberland*   138
Belton House, *Lincolnshire*   107
Belvoir Castle, *Leicestershire*   105
Beningbrough Hall, *North Yorkshire*   206
Benington Lordship Gardens, *Hertfordshire*   78
Benmore Younger Botanic Garden, *Strathclyde*   256
Benthall Hall, *Shropshire*   153
Bentley House & Gardens, *East Sussex*   176
Berkeley Castle, *Gloucestershire*   55
Berney Arms Windmill, *Norfolk*   125
Bernithan Court, *Hereford & Worcester*   70
Berri Court, *West Sussex*   184
Berrington Hall, *Hereford & Worcester*   70
Berwick Upon Tweed Barracks, *Northumberland*   138
Beth Chatto Gardens, *Essex*   51
Beverley Guildhall, *Humberside*   81
Bickleigh Castle, *Devon*   37
Bicton Park Gardens, *Devon*   38
Biddulph Grange Garden, *Staffordshire*   162
Birr Castle Demesne, *Ireland*   229
Bishop's Palace, *Lincolnshire*   108
The Bishop's Palace, *Somerset*   158

Bishop's Waltham Palace, *Hampshire*   63
Black Charles, *Kent*   87
Blackthorn Nursery, *Hampshire*   263
Blairquhan Castle and Gardens, *Strathclyde*   256
Blaise Castle House Museum, *Avon*   1
Blakeney House Nurseries Ltd, *Kent*   263
Blakenham Woodland Garden, *Suffolk*   165
Blakesley Hall, *West Midlands*   197
Blarney Castle and Blarney House, *Ireland*   231
Blaydes House, *Humberside*   81
Blenheim Palace, *Oxfordshire*   145
The Blewcoat School, *Greater London*   110
Blickling Hall, *Norfolk*   125
Bluecoat Chambers, *Merseyside*   124
Bodelwyddan Castle, *Clwyd*   221
Bodiam Castle, *East Sussex*   177
Bodiam Nursery, *East Sussex*   263
Bodnant Garden, *Gwynedd*   226
Bodnant Garden Nursery Ltd, *Clwyd*   264
Bolsover Castle, *Derbyshire*   33
Borde Hill Garden, *West Sussex*   185
Boscobel House, *Shropshire*   154
Boston Manor, *Greater London*   110
Bosvigo House (Gardens), *Cornwall*   21
Bosvigo Plants, *Cornwall*   264
Bosworth Battlefield Visitor Centre & Country Park, *Leicestershire*   105
Botanic Garden, University of Durham, *County Durham*   49
Botanic Gardens, *Oxfordshire*   145
Botanic Gardens, *Strathclyde*   256
Bothwell Castle, *Strathclyde*   256
Boughton House, *Northamptonshire*   130
Boughton Monchelsea Place, *Kent*   87
Bourton House Garden, *Gloucestershire*   55
Bowhill, *Borders*   237
Bowood House & Gardens, *Wiltshire*   199
J.W. Boyce, *Cambridgeshire*   264
Brackenwood Garden Centre, *Avon*   264
Bradley Manor, *Devon*   38
Braemar Castle, *Grampian*   246
Bramdean House, *Hampshire*   63
Bramham Park, *West Yorkshire*   217
Branklyn Garden, *Tayside*   260
Brantwood, *Cumbria*   27
Breamore House, *Hampshire*   63
Bressingham Gardens, *Norfolk*   125
Bressingham Plant Centre, *Norfolk*   264
Brickwall House, *East Sussex*   177
Bridgemere Garden World, *Cheshire*   264
Bridgemere Garden World, *Cheshire*   264
Brinkburn Priory, *Northumberland*   139
British Wild Flower Plants, *Norfolk*   265
Broadlands, *Hampshire*   64
Broadleas Gardens (Charitable Trust), *Wiltshire*   200
Brodick Castle, Garden and Country Park, *Strathclyde*   257
Brodie Castle, *Grampian*   246
Bromages Bonsai Centre, *Surrey*   265
Brook Cottage, *Oxfordshire*   145
Brough Castle, *Cumbria*   27
Brougham Castle, *Cumbria*   28
Broughton Castle, *Oxfordshire*   145
Browsholme Hall, *Lancashire*   103
Bryn Bras Castle, *Gwynedd*   226
Buckland Abbey, *Devon*   39

Buildwas Abbey, *Shropshire*   154
Bunratty Castle & Folk Park, *Ireland*   231
Burford House Gardens, *Hereford & Worcester*   71
Burgh House, *Greater London*   111
Burghley House, *Lincolnshire*   108
Burnby Hall Gardens, *Humberside*   81
Burncoose Nurseries and Garden, *Cornwall*   265
Burns Cottage, *Strathclyde*   257
Burton Agnes Hall, *Humberside*   82
Burton Constable, *Humberside*   82
Burton Court, *Hereford & Worcester*   71
Buscot Old Parsonage, *Oxfordshire*   145
Buscot Park, *Oxfordshire*   147
Bushmead Priory, *Bedfordshire*   3
Byland Abbey, *North Yorkshire*   206

C

Cadhay, *Devon*   39
Caerlaverock Castle, *Dumfries & Galloway*   243
Caerleon Roman Fortress, *Gwent*   224
Caernarfon Castle (World Heritage Listed Site), *Gwynedd*   226
Caerphilly Castle, *Mid Glamorgan*   223
Calke Abbey and Park, *Derbyshire*   33
Calshot Castle, *Hampshire*   64
Cannon Hall, *South Yorkshire*   216
Canons Ashby House, *Northamptonshire*   131
Capel Manor, *Hertfordshire*   78
Capesthorne, *Cheshire*   15
Cardiff Castle, *South Glamorgan*   224
Carding Mill Valley & Long Mynd, *Shropshire*   154
Carew Manor and Dovecote, *Greater London*   111
Carisbrooke Castle, *Isle of Wight*   85
Carlisle Castle, *Cumbria*   28
Carlton Hall, *Nottinghamshire*   142
Carlyle's Birthplace, *Dumfries & Galloway*   243
Carlyle's House, *Greater London*   111
Carreg Cennen Castle, *Dyfed*   221
Carrigglas Manor, *Ireland*   231
Carshalton House (Daughters of the Cross) St Philomena's School, Pound Street, *Greater London*   111
Castell Coch, *South Glamorgan*   224
Castle Acre Priory, *Norfolk*   125
Castle Bromwich Hall Gardens, *West Midlands*   197
Castle Campbell, *Central*   242
The Castle, Castle Eden, *Cleveland*   20
Castle Coole, *Northern Ireland*   235
Castle Drogo, *Devon*   39
Castle Fraser, *Grampian*   246
Castle Gates Library, *Shropshire*   154
Castle Howard, *North Yorkshire*   207
Castle Kennedy Gardens, *Dumfries & Galloway*   243
Castle Menzies, *Tayside*   260
Castle Rising Castle, *Norfolk*   125
Castle Ward, *Northern Ireland*   236
Castletown House, *Ireland*   231
Castletown House, *Cumbria*   28
Cawdor Castle, *Highlands*   248
Champs Hill, *West Sussex*   185
Chapter House and Pyx Chamber of Westminster Abbey, *Greater London*   111
Charlecote Park, *Warwickshire*   190

Charleston Farmhouse, *East Sussex*　178
Charlton Park House, *Wiltshire*　200
The Charterhouse, *Humberside*　83
Chartwell, *Kent*　89
Chatsworth, *Derbyshire*　33
Chavenage, *Gloucestershire*　55
Chedworth Roman Villa, *Gloucestershire*　56
Chelsea Physic Garden, *Greater London*　111
Chenies Manor House, *Buckinghamshire*　7
Chepstow Castle, *Gwent*　224
Cherryburn, *Northumberland*　139
Chester's Roman Fort and Museum, *Northumberland*　139
Chettle House, *Dorset*　44
Chicheley Hall, *Buckinghamshire*　8
Chichester Cathedral, *West Sussex*　185
Chicksands Priory, *Bedfordshire*　3
Chiddingstone Castle, *Kent*　88
Chilham Castle Gardens, *Kent*　89
Chillingham Castle and Gardens, *Northumberland*　139
Chillington Hall, *Staffordshire*　162
Chiltern Open Air Museum, *Buckinghamshire*　8
Chilworth Manor, *Surrey*　171
Chirk Castle, *Clwyd*　221
Chiswick House, *Greater London*　112
Cholmondeley Castle Gardens, *Cheshire*　16
Christchurch Mansion, *Suffolk*　166
The Church House, *Somerset*　158
Chysauster Ancient Village, *Cornwall*　21
Cilgerran Castle, *Dyfed*　221
Clandon Park, *Surrey*　172
Clapton Court Gardens and Plant Centre, *Somerset*　158
Claremont, *Surrey*　172
Claremont Landscape Garden, *Surrey*　172
Claverton Manor, *Avon*　1
Claydon House, *Buckinghamshire*　8
Cleeve Abbey, *Somerset*　158
Clevedon Court, *Avon*　2
Clifford's Tower, *North Yorkshire*　207
Dorothy Clive Garden, *Staffordshire*　162
Cliveden, *Buckinghamshire*　9
Cloghan Castle, *Ireland*　231
Clonalis House, *Ireland*　231
Clouds Hill, *Dorset*　44
Clumber Park, *Nottinghamshire*　143
Cobblers Garden, *East Sussex*　178
Cobham Hall, *Kent*　90
Cochwillan Old Hall, *Gwynedd*　226
Coity Castle, *Mid Glamorgan*　223
Coke's Barn, *West Sussex*　185
Colby Woodland Garden, *Dyfed*　221
Coleridge Cottage, *Somerset*　158
Coleton Fishacre Garden, *Devon*　39
College of Arms, *Greater London*　112
Combe Sydenham Country Park, *Somerset*　158
Compton Castle, *Devon*　39
Condover Hall, *Shropshire*　154
Conisbrough Castle, *South Yorkshire*　216
Conishead Priory, *Cumbria*　28
Constable Burton Hall, *North Yorkshire*　208
Conwy Castle (World Heritage Listed Site), *Gwynedd*　226
Corbridge Roman Site, *Northumberland*　140
Corfe Castle, *Dorset*　44
Corsham Court, *Wiltshire*　200
Cotehele, *Cornwall*　21

Coton Manor Gardens, *Northamptonshire*　131
The Cottage Garden, *Essex*　265
The Cottage Herbery, *Hereford & Worcester*　265
Cottesbrooke Hall and Gardens, *Northamptonshire*　131
Coughton Court, *Warwickshire*　191
The Courts Garden, *Wiltshire*　200
Coverwood Lakes, *Surrey*　172
Cowper & Newton Museum, *Buckinghamshire*　9
Craggaunowen - The Living Past, *Ireland*　232
Cragside House, Garden and Grounds., *Northumberland*　140
Cranborne Manor Gardens, *Dorset*　44
Crathes Castle & Garden, *Grampian*　247
Cratloe Woods House, *Ireland*　232
Criccieth Castle, *Gwynedd*　227
Crittenden House, *Kent*　90
Croft Castle, *Hereford & Worcester*　71
Cromer Windmill, *Hertfordshire*　78
Oliver Cromwell's House, Ely, *Cambridgeshire*　11
Crosswater Farm, *Surrey*　172
Crowe Hall, *Somerset*　158
Croxteth Hall & Country Park, *Merseyside*　124
Cruck Cottage Cacti, *North Yorkshire*　265
Culzean Castle, Garden and Country Park, *Strathclyde*　257
Cwmmau Farmhouse, Brilley, *Hereford & Worcester*　72
Cymer Abbey, *Gwynedd*　227

D

Dalemain, *Cumbria*　28
Dalmeny House, *Lothian*　250
Danny, *West Sussex*　185
Dartmouth Castle, *Devon*　39
Dawyck Botanic Garden, *Borders*　238
De Morgan Foundation, *Greater London*　112
Deacons Nursery (H.H.), *Isle of Wight*　265
Deal Castle, *Kent*　90
Deans Court, *Dorset*　45
Deene Park, *Northamptonshire*　132
Delapre Abbey, *Northamptonshire*　132
Denmans, *West Sussex*　185
Denny Abbey, *Cambridgeshire*　12
The Dickens House Museum, *Greater London*　112
Dinmore Manor, *Hereford & Worcester*　72
Dirleton Castle & Garden, *Lothian*　250
Ditchley Park, *Oxfordshire*　147
Dochfour Gardens, *Highlands*　248
Docwra's Manor, *Cambridgeshire*　12
Doddington Hall, *Lincolnshire*　108
Doddington Place Gardens, *Kent*　90
Dodington Hall, *Somerset*　159
Dorfold Hall, *Cheshire*　16
Dorney Court, *Buckinghamshire*　9
Dover Castle, *Kent*　91
Downhill, *Northern Ireland*　236
Drum Castle, *Grampian*　247
Drumlanrig Castle and Country Park, *Dumfries & Galloway*　244
Dryburgh Abbey, *Borders*　238
Dudmaston, *Shropshire*　154
Dumbarton Castle, *Strathclyde*　257
Duncombe Park, *North Yorkshire*　208
Dunguaire Castle, *Ireland*　232
Dunham Massey, *Cheshire*　16
Dunkathel, *Ireland*　232

Dunloe Castle Hotel Gardens, *Ireland*　232
Dunrobin Castle, *Highlands*　249
Dunstanburgh Castle, *Northumberland*　140
Dunster Castle, *Somerset*　159
Dunvegan Castle, *Highlands*　249
Durham Castle, *County Durham*　50
Dyrham Park, *Avon*　2

E

East Riddlesden Hall, *West Yorkshire*　217
Eastgrove Cottage Garden Nursery, *Hereford & Worcester*　72
Eastnor Castle, *Hereford & Worcester*　72
Ebberston Hall, *North Yorkshire*　208
Edinburgh Castle, *Lothian*　252
Edmondsham House and Gardens, *Dorset*　45
Edzell Castle & Gardens, *Tayside*　261
Eilean Donan Castle, *Highlands*　249
Elgin Cathedral, *Grampian*　247
Elsham Hall Country and Wildlife Park, *Humberside*　83
Elton Hall, *Cambridgeshire*　12
Emmetts Garden, *Kent*　91
Emo Court, *Ireland*　232
Endsleigh House, *Devon*　39
Epworth, *Humberside*　83
Erddig, *Clwyd*　221
Euston Hall, *Suffolk*　166
Ewloe Castle, *Clwyd*　221
Exbury Gardens, *Hampshire*　65
Eyam Hall, *Derbyshire*　35

F

Fairfax House, *North Yorkshire*　209
The Fairhaven Garden Trust, *Norfolk*　125
Falkland Palace & Garden, *Fife*　245
Farleigh Hungerford Castle, *Somerset*　159
Farnborough Hall, *Warwickshire*　192
Farnham Castle, *Surrey*　172
Farnham Castle Keep, *Surrey*　173
Fasque, *Grampian*　247
Fawley Court - Marian Fathers Historic House & Museum, *Oxfordshire*　147
Felbrigg Hall, *Norfolk*　126
Fenton House, *Greater London*　112
Fernhill Garden, *Ireland*　232
Finchcocks, *Kent*　91
Finlaystone House and Gardens, *Strathclyde*　257
Firle Place, *East Sussex*　179
Fitz House Garden, *Wiltshire*　200
Flete, *Devon*　40
Floors Castle, *Borders*　238
Florence Court, *Northern Ireland*　236
Forde Abbey and Gardens, *Dorset*　45
Fort Brockhurst, *Hampshire*　65
Fort George, *Highlands*　250
Fota, *Ireland*　232
Fountains Abbey & Studley Royal, *North Yorkshire*　209
Framlingham Castle, *Suffolk*　167
Frogmore Gardens, *Berkshire*　5
Frogmore House, *Berkshire*　5
Fruit for the Connoisseur, *Hampshire*　265
Fulbeck Hall, *Lincolnshire*　108
Fulham Palace, *Greater London*　113
Furness Abbey, *Cumbria*　28
Fursdon, *Devon*　40
Fyvie Castle, *Grampian*　247

G

G. Reuthe Ltd, *Kent*　265
Gad's Hill Place, *Kent*　91
Gainsborough's House, *Suffolk*　167
The Gardens of the Rose, *Hertfordshire*　266
Gaulden Manor, *Somerset*　159
Gawsworth Hall, *Cheshire*　16
Gawthorpe Hall, *Lancashire*　103
The Georgian House, *Lothian*　252
Georgian Theatre Royal, *North Yorkshire*　209
Gibside Chapel & Grounds, *Tyne & Wear*　189
Gilbert White's House & Garden and the Oates Exhibitions, *Hampshire*　65
Gisborough Priory, *Cleveland*　20
Gladstone's Land, *Lothian*　252
Glamis Castle, *Tayside*　261
Glendurgan Garden, *Cornwall*　21
Glin Castle, *Ireland*　232
Glynde Place, *East Sussex*　179
Goddards, *Surrey*　173
Godinton Park, *Kent*　92
Godolphin House, *Cornwall*　21
Goodnestone Park, *Kent*　92
Goodrich Castle, *Hereford & Worcester*　73
Goodwood House, *West Sussex*　185
Gorhambury, *Hertfordshire*　78
Gosfield Hall, *Essex*　52
Gosford House, *Lothian*　252
Gpa-Bolton Library, *Ireland*　232
Grantham House, *Lincolnshire*　108
Gray's Printing Press, *Northern Ireland*　236
The Great Barn, *Oxfordshire*　148
Great Chalfield Manor, *Wiltshire*　200
Great Comp Garden, *Kent*　93
Great Dixter, *East Sussex*　180
Great Maytham Hall, *Kent*　93
Greathed Manor, *Surrey*　173
Greenbank Garden, *Strathclyde*　257
Gregynog, *Powys*　227
The Greyfriars, *Hereford & Worcester*　73
Greys Court, *Oxfordshire*　148
Grime's Graves, *Norfolk*　126
Grimsthorpe Castle and Gardens, *Lincolnshire*　108
Groombridge Place, *Kent*　93
Guildhall of Corpus Christi, *Suffolk*　167
Gunby Hall, *Lincolnshire*　110
Gunnersbury Park Museum, *Greater London*　113
Gwydir Uchaf Chapel, *Gwynedd*　227
Gyrn Castle, *Clwyd*　221

H

Haddo House, *Grampian*　247
Haddon Hall, *Derbyshire*　36
Hadrian's Roman Wall in Northumberland and Tyne and Wear, *Northumberland*　140
Hadrian's Wall, *Cumbria*　29
Hadspen Garden, *Somerset*　266
Hadspen Garden & Nursery, *Somerset*　159
Hagley Hall, *West Midlands*　198
Hailes Abbey, *Gloucestershire*　56
Hall i' th' Wood, *Greater Manchester*　123
Hall Place, *Greater London*　113
Hall's Croft, *Warwickshire*　192
Ham House, *Greater London*　113
Hammerwood Park, *West Sussex*　186

The Hampshire Hydroponicum, *Hampshire* 266

Hampton Court Palace, *Greater London* 114

Hamptworth Lodge, *Wiltshire* 200

Hanbury Hall, *Hereford & Worcester* 73

Hanch Hall, *Staffordshire* 163

Handforth Hall, *Cheshire* 17

Hardwick Hall, *Derbyshire* 35

Hardwicke Court, *Gloucestershire* 56

Hardy's Cottage, *Dorset* 45

Hare Hill Garden, *Cheshire* 17

Harelaw Farmhouse, *Lothian* 253

Harewood House and Bird Garden, *West Yorkshire* 218

Harlech Castle (World Heritage Listed Site), *Gwynedd* 227

Harlow Carr Botanical Gardens, *North Yorkshire* 209

Hartland Abbey, *Devon* 40

Hartlebury Castle, *Hereford & Worcester* 73

Harvington Hall, *Hereford & Worcester* 73

Harwich Redoubt, *Essex* 52

Hastings Castle and 1066 Story, *East Sussex* 180

Hatch Court, *Somerset* 160

Hatchlands Park, *Surrey* 173

Hatfield House, *Hertfordshire* 80

Anne Hathaway's Cottage, *Warwickshire* 192

Haughley Park, *Suffolk* 167

Haughmond Abbey, *Shropshire* 154

Haxted Mill & Museum, *Kent* 95

Hazelbury Manor Gardens, *Wiltshire* 201

Heale Gardens and Plant Centre, *Wiltshire* 201

Heale Gardens, Plant Centre and Shop, *Wiltshire* 266

Hedingham Castle, *Essex* 52

Hellen's, *Hereford & Worcester* 74

Helmingham Hall Gardens, *Suffolk* 168

Helmsley Castle, *North Yorkshire* 209

Hemerdon House, *Devon* 40

The Herb and Heather Centre, *North Yorkshire* 266

Hergest Croft Gardens, *Hereford & Worcester* 74

Heritage Centre, *Greater London* 114

Hermitage Castle, *Borders* 238

Hever Castle & Gardens, *Kent* 94

Hezlett House, *Northern Ireland* 236

Hidcote Manor Garden, *Gloucestershire* 56

Cecil Higgins Art Gallery & Museum, *Bedfordshire* 3

High Beeches Gardens, *West Sussex* 186

Highbury, *Dorset* 45

Highclere Castle, *Hampshire* 66

Hill Court Gardens & Garden Centre, *Hereford & Worcester* 75

The Hill House, *Strathclyde* 257

Hill of Tarvit, *Fife* 245

The Sir Harold Hillier Gardens and Arboretum, *Hampshire* 66

Hinton Ampner, *Hampshire* 66

The Hirsel Grounds & Dundock Wood, *Borders* 238

Hodnet Hall Gardens, *Shropshire* 155

Hodsock Priory Gardens, *Nottinghamshire* 143

Hogarth's House, *Greater London* 114

Hoghton Tower, *Lancashire* 103

Holdenby House Gardens, *Northamptonshire* 133

Holker Hall, *Cumbria* 29

Holkham Hall, *Norfolk* 126

Holme Pierrepont Hall, *Nottinghamshire* 143

Honington Hall, *Warwickshire* 192

Hopetoun House, *Lothian* 253

Horn Park, *Dorset* 45

Horton Court, *Avon* 2

Houghton Hall, *Norfolk* 127

Houghton Lodge Gardens, *Hampshire* 67

House of Dun, *Tayside* 261

The House of the Binns, *Lothian* 253

Housesteads Roman Fort, *Northumberland* 140

Hovingham Hall, *North Yorkshire* 210

How Caple Court Gardens, *Hereford & Worcester* 75

Howick Hall Gardens, *Northumberland* 140

Hughenden Manor, *Buckinghamshire* 9

Huntingtower Castle, *Tayside* 261

Huntly Castle, *Grampian* 247

Hurst Castle, *Hampshire* 67

Hutchesons' Hall, *Strathclyde* 258

Hutton-in-the-Forest, *Cumbria* 29

I

Ickworth, *Suffolk* 168

Iford Manor Gardens, *Wiltshire* 201

Ightham Mote, *Kent* 95

Ilsington, *Dorset* 46

Inveraray Castle, *Strathclyde* 258

Inveresk Lodge Garden, *Lothian* 253

Inverewe Garden, *Highlands* 250

Ipswich Museum, *Suffolk* 168

19/20 Irish Street, *Cumbria* 29

Island Hall, *Cambridgeshire* 13

J

Japanese Gardens, *Ireland* 233

Jedburgh Abbey, *Borders* 238

Jenkyn Place, *Hampshire* 67

Johnstown Castle Demesne, *Ireland* 233

The James Joyce Tower, *Ireland* 233

Jungle Giants Bamboo Nursery, *Hereford & Worcester* 267

K

Kayes Garden Nursery, *Leicestershire* 267

Keats House, *Greater London* 114

Kedleston Hall, *Derbyshire* 35

Kelburn Country Centre and Kelburn Castle, *Strathclyde* 259

Kellie Castle and Garden, *Fife* 245

Kelways Nurseries Ltd, *Somerset* 160

Kelways Nurseries Ltd, *Somerset* 267

Kenilworth Castle, *Warwickshire* 192

Kensington Palace, *Greater London* 114

Kentchurch Court, *Hereford & Worcester* 75

Kentsford House, *Somerset* 160

Kentwell Hall, *Suffolk* 169

Kenwood, The Iveagh Bequest, *Greater London* 115

Kew Gardens, *Greater London* 115

Kew Palace (Dutch House), *Greater London* 115

Kidbrooke Park with Repton Grounds, *East Sussex* 180

Kidwelly Castle, *Dyfed* 223

Kiftsgate Court, *Gloucestershire* 56

Kildrummy Castle Garden, *Grampian* 248

Killerton, *Devon* 40

Kimbolton Castle, *Cambridgeshire* 13

Kingston Bagpuize House, *Oxfordshire* 148

Kingston Lacy, *Dorset* 46

Kinnersley Castle, *Hereford & Worcester* 75

Kirby Hall, *Northamptonshire* 133

Kirby Muxloe Castle, *Leicestershire* 105

Kirkham Priory, *North Yorkshire* 210

Kirkley Hall Gardens, *Northumberland* 140

Knappogue Castle, *Ireland* 233

Knebworth House, *Hertfordshire* 80

Knightshayes Court, *Devon* 40

Knole, *Kent* 95

Kylemore Abbey, *Ireland* 233

L

Lacock Abbey, *Wiltshire* 201

Ladham House, *Kent* 95

Lamb House, *East Sussex* 180

Lamb's House, *Lothian* 253

Lamphey Bishop's Palace, *Dyfed* 223

Lamport Hall and Gardens, *Northamptonshire* 134

Lanercost Priory, *Cumbria* 29

Langley Boxwood Nursery, *Hampshire* 267

Langstone Court, *Hereford & Worcester* 75

Lanhydrock, *Cornwall* 22

Launceston Castle, *Cornwall* 22

Lauriston Castle, *Lothian* 254

Layer Marney Tower, *Essex* 52

Lea Gardens, *Derbyshire* 267

Ledston Hall, *West Yorkshire* 218

Leeds Castle, *Kent* 96

Leighton Hall, *Lancashire* 103

Leighton House Museum, *Greater London* 116

Leith Hall and Garden, *Grampian* 248

Lennoxlove, *Lothian* 254

Leonardslee Gardens, *West Sussex* 186

Levens Hall, *Cumbria* 30

Lincoln Castle, *Lincolnshire* 110

Lindisfarne Castle, *Northumberland* 140

Lindisfarne Priory, *Northumberland* 141

Linley Sambourne House, *Greater London* 117

Linlithgow Palace, *Central* 242

Linn Park, *Strathclyde* 259

Lismore Castle, *Ireland* 233

Lissadell, *Ireland* 233

Little Dean Hall, *Gloucestershire* 56

Little Hall, *Suffolk* 169

Little Holland House, *Greater London* 117

Little Malvern Court and Gardens, *Hereford & Worcester* 75

Little Moreton Hall, *Cheshire* 17

Llancaiach Fawr, *Mid Glamorgan* 224

Llawhaden Castle, *Dyfed* 223

Logan Botanic Garden, *Dumfries & Galloway* 244

Longleat House, *Wiltshire* 202

Longthorpe Tower, *Cambridgeshire* 13

Loseley House, *Surrey* 174

Lotherton Hall, *West Yorkshire* 219

Lough Gur Visitor Centre, *Ireland* 233

Lough Rynn Estate & Gardens, *Ireland* 233

Lower Brockhampton, *Hereford & Worcester* 75

Lower Dairy House Garden, *Essex* 52

Luckington Court, *Wiltshire* 202

Ludford House, *Shropshire* 155

Ludlow Castle, *Shropshire* 155

Luffness, *Lothian* 254

Lullingstone Castle, *Kent* 96

Lullingstone Roman Villa, *Kent* 96

Luton Hoo, *Bedfordshire* 3

Lyddington Bede House, *Leicestershire* 106

Lydiard House, *Wiltshire* 202

Lydney Park, *Gloucestershire* 57

Lyme Park, *Cheshire* 17

Lympne Castle, *Kent* 96

Lytes Cary Manor, *Somerset* 160

Lyveden New Bield, *Northamptonshire* 134

M

Macpennys, *Dorset* 46

Macpennys of Bransgore, *Dorset* 267

The Magnolias, *Essex* 52

Maister House, *Humberside* 83

Malahide Castle, *Ireland* 233

Malleny Garden, *Lothian* 254

Malt House, *West Sussex* 187

Manderston, *Borders* 240

Mannington Gardens and Countryside, *Norfolk* 127

The Manor House, *Leicestershire* 106

The Manor House, *Avon* 2

The Manor House, *Hampshire* 67

Mapledurham House and Watermill, *Oxfordshire* 150

Mapperton, *Dorset* 46

Marble Hill House, *Greater London* 117

Margam Park, *West Glamorgan* 224

Markenfield Hall, *North Yorkshire* 210

Marston Hall, *Lincolnshire* 110

Martholme, *Lancashire* 103

Marwood Hill, *Devon* 40

Maunsel House, *Somerset* 160

Mawley Hall, *Shropshire* 155

Maxwelton House, *Dumfries & Galloway* 244

Meads End Bonsai, *East Sussex* 267

Meare Close Nurseries Ltd, *Surrey* 267

Medieval Merchants House, *Hampshire* 67

Melbourne Hall and Gardens, *Derbyshire* 35

Melford Hall, *Suffolk* 169

Mellerstain, *Borders* 240

Melrose Abbey, *Borders* 240

Meols Hall, *Merseyside* 124

Mertoun Gardens, *Borders* 240

Michelham Priory, *East Sussex* 181

Middleham Castle, *North Yorkshire* 210

Midelney Manor, *Somerset* 160

Millais Nurseries, *Surrey* 267

Hugh Miller's Cottage, *Highlands* 250

Milton Abbey, *Dorset* 46

Milton Lodge Gardens, *Somerset* 161

Milton Manor House, *Oxfordshire* 149

Milton's Cottage, *Buckinghamshire* 9

Minster Lovell Hall and Dovecote, *Oxfordshire* 150

Minterne, *Dorset* 46

Mirehouse, *Cumbria* 30

Misarden Park Gardens, *Gloucestershire* 57

Moat House, *Shropshire* 156

Moccas Court, *Hereford & Worcester* 76

Mompesson House, *Wiltshire* 203

Monk Bretton Priory, *South Yorkshire* 216

Monks House, *East Sussex* 181

Montacute House, *Somerset* 161

Moor Park Mansion, *Hertfordshire* 80

Moorlands, *East Sussex* 181

Moseley Old Hall, *Staffordshire* 163

Mottisfont Abbey Garden, *Hampshire* 68

Mount Edgcumbe House & Park, *Cornwall* 22

Mount Ephraim, *Kent* 97

Mount Grace Priory, *North Yorkshire* 210

Mount Stewart House, Garden and Temple, *Northern Ireland* 236

Mount Usher Gardens, *Ireland* 234

Muckross House and Gardens, *Ireland* 234

Muncaster Castle, *Cumbria* 31

Sir Alfred Munnings Art Museum, *Essex* 53

Museum of Garden History, *Greater London* 117

N

National Botanic Gardens, *Ireland* 234

Naworth Castle, *Cumbria* 31

Neath Abbey, *West Glamorgan* 224

The Needles Old Battery, *Isle of Wight* 85

Neidpath Castle, *Borders* 240

Nether Alderley Mill, *Cheshire* 18

Nether Hall, *Suffolk* 169

Nether Winchenden House, *Buckinghamshire* 9

Netley Abbey, *Hampshire* 68

New College of Cobham, *Kent* 97

New Place/Nash's House, *Warwickshire* 193

Newark Park, *Gloucestershire* 57

Newark Town Hall, *Nottinghamshire* 143

Newbridge House, *Ireland* 234

Newburgh Priory, *North Yorkshire* 211

Newby Hall & Gardens, *North Yorkshire* 211

Newhouse, *Wiltshire* 203

Newstead Abbey House and Grounds, *Nottinghamshire* 144

Newtimber Place, *West Sussex* 187

Newtown Old Town Hall, *Isle of Wight* 85

Norham Castle, *Northumberland* 141

Northbourne Court Gardens, *Kent* 97

Norton Conyers, *North Yorkshire* 212

Norton Priory Museum, *Cheshire* 18

Norwich Castle, *Norfolk* 127

Norwood Park, *Nottinghamshire* 144

Nostell Priory, *West Yorkshire* 219

Nuffield Place, *Oxfordshire* 150

Number One, Royal Crescent, *Avon* 2

Nunnington Hall, *North Yorkshire* 212

Nunwell House and Gardens, *Isle of Wight* 85

Nymans Garden, *West Sussex* 187

O

Oakham Castle, *Leicestershire* 106

Oakwell Hall, *West Yorkshire* 219

The Octagon, Orleans House Gallery, *Greater London* 117

Okehampton Castle, *Devon* 40

Old House Museum, *Derbyshire* 35

The Old Palace, *Greater London* 118

The Old Rectory, *Berkshire* 5

Old Royal Observatory, *Greater London* 118

Old Sarum, *Wiltshire* 203

Old Wardour Castle, *Wiltshire* 203

Orchard Wyndham, *Somerset* 161

Orford Castle, *Suffolk* 169

Ormesby Hall, *Cleveland* 20

Osborne House, *Isle of Wight* 86

Osterley Park, *Greater London* 118

Otley Hall, *Suffolk* 169

Overbecks Museum & Garden, *Devon* 40

Owl House Gardens, *Kent* 97

Owlpen Manor, *Gloucestershire* 57

Oxburgh Hall, *Norfolk* 127

P

Packwood House, *Warwickshire* 193

Painshill Park, *Surrey* 174

Painswick Rococo Garden, *Gloucestershire* 58

Palace of Holyroodhouse, *Lothian* 255

Papplewick Hall, *Nottinghamshire* 144

Parham House and Gardens, *West Sussex* 187

Park Farm (Garden), *Essex* 53

Parnham, *Dorset* 47

Pashley Manor, *East Sussex* 181

Paxton House, *Borders* 240

Paycocke's, *Essex* 53

Peckover House and Garden, *Cambridgeshire* 13

Pencarrow House and Garden, *Cornwall* 23

Pendennis Castle, *Cornwall* 23

Penhow Castle, *Gwent* 225

Penrhyn Castle, *Gwynedd* 227

Penshurst Place, *Kent* 98

Peover Hall, *Cheshire* 18

Perhill Nurseries, *Hereford & Worcester* 268

Perrott's Folly, *West Midlands* 198

Perryhill Nurseries, *East Sussex* 268

Perry's Plants, River Gardens, *North Yorkshire* 268

Petworth House, *West Sussex* 187

Pevensey Castle, *East Sussex* 182

Peveril Castle, *Derbyshire* 35

Philipps House, *Wiltshire* 203

Pickering Castle, *North Yorkshire* 212

Picton Castle, *Dyfed* 223

Pitmedden Garden, *Grampian* 248

Pitshanger Manor Museum, *Greater London* 118

Plants from a Country Garden, *Buckinghamshire* 268

Plas Brondanw Gardens, *Gwynedd* 227

Plas Mawr, *Gwynedd* 227

Plas Newydd, *Gwynedd* 227

Polesden Lacey, *Surrey* 174

Pollok House & Park, *Strathclyde* 259

Port Lympne Zoo Park, Mansion & Gardens, *Kent* 99

Portchester Castle, *Hampshire* 68

Portland Castle, *Dorset* 47

Powderham Castle, *Devon* 41

Powerscourt Gardens & Waterfall, *Ireland* 234

Powerscourt Townhouse Centre, *Ireland* 234

Powis Castle, *Powys* 228

The Prebendal Manor House, *Northamptonshire* 134

Preen Manor Gardens, *Shropshire* 156

Preston Manor, *East Sussex* 182

Preston Mill, *Lothian* 255

Preston Tower, *Northumberland* 141

Prideaux Place, *Cornwall* 23

Priest's House, *Northamptonshire* 134

Priest's House Museum and Garden, *Dorset* 47

Princes Risborough Manor House, *Buckinghamshire* 10

Prior Crauden's Chapel, *Cambridgeshire* 13

Priorwood Garden, *Borders* 240

The Priory, *Hereford & Worcester* 76

The Priory, *Suffolk* 170

Provost Ross's House, *Grampian* 248

Prudhoe Castle, *Northumberland* 142

Purse Caundle Manor, *Dorset* 47

Pyrford Court, *Surrey* 175

Pythouse, *Wiltshire* 203

Q

Quarry Bank Mill, *Cheshire* 19

Quebec House, *Kent* 99

Queen Charlotte's Cottage, *Greater London* 118

The Queen's House, *Greater London* 119

Quex House, Quex Park, *Kent* 99

R

Raby Castle, *County Durham* 50

Raglan Castle, *Gwent* 225

Ragley Hall, *Warwickshire* 194

Rainthorpe Hall & Gardens, *Norfolk* 128

Rammerscales, *Dumfries & Galloway* 244

Ramster, *Surrey* 175

Ranger's House, *Greater London* 119

Raveningham Hall Gardens, *Norfolk* 128

Red House, *West Yorkshire* 219

Restormel Castle, *Cornwall* 23

Richborough Castle, *Kent* 100

Richmond Castle, *North Yorkshire* 212

Rievaulx Abbey, *North Yorkshire* 213

Rievaulx Terrace, *North Yorkshire* 213

Ripley Castle, *North Yorkshire* 214

Riverhill House, *Kent* 100

Roche Abbey, *South Yorkshire* 216

Rochester Castle, *Kent* 100

Rockingham Castle, *Northamptonshire* 135

Rode Hall, *Staffordshire* 163

The Roger Plant Centre, *North Yorkshire* 268

Rokeby Park, *County Durham* 51

Rosemoor Garden, *Devon* 41

Ross Hall Park, *Strathclyde* 259

Rotherfield Park, *Hampshire* 68

Rousham House, *Oxfordshire* 151

Rowallane Garden, *Northern Ireland* 237

Royal Botanic Garden, *Lothian* 255

The Royal Horticultural Society's Garden, Wisley, *Surrey* 175

The Royal Hospital Kilmainham/The Irish Museum of Modern Art, *Ireland* 234

Royal Institute of British Architects: Drawings Collection and Heinz Gallery, *Greater London* 119

Royal Pavilion, *East Sussex* 182

RSA (The Royal Society for the encouragement of Arts, Manufactures and Commerce), *Greater London* 119

Rufford Old Hall, *Lancashire* 103

Rushton Hall, *Northamptonshire* 135

Rushton Triangular Lodge, *Northamptonshire* 135

Russborough, *Ireland* 234

Rydal Mount, *Cumbria* 32

The Sue Ryder Home, Hickleton Hall, *South Yorkshire* 216

Ryelands House, *Gloucestershire* 58

Ryton Organic Gardens, *West Midlands* 198

Ryton Organic Gardens, *West Midlands* 268

S

Sackville College, *West Sussex* 187

Saling Hall, *Essex* 54

Saltram House, *Devon* 41

Samarès Herbs-a-Plenty, *Channel Islands* 268

Sand, *Devon* 41

Sandford Orcas Manor House, *Dorset* 47

Sandham Memorial Chapel, *Hampshire* 69

Sandringham House & Grounds, *Norfolk* 128

Savill Garden, *Berkshire* 6

Saxtead Green Post Mill, *Suffolk* 170

Scarborough Castle, *North Yorkshire* 214

Scone Palace, *Tayside* 262

Scotney Castle Garden, *Kent* 100

Scott's Grotto, *Hertfordshire* 80

Seaforde Nursery and Butterfly House 268

Seaton Delaval Hall, *Northumberland* 142

Sewerby Hall, *Humberside* 83

Sezincote, *Gloucestershire* 58

Shaftesbury Abbey Ruins and Museum, *Dorset* 47

The Shakespeare Birthplace Trust Properties, *Warwickshire* 195

The Shakespeare Countryside Museum at Mary Arden's House, *Warwickshire* 195

Shakespeare's Birthplace, *Warwickshire* 196

Shalom Hall, *Essex* 54

Shandy Hall, *North Yorkshire* 214

Sheffield Botanic Gardens, *South Yorkshire* 217

Sheffield Park Garden, *East Sussex* 182

Sheldon Manor, *Wiltshire* 204

Sherborne Castle, *Dorset* 48

Sherborne Garden (Pear Tree House), *Avon* 3

Sherborne Old Castle, *Dorset* 48

Shibden Hall, *West Yorkshire* 220

Shipton Hall, *Shropshire* 156

Shugborough, *Staffordshire* 164

Shute Barton, *Devon* 41

Sion Hill Hall, *North Yorkshire* 214

Sissinghurst Garden, *Kent* 100

Sizergh Castle and Garden, *Cumbria* 32

Skipton Castle, *North Yorkshire* 215

Slane Castle, *Ireland* 234

Sledmere House, *Humberside* 84

Smailholm Tower, *Borders* 240

Robert Smail's Printing Works, *Borders* 242

Smallhythe Place, *Kent* 100

Smithills Hall, *Greater Manchester* 123

Snowshill Manor, *Gloucestershire* 58

Sir John Soane's Museum, *Greater London* 120

Somerleyton Hall, *Suffolk* 171

Sorn Castle, *Strathclyde* 259

Souter Johnnie's Cottage, *Strathclyde* 259

Souter Lighthouse, *Tyne & Wear* 189

South Foreland Lighthouse, *Kent* 100

Southside House, *Greater London* 120

Southwick Hall, *Northamptonshire* 135

Speke Hall, *Merseyside* 124

Spencer House, *Greater London* 120

Spetchley Park, *Hereford & Worcester* 76

Spinners, *Hampshire* 268

Springhill, *Northern Ireland* 237

Squerryes Court, *Kent* 101

St. Augustine's Abbey, *Kent* 100

St. Davids Bishop's Palace, *Dyfed* 223

St. John's Gate, *Greater London*   119

St. Mary's House and Gardens, *West Sussex*   188

St. Mawes Castle, *Cornwall*   24

St. Michael's Mount, *Cornwall*   24

St. Osyth Priory, *Essex*   54

Standen, *West Sussex*   188

Stanford Hall, *Leicestershire*   107

Stanton Harcourt Manor, *Oxfordshire*   151

Stanway House, *Gloucestershire*   58

Stapeley Water Gardens, *Cheshire*   268

Stapeley Water Gardens Ltd, *Cheshire*   19

Starborough Nursery, *Kent*   269

Stevenson House, *Lothian*   255

Stirling Castle, *Central*   242

Stockeld Park, *North Yorkshire*   215

Stoke Park Pavilions, *Northamptonshire*   136

Stokesay Castle, *Shropshire*   156

Stoke-sub-Hamdon Priory, *Somerset*   161

Stone House Cottage Gardens, *Hereford & Worcester*   76

Stoneacre, *Kent*   101

Stonehenge, *Wiltshire*   204

Stonor Park, *Oxfordshire*   152

Stonyhurst College, *Lancashire*   104

Stott Park Bobbin Mill, *Cumbria*   32

Stourhead, *Wiltshire*   204

Stowe Landscape Gardens, *Buckinghamshire*   10

Stowe (Stowe School), *Buckinghamshire*   10

Strata Florida Abbey, *Dyfed*   223

Stratfield Saye House, *Hampshire*   69

Strokestown Park House, *Ireland*   234

Sudbury Hall and Museum of Childhood, *Derbyshire*   37

Sudeley Castle, *Gloucestershire*   59

Sulgrave Manor, *Northampton*   136

Swallowfield Park, *Berkshire*   6

Sweetheart Abbey, *Dumfries & Galloway*   244

Syon House, *Greater London*   121

Syon Park Gardens, *Greater London*   121

T

Tabley House Collection, *Cheshire*   19

Talley Abbey, *Dyfed*   223

Tamworth Castle, *Staffordshire*   165

Tantallon Castle, *Lothian*   255

Tattershall Castle, *Lincolnshire*   110

Temple Newsam, *West Yorkshire*   220

The Tenement House, *Strathclyde*   260

The Thatched Cottage, *Buckinghamshire*   10

Thirlestane Castle, *Borders*   242

Thoor Ballylee, *Ireland*   235

Thornton Abbey, *Humberside*   84

Thorp Perrow Arboretum, *North Yorkshire*   215

Threave Garden, *Dumfries & Galloway*   244

Thrumpton Hall, *Nottinghamshire*   145

Tilbury Fort, *Essex*   55

Timoleague Castle Gardens, *Ireland*   235

Tintagel - The Old Post Office, *Cornwall*   24

Tintagel Castle, *Cornwall*   24

Tintern Abbey, *Gwent*   225

Tintinhull House Garden, *Somerset*   161

Tiverton Castle, *Devon*   42

Tolson Memorial Museum, *West Yorkshire*   220

Tonbridge Castle, *Kent*   101

Torosay Castle and Gardens, *Strathclyde*   260

Torre Abbey, *Devon*   42

Totnes Castle, *Devon*   42

Tottenham House, *Wiltshire*   205

HM Tower of London, *Greater London*   122

The Town House & The Study, *Fife*   245

Towneley Hall Art Gallery & Museum and Museum of Local Crafts & Industries, *Lancashire*   104

Townend, *Cumbria*   32

Traquair, *Borders*   242

The Travellers' Club, *Greater London*   122

Treasurer's House, *North Yorkshire*   216

Tredegar House, *Gwent*   225

Tregrehan, *Cornwall*   24

Trehane Camellia Nursery, *Dorset*   269

Trelissick Garden, *Cornwall*   25

Trelowarren House & Chapel, *Cornwall*   25

Trengwainton Garden, *Cornwall*   25

Trerice, *Cornwall*   25

Tretower Court & Castle, *Powys*   228

Trewithen House and Gardens, *Cornwall*   25

Trinity Hospital, *Norfolk*   129

Tudor Merchant's House, *Dyfed*   223

Tullynally Castle, *Ireland*   235

Ty Mawr Wybrnant, *Gwynedd*   227

Tynemouth Castle and Priory, *Tyne & Wear*   189

U

Ugbrooke House, *Devon*   42

Upnor Castle, *Kent*   101

Upton Cressett Hall, *Shropshire*   156

Upton House, *Warwickshire*   196

Urquhart Castle, *Highlands*   250

V

Valle Crucis Abbey, *Clwyd*   221

Valley Gardens, *Berkshire*   6

Vann, *Surrey*   175

Victoria Park, *Strathclyde*   260

Vine House, *Avon*   3

The Vyne, *Hampshire*   69

W

Waddesdon Manor, *Buckinghamshire*   10

Wakehurst Place Garden, *West Sussex*   188

Walcot Hall, *Shropshire*   156

Wall (Letocetum) Roman Site, *Staffordshire*   165

Wallingford Castle Gardens, *Oxfordshire*   152

Wallington House, Walled Garden and Grounds, *Northumberland*   142

Walmer Castle, *Kent*   102

Warkworth Castle and Hermitage, *Northumberland*   142

Warwick Castle, *Warwickshire*   196

Washington Old Hall, *Tyne & Wear*   189

Waterperry Gardens, *Oxfordshire*   153

The Weald and Downland Open Air Museum, *West Sussex*   189

Weaver's Cottage, *Strathclyde*   260

Webbs of Wychbold, *Worcestershire*   269

The Weir, *Hereford & Worcester*   76

Welford Park, *Berkshire*   6

Wellbrook Beetling Mill, *Northern Ireland*   237

Wenlock Priory, *Shropshire*   156

Weobley Castle, *West Glamorgan*   224

West Dean Gardens, *West Sussex*   189

West Wycombe Park (1750), *Buckinghamshire*   11

Westbury Court Garden, *Gloucestershire*   59

Weston Park, *Shropshire*   156

Westwood Manor, *Wiltshire*   205

Whitby Abbey, *North Yorkshire*   216

White Castle, *Gwent*   226

White Cottage, *Hereford & Worcester*   76

Whitehall, *Greater London*   123

Whitmore Hall, *Staffordshire*   165

Whittington Court, *Gloucestershire*   59

Wightwick Manor, *West Midlands*   198

Wilberforce House, *Humberside*   84

Wilderhope Manor, *Shropshire*   157

Willesborough Windmill, *Kent*   102

Wilton House, *Wiltshire*   205

Wimpole Hall, *Cambridgeshire*   13

Wimpole Home Farm, *Cambridgeshire*   14

Windsor Castle, *Berkshire*   7

Wingfield College, *Suffolk*   171

Winkworth Arboretum, *Surrey*   175

Winslow Hall, *Buckinghamshire*   11

Winster Market House, *Derbyshire*   37

Winton House, *Lothian*   255

Witley Court, *Hereford & Worcester*   77

Woburn Abbey, *Bedfordshire*   4

Wolfeton House, *Dorset*   48

Wollaton Hall, *Nottinghamshire*   145

Wolterton Park, *Norfolk*   129

Wolvesey: Old Bishop's Palace, *Hampshire*   69

Woodchester Park Mansion, *Gloucestershire*   60

Woodhey Chapel, *Cheshire*   20

Woolsthorpe Manor, *Lincolnshire*   110

Worcester Cathedral, *Hereford & Worcester*   77

Wordsworth House, *Cumbria*   32

Wotton House, *Buckinghamshire*   11

Wrest Park House and Gardens, *Bedfordshire*   4

Wroxeter (Viroconium) Roman City, *Shropshire*   157

Wychwood Carp Farm, *Hampshire*   269

Wygston's House, Museum of Costume, *Leicestershire*   107

Y

Yarde, *Devon*   43

Yarmouth Castle, *Isle of Wight*   86

NOTES

Page Index

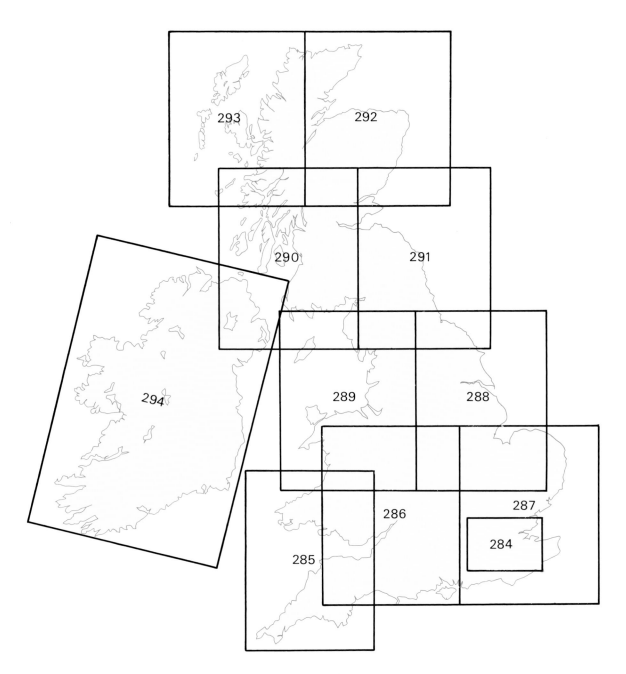

293

292

290

291

294

289

288

286

287

284

285

Legend

═══ Motorway

⬦ Motorway Intersections

─── Primary route

─── Major Roads

🏠 **House with or without garden**

🏰 **Castle with or without garden**

✾ **Garden**

⊞ **Property in the care of English Heritage**
(see supplement)

⋈ **Property in the care of the National Trust**

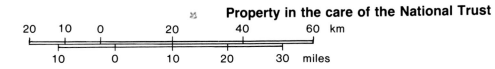

| 20 | 10 | 0 | | 20 | | 40 | | 60 | km |

| | 10 | | 0 | | 10 | | 20 | | 30 | miles |

© Cook, Hammond & Kell Ltd

See Inset on Page 5

19

18

17

16

15

A

B

C

Port of Ness

Carloway

Stornoway

Portnaguran

Balallan

Loch Langavat

Loch Erisol

Tarbert

THE MINCH

Lochinver

Inchnadamph

Ullapool

Rodel

Inverewe

Poolewe

Gairloch

Loch Maree

HIGHLAN

Tigharry

Lochmaddy

Staffin

Uig

Kinlochewe

Achnasheen

R Meig

Creagorry

Dunvegan Castle

Dunvegan

Portree

Bracadale

Shieldaig

R Orrin

R Farrar

Cannich

Urqu

Lochboisdale

Sligachan

Kyle of Lochalsh

Eilean Donan
Castle

Broadford

SEA OF THE HEBRIDES

Ardvasar

Invergar

Mallaig

Loch Arkaig

Loch Lochy

Arisaig

Glenfinnan

R Lochy

Spean Bridge

Loch Shiel

Corpach

Fort William

Acharacle

Corran

Kinlochleven

Tobermory

Loch Sunart

Glencoe

Lochaline

Loch Linnhe

Portnacroish

Salen

Bridge of Orchy

Torosay Castle
and Gardens

Connel

Craignure

Oban

Taynuilt

Crianlar

Fionnph

Bunessan

Kilninver

Awe

Ty

Pentland Firth

John O Groats

Thurso
Reay
Castletown
Bettyhill

Wick

R Thurso

Kinbrace
Latheron

R Helmsdale

Helmsdale

Brora
Dunrobin Castle
Golspie

Bonar Bridge
Dornoch

Tain

Cromarty Firth
Hugh Miller's Cottage
Cromarty
Rosemarkie
Fort George
Nairn
Cawdor Castle

Moray Firth

Lossiemouth
Elgin Cathedral
Elgin
Lhanbryde
Brodie Castle
Forres
Fochabers

Cullen
Buckie
Portsoy
Banff

Fraserburgh

Aberchirder

R Deveron
Turriff
Mintlaw
Peterhead

Keith

Balvenie Castle
Dufftown

R Spey

Huntly Castle
Huntly

Fyvie Castle

Haddo House

Ellon
Pitmedden

GRAMPIAN

Leith Hall

Druminnor Castle
Rhynie

Old Meldrum

Inverness

R Nairn

Tomatin

Grantown on Spey

Carrbridge

R Findhorn

Tomintoul

Kildrummy Castle Garden

Alford

Inverurie

Castle Fraser

Craigievar Castle

Aviemore

R Spey

Provost Ross's House
ABERDEEN

Drum Castle
Peterculter

Kingussie

Crathes Castle & Garden

Aboyne
Banchory

Braemar Castle
Braemar

Balmoral Castle
Ballater

R Dee

Fasque

Stonehaven

Inverbervie

R South Esk

Laurencekirk

TAYSIDE

Edzell Castle & Gardens

Blair Atholl

Brechin
House of Dun
Montrose

Pitlochry

R Tummel

Kirkmichael

Barrie's Birthplace

Aberfeldy
Castle Menzies
Kenmore

R Tay

Bridge of Cally

Blairgowrie

Angus Folk Museum
Glamis Castle
Forfar

Glamis

Meigle

Arbroath

Dunkeld

Rattray
Coupar Angus

Amulree

DUNDEE

Carnoustie

Killin

Loch Tay

R Tay

Scone Palace

Newport-on-Tay

Huntingtower Castle
Perth
Branklyn Garden

Comrie

Crieff

Drummond Castle Gardens

R Earn

Cupar

ST. ANDREWS

E   F   G   H

19

18

17

16

15

293

(V)

(IV)

(III)

(II)

(I)

294

W   X   Y   Z